# FUNK &
# WAGNALLS
# NEW
# ENCYCLO-
# PEDIA

fw

# FUNK & WAGNALLS NEW ENCYCLO- PEDIA

VOLUME 5

CALIGULA

to CHILLON

LEON L. BRAM
Editorial Director

ROBERT S. PHILLIPS
Editor

NORMA H. DICKEY
Executive Editor

FUNK & WAGNALLS, INC., NEW YORK

Funk & Wagnalls
New Encyclopedia
Copyright © MCMLXXI, MCMLXXV
By Funk & Wagnalls, Inc.

**ISBN** 0-8343-0003-6
Library of Congress Catalog
Card Number 72–170933

# FUNK & WAGNALLS NEW ENCYCLO- PEDIA

fw

# LIST OF ABBREVIATIONS USED IN THE TEXT*

| abbr. | abbreviated |
|---|---|
| AC; a-c | alternating current |
| A.D. | *anno Domini* (Medieval Lat., in the year of the Lord) |
| alt. | altitude |
| A.M. | *ante meridiem* (Lat., before noon) |
| AM | amplitude modulation |
| amu | atomic mass unit |
| anc. | ancient |
| Ar. | Arabic |
| AS. | Anglo-Saxon |
| A.S.S.R. | Autonomous Soviet Socialist Republic |
| at.no. | atomic number |
| at.wt. | atomic weight |
| b. | born |
| bbl | barrel |
| B.C. | before Christ |
| bd.ft. | board feet |
| bev | billion electron volts |
| b.p. | boiling point |
| B.T.U. | British Thermal Unit |
| bu. | bushel |
| Bulg. | Bulgarian |
| C. | centigrade |
| cent. | century |
| Chin. | Chinese |
| cm | centimeter |
| Co. | County |
| colloq. | colloquial |
| cu. | cubic |
| Czech. | Czechoslovakian |
| d. | died |
| Dan. | Danish |
| DC; d-c | direct current |
| Du. | Dutch |
| E. | east; eastern |
| ed. | edition; editor |
| Egypt. | Egyptian |
| Eng. | English |
| est. | estimated |
| ev | electron volt |
| F. | Fahrenheit |
| fl. | flourished |
| FM | frequency modulation |

| fr. | from |
|---|---|
| Fr. | French |
| ft. | foot |
| g | gram |
| Gael. | Gaelic |
| gal. | gallon |
| Ger. | German |
| Gr. | Greek |
| Heb. | Hebrew |
| Hind. | Hindustani |
| h.p. | horsepower |
| hr. | hour |
| Hung. | Hungarian |
| Hz | hertz or cycles per second |
| I. | Island |
| i.e. | *id est* (Lat., that is) |
| in. | inch |
| Ind. | Indian |
| Ir. | Irish |
| It. | Italian |
| K. | Kelvin |
| kg | kilogram |
| km | kilometer |
| kw | kilowatt |
| kw hour | kilowatt hour |
| lat. | latitude |
| Lat. | Latin |
| lb. | pound |
| long. | longitude |
| m | meter |
| M. | Middle |
| mev | million electron volts |
| mg | milligram |
| mi. | mile |
| min. | minute |
| M.L. | Medieval Latin |
| mm | millimeter |
| mod. | modern |
| m.p. | melting point |
| m.p.h. | miles per hour |
| Mt(s). | Mount, Mountain |
| N. | north; northern |
| N.T. | New Testament |
| OE. | Old English |
| OF. | Old French |
| OHG. | Old High German |
| ON. | Old Norse |
| ONF. | Old Norman French |

| O.T. | Old Testament |
|---|---|
| oz. | ounce |
| P.M. | *post meridiem* (Lat., after noon) |
| Pol. | Polish |
| pop. | population |
| Port. | Portuguese |
| prelim. | preliminary |
| pron. | pronounced |
| q.v. | *quod vide* (Lat., which see)** |
| r. | reigned |
| R. | River |
| rev. | revised, revision |
| R.R. | railroad |
| Rum. | Rumanian |
| Russ. | Russian |
| Ry. | railway |
| S. | south; southern |
| sec. | second |
| S.F.S.R. | Soviet Federated Socialist Republic |
| Skr. | Sanskrit |
| Sp. | Spanish |
| sp.gr. | specific gravity |
| sq. | square |
| sq.mi. | square mile |
| S.S.R. | Soviet Socialist Republic |
| St.; Ste. | Saint |
| Sum. | Sumerian |
| Sw. | Swedish |
| temp. | temperature |
| trans. | translation |
| Turk. | Turkish |
| U.A.R. | United Arab Republic |
| U.K. | United Kingdom |
| U.N. | United Nations |
| U.S. | United States |
| U.S.A. | United States of America |
| U.S.S.R. | Union of Soviet Socialist Republics |
| var. | variant |
| vol. | volume |
| vs. | versus or against |
| W. | west; western |
| yd. | yard |

*For a more extensive listing of abbreviations, widely used by authoritative sources in many fields, *see* ABBREVIATION. Charts of pertinent abbreviations also accompany the articles BIBLE, CANON OF THE; DEGREE, ACADEMIC; ELEMENTS, CHEMICAL; MATHEMATICAL SYMBOLS; and WEIGHTS AND MEASURES. Accent marks and special letters are explained in the article DIACRITIC MARK.

**The abbreviation (q.v.) stands for the Latin words "quod vide," meaning "which see". The placement of this abbreviation after a word—or a name or term—indicates that the word itself is the title of a separate article in the encyclopedia. By looking up the article on this word, or the entries on each word in a series that is followed by the plural form (qq.v.) of the abbreviation, the reader will find specific information about the words used as well as data about the main topic of the article he is reading.

dgg

# FUNK & WAGNALLS
# NEW ENCYCLOPEDIA

**CALIGULA,** real name GAIUS CAESAR (12–41 A.D.), Roman emperor (37–41), born probably in Antium (now Anzio, Italy), the youngest son of the Roman general Germanicus Caesar (q.v.), and the grandnephew of the Roman Emperor Tiberius (q.v.). His early life in military camps earned him the nickname Caligula (Lat., *caliga,*

*A bust of Caligula, 1st-century Roman emperor (from the Capitoline Museum, Rome).*　　Bettmann Archive

"little boot") because of the military shoes he wore. Tiberius named his grandson, Tiberius Gemellus (19–38), and Caligula joint heirs to the throne, but the Roman Senate and people chose Caligula as sole emperor. Caligula adopted Gemellus as his son, but subsequently had him murdered. Although Caligula ruled with gener-osity and mercy during the first six months of his reign, he became a vicious tyrant after a severe illness. Historians believe that he probably went insane. He squandered his fortune on public entertainment and building projects; banished or murdered most of his relatives; enjoyed having people tortured and killed while he dined; made his favorite horse a consul; declared himself a god; and had temples erected and sacrifices offered to himself. In 41 the officers of his guard (*see* PRAETORIAN GUARD) formed a conspiracy against him, and he was assassinated.

**CALIPH,** title formerly given to the supreme leader of the Muslim community and successor of the Prophet Muhammad (q.v.). Under Muhammad the Muslim state was a theocracy, with the shari'a, the religious and moral principles of Islam (q.v.), as the law of the land. The caliphs, Muhammad's successors, were both secular and religious leaders. They were not empowered, however, to promulgate dogma, because the revelation of the faith was considered to have been completed by Muhammad.

The Sunnites (followers of the Sunna, the body of Islamic custom or the Way of the Prophet), who comprise a majority of Muslims, generally consider the period of the first four caliphs to be the golden age of Islam. Other sects, however, as they were formed, came to regard this period and subsequent caliphates differently, and as a result great hostility has frequently arisen between the Sunnites and other Muslims concerning the caliphate; *see* MUSLIM SECTS. During the course of Islamic history the issue of the caliphate probably has created more dissension than any other article of faith.

Based on the examples of the first four "rightly-guided" caliphs and companions of the Prophet, the Sunnites formulated the following requirements of the caliphate: the caliph should be an Arab of the Prophet Muhammad's tribe,

7

the Quraish; he should be elected to his office and approved by a council of elders representing the Muslim community; and he should be responsible for the enforcement of divine law and the spread of Islam by whatever means necessary, including war. In the history of the caliphate, however, all of these requirements were rarely met.

**The Immediate Successors.** Muhammad died in 632, leaving no instructions for the future government of the Muslim community. A group of Islamic leaders met in Medina, now in Saudi Arabia, the capital of the Muslim world at that time, and elected abu-Bakr (q.v.), the Prophet's father-in-law and closest associate, to lead the community. Abu-Bakr took for himself the title *khalifat rasul-Allah* (Ar., "successor to the Messenger of God"), from which the term caliph (Ar. *khalīfah*, "successor") is derived.

Omar I (581?–644) became the second caliph in 634. On his deathbed, abu-Bakr had designated Omar as his successor, and all the important members of the Muslim community immediately accepted Omar's succession. Under his leadership, the first great expansion of Islam outside of Arabia took place. Egypt, Syria, Iraq, and the northern part of Mesopotamia became Islamic territories, and the armies of the Persian Empire were routed several times. Omar added the title *amir-al-mum-inin* (Ar., "commander of the believers") to that of caliph.

After Omar's death in 644, Othman (575?–656), Muhammad's son-in-law and one of his first converts, was appointed the third caliph by a panel of six Meccan electors. Although an aged man, he carried on Omar's policy of territorial expansion. Eventually, however, Othman earned the enmity of many of his subjects who felt he favored the Meccan aristocracy in political and commercial affairs. Othman also antagonized the Islamic preachers by issuing an official text of the Koran (q.v.) with an accompanying order to destroy all other versions. Rebellious Muslim troops from Al Kufa (Iraq) and Egypt besieged Othman in Medina and assassinated him in 656.

Ali (q.v.), a cousin and son-in-law of Muhammad, was acknowledged as the fourth caliph by the Medinians and the rebellious Muslim troops. Muawiyah I (d. 680), then governor of Syria, refused to recognize Ali as caliph and called for vengeance for the death of Othman (who was Muawiyah's kinsman). In 657 the rival parties met at Siffin, on a plain in northern Syria, near the site of the modern city of El Rachid. There, after an inconclusive battle, they agreed to arbitrate the dispute. Ali found himself being considered as a mere candidate for the caliphate on equal grounds with Muawiyah. Angered by this indignity, and with Ali for submitting to it, a group of his followers, later known as the Kharijites, deserted and vowed to assassinate both Ali and Muawiyah. They succeeded in killing only Ali. Ali's son Hasan (about 624–69) then claimed (661) the still disputed caliphate, but Hasan abdicated within a few months under pressure from Muawiyah's supporters, who greatly outnumbered the Shi'ites.

**The Umayyad Caliphs (661–750).** The Umayyad, formerly Ommiad, caliphs were descendants of aristocratic caravan merchants, the Umayya, to which Muawiyah, the first Umayyad caliph, belonged. Muawiyah (r. 661–80) restored stability to the Muslim community after Ali's assassination. He moved the capital of Islam from Medina to Damascus, bringing the Muslim rulers into contact with the more advanced cultural and administrative traditions of the Byzantine Empire (q.v.). Muawiyah also dispensed with the practice of electing the caliphate by designating his son Yazid (d. 683) as heir apparent. The principle of election was acknowledged formally, however, by having the council of elders pledge to support the designated heir. The practice of hereditary succession continued throughout the Umayyad dynasty and in subsequent dynasties as well. Many Muslims, however, later disapproved of it as a deviation from the essential nature of Islam.

Yazid I (r. 680–83) succeeded his father but immediately was faced with two rebellions, each one supporting rival claimants to the caliphate. The Kufan Shi'ites recognized Ali's second son (and the Prophet's grandson), Husain (about 629–69) as caliph. Thus encouraged, Husain left Medina for Al Kufa, despite warnings that Yazid's troops had quelled the Kufic uprising. On the plain of Karbala', in Iraq, he and his small escort were intercepted and slaughtered. This event, more than any other, marks the true beginning of the Shi'ite schism. A second rebellion by Meccans was not finally quelled until the caliphate of Abd-al-Malik (r. 685–705), Yazid's third successor.

Shi'ite, Kharijite, and other groups of Muslims and non-Arabic converts (Ar., *mawāli*), frequently revolted against the Umayyads. The mawāli accused the Umayyads of religious laxity and of indifference to their demands for full brotherhood in the Muslim community. Umayyad caliphs, nevertheless, vastly enlarged the Islamic empire and created a bureaucracy capable of administering it. Under the Umayyads, Islamic armies swept eastward to the

Harun al-Rashid, fifth Abbasid caliph of Baghdad, receiving emissaries from Charlemagne. Granger Collection

borders of India and China, westward across North Africa to the Atlantic Ocean, then northward through Spain and over the Pyrenees Mts. into France, where the Frankish infantry under the Carolingian ruler Charles Martel (q.v.) checked them near Poitiers in 732.

**The Abbasid Caliphs (750–1258).** The Umayyads were overthrown by a combination of Shi'ite, Iranian, and other Muslim and non-Muslim groups dissatisfied with the Umayyad regime. The rebels were led by the Abbasid family, descendants of the Prophet's uncle Abbas (q.v.). From about 718 the Abbasids had plotted to take the caliphate, sending agents into various parts of the Islamic empire to spread propaganda against the Umayyads. By 747 they had secured enough support to organize a rebellion in northern Iran, which led to the defeat of the

Umayyad caliphate three years later. The Abbasids executed most of the Umayyad family, moved the capital of the Islamic empire to Baghdad, and assimilated much of the pomp and ceremony of the former Persian monarchy into their own courts.

Beginning in 750 with abu-al-Abbas (721?–54), thirty-seven Abbasid caliphs ruled. The Abbasid caliphate, which lasted five centuries, is the longest and most famous Islamic dynasty. The Abbasids became patrons of learning and encouraged religious observance. They were the first Muslim rulers to become leaders of an Islamic civilization and protectors of the religion rather than merely an Arab aristocracy imposing an Arab civilization on conquered lands. Under

9

their caliphate Baghdad replaced Medina as the center of theological activity, industry and commerce developed greatly, and the Islamic empire reached a peak of material and intellectual achievement.

The 8th- and 9th-century caliphs Harun-al-Rashid (q.v.) and his son Abdullah al-Ma'mun (r. 813–33) are especially renowned for their encouragement of intellectual pursuits and for the splendor of their courts. During their reigns scholars were invited to the court to debate various topics and translations were made from Greek, Persian, and Syriac works. Embassies also were exchanged with Charlemagne (q.v.), King of the Franks and Emperor of the West.

Later in the 9th century, the Abbasid caliphs increasingly began to delegate administrative responsibility to ministers of state and other government officials and to lose control over their Baghdad guards. As they gradually gave up personal political power, the caliphs placed more and more emphasis on their role as protectors of the faith. One of the results of the change in emphasis was the increased persecution of heretics and non-Muslims. About the same time, several successful revolts in the eastern provinces led to the establishment of independent principalities; and independent states were subsequently established in North Africa and in Spain. Eventually the power of the Abbasids barely extended outside Baghdad, and by the middle of the 10th century, the Abbasid caliphs had virtually no power, serving merely as figureheads at the mercy of the military commanders. The final defeat of the Abbasid dynasty came from outside the Islamic empire, when Mustasim (r. 1242–58), was put to death by the invading Mongols at the order of Hulagu (1217–65), the grandson of Genghis Khan (q.v.).

**The Abbasids in Cairo (1261–1517).** When the Mongols captured (1258) Baghdad, two members of the Abbasid family escaped to Egypt, where they took refuge with Baybars, the Mameluke sultan (see under BAYBARS; MAMELUKES). Each was named caliph, successively, by the sultan; but they were allowed to assume only religious duties, and the descendants of the second caliph remained politically powerless under the Mameluke sultans.

**The Fatimid Dynasty and the Umayyads of Spain.** During the decline of Abbasid power, two rival caliphates were established, one in North Africa, and another in Spain. The first, the Fatimid dynasty, was founded by Ubaydullah (d. 933), who proclaimed (909) himself caliph in Tunisia. The Fatimids were Shi'ites, claiming descent from Fatima (thus the name Fatimid), Muhammad's daughter, and her husband Ali, the fourth caliph of Islam. At the height of their power, in the latter half of the 10th century, the Fatimid caliphate constituted a serious threat to the Abbasids in Baghdad. The Fatimids ruled most of northern Africa from Egypt to present-day Algeria, as well as Sicily and Syria. In addition the Fatimids claimed the allegiance of other Shi'ites, both within and outside their domain. They sent missionaries from their capital in Cairo to the rest of the Muslim world proclaiming the Fatimid caliphs to be infallible and sinless and the bearers of divine illumination handed down directly from Ali. Their dynasty was overthrown in 1171 by Saladin (q.v.), Sultan of Egypt.

The second rival caliphate was established by Abd-er-Rahman III, who proclaimed himself caliph in Spain in 929; see under ABD-ER-RAHMAN. He was the grandson of an Umayyad prince who fled the Abbasid massacre of his family and settled (755) in Spain. The Umayyad dynasty of Spain, responsible for a brilliant period in Spanish history, ruled from its capital in Córdoba until 1031, when Córdoba was proclaimed a separate republic; see SPAIN: History.

**The Ottomans and the Modern Period.** From about the 13th century various monarchs throughout the Muslim world, particularly the Ottoman sultans (see TURKEY: History), assumed the title caliph indiscriminately without regard to the prescribed requirements of the caliphate. The title held little significance for the Ottoman sultans until their empire began to decline. In the 19th century, with the advent of Christian powers in the Near East, the sultan began to emphasize his role as caliph in an effort to gain the support of Muslims living outside the Ottoman Empire. The Ottoman Empire collapsed during the First World War (1914–18). After the war, Turkish nationalists deposed the sultan, but they allowed his successors to remain as caliphs, without temporal power. Finally, in March, 1924, the Turkish Grand National Assembly abolished the caliphate entirely.

The abolition of the caliphate brought consternation to many sections of the Muslim world, and protests were directed against the action of the Turkish government. Subsequently, King Husein ibn-Ali (1854–1931) of Hejaz (now part of Saudi Arabia) laid claim to the title by virtue of his direct descent from the Prophet and his control of the two holy cities, Mecca and Medina. His claim received little attention outside of Palestine, Syria, and parts of Arabia. The conquest (1925) of Hejaz by Abdul-

Aziz ibn-Saud (*see under* IBN-SAUD), ruler of Nejd, Arabia, made Husein's claim even less significant.

An international caliphate congress held in Cairo in 1926 to choose an acceptable caliph proved abortive, resulting only in an appeal to the Muslims of the world to work together to reestablish a caliphate. In the mid-20th century, preoccupation with national independence and economic problems in Muslim nations has diverted attention from the issue of the caliphate.

**CALIPHATE.** *See* CALIPH; ISLAM.

**CALISTHENICS.** *See* GYMNASTICS.

**CALIXTUS II.** *See* CALLISTUS II.

**CALLA,** genus of plants of the Arum family (Araceae). The only species of this genus, *C. palustris,* the water arum, is a perennial herb found in the North Temperate Zone in cold bogs of Canada, Eurasia, and the United States. The calla is about 10 in. tall, has heart-shaped leaves, and bears an oval white leaf surrounding a cluster of yellow blossoms that develop into red berries. The name calla is applied also to other plants of the same family, especially the golden calla, *Zantedeschia elliottiana,* and the so-called calla lily, *Z. aethiopica,* both native to southern Africa. The calla lily, also called lily of the Nile, is a herb that grows about 2½ ft. high and has large spear-tip leaves and a flower with a white flaring leaf around a cluster of tiny flowers. The black calla, *Arum palaestinum,* found in Palestine and Syria, has beautiful black-purple flowers. *See* ARUM.

**CALLAGHAN, Morley Edward.** *See* CANADIAN LITERATURE: *English-Canadian Literature.*

**CALLAO,** city and chief seaport of Peru, and capital of Callao Province, on Callao Bay on the Pacific coast, about 8 miles w. of Lima. The harbor, sheltered by the island of San Lorenzo, is one of the safest and most spacious in South America. Cargo-handling facilities include side wharves sufficient for the simultaneous berthage of more than ten ships, and steam cranes, modern warehouses, and cold-storage plants. The port is also equipped with extensive drydock facilities. More than 2000 vessels are cleared through the port annually. Among the chief exports are minerals, ores, cotton and cottonseed cake, sugar, cocoa, wool, and hides. The principal imports consist of textiles, grain, machinery, paper, coal, foodstuffs, and hardware. In addition to numerous commercial establishments, Callao has various manufacturing industries, including lumber making, sugar refining, brewing, and iron making.

Callao was founded by the Spanish in 1537, and thereafter it developed as one of the most active ports on the w. coast of South America. Frequently raided by British buccaneers, the town was destroyed by an earthquake and tidal wave in 1796, with the loss of 6000 lives. It was later rebuilt, and remained a possession of Spain until 1821, when Peruvian independence from Spain was proclaimed. Pop. (1970) 355,400.

**CALLAS, Maria** (1923– ), American operatic soprano, born Maria Calogeropoulos in New York City. At the age of thirteen she was enrolled in the Royal Conservatory in Athens, Greece, to continue vocal studies begun five years earlier in the United States. She made her professional debut in Athens at fifteen. In 1950 she sang at La Scala (q.v.) in Milan; in 1954 she made her American debut with the Lyric Opera in Chicago, Ill.; and in 1956 she appeared with the Metropolitan Opera Company (q.v.) in New York City. Miss Callas announced her retirement from performing in 1965; but in 1973 she announced her return to the concert stage. Meanwhile she had appeared (1969) in the nonsinging title role of the film *Medea;* begun teaching in 1971 at the Juilliard School of Music (q.v.); and in 1973 served as co-director of the opera *I Vespri Siciliani* in Turin, Italy. Praised by critics for both the beauty of her voice and her acting ability, she specialized in coloratura roles in the bel canto repertory. *See* OPERA; SOPRANO.

**CALLES, Plutarco Elías** (1877–1945), Mexican soldier and statesman, born in Guaymas, in the State of Sonora. Calles gave up a teaching career to help the revolt of General Venustiano Carranza against President Victoriano Huerta (qq.v.) in 1914. During the Carranza administration Calles was governor of Sonora, and secretary of industry, commerce, and labor from 1919 to 1920. In 1920 Calles assisted General Álvaro Obregón (q.v.) in overthrowing Carranza, and was made secretary of the interior from 1920 to 1923, when Obregón became president. In 1924 Calles succeeded Obregón as president of Mexico. Notable among the achievements of his administration were the construction of many new highways and a number of irrigation projects; the founding of the Bank of Mexico; amortization of the public debt; encouragement of public education and the organization of labor; and the effective application of agrarian reform laws, including division of large estates among small farmers. In 1928 Calles retired to private life, but in subsequent years he served in various offices and was an adviser to the three presidents who succeeded him. In 1936 Calles was exiled because of his criticism of the social reform policies of President Lázaro Cárdenas (q.v.) but he returned to Mexico in 1941.

**CALLICRATES** (fl. 5th cent. B.C.), Greek architect. Callicrates designed the Temple of Athena Nike, or the Wingless Victory, on the Acropolis (q.v.) in Athens about 427 B.C. He collaborated with the Greek architect Ictinus (q.v.) in designing the Parthenon (q.v.) in Athens, under the direction of the Greek sculptor Phidias (q.v.).

**CALLIGRAPHY,** art of formally elegant or ornate handwriting. A revered skill in the East, calligraphy was practiced in China from the 5th century B.C. and later by the professional scribe (q.v.) in Greece, and through history evolved into various scripts. It has been especially important in the civilization of Islam (q.v.), in which decorated mosques and elaborately written copies of the Koran are a tradition. In the West calligraphy reached its peak during the Middle Ages and the Renaissance (q.v.), notably in the Gothic script of European monastic art; *see* ILLUMINATED MANUSCRIPTS. *See also* WRITING.

**CALLIMACHUS** (fl. 3rd cent. B.C.), Alexandrian poet and grammarian, born in Cyrene (now Shahat, Libya), Africa, and educated in Athens. After teaching at Eleusis, near Alexandria, Egypt, Callimachus was appointed by King Ptolemy II (*see under* PTOLEMY) as chief librarian of the famous library in Alexandria, an office he held for about twenty years; *see* ALEXANDRIAN LIBRARY. By his teaching and writing Callimachus exerted a great influence on the celebrated scholars and poets of the day. Callimachus reputedly wrote more than 800 books. Of his learned works in prose one of the most important was the *Pinakes,* a huge catalog of the works contained in the Alexandrian library. Through this catalog Callimachus became the founder of the critical study of Greek literature. As a poet he won distinction chiefly through his elegies and other short poems, of which six hymns and about sixty epigrams are extant. Also surviving are fragments of his most outstanding poetic work, *Aetia,* a collection of Greek legends in elegiac verse (*see* GREEK LITERATURE: *The Early Period*), and the short epic *Hecale; see* EPIC POETRY. He extolled the short, highly elaborated poem in preference to the lengthier forms in which his rival and former pupil Apollonius of Rhodes (q.v.) excelled. In this field Callimachus greatly influenced the Roman poets, especially Catullus, Ovid, and Propertius (qq.v.). *See also* ALEXANDRIAN AGE; GREEK LITERATURE: *The Hellenistic Period.*

**CALLIONYMUS.** *See* DRAGONET.

**CALLIOPE.** *See* MUSES.

**CALLISTUS II** *or* **CALIXTUS II,** original name GUY OF BURGUNDY (d. 1124), pope from 1119 to 1124. He expelled from Rome the antipope Gregory VIII (r. 1118–21) and in 1122 concluded the Concordat of Worms with Holy Roman Emperor Henry V (q.v.). The latter action ended the controversy between the Western Christian Church and the Holy Roman Empire over the question of lay investiture (*see* INVESTITURE).

**CALLOT, Jacques** (1592–1635), French engraver and etcher, born in Nancy. At the age of sixteen Callot was apprenticed in Italy as an engraver, but he abandoned engraving for etching, and became a renowned master of the art; *see* ENGRAVING; ETCHING. Noted for his realism, Callot depicted scenes of gypsies, court life, and the horrors of war. In the early part of his career he etched scenes of the *commedia dell' arte* (q.v.) for his patron, Cosimo II de' Medici, Grand Duke of Tuscany (1590–1621). Returning to France in 1622, Callot was subsequently commissioned by several contemporary rulers, including Louis XIII (q.v.), King of France, for whom he etched the siege of La Rochelle (q.v.) and the series entitled "Views of Paris". His masterpiece, "The Miseries of War", was completed shortly before his death.

**CALLUNA.** *See* HEATH.

**CALLUS,** thickened, horny area on the outer layer of the skin (q.v.), caused by local abrasion or friction against hard surfaces. The hands and feet are particularly susceptible to calluses, which commonly form as a result of heavy footwork or exertion in manual work or sports. Calluses on the hand are usually caused by prolonged gripping of implements such as garden tools or athletic equipment, for example, tennis rackets or baseball bats. *See also* BUNION.

**CALMAR.** *See* KALMAR.

**CALOCHORTUS,** genus of about forty plants of the Lily family (Liliaceae), closely related to the tulips. The various species are native to western North America, where they are variously known as Mariposa lily, star tulip, globe tulip, and butterfly tulip. The plants have corms (bulblike roots) from which grow leafy, branched stems bearing showy flowers of white, red, yellow, and lilac, often darker toward the center. *Calochortus venustus,* the butterfly tulip, is one of the handsomest and most variable species. *Calochortus nuttali,* the sego lily, is a desert species with beautiful bell-shaped flowers and edible corms; it is the State flower of Utah.

**CALORIE,** unit of measurement for heat. The small or gram calorie (cal.) is usually specified in science and engineering as the amount of heat required to raise the temperature of 1 gram of water from 14.5° C. to 15.5° C. The temperature interval is sometimes specified in other ways. One small calorie is equivalent to 4.1840 absolute joules, or 0.003966 British thermal unit (q.v.) or B.T.U. This definition is now generally accepted in the United States, and is standard in thermochemistry (q.v.).

A slightly different calorie is used in engineering, the international (I.T.) calorie, which equals $\frac{1}{860}$ international watt-hour. A large or kilocalorie (Cal.), sometimes referred to as kilogram calorie, equals 1000 small calories, and is the unit generally used to express the energy-producing value of food in the calculation of diets. *See* CALORIMETRY; HEAT; NUTRITION, HUMAN.

**CALORIMETRY,** science of measuring quantity of heat (expressed in calories), as distinct from thermometry, science of measuring intensity of heat (expressed as temperature). A calorimeter is the instrument used to measure the amount of heat; one widely used type consists of an insulated container of water, a stirring device, and a thermometer (q.v.). A heat source is placed in the calorimeter, the water is stirred until equilibrium is reached, and the rise of temperature is noted by reading the thermometer. Since the heat capacity of the calorimeter is known (or can be measured by using a standard heat source), the amount of heat liberated is readily calculated. When the heat source is a hot object of known temperature, the specific and latent heat may be measured as the object cools. When the heat source is a chemical reaction, such as the burning of a fuel, the reacting substances are placed in a heavy steel vessel called a bomb. The bomb is placed within the calorimeter, and the reaction started by ignition with an electric spark. *See* HEAT; TEMPERATURE.

**CALPE.** *See* PILLARS OF HERCULES.

**CALTANISETTA,** city of Italy, on the island of Sicily, capital of Caltanisetta Province, on a hill, 1930 ft. above sea level, about 60 miles S.E. of Palermo. Caltanisetta has a castle, a cathedral, a school of technology, and a school of mines. Two miles to the E. is a Norman monastery erected in 1153 by Roger II. Nearby, at Terra Pilata, are a mud volcano and an oil well. Caltanisetta is the center of the sulfur industry of Sicily. Pop. (1971 prelim.) 60,473.

**CALTHA.** *See* MARSH MARIGOLD.

**CALUMET CITY,** formerly WEST HAMMOND, city of Illinois, in Cook Co. It is a suburb of Chicago, about 5 miles S.W. of Lake Michigan, and, to the E., adjoins Hammond, Ind. Canning, bottling, meat packing, and the manufacture of fertilizers and chemicals are the principal industries. The city was incorporated in 1925. Pop. (1960) 25,000; (1970) 32,956.

**CALVARY** (Lat. *calvaria*, "skull"), hill just outside of Jerusalem on which the crucifixion of

*"The Crucifixion", an oil painting by the Flemish artist Hubert van Eyck (1366?–1426), depicts the traditional scene on the hill of Calvary.* Metropolitan Museum of Art

Jesus Christ took place. It has been identified as a place of execution where malefactors were flung from cliffs and stoned to death.

In Roman Catholic countries a calvary is a representation, either in a chapel or outside a church, of the scenes of the Passion and crucifixion of Jesus Christ. The representation is usually of three crosses with the life-size figures of Christ and the thieves, surrounded by figures of the various personages who took part in the crucifixion. Representations of Christ's sufferings on His way to be executed, known as Stations of the Cross (q.v.), line the way to Calvary. The Via Dolorosa is the name given to the approach to Calvary. *See also* GOLGOTHA.

**CALVE, Emma,** stage name of EMMA DE ROQUER (1858–1942), French dramatic soprano, born in Decazeville. She studied under the German mezzo-soprano Mathilde Marchesi (1821–1913), and made her operatic debut in Brussels in 1882 as Marguerite in *Faust,* by the French composer Charles François Gounod (q.v.). In 1884 Calvé created the part of Bianca in *Aben Hamet* by the French composer Théodore Dubois (1837–1924). She made her New York debut in 1893 as Santuzza in *Cavalleria Rusticana,* by the Italian composer Pietro Mascagni (q.v.). The French composer Jules Émile Fréderic Massenet (q.v.) wrote the part of Anita in his opera *La Navarraise* especially for her in 1894. After 1910 she devoted most of her time to concert tours. Known particularly for her performances of the leading role in *Carmen,* she sang the part first in New York in 1893. Her dramatic powers gained for her the reputation of being the greatest Carmen who had ever performed the role.

**CALVERT,** name of an English family, the members of which, under the title Baron Baltimore, played an important part in the colonization of Maryland; see MARYLAND: *History.*

**George Calvert, 1st Baron Baltimore** (1580?–1632), born in Yorkshire, and educated at Trinity College, University of Oxford. After being elected to Parliament in 1609, George Calvert was knighted in 1617 by James I (q.v.), King of England, and became his secretary of state in 1619. In 1625 Calvert became a Roman Catholic and, because no Catholics were then permitted to hold public office in England, resigned from Parliament. James rewarded him for his public service, however, by granting him large estates in Ireland and giving him the title Baron Baltimore. Thereafter Lord Baltimore devoted himself to establishing colonies in the New World. In 1623 Calvert received a charter for the colony of Avalon, Newfoundland (q.v.), which he had founded in 1621. In 1628 he and his family went to live in Avalon, but because of the harsh climate he decided to establish a colony farther to the south. In 1632 Charles I (q.v.), King of Eng-

*An engraving of the English colonist George Calvert, 1st Baron Baltimore.*      Bettmann Archive

land, granted him a tract of land to the northeast of the colony of Virginia. The grant comprised the present-day Sates of Maryland and Delaware and was named Maryland in honor of Charles' wife, Henrietta Maria (q.v.), Queen Consort of England. Calvert wrote the charter for the new colony, but died before it was granted to him officially.

**Cecilius Calvert, 2nd Baron Baltimore** (1605–75), elder son of George Calvert. After his father's death, the charter for Maryland was issued to Cecilius. He is considered the real founder of Maryland and although he never visited the region, he sent settlers there under his brother Leonard Calvert (see below) and after its settlement supervised the affairs of the colony from England. As the first Lord Proprietor of Maryland, Calvert founded the colony as a haven where Roman Catholics and other religious groups could worship together without being persecuted.

**Leonard Calvert** (1606–47), second son of George Calvert and younger brother of Cecilius. In 1634 he led a company of 200 colonists to Maryland. He became the first governor of the proprietary province of Maryland in 1634, and served in that capacity until his death.

**Charles Calvert, 3rd Baron Baltimore** (1637–1715), son of Cecilius Calvert. Charles became the second Lord Proprietor of the colony of Maryland in 1675 upon the death of his father. As the Roman Catholic proprietor of a predominantly Protestant colony, Charles was accused of undemocratic policies. He was deprived of the colonial charter following the Glorious Revolution (q.v.) of 1688, after which a royal government was established in the colony.

**CALVIN, John,** originally JEAN CHAUVIN or JEAN CAULVIN (1509–64), French theologian and religious reformer, born in Noyon, Picardy, and educated at the Collège de la Marche and Collège de Montaigu, in Paris. He was appointed to the curacy of Saint Martin de Martheville at the age of eighteen and later to the curacy of Pont l'Évêque. Because of his skill at disputation, his father sent him to study law at the University of Orléans in 1528 and later in Bourges. After his father's death in 1531, however, he returned to Paris to study the classics and Hebrew. At that time, he became interested in the principles of the Reformation (q.v.) and, after experiencing what he later termed a sudden conversion, variously dated from 1529 to 1534, he began preaching Reformation doctrines in Paris. To avoid government persecution, Calvin traveled from place to place and in 1536 settled in Switzerland. In Basel, in that year, he completed the first version of his *Institutes of the Christian Religion,* which had a profound effect on the course of the Reformation. Intended only as a brief manual stating the doctrines of the persecuted Protestants, it in fact contained a complete outline of his system of theology. The work, based on the principle that the Scriptures are the sole source of Christian truth, was later revised and enlarged.

In 1536, at the request of the religious reformer Guillaume Farel (1489–1565), Calvin settled in Geneva (q.v.), where he acquired a large following and was elected preacher by the city magistrates. He compiled a systematic Protestant confession of faith of twenty-one articles, which the citizens were required to profess under oath, and wrote the first Geneva *Catechism* (1536) for use in religious instruction. The reforms he advocated were so extreme, however, that he alienated many of his adherents and provoked strong political opposition. Exiled from Geneva in 1538, Calvin went to Strasbourg, France, and became a pastor and professor of theology. He represented that city at the imperial diets of Worms and Regensburg (qq.v.). In Geneva, irreligion and disorder became prevalent during Calvin's absence, and he was persuaded to return in 1541. He revised the laws of the city, organizing a theocratic form of government for the control of both the social and the religious life of the citizens. His second Geneva *Catechism* (1542) became the standard of doc-

*John Calvin*　　　　　Swiss National Tourist Office

trines for most of the Reformed churches in Europe. Calvin's rigid dogmatism and severe discipline led to controversies, not only with Roman Catholics, but with other religious reformers of the time. His differences with the German reformer Martin Luther (q.v.) about the nature of the Lord's Supper (q.v.) resulted in the splitting of the evangelical churches into the two great Lutheran (see LUTHERANISM) and Reformed (see REFORMED CHURCHES) groups, and Calvin's strictness gave rise to discontent even among his followers in Geneva. One of the most acrimonious disputes of this period was his controversy on the nature of the Trinity (q.v.) with the Spanish theologian Michael Servetus (q.v.), who, through Calvin's influence, was burned at the stake in 1553.

Calvin's political foes, known as the "Libertines", were expelled from Geneva in 1555, and for the next six years, with that city as a center, Calvin deepened and extended his influence and that of Protestantism throughout Europe. He both systematized the doctrines of Protestantism and organized its ecclesiastical discipline, constructing and making firm a new church polity that consolidated the scattered forces of the Reformation. Among Calvin's most important works are *Institutio Religionis Christianae* (1559; *Institutes of the Christian Religion*), *De Necessitate Reformandae Ecclesiae* (1544; *The Necessity of Reforming the Church,* 1843), *Commentaires sur la Concordance ou Harmonie des Evangélistes* (1561; *Commentary on a Har-*

*mony of the Evangelists,* 1846), *In Novum Testamentum Commentarii* (*New Testament Commentaries*), *In Libros Psalmorum Commentarii* (1557; *Commentary on the Psalms*), and *In Librum Geneseos Commentarii* (*Commentary on the Book of Genesis,* 1578). *See* CALVINISM.

**CALVIN, Melvin** (1911– ), American chemist, born in Saint Paul, Minn., and educated at the Michigan College of Mining and Technology (now Michigan Technological University) and at the universities of Minnesota and of Manchester, England. He joined the department of chemistry of the University of California, at Berkeley, in 1937. During the 1940's Calvin started his experiments in photosynthesis. Using radioactive carbon-14, Calvin was able to detect the sequence of chemical reactions produced by plants in converting gaseous carbon dioxide and water into oxygen and carbohydrates. For this discovery he was awarded the 1961 Nobel Prize in chemistry. He wrote *Chemical Evolution* (1961).

**CALVINISM,** religious system based on the teachings of the French theologian and reformer John Calvin (q.v.) and his associates. Generally, the system may be said to be distinctive of the Reformed churches other than the Lutheran and Anglican churches; *see* CHURCH OF ENGLAND; LUTHERANISM.

The core of Calvinist doctrine is the belief in the absolute, divine sovereignty of God, in His election of some individuals to salvation, and in His rejection of others, according to His inscrutable will. The teachings of Calvin include many other tenets that are held in common by numerous Protestant communions, including, for example, the doctrine of original sin and that of the fall of man; belief in Jesus Christ, and in His incarnation and death on the cross as the basis of salvation; belief in the possibility of achieving saving grace through Christ, and through the Church and sacraments (symbols of grace) as His selected channels; and belief that the chief end of man is the glorification of God.

Many of Calvin's tenets had profound social implications, in particular, the developed doctrine that thrift, industry, and hard work are forms of moral virtue and that business success is an evidence of God's grace. Of equal social significance was Calvin's attack on the traditional Christian prohibition against collecting interest on borrowed money. Because widespread acceptance of these views helped to create a climate favorable to commerce and industry, Calvinism played an important role in the overthrow of feudalism and the establishment of capitalism (qq.v.). In addition, Calvinist emphasis on the importance of the individual and on self-rule by individual churches is widely interpreted as having encouraged the rise of democracy.

The most authentic and formal expression of Calvinist doctrines is the Westminster Confession of Faith, which was promulgated in 1646 by an assembly of English clergymen and laymen. With some revisions and reinterpretations, the Confession forms the basic creed of the Church of Scotland and of numerous other Presbyterian groups in the United Kingdom and the United States.

Both before and after the death (1564) of its founder, Calvinism became the creed of Protestant communions in many lands. In addition to the theocracy founded (1536) by John Calvin and his followers in Geneva, Switzerland, the Calvinists founded the Huguenot (*see* HUGUENOTS) movement in France, the Reformed Churches of the Rhineland, and the Presbyterian Church and other Reformed churches in Scotland and North America. During the 17th century the Church of England passed through a Calvinist phase known as Puritanism (*see* PURITANS). Many of the Puritans, dissatisfied with the policies of the Church of England, migrated to North America, notably to the New England area, which they dominated until the 18th century. Calvinist doctrines subsequently continued, under various names, to exercise a powerful influence on Protestantism. In the late 1960's various religious groups in the U.S. that were basically Calvinist in theology and form of government numbered approximately 4,600,000.

*See* PRESBYTERIANISM; REFORMED CHURCHES.  V.F.

**CALVO, Carlos** (1824–1906), Argentine diplomat, historian, and specialist in international law, born in Buenos Aires. As a diplomat Calvo represented at various times both Paraguay and Argentina as minister to Berlin, Belgium, Paris, London, Saint Petersburg (now Leningrad), and Vienna. Today he is remembered for his writings on international law (q.v.) and as one of the founders of the Institute of International Law at Ghent, Belgium, in 1873. His principal work, *The Theoretical and Practical International Law of Europe and America,* was first published in 1863. Calvo also compiled a fifteen-volume collection of Latin American treaties, published from 1862 to 1867. In the latter part of his career Calvo enunciated the so-called Calvo Doctrine that has since become a part of several Latin American constitutions. This doctrine states that people living in a foreign nation should settle claims and complaints by submitting to the jurisdiction of local courts and not by using either diplomatic pressure or armed intervention from their own government. The Calvo Doctrine is sometimes confused with the Drago Doctrine (*see* DRAGO, LUIS MARÍA), which is a narrower application of the same principle. Calvo justified his doctrine as necessary to prevent the abuse of the jurisdiction of weak nations by more powerful nations. Calvo's writings had a decided influence on the development of international law in the 20th century.

**CALVO DOCTRINE.** *See* CALVO, CARLOS.

**CALYCANTHUS,** genus of aromatic shrubs native to North America, of the family Calycanthaceae, also known as shrub, sweet-shrub, or strawberry-shrub. These shrubs are bushy, with opposite leaves and fragrant flowers. The best-known species is *C. floridus,* which usually grows more than 6 ft. high and produces attractive mahogany-colored flowers. It is found in the southern region of the Allegheny Mts. Also growing in this region is *C. fertilis,* which has purple-brown flowers. These eastern species are popularly called Carolina allspice. The tallest species of this genus, *C. occidentalis,* is native to the Pacific region of the United States and is known as California allspice or spicebush. It has light brown flowers and sometimes reaches a height of 10 ft. The bark of all the known species of *Calycanthus* is aromatic.

**CALYPSO,** form of folk music developed in Trinidad, West Indies, and originally sung at carnivals. The derivation of the name and of the musical form is uncertain. Frequently improvised, the words of calypso songs usually deal with topical or satirical themes, and they are characterized technically by arbitrary shifts in the accentuation of everyday English words. In Trinidad calypso music is generally sung to a guitar accompaniment that establishes a complex counterrhythm with the voice of the singer in a style probably based upon the percussive rhythms of native African music.

**CALYPSO,** in Greek mythology, a sea nymph and daughter of the Titan Atlas (q.v.). Calypso lived alone on the mythical island of Ogygia in the Ionian Sea. When the Greek hero Odysseus (*see* ULYSSES) was shipwrecked on Ogygia, she fell in love with him and kept him a virtual prisoner for seven years. Although she promised him immortality and eternal youth if he would stay with her, she could not overcome his desire to return home. At the bidding of the god Zeus (q.v.) she finally released Odysseus and gave him materials to build a raft to leave the island. She died of grief after he departed. *See* ODYSSEY.

**CAM,** part of a machine used to provide a repetitive straight-line or back-and-forth motion to a second part, known as the follower. Cams are used to open and close the inlet and exhaust valves of an automotive engine, to index parts of automatic machinery for mass production, to operate a sequence of control switches in electrical equipment, and in many other machines. Complex cam shapes may be required to produce a desired motion.

Three types of cams are in common use, the most common being the disk cam illustrated in Fig. (a). The cam profile here is cut from a disk mounted on a rotating shaft. The follower can be a flat plate moving vertically in a straight line, or a roller or a knife-edge that moves in a straight line or is pivoted. The follower is usually spring-loaded to retain contact with the cam. The second type of cam commonly used is the cylinder cam shown in Fig. (b), the follower in which is a pivoted roller moving along a groove cut into a cylindrical cam rotor. The third type is the translation cam shown in Fig. (c), in which the required profile that defines the motion is cut into a flat plate that moves back and forth. The follower shown in the figure is a spring-loaded knife-edge that moves up and down. It can be observed from the figures that the motion of the follower can be changed easily, to obtain a desired sequence, by altering the shape of the cam profile.

*Three types of cams. (a) Disk cam; (b) Cylinder cam; (c) Translation cam.*

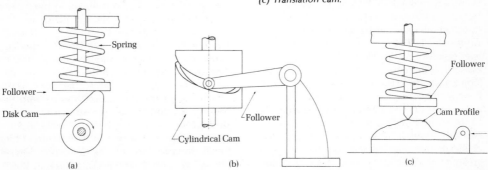

| (a) | (b) | (c) |

**CAM, Diogo** *or* **CÃO, Diogo** (fl. 15th cent.), Portuguese navigator and explorer. During voyages made between 1482 and 1484 and again in 1485 and 1486, he discovered the mouth of the Congo R. and was the first white man to explore the western coast of Africa as far south as Cape Cross, near what is now Walvis Bay, in southwestern Africa. He marked the territories he discovered by erecting four pillars inscribed with the Portuguese royal arms, three of which have since been transferred to museums. In recognition of his services, John II (q.v.), King of Portugal, made Cam a noble in 1484, promoted him to the rank of cavalier, and granted him an annuity.

**CAMACHO.** See ÁVILA CAMACHO, MANUEL.

**CAMAGÜEY,** formerly PUERTO PRÍNCIPE, city in Cuba, and capital of Camagüey Province, about 315 miles S.E. of Havana, and about 40 miles S.W. of Nuevitas, its port. It is the largest inland city of Cuba. Lying at the junction of railroads and highways, it is an important commercial center with a large trade in cattle, hides, and sugar, which the province produces. Industries in the city include sawmilling, distilling, tanning, and processing of meat and dairy products. The city has a cathedral and many beautiful churches and mansions. Founded in 1514 by the Spanish governor of Cuba, Diego Velásquez (q.v.), the original settlement occupied a site on the N. coast of Cuba; it was moved to its present site about 1530. In 1668 the city was seized and sacked by pirates under the English buccaneer Sir Henry Morgan (q.v.). Pop. (1970) 196,854.

**CAMBACÉRÈS, Jean Jacques Régis, Duc de** (1753–1824), French statesman and jurist, born in Montpellier. Educated as a lawyer, Cambacérès became president of the criminal court in Montpellier in 1791. During the French Revolution (q.v.), he was elected to the National Convention and voted somewhat reluctantly for the execution of Louis XVI (q.v.), King of France. Avoiding party politics, Cambacérès concentrated on legal matters and formulated the civil code from which the Code Napoléon (q.v.) was eventually derived. In 1796 he became a member of the Council of Five Hundred, the lower house of the new legislature set up by the constitution of 1795. In June, 1799, he became minister of justice, and in November of that year he assisted in the coup d'etat that brought Napoléon Bonaparte to power as First Consul; in 1804 Bonaparte became emperor of France as Napoleon I (q.v.). In 1799 Cambacérès was appointed to the second highest position in the nation as Second Consul, in 1804 he was made archchancellor of the empire, and in 1808 Napoleon created him Duke of Parma. In 1813–14 Camba-

cérès directed civil affairs as president of the Council of Regency, finally voting for Napoleon's abdication. During the Hundred Days, however, he again served Napoleon as minister of justice and president of the House of Peers. After the second Bourbon restoration (see LOUIS XVIII), Cambacérès returned to Paris, but he was exiled in 1816 because of his involvement in the death of Louis XVI. His legal and political rights were restored to him in 1818, and he returned to France.

**CAMBAY, GULF OF,** inlet of the Arabian Sea on the western coast of the Republic of India, between the Kathiawar Peninsula and the mainland of India. The gulf, which is cornucopia-shaped, is 130 mi. long and about 125 mi. wide at the mouth, and is noted for high tides of from 30 to 40 ft. Four rivers empty into the gulf, the Sabarmati, Mahi, Narmada, and Tapti. The city of Cambay at the head of the gulf was a prosperous port in the 15th century, but later lost its importance when silting almost sealed it off from the gulf. Surat (q.v.), a port on the mouth of the Tapti R., has also been affected by silting. The most important trading center today is the deep-sea port of Bhavnagar (q.v.) on the Kathiawar Peninsula.

**CAMBERWELL,** city of Australia, in Melbourne Statistical Division, in Victoria State, 6 miles E. of Melbourne. The city, center of a fruit-growing area, was named for a former metropolitan borough of London.

**CAMBIUM.** See TREE: *Life Processes.*

**CAMBODIA,** officially DEMOCRATIC KAMPUCHEA, nation of Southeast Asia, bounded on the N.E. by Laos, on the E. and S.E. by Vietnam, on the S.W. by the Gulf of Siam, and on the W. and N.W. by Thailand. The country is situated between lat. 10° N. and lat. 15° N. and long. 102° E. and long. 107°40′ E. The area is 69,884 sq.mi.

*THE LAND*

Cambodia comprises three physical regions: a large alluvial plain that occupies the N. and most of the center and S., a low, undulating plateau in the E., and a mountainous region in the W. The main features of the alluvial plain are the Mekong R., which flows from N. to S. through Cambodia, and the Tonle Sap (Cambodian, "great lake"), which covers an area of 1000 to 4000 sq.mi., depending on the season. The outlet of Tonle Sap is a river of the same name, which during the dry season flows S. into the Mekong R.; during the rainy season the waters of the Mekong R. back into the Tonle Sap, inundating the central part of the country. Chief mountain ranges include the Cardamom Mts. in the S.W. and the Phanom Dang Raek in the N.

cranes, pheasants, and wild ducks. Snakes and insects are widespread.

### THE PEOPLE

About 85 percent of the people are Cambodians, ethnically known as Khmers. The Chinese and Vietnamese comprise about 10 percent. The remainder includes Laotians, Thais, Europeans, Japanese, and the Cham-Malays, who inhabit the mountainous regions. The population is primarily rural.

**Population.** The population of Cambodia (census 1962) was 5,728,771; the United Nations estimated (1969) 6,701,000. The overall population density is 96 per sq.mi. (U.N. est. 1969).

**Political Divisions and Principal Cities.** The country is divided into seventeen provinces, which are subdivided into districts, townships, or village groups.

The capital and largest city is Phnom Penh (pop., 1970 est., 600,000), situated at the junction of the Mekong and Tonle Sap rivers. Other major cities are Battambang (40,000), Kompong

About 50 percent of the land is forested, and an additional 14 percent is cultivated. Some small but valuable mineral deposits are found. Cambodia has an enormous waterpower potential, but development of this resource was only in the stage of preliminary planning in the late 1960's.

**Climate.** Cambodia is within the Torrid Zone, but the climate is not excessively hot, as the heavy rains have a moderating influence. The annual temperatures range between 70° and 90° F. The rainy season extends from mid-April through mid-October. Average annual rainfall is 58 in. on the central plains, and 150 to 200 in. in the mountainous areas and along the rivers.

**Plants and Animals.** The mountainous regions support dense virgin forests, and the savannas are covered with high, sharp grass. Such trees as rubber, kapok, palm, coconut, and banana are common.

Elephants, deer, wild oxen, buffalo, panthers, bears, and tigers abound. The bird life includes

*A Cambodian princess, wearing a ceremonial costume that includes a mokot or tiara, takes part in a traditional Cambodian dance.* UPI

*A family of Cambodian farmers work in their rice paddies near Phnom Penh.*

Cham (30,000), and Kampot (13,000). The major port is Kompong Som, formerly Sihanoukville, on the Gulf of Siam.

**Language and Religion.** The official language is Khmer, or Cambodian; the secondary language is French.

About 90 percent of the people practice Theravada (formerly Hinayana) Buddhism, the state religion. The remainder are Roman Catholics, Muslims, and adherents of religions related to Buddhism. The mountain tribes are animists.

**Education.** About 45 percent of the population is literate, and the number is increasing. Government plans to modernize the entire educational system are being realized; and educational assistance is provided by foreign countries. All public education is free. In the late 1960's about 1,000,000 pupils attended some 5000 primary schools; and approximately 107,000 students attended some 200 secondary schools. UNIVERSITIES AND COLLEGES. The National University of Phnom Penh has seven faculties and about 4000 students. Other institutions of higher learning include schools of administration and public works. In the late 1960's annual student enrollment totaled about 14,500.

**Culture.** The cultural heritage of the Khmer dynasties is reflected in many facets of contemporary Cambodia. Many buildings, such as the Royal Palace in Phnom Penh, are decorated in the Khmer architectural style and use such motifs as the garuda, a mythical symbolic bird in the Hindu religion. Handicraft items, often in woven gold or silver lamé, also reflect ancient motifs. The classical Cambodian dance mimes in the most traditional style the legendary lives of ancient religious deities.

**Archeology.** The ruins of the ancient Khmer empire, found in N.W. Cambodia, constitute one of the richest and most remarkable archeological sites in the world. Hundreds of magnificently preserved temples, monuments, stelae, and friezes have been reclaimed from the forest. Particularly noteworthy are the ruins of the Khmer capital of Angkor Thom, built about 850 A.D., and, to the s., the temple of Angkor Wat (or Angor Vat), built between 1112 and 1152.

The buildings in Angkor Thom are characterized by magnitude, unity and grandeur of design, and delicate, profuse ornamentation. In the center of the city, which was enclosed by a moat and wall, stands Bayon, the national temple. This monumental building has a large central tower with encircling galleries and four enormous portals. Each of the gates is a carved representation of the face of Siva, one of the supreme deities of Hinduism (qq.v.). Well-preserved ruins of other temples, the ancient royal palace, and other notable buildings are scattered over the site of Angkor Thom. Angkor Wat, a temple dedicated to the composite god-king Vishnu-Siva, is generally regarded as the most magnificent product of Khmer architecture and contains priceless examples of Khmer art. The temple, a three-stepped pyramid constructed of varicolored sandstone and limonite blocks, is surmounted by five impressive pineapple-shaped towers.

## THE ECONOMY

Agriculture is the mainstay of the economy. To

expand other sectors of the economy, the government is trying to develop natural resources, improve agricultural and related activities, and initiate new industrial enterprises. Joint control or total nationalization of certain enterprises is in effect, and all exports and imports are state-controlled. The development of the resources of the lower Mekong basin is expected to be of major economic importance. In a recent year budget figures showed about $150,000,000 in revenue and $190,000,000 in expenditures. Because of the war in Indochina, however, revenues have fallen and expenditures have risen; and the United States has supplied important economic aid.

**Agriculture.** More than half of the 4,000,000 acres of cultivated land is devoted to the production of rice. In 1970 some 3,800,000 metric tons of rice and 12,800 tons of crude rubber were produced annually. Other important products include corn, soybeans, sesame, palm sugar, and pepper.

**Forest, Fishing, and Mining Industries.** Of the extensive potentially valuable forests, only a small proportion is being exploited, mainly because of poor transportation facilities. Pine, mangrove, bamboo, and teak are among the exploited hardwoods.

The Tonle Sap provides one of the largest freshwater fishery resources in Southeast Asia. About 25,000 tons of carp are caught annually.

Zircons, sapphires, and rubies are mined in limited amounts in the w., and salt is found in the central provinces. A phosphate plant was built in 1966 to begin the exploitation of deposits estimated at 700,000 tons.

**Manufacturing.** In the early 1970's industries included motor-vehicle assembly, distilling, sawmilling, rice-milling, fish canning, and the manufacture of cigarettes, matches, textiles, plywood, paper, cement, tires, pottery, and glassware.

**Currency and Banking.** The unit of currency is the riel, consisting of 100 sen (1 riel equals U.S.$0.0075; 1973). The Cambodian National Bank is the sole bank of issue. In 1964 all banks were nationalized and the National bank assumed all banking functions.

**Commerce and Trade.** The principal exports are rice and rice products, rubber, corn, and wood products. The total value of exports in the early 1970's was about $63,000,000 annually. The chief imports are metals, machinery, textiles, mineral products, and foodstuffs; their total value was about $76,000,000 annually.

**Transportation.** Cambodia has about 7000 mi. of roads of all types. A modern highway links

*Cambodian peasant cleans and prepares for cooking fish caught in the Mekong River.* UPI

the capital with the new port of Kompong Som. A railway links Phnom Penh with Battambang and extends northwestward to the Thai frontier. A link completed in 1969 connects Phnom Penh with Kompong Som. The aggregate rail mileage is about 565 mi. Inland waterways, including navigable sections of the main rivers, aggregate about 870 mi. in the rainy season, but diminish to less than 400 mi. at other times. The country is served by international and domestic airlines.

**Communications.** All major communications systems are controlled by the government. Radio services link the large cities, and radio-telephones provide international communications. The country also has some 8000 telephones, 1,000,000 radios, and 50,000 television receivers.

**Labor.** About 80 percent of the total labor force is engaged in agriculture. Organized industrial workers number only about 8000. The first labor unions were established in 1956, but most labor disputes are handled by the government.

### GOVERNMENT

Cambodia is a republic. The chief of state of the republic is a president. The head of government is the premier of the Council of Ministers.

A view of the causeway leading to Angkor Wat; the balustrades in foreground represent the naga, or cobra, of Hindu mythology. UPI

**Health and Welfare.** Dispensaries and first-aid stations are being established throughout the country to help combat such widespread illnesses as yaws, trachoma, tuberculosis, malaria, and dysentery. Welfare programs are still limited.

**Legislature.** Legislative power resides in the National Assembly; the seventy-two deputies are popularly elected to four-year terms.

**Local Government.** Each province is headed by a governor, and each district is headed by a district chief. Governors and district chiefs are appointed by the national government. Each local village council selects a mayor. Large cities are organized as autonomous municipalities. The capital is organized as a province, with a governor and an appointed municipal commission.

**Judiciary.** The Court of Review functions as the supreme court. The judicature also includes courts of appeal, nationally administered criminal courts, and conciliatory justices at the village level.

**Defense.** In 1970 Cambodia had 49,000 men in its army, navy, and air force. The armed forces were being expanded as a result of the spreading war in Southeast Asia, for which see *History*, below.

### HISTORY

Hindus from eastern India settled in Cambodia several hundred years B.C., bringing with them the Sanskrit language and the worship of Brahma. The Khmers gradually developed a national culture under Hindu influences and, in the 5th century A.D., established a kingdom. From the early 9th century to the latter part of the 12th century the Khmer kingdom was at its zenith. The period of Khmer political ascendancy was marked by great cultural achievements, especially in the areas of art and architecture (see *Archeology*, above).

In the 13th century the Thais, then subject to the Khmers, conducted a series of revolutionary wars against the overlords, and by the end of the 16th century the power of the Khmer kings had been destroyed. Rival kingdoms were subsequently established within Cambodia, and during the 17th and 18th centuries the sovereigns were frequently at war. Finally (1863) the French, then engaged in extending their sphere of influence, proclaimed a protectorate over Cambodia, and in 1887 they incorporated Cambodia into the Union of Indochina (see INDOCHINA: *History*).

In 1940 the pro-Axis Vichy regime of France granted Japan important concessions in Indochina. Abetted by the Japanese, Thailand soon invaded virtually defenseless Cambodia. Japan mediated the peace settlement of May, 1941, whereby the Cambodian provinces of Battambang and Siem Reap were ceded to Thailand. Shortly thereafter Japan occupied the dismembered kingdom and upheld a puppet regime until the return of the French in August, 1945, with Allied backing.

Cambodia remained a French protectorate for about a year, despite a declaration of independence by King Norodom Sihanouk (1922– ), who had acceded to the throne in 1941. In 1946 France granted a measure of autonomy, and a Franco-Thai agreement ensured Cambodia the return of the annexed provinces. In 1949 the kingdom was made an associate state within the French Union (q.v.). Four years later France gave the king full military control in Cambodia.

**Independence.** In order to advance his nationalist aims, in 1955 Norodom Sihanouk abdicated in favor of his father, Prince Norodom Suramarit (1896–1960), who later that year peacefully withdrew the kingdom from the French Union in accordance with the separate Cambodian agreement drawn up at the Geneva Conference on Far Eastern Affairs (begun in April, 1954). By the terms of the agreement Cambodia was to hold popular elections in 1955; in return, the country was assured of full independence. On Dec. 14, 1955, Cambodia became a member of the United Nations.

On the death of Suramarit in 1960, the office of king was replaced by that of chief of state and was assumed by Sihanouk.

During the 1960's Cambodia was involved in frequent disputes with neighboring Thailand and South Vietnam and early in the decade severed diplomatic relations with both countries. Relations were marked by sporadic flare-ups over disputed territory and alleged Thai and Vietnamese support to Cambodian subversive groups. In 1963 Cambodia renounced United States aid, charging that the U.S. was engaged in subversive activities in the country.

As the war in Vietnam intensified, Cambodian neutrality became seriously endangered; *see* VIETNAM, WAR IN. For example, Cambodian border areas were used by North Vietnamese forces and Vietcong guerrillas as bases from which to launch attacks in South Vietnam.

In March, 1970, Sihanouk was ousted as chief of state in a bloodless coup led by the conservative premier, Lieutenant General Lon Nol (1913– ), and later in the spring a combined U.S.-South Vietnamese force invaded Cambodia to destroy the Vietcong bases and supply dumps. The U.S. troops were later withdrawn, but some South Vietnamese forces remained in areas east of the Mekong R. On Oct. 9, 1970, Cambodia was proclaimed the Khmer Republic.

In the early 1970's left-wing groups began to mount an effective guerrilla campaign against the government of Lon Nol. The groups were loosely united in the Khmer Rouge, a political front founded about 1964, whose leaders were believed to favor a Communist form of government. The guerrilla forces attacked numerous towns and frequently threatened the capital.

In April, 1972, a new constitution was promulgated, and in June, Lon Nol was elected to a five-year term as president. The civil war continued to intensify, and by early 1975 the Khmer Rouge controlled virtually all of the country except Phnom Penh. Lon Nol went into exile on April 1, 1975, leaving the government largely in the hands of Prime Minister Long Boret (1933–75?). On April 16, Long Boret surrendered to the Khmer Rouge. According to Western analysts, the new regime immediately embarked on a massive campaign to reorganize Cambodian society and to reconstruct its economy. All city dwellers reportedly were forcibly moved to rural areas to work on agricultural projects. In May, Cambodians seized a U.S. merchant ship, the *Mayagüez*, in the Gulf of Siam (Thailand). American troops were dispatched to the region, and the ship and its crew were quickly released. In 1976 Cambodia was renamed Democratic Kampuchea when a new constitution came into force. Khieu Samphan became head of state, and Pol Pot was named as premier.

**CAMBRAI,** earlier CAMBRAY (Flemish *Kambryk;* anc. *Cameracum*), city of France, in Nord Department, on the Scheldt R., about 35 miles S.E. of Lille. It is an important textile-manufacturing and commercial center. Cambric and cambresine linen fabrics, which are named for the city, are the principal manufactures. Others include lace, leather products, soap, and beet sugar. Livestock, grain, and coal are chief articles of trade. Cambrai is an archiepiscopal see. Besides the Cathedral of Notre Dame, noteworthy edifices include the 18th-century church of Saint Géry and the town hall. In Roman times Cambrai was one of the leading towns of the Nervii, a Celtic-German tribe, which was defeated by the legions of the Roman soldier and statesman Gaius Julius Caesar (q.v.). Retaining its importance under the Franks, it became the capital of a Frankish kingdom in 445 and was fortified during the reign (768–814) of Charlemagne (q.v.), Holy Roman Emperor. In 870 the Northmen sacked the town; an attack by Hungarian invaders was repulsed in 953. Much of the medieval history of Cambrai is a record of strife between the ruling bishops and the citizenry. Late in the 15th century the town became a possession of the Holy Roman Emperor. There, in 1508, the kings of France and Spain, the pope, and the Holy Roman Emperor formed the League of Cambrai, an alliance aimed at the Venetian republic. In Cambrai, also, was signed (1529) the Peace of Cambrai, which concluded the war (1527–29) of Francis I, King of France, against Charles V (qq.v.), Holy Roman Emperor. The treaty is often referred to as the *Paix des Dames* ("Ladies' Peace"), the preliminary negotiations having been conducted by Louise of Savoy (1476–1531), mother of the French king, and Margaret of Austria (1480–1530), aunt of the Holy Roman emperor. Cambrai has been a possession of France since 1677. The city sustained severe damage in both world wars. Pop. (1968) 39,922.

**CAMBRIAN MOUNTAINS.** See WALES: *The Land.*

**CAMBRIAN PERIOD,** the earliest geological time period of the Paleozoic Era, preceded by the Precambrian Era and followed by the Ordovician 'Period (qq.v.). The Cambrian Period began about 600,000,000 years ago and lasted about 100,000,000 years.

Strata of Cambrian rock were first studied in Wales by the British geologist Adam Sedgwick (1785–1873), who named the period for ancient Wales (Lat. *Cambria*). In European classifications, geologists subdivide the rock system of the period into three series (Lower, Middle, Upper), named after, and characterized by the presence of, the trilobites *Olenellus, Paradoxides,* and *Olenus,* respectively. Although the Cambrian beds of North America are also subdivided into three series, these neither exactly coincide chronologically with the European divisions nor are definitely characterized by the presence of fossil trilobites. See GEOLOGY, HISTORICAL.

When the Cambrian Period began, most of the area now occupied by North America and its adjacent waters was dry land. Exceptions were two broad strips of depressed land surface in locations corresponding approximately to the Appalachian and Rocky mountains. In these areas downward warping of the crust of the earth caused extensive, troughlike depressions, called geosynclines, which were filled by shallow seas. The Appalachian geosyncline isolated a large land mass, called Appalachia, from the mainland. Appalachia included the present eastern seaboard of the United States and Canada, and the islands and continental shelf adjacent to this land area. Another body of land, Cascadia, which was either an island or a peninsula, was separated from the western mainland by the Cordilleran geosyncline in the present area of the Rocky Mts. Cascadia included approximately the area now occupied by Alaska, British Columbia, Washington, Oregon, and northern California, and an area of undetermined extent now lying under the Pacific Ocean. Appalachia and Cascadia were mountainous; the large land

area between the Appalachian and Cordilleran geosynclines was, however, relatively flat. During the Cambrian Period erosion reduced the elevation of Cascadia, and the Appalachian geosyncline became linked to the Cordilleran by the formation of the Ouachita geosyncline, which included present-day Oklahoma, Texas, and northern Mexico. During the remainder of the Cambrian Period most of the land area bordered by the three geosynclines and the present Canadian border was submerged in shallow seas. These seas receded before the close of the period.

Eroded sediment of the period was deposited in greatest abundance in the troughlike geosynclines. In eastern New York State the thickness of these beds is as great as 7000 ft. and in British Columbia, 40,000 ft. Cambrian rocks include sandstones, limestones, shales, and conglomerates; slates, marbles, and quartzites; and occasional igneous rocks.

North American Cambrian rocks are found in Newfoundland and eastern Canada; in New England and along the flanks of the Appalachians to Alabama; and in Wisconsin, South Dakota, Colorado, Arizona, and California. Cambrian rocks are found also in various countries of South America, Europe, and Asia. In the U.S., economically valuable products of Cambrian strata include slate, manganese, and limonite in the Appalachian States, sandstone in New York, and gold-bearing ores in the Black Hills.

The Cambrian is the earliest geological system containing a large assortment of fossil organisms. Cambrian fossils known to geologists lived in salt water. All plant fossils of the period are seaweeds, and all Cambrian animal fossils are invertebrates. Animal remains, in approximate order of their abundance, include Crustacea, Brachiopoda, Annelida (certain classes), Gastropoda, Bryozoa, Cephalopoda (qq.v.), and Porifera (certain classes). See PALEONTOLOGY; SPONGE.

**CAMBRIDGE,** city in Maryland, and county seat of Dorchester Co., E. of the Chesapeake Bay, on the Choptank R., about 38 miles S.E. of Annapolis. The city is a port of entry in a fishing and agricultural area. Cambridge is a processing center for flour, lumber, seafood, and vegetables. Manufactures include steel and copper-wire products, boats, clothing, and electrical equipment. Pop. (1960) 12,239; (1970) 11,595.

**CAMBRIDGE,** city in Massachusetts, and county seat of Middlesex Co., on the N. side of the Charles R., opposite Boston. The city is connected with Boston by nine bridges and a subway, is served by three railroad systems, and ranks second only to Boston among the manufacturing centers of the State. The chief industries include printing, publishing, and the manufacture of ink, chemicals, machine tools, machinery, furniture, mortuary equipment, paper products, rubber products, soap, and confections. A nationally famous educational center, Cambridge is the site of Harvard University, Radcliffe College, Massachusetts Institute of Technology, Episcopal Theological Seminary, and other educational institutions. The city was founded in 1630 as New Towne, and was renamed in 1638 in honor of Cambridge, England. Originally 35 mi. long and about 1 mi. wide, Cambridge was reduced in size by the separation of parts of its territory to form Newton in 1691, Lexington in 1713, Brighton in 1837, and Arlington in 1846. In 1846 Cambridge was incorporated as a city. After 1912, following the construction of the underground transit system and the development of the trucking industry, the industrial growth of the city was rapid.

**History.** Cambridge is rich in historical and literary traditions. The first printing press in America was established here in 1639. After the American Revolution (q.v.) began, American headquarters was organized in Cambridge. American troops encamped in the town were dispatched on June 16, 1775, to defend Bunker Hill (*see* BUNKER HILL, BATTLE OF) against the British; General George Washington took active command of the Continental Army in Cambridge on July 3. The city was the home of Henry Wadsworth Longfellow (q.v.), James Russell Lowell (*see under* LOWELL), Oliver Wendell Holmes (*see under* HOLMES), and other distinguished contributors to American letters and scholarship. Pop. (1960) 107,716; (1970) 100,361.

**CAMBRIDGE,** city in Ohio, and county seat of Guernsey Co., on Wills Creek, about 22 miles N.E. of Zanesville. Cambridge is situated in an agricultural area. Clay, gas, and coal are in the vicinity. Manufactures include furniture, plastics, steel, pottery, glass, and clothing. Pop. (1960) 14,562; (1970) 13,656.

**CAMBRIDGE,** Great Britain, municipal borough and administrative center of Cambridgeshire and the Isle of Ely, England, on the Ouse R., about 50 miles N.E. of London. The borough is the market center for the surrounding agricultural region. The site of the University of Cambridge (*see* CAMBRIDGE, UNIVERSITY OF), one of the great educational institutions of England, Cambridge is important as a center of learning. The borough also is an important center of research-based industries, the chief manufactures including radio and television equipment and scientific instruments. In addition to the university buildings, points of interest in Cambridge include a number of noteworthy ecclesiastical edifices, especially the Church of Saint Benedict, a 10th-century Saxon structure; and the Church of the Holy Sepulcher, one of the four round Norman churches in England. The parish Church of Great Saint Mary is the church of the university.

Ruins in the vicinity indicate that the Romans maintained a military outpost, possibly ancient *Camboritum,* on the site of present-day Cambridge. Written records disclose that by 1086 Cambridge had a castle and a mint and that in 1201 the town received its first charter. During the 12th century various religious orders established monasteries and affiliated schools in Cambridge. The university developed around these institutions. Pop. (1971) 98,519.

**CAMBRIDGE PLATONISTS,** school of English Christian philosophers, centered at the University of Cambridge, in the late 17th century. Derived from a group known as the Latitudinarians that reacted against Calvinism (q.v.), and basing their doctrines largely on the teachings of the Greek philosopher Plato (q.v.), the Cambridge Platonists were the theological liberals of their age. Stressing morality rather than dogma, they sought to reconcile fundamental Christian ethics with the new rationality of Renaissance philosophy, science, and humanism. Although their theological background was Puritan, they rejected the Puritan separation of theology and morals; *see* PURITANS. The school was fundamentally antagonistic to the doctrines of the English philosopher Thomas Hobbes (q.v.), who founded his dogma on the senses and ignored the moral and religious postulates of human nature. The extent of their liberalism often caused the Cambridge Platonists to be condemned as atheists, and they generally were viewed with suspicion. The two best-known Cambridge Platonists are the English philosophers Ralph Cudworth (q.v.) and Henry More (1614–87). *See* NEOPLATONISM.

**CAMBRIDGESHIRE AND THE ISLE OF ELY,** Great Britain, county of E. England, comprising the once-separate administrative divisions of Cambridgeshire and the Isle of Ely, which were amalgamated in 1965. Originally fen and marsh, the area was canalized and drained during the 17th century to create fertile farmland. Although the county has some industry, the economy is largely agricultural. The chief crops are wheat and other grains and sugar beets; other agricultural products are potatoes, carrots, kale, fruits, and bulbs. The Nene, the Ouse, and its tributary the Cam are the principal rivers. The section known as the Isle of Ely is not truly an island; it is named for the low hill on which the city of Ely is built, which dominates the surrounding flatlands. The flatness is also broken by rolling chalk hills in the E. and S.E. parts of the county. The most important town is Cambridge (q.v.), county town and the site of the University of Cambridge. Area, 867 sq.mi.; pop. (1971) 302,507.

**CAMBRIDGE, UNIVERSITY OF,** second-oldest institution of higher learning in England, located in Cambridge, Cambridgeshire. The exact origins of the university are obscure, but it is known that various religious orders, including the Franciscans and Dominicans (qq.v.), established monasteries and affiliated schools in Cambridge very early in the 12th century. The fame of the town as an educational center was unquestionably widespread by 1209, for in that year students transferred there from the *Studium Generale* (university) at Oxford, then temporarily closed down. Another influx of students, from Paris, occurred in 1229. In 1231 King Henry III (q.v.) officially approved a document containing a number of scholastic regulations for Cambridge. The next significant development was the appearance of voluntary student associations distinct from the groups affiliated with the religious organizations. These new associations consisted of groups of students who lived together in independent hostels or halls. Private benefactors presently began to endow the halls, or to establish colleges, often by consolidating several halls. The first of the Cambridge colleges was Peterhouse, founded in 1284 by Hugh de Balsham, Bishop of Ely (d. 1286), as a purely academic organization, with no monastic discipline.

**Papal Recognition.** In 1318 Pope John XXII (*see under* JOHN) issued a bull recognizing Cambridge as a *Studium Generale*. By this time the school had a constitution, similar to that of the University of Oxford and of the University of Paris (qq.v.), according to which it was governed by a corporation of resident teachers, called regents, and resident masters not engaged in teaching, called nonregents. The presiding officer, or chancellor, was elected by the regents. Besides the faculty of arts, the university maintained at this time the advanced faculties of theology, civil and canon law, and medicine. During the 14th century five new colleges were established at Cambridge. The university continued to expand in the 15th and 16th centuries (see table, page 28), acquiring ten new colleges. No colleges were founded in the 17th and 18th centuries. In the 19th century, seven were established, including two for women. The second half of the 20th century saw a marked growth in the size of the colleges and in the attention given to research and graduate students. New colleges were established to serve these students, notably Darwin College, University College, renamed Wolfson College, and Lucy Cavendish Collegiate Society, and Clare Hall. The older colleges also increased their number of graduate students.

**Religious Reform.** The university figured prominently in the Protestant Reformation. The Dutch scholar Desiderius Erasmus (q.v.), who was Lady Margaret professor of divinity (1511–14), translated the New Testament from Greek into Latin there. The English religious reformers William Tyndale and Hugh Latimer were educated at Cambridge, as was the prelate Thomas Cranmer (qq.v.); each made notable contributions to the English Reformation. The decrees of King Henry VIII (q.v.), which ended the power of the Roman Catholic Church in England, began a new epoch in the history of the university. The study of canon law was discontinued, public lectures in Greek and Latin were initiated in the colleges, the Bible was studied in the light of contemporary Renaissance knowledge, and the humanistic method replaced the scholastic. As elsewhere, recognition of royal supremacy was enforced at the university. With these changes and the replacement of clerical personnel by lay students and teachers, the medieval history of Cambridge came to a close, and the modern university began to emerge.

In the reign (1558–1603) of Queen Elizabeth I (q.v.), Cambridge became a stronghold of advanced Puritanism, particularly under the influence of Thomas Cartwright (1535–1603), professor of divinity (1569–70). As a result of the disturbances that ensued, restrictive legislation was enacted, in 1570, vesting government of the university in the heads of the colleges. They alone were empowered to elect the vice-chancellor, or executive head of the university, and the *Caput,* or supervising board. These statutes, which virtually converted Cambridge into a close corporation, remained in effect until the 19th century. In 1604, during the reign of King James I (q.v.), the university was granted the right of electing two members to Parliament, a right that ceased in the 1950's. The next development of historic importance at the university was the rise, late in the 17th century, of the Cambridge Platonists (q.v.), and the beginnings, through the influence of such members of the faculty as the British scientists Isaac Newton and Isaac Barrow (qq.v.), of an emphasis on the cul-

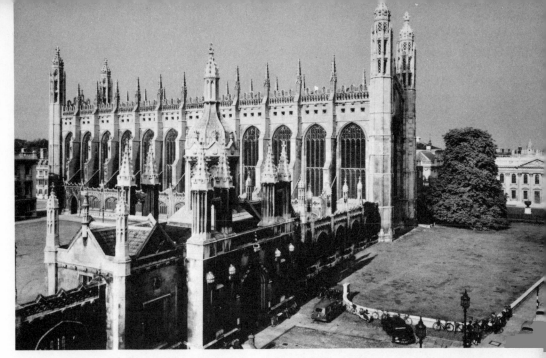

King's College Chapel.

tivation of mathematics and the natural sciences, which continues to be one of the university's chief distinctions.

A number of important changes were effected at Cambridge in the 19th century, including the reorganization of the colleges (as a result of the Universities of Oxford and Cambridge Act, approved in 1882), the repeal of the Elizabethan statutes of 1570, the inauguration of greater freedom in academic matters, the abolition (1871) of religious tests for admission, and the adoption of a broader and more liberal curriculum. Girton College and Newnham College, for women, were established in 1869 and 1871, respectively, but each remained separate from the formal university structure until 1947.

**The University Today.** Cambridge University today is a self-governing corporation. The legislative body is a senate, composed of the chancellor, vice-chancellor, and masters and doctors in various fields. Administration of the university is conducted by a regent house, a body that includes the university officers, faculty members and faculty secretaries, and heads of houses. University funds, derived mainly from tuition fees, contributions from the colleges, and an annual grant from the British government, are administered by an elected board, which also includes the vice-chancellor. This official, who is the actual head of the university, is elected by the senate and serves for two years. In his general duties he is assisted by various deputies and by two proctors. The latter also

have charge of university discipline. The university chancellor is a lifetime honorary official elected by the senate and is usually, as at Oxford, some dignitary of the realm.

Cambridge University, with its system of independent colleges, is (excepting Oxford University) a unique educational organization. Although the colleges and the university are separate corporations, in large measure independent of one another, all are closely connected in the sense that each is an interacting part of an integrated educational system. The university is essentially an examining and degree-conferring body; it conducts entrance examinations, examines candidates for degrees during their residence and at the conclusion of their studies, and confers degrees on those who meet its requirements. It regulates the system of education, enforces general discipline, and provides facilities, such as the university library, lecture rooms, and laboratories for teaching and research, beyond the scope of the colleges. The colleges receive the entering student, provide him with lodgings, meals, and other services, prepare him for the university examinations, afford him social contacts and recreation, and supervise his activities.

The university year is divided into three terms: the Michaelmas term, the Lent term, and the Easter term. The terms average about eight weeks each of required residence; during the vacations much of the actual work or reading, as it is called, is done. The students are under the direct supervision of tutors, who maintain personal relations with each student in their charge. The supervisor guides the studies of a small group of students allocated to him by the director of studies. The supervisors and directors of studies are usually university teaching officers and ensure that the students are prepared for examinations.

The colleges and dates of founding follow:

| College | Founded |
|---|---|
| Christ's | 1505 |
| Churchill | 1960 |
| Clare | 1326 |
| Clare Hall | 1966 |
| Corpus Christi | 1352 |
| Darwin | 1964 |
| Downing | 1800 |
| Emmanuel | 1584 |
| Fitzwilliam | 1966 |
| Girton (women) | 1869 |
| Gonville and Caius | 1348 |
| Hughes Hall (graduate women) | 1885 |
| Jesus | 1496 |
| King's | 1441 |
| Lucy Cavendish Collegiate Society (graduate women) | 1965 |
| Magdalene | 1542 |
| New Hall (women) | 1954 |
| Newnham (women) | 1871 |
| Pembroke | 1347 |
| Peterhouse | 1284 |
| Queens' | 1448 |
| Saint Catharine's | 1473 |
| Saint Edmund's House (graduate) | 1896 |
| Saint John's | 1511 |
| Selwyn | 1882 |
| Sidney Sussex | 1596 |
| Trinity | 1546 |
| Trinity Hall | 1350 |
| Wolfson (coeducational graduate) | 1965 |

The degree of bachelor of arts may be conferred, after the required examinations have been passed, at the end of nine terms or three years of residence. For the great majority of students, who are candidates for honors, special examinations called triposes are provided in mathematics, classics, philosophy, natural sciences, law, history, theology and religious studies, Oriental studies, medieval and modern languages, engineering, economics, archeology and anthropology, architecture, computer science, English, geography, land economy, medical sciences, music, and social and political sciences. Successful candidates in the triposes are classified according to their standing: first, second, and third class. The honor men in mathematics, however, were formerly known as wranglers, senior optimes, and junior optimes, and the head of the first list, the best man of the year, was called the senior wrangler. The university also confers higher degrees in law, theology, medicine, and music and advanced degrees in science. Certain honorary degrees are conferred also, notably that of doctor of laws (LL.D.).

The university proper, as distinguished from the colleges, has a number of outstanding institutions. The Fitzwilliam Museum, founded by the British statesman William Wentworth Fitzwilliam (1748–1833) in 1816, is one of the largest and finest museums of art in England. The university library contains more than 3,000,000 bound volumes, as well as more than 12,000 manuscripts and 600,000 maps. Among other notable university institutions are the Cavendish Laboratory of Experimental Physics, the Sedgwick Museum of Geology, a solar physics observatory, and the Scott Polar Research Institute.

In 1972–73 student enrollment at Cambridge University was about 10,800; the faculty numbered about 1200.

**CAMBYSES,** name of two rulers of the ancient Persian dynasty of the Achaemenidae. This dynasty was descended from Achaemenes, or Hakhamanish, ruler in the 7th century B.C. of an area now comprising southwest Iran. The Achaemenidae established the Persian Empire, which eventually extended from Mesopotamia (now Iraq) to India; see PERSIA.

**Cambyses I** (fl. 6th cent. B.C.), ruled about 600 to 559 over Anshan (now Baghdad Province, Iraq) as a vassal of the Medes, who ruled Persia at that time; see MEDIA. Little is known of Cambyses I, except that he was the son of Cyrus I (r. about 640–600), whom he succeeded, and the father of Cyrus the Great (q.v.), who founded the Persian Empire. According to the Greek historian Herodotus (q.v.), Cambyses I married the daughter of Astyages, King of the Medes (r. about 584–550).

**Cambyses II** (r. 529–22 B.C.), son of Cyrus the Great, whom he succeeded as King of Persia. In order to maintain control over the Persian Empire, Cambyses II had his younger brother Smerdis (d. about 525) murdered. He then led an expedition to conquer Egypt, the sole remaining independent kingdom of the East after the conquest of Asia by his father. Cambyses defeated Psamtik III, King of Egypt (r. 593–88), and succeeded in conquering Egypt as far south as Nubia (q.v.), but failed in later attacks on the Egyptian oasis of Ammonium (now Siwa) and in campaigns in Ethiopia. During his absence in Egypt, a usurper, Gaumata (r. 522), claimed to be Smerdis and seized the throne of Persia. The death of Smerdis had been kept secret, so Gaumata's claim was believed and he was acknowledged king throughout Persia for about seven months. Cambyses was on his way to Persia to punish Gaumata when he died either by accident or by suicide. According to Herodotus,

Cambyses II was a dissolute and inhuman despot, prone to drunken or insane rages in which he committed sacrilegious and cruel acts.

**CAMDEN,** city in Arkansas, and county seat of Ouachita Co., on the Ouachita R. Camden is a trade and distributing center for the surrounding agricultural area. Manufactures include furniture, wood products, paper, fertilizer, house trailers, and air conditioners. Pop. (1960) 15,823; (1970) 15,147.

**CAMDEN,** city in New Jersey, and county seat of Camden Co., on the E. bank of the Delaware R., opposite Philadelphia, Pa., and about 25 miles S.W. of Trenton. The Cooper R., an arm of the Delaware, bisects the city, dividing it into sections known as East Camden and Camden. One of the chief industrial and commercial centers of New Jersey, Camden is served by two railroads, by ferry and rapid-transit lines operating to Philadelphia (with which it is connected by the Delaware River Bridge), and by coastwise and transoceanic steamship lines. Port facilities include a large municipal pier and over 12 mi. of water frontage, about half of it along the Delaware. A noted shipbuilding center, Camden has shipyards engaged in the production of naval and commercial vessels of many types and sizes. Among the leading manufactures of the city are television, radio, and electronic equipment, sound apparatus, chemicals, phonograph records, pens, linoleum and oilcloth, leather, soap, and licorice products.

Beginning about 1681 a settlement known as Cooper's Ferry developed on the site of Camden. Formally established as a town in 1773, Cooper's Ferry was renamed in honor of the British jurist and political leader Charles Pratt, Lord Camden (1714–94), a vigorous opponent of the taxation policy of the British government in America. Camden was incorporated as a city in 1828, and in 1844 became the county seat of newly organized Camden County. After 1873 the American poet Walt Whitman (q.v.) resided in the city, where his home is preserved as a museum. Pop. (1960) 117,159; (1970) 102,551.

**CAMDEN,** city in South Carolina, and county seat of Kershaw Co., near the Wateree R., about 28 miles N.E. of Columbia. The city is a commercial and industrial center and a popular winter resort. It lies in an agricultural region especially noted for the training of Thoroughbred horses. Cotton, corn, peanuts, oats, tobacco, melons, and peaches are the chief crops of the surrounding area. The leading manufactures of the city are textiles, cottonseed oil, iron castings, farm implements and machinery. Camden is one of the oldest inland communities in South Carolina. The town was settled by Irish Quakers in 1758 and called Pine Tree Hill. In 1791 it was chartered and renamed in honor of British jurist and political leader Charles Pratt, 1st Earl of Camden (1714–94), an outspoken opponent of the policies of the British government toward the American colonies. Two battles of the American Revolution were fought in and around Camden (see CAMDEN, BATTLE OF). During the Civil War, Camden was an important Confederate supply base and hospital center. The city was captured and burned on Feb. 24, 1865 by troops of the Union army under General William Tecumseh Sherman (q.v.). Pop. (1960) 6842; (1970) 8532.

**CAMDEN, BATTLE OF,** engagement of the American Revolution (q.v.) fought on Aug. 16, 1780, about 3 miles N. of Camden, S.C., then occupied by the British. The American force, of about 1500 regulars and 2000 poorly trained militiamen, was commanded by General Horatio Gates (q.v.). General Charles Cornwallis (q.v.) commanded the British force, numbering about 2000 men. Shortly after the action began the American militiamen, many of whom were ill with dysentery, broke ranks, left their arms, and fled in disorder. The regulars, under General Johann Kalb, (q.v.), known as Baron de Kalb, stood firm and were almost annihilated. De Kalb was wounded and captured; he died three days later. Through their victory the British gained temporary control of the entire South. American casualties were about 1000 killed and wounded and about 1000 taken prisoner. British losses were about 325 killed and wounded. After the battle Gates was replaced as commander of the Army of the South by General Nathanael Greene (q.v.).

**CAMEL,** common name for two species of large ruminant, constituting the typical genus, *Camelus,* of the family Camelidae, and native to the desert regions of Asia and northern Africa. Both species have been domesticated since remote antiquity. The dromedary or Arabian camel, *C. dromedarius,* has one hump, and the Bactrian camel, *C. bactrianus,* has two humps. The humps are stores of flesh and fat, absorbed as nutrition when food is unavailable. A camel can subsist without water for several days. Its stomach has many diverticular or pouches, each closed by a sphincter muscle; water is stored in these pouches and is released as required. The Arabian camel usually stands 6 ft. tall at the shoulders. The hump rises about 1 ft. above the back. The Bactrian camel has shorter legs, is about 5 ft. in height at the shoulders, but usually has a heavier torso than the dromedary.

Arabian camel and its Bedouin owner near Beersheba, Israel.
**Trans World Airlines**

The Arabian camel, unknown in the wild state, is found from northwestern India and the lowlands of Afghanistan to the extremity of the Arabian peninsula and the Somali Republic to the south, and westward across the African deserts. Attempts have been made to introduce the species into Australia, Spain, Zanzibar, and the southwestern United States, but without lasting success. The Arabian camel is singularly adapted to subsistence in the desert by its structural qualities and by its ability to bite off and consume the thorny plants that grow there. Thick and broad sole pads and thick callosities on the joints of the legs and on the chest, upon which it rests in a kneeling position, enable it to withstand the heat of the desert sand. Moreover, its nostrils may be closed against flying dust, and its eyes are shielded by very long eyelashes. Its acute sense of smell is valuable in locating supplies of water.

The Bactrian camel is better adapted, by virtue of its smaller size and heavier build, harder and more cloven feet, longer and finer wool, and other qualities, to a rocky and cooler region, and its home is Central Asia, from northern Chinese Turkistan (now part of Sinkiang Province) to Mongolia. Its endurance is equally as remarkable, under different circumstances, as that of the Arabian camel, for it withstands the rigorous climate of the Tibetan Plateau where the temperature rises to 140° F. in summer and sinks to arctic cold in winter. A wild race of the Bactrian species is found in Central Asia.

The camel's endurance and strength have made it a valuable beast of burden. Loads as great as 1000 lb. can be carried by the Bactrian camel, and though its pace is slow (about 1½ mi. per hour), it will travel as many as 30 mi. in a day. Arabian camels, generally used as saddle animals, can cover more than 100 mi. in a day. The flesh and milk of the camel are used as food, and the hide for leather. The long hair, shed every summer, is made into cordage, fine paint brushes, and a light, warm, long-napped cloth.

**CAMELLIA,** genus of about ten species of evergreen shrubs or trees of the Tea family (Theaceae), native in tropical and subtropical Asia. The best-known and most-valued variety is *C. japonica,* cultivated in China and Japan for its beautiful, fragrant, waxlike flowers. In the wild state this species grows up to 40 ft. high and has red flowers; white, red, pink, and double varieties also have been developed. Camellias are grown in warm, damp regions in southern and western areas of the United States. Popular as ornamental plants, the camellia is also the State flower of Alabama.

**CAMELOT,** legendary site of the castle and court of King Arthur (q.v.) and the knights of the Round Table. The origin of the name is unknown, and scholars do not agree about whether Arthur actually lived or where Camelot might have been located. It has been placed variously in England at Winchester and Camelford, and in Wales at Caerleon (q.v.). The name occurs frequently in English literature, notably in the literature of the Arthurian Cycle (q.v.), which includes *Le Morte d'Arthur* by the 15th-century English writer Sir Thomas Malory and in *Idylls of the King*, by the 19th-century British poet Alfred, Lord Tennyson (qq.v.).

**CAMEO,** precious or semiprecious gemstone (such as onyx or sardonyx), shell, or artificial material (such as colored glass or porcelain), engraved in relief. Cameos are used as ornaments and are usually engraved with a profile portrait head. Most cameos consist of two or more layers of different colors. The top layer is carved and the darker lower layer forms a background. The term cameo is contrasted with intaglio, which consists of a sunken engraving on material of a uniform color. Although the art of gem carving in relief was known in very early times, the true development of the cameo did not begin until the 3rd or 4th century B.C. in Greece. It was also popular in ancient Rome. Examples of ancient cameos are found in many museum gem collections, including those in the British Museum in London and the Metropolitan Museum of Art in New York City. *See also* GEM ENGRAVING.

**CAMERA.** *See* PHOTOGRAPHY: *Cameras.*

**CAMERON, Richard** (1648?–80), Scottish Covenanter, born in Falkland, Fife County. During his early career Cameron was a schoolteacher and private tutor. Subsequently he espoused the cause of the Covenanters (q.v.), who worked to maintain Presbyterianism as the only religion in Scotland. Because Covenanters were being persecuted during the reign of Charles II (q.v.) King of England, who was Roman Catholic, Cameron went into exile in 1678 and joined other exiled friends in Holland. Returning in 1680, he and others antagonized the government by strenuously resisting the measures that reinstated the Episcopal Church in Scotland and proscribed the meetings for public worship of unauthorized religious bodies. In June, 1680, with twenty well-armed companions, he entered the town of Sanquhar and publicly renounced allegiance to Charles II for abuse of power and declared war against him and his followers. Cameron and his men were surprised by royal troops in Ayr County in July, 1680, and Cameron was killed.

*Crucifixion with the Virgin and Saint John on a 17th-century cameo pendant mounted in a gold and enamel frame.* Metropolitan Museum of Art – Gift of Mrs. Ethel Weil Worgelt

His hands and head were cut off and publicly displayed in Edinburgh. In 1689 the survivors of the skirmish organized a military unit that became the nucleus of the Cameronians, a famous regiment of the British army. In 1681 Cameron's followers organized the religious group later known as the Reformed Presbyterians; *see* CAMERONIANS.

**CAMERON, Simon** (1799–1889), American businessman, politician, and diplomat, born in Lancaster County, Pa. Apprenticed at an early age to a printing firm in Harrisburg, Cameron was a newspaper editor, State printer, and adjutant general of Pennsylvania. By this time he had become influential in both State and national politics and had built a fortune in banking, railroads, and the iron industry. In 1845 he was elected as a Democrat to the United States Senate, replacing James Buchanan (q.v.), who had just resigned. After his term expired in 1849 he became a leader of the new Republican Party (q.v.). In 1857 he was elected as a Republican to the Senate. During the period from 1857 to 1877 he controlled the Republican political machine in Pennsylvania. In 1860 he was an unsuccessful candidate for the Republican Presidential nomination. The managers of Abraham Lincoln (q.v.) secured his support by promising him a position in Lincoln's cabinet, and in 1861 he became secretary of war. Evidence was eventually presented in Congress against Cameron to prove corruption and favoritism in his letting of government contracts, and he was asked to resign in January, 1862. From then until November of the same year he was U.S. minister to Russia. He was reelected U.S. Senator in 1867 and served until 1877 when he resigned so that his son, James Donald Cameron (1833–1918), might be elected in his place. Because he controlled political patronage (see SPOILS SYSTEM) in his State, Cameron is considered the first powerful State "boss" in American politics.

**CAMERON, Verney Lovett** (1844–94), British explorer, born near Weymouth, Dorsetshire, England. Cameron entered the British navy in 1857, and in 1873 was sent to Africa by the Royal Geographical Society on a second expedition to relieve the British missionary and explorer David Livingstone (q.v.). Soon after the expedition landed at Zanzibar (q.v.) and began its journey inland, Cameron and his party met servants bearing Livingstone's body. Cameron continued on, becoming the first European to cross tropical Africa from east to west when he reached the Atlantic Ocean in November, 1875. On this expedition he found some of Livingstone's papers, which he sent back to England, and also explored the southern half of Lake Tanganyika (q.v.). When he returned home Cameron was made a commander in the British navy and a Companion of the Order of the Bath (see BATH, ORDER OF THE). In 1878–79 he traveled in Turkey, and in 1882, with the British explorer Sir Richard Burton (q.v.), he visited the African Gold Coast in search of gold. Cameron retired from the navy in 1883 and spent the rest of his life directing commercial projects in Africa. His writings include *Across Africa* (2 vol., 1877).

**CAMERONIANS,** followers of Richard Cameron (q.v.), one of the Covenanters (q.v.) of Scotland. The Cameronians were known officially as Reformed Presbyterians and date from 1681; except for a few seceding congregations, they united with the Free Church of Scotland (q.v.) in 1876 and, therefore, became part of the Church of Scotland in the 1929 reunion. The Cameronians refused to recognize the civil government of 17th-century Scotland. Moderate Calvinists (see CALVINISM), they asserted that the will of man is determined only by the practical judgment of the mind; that the cause of man's doing good or evil proceeds from the knowledge that God infuses into him; and that God does not move the will physically, but only morally, by virtue of its dependence on the mind.

**CAMEROON.** See CAMEROONS; CAMEROON, UNITED REPUBLIC OF.

**CAMEROONS** (Ger. *Kamerun;* Fr. *Cameroun;* Port. *Camerões*), region in w. Africa that covers the area of the United Republic of Cam-

eroon and part of E. Nigeria, bounded on the N. by Lake Chad, on the E. by Chad, on the S. by the People's Republic of the Congo, Gabon, and Equatorial Guinea, on the s.w. by the Gulf of Guinea, and on the w. by Nigeria.

The coast of the region was explored late in the 15th century by the Portuguese, who named the estuary to the south of Mt. Cameroon *Rio das Camerões* ("River of Prawns"). Merchants established trading stations along the coast in the 17th century, buying slaves, ivory, and rubber. British traders and missionaries were especially active in the area after 1845. Germans began to explore inland after 1860 and in 1884 established a colony; the British, taken by surprise, offered no resistance to their claim.

Transportation difficulties and local resistance slowed development of the area by the Germans, although they had managed to cultivate large cacao, palm, and rubber plantations, build roads, and begin the construction of a railroad and of the port of Douala on the Atlantic Coast. In 1911 France, in exchange for recognition of a protectorate in Morocco, ceded to Germany about 100,000 sq.mi. in the region, later reincorporated into French Equatorial Africa during World War I. Anglo-French forces invaded the German colony in 1916. In 1919 one fifth of the territory, which was contiguous with E. Nigeria, was assigned to Great Britain and the remaining four fifths were assigned to France as mandates under the League of Nations.

The British Cameroons consisted of the Northern Cameroons (17,500 sq.mi.) and the Southern Cameroons (16,580 sq.mi.), which were separated from each other by a 45-mi. strip along the Benue R. The N. territory, peopled by tribes of Sudan origin, was always administered as a part of Northern Nigeria. The Southern Cameroons, peopled by Bantu (q.v.) tribes, was administered as part of the Nigerian federation but had a locally elected legislature. The French Cameroons comprised an area of about 167,000 sq.mi. For the composition of the population of the area, see CAMEROON, UNITED REPUBLIC OF.

The mandated areas were made trust territories of the United Nations in 1946. The French Cameroons became an independent republic, the Cameroon Republic, in 1960. In a U.N.-sponsored plebiscite held in February, 1961, the Northern Cameroons voted to join Nigeria and the Southern Cameroons voted for union with the Cameroon Republic. The Cameroon Republic became the province of East Cameroon and the Southern British Cameroons became the province of West Cameroon in the newly constituted Federal Republic of Cameroon in October, 1961. In 1972 a national referendum voted overwhelmingly to change the Federal Republic to the United Republic of Cameroon.

**CAMEROON, UNITED REPUBLIC OF,** independent country, in w. Africa, bounded on the N. by Lake Chad; on the E. by Chad and the Central African Republic; on the S. by the People's Republic of Congo, Gabon, and Equatorial Guinea; on the s.w. by the Bight of Biafra in the Gulf of Guinea, and on the w. by Nigeria. The country is shaped like an elongated triangle. The base of the country extends for 435 mi. at lat. 2° N. between long. 8° E. and long. 16° E. and its apex reaches Lake Chad at lat. 13° N. and long. 14° E. It includes almost all the area that was in the Cameroons region. Until 1972 the republic was divided into two States, East Cameroon, the former French Cameroons, and West Cameroon, part of the former British Cameroons. The country has a total area of 183,380 sq.mi. *See* CAMEROONS.

### THE LAND

The country has four distinct topographical regions. In the S. is a coastal plain, a region of dense equatorial rain forests. In the center is the Adamawa Plateau, with heights reaching 4500 ft. above sea level. This is a transitional area where forest gives way to savanna country. In the N. the savanna gradually slopes into the marshland surrounding Lake Chad. In the w. is an area of high, forested mountains. Mount Cameroon (13,350 ft.), the highest peak in w. Africa, is an active volcano. The Sanaga and Nyong rivers flow S. to the Atlantic Ocean, the Mbere (Logone) R. flows N. from the central plateau into Lake Chad. A network of rivers in the Chad basin, including the Benue R., links the country with the vast Niger R. system to the E. and N.

**Climate.** On the coast the average annual rainfall is 153 in. On the exposed slopes of the Cameroon Mts. in the w., rainfall is almost constant and sometimes reaches 400 in. a year. In the semiarid N.W. annual rainfall averages 15 in. The dry season in the N. is from October to April. The average temperature in the S. is 77° F., on the plateau it is just under 70° F., and in the N. it is 90° F.

**Natural Resources.** Cameroon is dependent primarily on its agricultural resources. High-yield deposits of bauxite exist in N. Cameroon. A small amount of gold is mined. Deposits of iron, diamonds, manganese, mica, columbo-tantalite, cassiterite, lignite, and rutile are found in the country, but few are exploited. Natural gas was discovered near Douala in 1955.

Six hydroelectric stations and nine thermal

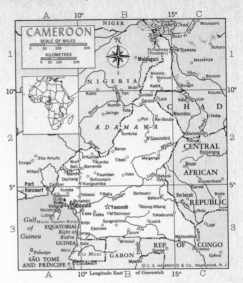

stations produced approximately 1,170,000,000 kw hours annually in 1970.

**Plants and Animals.** Cameroon has valuable stands of oil palms, bamboo palms, mahogany, teak, ebony, rubber, and kola. All animals found in tropical Africa, as well as chimpanzees and gorillas found only in rain forests, exist in Cameroon. Venomous snakes abound.

### THE PEOPLE

The majority of the people are farmers who live in small towns or villages in s. and central Cam-

*The falls of the Sanaga at Edéa.*      United Nations

eroon. Herdsmen are the principal inhabitants in the N.

**Population.** The population of Cameroon (census 1965) was 5,017,000; the United Nations estimated (1973) 6,167,000. The overall population density is 34 per sq.mi. (U.N. est. 1973). Some 11,000 French settlers and technicians also live in the country.

The capital is Yaoundé (pop., 1972 est., 190,000). Douala, on the Bight of Biafra, with an estimated population of 252,000, is the chief port.

About one half of the people adhere to the traditional animist religions, 15 percent of the peoples in the N. are Muslim, and 30 percent of the Bantu (q.v.) of the S. are Christian. Both Muslims and Christians continue to be influenced by animist practices.

Under the unitary republic established in 1972, French continued to be the official language of the former East Cameroon and English that of the former West Cameroon. Both are official languages of the national government. Located at the racial crossroads of Africa, Cameroon contains 140 ethnic groups speaking twenty-four languages. The languages fall into the Bantu and West Atlantic branches of the Niger-Congo family, the Central Saharan family, and the Chadic branch of the Afro-Asiatic family. *See also* AFRICAN LANGUAGES; AFRICAN LITERATURE.

**Education.** French principles of education predominate in secondary and technical schools. Mission schools play an important role in education and are partially subsidized by the government. At the start of the 1970's annual enrollment in primary schools totaled some 700,000 and in secondary schools about 37,000. The University of Yaoundé, which was established in 1962, has faculties of law, arts, education, and agriculture. The university and a college of arts and science at Bamenda, West Cameroon, which opened in 1963, had a combined enrollment of about 3500 students in the early 1970's. More than 1000 students in higher education were studying in institutions in other countries.

### THE ECONOMY

Agricultural activities are the main occupation of the vast majority of the population. Agricultural products constitute almost 80 percent of all exports. In a recent year the budget showed balanced revenue and expenditures of about $214,000,000.

**Agriculture.** The goal of the economic planning of Cameroon is to transform traditional farming into a modern production and processing industry, with special emphasis on increases in the major export crops of coffee, cocoa, palm oil, cotton, and bananas. The production of coffee and cocoa, the leading export commodities, amounted to about 85,000 metric tons and 112,000 metric tons, respectively, in the early 1970's. A rural exodus has created a growing amount of unemployment in the larger cities. Resettlement of unemployed persons to rural centers is being undertaken, and more than thirty rural centers for organizing and training the farm population are in existence.

Livestock raising is important in the Adamawa Plateau region. In the early 1970's the livestock population included about 1,800,000 head of cattle, 3,500,000 goats, 350,000 pigs, 1,180,000 and sheep, and 5,000,000 poultry.

**Forest and Fishing Industries.** In the early 1970's timber was the fifth most valuable export. Timber exports, mainly mahogany, ebony, and teak, were valued at about $17,000,000 annually. Deep-sea fishing activity is increasing, especially around Douala. About 72,000 tons of fish are caught annually; about 700 tons are exported to the American market.

**Mining and Manufacturing.** The largest single industrial enterprise is the aluminum plant at Edéa, which produces over 50,000 tons annually from imported bauxite. Bauxite deposits in Cameroon are estimated at 1,090,000,000 tons in the Adamawa region and 40,000,000 tons in the Bamileke region in the south, but are not being exploited. Annual gold production continued to decline; peak production of 617 lb. was reached in 1949. A rapid growth in food processing, consumer-item production, and the forestry industries has occurred recently.

**Currency and Banking.** The unit of currency of Cameroon is the C.F.A. franc, consisting of 100 centimes (253 C.F.A. francs equal U.S.$1; 1972). The currency is guaranteed by France and issued by the Central Bank of the States of Equatorial Africa and of Cameroon.

**Transportation and Communications.** Cameroon is engaged in an effort to improve the inadequate transportation network. Of the approximately 16,000 mi. of roads, about 1200 are paved. The country has about 500 mi. of railroad. About 90 percent of port traffic is handled at Douala. The port of Garoua on the Benue R. in the N. is open two to three months a year and normally handles most of the trade with Nigeria.

*Women husk yellow corn in the marketplace.*

Of some forty-five airfields in operation, only those in Douala, Yaoundé, Garoua, and Tiko have permanently surfaced runways. The national broadcasting system has its main station at Yaoundé and local stations in Douala, Garoua, and Buea.

## GOVERNMENT

The president of the republic is chief of state and commander of the armed forces. The president and vice-president are elected for five-year terms by universal suffrage. The federal ministers are appointed by the president and by statute are not permitted to be members of the legislature.

**Legislature.** The National Assembly, established in 1972 after reorganization of the government of Cameroon into a unitary republic, consists of 120 members. The cabinet comprises 19 ministers and 4 vice-ministers, including 8 from the English-speaking former West Cameroon.

**Judiciary.** Cameroon has two separate judicial systems. In the former East Cameroon the French system has been joined with traditional institutions to produce two co-existent jurisdictions: the local tribunals, which apply customary law; and the tribunals of modern law, which

35

*Terraced fields on the Mandara Mts. in northern Cameroon during the dry season.* United Nations

apply modern civil, criminal, and administrative codes. The judicial system in the former West Cameroon is based on the British legal system and is a dual system.

## HISTORY

For the history of Cameroon before independence in 1960 and the incorporation of British Southern Cameroons into the republic after independence, *see* CAMEROONS. When Cameroon became independent, the central government was faced with a rebellion incited by the Cameroon People's Union, a pro-Communist party. The revolt was suppressed in 1963. As President Ahmadou Ahidjo (1924–  ) succeeded in establishing the authority of the central government and of his regime, the opposition political parties lost strength. In 1966 the four major parties merged into the National Cameroonian Union, which was declared the only legal party.

In 1972 President Ahidjo sponsored a national referendum that changed Cameroon from a federal to a unitary state, called the United Republic of Cameroon. The first cabinet of this unitary state was appointed in July.

Cameroon is a member of the United Nations and the West African Economic-Customs Union and is an associate member of the European Economic Community. In the early 1970's Ahidjo attempted to reduce the country's ties with France and increase its role in African affairs.

**CAMILLUS, Marcus Furius** (477?–365 B.C.), Roman soldier and statesman. During the period of the Roman Republic, Camillus was made military tribune of Rome several times, as well as censor, and finally dictator about 403 B.C. He led the Roman army against rival cities in Etruria (q.v.), conquering Veii in 396, Capena in 395, and Falerii in 394. Shortly thereafter it is believed that he went into exile near Rome, because he had mishandled distribution of booty after his Etruscan campaigns. While he was in exile, the Gauls (*see* GAUL), about 387, plundered and burned Rome. During the recovery of Rome, Camillus became a folk hero, and it is believed that he again served as military tribune and dictator several times, although legends have obscured the facts about his life. According to legend he raised an army and forced the Gallic leader Brennus (q.v.) out of Rome. In fact, however, the Gauls retired unharmed after Rome ransomed itself with gold. Afterward Camillus resisted efforts of the plebs (q.v.) to move the Capitol building to Veii, and worked instead to rebuild and fortify Rome. He reorganized the Roman army and made administrative reforms. His military exploits assured Roman supremacy in central Italy. Camillus is also credited with persuading the Roman patricians (q.v.) to make concessions to the plebs, thus keeping peace between the two groups. *See also* ROME, HISTORY OF: *The Republic.*

**CAMISARDS** (Fr. dialect *camiso,* "shirt"), name applied to the French Huguenot peasants of the Cévennes mountain region who rose in rebellion in 1702 against Louis XIV (q.v.), King of France. The Camisards, so called because of the black smocks they wore during night raids, had sought refuge in the Cévennes after Louis XIV in 1685 had revoked the religious freedom granted to them by the Edict of Nantes (q.v.). The revolt was an attempt to restore the decree. Led principally by the French soldier Jean Cavalier (q.v.), the Camisards conducted guerrilla warfare from mountain strongholds against the royal troops sent to crush them. Roman Catholic churches were burned and their priests were killed or forced to flee. Urged on by Pope Clement XI (1649–1721), who issued a Papal Bull excoriating the Camisards, the Catholics razed more than 450 villages and exterminated most of the inhabitants. In 1704 the Royalist commander Duc Claude Louis Hector de Villars (1653–1734) met with Cavalier and persuaded the rebel leader to surrender in return for a commission in the royal army and certain religious liberties for the Camisards. These terms of surrender were rejected by the mass of the Camisards, who demanded full restoration of the rights granted by the Edict of Nantes. The struggle continued sporadically until about 1710. *See* HUGUENOTS.

**CAMMAERTS, Émile** (1878–1953), Belgian poet, born in Brussels. Although he remained a citizen of Belgium, in 1908 he settled in England and taught at the University of London. He excelled in poetic representation of the emotional upheaval during both world wars. His many works included *Belgian Poems* (1915); *New Belgian Poems* (1916); *Upon This Rock* (1942), a sketch of a son killed during World War II; *The Flower of Grass* (1944), his autobiography; and several histories and commentaries.

**CAMÕES, Luiz Vaz de,** usually known in English as LUIS VAS DE CAMOËNS (1524?–80), Portuguese poet, probably born in Lisbon, and educated possibly at the University of Coimbra. His adventurous life included service from 1547 to 1549 with the Portuguese army in North Africa, where he lost an eye, and army service and a civil service post in India from 1553 to 1569. He wrote numerous sonnets, eclogues, elegies, odes, satires, epigrams, canzoni, and plays. In the epic *Os Lusiadas* (1572, "The Lusiads"), Camoëns brought the Portuguese lyric to the point of perfection. This work is considered one of the greatest written in Europe during Renaissance times and is regarded as the Portuguese national epic.

**CAMOMILE,** or CHAMOMILE, common name for a herb of the family Compositae (q.v.). The three genera of camomiles are *Anthemis, Boltonia,* and *Matricaria.* Two species are *A. nobilis,*

*Camomile,* Anthemis nobilis          Edith A. Schmitz

or garden camomile, a European perennial, and *M. chamomilla,* or sweet false camomile, a European annual. Both species bear flowers with white rays and yellow disks, and have a strong scent and a bitter taste. The dried flowers of *A. nobilis* are often used to make camomile tea. Also, oil may be extracted from the flowers for use in perfume, medicine, and hair rinses.

**CAMORRA,** secret criminal and terrorist society in the former Italian Kingdom of the Two Sicilies, the members of which, called Camorristi, plundered and terrorized the country for many years. The society, originating from a fraternal organization among prisoners, become prominent about 1830. During the turmoil in Italy in the fight for Italian unity, the Camorra prospered. The society allied with the forces of the Italian patriot Giuseppi Garibaldi (q.v.) and helped expel the ruling House of Bourbon from Italy (*see* BOURBON: *Italian Bourbons*). In the period after unification in 1870, a brief, unsuccessful attempt was made to employ the Camorristi in police service. The society continued to terrorize the country and during the early 1900's it practically dominated the city of Naples. The power of the Camorra was ended in 1911 when the Camorristi were brought to trial for murder.

**CAMOUFLAGE** (Fr. *camoufler,* "to disguise"), word introduced by the French at the beginning of World War I to designate scientific disguise of objects through imitation of natural surroundings. Early in the war front-line camouflage, or concealment from ground observation, played the principal role. Later the development of the bomber plane made camouflage of industrial centers far in the rear of the fighting front a necessity. To camouflage an object, the surrounding landscape is imitated by the use of fabric screens, grass, or shrubs, genuine or artificial. Fortifications or factories may be given the appearance of farm buildings, and well-known landmarks may be altered or duplicated. During World War II the use of aerial survey (q.v.) and the development of infrared (q.v.) photography, which distinguishes between natural and artificial vegetation, led to the development of sophisticated devices for camouflage.

For information about protective coloration in animals, see ADAPTATION.

**CAMP, Walter Chauncey** (1859–1925), American football authority and writer, born in New Britain, Conn., and educated at Yale University. He became the general athletic director and head football coach at Yale in 1888. He was active in revising the rules by which football was played. He invented the system of downs, created the position of quarterback, and set the number of players at eleven. In 1889 he initiated the practice of honoring the best college football players of each season by naming them to an "All-American Team." Camp was the author of many books on football. See FOOTBALL.

**CAMPAGNA DI ROMA,** undulating plain of central Italy, surrounding Rome, in the modern region of Latium (q.v.). The name is applied to the district of about 800 sq.mi. extending about 90 miles S. along the coast of the Tyrrhenian Sea from the city of Civitavecchia to the city of Terracina. From the coast the district extends inland to the Alban and the Sabine hills, a distance of between 25 and 40 mi. The ground, which never rises higher than 200 ft. above sea level, is almost entirely volcanic. The many lakes were formed in craters of extinct volcanoes. Until the 5th and 6th centuries A.D. the Campagna di Roma was well inhabited and was filled with luxurious villas, ruins of which have been found. During the Middle Ages the political insecurity of the region following the fall of Rome, as well as the poor soil resulting from misuse of the land and the misuse of the water supply, led to a gradual depopulation and to an increase of unhealthful conditions, including malaria. Reclamation of the district was begun in the 19th century and largely completed in the 1930's. Today the district has grazing land for sheep and cattle and land suitable for growing grain, vegetables, and fruit.

**CAMPANELLA, Tommaso,** real name GIOVANNI DOMENICO CAMPANELLA (1568–1639), Italian philosopher, born in Stilo, and educated in the order of the Dominicans (q.v.). He dissented from the teaching of his time, and in 1599 he was arrested on charges of heresy and of conspiring against the Spanish government in Naples. He spent the next twenty-seven years in prison in Naples, where he wrote *Civitas Solis,* ("City of the Sun", 1623), a description of an ideal society patterned after the *Republic* of the Greek philosopher Plato (q.v.). He was released from prison in 1634, but renewed persecutions compelled him to seek refuge in France. Many of the tenets of his philosophy were similar to the views of the French philosopher René Descartes (q.v.) and the later German philosopher Immanuel Kant (q.v.). His works, eighty-two in all, treated many different philosophical subjects.

**CAMPANIA,** Region of Italy, on the Tyrrhenian Sea, between Latium and Basilicata, and comprising the provinces of Avellino, Benevento, Caserta, Naples, and Salerno. The islands of Capri and Ischia (qq.v.) in the Bay of Naples form part of the Region. The capital is Naples (q.v.). In the E. section Campania is crossed by the Apennines. The coastal plain, which is exceptionally fertile and thickly populated, is noted for the production of citrus fruits and garden vegetables. Corn, oats, tobacco, olives, and wine grapes also are grown in Campania. Other leading regional industries are livestock raising, fishing, lumbering, tanning, canning, oil refining, shipbuilding, and the manufacture of glass, ceramics, chemicals, machinery, textiles, and iron and steel. The tourist industry is important also. Among the notable landmarks are Mount Vesuvius (see VESUVIUS) and Lake Avernus (see AVERNUS, LAKE). Area, 5249 sq.mi.; pop. (1971 prelim.) 4,997,401.

**History.** Greeks settled on the Campanian coast about 1030 B.C. and founded, among other colonies, the cities of Cumae (q.v.) and Neapolis (Naples). In the 4th century B.C. the district fell under Roman rule and became a favorite resort of wealthy Romans. After the fall of the Western Roman Empire in the 5th century A.D., Campania was occupied successively by Goths, Byzantines, and Lombards. The Normans, who conquered it in the 11th century, ruled it as part of the Kingdom of the Two Sicilies (see SICILY). The Region was incorporated subsequently in the Kingdom of Naples and united in 1861 with the Kingdom of Italy. During the invasion of Italy by the Allies in World War II Campania suffered extensive destruction (see WORLD WAR II: *The Italian Campaign*).

**CAMPANILE.** See BELL TOWER.

**CAMPANULA** (Lat., "little bell"), type genus of widely distributed flowering herbs of the

*The waterfront of Naples, the capital of Campania, with Mt. Vesuvius in the background.*
Italian State Tourist Office

Bellflower family (Campanulaceae). The species of this genus number about 250, and are found in the Northern Hemisphere, chiefly in Europe. Characterized by their hardiness and by the beauty of their flowers, they are among the most widely cultivated of the garden plants. The bluebell (q.v.), *C. rotundifolia,* made popular in the literature of the British Isles, is probably the best-known species of the genus. It is a perennial, varying in height from about 6 to 20 in. and bearing attractive blue-violet flowers. Other popular perennial species are *C. carpatica,* the Carpathian harebell; *C. pyramidalis,* the chimney plant; and *C. persicifolia,* the peach-leaved bellflower. The popular Canterbury bell, *C. medium,* is a biennial, native to central Europe and cultivated in the United States to produce varieties greatly diversified in color and size. A common annual species is *C. americana,* the tall bellflower, which grows throughout the U.S. This species is taller than most, often growing to more than 6 ft. in height.

**CAMPBELL,** city of California, in Santa Clara Co., about 5 miles S.W. of San Jose. Situated in an agricultural area, the city is a food-processing center. Manufactures include electrical supplies, furniture, and aluminum products. It is the site of West Valley College, established in 1963. Pop. (1960) 11,863; (1970) 24,770.

**CAMPBELL,** city of Ohio, in Mahoning Co., on the Mahoning R., about 3 miles S.E. of Youngstown. Campbell is an industrial city whose manufactures include iron and steel products. Originally known as East Youngstown, the city was renamed in 1926. Pop. (1960) 13,406; (1970) 12,577.

**CAMPBELL,** noble Scottish family of the county of Argyll (q.v.) having the hereditary titles of the earls, marquises, and dukes of Argyll. The lineage of the family has been traced to Sir Colin Campbell of Loch Awe, who was knighted in 1286, and who bequeathed to the chiefs of his line the title *Mac Callum More* ("great Colin's son"). Sir Duncan Campbell was made a peer, Lord Campbell, in 1445, and his son Colin (d. 1493) was created the 1st Earl of Argyll in 1457. Other important members of the family are the following.

**Archibald Campbell, 2nd Earl of Argyll** (d. 1513), son of the first earl. While commanding the right wing of the Scottish army in the battle against the English at Flodden (q.v.), England, he was killed.

**Archibald Campbell, 4th Earl of Argyll** (d. 1558), grandson of the second earl. He was an early follower of the Scottish religious reformer John Knox (q.v.) and one of the first Scottish nobles to espouse the cause of the Reformation (q.v.).

**Archibald Campbell, 5th Earl of Argyll** (1530–73), son of the fourth earl. He was a supporter of Mary, Queen of Scots (q.v.), and was implicated in the murder in 1567 of her husband Henry Stewart, Lord Darnley (q.v.). In 1568 Argyll, commanding the army of the queen, was defeated at Langside by the forces of the regent of Scotland, the Earl of Moray (1531?–70). Argyll later made peace with Moray and was made lord high chancellor of Scotland in 1572.

**Archibald Campbell, 1st Marquis and 8th Earl of Argyll** (1598–1661), great-grandson of the fifth earl. A Puritan, he was a leader of the Covenanters (q.v.), and at the onset of the first phase of the Great Rebellion (q.v.), he forced Charles I (q.v.), King of England, to submit to the demands of the Scottish Parliament. In 1645 Argyll and his forces were defeated at Inverlochy by Scottish Royalist nobles led by the Scottish soldier James Graham Montrose (q.v.). After the execution of Charles I in 1649, Argyll invited Charles II (q.v.) to Scotland, and crowned him King of Scotland at Scone in 1651. In 1660, upon the restoration of Charles II as King of England, Argyll was arrested on a charge of having collaborated with the Commonwealth leader Oliver Cromwell (*see under* CROMWELL) in the latter's invasion of Scotland in 1650. Argyll was tried by the Scottish Parliament, and was convicted and beheaded.

**Archibald Campbell, 9th Earl of Argyll** (1629–85), son of the eighth earl. During the second phase of the Great Rebellion (q.v.) he fought for Charles II against Oliver Cromwell at Dunbar, Scotland, in 1650. After the Restoration Argyll increasingly criticized the government. Subsequently, he was arrested for treason and his estates were seized. He escaped to the Netherlands, where he joined the conspiracy to capture the English throne for James Scott, Duke of Monmouth (q.v.). Argyll and Monmouth led an invasion of Scotland in 1685, but both were captured and beheaded.

**Archibald Campbell, 10th Earl and 1st Duke of Argyll** (1651?–1703), son of the ninth earl. During the Glorious Revolution (*see* ENGLAND: *History*), he helped the Dutch royal couple to gain the thrones of the British Isles as William III and Mary II (qq.v.). Argyll recovered the lands that had been seized from his father and had been denied Argyll by the deposed monarch James II (q.v.), King of England. Argyll was instrumental in the submission of the Scottish nobles to the joint sovereigns and in 1701 he was rewarded with a dukedom.

**John Campbell, 2nd Duke of Argyll and Duke of Greenwich** (1678–1743), son of the first duke. He distinguished himself as a soldier, fighting under John Churchill (q.v.), 1st Duke of Marlborough, at the Battle of Malplaquet (France) during the War of the Spanish Succession (*see* SPANISH SUCCESSION, WAR OF THE). Later, as high commissioner, Argyll furthered the union of England and Scotland. In his political activities he several times changed his views and alternated in favor and disfavor at court. He was made Duke of Greenwich in the English peerage in 1719.

**Archibald Campbell, 3rd Duke of Argyll** (1682–1761), brother of the second duke. He was treasurer of Scotland in 1705; he aided in the union of England and Scotland; and in 1707 he became one of the original Scottish peers in the first Parliament of Great Britain. In Parliament he later became the adviser on Scottish affairs for the British statesman Sir Robert Walpole (*see under* WALPOLE). Argyll was Keeper of the Great Seal from 1734 until his death.

**George John Douglas Campbell, 8th Duke of Argyll** (1823–1900), descendant of a younger son of the ninth earl. He served as Lord Privy Seal from 1853 to 1855 and again from 1880 to 1881, postmaster general in 1855, and secretary of state for India from 1868 to 1874. He wrote a variety of scientific papers, a series of pamphlets on patronage in the Church of Scotland, and a series of works to reconcile the doctrines of Christianity with current scientific thought.

**John Douglas Sutherland Campbell, 9th Duke of Argyll and Marquis of Lorne** (1845–1914), son of the eighth duke. In 1871 he married Princess Louise (1848–1939), fourth daughter of Victoria (q.v.), Queen of Great Britain. From 1878 to 1883 he was governor-general of Canada. He wrote a number of works in both prose and poetry, including the biography of Queen Victoria (1902).

**CAMPBELL, Alexander** (1788–1866), American minister and a founder of the Christian Church (Disciples of Christ), or Campbellites. He was born in Ireland and studied for one year at the University of Glasgow. After emigrating to the United States in 1809, he later settled in Bethany, W.Va. At first a member of the Baptist church, he organized the Disciples of Christ about 1827.

Campbell founded Bethany College in 1840 and served as its president until his death. In 1823 he established the *Christian Baptist*, which became the *Millennial Harbinger* in 1830;

Campbell continued the magazine until 1863. He also engaged in many public debates and published approximately sixty volumes, including hymn books and a translation of the New Testament. His most important doctrinal work is *The Christian System* (1839). Campbell also wrote a biography of his father, Thomas Campbell (1763–1854), *Memoirs of Elder Thomas Campbell* (1861). The elder Campbell was associated with his son in organizing the Disciples of Christ and in writing for the *Christian Baptist* and the *Millennial Harbinger.*

**CAMPBELL, Beatrice Stella Tanner,** known usually as MRS. PATRICK CAMPBELL (1865–1940), British actress, born in London, England. Her first important stage success was in 1893 in the title role of *The Second Mrs. Tanqueray* by the British dramatist Sir Arthur Wing Pinero (q.v.). Mrs. Campbell was noted for her performances of the Shakespearean roles of Juliet, Ophelia, and Lady Macbeth. She also appeared in a number of dramas by the Norwegian playwright Henrik Ibsen (q.v.), the most notable being the title role in *Hedda Gabler* in 1907. After she met the British dramatist George Bernard Shaw (q.v.), Shaw wrote the role of Eliza Doolittle in *Pygmalion* (1912) for her. Mrs. Campbell made several tours of the United States; she retired from the stage in 1938. She wrote an autobiography, *My Life and Some Letters* (1922); her correspondence with Shaw was published in 1952.

**CAMPBELL, Sir Colin, Baron Clyde** (1792–1863), British field marshal, born in Glasgow, Scotland. His original surname was Macliver, but he took the surname of his maternal uncle, Campbell. Entering the army in 1808, he fought in the Peninsular War (*see* SPAIN: *History*) with distinction and was badly wounded. He served in 1842 in China during the Opium War (q.v.) and from 1854 to 1855 he was a field commander in the Crimean War (q.v.). He was largely responsible for the British victory at the Alma R. and for driving back the Russian attack on Balaklava (q.v.). In 1856 Campbell was promoted to the rank of lieutenant general and knighted. Called to India at the outbreak of the Indian Mutiny (q.v.) in 1857, he effected the relief of Lucknow (q.v.) and quelled the revolt of the sepoys, or native soldiers. For these services he was created Baron Clyde in 1858 and appointed field marshal in 1862.

**CAMPBELL, Sir Malcolm** (1885–1948), British corporation director and automobile racer, born in Chislehurst, Kent, England, and educated in Uppingham and abroad. He was prominent in the business world of England as a director and

*Beatrice Campbell on her first American tour, in 1896.*

officer in a number of corporations, but he is known in the United States chiefly for the world speed records he set, beginning in the 1920's, in his specially constructed racing cars on the flat sands in Daytona Beach, Fla.; and near Bonneville, Utah. He was knighted in 1931. Campbell is the author of *Speed* (1931), *The Romance of Motor-Racing* (1936), *The Roads and the Problem of their Safety* (1937), and *Drifting to War* (1937).

**CAMPBELL, Mrs. Patrick.** *See* CAMPBELL, BEATRICE STELLA TANNER.

**CAMPBELL, Robert.** *See* ROB ROY.

**CAMPBELL, Thomas** (1777–1844), British poet, born in Glasgow, Scotland, and educated at the University of Glasgow. He served briefly as a tutor and studied law before settling in Edinburgh and embarking on a literary career. His first work, "The Pleasures of Hope" (1799), a poem in couplets, met with immediate success. Other successes followed, and in 1805, through the influence of the British statesman Charles James Fox (q.v.), he was granted a royal pension. Campbell served as lord rector of the University of Glasgow from 1826 to 1829 and was later instrumental in founding the University of London. He was buried in Westminister Abbey (q.v.). Much of his fame rests on the war poems "Hohenlinden", "Ye Mariners of England", and

"The Battle of the Baltic", all of which abound in memorable lines that are often quoted. His volumes of poetry include *Gertrude of Wyoming* (1809), *Theodoric* (1824), and *The Pilgrim of Glencoe* (1842). In addition, he compiled *Specimens of the British Poets* (7 vol., 1819).

**CAMPBELL, William Wallace** (1862–1938), American astronomer, born in Hancock County, Ohio, and educated at the University of Michigan. He taught astronomy at the University of Michigan, and in 1891 he joined the staff of the Lick Observatory of the University of California, serving as its director from 1901–1930. Campbell also was president of the University of California (1923–30) and led research into many fields of astronomy including studies of various nebulae and bright-line stars, eclipses, atmosphere of Mars, and computation of astronomical calendars. He wrote *The Elements of Practical Astronomy* (1899) and *Stellar Motions* (1913), and many papers.

**CAMPBELL-BANNERMAN, Sir Henry** (1836–1908), British statesman, born in Glasgow, Scotland, and educated at Trinity College, University of Cambridge. He entered Parliament as member for Stirling, Scotland, in 1868 and allied himself with the Liberal Party of Prime Minister William Ewart Gladstone (q.v.). In 1886 Campbell-Bannerman was secretary for war under Gladstone and from 1892 to 1895 in the ministries of Gladstone and Archibald Philip Primrose, 5th Earl of Rosebery (1847–1929). Campbell-Bannerman was chosen leader of the Liberal Party in 1899 and became prime minister in 1905. During his ministry he granted responsible government to the Transvaal and Orange Free State (qq.v.), but he failed in his ambition to gain home rule for Ireland. He resigned his post two weeks before his death, because of illness.

**CAMPBELL ISLAND,** mountainous island in the South Pacific Ocean, about 450 mi. s. of New Zealand, to which it belongs. Although only about 30 mi. in circumference, the semicircular island has good harbors that are used as provision depots but are not permanently inhabited. Campbell Island is rich in fur seals. Area, 64 sq.mi.

**CAMPBELLITES.** *See* Campbell, Alexander; Christian Church (Disciples of Christ Church).

**CAMPEACHY WOOD** *or* **CAMPECHE WOOD.** *See* Logwood.

**CAMPERDOWN,** broad tract of sandy hills located near the North Sea in the village of Camp, North Holland Province, the Netherlands. Off Camperdown, on Oct. 11, 1797, during the French Revolution (q.v.) a British fleet defeated a Dutch fleet in the service of France.

**CAMP FIRE GIRLS, INC.,** national nonsectarian organization for girls seven through high-school age, founded in 1910 by the American physical-education specialist Luther Halsey Gulick (1865–1919). Camp Fire Girls pioneered in numerous fields, including group camping for girls. In groups varying in size from 8 to 30 girls, with trained adult volunteer leadership, girls develop skills in seven crafts: home, outdoors, creative arts, science, business, sports and games, and citizenship. The groups are composed of Blue Birds, ages 7 and 8; Camp Fire Girls, 9 to 11; Junior Hi' Camp Fire Girls, 12 and 13; and Horizon Club members, 14 through high school. As they grow older, girls advance into more specialized activities, explore possibilities for careers, participate in activities with boys, become involved in community affairs, and travel in the United States and abroad.

The watchword of Camp Fire Girls is Wo-He-Lo, composed of the first two letters of work, health, and love. The insignia is crossed logs and flame, symbolizing the fire of the outdoor camp and the flame of the hearth. The program stresses femininity, individuality, and understanding of others and oneself.

The President of the U.S. is the Honorary President of Camp Fire Girls, Inc. The policy-making body, the national council, is composed of 50 to 150 members chosen from seven regional councils. More than 400 chartered councils and associations exist, and membership is over 600,000.

Financial support comes from community fund agencies and other organizations, from individuals, and from membership dues. The national headquarters are in New York City.

**CAMPHOR,** volatile, white, crystalline compound, $C_{10}H_{16}O$, with a characteristic aromatic odor. Camphor is insoluble in water, soluble in organic solvents, and has m.p. 176° C. (349° F.), b.p. 209° C. (405° F.), and sp.g. 0.99. The compound occurs in three slightly different forms. Ordinary camphor is obtained from the camphor tree, *Cinnamomum camphora*, which grows in Taiwan, Japan, parts of China, Java, Sumatra, and Brazil. The camphor is distilled by steaming chips of the root, stem, or bark. The leaves of certain plants, such as tansy and feverfew (qq.v.), contain a second form of camphor, which is not used commercially. Racemic camphor is the form that is produced synthetically; it is also present in the oil of an Asian chrysanthemum (q.v.).

Most camphor used commercially is made synthetically. It is used in the manufacture of celluloid and explosives (qq.v.), and medicinally

in liniments and other preparations for its mild antiseptic and anesthetic qualities. Camphor is poisonous if ingested in large amounts.

**CAMPI,** family of 16th-century Italian painters of Cremona. The most important members of the family were the four sons of Galeazzo Campi (1477–1536), who was a painter of religious pictures. They were the following.

**Giulio Campi** (1502?–72). Trained by his father and the Italian painter Giulio Romano (q.v.), he is best known for building and decorating Santa Margherita, a church in Cremona. He also painted frescoes in the cathedral in Cremona and in other churches in Cremona and Milan. Among his art students were his three brothers.

**Bernardino Campi** (1522–90?). He is best known for the frescoes in the cupola of the Church of San Sigismondo in Cremona.

**Antonio Campi** (1530?–91?). He was one of the artists commissioned by Philip II (q.v.), King of Spain, to decorate the Escorial (q.v.) in Spain. He painted the "Birth of Christ" in the Church of San Paolo, Milan.

**Vincenzo Campi** (1536–91). He specialized in still lifes and portraits, some of which are in the Bergamo Gallery, Bergamo, and the Brera Gallery, Milan.

**CAMPIN, Robert.** *See* FLÉMALLE, LE MAÎTRE DE.

**CAMPINA GRANDE,** city of Brazil, in Paraíba State, at the edge of the arid Borborema Plateau, 70 miles w. of João Pessoa and 100 mi. N.W. of Recife. It is an industrial processing and export center for a large cotton-growing region that also produces sugar, oranges, pineapples, cassava, tobacco, and agave. Deposits of tantalite and columbite are nearby. Campina Grande is the site of a thermoelectric station. Pop. (1970) 163,206.

**CAMPINAS,** city of Brazil, in São Paulo State, on the Piracicaba R., about 65 miles N.W. of the city of São Paulo. Connected by rail with São Paulo and the port of Santos, it is the trading and shipping center of a region producing coffee, sugar, grain, and cotton. Pop. (1970) 328,629.

**CAMPING,** living in tents or other temporary shelters, including special vehicles, primarily as a form of outdoor recreation in parks or forests, on beaches, in mountains, or in similar remote environments. The relative comfort and style of camping depends upon the preference of the individual camper, whose equipment may be rudimentary or considerable. Camping may consist of backpacking, or hiking with a knapsack, whereby one sleeps unsheltered on the ground and cooks food over an open wood fire; or of traveling in a camping vehicle having amenities such as insulated walls, gas heating, built-in beds, kitchen range and refrigerator, and bathroom facilities. *See* RECREATIONAL VEHICLE. Boats are also used on lakes or waterways for camping.

**Campsites and Facilities.** In the United States more than 10,000 campgrounds, public and private, provide a wide range of facilities such as water taps, public toilets and showers, tables and cooking stoves, and electrical outlets. Private campgrounds tend to be more expensive than public sites, which are free or available at a nominal charge, but frequently offer special recreational facilities such as swimming, fishing, archery (qq.v.), boating (*see* YACHTING), and other outdoor sports. Families that use private campgrounds usually stay a week or more at a single site, whereas public campgrounds are preferred by the more nomadic, self-sufficient campers. Many campsites are available in national forests and parks throughout the U.S. So-

43

called raw campsites are those requiring that the camper pack on his back, or on horse or muleback, whatever is needed for his subsistence, such as water, food, and a sleeping bag.

Detailed topographic maps distributed by the National Park Service and Forest Service (qq.v.) are used by recreationists who prefer the raw campsites. Special hiking maps also are available for backpacking campers who use the many established trails. The route of the Appalachian Trail (q.v.), for example, can be followed from Georgia to Maine with carefully documented maps; distances are calculated to the hundredth of a mile, shelters and raw campsites are marked, and nearby sources of food and supplies are indicated. See MAP: Types of Maps; Map Scales.

**Camping Equipment.** Experienced campers plan their outings with considerable care, economy, and daily scheduling regarding destination. Optimal clothes for campers are generally layers of light garments which can be added or removed as comfort or weather demands. A man, for example, may wear a cotton shirt and trousers, and add a sweater if the temperature drops in the evening, plus a nylon parka if a cold wind develops. Socks worn are usually of wool and should be long enough to reach the calf of the leg. Suitable shoes include sneakers, ankle-high boots, and moccasins with tough, composition soles. For sleeping, air mattresses, foam pads, sleeping bags, or folding cots are used.

Eating and cooking equipment chosen by the camper depend on weight and space limitations. For eating utensils he may use plastic dinnerware, paper plates, or metal kit and canteen. For cooking most campers use durable ware such as heavy aluminum pots, skillets, coffee makers, and griddles, although backpackers may prefer lightweight aluminum gear. Meals can be prepared over a wood fire or on portable ranges using kerosene, alcohol, gasoline, or liquid petroleum as fuel. Today many foods, from coffee to meat dishes, are available in dehydrated or freeze-dried form, providing the camper with canned meals of reduced weight and bulk. Aluminum foil is widely used for packaging and cooking foods in camp and, with some ingenuity, can also be fashioned into makeshift cooking utensils themselves. Other equipment useful in camping includes knives or axes, compasses, first-aid kits, binoculars, cameras, and various survival handbooks.

**Pleasures and Value of Camping.** Camplife consists essentially of two activities, working to maintain eating and sleeping facilities and

enjoying the recreational benefits of the campsite area. With adequate equipment and proper organization, the necessary work can be held to a minimum so that more time is available for recreation.

Walking for pleasure or hiking for physical activity enables the outdoorsman to view at close range the native plants and animals of the area. If not prohibited by regulations of a park or forest preserve, he can collect specimens of flowers and insects; see CONSERVATION. Larger forms of animal life can be observed in their habitats through binoculars or photographed. By following the runoff of rainwater into streams and lakes, the camper can observe the feeding activity of fish, which is stimulated by the appearance of worms, insects, and other organisms washed into their habitat by the rainwater. A deeper appreciation of the role of weather in nature can also be acquired, and the camper can learn how to make his own forecast by observing wind directions and cloud formations and movements; see METEOROLOGY. By living close to nature through camping, one gains new insights into the important relationships and dynamic factors in the ecological environment. See ECOLOGY. See also HOSTEL.

**CAMPION, Edmund** (1540–81), English Jesuit, born in London and educated at the University of Oxford. Although ordained a deacon in 1567, he could not accept the Protestant formulary as required by the Church of England. Accordingly, he left England for Ireland in 1569; later he went to France, where he joined in 1573 the Roman Catholic Church, and to Rome. Returning to England in 1580 on a mission to establish Catholicism, he was hunted and harassed in his work. Despite persecution he wrote a bold attack on the Church of England, *Decem Rationes* ("Ten Reasons"), which was distributed at the Oxford commencement in 1581. A few weeks later he was captured and brought before Elizabeth I (q.v.), Queen of England, who offered him honors and fortune if he would recant. When he refused the offer, he was imprisoned, tortured, and hanged as a traitor. He was beatified by Pope Leo XIII (see under LEO) in 1886.

**CAMPION, Thomas** (1567–1620?), English poet and musician, born in London, and educated at the University of Cambridge. Although he was a London physician with a large practice, Campion was active in literature and music. His reputation rests chiefly on his lyric poems, which are distinguished for their musical quality and charm; among them are "Cherry Ripe" and "Whether Men Do Laugh or Weep". His other works include *Poemata* (1595), poems in Latin;

the words and music for such court masques as *The Lord's Masque* (1613); *Observations on the Arte of English Poesie* (1602); four books of *Ayres* ("Airs", 1601–about 1617); and *A New Way of Making Four Parts in Counterpoint* (1613).

**CAMPOAMOR Y CAMPOOSORIO, Ramón de** (1817–1901), Spanish poet, philosopher, and statesman, born in Navia, educated at the University of Santiago and at the Jesuit College of Saint Thomas. The political offices he held included those of governor of the provinces of Alicante and Valencia in 1854, and councilor of state after 1874 under Alfonso XII, King of Spain (*see under* ALFONSO). Campoamor is best known as one of the most popular poets of his day. He wrote short, philosophical verse epigrams called *doloras;* these poems were usually sentimental and humorous, and were based on an unsophisticated philosophy of life. Campoamor's poetry is typified by *Doloras* (1846), *Pequeños Poemas* ("Little Epics", 1872–94), and *Humoradas* ("Humorous Sayings", 1886–88).

**CAMPOBELLO.** *See* ROOSEVELT-CAMPOBELLO INTERNATIONAL PARK.

**CAMPOFORMIO, TREATY OF,** peace agreement between Austria and France, signed in the village of Campoformio (now Campoformido), in northern Italy, on Oct. 17, 1797. This treaty ended the Italian campaign of Napoléon Bonaparte, later Napoleon I (q.v.), Emperor of France. The campaign, generally regarded as the initial phase of the Napoleonic Wars (q.v.), began in 1796 in northern Italy. Preliminary negotiations for the treaty had been completed in Leoben, Austria, on April 18. By the principal terms of the treaty Austria ceded to France the Ionian Islands (q.v.) and the Austrian Netherlands (Belgium). In compensation, most of the territories of the Republic of Venice were awarded to Austria; *see* VENICE: *History.* Austria also agreed to recognize the two Italian, French-sponsored states known as the Ligurian Republic (*see* LIGURIA) and the Cisalpine Republic (q.v.).

**CAMPOS,** city of Brazil, in Rio de Janeiro State, on the Paraíba R., about 30 mi. from its mouth, and 70 miles N. of Niterói. Coffee, tobacco, sugarcane, and tropical fruits are grown in the surrounding region. Among industries in the city are sugar refining, alcohol distilling, and fruit preserving. Pop. (1970) 153,310.

**CAMULODUNUM.** *See* COLCHESTER.

**CAMUS, Albert** (1913–60), French novelist, essayist, and dramatist, born in Mondovi (now Drean), Algeria, and educated at the University of Algiers. Camus lived in Algeria until 1940, when he moved to Paris and joined the staff of

Albert Camus          French Embassy Press & Information Div.

the newspaper *Paris-Soir.* He was active in the French Resistance, especially as editor of the clandestine newspaper *Combat.*

An Algerian background provides the setting for Camus' first published novel, *L'Étranger* (1942; Eng. trans., *The Stranger,* 1946), and for most of his subsequent fiction. *L'Étranger* and the essay *Le Mythe de Sisyphe* (1942; Eng. trans., *The Myth of Sisyphus,* 1955), in which he sees the existence of man in the universe as meaningless and absurd, reveal the influence of Existentialism (q.v.) on his thought. Of the plays that develop these themes, *Caligula* (1944), produced in New York City in 1960, is one of the best known. Although in the novel *La Peste* (1947; Eng. trans., *The Plague,* 1948) Camus still is concerned with the fundamental absurdity of existence, he recognizes the heroism of man in the face of disasters. His later works include the novel *La Chute* (1957; Eng. trans., *The Fall,* 1957). *Lyrical and Critical Essays* (1968) includes some of his earliest works, while *Une Morte Heureuse* (1971; Eng. trans., *A Happy Death,* 1972), although posthumously published, was actually his first novel. Regarded as one of the finest philosophical writers of modern France, he was awarded the 1957 Nobel Prize in literature.

**CANAAN,** in the Old Testament, designation of the land to the west of the Jordan R., later known as Palestine (*see* PALESTINE: *History*), and the name of the reputed ancestor of the Canaanites (q.v.), the original inhabitants of that land. The Israelites (see JEWS) gradually conquered and occupied this territory during the 2nd millennium B.C. or earlier. It was probably the Canaanites who gave the Israelites the language now known as Hebrew.

**CANAANITES,** in the Old Testament, original inhabitants of the land of Canaan (q.v.). According to the book of Judges (q.v.), the Israelites, during the 2nd millennium B.C. or earlier, gradually subjugated the Canaanite cities. By the end of the reign of Solomon (q.v.), King of Israel, the Canaanites virtually had been assimilated into the Hebrew people, among whom they appear to have exerted a reactionary religious influence. The Canaanite religion itself was based on the worship of the divinities Baal (q.v.) and Ashtoreth (see ASTARTE). Biblical scholars now believe that the Hebrew language (q.v.) was derived from Canaanite sources, and that the Phoenician language (q.v.) was an early form of Hebrew. Recent discoveries indicate that the Canaanites and the Phoenicians formed, in fact, one nation before the Hebrew conquest of the south of Canaan, and that the people we now know as the Phoenicians subsequently developed as a separate nation. See PHOENICIA.

**CANADA,** federated state of North America, known for many years as the Dominion of Canada although the term "Dominion" is no longer in common use. Canada is the largest member of the Commonwealth of Nations (q.v.) and ranks second in area (after the U.S.S.R.) among the nations of the world. Canada is bounded on the N. by the Arctic Ocean, on the N.E. by Baffin Bay and Davis Strait, which separate it from Greenland, on the E. by the Atlantic Ocean, on the S. by the United States, and on the W. by the Pacific Ocean and Alaska. Occupying all of North America N. of the U.S., except Alaska, Greenland, Saint Pierre, and Miquelon, Canada includes many islands, notably the Canadian Arctic Islands (Arctic Archipelago) in the Arctic Ocean. Among the larger islands of this group, which aggregates over 575,000 sq.mi. in area, are Baffin, Victoria, Ellesmere, Banks, Devon, Axel Heiberg, and Melville. Cape Columbia, a promontory of Ellesmere Island at lat. 83°07′ N., is the northernmost point of Canada; its southernmost point is Middle Island, in Lake Erie, at lat. 41°41′ N. The easternmost and westernmost limits are delineated respectively by long. 52°37′ W., which lies along Cape Spear, Newfoundland, and long. 141° W., which coincides with part of the Alaskan-Canadian frontier. Canada has a total land area of 3,560,238 sq.mi.; areas occupied by rivers, lakes, including those portions of the Great Lakes (q.v.) under Canadian jurisdiction, and other bodies of fresh water total 291,571 sq. mi.

### THE LAND

The Canadian mainland coastline, about 36,500 mi. in length, is extremely broken and irregular. Large bays and peninsulas alternate, and Canada has numerous coastal islands, in addition to the Arctic Archipelago, with a total coastline of almost 150,000 mi. Off the E. coast the largest islands are Newfoundland, Cape Breton, Prince Edward, and Anticosti. Off the W. coast, which is fringed with fjords, are Vancouver and Queen Charlotte islands. Southampton Island, covering about 15,900 sq.mi., and many smaller islands are situated in Hudson Bay (q.v.), a vast inland sea in east-central Canada.

Canada contains more lakes and inland waters than any other country. In addition to the Great Lakes on the U.S. border (all partly within Canada except Lake Michigan), the country has over thirty lakes more than 500 sq.mi. in area. Largest among these lakes are Great Bear, Great Slave, Dubawnt, Baker, and Yathkyed in the mainland Northwest Territories; Nettilling and Amadjuak on Baffin Island; Athabasca in Alberta and Saskatchewan; Wollaston in Saskatchewan; Reindeer in Saskatchewan and Manitoba; Winnipeg, Manitoba, Winnipegosis, and Southern Indian in Manitoba; Nipigon and Lake of the Woods in Ontario; Mistassini in Québec; and Melville in Newfoundland.

Among the many great rivers of Canada are the Saint Lawrence, draining the Great Lakes, and emptying into the Gulf of St. Lawrence; the Ottawa and the Saguenay, the principal affluents of the St. Lawrence; the Saint John, emptying into the Bay of Fundy, between Nova Scotia and New Brunswick; the Saskatchewan, flowing into Lake Winnipeg, and the Nelson, flowing from this lake into Hudson Bay; the system, formed by the Athabasca, Peace, Slave, and Mackenzie rivers, which empties into the Arctic Ocean; the upper course of the Yukon, which flows across Alaska into the Bering Sea; and the Fraser and the upper course of the Columbia, emptying into the Pacific Ocean.

Excluding the Arctic Archipelago, five physiographic regions are distinguishable in Canada. The largest region, variously designated as the Canadian Shield (q.v.), the Laurentian Shield, and the Laurentian Plateau, extends from Labrador to the Mackenzie R. and from the Arctic Ocean to the Thousand Islands in the St. Lawrence R. and into the U.S. at Lake Superior. This region of ancient granite rock, sparsely covered with soil and deeply eroded by glacial action, comprises all of Labrador, most of Québec, N. Ontario, Manitoba, and most of the Northwest Territories, with Hudson Bay in the center.

Eastern Canada consists of the Appalachian-Acadian region and the St. Lawrence and Lower Lakes region. The former embraces Newfoundland, Nova Scotia, New Brunswick, and Prince Edward Island, and the Gaspé Peninsula of Québec. This region is an extension of the Appalachian Mts. system (continuations of the Green Mts. of Vermont and the White Mts. of New Hampshire), and of the Atlantic Coastal Plain. The St. Lawrence and Lower Lakes region, covering an area of about 38,000 sq.mi. in s. Québec and Ontario, is a generally level plain. In this region is the largest expanse of cultivable land in E. Canada and about 80 percent of the manufacturing industries of the nation.

Bordering the Canadian Shield on the w. is the Interior Plain, an extension of the Great Plains of the U.S. About 800 mi. wide at the U.S. border, it narrows to about 200 miles w. of Great Bear Lake and widens again at the mouth of the Mackenzie R. on the coast of the Arctic Ocean to 300 mi. Within the Interior Plain are the N.E. corner of British Columbia, most of Alberta, the s. half of Saskatchewan, and the s. third of Manitoba, the most fertile sections of Canada.

The fifth and westernmost region of Canada embraces the uplifts w. of the Interior Plain. The region belongs to the Cordillera (q.v.), the vast mountain system extending from the southernmost extremity of South America to westernmost Alaska. In Canada the Cordillera has an average width of 500 mi. Part of w. Alberta, much of British Columbia, w. Mackenzie District in the Northwest Territories, and practically all of Yukon Territory lie within this region. The E. portion of the Cordillera in Canada consists of the Rocky Mountains (q.v.) and related ranges, including the Mackenzie, Franklin, and Richardson mountains. Mount Robson (12,972 ft.) is the highest summit of the Canadian Rockies, and many other peaks reach elevations over 11,000 ft. To the w. of the Canadian Rockies is a region occupied by numerous isolated ranges, notably the Cariboo, Stikine, and Selkirk mountains, and a vast plateau region. Deep river valleys and extensive tracts of arable land are the chief features of the plateau region, particularly in British Columbia. Flanking this central belt on the w. and generally parallel to the Pacific Ocean is another great mountain system. This system includes the Coast Mts., an extension into British Columbia of the Cascade Range (q.v.) of the U.S., and various coastal ranges. The loftiest coastal uplift is the Saint Elias Mts., on the

The Château Frontenac, a landmark of Québec City, was built in 1890 by the Canadian Pacific Railway.
Canadian Pacific photo from Québec National Tourist Office

boundary between Yukon Territory and Alaska. Among noteworthy peaks of the w. Cordillera in Canada are Mt. Logan (19,850 ft.), the second-highest mountain in North America, Mount St. Elias (18,008 ft.), Lucania Mt. (17,147 ft.), and King Peak (17,130 ft.), all in the St. Elias Mts.

**Geology.** The most ancient rocks found in Canada are the granites, gneisses, and schists that underlie the Canadian Shield, a great U-shaped area with Hudson Bay in the center, extending from the Great Lakes N.E. to the Labrador coast and N.W. to the shores of the Arctic Ocean. The age of the granites and banded rocks is Archean. On the borders of this primitive land area, stratified beds were deposited during all the succeeding geological periods. The Cambrian and Silurian systems are represented by great thicknesses of strata that outcrop in Nova Scotia, New Brunswick, Newfoundland, along the St. Lawrence valley, and on the shores of Lake Ontario. These outcroppings also appear in Manitoba, extending thence in a northwesterly direction toward the Arctic Regions and into British Columbia. The Devonian system is less extensively developed in the E. provinces, but it constitutes a wide belt in the plains regions that border the Cambrian and Silurian strata.

Between this Devonian belt and the E. Rocky Mts. the surface is formed by Cretaceous and

Tertiary beds that are a part of the great system reaching northward from Texas across the U.S. The Rocky Mts. of Canada are similar in structure to the mountains of Colorado, Wyoming, and Montana and have been built up by upheaval and folding of sediments and, to a lesser extent, by volcanic action. The strata of which they are composed range in age from Paleozoic to Tertiary, and in the Selkirks even the Archean may be exposed. The Carboniferous system is not especially important in respect to area, but it contains the valuable coal deposits of Nova Scotia and New Brunswick, and is known to occur also in the central plains region, in British Columbia, and along the arctic coast. The coal beds of Vancouver Island and those found in the Rocky Mts. are of Cretaceous and Tertiary age. In recent geological times nearly the entire area of Canada was covered by an ice sheet, the Laurentian glacier, that terminated in the northern U.S. Surface features were profoundly modified by the erosive action of this vast mass of moving ice, as is evidenced by the numerous great lakes and by the large deposits of sands, gravels, and clays that rest upon the older formations. See NORTH AMERICA: The Land: Geology.

**Climate.** Part of the Canadian mainland and most of the Arctic Archipelago fall within the Frigid Zone, and the remainder of the country lies in the N. half of the North Temperate Zone. In consequence general climatic conditions range from the extreme cold characteristic of the Arctic Regions to the moderate temperatures of more southerly latitudes. The Canadian climate is marked by wide regional variations. In the Maritime Provinces extremes of winter cold and summer heat are modified by oceanic influences, which also cause considerable fog and precipitation. Along the w. coast, which is under the influence of warm ocean currents and moisture-laden winds, mild, equable summers and winters, high humidity, and abundant precipitation are characteristic. In the Cordilleran region the higher w. slopes of certain uplifts, particularly the Selkirks and the Rockies, receive copious amounts of rain and snow, but the E. slopes and the central plateau region are extremely arid. A feature of the Cordilleran region is the chinook, a warm, dry westerly wind that substantially ameliorates winter conditions in the Rocky Mt. foothills and adjoining plains, often causing diurnal changes of 40° F. For further information see articles on the individual provinces.

**Natural Resources.** Canada is richly endowed with valuable natural resources that are com-

mercially indispensable to the economy. The country has enormous areas of fertile, low-lying land bordering the Great Lakes and St. Lawrence R. in s. Québec, Ontario, and the Prairie Provinces. Canadian forests cover over 1,240,000 sq.mi. and abound in commercially valuable stands of timber. Commercial fishing in Canada dates back nearly 500 years. The waters of the Atlantic and Pacific oceans, inland lakes, and rivers continue to yield abundant catches. The mining industry of Canada has a long history of exploration and development that predates confederation in 1867. The Canadian Shield contains a wealth of minerals; the nation is also rich in reserves of crude oil and natural gas. The river and lake systems of the country combine with the mountainous topography to make energy produced by waterpower one of the permanent natural assets of Canada. The wildlife of the country is varied, and fur farming is of considerable value.

**Plants.** The flora of the entire N. part of Canada is arctic and subarctic (see TUNDRA). The St. Lawrence R. valley and the Maritime Provinces are comparatively treeless as far N. as the Saskatchewan R. Prairie grasses, herbage, and the bunchgrasses are the chief forms of vegetation. North of the Saskatchewan a broad belt of rather small and sparse trees extends from Hudson Bay to Great Slave Lake and the Rocky Mts. Spruce, tamarack, and poplar are the principal species. The dry slopes and valleys of the Rocky Mts. support thin forests, mainly pine, but the forests increase in density and the trees in size westward toward the region of greater rainfall. On the coast ranges, especially their w. slopes, are dense forests of mighty evergreen trees. The principal trees are the spruce, hemlock, Douglas and balsam firs, jack and lodgepole pines, and cedar. See NORTH AMERICA: The Land: Natural Resources.

**Animals.** The animals of Canada bear a close resemblance or are identical to those of N. Europe and Asia. Among the carnivores are several species of the weasel subfamily, such as the ermine, sable, fisher, wolverine, and mink. Other representative carnivores include the black bear, grizzly bear, lynx, wolf, coyote, fox, and skunk. The polar bear is distributed throughout the Arctic Regions; the puma, or American lion, is found in British Columbia. Of the rodents, the most characteristic is the beaver. The Canada porcupine, muskrat, hare, and many smaller rodents are numerous, and in the w. plains is found a variety of burrowing gopher.

Several varieties of Virginia deer are indigenous to s. Canada; the black-tailed deer occurs

# INDEX TO MAP OF CANADA

**Continued on page 52**

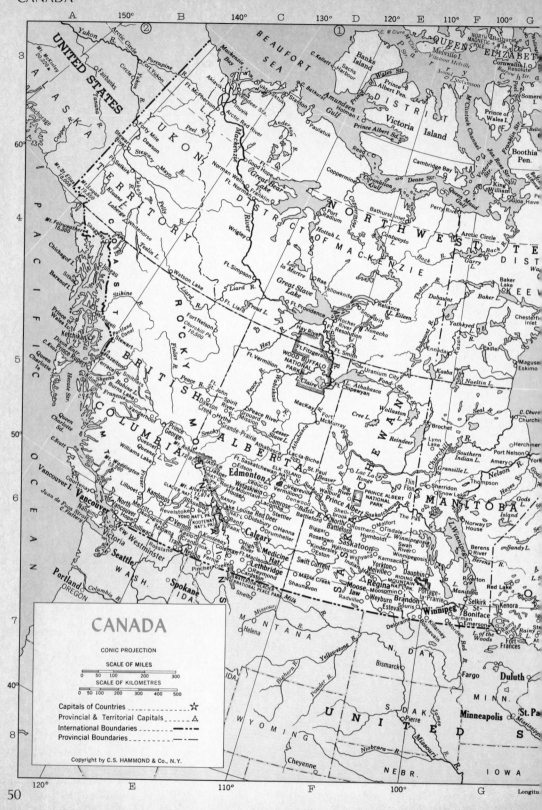

CANADA

CONIC PROJECTION

SCALE OF MILES

0 50 100 200 300

SCALE OF KILOMETRES

0 50 100 200 300 400 500

Capitals of Countries ............ ☆
Provincial & Territorial Capitals .... △
International Boundaries .......... ▬ ▬ ▬
Provincial Boundaries .......... ▬ ▬ ▬

Copyright by C.S. Hammond & Co., N.Y.

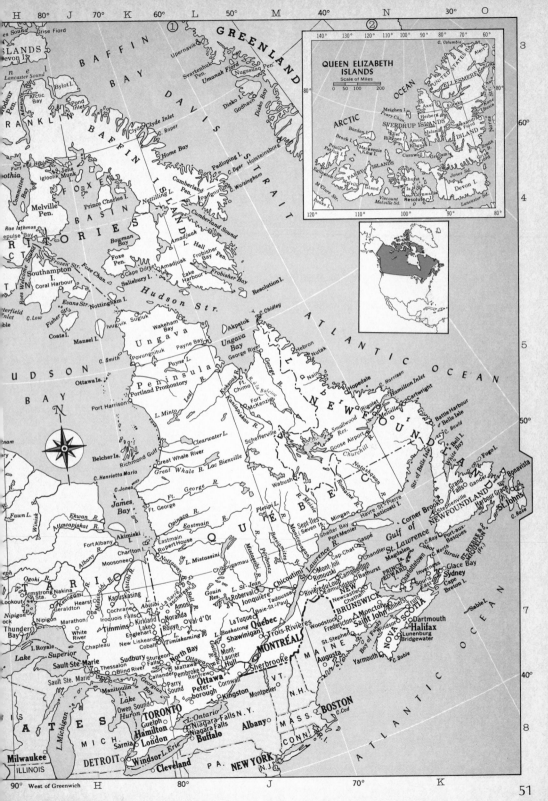

in British Columbia and parts of the plains region. This region is also the habitat of the pronghorn antelope. The woodland caribou and the moose are numerous and widely distributed, but the Barren Ground caribou is found only in the more northerly areas, which are the habitat also of the musk ox. Elk and bison are found in various w. areas. In the mountains of British Columbia bighorn sheep and Rocky Mountain goats are numerous. An immense va-

Montréal, in the province of Québec, is Canada's largest city as well as its commercial and industrial center.   Dick Huffman–Monkmeyer Press

riety of birds abounds, and fish are numerous in all the inland waters and along all the coasts. Reptiles and insects are scarce, except in the most southerly part of the country.

**Soils.** Large areas of Canada are covered by boggy peat characteristic of the tundra and adjoining forest areas. It is generally infertile and frequently mossy. A formation of rich, black prairie soil runs from s. Manitoba westward across Saskatchewan and into Alberta, forming Canada's best farming land. The gray-brown soil of the St. Lawrence basin and the Great Lakes is also good farmland. However, only about 7 percent of Canada's land is suitable for farming, the remainder being too mountainous, rocky, wet, or infertile.

**Waterpower.** Canada ranks second, after Norway, among the countries of the world in per capita production of hydroelectricity. The chief sources of this power are the numerous fast-flowing rivers, found in almost every section of the nation, which supply about 66 percent of the installed generating capacity. Many areas, however, are increasingly developing thermal electric power, using coal, oil, gas, or uranium as sources of energy. In recent years, according to latest available statistics, generating facilities annually produced a total of about 216,500,-000,000 kw hours of electrical energy. In 1962 the Nuclear Power Demonstration Station at Rolphton, Ontario, first produced thermal electric power from uranium. In 1967 a full-scale 220,000-kw nuclear station went into operation at Douglas Point on Lake Huron, followed by the huge nuclear plant at Pickering, Ontario, which has an installed capacity of 2,205,000 kw. An even larger plant is under construction on the Bruce Peninsula, which will have an installed capacity of 3,200,000 kw by 1978.

## THE PEOPLE

The racial and national makeup of the Canadian people is diversified. About 45 percent of the population, which consists predominantly of native-born citizens, is composed of persons of British origin. Persons of French origin total about 29 percent of the population. The vast majority of French-speaking Canadians resides in Québec, where they make up about 80 percent of the population; large numbers also live in Ontario and New Brunswick, and smaller groups inhabit the remaining provinces. French-speaking Canadians maintain their language, culture, and traditions. The Federal government

53

and most provincial governments follow the policy of a bilingual and bicultural nation, with the French language becoming a practical as well as official language, with English, throughout Canada. The remainder of the population is composed of people of various ethnic origins, chiefly German, Italian, Ukrainian, Netherlands Dutch, Scandinavian, Polish, Native Indian, Jewish, Hungarian, and Greek.

Negroes have never constituted a major segment of the Canadian population, but their history has been an interesting one. Although Louis XIV in 1689 authorized the importation of slaves from the West Indies, Negro immigration into Canada has been almost entirely from the U.S. Some Loyalists brought slaves north with them during and after the American Revolution. The British troops that burned Washington in the War of 1812 (q.v.) brought many slaves back with them to Halifax. As early as 1787, however, Nova Scotia, and six years later, Upper Canada, abolished slavery, thus setting precedents for the whole British Empire. The fact of free soil in Canada was a major factor in the operation of the Underground Railroad (q.v.), which, during the abolition campaign in the U.S., transported many slaves into Canada, particularly to Chatham and Sarnia. Negroes in Canada (1971 census) numbered 34,000 and West Indians, 28,000.

American Indians and Eskimos (*see* ESKIMO) in Canada number respectively about 297,000 and 18,000. Close ethnic relatives of the aborigines of the U.S. (*see* AMERICAN INDIANS), the Indians of Canada belong predominantly to the Algonquian linguistic group; other representative linguistic stocks are the Iroquoian, Salishan, Athapaskan, and Eskimoan. Tribal groupings total about forty-five.

**Population.** The population of Canada (1971) was 21,568,311, compared with 20,014,880 in 1966. The 1971 population density was 6.06 per sq.mi.

Approximately three quarters of the people of Canada inhabit a relatively narrow belt along the U.S. frontier, with close to 64 percent concentrated in Québec and Ontario. About 17 percent of the population lives in the Prairie Provinces of Alberta, Manitoba, and Saskatchewan; nearly 10 percent in the Atlantic Provinces, which include Newfoundland and Labrador, and the Maritime Provinces of Prince Edward Island, Nova Scotia, and New Brunswick; and about 10 percent in British Columbia. Yukon Territory and Northwest Territories are sparsely inhabited, having only about 0.3 percent of the total population. About 76 percent of the population lives in urban centers.

**Political Divisions.** Canada comprises ten provinces, each with a separate legislature and administration, and the Yukon Territory and Northwest Territories, which are governed by commissioners, assisted by councils. In descending order of population (1971 official census) the provinces are Ontario, Québec, British Columbia, Alberta, Manitoba, Saskatchewan, Nova Scotia, New Brunswick, Newfoundland, and Prince Edward Island.

**Principal Cities.** The leading cities in descending order of population (1971 official census for metropolitan areas) are Montréal, Québec, seaport and major commercial center (2,743,208); Toronto, Ontario, seaport and manufacturing city (2,628,043); Vancouver, British Columbia, railroad terminal, shipbuilding and lumber center (1,082,352); Ottawa, Ontario, the capital of Canada and noted for lumbering and forest-product production (602,510); Winnipeg, Manitoba, world wheat market and agricultural city (540,262); Hamilton, Ontario, important metallurgical manufacturing center (498,523); Edmonton, Alberta, farming, dairying, and oil-producing center (495,702); Québec, Québec, market of an agricultural and dairy region (480,502); Calgary, Alberta, noted for its ranching, lumber mills, and tanneries (403,319); London, Ontario, railroad terminal and agricultural and chemical center (286,011); Windsor, Ontario, center of an auto-manufacturing and agricultural region (258,643); and Halifax, Nova Scotia, seaport and machinery-producing city (222,637). See separate articles for each of the cities mentioned above.

**Religion.** The largest religious community in Canada is Roman Catholic. Considerably more than half of the communicants of the Roman Catholic faith live in Québec. Of the Protestant denominations in Canada the largest is the United Church of Canada (q.v.), followed by the Anglican Church. Other important religious groups are the Presbyterian, Lutheran, Baptist, Greek Orthodox, Jewish, Ukrainian Catholic, and Pentecostal.

**Education.** The educational system in Canada is derived from the British and American traditions and the French tradition, particularly in the Province of Québec. English or French is the language of instruction, but more schools are instituting instruction in both official languages. Present-day Canadian education is administered under the terms of the British North America Act of 1867, which charged each of the ten provinces with responsibility for establishing and maintaining its own school system. In Québec the French-Canadian tradition is followed with Roman Catholic schools. However, the province also maintains Protestant schools, which are widely attended. Although Canada does not have a central ministry of education, the Federal government provides schools for Indian and Eskimo children, inmates of Federal penitentiaries, and the children of servicemen in Europe.

The earliest Canadian schools, which were conducted by French Catholic religious orders, date from the early 17th century. Higher education was inaugurated in 1635 with the founding of the Collège des Jésuites in the city of Québec. It was not until the transfer of Canada from French to British jurisdiction in 1759 that an educational system began to emerge, which encompassed church, governmental, and private secular schools. The early 19th century saw the founding of the large universities, beginning with McGill in 1821 and followed by Ottawa in 1848 and Toronto in 1904. Since World War II there has been a notable expansion in higher education. Many new institutions have been founded, and the older universities have increased in size, scope, and influence. Universities still are the predominant institutions offering tertiary education, but nonuniversity postsecondary institutions, particularly community colleges, have increased sharply in recent years. ELEMENTARY AND SECONDARY SCHOOLS. Education is generally compulsory for children from ages six to fourteen or sixteen, depending on the province in which they live, and it is free until the completion of secondary-school studies. According to latest available figures, in the early 1970's Canada had about 16,700 elementary schools (including public, Federal, and private schools, except private kindergartens) and secondary schools (including vocational high schools), with about 271,000 teachers. Annual enrollment was about 5,790,000.

SPECIALIZED SCHOOLS. In the early 1970's, according to latest available figures, the country had over twenty specialized schools for the blind and the deaf, which were annually attended by about 3900 students who were taught by nearly 800 teachers. About 140 schools offered diploma courses in nursing; enrollment averaged about 20,000 annually, with about 2000 teachers. In this period Canada had over twenty-five teachers colleges, annually attended by about 10,500 students, with about 550 instructors. Private trade schools and private business colleges averaged annual enrollments of about 12,000 students.

UNIVERSITIES AND COLLEGES. Large universities, with numerous faculties and extensive graduate study, are comparatively recent phenomena in Canada and have largely developed since the end of World War II. The country has about 350 institutions of postsecondary education, about 70 of them degree-granting universities and the remainder community colleges, teachers colleges, and hospital schools. More than 323,000 students were annually enrolled at the university level in the early 1970's, with an additional 179,000 at the other postsecondary nonuniversity institutions. Among the larger and internationally famous universities of Canada are the University of Toronto; Université de Montréal; Université Laval, in Québec City; McGill University, Montréal; Queens University, Kingston, Ontario; University of Western Ontario, London; Dalhousie University, Halifax; and provincial universities of Western Canada: Manitoba, Winnipeg; Saskatchewan, Saskatoon; Alberta, Edmonton; British Columbia, Vancouver.

## CULTURE

The cultural pattern of Canada has been derived from Anglo-American, French, and European influences. The cultural development of the country has been complex throughout a period of 300 years and has reflected the diversity of the ethnic distribution of the population. Predominant is the Anglo-American tradition, chiefly brought to Canada by generations of British colonial officials, soldiers, and settlers who laid the foundation in aesthetic and intellectual matters. At the beginning of the 20th century British literature, theater, music, and art were solidly established in Canada. American tastes, traditions, and media have crossed the 3000-mi. border, as have a steady influx of American immigrants and tourists; in combination, the American cultural environment made strong inroads in Canada. Almost 30 percent of the population is of French ethnic and cultural background. For more than three centuries French-speaking Canadians have maintained a separate French-inspired cultural identity. In the great migration between 1885 and 1914 families from Germany, Poland, Scandinavia, Italy, Hungary, the Ukraine, and the Netherlands brought their deep-rooted national customs, music, dances, and literature to Canada. This European influence merged with the Anglo-American and French influences to complete the mosaic of Canadian culture. See CANADIAN LITERATURE.

**Libraries and Museums.** The National Library of Canada came into existence formally on Jan. 1, 1953, by the proclamation of the National Library Act. The act established a National Library Advisory Board, comprising the national librarian; dominion archivist; librarian of the Na-

A farm in Saskatchewan, in west-central Canada. Saskatchewan, Manitoba, and Alberta are known as the Prairie Provinces.                    Annan Photo Features

tional Science Library; one member representing the Canada Council; one member representing the Association of Universities and Colleges of Canada; and nine other members, four of whom must be professional librarians. Provincial governments have jurisdiction over public libraries, which are generally administered by municipal authorities. The cities are served by municipal libraries, and the provincial and regional libraries serve the more widely dispersed population.

Museums and art galleries are to be found in virtually all of the provinces and major cities of Canada. Among the most important are the National Gallery of Canada in Ottawa, which contains important collections, including paintings of the old masters and the French school. It also houses the most extensive collection of Canadian art in existence. The National Museums of Canada are the most important in the country and comprise three distinct entities: the National Museums of Natural Sciences (botany, zoology, geology, and paleontology); the National Museum of Man (archeology, ethnology, history, folk culture studies, and Canadian War Museum); the National Museum of Science and Technology (agriculture, transportation, and industrial technology; National Aeronautical Collection; scientific demonstrations). The Royal Ontario Museum in Toronto is another internationally known institution.

**Archeology.** Three basic kinds of archeological discovery have been made in Canada. Throughout the country, relics of American Indian tribes have been found. In the N. discoveries linked to the Eskimos have been made, and in the E. evidence of pre-Columbian Viking settlements have been unearthed.

Material assembled by the National Museum in Victoria, B.C., from sites in the Maritime Provinces, Ontario, and British Columbia, shed light on the prehistory of the Algonquian and Iroquoian tribes. On Canada's w. coast some of the

***Canada. Plate 1.*** *The Toronto City Hall, a structure of innovative design involving curved surfaces and comprising two office buildings "wrapped" around a domed council chamber, was dedicated in 1965.*

In the town of Saint Phillips, a chapel of the Church of England overlooks Conception Bay. The bay, an inlet of the Atlantic Ocean, is on the southeastern coast of the island of Newfoundland.

*Canada. Plate 2.*

River drivers on the Rivière-du-Loup in Québec Province. Forestry ranks high in the national wealth of Canada, and Québec is the leader among the provinces in the production of pulp and paper.

most remarkable finds are the dramatic carvings of the Haida and Kwakiutl groups. The Royal Ontario Museum is doing research on the local archeology of the Huron Indians. Considerable information about the prehistoric migrations of Eskimo and pre-Eskimo groups has been gathered in the arctic area; notable Eskimo decorative work in bone and ivory, which reached its peak before 1000 A.D., has been found. Discoveries at L'Anse-au-Meadow, on the northern tip of Newfoundland, revealed ruins of a Norse settlement dating from 1000 A.D. Similar finds on the Ungava Peninsula in N. Québec include a Norse longhouse and a group of stones thought to be navigational beacons, dating from before 1200.

## THE ECONOMY

Until the early 20th century, Canada was primarily an agricultural nation. Since then it has become one of the most highly industrialized countries in the world. Manufacturing is by far the leading economic activity. To a large extent the manufacturing industries are supplied with raw materials produced by the Canadian agricultural, mining, forestry, and fishing sectors.

Between 1950 and 1972 the gross national product increased from $18,491,000,000 to $102,935,000,000. In the 1972–73 fiscal year the national budget showed revenues of $16,601,603,475 as compared with $2,744,592,000 in 1950. (All monetary values in this article are given in Canadian dollars.)

**Agriculture.** The Canadian economy is heavily dependent upon agriculture. About 5 percent of the labor force is engaged in agricultural pursuits. Farm cash receipts annually totaled about $5,384,228,000 in the early 1970's, according to latest government statistics. Because of the high volume of production and a relatively small population, Canada is one of the leading world exporters of food products. Field crops account for about 39 percent of cash receipts from farming operations. Wheat is the most important single crop, and the Prairie Provinces of Alberta, Manitoba, and Saskatchewan form one of the greatest wheat-growing areas of the world, producing about 96 percent of Canadian wheat. These provinces also grow a large percentage of the coarse grains and oilseeds produced in Canada. After wheat, the major cash receipts from field crops are obtained from sale of barley, rapeseed, tobacco, vegetables, potatoes, fruits, corn, flaxseed, soybeans, and oats.

Livestock and livestock products account for about 58 percent of farm cash receipts. Ranching prevails in the w., and livestock raising is a general enterprise, except in parts of Alberta and Saskatchewan, where beef cattle form a specialized industry. Ontario and Québec rank highest in production of dairy products, with about 75 percent of the national output; in poultry farming, with 68 percent; and in egg production, with 55 percent. Québec produces 65 percent of the maple products, and Ontario produces 95 percent of the nation's tobacco crop.

In the early 1970's the livestock population of Canada included about 2,147,000 milk cows; 3,902,800 calves; 6,676,200 cattle; 7,301,000 hogs; 587,100 sheep and lambs; 340,000 horses; and 84,147,800 poultry. Fruit farming is carried on principally in Ontario, British Columbia, and Québec, with apples contributing about one third the total value. Berries, peaches, grapes, and cherries are other important crops. Tomatoes, onions, carrots, turnips, peas, and beans are major vegetable crops, with Ontario producing about 57 percent of the total crop, followed by Québec and British Columbia.

**Forest and Fishing Industries.** Forestry is a major source of national wealth, and forest products annually accounted for about 18 percent of Canadian exports in the early 1970's, according to latest available statistics. Forests cover about 1,240,000 sq.mi., about 74 percent of which are suitable for regular harvest. Canada has over 150 varieties of native trees, 20 percent of which are softwoods, such as spruce, Douglas fir, hemlock, cedar, pine, and balsam. The annual forest harvest in the early 1970's was about 4,287,890,000 cu.ft. It sustains a complex and diversified export and domestic industry, which employs about 400,000 persons and supports about 1770 sawmills and planing mills and 3330 wood-using plants. Canada leads the world in the production of newsprint with about 40 percent and probably accounts for 65 percent of world exports; most of the Canadian export is sent to the U.S. The sawmill and planing-mill industry is centered in British Columbia; Québec and Ontario lead the nation in pulp and paper production.

The fishing resources of the country are harvested from the N.W. Atlantic and N.E. Pacific oceans and from the most extensive bodies of fresh water in the world. In the early 1970's, according to the latest available statistics, the number of people employed in primary fishing operations was 51,000 in the sea fisheries and 8100 in the inland fisheries. Another 18,500 worked in fish-processing plants. Two thirds of the yearly output of the industry, which had a market value of about $463,000,000, is exported, making Canada one of the top three fish-exporting nations. The catch includes cod, haddock, herring, salmon, flounder, lobster, halibut, and whitefish.

**Furs.** A minor Canadian industry is fur farming and trapping. The farming operations consist mainly of raising mink, which contributes 99 percent of the annual value of pelts from fur farms, and small quantities of chinchilla, fox, and nutria. The fur farms are mainly concentrated in Ontario, British Columbia, Manitoba, and Alberta. According to latest statistics, in the early 1970's a seasonal average of about 1,156,-000 pelts were taken, with a value of about $14,689,000. Trapping is carried on primarily in the N. region of Canada, with Ontario, Québec, and Manitoba accounting for over half the total annual catch, in the early 1970's, of some 4,324,000 pelts, with a value of approximately $33,010,000.

**Mining.** The mining industry of Canada has a long history of exploration. The most significant period of growth, however, has been since World War II, with mineral discoveries in almost every region of the country. Mining is a significant source of national wealth and is the leading export industry of Canada. The value of annual mineral production reached about $6,341,-000,000 in the early 1970's and exports of mineral materials, in crude and fabricated forms, reached an annual value of about $5,318,000,000. Among the factors contributing to the impetus in the mining industry are: oil and gas discoveries in W. Canada; development of huge iron-ore deposits in Labrador and Québec; the discovery and development of large deposits of nickel in Manitoba, uranium in Ontario and Saskatchewan, and potash in Saskatchewan; extraction of sulfur from natural gas in the W. provinces; development of copper, lead, and zinc deposits; and the increased production of asbestos in Québec, British Columbia, and Newfoundland. The leading minerals of Canada are crude petroleum, copper, nickel, iron ore, zinc, natural gas and natural gas by-products, asbestos, cement, sand and gravel, and coal, all of which accounted for over 85 percent of the total annual value of production in the early 1970's. Canada leads in the world production of asbestos, nickel, silver, and zinc; is second in gypsum, molybdenum, potash, sulfur, and uranium; and ranks high in the production of cadmium, cobalt, copper, gold, iron ore, lead, magnesium, natural gas, platinum-group metals, and titanium. The Canadian mineral industry is strongly export-oriented, about 84 percent of output going to foreign markets. Canada is the largest world exporter of minerals and mineral products; it is the third-largest world mineral producer, following the U.S. and U.S.S.R. Alberta leads in mineral production, followed by Ontario, Québec, Saskatchewan, British Columbia, and Newfoundland.

**Manufacturing.** The national economy of Canada is largely dependent on manufacturing, which employs about 22 percent of the labor force and accounts for over 56 percent of the value added by goods-producing industries. Manufacturing has grown remarkably since World War II, with total value of shipments increasing more than sixfold. The leading industries in order of the dollar value of shipments are motor-vehicle manufacturing, pulp and paper mills, meat packing, petroleum refining, iron and steel manufacturing, dairy products, sawmills and planing mills, and miscellaneous machinery and equipment manufacturing. The most important manufacturing provinces are Ontario, which accounts for more than half of the manufacturing production of Canada, and Québec, which accounts for about 30 percent. The chief manufacturing cities are Toronto, Montréal, Hamilton, Vancouver, Windsor, Winnipeg, and Kitchener.

**Tourism.** The natural variety of seasons and scenic wonders draws tourists. In the spring, blossom festivals flourish across Canada, especially in the Annapolis valley of Nova Scotia and the Okanagan valley in British Columbia. Noteworthy is the Canadian Tulip Festival in Ottawa in May. The Niagara Grape and Wine Festival and autumn-color tours in central Ontario and the Laurentian Mts. of Québec are among the attractions. In the winter the abundant snowfall has been exploited; skiing centers are rapidly expanding. About 105,000 sq.mi. of scenic countryside have been preserved in the natural state for use as national, provincial, and roadside parks.

Tourism has become one of the leading industries of Canada, and receipts now rank second to dollar earnings of domestic exports of motor vehicles and parts. An annual average of 38,000,000 travelers visit the country, of whom about 99 percent come from the U.S. Expenditures are about $1,200,000,000 a year; U.S. residents spend some 90 percent of the total.

**Currency and Banking.** The unit of currency is the Canadian dollar, which consists of 100 cents (1 Canadian dollar equals U.S.$1.00; 1973). The Bank of Canada has the sole right to issue paper money for circulation. The commercial banking system of Canada consists of ten privately owned banks, which have been chartered by parliament and which operate under the provisions of the Bank Act. Of the ten banks in oper-

*Canada. Plate 3.* Manufacturing provides more than 56 percent of the value added by the goods-producing industries in Canada. Among key products are aviation equipment, shown being made (above), and iron, being poured (left) in a foundry.

National Film Board of Canada

**Canada. Plate 4.** Most of the Eskimo population of Canada, numbering only about 18,000 persons, live in the Northwest Territories and northern Québec. Top: An Eskimo family group. Left: An Eskimo sculptor works on a soapstone figure, a popular art among Canadian Eskimos. Above: A walrus herd on an island in the Northwest Territories.

ation, five are nationwide, with branches in all ten provinces and the two territories; one has branches in six provinces only; two operate chiefly in Québec and in other French-speaking regions; one has branches only in Ontario; and one has branches only in British Columbia. A distinctive feature of the Canadian banking system is the relatively limited number of large banks, having a widespread network of branches (totaling over 6564 in Canada and 256 branches in other countries), functioning under Federal legislative jurisdiction and under one comprehensive statute, the decennially revised Bank Act.

**Commerce and Trade.** From the 16th century to the 18th century the chief Canadian items of export were fish and furs. During the 19th century exploitation of the white-pine forests of the Laurentian region was initiated, and timber became the staple item of export. With the improvement of railroad communications early in the 20th century, the w. prairie regions were opened, and wheat became the chief item of export. The mining industry began to grow at about the same time; valuable mineral deposits were discovered in the Laurentian region (previously mining had been confined largely to iron and coal in Nova Scotia, and gold, silver, and copper in British Columbia); and exploitation began of the spruce timber of N. Ontario and Québec. Manufacturing industries developed to supply and process the goods of the three primary industries, agriculture, forestry, and mining. Aiding economic expansion in the Canadian North was the advance of hydroelectric and thermal-electric technology.

Canada has the largest per capita export and import trade of any nation in the world. The growth in external trade in the past twenty-five years has been remarkable. The value of exports for 1946 was $2,272,005,000; in 1950, $3,104,-016,000; in 1960, $5,255,575,000; in 1970, $16,401,-091,000; and in 1972 the total reached $19,-500,135,000. Imports showed a comparable increase in dollar value from the 1946 figure of $1,841,267,000 to $3,125,231,000 in 1950; $5,482,695,000 in 1960; $13,951,903,000 in 1970; and $18,736,066,000 in 1972.

The U.S. in the early 1970's took about 69 percent of Canadian exports and supplied about 69 percent of its imports. Great Britain was second in exports, with about 7 percent, and Japan was second in imports, with about 6 percent. Other leading recipients of Canadian export trade were Japan, the Soviet Union, China, West Germany, the Netherlands, Belgium and Luxembourg, Australia, Italy, India, Norway, France,

and Venezuela, all receiving over $100,000,000 in Canadian goods. After the U.S. and Japan, the leading nations from which Canada imported goods were Great Britain, West Germany, Venezuela, France, and Italy.

The three leading commodities exported in the early 1970's were motor vehicles and parts, lumber, and newsprint. Other major commodities were crude petroleum, wheat, wood pulp, nickel ores and alloys, and copper ores and alloys. Motor vehicles and parts, nonfarm machinery, and crude petroleum were the principal items imported, followed by communications equipment, steel, electrical equipment, wearing apparel and accessories, tractors and parts, and aircraft and parts.

**Transportation.** The natural water and mountain barriers of Canada, combined with a dispersed population, necessitate efficient and economical transportation facilities. Since the earliest explorations of the country, water transportation has been indispensable. The St. Lawrence–Great Lakes navigation system extends some 2280 mi. from the Gulf of St. Lawrence into the center of the continent. The opening of the St. Lwrence Seaway in 1959 contributed greatly to industrial expansion. In the early 1970's some 7000 transits were made; cargo carried totaled more than 51,000 tons. Some 25,000 vessels engaged in foreign trade entered and cleared Canadian ports annually; cargo unloaded totaled more than 61,000,000 tons, and about 106,000,000 tons were loaded. Vancouver, Sept Îles, Port Cartier, Montréal, Halifax, Québec, Saint John (New Brunswick), and Hamilton handled more than 50 percent of the total. Vessels of Canadian registry numbered about 28,000 with a gross tonnage of 3,805,000.

The government-owned Canadian National Railways is the largest public utility in Canada and operates more than 23,300 mi. of the 44,000 mi. of first main track in the country. The system serves all ten provinces and the Northwest Territories. The privately owned Canadian Pacific Railway Company serves all provinces except Newfoundland, Prince Edward Island, and the two territories. The two railways operate about 340 mi. of track in the U.S. and operate 16,100 mi. of first main track. Canadian railroads carried about 23,100,000 passengers over more than 2,042,808,000 passenger-miles annually in the early 1970's. Total freight exceeded 288,000,000 tons, carried over 126,500,000,000 ton-miles.

The total mileage of the Canadian highway and rural road system in the early 1970's was about 516,000 mi. Included in this total are about 76,000 mi. of paved highways and 274,000

*Seal Cove, on Grand Manan Island, a popular resort area in southwest New Brunswick, one of the Maritime Provinces.*                    Burdick, Leo DeWys Inc.

mi. of gravel roads. The 4860-mi. Trans-Canada Highway, completed in 1962, stretches from Saint John's, Newfoundland, to Vancouver, British Columbia. In the early 1970's about 6,967,000 passenger automobiles, 1,856,000 commercial vehicles, and 199,000 motorcycles were in use.

Two major airlines, Air Canada and Canadian Pacific Air Lines Limited (CP Air), maintain a broad network of domestic and international routes. Other small carriers are licensed.

**Communications.** The government-owned Canadian Broadcasting Corporation (CBC) operated some 48 radio stations, including AM, FM, and shortwave, and about 29 television stations, in the early 1970's. About 385 private radio stations and about 70 private television stations also were operating. The CBC has no supervisory function over the private stations. In 1968 the Canadian Radio-Television Commission was created to regulate all aspects of Canadian broadcasting. In September, 1969, the Canadian Domestic Satellite Communication System (Telesat Canada) was established to provide telecommunications on a commercial basis. The company is owned jointly by the government of

Canada, the telecommunications companies, and the general public. Telesat Canada launched the world's first stationary communications satellite designed for domestic commercial use in December, 1972. Known as ANIK I, an Eskimo word meaning. "brother", the satellite orbits over the equator at long. 114° W. and an altitude of 22,300 mi. Because it rotates with the earth every 24 hr., its position over the equator remains constant.

The government maintains about 8994 post offices; over 10,268,000 telephones are in use.

**Labor.** The labor force of Canada in 1972 averaged about 8,891,000 workers. Union membership during this period totaled about 2,371,000. It included about 34 percent of the approximately 7,848,000 nonagricultural paid workers in the country and nearly 28 percent of the overall labor force. About three quarters of all union members belonged to organizations affiliated with the Canadian Labour Congress (C.L.C.); these unions generally are also affiliated with the American Federation of Labor and Congress of Industrial Organizations (A.F.L.–C.I.O.). An additional 9.2 percent of total union membership was affiliated with the Confederation of National Trade Unions (C.N.T.U.). Some 18 percent belonged to unaffiliated unions and the remainder were in independent local organizations.

## GOVERNMENT

Canada is governed according to the constitution embodied in the British North America Act of 1867 and its amendments. Under the terms of the constitution Canada is a Federal union, with a definite division of powers between the central and provincial governments.

**Central Government.** The central government exercises all powers not specifically assigned to the provinces; it has exclusive jurisdiction over administration of the public debt, currency and coinage, taxation for general purposes, organization of national defense, fiscal matters, banking, fisheries, commerce, navigation and shipping, postal service, census, statistics, patents, copyright, naturalization, aliens, Indian affairs, marriage, and divorce. Among the powers assigned to the provincial governments are education, hospitals, property and civil rights, taxation for local purposes, the regulation of local commerce, and the borrowing of money. With respect to certain matters, such as immigration, the Federal and provincial governments possess concurrent jurisdiction.

The nominal head of the government is the governor-general, the representative of the crown, who is appointed by the queen on the recommendation of the prime minister of Canada. In the performance of his duties the governor-general is assisted by a privy council consisting of members of the Canadian cabinet.

**Health and Welfare.** All levels of government share the responsibility for social welfare in Canada. The Federal government administers comprehensive income-maintenance measures, such as the Canada Pension Plan, Canada Assistance Plan, old-age security pensions, family allowances, youth allowances, and unemployment insurance, in which nationwide coordination is necessary. The Federal government also gives aid to the provinces in meeting the costs of public assistance; it also provides services for special groups, such as Indians, Eskimos, veterans, and immigrants. Administration of welfare services is mainly the responsibility of the provinces, but local authorities, generally with financial aid from the province, often assume the provision of services. Provincial governments have the major responsibility for health services in Canada, with the municipality also assuming authority over matters delegated to it by provincial legislation. The department of national health and welfare is the chief Federal agency in health matters.

The Medical Care Act, passed in 1968, has permitted the Federal government to contribute about half the cost of the Medical Care Insurance Program ("medicare"), with the respective province contributing the remainder. The program establishes the following minimum criteria: (1) comprehensive coverage, to cover all medically required services rendered by physicians and surgeons; (2) universal availability to all residents; (3) portability, to cover temporary or permanent change in residence to another province; (4) nonprofit basis, regulated by a public authority.

**Legislature.** Actual executive and legislative authority is vested in the prime minister. The governor-general is guided by the advice of this official. The prime minister and members of the cabinet must be members of parliament, which consists of two houses, a Senate composed of 102 members appointed by the governor-in-council (cabinet) to hold office until the age of seventy-five, and a House of Commons composed of 264 members apportioned according to provincial population. Members of the House are elected for five years (or until the House is dissolved) by popular vote. Women have the franchise and are eligible for election to the House of Commons or appointment to the Senate. Elections are held at the discretion of the prime minister. The prime minister is the leader of the largest party in the House of Commons. Laws must be passed by both houses and signed by the governor-general.

**Political Parties.** The two strongest political parties in Canada today are the Progressive Conservatives (P.C.) and the Liberals. The P.C. urges the maintenance of close ties with other members of the Commonwealth and advocates tariff protection for industry. While not differing from the P.C. essentially, the Liberals emphasize the development of closer relationships with the countries of the North Atlantic community, particularly the U.S., and are more disposed toward free trade. Some of the factions within each party differ more ideologically than the two parties themselves do.

A third party, the New Democratic Party, has considerable support in the trade-union movement and among the voters of British Columbia, Saskatchewan, Manitoba, and Ontario; it stands for extensive economic planning. The fourth party in the House of Commons is the Social Credit Party, whose members are all from the province of Québec.

**Judiciary.** The judicial system consists of the Supreme Court, which possesses appellate, civil, and criminal jurisdiction, and the Federal Court of Canada, which has jurisdiction over claims made by, or against, the government of Canada; both are located in Ottawa. Superior courts sit in each province, and county courts have limited jurisdiction. English common law is used, except in Québec, where French civil law is used in civil cases. All judges are appointed officials. The Royal Canadian Mounted Police is maintained by the Canadian government to enforce Federal laws throughout the country and to perform the function of provincial police in all provinces except Ontario and Québec.

**Defense.** The Canadian armed forces are integrated and headed by the chief of defense staff, who reports to the civilian minister of defense. Under the staff are seven separate commands, organized according to their function. For example, the Mobile Command is to protect Canadian territory and to support United Nations or other peace-keeping operations. Maritime Command has the role of defending Canadian interests from assault by sea and to support NATO with antisubmarine duties in the North Atlantic. Air Defense Command participates with the U.S. in the air defense of North America (NORAD); see COAST DEFENSE. Canadian Forces Europe comprise the land and air elements allocated to support NATO in Europe. Other commands are Air Transport Command, Training Command, and the Canadian Forces Communications Command. At the end of 1972 the regular forces consisted of 83,048 men and women. The 1973–74 budget estimated defense expenditures at about $2,130,572,000.

## HISTORY

According to medieval Icelandic literature, the Norse mariner Leif Ericson (q.v.) crossed the Atlantic Ocean and reached the North American mainland in about 1000 A.D. He explored a region that he called Vinland (q.v.) because of the abundance of grapes he found growing there. The location of Ericson's Vinland has not been determined conclusively. Some geographers believe that it lay on the eastern coast of present-day Canada, probably in Labrador; critics of this view hold that Vinland was on the coast of Nova Scotia or in northern New England, because of the fact that wild grapes are unknown north of Passamaquoddy Bay.

**Early Exploration.** The first European of whom there is authentic record to reach this part of North America was the Italian navigator John Cabot (see under CABOT). Seeking a westward route to Asia in the service of King Henry VII (q.v.) of England, he made a landfall on June 24, 1497, probably at Cape Breton Island. Before returning to England, Cabot made additional explorations, notably of Newfoundland and the Grand Banks fisheries off Newfoundland. Later England claimed the entire continent on the basis of this voyage. Cabot revisited the northeast coast of North America in the following year. His enthusiastic reports on the Newfoundland fisheries evoked widespread interest in Europe; within a few years the fishermen of several European nations, especially France, were voyaging regularly to the Grand Banks.

Systematic investigation of the coast began when, in 1534, the French mariner Jacques Cartier (q.v.) was commissioned by his government to find a northwest passage to Asia. Guided by fishermen's reports of a vast bay between Newfoundland and Labrador, Cartier reached the present-day Strait of Belle Isle on June 10, 1534. He subsequently entered and explored the gulf that became known as the Gulf of St. Lawrence. On July 24, during a visit to the Gaspé Peninsula, Cartier claimed the surrounding territory in the name of King Francis I (q.v.) of France. The French government authorized another expedition to the region in 1535. On this voyage Cartier explored the course of what became known as the St. Lawrence R. as far inland as Hochelaga (now Montréal).

**The French Colonial Period.** The French government dispatched a third expedition to the St. Lawrence R. in 1541. Cartier and an advance party spent the winter of 1541–42 a few miles southwest of the site of the present city of Québec. Because of illness, the rigorous climate, and poor planning and organization, the enterprise was abandoned later in 1542.

Owing mainly to domestic disturbances arising from the Protestant Reformation at home, French interest in the area lagged for over sixty years. More and more French fishing vessels were attracted to the fisheries, however, and the fishermen soon began to barter with the Indians of the coastal areas for furs. Eventually the profits from these trading activities engaged the attention of French commercial interests. A prosperous merchant obtained monopoly rights to the fur trade in 1599, on condition that he transport no less than fifty colonists annually to the St. Lawrence region. At about the same time the region was officially designated New France. The name Canada is derived from *kanata,* an Indian word for village.

A tiny settlement, called Tadoussac, was founded near the mouth of the Saguenay R. in the first year of the monopoly. Most of the colonists perished during the ensuing winter, and the settlement was abandoned. Failure of the monopolist to meet the terms of his contract and the protests of excluded traders finally forced the government to intervene. In 1603 the French explorer Samuel de Champlain (q.v.), under orders to locate an area suitable for settlement, explored the coast of Acadia (Nova Scotia and New Brunswick) and part of the St. Lawrence valley. A group of merchants headed by the Sieur de Monts (q.v.) obtained monopoly rights to the fur trade of New France in 1603. The following year the traders established a settlement on Saint Croix (now in Maine), an islet in the St. Croix R. The next year the settlement was moved to the site of present Annapolis Royal, Nova Scotia. Called Port Royal, it endured until 1607, when revocation of the monopoly forced its abandonment.

De Monts then secured monopoly rights for one year to the fur trade in the St. Lawrence valley. Employed by De Monts, Champlain chose an easily defensible site on the St. Lawrence in the summer of 1608 and founded there a trading post called Québec. In the following year Champlain, accompanied by friendly Indians, mainly Algonquins and Hurons, explored the region south of Québec and discovered the lake now known by his name. During the expedition, the Hurons and Algonquins attacked a party of Iroquois Indians, a traditional enemy. Champlain joined the battle against the Iroquois, and as a consequence the Five Nations, a powerful confederation of Iroquoian tribes, became implacable foes of New France.

In 1610 the French government, refusing to renew De Monts' monopoly, lifted all restrictions on the Canadian fur trade, but a new monopoly was granted late in 1612. The holders of the monopoly failed to meet their colonizing obligations, but during this period Champlain penetrated deep into the interior of New France, exploring (1613) the Ottawa R. and reaching (1615) Lake Huron and Lake Ontario.

In 1615 four Franciscan (Récollet) missionaries arrived in Québec. The event signalized the beginning of a protracted and zealous campaign by the Roman Catholic Church to Christianize the Indians. For an extended period after 1625, when five members of the Society of Jesus reached the colony, the Jesuits profoundly influenced secular and religious affairs in New France.

Meanwhile, the monopoly charter of 1612 was revoked and a new one was conferred on another company in 1622. Mismanagement of colonial affairs continued, with the result that in 1627 the French government organized the Company of New France (usually called the Company of One Hundred Associates), a quasi-official body endowed with broad economic and political powers. The charter provided that the company should transport three hundred settlers annually to the colony. It also prohibited the immigration of Huguenots (q.v.) to New France, thus excluding from the colony the most active members of the commercial community and seriously retarding economic growth in the French areas of North America.

In 1629, during the Thirty Years' War, an English naval force captured Acadia and Québec. The possessions were restored to France by the Treaty of Saint-Germain-en-Laye, concluded in 1632, but their seizure presaged the relentless struggle between England and France for mastery in North America.

During the administration of the Company of One Hundred Associates, a few new settlements were founded, notably Trois Rivières in 1634 and Ville Marie (Montréal) in 1642. Between 1657 and 1659 the French fur trader and explorer Pierre Esprit Radisson (1636?–1710?) explored the western region around Lake Superior. Radisson later conducted surveys for the English in the Hudson Bay region and helped to found the Hudson's Bay Company (q.v.). But the colony continued to languish. By 1659 French colonists in New France still numbered fewer than two thousand.

With the arrival in Québec of the vicar apostolic François Xavier de Laval-Montmorency (1623–1708) in 1659, the Roman Catholic clergy began aggressively to challenge the authority of the colony's temporal rulers. The Company of One Hundred Associates resisted his proposed reforms, mainly measures designed to benefit the Indians. In 1663, at the height of the struggle, King Louis XIV (q.v.) revoked the company's charter and constituted New France as a royal province. A feudal regime similar to the system then prevailing in France was established.

The most important period of French exploration and colonization in North America began after the appointment in 1672 of the Comte de Frontenac (q.v.), a soldier, as governor. A progressive administrator, Frontenac founded Fort Frontenac (Kingston) and sponsored many expeditions into the interior. He initiated the expedition, under the explorers Louis Jolliet and Jacques Marquette (qq.v.), which in 1673 discovered the Mississippi R. Frontenac also gave help to the explorer Robert Cavelier, Sieur de La Salle (see LA SALLE), who made the descent of the Mississippi in 1682 and claimed the entire Mississippi valley for France; see LOUISIANA: History.

Besides expanding the territory of New France, Frontenac subdued the Iroquois, forcing

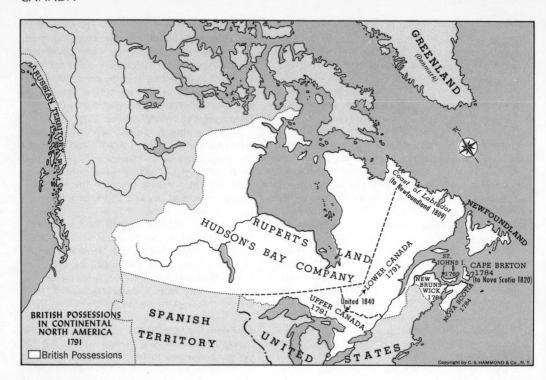

BRITISH POSSESSIONS
IN CONTINENTAL
NORTH AMERICA
1791

☐ British Possessions

GREENLAND
(Denmark)

RUSSIAN TERRITORY

HUDSON'S BAY COMPANY

RUPERT'S LAND

Coast of Labrador
(to Newfoundland 1809)

NEWFOUNDLAND

LOWER CANADA
1791

United 1840

UPPER CANADA
1791

ST. JOHNS I.
1784
1769

CAPE BRETON
1784
(to Nova Scotia 1820)

NEW BRUNS WICK
1784

NOVA SCOTIA
1784

SPANISH TERRITORY

UNITED STATES

Copyright by C. S. HAMMOND & Co., N. Y.

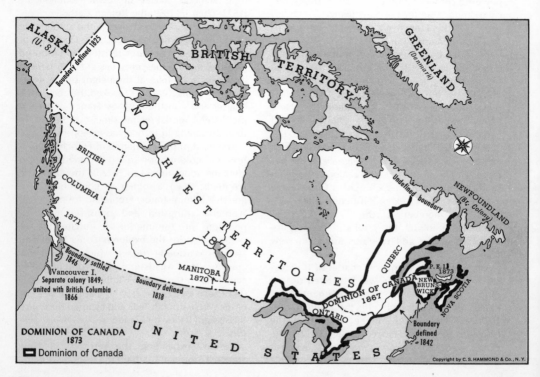

DOMINION OF CANADA
1873

☐ Dominion of Canada

ALASKA
(U. S.)

Boundary defined 1825

GREENLAND
(Denmark)

BRITISH TERRITORY

NORTHWEST TERRITORIES 1870

BRITISH COLUMBIA
1871

Boundary settled
1846

Vancouver I.
Separate colony 1849;
united with British Columbia
1866

MANITOBA
1870

Boundary defined
1818

Undefined boundary

NEWFOUNDLAND
(Br. Colony)

QUEBEC

P.E.I.
1873

NEW BRUNS WICK

NOVA SCOTIA

DOMINION OF CANADA
1867

ONTARIO

Boundary
defined
1842

UNITED STATES

Copyright by C. S. HAMMOND & Co., N. Y.

them to maintain peace for nearly two decades. His differences with the ecclesiastical authorities led in 1682 to his recall. Soon after his departure the Iroquois resumed their depredations. The fur trade came to a standstill, frontier outposts were destroyed, and, in August, 1689, most of the inhabitants of Lachine, near Montréal, were massacred. Following the Lachine disaster Frontenac was reappointed governor. His second term began on the eve of a major crisis in Anglo-French relations.

**Anglo-French Struggle for North America.** Rivalry for colonial empire, especially in North America, was a principal cause of the 18th-century wars between England and France. Aggravated by French military aggressiveness in Europe and other areas, the rivalry became particularly acute after France added the Mississippi valley to its Canadian domain. French domination of this region confronted the English with a number of grave threats, especially containment east of the Appalachian Mts. and eventual expulsion from their holdings along the Atlantic seaboard. Northeastern North America became one of the most fiercely contested battlegrounds of the resultant war, which continued in various phases and many parts of the world over almost three quarters of a century.

Fundamentally, the first phase of the conflict, known in Europe as the War of the Grand Alliance (1689–97) and in North America as King William's War (q.v.), represented an attempt by a coalition of European powers, including England, to halt French aggression in Europe. In North America the fighting was limited in scope, but nonetheless sanguinary. Frontenac quickly mobilized the numerous Indian tribes friendly to France; English colonial leaders obtained the services of the anti-French Iroquois. Thus reinforced, each side conducted guerrilla warfare in the border regions between New France and the English colonies. The pattern of struggle that evolved in the frontier areas prevailed through all the subsequent phases of the general conflict. Under the terms of the Peace of Ryswick (now Rijswijk) of 1697, Acadia, seized by an English naval force in 1690, was restored to France; see RYSWICK, PEACE OF.

During the ensuing interlude of peace the French hastily improved their defense system in New France. Colonization of the lower Mississippi valley was begun in 1699. In 1701 Fort Pontchartrain du Detroit, commanding the passage between lakes Huron and Erie, was established on the site of present-day Detroit. The conflict was renewed in 1702. Known in America as Queen Anne's War (q.v.), this phase was highlighted by the capture (1710) of Acadia by New England colonial troops. The French repulsed another expedition against Québec and destroyed Saint John's, Newfoundland. Under the provisions of the Peace of Utrecht (1713) ending the war, Great Britain obtained French recognition of its claims to the Hudson Bay region and cession of Acadia and Newfoundland. Cape Breton Island and Île Saint-Jean (Prince Edward Island), adjoining Acadia, were retained by France.

Thirty years elapsed before the outbreak of the conflict's next phase, known in America as King George's War (q.v.). Like the preceding war, King George's War was indecisive. Bloody fighting raged in the frontier areas, however, and in 1745 the fortress of Louisbourg on Cape Breton Island was captured by an expedition consisting of British naval units and New England troops. Louisbourg was restored to France by Great Britain in exchange for Madras, India, at the end of the war in 1748. But the city was recaptured by the British and colonial forces on June 26, 1758, thus releasing men and ships for the ultimate attack on Québec.

Competition between British America and New France for possession of the Ohio R. valley precipitated in 1754 the French and Indian War (q.v.), the final phase of the prolonged struggle for dominance in North America. The French, skillfully utilizing their Indian allies, inflicted many severe defeats on the American colonials, who were largely dependent on their own resources because of Britain's preoccupation with the European aspect of the war (see SEVEN YEARS' WAR). However, handicapped by sparse population and threatened by the Iroquois, New France weakened steadily as the war progressed, and the British navy repeatedly severed the colony's lines of communication with France. On Sept. 18, 1759, after a long sequence of defeats, the French surrendered Québec to a British army. With the capture (Sept. 8, 1760) of Montréal, the British were in effective control of the whole of New France. The victors imposed harsh peace terms on France in the Treaty of Paris (Feb. 10, 1763). With the exception of territories west of the Mississippi and New Orleans, which had been ceded previously to Spain, the entire French domain on the North American mainland was ceded to Great Britain. The only Canadian holdings left to France were the tiny islands of Saint Pierre and Miquelon. France was, however, allowed to retain her historic fishing rights on the Newfoundland banks, including the right to dry fish on the coast itself.

*Logs are stacked on a truck for shipment to paper mills.*
National Film Board of Canada

Those French colonists who decided to remain in the conquered areas were also permitted to continue the practice of the Roman Catholic religion.

**British Rule to Confederation.** From 1764 to 1774 New France was controlled by a provisional government proclaimed by King George III. The majority of French Canadians willingly accepted British rule; those who returned to France were mainly feudal landlords and other prominent persons. In 1774 the British Parliament passed the Québec Act, which confirmed safeguards to the Roman Catholic Church in Canada, recognized the validity of French civil law, and made various concessions to the French Canadians. The act also provided for the establishment of a royal province officially styled Québec and consisting of virtually all the formerly French territory north of the Ohio R. Governmental authority was vested in a royally appointed governor and legislative council. Prevailing relations between landowners and tenants remained undisturbed.

Largely as a result of the privileges retained and acquired through the Québec Act, the French Canadians remained loyal to Great Britain after the outbreak of the American Revolu-

tion (q.v.). Early in the conflict the Continental Congress employed the services of the American diplomat and statesman Benjamin Franklin (q.v.) and others in strenuous efforts to obtain Canadian support. These efforts failed, however, and late in 1775 American troops were dispatched to the province. Montréal was captured on Nov. 12, 1775, but following reverses suffered on Dec. 31 at the city of Québec the Americans withdrew into New York.

Canada's ethnic composition and frontiers underwent profound changes as a result of the American Revolution. During and immediately after the war large numbers of Americans who remained loyal to the British cause fled across the Canadian frontier. Most of the immigrants, totaling between 40,000 and 50,000, took refuge in Nova Scotia, in New Brunswick (detached from Nova Scotia in 1784), and in the wilderness west of Montréal, where they laid the foundations of the present-day province of Ontario. Canadian territory ceded by Great Britain to the United States at the close of the war in 1783 consisted of the region now occupied by the States of Wisconsin, Michigan, Ohio, Indiana, and Illinois.

The newly arrived English-speaking section of the Canadian population, living in the regions that are now Québec and Ontario, soon became restless under the institutions and procedures provided by the Québec Act. Accordingly, in June, 1791, the British Parliament passed the Constitutional Act providing for the division of the province into Upper Canada, the region inhabited mainly by British stock, and Lower Canada, the center of the French population. The Ottawa R. was made the boundary between the provinces. Most of the privileges bestowed on the French Canadians under the Québec Act were approved for Lower Canada. The legislation authorized Upper Canada to allocate one seventh of all new land grants to the Anglican Church. Each province was given the same form of government, consisting of a popularly elected legislative assembly and a royally appointed governor, executive council, and legislative council.

Vast tracts of territory in the west and northwest were explored during the final decade of the 18th century. The Scottish explorer Alexander Mackenzie (q.v.) journeyed overland to the west coast in 1793, and various regions, especially in what is now west central Canada, were investigated by the Canadian surveyor and explorer David Thompson (q.v.). Thompson founded a settlement on the Columbia R. in 1807. Colonization of the region comprising present-day Manitoba began in 1812.

Meanwhile, relations between Canada and the U.S. deteriorated. British-inspired Indian raids on American outposts and American designs on Canadian territory were mainly responsible for the friction and were among the contributory causes of the War of 1812. Fighting took place during the war in Canadian-American frontier areas, and a number of towns and areas fell to one side or the other. But under the terms of the Treaty of Ghent (December, 1814), all occupied territories were restored to their previous owners. Thereafter, aside from several sharp boundary disputes, relations between Canada and the U.S. were generally harmonious.

During the next two decades Canadian domestic affairs were marked by a mounting struggle for reform. In Upper Canada the discontent was caused primarily by the arbitrary conduct of the crown's appointees, most of whom were representatives of landed or commercial interests. Other grievances included the ineffectuality of the popularly elected legislative assembly, and favoritism toward the Anglican Church in the distribution of crown lands. In Lower Canada identical grievances were compounded by French nationalist antagonisms, which were aggravated by the crown's practice of restricting most official posts to persons of British extraction. At last, in November, 1837, an ardent group of Lower Canada reformers, led by the French-Canadian political leader Louis Joseph Papineau (1786–1871), rose in revolt against British rule. The Upper Canadian radicals, under the leadership of Scottish-born William Lyon Mackenzie (q.v.), resorted to armed insurrection early in December. Both uprisings were swiftly quelled by the authorities. Captured rebels were given extremely lenient treatment, however, by John George Lambton (q.v.), Earl of Durham, newly appointed governor-general of British North America.

In February, 1839, Lord Durham submitted to the British government a comprehensive report on the political situation in Canada, recommending unification of Upper and Lower Canada and the institution of an executive department responsible to the legislature. On July 23, 1840, the British Parliament adopted legislation, known as the Act of Union, merging the provinces of Lower Canada (Québec) and Upper Canada (Ontario). The measure provided for the establishment of a single government including a royally appointed governor and a legislative council and a popularly elected legislative assembly. Representation in the legislative assembly was apportioned equally between the former provinces. Provisions were made for an executive council, or cabinet, consisting of assembly and council members selected by the governor. Durham's recommendation of executive responsibility to the legislature was ignored in the act, but was granted in 1849. Although the act established a single government for Canada, the provinces remained disunited, and sectional antagonisms were actually aggravated.

Among the chief sources of political discord in the postunification period were feudal-type land rights dating from the French period and the land reserves of the Anglican Church. The union legislature finally resolved these issues through legislation (1854) secularizing the land reserves and abolishing certain of the land rights.

Meanwhile, the British and U.S. governments had settled two Canadian-American boundary disputes. In the first settlement (1842) Great Britain relinquished claims to considerable territory along the northeast frontier of the U.S. (Maine); in the second (1846) the American northwest boundary (Oregon) was delineated (see NORTHEAST BOUNDARY DISPUTE; NORTHWEST BOUNDARY DISPUTE). Canadian-American relations were further improved by the adoption (1854) of a ten-year reciprocal-trade agreement, which stimulated the economic development of the united provinces, especially after the outbreak of the American Civil War, in 1861.

The war had profound repercussions in Canadian politics. As a result of Great Britain's friendliness to the Confederate cause, political leaders throughout British North America were forced, as the war drew to a close, to consider the possibility of U.S. retaliation. This possibility, combined with mutual-defense and economic problems and the frustrating experience of the provinces under the Act of Union, gave rise to a movement for greater unity, or confederation of what are now the five provinces of Nova Scotia, Prince Edward Island, New Brunswick, Québec, and Ontario. The first step was taken in September, 1864, when representatives of a broad range of political views met at Charlottetown, Prince Edward Island. Delegates representing the various provinces convened again in Québec on Oct. 14, 1864, for the purpose of considering the advisability of union. A series of resolutions was directed to the imperial government. The resolutions, somewhat modified, were later incorporated into the British North America Act, passed by the British Parliament on March 29, 1867, and made effective on the following July 1. As constituted under this legislation, the Confederation, styled the Dominion of Canada, or simply Canada, consisted of the provinces of Québec (Lower Canada), Ontario (Upper Canada), Nova Scotia, and New Brunswick. (For various reasons Newfoundland and Prince Edward Island had not joined the confederation, and British Columbia was in its infancy and separated by hundreds of miles of unoccupied land.) The Scottish-born political leader John Alexander Macdonald (q.v.), an outstanding proponent of union, became the dominion's first prime minister. The population at confederation was 3,463,000, with only 92,000 people living west of Ontario. July 1, also known as Dominion, or Canada Day, is celebrated annually in Canada as a national holiday with various patriotic activities.

**From Confederation to World War I.** Most of Rupert's Land and North-Western Territory, vast tracts in northern and northwestern Canada under lease to the Hudson's Bay Company, was purchased by the Canadian government in 1870. Government surveys and other measures preliminary to final acquisition of the region, which was officially designated Northwest Territories, aroused suspicion and hostility in Red River Settlement, a colony situated in the valley of the Red R. of the North. People of French and Indian extraction, known as métis, made up a large majority of the settlement's inhabitants. In November, 1869, the métis, fearful that their lands would be confiscated, resorted to open rebellion. Under the guidance of their principal leader Louis David Riel (q.v.), they seized control of Fort Garry (now Winnipeg) and established a provisional government. The rebels dispersed shortly before the arrival of Canadian military units in the following summer. In July, 1870, the Red R. region was reorganized as the new Federal province of Manitoba.

The major domestic problems confronting Canada during the half century following the Red River Rebellion centered around commercial relations with other countries, particularly the U.S., development of the immense natural resources in western Canada, and the development of new areas into provinces within the Confederation. The tariff issue soon became an integral part of Federal politics. The Conservative Party, one of the country's two major political organizations, favored a protective policy. The Liberal Party, although not favoring free trade, has historically advocated somewhat lower tariff walls. From 1879 to 1898 the electorate endorsed the protective tariff, consistently returning Conservative governments to power.

Construction of a transcontinental railroad, a project prerequisite to settlement and exploitation of the interior and west, was promised in 1871. As a result, British Columbia joined Canada that year. Prince Edward Island joined in 1873. The transcontinental railroad was completed in May, 1887. Large numbers of immigrants settled in the fertile plains area and to the west of Manitoba after the railroad began operations. In 1905 the districts of Assiniboia, Saskatchewan, Alberta, and Athabasca and parts of the Northwest Territories became the provinces of Alberta and Saskatchewan.

The general election of 1896 was won by the Liberal Party, headed by the Québec statesman Wilfrid Laurier (q.v.). The period of Liberal ascendancy, lasting for fifteen years, was marked by industrial expansion and outstanding developments in foreign affairs, including an amicable settlement of disputes with the U.S. about the Bering Sea seal fisheries (see BERING SEA CONTROVERSY) and the frontier between British Columbia and Alaska. Conservative opposition to a reciprocal trade agreement with the U.S. caused the Liberal Party to be defeated in elections held in 1911. A Conservative government was formed on Oct. 10, with the Conservative Party leader Robert Laird Borden (q.v.) as premier.

**World War I.** Canada made impressive military and economic contributions to the British war effort in World War I. An expeditionary force numbering over 424,000 men was dispatched overseas, and Canadian troops figured significantly in a number of crucial campaigns, including the victorious assault on the Hindenburg Line in 1918. Canadian casualties during the war totaled almost 225,000. Some 60,661 men were killed in action or died of wounds. Canadian expenditures for war purposes amounted to more than $1,500,000,000. Until Aug. 28, 1917, when parliament passed legislation providing for compulsory military service, the nation's armed forces consisted of volunteers. Québec opposition to the conscription bill caused a serious split in the Liberal Party and disrupted national unity. The rupture was partially healed by formation of a coalition government, approved by the electorate at the so-called Khaki election of December, 1917. In March, 1918, the coalition government secured passage of legislation extending to all women over twenty-one years of age the right to vote in Federal elections.

**Post-World War I.** Canada's role in World War I, its representation at the Paris Peace Conference, and British recognition in 1920 of the country's right to diplomatic representation in foreign capitals all reflected the trend toward autonomy. Canadian nationhood was implicitly recognized at the Imperial Conference of 1926. The principles formulated at this conference were given legal status in the British Statute of Westminster of 1931, by which Canada and the other dominions became copartners with Great Britain in the Commonwealth of Nations.

Because of reduced demands on the world market for Canadian grain and raw materials, the country suffered a sharp economic crisis in the immediate postwar period. The effects of the crisis were disastrous in the western grain-growing areas. Crop prices fell to unprecedented levels, forcing many farmers into bankruptcy. Thousands of farmers turned to cooperatives as a way out of their predicament (see COOPERATIVE MOVEMENT). Political ferment engendered by the crisis had several important results. The Borden coalition government lost favor among the electorate; the Liberal Party, led by William Lyon Mackenzie King (q.v.), developed an opposition program that gained wide support; and several new parties, notably the farmer-supported National Progressive Party, were organized. A Liberal government, with King as prime minister, was formed following a general election in December, 1921. Liberal policies included a moderate lowering of tariff rates, subsidization of industry, and consolida-

tion of government-owned railroads. The railroads had not been functioning on a profitable basis in spite of large government subsidies. By 1921, therefore, the government was obliged to take over two privately owned transcontinental railways, the Canadian Northern and the Grand Trunk lines. These, added to the previously acquired Intercolonial Railway, were established as the Canadian National Railways in 1923. By 1925 rising grain prices and the general improvement in world business conditions stimulated a strong resurgence of industrial activity. After the national election of October, 1925, the Progressive Party held the balance of power in Parliament between the Liberal and Conservative parties, but Prime Minister King continued in office.

At the end of 1929, the Canadian economy suffered another disastrous decline. The crisis, part of the general world depression, soon attained catastrophic proportions. The export trade of Canada, chief source of national prosperity, decreased rapidly. The loss of export markets resulted in gradual paralysis of the entire industrial structure. Sharp wage cuts and mass layoffs accompanied the resultant industrial retrenchment. In retaliation against the imposition of protective tariffs by the U.S. and several other countries, the King government in May, 1930, placed correspondingly higher tariffs on various imports. Demands by the Conservatives for more drastic measures and popular resentment over the government's failure to provide adequate relief for the jobless were major factors in the victory won by the Conservative Party in the elections of July, 1930.

Headed by the Conservative leader Richard Bedford Bennett (q.v.), the new government assumed office on Aug. 7, 1930. Measures providing for an expanded unemployment-relief program and for higher tariff schedules were adopted by a special parliamentary session held in September. Upward revision of tariff schedules in 1931 further reduced the volume of imports, particularly from the U.S. In 1932, at an Imperial Economic Conference held in Ottawa, the government arranged preferential-trade treaties with Great Britain and several other member nations of the British Commonwealth. Prime Minister Bennett later initiated discussions with the U.S. about a reciprocal-trade agreement.

In 1932 the government created the Canadian Radio Broadcasting Commission, forerunner of the Canadian Broadcasting Corporation, to build a national broadcasting network. In 1934 an act was passed establishing the Bank of

Canada, a government-supervised, privately owned institution, which centralized banking operations throughout the country. The bank was subsequently nationalized by a Liberal government in 1938. In response to mounting demands for social security, parliament enacted in July, 1935, a program containing provisions for unemployment insurance, the forty-eight-hour week in industry, minimum wages, and other benefits. However, the Supreme Court of Canada in 1936 declared most of the program in violation of the British North America Act and therefore illegal.

Despite large-scale governmental intervention, economic stagnation persisted throughout Prime Minister Bennett's administration. The accompanying social unrest led to the founding of the Cooperative Commonwealth Federation (C.C.F.), a party which sought to unite labor and agriculture on a program of state socialism.

A general election, held in October, 1935, resulted in overwhelming victory for the Liberal Party and W. L. Mackenzie King succeeded Bennett as prime minister on Oct. 23.

The country's economic condition gradually improved under the King administration. A Canadian-American reciprocity agreement, signed on Nov. 15, heralded the beginning of a sustained foreign-trade revival, with resulting beneficial effects on industrial activity.

The sequence of events that culminated in the world diplomatic crises of 1937–39 engendered profound isolationist sentiments among Canadians. Although the government was noncommittal during most of this period of tension regarding its obligations in the event of British involvement in war, existing economic, political, and cultural ties with the mother country overcame the isolationism. Full support of Britain was promised in a formal pronouncement of the government on Aug. 24, 1939. With the German invasion of Poland on Sept. 1, Canada was placed on a war footing and parliament convened. On Sept. 10 Canada declared war in her own right for the first time in history.

**World War II.** Stabilization of the national economy, expansion of war-production facilities, and mobilization of economic resources were the chief objectives of the government during the early months of World War II. Transportation and industry, as well as foreign trade, prices, and the necessities of life, were immediately placed under governmental control. Initial military measures included the dispatch of a division to Great Britain and adoption of a British Commonwealth Air Training Plan. Under the terms of a program drafted jointly with Great Britain, Australia, and New Zealand, Canada became the advanced training center for pilots and other aviation personnel of the Commonwealth.

Canadian forces participated in campaigns in the Aleutian Islands, Hong Kong, Sicily, and Italy and the invasion (June, 1944) of western Europe. Although power to conscript forces for overseas duty had been granted in a plebiscite in 1942, the government chose to act with restraint because of strong opposition in Québec Province to compulsory overseas service. But heavy losses in the European invasion forced the Canadian government to abandon its anticonscription stand on Nov. 23, 1944. The collapse of German resistance early in 1945 rendered unnecessary a large-scale dispatch of draftees to the fighting fronts. Canada enlisted 1,086,771 men for participation in World War II and suffered 41,992 fatal casualties.

**Post-World War II.** Shortly after the fighting in Europe ended, Canada, a charter member of the United Nations, began the allocation of Canadian manufactures and foodstuffs to the international relief program of the U.N. Relief and Rehabilitation Administration and other foreign-aid agencies. This step, together with continued assistance to Great Britain and the extension of large credits to various European countries, helped to maintain a high level of industrial activity. Continued rationing of such basic commodities as meat and butter and the retention of price and rent controls retarded inflationary pressures. Thus the transition to a peacetime economy was accomplished with a minimum of political and social unrest.

When in 1947 the government relinquished wartime controls, except ceilings on rents, sharp increases in the cost of living resulted. In large measure, this inflationary trend stemmed from the country's dollar deficit, a result of the prevailing unfavorable trade balance with the U.S. By September, 1947, the deficit had reached an annual rate of nearly $1,000,000,000. The government, in November, 1947, obtained a $300,000,000 short-term loan from the U.S. Export-Import Bank to meet the emergency; stringent restrictions were imposed on many imports from the U.S.; and price ceilings were restored on meat and other foodstuffs. Gradually, the inflation was stemmed.

After serving for a total of twenty-two years as prime minister, Mackenzie King retired in November, 1948, at the age of seventy-four. He was succeeded as leader of the Liberal Party and as prime minister by Louis Stephen St. Laurent (q.v.), secretary of state for external affairs. In the general elections held the following June, the Liberals won an overwhelming majority of the seats in the House of Commons.

Meanwhile, in a referendum in July, 1948, Newfoundland voted by a small majority to join the Confederation, and became a member on April 1, 1949. Later in that year, the British Parliament acted on a Canadian request that the Canadian parliament have sole power to amend the Canadian constitution in all matters except those assigned to the exclusive jurisdiction of the provincial legislatures. This opened the way for enactment of the social security legislation declared unconstitutional by the Supreme Court in 1936.

Throughout the postwar period, Canadian foreign relations were marked by close ties with the U.S., Great Britain, and the British Commonwealth, and by continuing cooperation in the endeavors of the U.N. On April 29, 1949, the House of Commons unanimously ratified the North Atlantic Treaty, the original concept of which was, in part at least, a Canadian initiative, it having been first publicly suggested by Louis St. Laurent. Along with other participating members of the U.N. Security Council, the Canadian delegate voted, June 27, 1950, for military sanctions against North Korea following the North Korean invasion of South Korea. The Canadian government dispatched three destroyers to Korean waters, and a battalion of volunteers reached the fighting front later in the year. In July, 1954, Canada was represented at the "Big Four"–sponsored conference at Geneva, Switzerland, and was one of three nations chosen to supervise application of the Indochinese truce agreement. Following the Suez crisis of 1956 and the dispatch of Canadian troops to serve on the U.N. Emergency Force in Egypt, Lester Bowles Pearson (q.v.), minister of external affairs, became the first Canadian to be awarded the Nobel Peace Prize.

Two events of great economic significance occurred during the 1950's. In May, 1954, the U.S. Congress reversed its thirty-year refusal to approve the St. Lawrence Seaway and Power Project, and adopted legislation authorizing the U.S. government to join with Canada in construction of the facilities. Joint work on the project began in August of that year. The Seaway was opened to limited traffic in July, 1958, and to navigation by ocean vessels in June, 1959; see SAINT LAWRENCE SEAWAY. The second important event was the merger in April, 1956, of the two largest Canadian labor unions, the Canadian Congress of Labour and the Trades and Labour Congress, into the Canadian Labour Congress.

In the elections of June, 1957, the Liberal Party, which had been in power for almost a quarter of a century, was defeated. Prime Minister St. Laurent resigned and was succeeded by John George Diefenbaker (q.v.), leader of the Progressive Conservative (formerly Conservative) Party. Because his party had not obtained a clear majority, however, the House of Commons was dissolved on Feb. 1, 1958, at Diefenbaker's request. In the subsequent general elections the Progressive Conservatives won a record-breaking 209 of the 265 seats in the Commons.

**The 1960's and '70's.** Canada's role in world affairs changed little under Diefenbaker. In May, 1958, Canada and the U.S. established NORAD, and shortly afterward, a joint cabinet committee on defense was formed. But in July, 1960, Prime Minister Diefenbaker declared that no nuclear weapons would be allowed in Canada, even on U.S. bases, unless the weapons were entirely under Canadian control. Lester Pearson, leader of the Liberal Party, although he had agreed with Diefenbaker in opposing nuclear weapons in Canada, changed his position just before the election. Under pressure from many quarters, he agreed to accept nuclear warheads for the air-defense command. The controversy ended with the downfall of the Diefenbaker government on Feb. 4. In a general election held April 8, the Liberal Party won 129 seats and, with the pledged support of three Québec members of the Social Credit Party, gained a majority in parliament. Diefenbaker resigned on April 17, and Pearson became prime minister. In August a pact was signed with the U.S. providing for the acquisition of nuclear warheads and the stockpiling by the U.S. of warheads, which would be under U.S. control.

In other foreign relations, Canada continued to cooperate with the U.N. and supplied a force of 1000 volunteers to a U.N. peace-keeping effort in Cyprus in March, 1964. In the matter of the war in Vietnam the government proposed a four-point peace plan in September, 1967, and the foreign secretary, Paul Martin (1903–    ), attempted unsuccessfully to initiate negotiations between the two opposing sides. During the Arab-Israeli war of June, 1967, Canada's attempted mediation was again rejected.

In 1965 the decades-old campaign for adoption of a distinctive Canadian flag was finally successful. The new flag did not incorporate the British Union Jack; see FLAGS, NATIONAL.

A severe and recurring problem during the 1960's involved a number of separatist groups formed for the purpose of gaining full independence for the predominantly French-speak-

*Prime Minister Pierre Elliott Trudeau tours campaign headquarters in 1972, shortly before his indecisive victory at the polls.* UPI

ing province of Québec. Most militant of these groups was the Front de Libération du Québec (F.L.Q.), whose terrorist activities led to the arrest of a number of its members.

Although Federal-provincial relations improved somewhat in the mid-1960's, the controversy was given new life during a visit in July, 1967, of Charles de Gaulle (q.v.), then president of France, to Expo '67, the World's Exposition in Montréal. In a speech de Gaulle clearly gave strong support to the Québec separatist movement. The province moved in that direction later in the year by establishing a department of external affairs.

Prime Minister Pearson retired in April, 1968, at the age of seventy, and was succeeded by a French-Canadian, Pierre Elliott Trudeau (q.v.), who had been minister of justice. Federal-provincial disagreement continued on the ownership of offshore mineral resources of the continental shelf. In 1969 the Trudeau government announced a phased reduction of Canada's armed forces contribution to NATO in Europe and placed more emphasis on Canadian sovereignty and cooperation with the U.S. in the defense of North America. The Official Languages Act was proclaimed in the same year. It declared both English and French to be official languages in Canada and decreed that Federal services would be provided to the public in both languages. During 1970 the Trudeau ministry was faced with separatist terrorism in Québec as a provincial cabinet minister was kidnapped and eventually murdered by supporters of the F.L.Q.

The voting age was reduced from twenty-one to eighteen years, to take effect at the next Federal election.

The Trudeau government made major changes in foreign policy in 1971 with diplomatic recognition of the People's Republic of China and severance of relations with Taiwan. In March, 1971, the country set a new 12-mi. limit within which ocean fishing by foreign boats was sharply restricted; in 1977 Canada extended its fishing zone to 200 mi. offshore. Starting in 1971 the country undertook extensive programs to control coastal and inland water pollution.

In January, 1972, a new income-tax law, designed to stimulate the economy and to provide relief for persons with lower incomes, came into effect. The unemployment rate, however, reached a ten-year high of 7.1 percent of the labor force in September. Amid the economic slump and controversy over the government's efforts to promote the use of the French language, a general election was held in October. Prime Minister Trudeau's Liberal Party suffered a major setback in the voting, winning only 109 seats (46 fewer than in 1968) in the House of Commons. The Conservative Party won 107 seats, and the socialist-oriented New Democratic Party (N.D.P.) took 31 seats. After the election Trudeau formed a minority government dependent on N.D.P. support.

In the 1970's Canadians expressed great concern with foreign—especially U.S.—influence over the country's economic and cultural affairs. As a result, in 1973–74 Parliament tightened restrictions on the acquisition of Canadian firms by foreigners, and existing foreign-owned concerns came under closer scrutiny. A 1976 law sharply cut the revenue of Canadian editions of foreign-owned magazines by ending the policy of allowing domestic firms tax deductions for their advertising in these publications.

Canada was troubled by serious economic and social problems in the mid-1970's. Consumer prices increased by almost 11 percent in both 1974 and 1975, and more than 7 percent of the work force was unemployed in 1975 and 1976. Economic issues had a direct bearing on politics in 1974, as Trudeau's minority government was toppled in May after it lost a vote of confidence initiated by legislators dissatisfied with its proposed national budget. In the general election that followed in July, however, Trudeau's Liberal Party emerged with a clear majority of 141 seats in the House of Commons. In late 1975 Trudeau instituted mandatory wage and price guidelines, and the inflation rate declined to 7.5 percent in 1976. Despite great inflation-induced cost overruns and labor unrest, which for a time threatened to prevent the completion of necessary facilities, the Olympic Games (q.v.) were held in Montréal in the summer of 1976.

The country's most troublesome social issue involved relations between English and French Canadians. Forming only about one quarter of Canada's population and concentrated chiefly in Québec Province, the French Canadians felt submerged in the federation and sought increased recognition of their cultural heritage. In elections in late 1976, Québecers unexpectedly gave the separatist Parti Québécois (P.Q.) a large majority in the provincial legislature. Led by René Lévesque (1924– ), the P.Q. proposed to hold a referendum in Québec on whether the province should become a sovereign entity.

**CANADA BALSAM,** also called CANADIAN TURPENTINE, an oleoresin obtained from the balsam secreted by the bark of the evergreen fir tree *Abies balsamea,* or balsam fir; *see* RESINS. The balsam fir, a member of the Pine family (Pinaceae), grows in the forests of Canada and the northern United States. As it exudes from the tree, the balsam is a greenish-yellow liquid the consistency of honey. It becomes hard and transparent as it dries. Although balsam is sometimes an ingredient of varnishes, it is used chiefly as an adhesive for the mounting of microscopic specimens and the manufacture of lenses and optical systems. Balsam has two great advantages when used to cement the elements of compound lenses and other glass surfaces: it is transparent, and its index of refraction is so close to that of optical glass that it introduces little distortion.

**CANADA COMPANY,** private venture for the colonization of Upper Canada (now Ontario Province), organized in 1825 by the British novelist John Galt (*see under* GALT). The company, which received a royal charter in 1826, played an important part in settling southern Ontario between lakes Ontario and Huron, where large tracts of land were cleared and many English and Scottish settlers established farms. In 1827 the town of Guelph was founded by the company. Goderich and Saint Marys were established shortly thereafter. The region became one of the richest in Ontario.

**CANADA, THE UNITED CHURCH OF.** *See* UNITED CHURCH OF CANADA, THE.

**CANADIAN,** river of the United States, sometimes called the South Canadian R., a nonnavigable stream 906 mi. long. The Canadian R. is formed in N.E. New Mexico by the union of several branches from the southern Rocky Mts. The river flows S. through New Mexico and then turns E., crossing the panhandle of Texas into Oklahoma. Following a meandering course in Oklahoma, it finally joins the Arkansas River (q.v.). The only major tributary of the Canadian R. is the North Canadian R., 784 mi. long, which runs almost parallel to the Canadian R. in Oklahoma. The tributary joins the Canadian R. at Eufaula in McIntosh County to form the Eufaula Reservoir. In N.E. New Mexico, a semiarid region, the Canadian R. provides an important water source at the Conchas Dam, a flood-control and irrigation project.

**CANADIAN ART,** various kinds of art produced by Canadians in precolonial, colonial, and modern times, including handicraft work, painting, sculpture, architecture, photography, and films.

**Primitive Art.** Art in various forms was practiced among the primitive tribes of Canada, but their nomadic existence and the severe climate were responsible for the destruction of much of the early work. Pottery shards, ceremonial masks, and the tradition of geometric pattern are the only remaining evidence that primitive art once existed. Indians decorated all their tools of daily living, from valuable wampum belts to arrow quivers and skin teepees. Rock paintings have been found northwest of Lake Superior, but the only monumental art was produced by the coastal tribes of British Columbia. Although these tribes were the last to come under the domination of the white man, European trade goods did reach them before 1800. With metal tools of European manufacture Indian art and culture developed to a high creative level. The carved doorposts and great totem poles that stood before their houses are sculptures of great strength and beauty. Objects of daily use were made with particular care and decorated with stylized man-animal motifs. The materials that the Indians used in their art were horn, wood, walrus ivory, argillite (a clayey rock), and abalone shell. The cedar provided wood for carving and for constructing buildings; the fibrous inner bark was woven into baskets, rain hats, and capes, and wool from the mountain sheep was spun and woven into ceremonial blankets.

The Plains Indians (q.v.), who made up various North American Indian tribes, painted on buffalo hide, and early missionaries taught them to use trade beads to decorate their buckskin garments. Despite the attempt of Europeans to impose the stylized flower designs of peasant art on their Indian pupils, the more striking geometric patterns traditional in Indian culture persisted. Both styles of beadwork are seen today in the ceremonial dress of Indians participating in the Calgary Stampede, a rodeo that is the most popular annual event in the province of Alberta.

Throughout the Arctic Regions, a skillful North American aboriginal people, the Eskimo (q.v.) tribes, make clothing of skins fitted to the body and decorated with contrasting patterns of colored fur. The Eskimos use walrus ivory and soapstone as material for sculpture, and travelers have brought south small carvings and drawings of tundra animals and hunters worked in ivory. Under the supervision of the Federal Department of Northern Affairs, Eskimo artists have been encouraged to work on a larger scale and their distinctive style of sculpture is well known. Since the 1950's, when graphics were added to the repertory of artistic media used by the Eskimo, his prints, displaying a playful gaiety, have found a receptive market in southern Canada as well as the United States.

**French Regime.** During the period of French colonization beginning in the early 17th century, church decoration and the fashioning of religious objects occupied the artist-craftsman of the colony. François Xavier de Laval Montmorency (1623-1708), first bishop of Québec, encouraged the arts by founding a school, École des Arts et Métiers, at Cap Tourmente on the Saint Lawrence R. (about 30 mi. below the city of Québec) in 1675. Here, artists from France taught the men of the community. The traditions of wood sculpture executed in the French style, which were established at that time, can still be seen in village workshops along the shores of the lower St. Lawrence R.

Religious paintings adorning village churches in Québec are sincere expressions of 19th-century folk art. The journeying portrait painters also left a record of the Canadian 19th-century bourgeoisie. It is the work of Cornelius Krieghoff (1812-72), however, that recorded French Canadian life in its many varieties. Executed in the anecdotal style of the period, Krieghoff's numerous paintings, depicting activity on the farm, in the inn, and at winter and summer frolics, are valued as a rich historical account of 19th-century life.

Painters in 19th-century Québec usually studied in Paris. Among the most celebrated artists of the time were Joseph Légaré (1795-1855), Antoine Plamondon (1804-95), and Théophile Hamel (1817-70); these men were chiefly portrait painters whose work is exhibited in the art galleries of Québec, Montréal, and in the National Gallery of Canada in Ottawa, Ontario.

**English Period.** In the years following the French and Indian War (q.v.), topographers attached to the British army left valuable records of the country they were exploring and surveying. The watercolors and sketchbooks of men and women of this period convey the quality of a peaceful English countryside. Of the many topographers who worked in 19th-century Canada, Sir James Pattison Cockburn (1779-1847) and William Henry Bartlett (1809-54) are perhaps the best known. Bartlett came to Canada in 1836 and his scenes of various parts of Canada, published as *Canadian Scenery* (1842), are highly valuable prints today.

After confederation in 1867, when Canada became a dominion, the leading Canadian painters were Robert Harris (1849-1919) and Horatio Walker (1858-1938), whose work was chiefly the genre type (see GENRE PAINTING), in which scenes of everyday life were depicted. Lucius Richard O'Brien (1832-99), Homer Watson (1855-1936), and William Brymner (1855-1925) were primarily landscape painters. They all were adherents of European styles of painting. Maurice Galbraith Cullen (1866-1934), Aurèle Suzor Coté (1870-1937), and Ozias Leduc (1864-1955) began to experiment with color and to break with European traditions. James Wilson Morrice (1865-1939) studied abroad but often returned to his home in Montréal. Influenced by Henri Matisse (q.v.), he treated the winter scenes of the St. Lawrence R. and the tropical vistas of the West Indies in broad flat patterns reminiscent of that French artist.

North of the St. Lawrence valley and the gently rolling hills of southern Ontario is the Laurentian Shield of Precambrian hills, a vast, forested wilderness covered by rocks and interspersed with lakes. The tangled forms of evergreen and the brilliant autumn colors of maple and birch could not be painted in a photographic technique. The impressionistic techniques developed in Europe during the 1880's, however, were adapted to the painting of the northland. A group of young men working in Toronto were challenged by the dramatic landscape, and with sketch boxes and camping gear, traveled the northern lakes by canoe. Of this group, Tom Thomson (1877-1917) was self-taught; others, Arthur Lismer (1885-1969) and Frederick Horsman Varley (1881-1968), were Englishmen trained in Europe before they came to Canada; Lawren Harris, Sr. (1885-1970), Alexander Young Jackson (1882-1974), J. E. H. Macdonald (1873-1932), Frank Carmichael (1890-1945), and Franz Johnstone (1888-1949) were Canadians who had studied in Europe or in the European tradition. Each developed his own

*"The Ferry, Québec", oil painting (about 1909) by James Wilson Morrice.* The National Gallery of Canada-Ottawa

individual style in paintings that revealed the grandeur of the landscape, encompassing the rhythmic patterns of rock, the beauty of wind-swept pine forests, and the kaleidoscope of autumn color. These artists painted in a new way; breaking with the European traditions, they gave their countrymen and the world an image of the northland and in so doing, created the first Canadian school of painting.

On the west coast of Canada Emily Carr (1871–1945) worked alone, developing her interpretation of the grandeur of the forests of British Columbia. On large canvasses she painted totem poles, great sculptured forms of vegetation, and Indian villages. Emily Carr was unknown by collectors in eastern Canada and only through her Indian friends did Dr. Charles Marius Barbeau (1883–1969), an anthropologist from the National Museum of Canada in Ottawa, come to know of her work and introduce it to the art galleries of Toronto and Montréal.

In contrast to the powerful canvasses of Emily Carr, the work of David Bruce Milne (1882–1953) is delicate and poetic. A quality of gentleness is reflected in his watercolors of street scenes, landscapes, and still lifes.

Among the many painters in Québec who followed the same tradition were Jacques de Tonnancour (1917– ), Goodridge Roberts (1904– ), and John Fox (1927– ). Those who broke with this tradition were Paul Émile Borduas (1905–60), Alfred Pellan (1906– ), and Jean-Paul Riopelle (1923– ). Their nonfigurative works still provide inspiration for younger artists.

A significant contribution to Canadian painting has been made by women. Represented in the collections of the larger museums are the stylized landscapes of Anne Savage (1896–1971), the scientific panels of Marion Scott (1906– ), the figures and interiors of Ghitta Caiserman (1923– ), and the figures and landscapes of Molly Bobak (1922– ).

Alexander Colville (1920– ) on the east coast paints in a realistic, almost photographic, style. From the Vancouver school in British Columbia, Bertram Charles Binning (1909– ) paints seascapes in a stylized and geometric manner.

Montréal, Toronto, Regina, and Vancouver were the most active centers of painting during the 1950's and 1960's. Among the contemporary artists doing serious work there were Harold Town (1924– ), David Partridge (1919– ), Jean McEwen (1923– ), Albert Dumonchel (1916–71), and Yves Gaucher (1934– ), all of whom work in nonfigurative styles.

**Graphics.** In the graphics media, young artists have found a major art form. The low cost of production has brought the works of such graphic artists as Pierre Ayot (1943– ) and Toni Onley (1928– ) within the range of young collectors.

**Sculpture.** The wood sculpture of the west-coast Indians, the stone sculpture of the Eskimo, and the church wood sculpture of Québec have honored places in museums. Until recently, however, sculpture intended to adorn streets and parks was generally restricted to war memorials and representations of statesmen, the only exceptions being the work of Phillippe Hébert (1850–1917) and his son Henri Hébert (1884–1950). Their sculpture in Québec City, honoring the first pioneer, portrays the figure of a farmer lifting the first sheaf of grain high in the air; around the base of the monument are figures representing members of a family engaged in various farm activities.

In the 20th century the sculpture of Walter Allward (1876–1950) drew attention; he created the war memorial at Vimy Ridge, a point in France taken by Canadians during World War I.

Other important contemporary sculptors are Emanuel Hahn (1881–1957) and his wife Elizabeth Wyn Wood (1903–66), Florence Wyle (1881–1968), and Frances Loring (1887–1968). Their work consisted basically of memorials and building decorations.

The work of a younger generation, including Louis Archambault (1915– ) with his strange and amusing bird forms, Anne Kahane (1924– ) and her large wood sculptures, and Michael Snow (1930– ), with his "Walking Woman", has given sculpture a new spirit of gaiety and vitality and removed it from exclusive association with memorials.

A transient but interesting form of sculpture is the ice sculpture seen at mid-winter festivals. In the province of Québec, Mardi Gras is celebrated with contests of skill in sports and other activities. Both professional and amateur sculptors engage in creating large constructions of ice and snow, which, because of the nature of the materials with which they are made, are of limited duration. Canadians are privileged to have the works of major sculptors displayed in the squares of their cities and in parks throughout Canada. Sculpture is also prominently featured in the Man and His World exhibition in Montréal.

A medium that falls between painting and free-standing sculpture is embodied in the work of Eli Bornstein (1925– ) of Saskatoon and Gino Lorcini (1923– ) of London, Ontario. Building out from a vertical surface, they design in wood, plastic, and aluminum. The forms of aluminum vary in depth and size, creating patterns of shadows and reflections against the background and on each other. The patterns of light change constantly with the movement of the viewer. The work of Bornstein can be seen in provincial galleries and at the University of Saskatchewan in Saskatoon. Lorcini's work is on view in various public collections and in the Centre for the Performing Arts in Ottawa.

**Architecture.** Three main streams of architectural style influenced building in Canada. One was the provoncial style of northern France that early settlers adapted to the climate and materials of the St. Lawrence valley; another, the English baroque (q.v.) of the 18th century; and the third, a modified form of English baroque contributed by the United Empire Loyalists, a group of colonists from the United States who came to Canada after the American Revolution (q.v.).

The French settlers built in stone, and many fine examples executed in the 17th century survive in the cities of Québec and Montréal. The steep-pitched roofs with two rows of projecting dormer windows, the bell-shaped projecting eaves, and the casement windows that open inward like doors give a distinct style to the long farmhouses of Québec. The church and church spire dominate the village. Built of local stone, the spire rises from a square tower through two or more octagonal galleries to the cock weathervane. Many churches have twin spires rising from the west facade. In the 20th century the roof has generally been covered with aluminum; the windows are of clear glass, framed in white-painted wood.

Unlike the stone houses of the St. Lawrence valley, the houses of English-speaking Canada were constructed in the New England fashion with wooden clapboard. The shape of the house was square with the summer kitchen added as an ell, or else attached to the back, forming the so-called salt-box style. The classical revival in architecture dominated styles of building in the first decades of the 19th century. Saint Andrew's Presbyterian Church at Niagara-on-the-Lake, Ontario is a good example of this style.

Many towns were laid out by military engineers who surveyed the area of Upper Canada and Canada West (now Ontario). The town of Goderich, Ontario, with streets radiating from a central square, was one experiment in town-planning. Kingston, Ontario, built early in the English regime, reflects in the government buildings and churches the tradition of the English architect Sir Christopher Wren (q.v.).

The Neo-Gothic style was the current architectural idiom of the second half of the 19th century (*see* GOTHIC ARCHITECTURE). Churches and public buildings were modeled in this style and constructed of local materials of stone or wood. The Parliament buildings in Ottawa were built between 1859 and 1867 in the Neo-Gothic style, although only the library remains of the original structures. The Château Frontenac (q.v.) (1890) at Québec City and other hotels built by railway companies were designed in a variety of styles, although French Renaissance, a style that apparently pleased wealthy travelers at the turn of the century, was favored (*see* RENAISSANCE ART AND ARCHITECTURE: *France*).

Contemporary architecture prevalent elsewhere in the 1920's and 1930's made little headway in Canada. The requisite building materials were unsuited to the Canadian climate, and technical problems of heating had to be solved before large areas of glass could be used. The most important structures built during these years were the great terminal grain elevators made of concrete. These enormous cylinders rise like pillars on the waterfronts of port cities along the Great Lakes and St. Lawrence R.

Since the end of World War II (q.v.), housing needs for the rapidly expanding population has been met by increased suburban development and by the construction of high-rise buildings, both residential and commercial. A significant change in architecture can also be seen in the design of churches, where contemporary style is used in great variety.

Some of the outstanding modern Canadian buildings are: The Shakespearean Festival Theatre (1957) in Stratford, Ontario; Place des Arts (1964) in Montréal; City Hall (1965) in Toronto; and Theatre of the Performing Arts (1969) in Ottawa. Talented contemporary architects who have contributed to modern Canadian building design include Robert Fairfield (1918– ), the Finnish architect Viljo Revell (1910–64), and the architectural firm of Affleck, Dimakapoulous, Lebensold, Michaud, and Sise.

**Films and Photography.** The National Film Board of Canada is well known for the documentary films it has released that have won awards at international film festivals. The subjects of the films cover all aspects of Canada: the land and people, industry and art, sports and recreation, science, legends, and history. Award-winning films include: *Land of the Long Day* (1952), a film about the far North directed by Robert J. Flaherty (1884–1951); *Street to the World* (1958), a poetic study of a small boy watching ships pass up and down the St. Law-

rence R.; *The Backbreaking Leaf* (1960), a film on the tobacco harvest of southern Ontario; and *The Stratford Adventure* (1954), a film of the growth of the Stratford Shakespearean Festival. Norman McLaren (1914– ) is noted for his many experimental film animation techniques. He often works directly on film with ordinary pen and ink as in *Dots* (1940) and *Pen Point Percussion* (1950). In *Blinkity Blank* (1954), he made use of intermittent animation and spasmodic imagery and dealt with the laws relating to persistence of vision and afterimages on the retina of the eye. McLaren often uses folk songs and nonsense songs for themes as in *Le Merle* ("The Blackbird", 1958), or he utilizes specific situations, as in the film *Neighbors* (1952), a parable about two people who come to blows over the possession of a flower.

Yousuf Karsh (1908– ) is a Canadian photographer with an international reputation. He is primarily a portrait photographer and is interested in capturing on film impressions of leaders and outstanding people of the world. Among his published books are *Faces of Destiny* (1946) and his autobiography, *In Search of Greatness* (1962), both of which are valuable records of modern history.

Wilfred Roloff Beny (1924– ) is an artist-photographer well known outside of Canada for his books of photographs: *The Thrones of Earth and Heaven* (1958), *A Time of Gods* (1962), and *Pleasure of Ruins* (1965). He returned to Canada in time to prepare a volume of photographs, *To Everything There Is a Season* (1967) for the centennial year 1967. In these photographs he has sought the essence of Canada and the people of that nation, portraying them with the same skill and dramatic point of view that he developed and revealed about Europe and the Orient.

**Art and the Public.** Since the publication of the *Report of the Royal Commission on the National Development in Arts, Letters, and Science* (1949–1951), known as the *Massey Report,* the arts have been supported increasingly by all levels of government. Under the federal government, the Canada Council makes grants to practicing artists who wish to work abroad or pursue a specific program of work at home. The Federal Department of Transport has used the work of artists in airports. The provision of educational programs and traveling exhibitions by the National Gallery of Canada, Ottawa, has been particularly effective in western Canada.

Canadian business corporations and universities have become patrons of contemporary artists, for whom their collections are an important showcase. Large private collections also exist,

*Archibald Lampman, Canadian poet of the late 19th-century Confederation period.*

Photo Folios, Chemainus, B.C.

including the Mendel Collection at Saskatoon, Saskatchewan. The increase in the number of public galleries in small cities and the rapid growth of commercial galleries in large cities indicate the rising interest in art among the Canadian public.                                                A.E.J.

**CANADIAN LITERATURE,** literature written by both the English-speaking and French-speaking inhabitants of Canada. Both segments of the literature began with the accounts of explorers, missionaries, and colonizers of the 16th, 17th, and 18th centuries. Among the early works in French are the account of the explorer Jacques Cartier (q.v.) of his voyages of 1534–35; the books of the explorer Samuel de Champlain (q.v.), most notably his *Les Voyages de la Nouvelle France Occidentale* ("Voyages From Western New France", 1632); and *Les Relations des Jésuites*, a compilation of annual reports of French Jesuit missionaries from their stations in the Indian lands. The early English works include *An Account of a Journey from Prince of Wales's Fort in Hudson's Bay to the Northern Ocean* (1795) by the English explorer Samuel Hearne (1745–92), and *Voyages from Montreal to the Frozen and Pacific Oceans* (1801) by the Scottish explorer Sir Alexander Mackenzie (q.v.). *See* CANADA: *History*.

From such beginnings the literature continued to develop separately in French and Eng-lish. While the English-Canadian writers developed under the influence of English and American literature, the French-Canadians found their models in French works and their themes in the folkways of their largely rural communities.

### ENGLISH-CANADIAN LITERATURE

Because the English-speaking community in Canada is larger than the French, the English-Canadian literature is more abundant and varied than the French-Canadian. The first novel produced in North America was *The History of Emily Montague* (1769) written by an English woman, Frances Brooke (1724–89), whose husband was the chaplain of the army garrison at Québec. The first book-length poem was *The Rising Village*, written by Oliver Goldsmith (1794–1861) as a reply to *The Deserted Village* (1770) written by his granduncle, the British author Oliver Goldsmith (q.v.). Beginning in 1836 the humorous political essays of Thomas Chandler Haliburton (1796–1865) were issued in three successive volumes, the first of which was *The Clockmaker, or the Sayings and Doings of Sam Slick of Slickville*. The Sam Slick books proved popular in the United States as well as in Canada. Two outstanding books on pioneer life were written by Catherine Parr Traill (1802–99), author of *Backwoods of Canada* (1836), and her sister, Susanna Moodie who wrote *Roughing It in the Bush* (1852).

The Confederation of 1867, which ushered in Canadian nationhood, created a sense of national identity and stimulated literary activity. During this period also the English-Canadian writers came under the influence of the later English Romantics, whose enthusiasm for nature inspired Canadians to look for themes in the natural grandeur of their country. These trends found expression in the nature lyric and the regional prose romance. Today one of the most admired of the so-called Confederation poets who began writing in the late 19th century is Archibald Lampman (1861–99). *Among the Millet* (1888), *Lyrics of Earth* (1893), and other volumes portray the lonely splendor of the Ottawa country-side.

Better known abroad than Lampman was William Bliss Carman (q.v.), who was also a teacher and editor in the U.S. His three-volume *Songs from Vagabondia* (1894–1900), written in collaboration with the American poet Richard Hovey (1864–1900), was highly successful. Carman's best poems are found in *The Pipes of Pan* (5 vol., 1902–05). Another outstanding poet was Sir Charles George Douglas Roberts (1860–1943), whose best-known volumes of verse include

*Orion and Other Poems* (1880) and *Songs of the Common Day* (1893). Roberts also won fame for his animal stories and historical romances.

Roberts' Canadian scene is the product of close and cheerful observation. Carman's Canada is awesome, its atmosphere tinged with melancholy. A more dramatic view of nature is offered by Duncan Campbell Scott (1862–1947), whose volumes of poetry include *The Magic House and Other Poems* (1893), *New World Lyrics and Ballads* (1905), and *Beauty and Life* (1921). To Scott nature is a battleground in which insensate forces, like animate beings, war with one another. The leading Canadian woman poet of the 19th century, Isabella Valancy Crawford (1850–87), is noted for her dynamic portrayal of pioneer life; her *Collected Poems* appeared in 1905.

The two principal novelists of the early post-confederation period, William Kirby (1817–1906) and Sir Gilbert Parker (q.v.), deal with the difficulties and satisfactions of life in a vast and primitive country. Kirby's best-known novel is *The Golden Dog* (1877), a historical romance set in New France before the English conquest. *Seats of the Mighty* (1896), which is set in the same period, is Parker's most popular work.

Early in the 20th century the literary fashion began to shift from Romanticism to realism. Some of the noteworthy books of this period were *The Man from Glengarry* (1901) by Ralph Connor (1860–1937); *Anne of Green Gables* (1908), a popular girls' book by Lucy Maud Montgomery Macdonald (1874–1942); and the works on nature study and wood lore by Ernest Thompson Seton (q.v.), who grew up in Canada but later settled in the U.S. A widely read poet who emerged in this period was Robert William Service (q.v.), author of *Songs of a Sourdough* (1907), which includes "The Shooting of Dan McGrew", *Rhymes of a Red Cross Man* (1916), and many other volumes of verse. Some critics sought to raise esteem for his work by labeling his pictures of rough northwestern life as realism, but Service himself never pretended to be anything but a doggerel rhymester.

More highly respected in the literary world was Stephen Butler Leacock (q.v.), a professor of economics and political science at McGill University, in Montréal. A brilliant humorist and satirist, Leacock wrote the sharpest and wittiest social criticism Canada has yet produced. Among his books were *Literary Lapses* (1910), *Sunshine Sketches of a Little Town* (1912), and *Arcadian Adventures with the Idle Rich* (1914). A more serious book was *The Unsolved Riddle of Social Justice* (1920).

A pioneer writer of the sociological novel in Canada was Swedish-born Frederick Philip Grove (1871–1948), who wrote about life on the Canadian prairies. His work, although weak in style and characterization, has great strength and vigor. Some of his best writing is contained in *Over Prairie Trails* (1922), a volume of western sketches. *Settlers of the Marsh* (1925) and *Fruits of the Earth* (1933) are two of his most powerful novels. Another sociologically oriented novelist is Morley Callaghan (1903– ), whose novels deal with misfits in an urban society. Callaghan's stories are somewhat sentimental, but they are better plotted and his characters are more convincing than Grove's. Three of his best novels, *Such Is My Beloved* (1934), *They Shall Inherit the Earth* (1935), and *More Joy in Heaven* (1937), date back to the 1930's. His more recent novels, including *The Many Coloured Coat* (1960) and *A Passion in Rome* (1961), concentrate on the values of the Christian ethic in modern society.

Belonging to the same period but of a wholly different literary tradition is Mazo de la Roche (q.v.), probably the most widely read Canadian novelist. Her works resemble the regional romances of the late 19th century and include sixteen *Jalna* books, of which the first, *Jalna* (awarded the *Atlantic Monthly* prize in 1927), is recognized as the best.

In the post-World War II period Hugh MacLennan (1907– ) is generally considered the most important literary interpreter of the Cana-

*Duncan Campbell Scott*     Photo Folios, Chemainus, B.C.

dian scene. In his novels, which are not particularly outstanding artistically, he has investigated such matters as the emergence of a Canadian sense of identity, the clash of English and French cultures, and the impact of American mores on Canadian life. His most impressive novel is *The Watch That Ends the Night* (1959), which considers the impact of the social idealism of the 1930's in Canada. In his *Return of the Sphinx* (1967) he suggests that the conflict between English- and French-speaking Canadians is symptomatic of worldwide maladjustments. A writer who has made a literary career of irony and satire is Robertson Davies (1913– ), who has written a number of plays and several novels, including *Tempest-Tost* (1951) and *A Mixture of Frailties* (1950).

Other outstanding novels dating from World War II and after are *As for Me and My House* (1941) by Sinclair Ross (1908– ), *Day of Wrath* (1945) by Philip Child (1898– ), *Who Has the Wind?* (1947) by W. O. Mitchell (1914– ), *The Cruelest Month* (1962) by Ernest Buckler (1908– ), *Cocksure* (1968) by Mordecai Richler (1931– ), *The Equations of Love* (1952) and *Swamp Angel* (1964) by Ethel Wilson (1890– ), *The Second Scroll* (1951) by Abraham Moses Klein (1909–72), *The Sacrifice* (1956) by Adele Wiseman (1928– ), *The Luck of Ginger Coffey* (1960) by Brian Moore (1921– ), and *Beautiful Losers* (1966) by Leonard Norman Cohen (1934– ). Margaret Laurence (1926– ) is recognized as the best contemporary Canadian novelist. Her works include *The Stone Angel* (1964) and *A Jest of God* (1966).

One of the finest of the poets to emerge after World War I was Newfoundland-born Edwin John Pratt (1883–1964), whose earliest poems appeared in the 1920's. His work, which is vigorous and allegorical, is populated with whales, dinosaurs, and giants. It reflects his fascination with the sea, his sense of the impersonal violence of nature, and his fundamentally tragic vision of life. Pratt's long verse narratives include *Titanic* (1935) and *Brebeuf and His Brethren* (1940).

One of the most exciting and seminal periods in English-Canadian poetry occurred during the 1940's as a result of the activities and rivalries of two groups of Montréal poets. The older of the groups included Frank R. Scott (1899– ), A. J. M. Smith (1902– ), Leo Kennedy (1907– ), and Abraham Moses Klein. Of this group, the first two members have remained the most active. Scott's own collection of satirical works, *The Eye of The Needle: Satires, Sorties, Sundries,* appeared in 1957. Also in that year, in collaboration with Smith, he compiled *The Blasted Pine: An Anthology of Satire, Invective and Disrespectful Verse: Chiefly by Canadian Writers,* which perhaps belies the cliché that Canadians are incapable of self-criticism. Both these poets have issued their collected poems, Smith in 1962 and Scott in 1966.

This group became involved as well in the publication of a literary magazine called *Preview,* founded in 1941 and boasting among its contributors, in addition to the four poets previously cited, such notable Canadian poets as P. K. Page (1916– ), and Patrick Anderson (1915– ). In 1942 a rival magazine, *First Statement,* challenged the premises of *Preview,* accusing its poets of being artificial, precious, and British oriented, which was true to an extent. If it had not been for the rivalry between the magazines, a great deal of creative Canadian talent could have been siphoned off in either the American or British traditions. In 1945 the two magazines merged and became the *Northern Review,* which existed until 1955. Founded in 1959, *Canadian Literature* has become the most important and informative literary magazine in Canada. Brought to prominence in the magazines were a number of new poets, including Irving Layton (1912– ), Louis Dudek (1918– ), Raymond Souster (1921– ), Miriam Waddington (1917– ), and Anne Wilkinson (1910–61).

Two of the most colorful of these poets are Layton and Dudek, who collaborated in 1952 with *Canadian Poems 1850–1952,* a very useful anthology showing the development of a distinctive Canadian style. The more scatalogical appeal of Layton is best illustrated by his *The Laughing Rooster* (1964). His later work, *Periods of The Moon* (1967), is somewhat mellowed in tone, but still runs counter to middle-class morality. His *Collected Poems* appeared in 1965. As a contrast, Dudek reveals a scholarly concern with the progress of Canadian verse in *Poetry in Our Time* (1965). *Atlantis* (1968), based on the myth of the lost city, sincerely manifests the reflections of a thinking man upon modern life.

Souster examines the esoteric qualities of Canadian poets in *New Wave Canada: The New Explosion in Canadian Poetry* (1966), and Waddington revives an almost Wordsworthian emphasis upon the beneficial power of nature in *The Glass Trumpet* (1966). Both these poets may appear imitative, yet in their poetry is an essence which could only be Canadian.

Among the outstanding contemporary poets not already mentioned are: Robert Finch (1900– ), who wrote *Dover Beach Revisited and Other Poems* (1961), a reassessment of the famous poem by the British poet Matthew Arnold (q.v.), and *Silverthorn Bush and Other Poems* (1966). He creates an almost metaphysical exploration of his subject, yet the whole effect is lightened by his superb control of symbol. The descriptive verse of Earle Birney (1904– ), *Ice, Cod, Bell, or Stone* (1962) and *Near False Creek Mouth* (1964) is characteristically philosophical and lyrical. In *Colour of God's Face* (1964), which deals with her African experiences, and *The Unquiet Bed* (1967), Dorothy Livesay (1909– ) reveals the thoughts of a sensitive feminine mind. Three other poets who should be noted are James Reaney (1926– ), Jay Macpherson (1931– ), and Margaret Avison (1918– ), a very complex writer who expresses impressions of the senses and the range of human feeling with remarkable clarity.

## FRENCH-CANADIAN LITERATURE

For a long period after the English conquest of New France, French-Canadian culture revealed a defensive and ingrown character that tended to discourage originality. The earlier French-Canadian literature was produced by upper-class and clerical writers who looked to France for their models. Their main preoccupation was with history, and that tradition continued into the 19th century.

The first notable French-Canadian literary work was *Histoire du Canada* (1845–48), by François Xavier Garneau (q.v.), still the classic expression of French-Canadian nationalism. Garneau became the prophet for a school of patriotic French-Canadian writers that was organized about 1860 and centered around a bookshop in Québec City. The shopkeeper was Octave Crémazie (1822–79), who is considered the father of French-Canadian poetry; his *Oeuvres Complètes* ("Complete Works") was published in 1882. One of the members of the Québec group was the historian Abbé Henri Raymond Casgrain (q.v.), whose best-known works are *Montcalm et Lévis* (2 vol., 1891; Eng. trans., *Wolfe and Montcalm,* 1964) and *Une Seconde Acadie* ("A Second Acadia", 1894). Another follower was Philippe Aubert de Gaspé (1786–1871), author of the best-known French-Canadian novel of the 19th century, *Les Anciens Canadiens* ("The Old Canadians", 1863). Other important French-Canadian novels are *Charles Guérin, Roman de Mœurs Canadiennes* ("Charles Guérin, A Novel of Canadian Manners", 1846) by Pierre Joseph Olivier Chauveau (1820–90), one of the earliest works of fiction written by a French-Canadian; *Jean Rivard* (1864) by Antoine Gérin-Lajoie (1824–82); and *Pour la Patrie* ("For Our Country", 1895) by Jules

Paul Tardivel (1851–1905). Louis Honoré Fréchette (1839–1908) was an important nationalistic poet of the period.

During the early 20th century, nationalism continued to preoccupy French-Canadian writers, as in the work of Abbé Lionel Groulx (1878–1967). His *Vers l'Émancipation* ("Toward Freedom", 1921) speaks for the preservation of a French-Canadian culture free of English dominance. In poetry as well, opposition to assimilation with the English and pride in the French were the dominant themes. Patriotism was animated by a vivid re-creation of regional life, as in *Les Gouttelettes* ("Small Drops", 1904), a volume of sonnets by Pamphile Lemay (1837–1918); in *Floraisons Matutinales* ("Early Flowers", 1897) by Nérée Beauchemin (1850–1931); and in *La Vieille Maison* ("The Old House", 1920) and other works by Blanche Lamontagne Beauregard (1889–1958). A break with such parochial themes was made by members of an association founded in 1895, known as the *École Littéraire de Montréal* (Montreal Literary School). The most prominent poets of the school were Émile Nelligan (1879–1941) and Paul Morin (1889–1963).

In the early 1930's one of the most important literary events was the founding of the magazine *La Relève* ("Changing of the Guard") by the novelist and editor Robert Charbonneau (1911–67) and the poets François Hertel (1905– ) and Rodolphe Dubé, pen name of St. Denys Garneau (1912–43). Later in the decade, on the eve of World War II, the cultural isolation of French Canada and its rigid social system began to break down. Urbanization and the war disrupted established ways, giving rise to new conflicts and tensions, new attitudes, and new literary modes. Since 1940 many writers have been active in the fields of criticism, philosophy, poetry, and fiction. In *Le Combat contre Tristan* ("The Battle Against Tristan", 1951), a volume of poems by Pierre Trottier (1925– ), a tragic drama of love and death is enriched by symbolic and ironic evocations of the troubled disunity of Canada. Themes at once local and universal appear in the poetic works of Alain Grandbois (1900– ), Anne Hébert (1916– ), Rina Lasnier (1915– ), Jean Guy Pilon (1930– ), and Gatien Lapointe (1931– ), and in the novels of Robert Élie (1915– ), Yves Thériault (1915– ), André Giroux (1916– ), Germaine Guèvremont (1900–68), and André Langevin (1927– ). One of the outstanding novelists is Gabrielle Roy (1909– ). In her novels *Bonheur d'Occasion* (1945; Eng. trans., *The Tin Flute,* 1947), and *Alexandre Chenevert* (1954; Eng.

trans., *The Cashier,* 1955), she describes the way in which urban industrial life has disturbed family integrity and human dignity. Unlike some earlier writers, she does not advocate a return to the past. Instead, she suggests that French-Canadians may best withstand the pressures of their disrupted and expanding society by cultivating the basic human values of compassion, charity, and love. Another portrayal of life among the urbanized working class of French Canada is *Pierre le Magnifique* ("Pierre the Magnificent", 1952) and other novels by Roger Lemelin (1919– ). One of the most sensitive and well-written novels appearing in the 1950's was *Poussière sur la Ville* ("Dust on the Town", 1953), a study of despair by André Langevin.

Among the best French-Canadian novels of the 1960's were *Une Saison dans la Vie d'Emmanuel* ("One Season in the Life of Emmanuel", 1965), by Marie-Claire Blais (1939– ) and *La Patience des Justes* ("The Patience of the Just", 1967), a story about a returning expatriate, by Pierre de Grandpré (1920– ).

**CANADIAN SHIELD** *or* **LAURENTIAN PLATEAU,** geologic or physiographic region lying between the Saint Lawrence R. and the Arctic Ocean, extending westward to northern Minnesota and Great Bear and Great Slave lakes in the Northwest Territories of Canada, and eastward to western Greenland. It thus makes up most of eastern Canada, part of Greenland, and a small portion of the United States. About 2,800,000 sq.mi. in area and rudely circular in outline, the Shield is composed of granitic and metamorphic Precambrian rocks, representing the deeply eroded roots of ancient mountain chains.

**Precambrian Era.** Microscopic fossils 2,200,000,000 years old, recently discovered in this area, are evidence of the earliest life on earth yet known. Continental ice sheets that covered the region during the Pleistocene Epoch (*see* QUATERNARY PERIOD) stripped away soil, eroded thousands of lake basins, and deposited widespread glacial drift. Elevations are mainly below 1000 ft. except in the Québec-Labrador peninsula, where they rise to 3700 ft. Poorly integrated drainage follows, for the most part, depressions in the ice-grooved terrain. The climate is rigorous: in the northern part of the region, January mean temperatures drop below −40° F., the effective growing season is less than forty days a year, and the lakes are free of ice for as few as sixty days annually. Permanently frozen soil is sporadic south of Hudson Bay and continuous north of it. In the southern part of the Shield, forests of spruce, pine, hemlock, and northern hardwoods are found; these give way northward to bog and muskeg, and then to open country carpeted with sedges, grasses, lichens, dwarf shrubs, and tundra. Sparsely populated and with poor ground-transport facilities, the region is rich in minerals, water power, and timber. The Québec-Labrador iron belt contains the largest reserves of iron ore in the world. In this belt, only 100 mi. long, the reserve has been estimated at 10,000,000,000 tons, and another 10,000,000,000 tons are believed probable. Recent discoveries in the Northwest Territories at Ungava Bay and on Baffin Island suggest an enormous northward extension of the iron belt. Because of other mines in the Shield, Canada ranks first among the nations in the production of nickel, second in uranium, third in both cobalt and gold, and fourth in silver. *See* GEOLOGY, HISTORICAL.

**CANAIGRE,** common name for a perennial weedy herb, *Rumex hymenosepalus,* of the Buckwheat family (Polygonaceae), found wild in the southwestern United States. Canaigre is sometimes called wild rhubarb. The stem is often reddish in color and grows about 1 to 3 ft. high. The leaves are long, broad, and lance-shaped. Greenish-white flowers grow in clusters of 1 ft. or more. Tannin is obtained from the tuberous roots of this plant; for this reason canaigre is sometimes cultivated. *See also* DOCK; TANNINS.

**ÇANAKKALE,** city in Turkey, and capital of Çanakkale Province, on the narrowest part of the Dardanelles, about 150 miles S.W. of İstanbul. The province is on both sides of the Dardanelles, the smaller part in Europe and the larger in Asia. The E. part of the province constitutes the easternmost extremity of the mainland of Asia. The heavily fortified capital, formerly called Chanak, is in the Asian part of the province. In 1915 during World War I, an Allied expeditionary force made an unsuccessful attempt to take the city of Çanakkale. Pop. (1970) 27,074.

**CANAL,** artificial waterway constructed for purposes of irrigation, drainage (qq.v.), or navigation, or in connection with a hydroelectric dam (q.v.). This article deals only with navigational waterways, which are generally of two kinds: ship canals, which are deep enough to accommodate oceangoing vessels, and shallower canals used mainly by barges.

**Construction.** Canal construction consists chiefly of opencut excavation with ordinary power tools and construction machinery. The sides of the cut are often faced with masonry to prevent erosion of the banks by the wash of passing vessels and the subsequent blocking of the channel by silt.

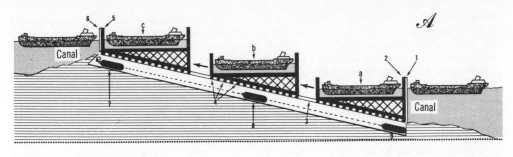

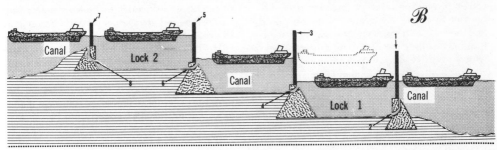

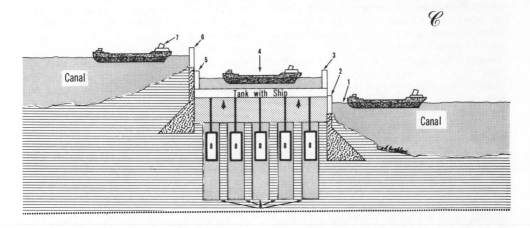

Types of canal. Part A, Incline: A ship traveling along a canal reaches the downstream side of the incline. The lower gate (1) and the incline tank gate (2) open to admit the ship. With the ship in the tank (a) and the gates closed, the tank begins traveling up the railroad rails (3) of the incline to the middle level (b), riding on steel wheels (4). At the upper level (c), the tank gate (5) and the incline gate (6) open and the ship enters the upper canal. The tank containing the ship is pulled up the incline by counterweights weighing up to 4000 tons. The counterweight is at top of the incline (7) when the tank is in lower position; at the middle of the incline (8) when the tank is halfway up or down; and at the lower end (9) when the tank is at the upper level. Part B, Locks: A ship moving through a canal reaches a lock. The lock gate (1) opens to admit the ship. A valve (4) opens and water flows into the lock, raising the ship to the level of the upper canal. The upper lock gate (3) opens and the ship moves out into the next canal section. The lower valve (2) opens to let water run out of the lock. The ship reaches Lock 2. The lower gate (5) opens to admit the ship, and the outlet valve (6) closes. The upper gate (7) opens to admit the ship into the next section of the canal after the valve (8) has opened and water has run into the lock to raise the ship to the next level. Part C, Hydraulic Lift: A ship sailing up a canal (1) reaches the hydraulic lift. The gate (2) and the lift tank gate (3) open to admit the ship, after which both gates close. The lift tank (4), shown midway between lower and higher canal sections, rises straight up until it reaches the level of the upper canal section, whereupon the tank gate (5) and the lift gate (6) open and the ship sails into the canal (7). Hydraulic lifts (8) raise and lower the tank.

Unlike roads and railways, canals cannot be made to conform to irregularities in terrain, but must consist of one or more level stretches, or reaches. Where reaches of different levels meet, vessels are transferred from one reach to the next usually by means of locks. A lock is a walled section of the channel, closed by water gates at both ends, in which the water level can be raised or lowered by means of valves or sluiceways to match the level in the upper or lower reach, as desired; when the levels are the same, the corresponding water gate is opened to permit a vessel to enter or leave the lock. Other devices sometimes used to raise and lower small vessels are inclines and lifts. Inclines are paved or railed ramps over which vessels are hauled from one reach to the other by means of cables. In a lift the vessel is floated into a movable tank from one reach, water gates are closed, and the tank with the floating vessel is raised or lowered to the level of the next reach. Locks, which are used in most multilevel canals, have certain disadvantages; frequently they are uneconomic because of the expense of construction and operation. Also, when traffic is heavy, the supply of water for the highest reach is difficult to maintain; in addition to the natural current flow, a lockful of water is lost from the upper reach in each locking operation. Consequently, to avoid construction of locks, canals are sometimes carried across depressions on embankments, over rivers on aqueducts, and through mountains in tunnels.

**History.** Canals date from a period long before the Christian era and served as means of navigation and communication for the Assyrians, Egyptians, Hindus, and Chinese. The royal canal of Babylon was built about 600 B.C., and the 1000-mi.-long Grand Canal of China, connecting Tientsin and Hangchow, was begun in the 6th century B.C. The lock was invented in Europe in the late 15th century. Several important French canals were built in the 17th century, including the Brière, Orléans, and Languedoc canals. During the 18th century in Russia a great system of canals connecting Saint Petersburg (now Leningrad) with the Caspian Sea was built. The Göta Canal (q.v.), a 240-mi.-long system of lakes, rivers, and canals, about 54 mi. of which can accommodate oceangoing vessels, connected Stockholm and Göteborg and was completed in 1832; the Ludwig Canal, joining the Danube with the Main and Rhine rivers and totaling about 110 mi., was built in 1832. The Suez Canal (q.v.), opened in 1869, links the Mediterranean and Red seas. The Panama Canal (q.v.), first used in 1914, joins the Atlantic and Pacific oceans. In Germany the opening of the Mittelland Canal system (290 mi. long) in 1938 completed the east-west link in a system of about 7000 mi. of inland waterways, extending from the Dortmund-Ems Canal east of the Rhine to the Elbe north of Magdeburg.

The first canal in England was completed in 1134, during the reign of King Henry I (q.v.); it joined the Trent and Witham rivers. Canal building in Great Britain and Ireland flourished in the late 18th and early 19th centuries. Two of the most notable canals of that period are the Grand Canal in Ireland (begun in 1756), which extends 83 mi. east-west between Dublin and the Irish town of Shannon Harbor on the Shannon R., and the Caledonian Canal ( completed 1847), a 60½-mi.-long waterway including 23 mi. of canals, across Scotland. The Manchester Ship Canal (opened 1894) opened Manchester port to oceangoing vessels.

The Canadian canal system includes the Saint Lawrence R. canals, the Ottawa R. canals, the Chambly Canal, the Rideau Canal, and the Trent Canal. Of these the St. Lawrence system has long been the most important, because it provides a waterway 14 ft. deep from the head of Lake Superior to the Gulf of St. Lawrence. As part of the St. Lawrence Seaway project, completed in 1959, the waterway was deepened to 27 ft. to permit oceangoing vessels with drafts up to 25½ ft. to sail from the Atlantic Ocean to such Great Lakes ports as Chicago and Duluth. *See* SAINT LAWRENCE SEAWAY AND POWER DEVELOPMENT.

The first navigation canal in the United States was built around the rapids of the Connecticut R. at South Hadley, Mass., in 1793. It had two levels connected by an incline over which boats were transported in tanks filled with water and dragged by cables operated by waterpower. The construction of the Erie Canal (q.v.), started in 1817, marked the beginning of an era of canal building, which produced an aggregate of more than 4500 mi. of canals, mostly in the Middle Atlantic and Central States, and which was largely responsible for opening the American Midwest to settlement. Many of these early canals are no longer in active service, having been superseded by railroads and by modern, enlarged waterways such as the Mississippi R. system, which is navigable for 1837 mi. and has thirty locks and dams; the Illinois Waterway, which links Lake Michigan with the Mississippi R.; the 981-mi. Ohio R. waterway system, extending from Pittsburgh, Pa., to the Mississippi R.; and the New York State Barge Canal (q.v.), which connects Lake Erie with the Hudson R. The intracoastal waterways along the Atlantic and Gulf coasts are an important part of the inland-waterway system of the U.S., which in the late 1960's totaled 25,380 mi.

**Barge Canals.** On most large canals barges are pushed or pulled by tugboats and towboats;

one towboat may pull as many as forty barges lashed together. Modern barges are designed to carry specific types of cargo: open-hopper barges carry coal, gravel, and large equipment; covered dry-cargo barges are used for grain, dry chemicals, and other commodities that must be kept dry; tank barges carry petroleum and liquid chemicals. On some European canals barges are towed in trains of two or more by gasoline- or diesel-powered tractors running on a towpath beside the canal. In primitive areas men and draft animals are still used for haulage.

**River Canalization.** Formerly, when important rivers were found to be unnavigable at certain points, shallow side canals running parallel to the river were built with pick and shovel so that vessels could bypass that part of the river and reenter it at a more suitable point. With the advent of power machinery, this practice has been largey discarded in favor of canalization of the river itself; that is, a river may be dredged at unnavigable points and provided with dams and bypass locks which control the level of the river from end to end. Construction of fifty-two locks and dams on the Ohio R. was completed in 1929; redevelopment to be completed about 1980 was begun in 1955 to replace the present system with nineteen high-lift locks. Canalization of the upper Mississippi R. from Minneapolis, Minn., to Alton, Ill. (just above Saint Louis, Mo.), was completed in 1939–40. In May, 1954, the Congress of the United States authorized the Federal government to join with Canada in the construction of the St. Lawrence Seaway; as its share of the project, the U.S. built two canals, three locks, and various other improvements along the St. Lawrence R. from Montréal, Québec, to Ogdensburg, N.Y. Canalization of the Arkansas R., which includes thirteen locks and dams and a 9-mi. canal linking the Arkansas to the White and Mississippi rivers, opened the river to navigation to Catoosa, Okla., in 1970. The Tennessee-Tombigbee Waterway, a 253-mi.-long project that began construction in 1970, will include five dams, ten locks, and a 45-mi.-long canal linking the two rivers in Alabama, Mississippi, and Tennessee. *See also* INTRACOASTAL WATERWAYS; SHIPPING.

**Ship Canals.** Ship canals are generally of two kinds: those which connect two lakes or oceans, such as the Suez Canal and the Panama Canal, and those which link an inland port to the ocean, such as the Manchester Ship Canal and the Houston Ship Canal. The list below includes the major ship canals of the world. In many cases the length given represents enlargement of the canal since it was opened.

## MAJOR SHIP CANALS OF THE WORLD

| Name and Location | Length (Miles) | Year Opened |
|---|---|---|
| Baltic-White Sea, U.S.S.R. | 141.00 | 1933 |
| Suez, U.A.R. | 100.76 | 1869 |
| Albert, Belgium | 81.00 | 1939 |
| Moscow-Volga, U.S.S.R. | 80.00 | 1937 |
| Nord-Ostsee, Germany | 61.00 | 1895 |
| Göta, Sweden | 54.00 | 1832 |
| Panama, Panama | 50.72 | 1914 |
| Houston Ship, U.S. | 50.00 | 1914 |
| Amsterdam-Rhine, Netherlands | 39.00 | 1947 |
| Manchester Ship, England | 35.50 | 1894 |
| Chicago Sanitary & Ship, U.S. | 30.00 | 1900 |
| Welland Ship, Canada* | 27.60 | 1932 |
| Juliana, Netherlands | 21.00 | 1934 |
| Chesapeake-Delaware, U.S. | 19.00 | 1829 |
| North Sea-Amsterdam, Netherlands | 18.00 | 1876 |
| Cape Cod, U.S. | 17.50 | 1914 |
| Kronshtadt-Leningrad, U.S.S.R. | 17.00 | 1885 |
| Lake Washington Ship, U.S. | 8.00 | 1916 |
| New Orleans Industrial, U.S. | 6.00 | 1923 |
| Sault Ste. Marie (N.), U.S. | 1.60 | 1919 |
| Sault Ste. Marie, Canada | 1.40 | 1895 |

\* Reconstructed from the old Welland Canal, which was originally completed in 1833.

**CANALETTO, Antonio,** or CANALE, Antonio (1697–1768), Venetian painter and etcher, born in Venice. Canaletto studied with his father, who was a scene painter, and later studied architecture in Rome. He is noted for his paintings and etchings of Venetian architecture, canals, and shipping. His work is distinguished by painstaking realism and luminous atmosphere, and he is regarded as one of the important artists of the late Venetian school. Canaletto was one of the first artists to use the camera obscura as an aid in drawing; *see* PHOTOGRAPHY: *Historical Development.* In 1746 and 1753 he visited England, where he painted a number of landscapes and architectural views. Among his

*"The Piazzetta", an oil painting by Antonio Canaletto.*
Metropolitan Museum of Art–Kennedy Fund

Canary, Serinus canarius, *a popular cage bird.*
Jeanne White—National Audubon Society

paintings, found in the principal museums of Europe and the United States, are "Regatta on the Grand Canal" (National Gallery, London), "Scene in Venice: The Piazzetta" (Metropolitan Museum of Art, New York City), and "Capriccio, a Tomb by the Lagoon" (Uffizi, Florence).

**CANAL ZONE.** *See* PANAMA CANAL ZONE.

**CANANDAIGUA LAKE,** lake of New York, in Ontario County, and forming part of the western border of Yates County, N.Y. One of the Finger Lakes (q.v.), it extends almost due N. and S., is 15 mi. long, about 2 mi. wide, and is 668 ft. aboye sea level. The area around the lake is noted for summer resorts. At the northern end of the lake is the town of Canandaigua, the seat of Ontario Co.

**CANARY,** common name for a small finch, *Serinus canarius,* native to the Azores, Madeira, and the Canary and Cape Verde islands. It is bred as a cage bird throughout the world. In its wild state, the canary builds its nest of moss, feathers, or hair in thick, bushy, high shrubs or trees and produces from two to four broods in a season; its plumage is olive green or greenish yellow, tinged with brown. The birds produced by selective breeding are predominantly yellow. In confinement the canary often breeds three or four times a year, laying from four to six pale blue eggs in each clutch. The canary can be taught various notes or series of notes, which it in turn will teach to its young. Many varieties of canaries have been produced by selective scientific breeding. Particularly noted as a songbird is the Harz Mountain canary, bred in Germany.

Some canaries are bred for beauty and trained to perch in a manner that will best display their attractiveness. These ornamental species include the crested Norwich; the Scotch fancy, a slender bird with high-arched shoulders; and the Manchester, a show variety noted for its size.

The canary songs consist of bass and flute notes, as well as "bell" and "bubbling water" sounds. The songs are classified as either "roller" or "chopper". The roller song is soft and is sung with a nearly closed beak. The chopper song is loud and natural and produced with an open beak; distinct "chop-chop" sounds are heard. Some breeds of canary sing a warbler-type song consisting of both roller and chopper notes.

**CANARY GRASS,** common name for an annual grass, *Phalaris canariensis,* of the Grass family (Gronineae), native to the temperate zones of Europe and the United States; *see* GRASSES. The grass is frequently cultivated commercially for the seeds, which are sold as birdseed. Canary grass grows to a height of 24 in. and has slender leaves about 6 in. long. The seeds are egg shaped and are about 1½ in. long. Reed canary grass, *P. arudinacea,* particularly the variety *picta,* is common in gardens of the U.S., and is called ribbon grass or gardener's garters. This variety grows to a height of 6 ft. and has yellow and white striped leaves.

**CANARY ISLANDS** *or* **CANARIES** (Sp. *Islas Canarias*), group of islands in the Atlantic Ocean, off the N.W. coast of Africa and forming the Spanish provinces of Las Palmas and Santa Cruz de Tenerife. The seven chief islands of the group, in descending order of size, are Tenerife; Fuerteventura, the nearest to the African mainland (about 60 mi.); Grand Canary; Lanzarote; La Palma; Gomera; and Hierro. In addition there are the barren islets of Alegranza, Roque del Este, Roque del Oeste, Graciosa, and Montaña Clara y Lobos.

The province of Las Palmas includes Grand Canary, Lanzarote, Fuerteventura, and the uninhabited islets. Its capital is Las Palmas (q.v.), on Grand Canary. Tenerife, La Palma, Gomera, and Hierro comprise Santa Cruz de Tenerife Province, the capital of which is Santa Cruz de Tenerife (q.v.), on Tenerife Island.

*Aerial view of Las Palmas, Canary Islands.*

The islands are of volcanic origin. Of the volcanic peaks the highest is the dormant Pico de Teide, or Pico de Tenerife, which rises to a greater height (12,172 ft.) than any other island mass found in the North or South Atlantic Ocean. The Canaries are noted for their scenery and mild, dry climate. Annual temperatures average about 65° F.; the average maximum and minimum temperatures are respectively 80° F. and 52° F. Precipitation is scant and occurs mainly during the winter season. The flora includes numerous species indigenous to both tropical and temperate zones. Climatic differences consequent on differences in altitude are responsible for this diversity. In areas below the 1300-ft. level the vegetation is typically N. African. Characteristic varieties are the date palm, dragon tree, and cactus. Growing at higher levels are laurels and other varieties of deciduous trees, various species of coniferous trees, and many types of flowering plants. The indigenous birds of the islands are the canary, chaffinch, goldfinch, titmouse, magpie, quail, raven, owl, sparrow hawk, kite, buzzard, falcon, and African vulture; the hog, goat, sheep, and dog are the only indigenous quadrupeds.

Farming and fishing are the principal industries. The soil of the Canaries, which is of volcanic origin, is extremely fertile. However, there are no rivers, and severe droughts are common in the islands; these circumstances make necessary the artificial irrigation of most cultivable areas. Among important crops are bananas, citrus fruits, peaches, figs, wine grapes, grain, tomatoes, onions, and potatoes. Manufactured products include textiles and fine embroideries. Tourism is another important industry in the Canaries, which are a popular winter-resort area. The islands are served by steamship and air-transport lines operating on regular schedules.

The aboriginal inhabitants of the Canaries comprised the Guanche, probably a North African people. Following the Spanish conquest of the islands in the 16th century, most of the Guanche became extinct, although some doubtless were absorbed into the Spanish population. The present-day population is overwhelmingly Spanish.

**History.** In the view of some authorities the Canaries are the *Fortunatae Insulae* of antiquity. The islands were probably known to the Phoenicians and Carthaginians and, according to an account written by the Roman scholar Pliny the Elder, were visited (about 40 B.C.) by a Mauretanian expedition. As described by Pliny, large numbers of wild dogs roamed the islands, which he therefore named *Canaria*. Arab mariners reached the group in the 12th century, and it was rediscovered in 1334 by the French. Pope Clement VI awarded the islands to Castile in 1344. In 1402 the French mariners Gadifer de la Salle and Jean de Béthencourt began the conquest of the Canaries, probably with the consent of Castile. Béthencourt was made king of the Canaries in 1404 by the Castilian ruler Henry III, but two years later he returned to the mainland. During the next three quarters of a century various claimants, including Prince Henry the Navigator of Portugal, contested ownership of the islands. Through a treaty negotiated in 1479 with Portugal, the group finally became a Spanish possession. Although the natives offered fierce resistance to Spanish rule, they were subdued after a struggle extending over fifteen years.

In 1927 the Canaries, previously a single province of Spain, were divided into two provinces. Area, 2807 sq.mi.; pop. (1970) 1,170,224. Area of Las Palmas Province, 1279 sq. mi.; pop. (1970) 579,710. Area of Santa Cruz de Tenerife Province, 1528 sq.mi.; pop. (1970) 590,514.

*See* separate articles for most of the persons mentioned. C.J.H.H.

**CANARY SEED.** *See* CANARY GRASS.

**CANASTA** (Sp., "basket"), variant of rummy played with a pack made up of two regular fifty-two card decks and four jokers. In the United States it is one of the most popular card games (*see* RUMMY). Of Uruguayan or possibly of Argentine origin, canasta apparently was devised to provide a common meeting ground between poker-playing husbands and wives devoted to rummy. As in all rummy games, the grouping of cards into melds is the main feature of canasta; but unlike other games of this family its object is not to match up cards as quickly as possible, but to build up melds of seven like cards, called canastas, because such cards have a high scoring value. In the two-handed games each player receives fifteen cards, dealt one at a time alternately; in the partnership game hands of eleven cards are distributed in clockwise rotation. The remainder of the pack is placed face down in the center of the table to form a drawing stock, with the top card turned face up alongside to begin a discard pile. If this top card is an ace, deuce, joker, or three, other cards must be turned until a card of any denomination from king to four appears.

Melds in canasta are restricted to sets of cards of the same denominations, and sequences are not played. Melds may start with three or four of a kind and may be added to as play progresses, players building always on their own and never

on the melds of an opponent. However, melds must contain at least two natural cards and not more than three wild cards, which consist of the deuces and jokers. The bonus for "going out" by matching the hand completely is small compared to the premiums for establishing canastas.

More complicated than those of other rummy games, the playing rules of canasta contain certain novel features that distinguish it from most other games of its family group. Thus, the three of diamonds or hearts, known as red three, may have either a plus or minus value. If obtained originally in a deal or in a draw from the stock, each such card must be turned face up in front of the holder and replaced by another card from the pack. If obtained in a discard pile, it is also turned up but no replacement is drawn. When play ends, red threes count as a plus of 100 each for the holding side, with an extra bonus of 400 for all four. Red threes are a minus or debit, however, if the holding side has put down no meld.

When the top card of the discard pile is taken to match a meld, all the cards of the pile must be taken; however, the top discard may not be taken if it is a black three or a wild card. Also, a side may not avail itself of the discard pile if it has not made an initial meld totaling a certain minimum count. This count is determined by computing the value of the cards in the meld according to the following schedule: each joker, 50; deuce, 20; ace, 20; king through eight, 10; seven through three, 5. When a side has a minus score, a meld of only 15 is required initially; from 0 to 1495 the required count is 50; from 1500 to 2995 it is 90; and over 3000 it is 120. The base score of a side is calculated thus: 100 for "going out", that is getting rid of the entire hand by meld or discard; for each red three, 100, provided a meld has been made; for each "natural" canasta, that is, one without wild cards, 500; for each mixed canasta, 300. Added to this base score is the total point value of melds less the point value of cards left in the hand.

When the discard pile contains a red three (originally turned) or any wild card, it is "frozen"; this situation is indicated by turning the lowermost freezing card sideways. A player may take a frozen discard pile by melding its top card with a natural pair from his hand. He may take an unfrozen pile by matching its top card with a natural card and a wild card, or with a meld already made by his side.

In a turn of play, a player has the alternative of drawing the top card of the stock (two in the two-handed game) or, if legally able to do so, of taking the discard pile. The player then makes as many new melds as desired, or adds to those already made, or does both. Finally, he makes a discard of one card from the hand. Wild cards may never be melded as a separate set, and black threes may be melded only when going out. The latter move is accomplished when a player finally gets rid of his cards by meld or discard or both, but only after at least one canasta has been melded (two in the two-handed game). Before going out a player may ask his partner for permission to do so and must consider the answer binding whether it is negative or positive.

Canasta lends itself to numerous variations, as do all rummy games. For example, in some games sevens, like black threes, may be used to freeze the discard pile. Another popular variation is samba, for which three decks of cards are used plus six jokers. In this game two cards are drawn from the stock instead of one; sequences may be melded from four up to the ace but without the use of wild cards. A seven-card sequence, known as samba, counts for 1500 and may be used for purposes of going out. The top discard may be matched only with a natural pair and, when unfrozen, used to extend a table meld. At least two seven-card melds are required to go out and to turn red threes into a plus. The bonus for going out is 200, and for six red threes, 1000; the game is 10,000. Initial meld requirements are 15 when minus, 50 under 1500, 90 under 3000, 120 under 7000, and 150 for 7000 or over.

**CANBERRA,** capital of the Commonwealth of Australia, coextensive with the Australian Capital Territory (q.v.), about 204 miles s.w. of Sydney and about 80 mi. inland from the Pacific Ocean. Located on an elevated plateau, the city is the site of the capitol, known as Parliament House, various Federal office buildings, and the Australian National University. Construction of the city began in 1913, after an international competition for the design of the city was won by Walter Burley Griffin, an American architect. Building activity was suspended during World War I, and the capitol was not completed until 1927, when the first Federal Parliament convened there. Pop. (greater city; 1972 est.) 156,100.

**CANBY, Henry Seidel** (1878–1961), American editor and writer, born in Wilmington, Del., and educated at Yale University. Canby taught English at Yale from 1900 to 1941, becoming full professor of English there in 1922. From 1920 to 1924 he was literary editor of the New York *Evening Post*. In 1924 he became a cofounder of the *Saturday Review of Literature* (now *Saturday Review/World*), and he edited the magazine until

"Moulin Rouge", the first poster (1891) designed by Henri Toulouse-Lautrec, advertises the cancan at the famous nightclub in Montmarte, the Bohemian section of Paris. **Museum of Modern Art**

1936. As a teacher and editor, and as chairman of the board of judges of the Book-of-the-Month Club for almost thirty years, Canby had an important influence in awakening interest in contemporary American writing. He wrote a number of works on American literature, including *Thoreau: A Biography* (1939), *Walt Whitman: An American* (1943), and *Turn West, Turn East: Mark Twain and Henry James* (1951). Canby was also editor of several textbooks on English, including the *Handbook of English Usage* (1942).

**CANCAN,** French dance in two-quarter time, derived from the quadrille, and noted for high kicking and suggestive bodily movements. The cancan, danced by women, became popular in the music halls of Paris about 1840. It was considered vulgar. The name of the dance is derived from the French word *cancan* ("scandal"). The French composer Jacques Offenbach (q.v.) wrote a well-known cancan melody for his light opera *Orpheus in the Underworld* (1858), and the French painter Henri de Toulouse-Lautrec (q.v.) produced several notable paintings of cancan dancers.

**CANCER** (Lat., "crab"), in astronomy and astrology, the fourth constellation of stars or sign of the zodiac (q.v.) in the ecliptic (q.v.), the apparent annual path of the sun through the stars. The name is derived from a Greek myth about a crab who fought the Greek hero Heracles as he attacked the Hydra, his second labor; see HERCULES. The ancient Greeks discovered that the sun entered Cancer at the summer solstice (q.v.), at which time the sun is 23½° N. of the equator (q.v.). For this reason the parallel 23½° N. lat. was called the Tropic of Cancer; see TROPICS. A loose cluster of more than 300 faint stars, known as Praesepe or the Beehive, is a prominent feature of the constellation.

**CANCER,** new growth of tissue resulting from a continuous proliferation of abnormal cells that have the ability to invade and destroy other tissues. This new growth, or neoplasm, may originate from a single cell or a single group of cells not controlled by the normal forces regulating cellular growth; see CELL. As these autonomous cells multiply, they may form a mass, called a tumor, which enlarges and continues to grow without regard to the function of the tissue of origin.

Almost all cancers form tumors, but not all tumors are cancers. The greatest number of tumors are benign; cancers are said to be malignant. Benign tumors are characterized by entirely localized growth and are usually separated from neighboring tissue by a surrounding capsule or, in the case of superficial benign tumors, such as warts or moles, by an underlying membrane. Benign tumors generally grow slowly and in structure closely resemble the tissue of origin. In some instances they may endanger the host by obstructing normal processes or by producing pressure on or causing displacement of neighboring structures, as in the brain.

The most significant attribute of a cancer is its ability to spread beyond its site of origin. Cancer may invade neighboring tissues by direct extension or may disseminate, forming secondary growths known as metastases, or colonies. Dissemination takes place through the lymphatic system, the bloodstream, or the direct implantation in adjacent organs of cancer cells dislodged from the original growth. The route and site of metastases vary with different cancers, depending on whether they spread through blood vessels or lymphatic vessels, and on the characteristics of certain cancers that tend to metastasize to particular tissues, such as bone or brain.

Cancer may arise from any type of cell, in any body tissue. It is not confined to a single organ, and it can affect any part of the body. Even though it takes different forms, it is basically a wild form of growth, ceaseless and often uncontrollable, that, if unchecked, destroys life. It is not a single disease but a general term that describes a whole galaxy of diseases, probably more than 100 in all.

Because various types of cancer tend to behave in characteristic ways, cancers are classified according to the tissue and type of cell origin. Several hundred such classifications exist, constituting three major subtypes. Sarcoma denotes those cancers arising from connective and supporting tissue, such as bone, cartilage, nerve, muscle, and fat. Carcinoma, which includes the more frequently occurring forms of human cancer, refers to all cancers arising from epithelial tissue, such as the skin and the lining of the body cavities and organs, and the glandular tissue of the breast or prostate. The leukemias and lymphomas include the cancers that involve blood-forming tissue and are typified by the enlargement of lymph nodes, the invasion of spleen and bone marrow, and the overproduction of immature white cells.

Cancer cells, even when widely disseminated, may retain the physical and biological characteristics of their tissue of origin. Thus the pathologist can often determine the site of origin of metastatic cancer by microscopic examination of the cancerous tissue. It is not uncommon for a distant deposit of thyroid cancer, for instance, to elaborate thyroid hormone, or for gastric cancer to secrete mucus. In general, the more closely a cancer resembles its tissue of origin, the less malignant and rapidly invasive it tends to be. The rate of growth of a cancer depends not only on cellular type and classification but also on various host factors, many of which are undefined, that influence the course of any particular instance of the disease.

**Historical Aspects.** Tumors are mentioned among the earliest records of Egypt, Greece, and India. In the period between 2000 and 1500 B.C. accessible tumors were treated in Egypt by excision or application of corrosive pastes. The Greeks termed the disease *karkinos* (crab) because of the clawlike extensions of spreading cancers. Thus the Romans gave the disease its common name, "cancer", which means "crab" in Latin. In the 1st century A.D. the Roman physician Aulus Cornelius Celsus (q.v.) attempted an elaborate classification of cancer. The Greek physician Galen (130–200) in the latter half of the 2nd century attributed cancer to concentration of black bile in the affected part of the body.

In the 18th century the British surgeon Percivall Pott (1714–88) correctly attributed the high incidence of cancer of the scrotum among London chimney sweeps to the collection of soot in scrotal skin; nearly two centuries later the cancer-causing agent was found to be benzopyrene, an ingredient of coal tar. The cellular basis of cancer was established in the 19th century largely by the work of the German physiologist Theodor Schwann (1810–82) and the German pathologist Rudolf Virchow (1821–1902). Effective treatment of internal cancer by surgery first began about 1880; the first successful operation for stomach cancer was performed in 1882, and the modern surgical procedure for breast cancer was devised in 1890. Radiation treatment of cancer commenced about 1900, soon after the discovery of X rays in 1895 and radium in 1898.

**Extent of the Problem.** More than 1,000,000 new cases of cancer occur in the United States each year. It is the second leading cause of death in the nation, accounting for more than 350,000 deaths annually, and is the leading cause of death from disease for children between the ages of one and fourteen. According to mortality statistics in the late 1960's, Scotland had the highest cancer death rate, with Austria and Denmark the next highest. Other nations with high cancer mortality rates are Belgium, England and Wales, Finland, West Germany, and the Republic of South Africa; all of which have a higher rate than that of the U.S.

Cancer treatments have improved significantly since the 1930's. At that time fewer than 20 percent of all cancer patients were cured. (For ordinary statistical purposes, a person who has no signs of disease five years after treatment is considered cured.) In the early 1970's more than one cancer patient in every three was being treated successfully, and an estimated 1,500,000 Americans who had been treated successfully for cancer five or more years previously were still living.

Despite the improvements in cure rates, total cancer mortality has risen, largely because of the increasing proportion of older people in the population. More than one half of all cancer deaths occur in persons over sixty-five. In addition, the absolute rate of lung cancer has increased dramatically, as, to a lesser extent, has that of leukemia. Since 1949 cancer mortality has been higher among men than women.

Five-year survival rates for six of the most important sites of cancer are as follows: female breast, 83 percent for localized disease and 52 percent for regionally involved disease; colon and rectum, 70 percent localized and 37 percent regional; lung, 27 percent localized and 7 percent regional; oral cancer, 76 percent localized and 23 percent regional; skin, 92 percent localized (no figures in regional involvement are available); uterus, 81 percent localized and 48 percent regional.

## COMMON CANCER TYPES

The most common types of cancer are those just named. In men prostate cancer (16%) could be added to the list; in men, women, and children leukemia and lymphoma account for between 7 and 9 percent of cancers. The number of stomach cancer cases has declined for no known reason, by 46 percent in men and 48 percent in women since 1949–51. On the other hand, cancer of the pancreas is increasing in both sexes, although it is still a relatively uncommon form of the disease.

**Lung Cancer.** This type is now the leading cause of death from cancer among men in the U.S., with a thirteenfold increase in the number of deaths since 1930. Almost 80 percent of lung-cancer cases are found among men. Common late symptoms are chest pain, cough, difficulty in breathing, and expectorated blood. Early lung cancer is usually asymptomatic. Treatment for operable cases is complete removal of the affected lung and the adjacent lymph nodes. Palliative treatment includes radiation therapy and the administration of nitrogen mustard. Lung cancer is difficult to diagnose in time for adequate surgical treatment; the current rate of cure is about 8 percent.

**Breast Cancer.** This most common form of cancer among women accounts for an estimated 90,000 new cases annually in the U.S. It occurs often in unmarried women. The usual symptom is a nonpainful lump in the breast; other symptoms include bleeding or discharge from the nipple, alterations in size or shape of the breast, and retraction of or scaly rash around the nipple. Surgery, sometimes followed by radiation therapy, is the most common form of treatment. Advanced cases may be treated by the administration of sex hormones or the removal of the ovaries or of the pituitary gland. Surgical-cure rates range between 47 and 82 percent, depending on the state of the disease at time of surgery.

**Skin Cancer.** This type of cancer, estimated to affect 300,000 persons annually, is common among older men, especially out-of-door workers continuously exposed to sunlight. It usually appears as a persistent sore, often on the face or the back of the hands. Most skin cancers are readily curable by surgery or X rays, the choice of treatment depending on the site and extent of disease. Melanoma is a highly malignant form of skin cancer, usually arising from a pigmented mole and treatable by surgery.

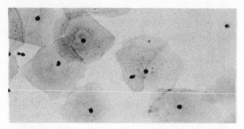 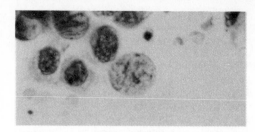

*Normal cells of the human cervix (left); cancerous cells (right).*                                    American Cancer Society

**Cancer of the Gastrointestinal Tract.** The gastrointestinal tract is the site of about one fourth of all cancers, and the organs most commonly affected, in the order of frequency, are the large bowel, stomach, pancreas, and rectum. For reasons that are unknown, the incidence of stomach cancers in the U.S. has decreased in recent years and the incidence of cancer of the pancreas has increased. Common symptoms are a slight but persistent indigestion, difficulty in swallowing, and blood in vomit or stool. Treatment is usually surgical.

**Uterine Cancer.** Cancer of the uterus is the third most common form of cancer among women in the U.S., with about 50,000 new cases occurring each year. The most common symptoms are unusual bleeding and discharge. The mortality rate for uterine cancer has declined more than 50 percent since 1930, largely as a result of earlier diagnosis and improved treatment. By use of the "Pap" smear (see *Detection and Diagnosis*, below), this type of cancer can be detected before symptoms appear; at this stage it is curable in more than 90 percent of the cases.

**Prostate Cancer.** This form of cancer is rare among men under forty years of age and occurs more frequently with advancing age. The commonest symptoms are urinary disturbances, such as increased frequency and difficulty in urination, and blood in the urine. Early cases are treated by surgery. Castration and the administration of female hormones may offer substantial palliation and often prolong life.

**Leukemias and Lymphomas.** These types of cancer are usually generalized, involving lymphatic tissues, blood, and bone marrow; see LEUKEMIA. Acute leukemia is more common among younger people and accounts for one half of cancers in children between the ages of three and fourteen; Hodgkin's disease (q.v.) is more often found in young adults and chronic leukemia in the aged; lymphosarcoma, a cancer having structural elements similar to those of a lymph gland, occurs at any age. Symptoms include paleness, fatigue, loss of appetite, persistent fever, and swelling in the armpit, groin, or abdomen. Treatment includes the use of X rays and chemotherapy (q.v.), depending on stage and type of the disease.

**Precancerous Lesions.** Carcinoma may arise on the site of a long-standing keratosis (warty overgrowth of the skin), leukoplakia (white spot) in the mouth, or unrepaired burn scar. Rectal or intestinal polyps are considered cancer precursors. Undescended testicle and benign tumors (adenomas) of the thyroid, and moles subject to irritation are also potential cancer sites. These conditions should be corrected by medical or surgical means to prevent the development of cancer.

### DETECTION AND DIAGNOSIS

Emphasis is placed on early diagnosis of cancer because cure is most possible in early cases.

The periodic examination of apparently healthy persons for cancer, either in special clinics or by the private physician, is generally recognized as the most efficient method of early cancer detection. Such an examination includes a complete medical history, visual inspection, and palpation of all accessible sites, the "Pap" test and breast and pelvic examination in women, as well as special laboratory examinations. The American Cancer Society also recommends a monthly self-examination of the breasts by women.

**Cytological Detection of Cancer.** The Papanicolaou technique, named for the American cytologist Dr. George N. Papanicolaou (1883–1962), who devised the procedure, involves the microscopic examination of fluids collected from a body cavity. Cancer cells cast off from the malignant growth may be detected in the fluid. The Papanicolaou, or "Pap", test has proved highly valuable in early detection of cancer of the uterine cervix and may also be used for lung, gastric, and other types of the disease. See CYTOLOGY.

**Diagnosis.** The diagnostic procedures vary according to location of the lesion. X-ray and fluoroscopy procedures are used to detect inaccessible growths. Bronchoscopy, cystoscopy, and proctoscopy are employed for the visualization and collection of suspicious tissue in the bronchial tubes, the bladder, and the rectum, respectively. An exploratory surgical operation is sometimes necessary to determine the exact site of a growth.

Biopsy is the only definitive method for deciding whether or not a suspicious lesion is malignant. It involves the microscopic examination of excised tissue by a trained pathologist.

### TREATMENT

Three basic forms of therapy for cancers are currently practiced: surgery, radiation, and prescription and experimental drugs. They may be used to cure the affliction (a former cancer patient is considered cured when he is free of cancer for five years and thus has the same life expectancy as someone of the same age-group who has never had the disease), or to palliate, or to prolong life and to ease pain. The physician may use one form of therapy, or a number of different forms, in order to produce the desired results.

**Surgery.** Surgical operation is the principal means for the cure of cancer. Because the success of the operation depends on the removal of all malignant cells, the trend in cancer surgery is to remove as much involved and potentially involved tissue as possible, including adjacent structures and lymph nodes. Operations based on this principle have been devised for most of the common types, including cancer of the stomach, breast, rectum, uterus, and bladder. With the advent of antibiotics, blood transfusions, and improved anesthetics, together with increased knowledge of physiology, operative mortality has declined, and even those patients who formerly might have been considered poor surgical risks can be operated on safely and routinely. Cancer surgery also is used palliatively to relieve obstruction or remove a bulky growth or metastases. Results of surgery are generally evaluated in terms of "five-year cures", arrest of the disease for five years following the operation. Recurrence of cancer after surgery usually may represent not a second attack of the disease but a regrowth from remaining cancer cells. In some forms of cancer a long latent period may pass before recurrence.

**Radiation Therapy.** X rays, radium, and manufactured radioactive isotopes (see ISOTOPE) are the principal agents in radiation therapy. Not all cancers are "radiosensitive", that is, adversely affected by radiation. The most accessible lesions, and those most readily treated by X ray, are those on the uterine cervix, skin, lip, tongue, and larynx. But new megavoltage equipment, by which radiation can be directed below the skin, allows treatment of deep-seated cancers in the brain, lungs, and other organs. Precision techniques for calculating tissue dosage of radiation make it possible to localize the effects of radiation in tumors without doing excessive damage to adjacent normal tissue. Radiation is often used postoperatively to destroy cancer cells that were beyond the reach of the surgeon's knife. Radiation therapy can be palliative in delaying the growth of localized inoperable cancers, in controlling metastatic lesions, and in the treatment of certain cancers of the blood-forming organs, such as chronic leukemia. Hodgkin's disease is often treated by radiation.

Among the man-made radioactive isotopes most commonly used in cancer treatment are iodine 131, phosphorus 32, cobalt 60, gold 198, and strontium 90. Like radium, isotopes may be used as a source for external radiation, as "seeds" for direct implantation in the diseased tissue, or for local application to surface lesions. Some functioning thyroid cancers selectively take up radioactive iodine in amounts sufficient to cause injury to the cancer cells. Radioactive phosphorus, which concentrates in the bloodstream, is similarly used in the transient control of leukemias. Small blocks of cobalt–60 used in cancer treatment deliver the equivalent of about 2,000,000 to 3,000,000 volts of X ray.

**Chemotherapy.** Since 1947 control and in some cases cure of certain cancers by the use of drugs has introduced a third method of cancer therapy. More than thirty different chemicals are now in prescription use in the treatment of cancer; others are still in the stage of clinical investigation. Almost without exception, these drugs are highly toxic. They can be used against cancer because they are slightly more toxic to some malignant cells than to normal cells. This narrow difference can be exploited in proper hands; cancers can be reduced or arrested with drugs that may make a patient ill but will not kill him. Alterations in the sex-hormone balance, achieved by the administration of such sex hormones as androgen or estrogen, may have temporary but definite benefit in patients with prostate or breast cancer. Cortisone (q.v.) and related adrenal hormones produce considerable temporary improvement in leukemia, particularly in children. Nitrogen mustard, a derivative of mustard gas, has temporary beneficial effects in the lymphomas and chronic leukemias and may be of benefit in cancers of the lung and ovary; chlorambucil, sarcolysin, cyclophosphamide, thio-tepa, and bisulfan are compounds with similar effects in those types of cancer. The drugs methotrexate, 6-mercapto-purine, and vinca alkaloids are useful in the treatment of acute leukemia in children. These drugs can produce a temporary remission of the disease with prolongation of life in nearly 100 percent of children with acute leukemia.

Drugs given in sequence, or in series, in varied combinations known acronymically as VAMP, POMP, and BIKE from the initials of agents used, are producing much longer remissions in leukemia and lymphoma than do single drugs. In the late 1960's more than 50 percent of children treated in one large hospital have been in remission for three years and 25 percent for four years. At that time the U.S. had nearly 200 five-year survivors of leukemia.

Methods have been developed for isolating an area of the body, such as the head or leg, from the general blood supply and flooding the area with an anti-cancer drug delivered directly into the bloodstream. This "regional perfusion" makes it possible to deliver high doses of a drug to solid tumors while protecting the rest of the body from the toxic effects.

In 1956 women with choriocarcinoma, a rare form of cancer arising from fetal tissue during pregnancy, were treated by chemotherapy for the first time. The results constituted the first cures achieved by cancer chemotherapy in a statistically significant number of patients. About 75 percent of all cases of choriocarcinoma can now be cured with drugs. Similarly, five-year survivals have been observed in children with inoperable Wilms' tumor, a cancer of the kidney, and in retinoblastoma, an eye cancer of infants, treated with a combination of chemotherapy and radiation.

In the early 1970's, some success was reported in the treatment of skin tumors in animals with the use of the Bacillus Calmette-Guérin (BCG) vaccine, which is normally used for protection against tuberculosis (q.v.). Much testing, however, remained to be done.

The development of better chemotherapeutic agents is one of the major current efforts in cancer research. Large-scale programs have been instituted for testing candidate agents using animal cancers grown under a variety of conditions. Laboratory and clinical studies being carried out in a large number of research centers are coordinated and expedited by the Cancer Chemotherapy National Committee, which was formed in 1955 under the auspices of the U.S. Public Health Service.

### CANCER RESEARCH

All forms of treatment, as well as methods of diagnosis, are the product of extensive research.

About $400,000,000 a year is spent on cancer research in the U.S. by the Federal government, the American Cancer Society, and leading cancer hospitals and the pharmaceutical industry. Such research attacks the disease at all levels. Cancer is being studied in human patients (clinical research), and in mammals, fish, plants, insects, and mollusks in the hope that findings will occur that may aid in the cure or prevention of cancer in man. Major research is carried on in about a dozen countries and scientists cooperate internationally on many projects.

In one form of cancer research, known as epidemiological research, large groups of people are observed to learn what in their living and working conditions may cause cancer to start and to grow. Such researchers for instance investigate why Japanese women have only one sixth the amount of breast cancer of U.S. women (it is thought to be inversely related to the amount of breast feeding) and why the rate of stomach cancer in Japan, Scandinavia, Poland, and Soviet Russia is high compared to the U.S., where stomach cancer is declining.

**Smoking and Cancer.** By the mid-1960's the correlation between cigarette smoking and the mounting incidence of lung cancer had been generally accepted by epidemiological authorities. The evidence came from several different lines of investigation. In the laboratory tobacco-tar condensates were shown to cause cancers on the skin of several different species of laboratory animal. Physical examinations of patients and human autopsy studies showed changes and abnormalities in the lungs of smokers (as compared with nonsmokers) that could be correlated with the number of cigarettes smoked. Numerous studies of lung-cancer patients conducted by many groups and organizations all over the world have shown unanimously that a lung-cancer patient was more likely to be a heavy smoker than another man of the same age who did not have lung cancer. Since 1948 several "prospective" studies have been undertaken. In these studies a segment of the population is selected and interviewed concerning a number of variables, such as diet and occupation as well as smoking; subsequent illnesses and deaths among the group are recorded over a period of years. One of the first of these studies was begun in 1951 by the American Cancer Society on 188,000 men between the ages of fifty and seventy in the U.S. During the forty-four month period of the study, 473 of the men died of lung cancer, only 25 of whom were nonsmokers. The study found that the death rate among cigarette smokers *from all causes* was much higher than that among nonsmokers or pipe and cigar smokers.

Another study was begun by the American Cancer Society in 1959. From a group of 442,079 men, 36,975 matched pairs of male smokers and nonsmokers were extracted by computer. Pairs were matched by race, height, nativity, residence, occupation, education, marital status, consumption of alcohol, etc. After three years, study of these pairs showed that twice as many cigarette smokers as nonsmokers had died *from all causes:* 1385 against 662; among smokers, 110 cases of lung cancer deaths occurred, as contrasted with 12 among nonsmokers; and 654 smokers died of coronary heart disease, compared with 304 nonsmokers.

Combined results of other studies showed that cigarette smokers are from five to twenty times as likely to contract lung cancer (depending on number of cigarettes smoked) as nonsmokers. Rates of cancer of the larynx, mouth, esophagus, and bladder are also significantly higher among cigarette smokers. In all cases risks were related to the number of cigarettes smoked.

Summarizing such studies, the Royal College of Physicians of Great Britain stated, in a report entitled *Smoking and Health,* that "cigarette smoking is an important cause of lung cancer". In 1964 after a year of study by ten scientists appointed with the approval both of those who favored and those who opposed the use of cigarettes, the Surgeon General of the United States concluded: "Cigarette smoking is causally related to lung cancer in men; the magnitude of the effect of cigarette smoking far outweighs all other factors. The data for women, although less extensive, point in the same direction". As a result of this report, the Congress of the U.S. passed the Public Health Cigarette Act, effective Jan. 2, 1971, prohibiting cigarette commercials on all broadcast media. Although the law has no effect on print media, several newspapers and magazines voluntarily decided to eliminate cigarette advertising. The law also demands, effective April 1, 1971, that the following text appears on all cigarette packages sold in the U.S. to read: "Warning: the Surgeon General has determined that cigarette smoking is dangerous to your health".

### ENVIRONMENTAL CAUSES OF CANCER

Cancer-causing factors have been found in industries where workers were exposed to tar, pitch, arsenic, benzol, asbestos, and chloropyrene. Similarly, the incidence of leukemia among doctors who work with X ray is eight times that of the medical profession as a whole.

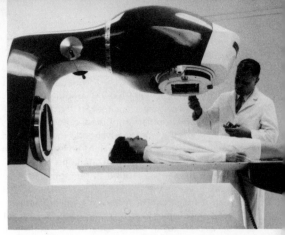

Cobalt 60 Rotation Therapy Unit bombards cancerous tissue with radiation equal to a 3,000,000-volt X-ray machine. The 360° rotation protects surrounding tissue from excess radiation.     Atomic Energy of Canada, Ltd.

Light-skinned people greatly exposed to sunlight often develop skin cancer. Circumcised men rarely develop penile cancer.

A report issued in 1972 by a committee of the National Research Council (q.v.) linked lung cancer to air pollution (q.v.). Urban residents were found to have twice as high an incidence of lung cancer as nonurban residents, and the incidence was even higher in urban areas where the air had concentrated amounts of fossil-fuel pollutants. The major sources of urban air pollutants are automobile-engine emissions, coal and wood-fired residential and industrial heating furnaces, coal refuse fires, and coke production by the iron and steel industries. A major source of indoor air pollutant is tobacco smoking, which could affect a nonsmoker in a smoke-filled room.

The air pollutant considered by the committee most dangerous to man, the polycyclic organic matter (POM) known as benzopyrene, $C_{20}H_{12}$, is a crystalline cancer-producing hydrocarbon found in coal tar (q.v.); *see* HYDROCARBONS.

In 1974 it was reported that American workers exposed to large amounts of vinyl chloride, a chemical widely used in the manufacture of plastics (q.v.), ran the risk of contracting a rare, fatal liver cancer called angiosarcoma. Among other cancer-causing agents under investigation in the mid-1970's were the polluted waters of rivers such as the Mississippi, the amines and diamines used in hair dyes, and ultrafine fiberglass particles.

**Soviet Statistics.** The role of environmental factors in the incidence of cancer was further underlined by the cancer statistics of the Soviet Union, first reported in 1974. Although the incidence of cancer in the U.S.S.R. had increased at a rate similar to that of the U.S. in the preceding twelve years, the Soviet rate of deaths in 1972 (129.6 per 100,000 population) was significantly lower than that of the U.S. (166.8 per 100,000 population). Breast cancer, which is typical of the more advanced, industrialized societies, was most prevalent in the Estonian S.S.R., which has a high standard of living. Cancer in men was found to be more common than in women in the U.S.S.R., and male deaths from cancer of the respiratory system, associated with smoking, increased by 15 percent between 1967 and 1972. Death rates from lung cancer were five times higher for men than for women, the same as those in the U.S. For unexplained reasons, however, both the U.S. and the U.S.S.R. reported a significant decrease in the number of deaths from stomach cancer during the period 1967–72.

**Viruses.** Viruses are submicroscopic (visible now by electron microscopy) parasites that can reproduce only inside a living cell. Some cause certain diseases in man: measles, influenza, poliomyelitis, and the common cold. Vaccines have been created against viral infections with attenuated (weakened) living viruses, or killed viruses. In 1911 at Rockefeller Institute, New York City, Dr. Peyton Rous (q.v.) discovered a cancer, in a Plymouth Rock hen, that contained a nonfilterable substance which caused similar cancers in other chickens. This was the first proof of an animal cancer caused by a virus; Dr. Rous won the Nobel Prize in 1966 for his discovery of the "Rous sarcoma virus". Since 1911 a number of researchers have isolated other animal cancer viruses, leading some scientists to believe that similar cancer viruses must exist in human beings. Some evidence points to the leukemias and lymphomas in human beings as being virus-caused, although no proof has yet been found. Recently it has been shown that a common virus in human beings, the adenovirus, will cause malignant changes in newborn hamsters and mice. The mechanism by which viruses may cause cancer is thought to be a merger of the virus with the DNA of the cell, creating false genetic information leading to the production of abnormal, malignant cells. See VIRUS.

**Immunology.** It is known that the human body has a number of systems which throw off disease bacteria, poisons, and other foreign substances including tissue transplants. Together, these are known as the immune mechanisms. These are now widely discussed as the result of publicity regarding heart and kidney transplants; patients often reject the new tissue in spite of the doctors' best efforts. Lately, information has developed that in transplant patients, in whom immune systems are deliberately repressed with drugs, there appear an abnormally high number of lymphatic cancers. Researchers have for some years theorized that the body has an immunological system protecting it against cancer; a research team at the Sloan-Kettering Institute in New York City injected both cancerous and noncancerous volunteers with cancer cells. The cells continued to grow in the cancer patients, but in those free of cancer the cells were trapped by local lymph nodes and eventually rejected spontaneously. The assumption of an immune mechanism against cancer is supported by these experiments; by animal experiments that show certain strains of mice highly susceptible to cancer while others are almost totally resistant; and by the new information developed in organ-transplant patients.

It was also reported early in 1972 that children who had been administered the BCG vaccine might develop an immunity against leukemia. Vigorous tests were being carried on in order to confirm this report.

### CANCER AGENCIES

The American Cancer Society was founded in 1913 as the American Society for the Control of Cancer; after reorganization in the mid-1940's it embarked on an expanded fund-raising program with emphasis on cancer research. In 1937 Congress passed the National Cancer Act, enabling the U.S. Public Health Service to establish the National Cancer Institute. In 1971 Congress voted an appropriation of $1,600,000,000 in an accelerated effort to conquer cancer within a few years. In the mid-1970's annual expenditures for cancer research totaled about $500,000,000 in the U.S., placing a heavy burden on volunteer groups such as the American Cancer Society, Inc., and private research centers. Additional funds were raised and spent for treatment of indigent cancer patients; aid to families of cancer patients; and for public and professional education to control the disease through the increased use of widespread physical examinations and prompt treatment.

H.A. & W.S.R.

**CANDIA.** See IRÁKLION.

**CANDLE,** illuminating device made of a fiber wick enclosed in a cylinder of wax or fatty material. Beeswax candles were used by the Romans, and tallow (animal fat) candles have been made in Europe since the Middle Ages. In the 18th century spermaceti, a wax obtained from the heads of whales, was introduced for candles. Since the middle of the 19th century ordinary candles have been made from mixtures of paraffin wax, stearic acid (a solid fatty acid), and beeswax. Stearic acid adds stiffening to the soft paraffin and gives candles greater illuminating power. Hydrogenated vegetable oils and other waxes, such as carnauba wax, are also used; *see* CARNAUBA PALM.

The earliest method of candle-making was by dipping the wick, usually made of flax or cotton fibers, into melted wax or fat and removing it to let it cool and solidify in the air. The candle was built up to the required thickness by successive dippings. Taper candles are still made by dipping, but the great majority of candles used today are molded, usually by machine. Beeswax candles, which are used in churches, cannot be molded because the wax shrinks during the cooling process. They are made by pouring wax around a wick, after which the candle is rolled to shape.

**CANDLEBERRY.** *See* BAYBERRY.

**CANDLEFISH,** or EULACHON, common name for a small, saltwater fish, *Thaleichthys pacificus,* of the Smelt family (Osmeridae). The candlefish is closely related to the capelin (q.v.) and is found in the N. Pacific Ocean. Used primarily as food fish, candlefish are about 12 to 15 in. long and are silvery in appearance. From February to April they swim up western freshwater streams to spawn. They derive their name from the fact that Alaskan Indians sometimes use the dried fish as a lamp. This is done by pushing a piece of bark through the fish as a wick. *See* SMELT.

**CANDLEMAS,** Christian festival observed on Feb. 2 in honor of the presentation of the infant Christ in the Temple (*see* TEMPLE: *Temple at Jerusalem*) and the purification of the Virgin Mary. The festival was probably meant to replace the great feast of expiation and purification (*Februa*) that was held in ancient Rome in mid-February. The date of the pagan feast was then transferred to Feb. 2, the fortieth day after Christmas; the forty-day period was in accordance with the Jewish law that required the ritual purification at the Temple of every mother of a male child forty days after its birth. The Candlemas festival is believed to have been instituted in 541 or 542 by the Byzantine Emperor Justinian I (q.v.).

**CANDY.** *See* CONFECTIONERY.

**CANDYTUFT,** common name for more than thirty species of *Iberis,* forming a genus of herbs of the Mustard family (Cruciferae). The species comprise both annual and perennial plants, na-

*Candytuft,* Iberis sempervirens

tives of Mediterranean countries, and are cultivated in gardens in both Europe and America. The perennial *I. sempervirens* is popular as edging for rock gardens because of its evergreen leaves and fragrant white flower clusters; *I. amara* and *I. umbellata* are the most popular annual species. The latter plant produces flowers of many colors.

**CANFIELD, Dorothy.** *See* FISHER, DOROTHY CANFIELD.

**CANISIUS, Saint Peter,** original name PIETER DE HONDT (1521–97), German Jesuit theologian, born in Nijmegen (now in the Netherlands). The first German to join (1543) the Jesuit order, he established Jesuit centers in many parts of Germany and taught at German universities, including those at Cologne and Vienna. Canisius was a leader of the Counter-Reformation, the reform movement that arose in the Roman Catholic Church in answer to the Protestant Reformation; *see* REFORMATION. He participated actively in the Council of Trent (*see* TRENT, COUNCIL OF) and the Diet of Augsburg (1556). His triple catechism, written for different age levels, is his most important work. He was canonized in 1925 and in the same year was named doctor of the Church; his feast day is Dec. 21. Canisius College in Buffalo, N.Y., a Jesuit institution founded in 1870, is named for him. *See also* JESUITS.

**CANIS MAJOR** and **CANIS MINOR** (Lat., "greater dog" and "lesser dog"), two constellations of stars lying respectively southeast and east of Orion (q.v.), and separated by the Milky

Way (q.v.). According to the mythology of the ancients, these constellations represent dogs trotting at the heels of the Greek hunter Orion. Canis Major contains Sirius (or dog star), the brightest star in the heavens, and Canis Minor contains Procyon, far less bright than Sirius, but still a star of the first magnitude. Midsummer, when Sirius rises at dawn, was associated by the ancients with the dog star, and is still known as the dog days or canicular days. *See* SIRIUS.

**ÇANKAYA,** former city in Turkey, now the S.E. part of greater Ankara, Ankara Province, 4 miles s. of the city center, with which it is connected by Atatürk Boulevard. Çankaya, which includes the residential section of Kavaklıdere, is the site of most of the foreign embassies and of the presidential palace. Textiles, mohair, and vetch are produced. Çankaya was formerly called Yenişehir, or New City. Pop. (1970) 496,953.

**CANKERWORMS,** common name for destructive caterpillars known as inchworms, especially *Paleacrita vernata,* the spring cankerworm, and *Alsophila pometaria,* the fall cankerworm belonging to the family Geometridae. They are found in the United States from Maine to Texas. The male moth of both species has silky wings, but the female is wingless. The females crawl up the trunks of fruit or shade trees to lay their eggs, and the caterpillars, which hatch about the time the tree comes into leaf, often skeletonize the leaves of an entire orchard in a few days. The common name of these two species is derived from the season in which the female lays eggs.

**CANNA,** single genus of almost fifty species of tropical herbs constituting the family Cannaceae, native to warm countries in both hemispheres. Before 1860 canna varieties such as *C. indica,* Indian Shot, were grown chiefly for their foliage. Since that time numerous hybrid varieties have been cultivated for their showy clusters of flowers of many colors. The stem is about 3 to 10 ft. high and the leaves are broad, long (up to 2 ft. in some varieties), and often bronze in color.

**CANNABIS,** genus of annual plants, the Indian Hemp, of the family Urticaceae. The plant ranges from 3 to 6 ft. in height, with coarsely toothed leaves. It has on the inner bark tough fibers of commercial importance (*see* HEMP). A resin, known as hashish or bhang, is extracted from the leaves and flowers of the oriental species, *C. indica.* This substance is a narcotic drug producing, in susceptible persons, intoxication, hallucinations, or torpor. Although its use in medicine and pharmacy is limited by its variability both in its potency and in its effect on dif-

ferent persons, it is sometimes substituted for opium as a sedative and hypnotic. An American species, *C. sativa* or *C. americana,* commonly called "marijuana" (q.v.), has properties similar to, but weaker than, those of the Oriental species. The English word "assassin" is derived from the Arabic *hashishin,* "hemp eaters". *See* ASSASSINS; DRUGS, ADDICTION TO.

**CANNAE,** ancient town of Italy, in the Apulia Region, near the mouth of the Aufidus (now Ofanto) R. In 216 B.C. the Carthaginian general Hannibal (q.v.) defeated the Romans in the Second Punic War at Cannae; *see* PUNIC WARS.

**CANNES,** city, resort, and seaport of France, in Alpes-Maritimes Department, on the Mediterranean Sea, about 16 miles s.w. of Nice. The city, renowned for a mild climate and fine beaches, is built on an elevation that slopes to the sea and is sheltered by a range of hills. The surrounding country is picturesque and fertile; oranges, lemons, olives, almonds, figs, peaches, and grapes are grown in abundance. The city exports olive oil, anchovies, fruit, and flowers; other occupations are fishing and the manufacture of soaps and perfumes.

Architectural features of the city include the tower of the Abbés of Lérins, built about 1070, the 15th-century Church of Notre-Dame d'Espérance, and the Musée Lycklama, which contains a fine collection of antiquities. Along the promenade, called La Croisette, are splendid hotels and shops.

For centuries Cannes was a small fishing village; since the 1830's, however, when British political leader Henry Peter Brougham, Baron Brougham and Vaux (1778–1868), built a villa there, Cannes has been a popular winter and summer resort. Later in the 19th century two gambling casinos were constructed. An important international motion-picture festival has been held in the city each spring since 1951. Pop. (1968) 68,021.

**CANNIBALISM,** eating of human flesh by human beings, and also eating by animals of members of their own species. The term cannibalism is derived from the name of the Carib (q.v.) Indians who lived in the West Indies when the Genoese-born navigator Christopher Columbus (q.v.) arrived. The Carib were maneaters and the Spanish name for the tribe was *Canibales,* meaning bloodthirsty and cruel. The practice of cannibalism is of great antiquity and has been reported in many parts of the world. Evidence indicates that it may have been practiced as early as Neolithic times (*see* ARCHEOLOGY: *Periods*). The Greek historian Herodotus (q.v.) and other ancient writers gave accounts of various ancient peoples who were cannibals. In medieval times the Italian traveler Marco Polo (q.v.) reported that tribes from Tibet to Sumatra practiced cannibalism. It was practiced among many North American Indians, especially the tribes of the western coast of the Gulf of Mexico. Until recent times cannibalism prevailed throughout much of central and western Africa, Australia, New Zealand, Melanesia, Sumatra, New Guinea, Polynesia, and remote parts of South America.

Sometimes cannibalism arose from the belief that the person who ate the dead body of another would acquire the desired qualities of the person eaten, particularly of a brave enemy. In a few instances cannibalism seems to have been dictated by no other motive than revenge. It was even believed that the existence of the ghost of an enemy would be utterly destroyed if his body were eaten, thus leaving nothing in which his spirit could live. Cannibalism was sometimes part of a religious practice. The Binderwurs of central India ate their sick and aged in the belief that the act was pleasing to their goddess, Kali. In Mexico thousands of human victims were sacrificed annually by the Aztecs to their deities; *see* AZTEC. After the ceremony of sacrifice, the Aztec priests and the populace ate the bodies of the victims, believing that the act brought those who ate closer to their gods.

Among Western peoples cannibalism is rare, although starvation has sometimes driven men to eat the flesh of other men. One instance in America involved members of the ill-fated Donner Party (q.v.) in the Sierra Nevada in California during the winter of 1846–47. Another occurred in Chile in 1972 when 16 members of a Uruguayan soccer team survived for 70 days after their airliner crashed in the Andes Mts.

Cannibalism also exists among animals. Wolves have been known to eat injured members of their packs, and rats and pigs have been observed to eat the young of their species. A well-known instance of cannibalism among insects is the habit of the female spider of eating the male after mating. Among the mantes, the larger insects often eat the smaller, and the female mantis devours the male.

**CANNING,** process of preserving food by heating and sealing in suitable containers. The process was invented in 1809 by François Appert (1752–1841), a French chef. In the Appert process, the food was cooked in open kettles and placed in glass jars, which were sealed by corks wired in place. The jars were then heated by submersion in boiling water. Canning was introduced into the United States soon after its in-

At sorting tables in a food-processing plant, tomatoes are inspected and sorted for ripeness and uniformity of shape.
Hunt-Wesson Foods

vention, and by 1825 lobster, salmon, pickles, fruit, and vegetables were canned for domestic use and export. In 1810 an Englishman, Peter Durand, patented the idea of using tin-plated cans instead of glass jars; in spite of their comparative cheapness, however, tin cans did not replace glass containers until the middle of the 19th century. The early form of tin can was sealed with a disk of metal soldered over a hole

*Field-ripened tomatoes go through a series of high-powered spray washes, inspections, and sortings before being placed in individual cups by automatic feeders; they are then checked and hand-oriented for proper position before they enter the peeler.*
Hunt-Wesson Foods

Tomatoes move along conveyors to rotary fillers, where they are packed in cans, ready for sealing and cooking.
Hunt-Wesson Foods

The U.S. has the highest per capita consumption of commercially canned foods in the world. About 75,000,000,000 cans were produced in the U.S. in 1972; 20 percent of the cans were used for beer and 19.4 percent for soft drinks. Vegetable and fruit packing accounted for nearly 24 percent of the output.

Home canning became an important method of preserving food in the 19th century, when John Landis Mason (1832–1902) an American, invented (1858) a practical glass jar and lid, now called the mason jar. Home canning is still popular in some areas of the U.S. because it is an economical means of preserving home-grown fruits and vegetables. The preferred method for canning foods at home is the hot-pack method, in which precooked, hot food and part of the liquid in which it was cooked are placed in a clean, hot mason jar. The mouth of the jar is covered with a metal disk that has a rubber ring seal. A screw-type lid is then partially screwed onto the glass jar. After the jar has been processed in boiling water for the length of time required for the type of food, the screw top is tightened completely. Heat and pressure during processing force most of the air from the jar and minimize the danger of multiplication of disease-causing organisms. Jams and jellies are usually prepared by the open-kettle method. The jam is cooked to the proper consistency, then poured into hot, sterilized jars, which are then sealed. Further heating is not required;

in the end of the can. Later, calcium chloride was added to the water used to sterilize the food sealed in the cans, to raise the temperature of the water above 212°. Although the food was heated faster, the increased internal pressure often burst the cans. In spite of this disadvantage, the improved sterilization and faster production that this process allowed led to expansion of the canning industry in the U.S., especially during the American Civil War. In 1874 the American Andrew Kayser Shriver of Baltimore, Md., patented the closed-vessel process, in which the cans were heated by steam under pressure; the pressure of the steam compensated for pressure that developed in the can, largely eliminating the bursting of cans. Gradual improvements in machinery and techniques for producing cans resulted in better lining materials, such as lacquers and enamels, and in the development of the sanitary open-top can in which the top is crimped to the can after filling, producing an airtight seal by means of a rubber gasket. During World War II the critical shortage of tin and the requirements of the U.S. armed forces for cans to pack ammunition caused many food packers to change to glass containers for their products.

Recent developments include the use of aluminum cans, very thin steel cans, and tin-free cans. Tin-free cans may be coated with plastic on the inner surface to eliminate a metallic taste. The use of can openers or slotted keys has been eliminated in many containers that are opened by pulling a metal tab or ring attached to the top of the can, which is designed to pull free of the can. The aerosol (q.v.) can, developed during World War II as an insecticide container, has been adapted to package more than 300 types of consumer products.

Pull-tape containers are used for a variety of vacuum-packed products.
American Can Company

jams and jellies do not ordinarily spoil because the sugar used in preparing them acts as a preservative. See BOTULISM; FOOD PRESERVATION.

**CANNING, George** (1770–1827), British statesman, born in London, England, and educated for the law at the University of Oxford. A Tory, he entered the House of Commons in 1794, as the protégé and supporter of Prime minister William Pitt, known as the Younger (*see under* PITT). In 1796 Canning was made undersecretary of state for foreign affairs. In 1801, when Pitt resigned, Canning left his post on the privy council. When Pitt again became prime minister in 1804, Canning was appointed treasurer of the navy, an office which he held until the death of Pitt in 1806. In 1807 Canning became foreign minister. His resignation three years later was prompted by his continuing feud with the secretary of war, Viscount Castlereagh (q.v.). Canning held a series of minor offices until 1822, when he was called by George IV (q.v.), King of Great Britain, to the foreign secretaryship and the leadership of the House of Commons, succeeding Castlereagh. From then until his death, Canning guided the foreign affairs of Great Britain. He supported nationalist movements throughout Latin America, discouraging foreign intervention in American affairs, a policy that accorded with the attitude of the United States (*see* MONROE DOCTRINE); he aided Portugal against Spanish aggression and the Greeks in their struggles against the Turks. At home, Canning worked for emancipation of Catholics. For the last four months of his life, he served as prime minister.

**CANNIZZARO, Stanislao** (1826–1910), Italian chemist, born in Palermo, Sicily. After participating in the 1848 Sicilian revolution (*see* SICILY: *History*), Cannizzaro worked in a laboratory in Paris (1849–51). He was appointed professor of chemistry at the institute in Alessandria in the Piedmont district of Italy (1851) and at the universities of Genoa (1855), Pisa (1861), and Rome (1871). At Alessandria he discovered the reaction that bears his name, Cannizzaro's reaction, which proves that aldehydes (q.v.) in the presence of concentrated alkali (*see* ALKALIES) are reduced to a mixture of their corresponding alcohol and acid; for example, benzaldehyde yields benzyl alcohol and benzoic acid. Cannizzaro made a great contribution to atomic theory by his clarification in 1858 of the distinction between atomic weight and molecular weight; *see* ATOM AND ATOMIC THEORY. He showed how unknown atomic weights of elements in volatile compounds can be arrived at from known molecular weights of the compounds. Cannizzaro also determined that atomic weights of elements in compounds can be determined if specific heats are known even though vapor densities are unknown; *see* SPECIFIC HEAT. His work on atomic theory was based on Avogadro's Law (q.v.), which states that equal volumes of any two gases contain an equal number of molecules when held under identical conditions of temperature and pressure.

**CANNON,** in military usage, general term for artillery weapons of all types and sizes. Early cannon were smooth-bore metal tubes mounted on simple carriages. They were loaded from the muzzle with a charge of powder, a cloth wad, and a spherical iron shot rammed into the bore; they were discharged by applying fire to the powder through a small hole near the breech. Such cannon were aimed by sluing the carriage, and elevated by means of wedges; recoil was absorbed by allowing the carriage to run backward. The modern cannon consists of a forged steel tube, rifled to give the projectile (q.v.) a spin in flight, and enclosed for strength in a steel jacket. Its carriage is equipped with recoil mechanism to absorb the force of recoil on firing, and a counterrecoil mechanism which returns the cannon to firing position after recoil. Elevating and traversing mechanisms provide for accurate aiming by hand, by electric power, or by a completely automatic system which locates and tracks the target by radar, makes corrections for range, wind, and target speed, and times the firing so that projectile and target will reach the same spot at the same time.

Ammunition for modern cannon is loaded through the breech. A complete round consists of the fuzed projectile, a propelling charge of smokeless powder, and a primer. In large cannon the parts are loaded separately; the projectile is rammed into place, the propelling charge is placed in the chamber, the breechblock is

*Gun practice by a squad of Federal soldiers during the American Civil War, from a photograph by Mathew B. Brady.* U.S. Army

An example of a 105-mm howitzer that was used by U.S. Marines to shell enemy positions during the war in Vietnam.                                    U.S. Army

closed, and the primer inserted. Ammunition for smaller cannon is "fixed": the propelling charge is contained in a metal cartridge case which has the primer inserted in one end and the projectile crimped in the other; the entire round is loaded as a unit. Cannon may fire high-explosive shells, shaped-charge antitank shells, white phosphorus, smoke, and signal shells, shells containing chemical agents, shells with nuclear warheads, or shells filled with propaganda leaflets. Shells have on occasion delivered vital medical supplies to isolated troops.

Early in 1975 the U.S. Army demonstrated a laser-guided artillery shell that could be fired by a standard 155-mm howitzer with great accuracy. The new "cannon-launched guided projectile" was expected to become part of the U.S. arsenal by the late 1970's. *See* ARTILLERY; LASER.

**CANNON, Annie Jump** (1863–1941), American astronomer, born in Dover, Del., and educated at Wellesley and Radcliffe colleges. She was an assistant at the Harvard College Observatory from 1897 until 1911, when she was appointed curator of astronomical photographs. She was responsible for the photographic discovery of five novae and about 300 variable stars; *see* NOVA; STARS: *Variable Stars.* She is best known for the compilation of a bibliography of about 200,000 references to variable stars, and the classification of about 250,000 stellar spectra to form the catalog that is still accepted as an international standard. Regarded as the first great woman astronomer, she was also the first woman to receive an honorary doctor's degree from the University of Oxford. *See* STARS: *Classification of Stellar Spectra.*

**CANNON, Joseph Gurney** (1836–1926), American lawyer and politician, born in New Garden, N.C., and educated at the Cincinnati Law School. In 1858 Cannon moved to Illinois and he was admitted to the Illinois bar. He was elected as a Republican to the United States House of Representatives in 1873 and served twenty-three terms in Congress, failing to be reelected for the two terms beginning in 1891 and 1913. From 1903 until 1911 he was Speaker of the House. Cannon was noted for his strong partisan leadership as speaker and his conservative political views. He was opposed to the so-called progressive reforms advocated by such political leaders as President Woodrow Wilson (q.v.), and was an outspoken opponent of the League of Nations (q.v.). Cannon's opponents in Congress felt that he had arbitrary power over legislative procedure in the House, and in 1910 they passed a resolution reducing the powers of the office of Speaker.

**CANO, Juan Sebastian Del,** also known as EL CANO (d. 1526), Spanish navigator, born in Guetaria. In 1519 he was made captain of the *Concepción,* one of the five vessels commanded by the Portuguese navigator Ferdinand Magellan (q.v.) during his expedition in the service of Spain. After the death of Magellan on April 27, 1521, Cano assumed command of the expedition. On Sept. 6, 1522, he arrived in Spain on board the *Victoria,* becoming the first man to circumnavigate the earth, although Magellan is usually given credit for the voyage. Cano died off the western coast of South America, while

Joseph G. Cannon                    UPI

he was in command of a subsequent expedition.

**CANOE,** light, narrow boat, generally with identically shaped bow and stern and curved sides, and usually propelled by at least one oar or paddle. The canoe was developed by primitive peoples throughout the world. It varies in shape, size, and construction, according to its origin. The oldest form of canoe was probably a tree trunk hollowed out by tools or fire.

The North American Indians created the birchbark canoe, a vessel with a frame of light wood that is covered with pieces of bark sewn together and made watertight with melted pitch. Similar in design to the birchbark is the canvas canoe created by the Penobscot (q.v.) Indians of Maine in the 19th century. Indians living in treeless regions made canoes of tule or other bulrushes lashed together; the Indians living on the shores of Lake Titicaca in South America still make them this way.

The Eskimo created two kinds of canoe, both of which had whalebone or wooden frames and were covered with animal skins, generally those from whales or seals. The kayak, a boat used only by the male Eskimo, is completely enclosed except for an opening for the occupant. The umiak, used only by the female, is open. The canoe of Greenland and Hudson Strait is flat bottomed and flat sided.

The dugout is still used by the peoples of Africa, South America, and Polynesia. Another type of canoe used by the natives of the Southwest Pacific islands is made of planks fastened together. This type is often equipped with an outrigger, a device that ensures stability in heavy seas. Many of the ancient war canoes used by natives of the Pacific islands were elaborately carved.

In recent years the canoe has been used increasingly by vacationists and sportsmen, and since 1886 canoeists have engaged in official competitions. Today canoes are constructed of plastic, aluminum and magnesium alloys, rubber, canvas, and other materials. A modern development is the faltboat, a small collapsible canoe of rubberized sailcloth stretched over a knockdown frame.

**CANON,** rule or standard, mentioned in the Bible in Gal. 6:16. By the middle of the 3rd century the meaning of the word had narrowed to denote the type of doctrine recognized as orthodox by the Christian Church. It was after-

English explorers trade with Indians for a birchbark canoe.                    Bureau of Public Roads

ward employed to designate collectively the list of books accepted as Scripture; see BIBLE, CANON OF THE. Canon is also used to denote the catalog or register of Catholic saints. The use of the plural form to denote church precepts originated about the year 300; this form began to be specifically transferred to the decrees of church councils about the middle of the 4th century; see CANON LAW. The term is also applied to the part of the Roman Catholic Mass (q.v.) that opens with the Preface, or prayer of thanksgiving, and closes just before the recitation of the Lord's Prayer or *Pater noster.*

**CANON** (Gk. *kanon*, "standard"), in music, composition of two or more voice parts, employing in a strict form the device of musical repetition known as imitation. In a canon one voice introduces the melody or subject and, after an interval of a specific number of beats or measures, a second voice repeats or answers the melody note for note, either on the same pitch (q.v.) with the first voice, or on any pitch above or below. A third voice may then repeat the melody exactly, entering at precisely the same interval after the second voice as the second entered after the first. A canon in which two voices are treated in exact imitation is called a canon "two in one"; when three voices are so treated, the composition is a canon "three in one". At times two or more canons are simultaneously combined into one composition. A canon may conclude with a single phrase or coda (q.v.). When the subject leads back to the beginning so that it may be endlessly repeated the canon is known as "circular" or "infinite". A well-known example of the circular canon is the round (q.v.) "Three Blind Mice". One of the earliest known canons is "Sumer Is Icumen In", probably written in the 13th century.

Canonic imitation is often employed for several measures in contrapuntal compositions; see COUNTERPOINT.

**CANON CITY,** city in Colorado, and county seat of Fremont Co., at the head of the Royal Gorge of the Arkansas R., about 160 miles S.W. of Denver. Canon City is encircled by mountains and is a health resort frequented for the hot and cold mineral springs in the vicinity. About 9 miles N.E. of Canon City, on Oil Creek, scientists have excavated fossil remains of prehistoric animals. The economy of the city depends on the surrounding agricultural region, which also contains quarries for building stone and mines that produce metals, coal, and semiprecious gems. Industrial establishments in the city include foundries, smelters, and brick and tile yards. Founded in 1859–60 during a gold rush, Canon

City grew rapidly after 1872, when oil was discovered nearby. By the beginning of the 20th century the oil deposits had been exhausted. Pop. (1960) 8973; (1970) 9206.

**CANONICAL HOURS** or **LITURGICAL HOURS,** stipulated times for daily corporate worship or private prayer in the Roman Catholic Church (q.v.), the Orthodox Church (q.v.), and, in greatly revised form, the various branches of Anglicanism (see CHURCH OF ENGLAND) and Lutheranism (q.v.). Observances for the seven traditional hours collectively form the Divine Office. They are derived from the original eight hours, with two combined so that the number corresponds with Psalm 119: "Seven times a day do I praise thee". The services for the canonical hours were originated to provide orderly recitation of the Psalter once a week and consecutive reading of the Bible, the Old Testament to be covered once a year and the New Testament twice.

In the Roman Catholic Church the hours bear Latin names: matins, about 2 A.M., said with lauds at daybreak; prime in the early morning; terce at 9 A.M.; sext at noon; none, from 2 to 3 P.M.; vespers about 6 P.M.; and compline about 8 P.M. Matins, lauds, and vespers are the major hours, and it is these, with matins and lauds combined, that have been retained in Anglican and Lutheran practice. Protestant reformer Martin Luther (q.v.) suggested the reduction of the office to prayers twice daily at church.

The psalms, other Scripture passages, hymns, prayers, versicles, and lives of saints used in the Roman Office are contained in the breviary (q.v.), and, before the reforms of Pope John XXIII (see under JOHN) in 1961 were printed in four volumes, one for each liturgical season.

Canonical hours are, ideally, to be observed by all Catholic priests, monks, some nuns, and other religious. Reforms have been made to meet 20th-century conditions. Some shorter offices are acceptable for particular persons. The custom of reciting the office has never been practical for the laity, and since at least the 9th century shorter and simpler forms have been provided.

The pattern of the hours developed in monasticism (q.v.), the definite form and content emerging in the 6th century in the Benedictine order. Saint Benedict of Nursia (q.v.) made use of a breviary from the Church in Rome. He added the offices of prime and compline. Although not called a "breviary" until the 11th century, the Benedictine Divine Office remained in general use and relatively unchanged until 1912. The place of the Divine Office be-

came secure throughout the Roman Church in the Middle Ages (q.v.). Today the full recitation of the revised hours is confined mainly to monasteries and some cathedral chapters. Monastic hours include more Old Testament canticles (q.v.) than others.

Observation of each hour contains common elements: psalms and canticles; antiphons, that is, Biblical or patristic sentences; responsories, that is, meditative Scripture passages; versicles; hymns; lessons; little chapters or short lessons, often from the New Testament Epistles; and collects. The selections for each day are set.

In the Orthodox Church, psalms for each hour are specified. The hours are named differently from those in the West, but the purpose is essentially the same. A more prominent part is given to religious poetry than in the Roman Divine Office.

**CANONIZATION,** in the Roman Catholic Church, an act by which the pope publicly proclaims the sanctity of a servant of God, whom he thereupon proposes for the veneration of the universal Church. Canonization is usually the final act of a lengthy process that begins with beatification (q.v.). The decree of beatification declares the worthy person to be among the citizens of Heaven, and accords him the title of "blessed"; canonization awards him the full title of "saint" (q.v.) and enjoins the entire Church to venerate him.

The beginnings of the modern custom of canonization are to be found in the early Christian practice of paying public honor to the martyrs. For many centuries thereafter, the appellation of saint was given to individuals by popular acclamation. Not until a comparatively late period was a procedure equivalent to canonization adopted.

The earliest acknowledged instance of a solemn decree of canonization is that of Udalric or Ulric, bishop of Augsburg, declared a saint by Pope John XV (*see under* JOHN) in 993. Pope Alexander III (*see under* ALEXANDER) in 1170 reserved the right of canonizing exclusively for the papacy. Pope Urban VIII (*see under* URBAN), in two constitutions promulgated in 1625 and 1634, made more stringent regulations and laid down the canonization procedure that, with slight modifications, is still followed.

Canonization, without a special dispensation, cannot be decreed until fifty years have elapsed since the claimant's death. The process that precedes the decree of canonization seeks to establish two characteristics of the claimant according to the testimony of competent witnesses; the two characteristics are eminent virtues, technically called virtues in a "heroic degree", and the performance of miracles.

If the initial investigation is satisfactory, the pope takes the cause into his own hands and issues letters assigning the cause to a committee of the Congregation of Rites, which then examines the virtues and miracles specifically. The claimant's cause is now said to be introduced. The introduction of the cause, that is, of the pontifical process, entitles the *beatificandus,* or candidate for beatification, to be called "venerable". Many candidates have reached this point in the proceedings and have failed to go beyond it. If the candidate passes successfully through the proceedings, a decree of beatification is pronounced. Before the further process of canonization can be instituted, witnesses must testify that the candidate has worked a certain number of miracles since his beatification. The case then once more passes through the hands of several congregations, the last of which is held in the presence of the pope, when the final decree is drawn up and agreed upon.

The ceremony of canonization takes place in the Vatican basilica, and is one of the most solemn and imposing of all papal functions.

Equipollent or equivalent canonization is founded upon proof of immemorial veneration, or of some papal sanction given to veneration, prior to the date of Urban VIII's constitution. In such cases the pope may at once pronounce the decree of canonization. Equipollent beatification is a summary process of a similar kind. The pope accepts the results of the preliminary process and at once decrees beatification.

**CANON LAW** (Lat. *jus canonicum*), the part of ecclesiastical legislation that is concerned with the moral and disciplinary government of a religious body, and is embodied in the form of canons, or rules; *see* CANON. Although the term "canon law" as used in this article and as applied generally refers to the law of the Roman Catholic and Greek Orthodox churches, in a broad sense it may be held to include the regulations governing any religious organization.

The canon law that governs the Roman Catholic and Greek Orthodox churches is distinguished from the ecclesiastical decisions embodied in decrees, which affect formularies and standards of doctrine; from papal law (*jus pontificium*); and from enactments of civil law upon ecclesiastical subjects (*jus ecclesiasticum*), although the last often overlaps the canon law proper. The earliest example of the enactment of canon law appears in Acts 15:6–29, in which the council of elders at Jerusalem framed rules of discipline for the Gentile converts to Christianity.

In the Greek Orthodox Church, canon law is composed of a small number of homogeneous, ancient regulations. Since the compilation of the *Nomocanon* (from Gr. *nomos,* "law" and *kanōn,* "rule") probably by Enantiophanes, renowned for his knowledge of international law, in about 629, canon law in the Greek Orthodox Church has remained unchanged.

In the Roman Catholic Church, canon law is of much greater extent. It includes papal law and has been subjected to continual accretion and interpolation. Canon law became the object of scientific research in the 12th and 13th centuries. Of the various compilations made during those centuries, the most important was the Five Books of the Decretals, promulgated by Pope Gregory IX (r. 1227–41) about 1234, to which a sixth book was added by Pope Boniface VIII (*see under* BONIFACE) in 1298. Additions, obsoletions, and interpolations continued to accumulate, until in 1904 Pope Pius X (*see under* PIUS) appointed a commission of cardinals to codify canon law. In 1917 Pope Benedict XV (*see under* BENEDICT) promulgated the New Code of Canon Law (*Codex Juris Canonici*), which took effect May 19, 1918.

The New Code of Canon Law consists of 2414 canons, arranged in five books. The first book contains general rules, the second, rules regarding ecclesiastical persons. The third book deals with sacred objects and rites, such as altars and sacramentals; the fourth, with canonical trials; and the fifth, with crimes and punishments.

By the 1960's, however, the Code of 1918 had grown out of date, and began to undergo a complete revision and adaptation. Except for a few officially decreed changes, the 1918 code was to retain the force of law until the revised code was promulgated.

The Church of England (q.v.) follows the canon law of England as it existed before the Reformation (q.v.) with the changes made necessary by the Reformation. Those changes introduced into the Roman Catholic Church canon law at the Council of Trent and thereafter necessarily do not affect the English church. In general, church law in the Anglican Communion (q.v.) is decided by institutions maintained within the individual church. Where the state has recognized the church as an established church, state participation may be required in making church law.

*See also* CHURCH DISCIPLINE.

**CANONSBURG,** borough of Pennsylvania, in Washington Co., about 23 miles s.w. of central Pittsburgh. Manufactures include metal products, radio equipment, steel, and pottery. The Log Academy, built in 1780, is the oldest school building west of the Allegheny Mts. Pop. (1960) 11,877; (1970) 11,439.

**CANOPUS,** star of the first magnitude, the second most brilliant star in the heavens, located in the southern constellation Argo. Although Canopus is about 98 light-years away from the earth, it is only half a magnitude fainter than the brightest star, Sirius (q.v.), which is 8.8 light-years distant. Because of its brightness, Canopus is used as a reference point for navigation of spacecraft launched on interplanetary missions. The star is in the extreme southern part of the sky and cannot be seen at latitudes north of Norfolk, Va.

**CANOSSA,** castle in Italy, destroyed in 1255, in the village of Canossa, in Reggio nell'Emilia Province, about 12 miles s.w. of the city of Reggio nell'Emilia. In January, 1077, Henry IV (q.v.), Holy Roman Emperor, who had been excommunicated, went to Canossa, then the papal residence, for an audience with Pope Gregory VII (*see under* GREGORY). The emperor stood for three days in the courtyard of the castle, bareheaded and barefooted. Following this display of humility, the pontiff granted Henry absolution. "Going to Canossa" is a phrase that was probably coined by the Prussian statesman Prince Otto Eduard Leopold von Bismarck (q.v.) during the Kulturkampf (q.v.), his struggle with the Roman Catholic Church. The phrase has since characterized a place or occasion of submission, penance, or humiliation.

**CANOVA, Antonio** (1757–1822), Italian sculptor, born in Possagno, Treviso Province. He was regarded as a leader of the Classic Revival, a style imitative of ancient Greek and Roman art. He studied in Venice and won distinction with his first marble statues, especially "Daedalus and Icarus" (Louvre, Paris). After 1779 he went to study in Rome, where the revival of the classical style was gaining in importance. He was soon recognized as the foremost sculptor of the classical style for his "Perseus" (Vatican, Rome) and "Theseus Vanquishing the Minotaur" (Louvre). Thereafter he was commissioned to sculpt a monument of Pope Clement XIV (*see under* CLEMENT), which is in the Church of the Santi Apostoli, Rome.

Canova also received commissions from Napoleon I (q.v.), Emperor of France. Among the works of the sculptor were a bust of Napoleon (Pitti Palace, Florence) and the sculpture portrait "Venus Borghese" (Villa Borghese, Rome). After the fall of Napoleon Canova was sent to Paris to bring back the art treasures that the emperor had taken from Italy. Succeeding in his mission, he was made Marquis of Ischia.

**CANSO, STRAIT OF,** strait separating Cape Breton Island and the mainland of Nova Scotia,

*"Perseus holding the Head of Medusa", a marble statue by Antonio Canova.* Metropolitan Museum of Art — Fletcher Fund

and connecting Northumberland Strait to the Atlantic Ocean. It is 17 mi. long and about 2 mi. wide. In 1955 the strait was spanned by the Canso Causeway. The causeway carries railroad and highway traffic and is broken by a ship canal on the Cape Breton Island side.

**CANTABRIAN MOUNTAINS,** mountain range of N. Spain, extending about 300 mi. westward from the Pyrenees to the Atlantic Ocean along the s. shore of the Bay of Biscay. Torre de Cerredo, 8687 ft. above sea level, is the highest peak; many others exceed 7000 ft. The range is rich in coal and iron deposits.

**CANTAB TERRIER.** *See* NORWICH TERRIER.

**CANTACUZENE** or (Rum.) **CANTACUZINO,** name of a Rumanian family descended from the Byzantine emperor John VI Cantacuzene (q.v.). The more important members of the family were the following.

**Serban Cantacuzino** (1640–88), statesman. He was hospodar or governor of the Rumanian region of Walachia from 1679 to 1688, while the region was part of the Ottoman Empire; *see* TURKEY: *History.* In 1683 he was forced to help the Turks in their unsuccessful siege of the city of Vienna (q.v.). In return for his aid, the Turkish emperor recognized the descendency of the Cantacuzino family from John VI Cantacuzene.

Serban is noted for introducing the cultivation of Indian corn into his country; for establishing the first Rumanian school in the city of Bucharest; and for replacing the Slavonic language with the Rumanian in the liturgy (q.v.).

**Gheorge Cantacuzino** (1837–1913), statesman. In 1889 he became president of the lower house in the Rumanian parliament and three years later president of the upper house. In 1899 he became the leader of the Conservative Party. From 1905 to 1907 he served as prime minister of Rumania.

**CANTALOUPE,** name applied commonly in the United States to a variety of muskmelon, *Cucumis melo reticulatus,* belonging to the family Cucubitaceae. The term cantaloupe is applied to a similar variety, *C. melo cantalupensis,* in Europe.

The common American type of cantaloupe grows on vines which frequently attain 7 ft. in length. It has a thin, reticulated rind and yellowish-orange flesh. The seeds are attached to a netlike fiber in the center of the melon. The cantaloupe has a sweet flavor and gives off a musklike odor when it is ripe.

The European variety, first cultivated in the Italian town Cantalupo, has a hard, deep-ribbed rind and a reddish-orange flesh with a delicate flavor. It is seldom grown in the U.S. *See also* MUSKMELON.

**CANTATA,** in music, a vocal composition with instrumental accompaniment. The cantata originated in the early 17th century simultaneously with opera and oratorio (qq.v.). The earliest type of cantata, known as the *cantata da camera,* was written for solo voice on a secular text. It contained several sections in contrasting vocal styles, such as recitative and aria (qq.v.). Italian composers who wrote in this form include Giulio Caccini, Claudio Monteverdi (qq.v.), and Jacopo Peri (1516–1633). During the late 17th century, the *cantata da camera* developed into a composition for two or three voices written mainly for churches and known as the *cantata da chiesa.* Its chief Italian exponents were Giacomo Carissimi and Alessandro Scarlatti (qq.v.). In Germany during this period, the *cantata da chiesa,* under the leadership of Heinrich Schütz (1585–1672), Georg Philipp Telemann, Dietrich Buxtehude, Johann Sebastian Bach (qq.v.) and other composers, developed into a far more elaborate form than its Italian model.

Since the time of Bach the cantata has usually been a choral composition with instrumental accompaniment, containing choruses, solos, arias, recitatives, and instrumental interludes.

The text may be sacred, in which case the cantata resembles the oratorio, or secular, in which case it resembles an opera. In its sacred form it differs from an oratorio by being considerably shorter and less elaborate in both its vocal writing and its accompaniment. In its secular form it differs from the opera by being sung without scenery, costumes, or staged action. Among composers of the cantata since the period of Bach are Felix Mendelssohn, Franz Liszt, Robert Schumann, Johannes Brahms, Louis Hector Berlioz, Aaron Copland, Béla Bartók, and Sergei Prokofiev (qq.v.). W.M.

**CANTERBURY,** Great Britain, county borough of Kent, England, on the Stour R., about 54 miles S.E. of London. It is the ecclesiastical metropolis of England, and a center of trade in grains and hops, the chief crops of the surrounding region. Among the industrial establishments in the city are textile mills, brickworks, breweries, and plants manufacturing leather products. Canterbury, one of the oldest cities in England, was an important town in Roman times, and the remains of the ancient Roman city wall and the west gate (now a museum for arms and armory) are still evident. Saint Martin's, one of the most beautiful of the fourteen parish churches of the borough, was also originally built by the Romans. In the 15th century, the community was incorporated by King Henry VI (q.v.), and during the 17th century it had a flourishing silk-weaving industry.

Canterbury is dominated by the huge cathedral, seat of the primate of the Church of England (q.v.) since the time of Saint Augustine (q.v.), the first Christian missionary to, and first archbishop of, England. Augustine consecrated an existing Roman church, Christ's Church, as his cathedral in 601, but no part of the original structure remains. The edifice was destroyed by fire in 1067 and again in 1174, and was subsequently rebuilt. The present cathedral is 522 ft. long, and is flanked by a large central tower 235 ft. high, dating from the 15th century, and by two towers on the w. side of the nave, dating from the 12th and 19th centuries, all in the Perpendicular (q.v.) style. The choir, separated from the nave by an imposing screen, is in the Norman style (*see* ROMANESQUE ART AND ARCHITECTURE), and is flanked by two projecting chapels. Trinity Chapel to the rear of the altar contains the shrine of Saint Thomas à Becket (q.v.), who was murdered there in 1170. During the centuries following his canonization in 1172, the shrine became the mecca of thousands of pilgrims. A representative group of 14th-century pilgrims is vividly portrayed in *The Canterbury*

*Canterbury Cathedral seen through Christ Church Gate.* **British Information Services**

*Tales* (q.v.) by the English poet Geoffrey Chaucer (q.v.). Several old inns visited by pilgrims of that time can still be seen in Canterbury. Becket's shrine, dismantled in 1538 by command of Henry VIII (q.v.), King of England, who confiscated the accumulated treasures deposited there by the devout, has been reconstructed. The tomb and effigy of Edward (q.v.), Prince of Wales, commonly known as the Black Prince, are also in Trinity Chapel. At the eastern terminus of the cathedral is the circular tower known as Corona Chapel or Becket's Crown. The chapel contains a large marble chair of undetermined date known as St. Augustine's chair, on which the archbishops of Canterbury are enthroned. On the N. side of the cathedral are the cloisters, chapter house, baptistery, deanery, the King's School, and library. On the site of the Benedictine abbey founded by Augustine in the 6th century stands St. Augustine's College for training Anglican clergy (founded 1848). The cathedral and the surrounding buildings were severely damaged in 1942 during the German air raids of World War II. Pop. (1971) 35,530.

**CANTERBURY BELL.** *See* CAMPANULA.

**CANTERBURY TALES, THE,** long narrative poem written by the English poet Geoffrey Chaucer (q.v.), probably after 1387, **and styled**

after *The Decameron* (q.v.) by the Italian writer Giovanni Boccaccio (q.v.). *The Canterbury Tales* has about 17,000 lines of verse, mostly in iambic pentameter rhyming couplets. Although Chaucer originally intended the poem to contain 120 tales, the finished work has twenty-three tales, several of which are incomplete. In the lengthy General Prologue at the beginning of the poem, Chaucer humorously but realistically introduces his characters and creates the frame for the stories, which are linked together by shorter prologues to make a continuous narrative.

The poem concerns a group of thirty-one pilgrims, including the author, who have gathered at Tabard Inn (*see* TABARD) in Southwark before setting out on their way to the shrine of Saint Thomas à Becket (q.v.) in the city of Canterbury (q.v.). At the suggestion of the host of the inn, the pilgrims decide to relieve the tedium of their travel by telling stories. The best-known tales are those told by the Knight, the Nun's Priest, the Pardoner, the Wife of Bath, and the Miller. The Knight's Tale, the first and longest story, is a quasi-historical romance set in ancient Athens; it is generally considered the most beautiful of the tales. The Nun's Priest Tale, the familiar beast fable of the fox and cock who match wits, is the first important mock-heroic tale in English. The Pardoner's Tale is an *exemplum,* or illustrative sermon of three revelers who meet death. The Wife of Bath's Tale is an Arthurian fairy tale preceded by a long prologue in which she condemns celibacy by giving a frank account of her life with five successive husbands. The Miller's Tale is a bawdy story of deception of an aged husband by his young wife and a young scholar. Other tales are contributed by remaining members of the group, including a Nun, a Lawyer, a Student, a Cook, a Merchant, a Squire, a Physician, and Chaucer himself.

Most of the tales are borrowed and the sources and literary forms are varied, so that Chaucer gives not only a picture of contemporary England, but also a 14th-century view of ancient Greece and Rome, of Asia, and of continental Europe. Chiefly concerned with the character of men as revealed in their conduct, Chaucer satirizes social class and sex and broadly ridicules human weaknesses. *The Canterbury Tales* are regarded as the most brilliant achievement of the "Father of English Poetry". *See* ENGLISH LITERATURE: *Middle English Period.*

**CAN THO,** city in South Vietnam, and capital of Phong Dinh Province, at the confluence of the Can Tho R. and Song Hau Giang (Bassac R.) in the Mekong delta, 80 miles S.W. of Saigon. A road hub in an important rice- and fruit-growing area, Can Tho has an agricultural experimental station. Industries include rice milling, sawmilling, coconut-oil extracting, and soap and cigarette manufacturing. Situated in an area of Cochin China formerly dominated by the Khmer people, Can Tho was captured by the Annamese in the 18th century and eventually became a part of French Indochina. Pop. (1973 est.) 182,500.

**CANTICLES** (Lat., *canticum*, "song"), specifically, the SONG OF SONGS in the Old Testament. In the Vulgate, the name of the book is *Canticum canticorum;* in the King James Version, it is Song of Solomon (q.v.). *See* BIBLE.

An unmetrical hymn (q.v.) in the church service arranged for chanting, such as the *Te Deum,* is also called a canticle. *See* RELIGIOUS MUSIC.

**CANTILEVER,** in engineering or construction, beam or truss rigidly supported at one end, or in the middle, but not at both ends, which has forces applied along the free arm or at the free end. A typical example of a cantilever is a diving (q.v.) springboard. Cantilever construction is used for canopies, balconies, large construction cranes, and in cantilever bridges where the span is supported not at the ends but towards the center of the bridge truss; *see* BRIDGE: *Cantilever Bridges.* A cantilever beam of given cross section is much weaker than a similar beam twice as long but supported at both ends. The cantilever end also deflects much more than the center of the beam supported at both ends.

**CANTINFLAS,** real name MARIO MORENO (1911– ), Mexican comedian, born in Mexico City. After leaving agricultural school he joined a *carpa,* or traveling tent show, and adopted the name Cantinflas. By 1940 he had left the carpa circuit and soon after became a popular stage comedian and later the leading Mexican motion-picture comedian. Cantinflas achieved his greatest fame in portraying fumbling characters and underdogs who, in spite of themselves,

triumph at the end. His technique in comedy is characterized by the use of nonsense words and phrases, non sequiturs, and satire. Two of his Spanish language films, *Ahí Está el Detalle* (1941; "Here's the Point") and *Ni Sangre Ni Arena* (1942; "Neither Blood Nor Sand") played to more Latin-American audiences than any other Mexican-made film. His best-known American films include *Around the World in 80 Days* (1956) and *Pepe* (1960).

**CANTON,** city of Illinois, in Fulton Co., about 23 miles S.W. of Peoria. Bituminous coal is mined. The city is an industrial and trade center for the surrounding agricultural region. Manufactures include wood products and farm implements. Pop. (1960) 13,588; (1970) 14,217.

**CANTON,** city in Ohio, and county seat of Stark Co., on Nimisillen Creek, about 15 miles S. of Akron. An important industrial center, the city contains plants engaged in the manufacture of steel ingots and bars, stainless steel, safes and vaults, motors, Diesel and gasoline engines, oil- and gas-well machinery, street-lighting standards, roller bearings, bells and gongs, vacuum cleaners, brick and tiles, enamelware, rubber products, and paper and paper products. William McKinley (q.v.), twenty-fifth President of the United States, resided in Canton after 1867, and his remains are interred there in the McKinley Memorial, constructed in 1907. Founded about 1805, Canton was incorporated as a village in 1822, as a town in 1838, and as a city in 1854. Pop. (1960) 113,631; (1970) 110,053.

**CANTON,** officially KWANGCHOW, city and seaport in the People's Republic of China, and capital of Kwangtung Province, on the Canton, or Pearl, R., at the N. edge of the delta of the Si Kiang R., 90 miles N.W. of Hong Kong. The surrounding area yields rice, sugar, tea, fruit, and silkworms. The city is an important commercial

*The Haichu Bridge in Canton, China.* China Photo Service

center, serving as a way station for cargoes bound to and from Hong Kong and inland points. Among the chief exports are tea, silk, sugar, chinaware, matting, and firecrackers. Industries include the manufacture of steel, machinery, chemicals, cotton, silk, refined sugar, paper, and jade, metal, and ivory products. The main section of the city is located on the N. bank of the Canton R., with the industrial district on the S. bank. Several hundred thousand Cantonese live in houseboats on the river. Canton was walled until 1921; since then it has been extensively rebuilt and modernized. Sun Yat-Sen University and several colleges are in Canton.

**History.** Canton was brought into the Chinese empire in the 3rd century B.C. The Portuguese began trading there in the 15th century, and were followed by British, French, and Dutch traders. Their offices were located on the island of Shameen, formerly the European quarter. Restrictions on foreign trade, imposed by the Chinese because of opium imports from India, were followed, in 1841, by a British declaration of war against China. By the terms of the Treaty of Nanking (1842), which terminated the so-called Opium War (q.v.), Canton became a port open to foreign trade, and the city was occupied by French and British troops from 1856 until 1861, when the Chinese government granted unrestricted trading and residential rights to foreign nations. Canton was a center of activity in the Chinese Revolution (1911), and in the subsequent establishment of the Chinese Republic. From 1917 until 1925 it was the headquarters for the Kuomintang (q.v.). The military forces of Japan occupied the city in October, 1938, and held it for the duration of World War II. During the Chinese civil war, Canton was the last mainland capital of Nationalist China. In October, 1949, Chinese Communist forces occupied the city. Pop. (1970 est.) 2,300,000.

**CANTON.** See SWITZERLAND: *The People: Political Divisions.*

**CANTON AND ENDERBURY ISLANDS.** See PHOENIX ISLANDS.

**CANTOR.** See JEWISH MUSIC: *Synagogue Music.*

**CANTOR, Eddie** (1892–1964), American comedian, born in New York City. Beginning his career in 1906, he worked first as a member of popular vaudeville and burlesque troupes, and later in productions of Jacob J. Schubert, Lee Shubert, and Florenz Ziegfeld (qq.v.). Cantor starred in the musical successes *Kid Boots* (1923–26), *Whoopee* (1929–30), *Kid Millions* (1934), and *Banjo Eyes* (1941). He appeared for the first time in motion pictures in 1926. His first radio program began five years later, and after

1950 he performed regularly on television. He was active in many philanthropic movements. His career was depicted in the film *The Eddie Cantor Story* (1953).

**CANTOR, Georg** (1845–1918), German mathematician, born in Saint Petersburg (now Leningrad, U.S.S.R.), of Danish parents. Cantor's family moved to Germany while he was a child, and he was educated in Frankfurt, Zürich, Berlin, and Göttingen. He taught at the University of Halle from 1869 to 1913 and was professor there after 1872. His early work dealt with the Fourier Series (*see* FOURIER, BARON JEAN BAPTISTE JOSEPH), which led to his development of a theory of irrational numbers. Cantor also formulated the theory of sets, upon which modern mathematical analysis is based. This theory extended the concept of number by introducing infinite or, as he called them, transfinite numbers; *see* INFINITE. Cantor's work was largely responsible for the subsequent critical investigation of the foundations of mathematics and mathematical logic. He wrote *Contributions to the Founding of the Theory of Transfinite Numbers* (1895–97; Eng. trans., 1915).

**CANUTE II** *or* **CNUT II** *or* **KNUT II,** known as CANUTE THE GREAT (994?–1035), King of England (1016–35), Denmark (1018–35), and Norway (1028–35). He was the son of Sweyn (q.v.), King of the Danes, and upon the death of his father in 1014 Canute was proclaimed king of England by the warriors of the Danish fleet who were then ravaging the country. The witenagemot, the English body of nobles who advised and elected kings, however, reinstated King Ethelred (q.v.), and Canute was forced to flee. He returned in 1015 with a powerful fleet. Within a year he subjugated all of England except the city of London. The witenagemot, after the death of Ethelred in 1016, elected Canute king, but the citizens of London proclaimed Edmund II (q.v.), a son of Ethelred, king. During the ensuing struggle between Canute and Edmund, the Londoners fought bravely, but in October, 1016, they were decisively defeated at Assandun (now Ashingdon, Essex). Canute and Edmund then agreed to divide the country between them, but within a month Edmund died and Canute gained the whole kingdom. His first acts were to execute some of the more powerful English chiefs and to banish the two young sons of Edmund. He increased the Danegeld, a heavy land tax, to pay his Danish warriors. To maintain order in England, he divided the kingdom into the four earldoms of Mercia, Northumberland, Wessex, and East Anglia.

Although Canute had inherited the crown of

Denmark upon the death of his brother Harold (d. 1018), he continued to live in England. He instituted a new English code of laws, and he enhanced the position of the Roman Catholic Church. Canute went to Rome in 1027 to do penance and to attend the coronation of Conrad II (q.v.), Holy Roman Emperor. Canute thus endeared himself to his Catholic subjects and ensured peace with the emperor. In 1028 Canute defeated Olaf II (q.v.), King of Norway, but instead of ruling he installed his son Sweyn (r. 1028–35) on the Norwegian throne. In 1031 Canute ended the long-standing border warfare between Northumberland and Scotland. During this era of peace he encouraged trade among his three kingdoms.

The famous legend, relating how he rebuked his flatterers by showing them that he could not order the advancing waves to stand still, was related by the English historian Henry of Huntingdon (1084?–1155).

**CANVASBACK,** North American bay or sea duck, *Aythya valisineria,* much esteemed as a table delicacy. It is named from the wavy or vermiculated dusky markings on the white feathers of its upper parts. It has a reddish-brown head and neck. It is larger than the redhead (*A. americana*), with a bill deeper at the base and larger. It nests only in the interior, being found from Minnesota and the Dakotas north to the Arctic Circle. It winters on the tidewaters of the middle and southern States. The canvasback has a length of 21 in. and weighs 3 lb. *See* DUCK.

**CANYON** (Sp. *cañon*), deep gorge created by the erosive action of a river. The best-known examples in North America are the Grand Canyon of the Colorado (q.v.) and the Grand Canyon of the Yellowstone (*see* YELLOWSTONE NATIONAL PARK).

**CANYON DE CHELLY NATIONAL MONUMENT,** region of historic interest, in N.E. Arizona, within the Navajo Indian Reservation. The monument contains Canyon de Chelly and Canyon del Muerto. The walls, decorated with pictographs, are sheer, red sandstone, and rise to a height of more than 1000 ft. above the canyon floor. On the floor and in wall caves are ruins of prehistoric cliff dwellings, some dating to the 4th century A.D. Later ruins of importance are the White House Pueblo, occupied from about 1060 to 1275, and the Mummy Cave, dating from 1253. The monument covering an area of 83,840 acres, was established in 1931, and is administered by the National Park Service (q.v.).

**CANYONLANDS NATIONAL PARK,** area of scenic interest in S.E. Utah, adjoining Glen Canyon Recreation Area (q.v.) in the S.W., including about 95 mi. of the Colorado and Green rivers. Spectacular sandstone formations line the river courses. Points of interest in the park include the Island in the Sky plateau, at the confluence of the two rivers, and Cataract Canyon on the Colorado R. Elevations range from 3600 ft. to spires and mesas over 7000 ft. high. Indian carvings in stone dating from about 900 A.D. are also found in the park. The park, covering 337,258 acres, was established in 1964. It is administered by the National Park Service (q.v.).

**CANZONE. 1.** In poetry, a short lyric poem that developed in Provence (q.v.), France, and became popular in Italy during the Middle Ages. The subject of the canzone (It., "song") was usually love, nature, or feminine beauty. In form the poem was comprised of stanzas of equal length and closed with an envoy, a shorter stanza. The number of lines in the stanzas varied from seven to twenty. The most famous writers of canzoni were the 14th-century Italians Dante Alighieri and Petrarch (qq.v.). **2.** In music, canzone denotes either the solo melody or the polyphonic vocal composition to which a literary canzone is set. The term also applies to an independent instrumental composition in a similar polyphonic style.

**CÃO, Diogo.** *See* CAM, DIOGO.

**CAPABLANCA Y GRANPERA, José Raoul** (1888–1942), Cuban chess grandmaster, born in Havana, and educated at Columbia University. He learned to play chess at the age of four and won the championship of Cuba at the age of twelve. Later, in international tournaments in Europe, he defeated a number of the best

*Canvasback,* Aythya valisineria
Arthur W. Ambler – National Audubon Society

players of the time, and established himself as a grand master. In 1921 he won the world championship from the German Emanuel Lasker (q.v.), but in 1927 Capablanca lost his title to the Russian grand master Alexander Alekhine (q.v.) in a match that lasted three months. Relying less on theory than on intuitive perceptions, intense concentration, and precise positional analysis, Capablanca was what is called a "natural player". See CHESS.

**CAPACITOR.** See CONDENSER, ELECTRICAL.

**CAPE AGULHAS** (Port., "needles"), the southernmost point of Africa, about 100 miles S.E. of the Cape of Good Hope in the Republic of South Africa. Fog, uncertain currents, and rocks make the point dangerous for ships.

**CAPE ANN,** peninsula on the N.E. coast of the United States, marking the N. limit of Massachusetts Bay, 31 miles N.E. of Boston, Mass. Two fixed lights located 900 ft. apart are visible for 19 nautical mi. The whole rocky peninsula, rich in stone quarries, projects about 10 mi. into the Atlantic Ocean. On the S. and E. shores are located many summer resorts.

**CAPE BON.** See TUNISIA: The Land.

**CAPE BRETON ISLAND,** rocky, irregularly shaped island of Canada, between the Atlantic Ocean and the Gulf of Saint Lawrence, that forms the N.E. part of the Province of Nova Scotia. The island is 110 mi. long and has a maximum width of 85 mi. It is separated from the mainland of Nova Scotia by the narrow Strait of Canso, and is divided into two parts by the Bras d'Or Lake (Fr., "Golden Arm"), a large tidal inlet of the Atlantic Ocean, and by a short ship canal connecting the lake with Saint Peters Bay on the S. The Canso Causeway, completed in 1955, connects the island by road and railway with the mainland.

The rugged scenery and cool summer climate of Cape Breton Island attract many tourists, especially to Cape Breton Highlands National Park (367 sq.mi.) in the N. Sydney, Glace Bay, and Sydney Mines are the largest towns. The island is rich in bituminous coal and iron and copper ores, and also contains deposits of slate, marble, gypsum, and limestone. Important industries are mining, lumbering, fishing, sheep farming, and the production of steel.

The Italian-born navigator and explorer John Cabot (see under CABOT) is believed to have discovered the island in 1497. In 1534 the French explorer Jacques Cartier (q.v.) called the island Breton because it resembled the French region of Brittany. The first English settlement was made in 1629 and was soon captured by the French. The island was formally assigned to

France in 1713, by the Peace of Utrecht, and renamed Île Royale (see UTRECHT, PEACE OF). At Louisbourg the French built a fortress that was believed to be the strongest in the New World. In 1745, however, during King George's War (q.v.), the fortress was seized by British colonial forces. When the war ended three years later, Cape Breton Island was again returned to France. The British in 1758, during the French and Indian War (q.v.), destroyed the fortress and gained possession of the island. Since 1763, except for the period from 1784 to 1820, when it was a separate British colony, Cape Breton Island has been united politically with Nova Scotia.

Area, 3975 sq.mi. Pop. (1971) 170,007 (chiefly of Highland Scottish descent, with about 15,000 descendants of the French and a small number of Micmac Indians).

**CAPE BUFFALO.** See BUFFALO.

**CAPE CANAVERAL,** easternmost point of a barrier beach on the E. coast of Florida about 150 miles S.E. of Jacksonville. It is part of Brevard County. Occupying the cape area and a part of Merritt Island is the John F. Kennedy Space Center, operated by the National Aeronautics and Space Administration (q.v.). Patrick Air Force Base is located on the same beach, to the S. The neighboring towns of Cocoa Beach, Titusville, and Melbourne have experienced great industrial expansion, largely space-oriented, and population growth as a result of the growth of the space center. From 1963 to 1973 the cape was known as Cape Kennedy in honor of President John F. Kennedy. See also ASTRONAUTICS.

**CAPE CHARLES,** promontory in E. Virginia, at the N.E. side of the entrance to Chesapeake Bay, comprising the southernmost part of Northampton Co. On Smith's Island, N.E. of the cape, is a lighthouse with revolving light 180 ft. above high water.

**CAPE CHELYUSKIN,** promontory in N. Siberia, on the Boris Vil'kitskiy Strait, forming the northernmost point of the Asiatic continent. It is a portion of the tundra extending northward from the Taymyr Peninsula to lat. 77°41' N.

**CAPE COAST,** city and port in Ghana, and capital of the Central Region, 80 miles W. of Accra. The city exports the products of the district, including frozen fish, cacao, coconuts, citrus fruits, corn, and cassava. It is the site of a university college. The area was settled by the Portuguese in 1610, and the city, formerly called Cape Coast Castle, is the site of an old castle and several forts. The Swedes in 1652 built the fort of Carolusberg, which passed to the Dutch

*Neils Harbour, Cape Breton Highlands National Park.*
Canadian Government Travel Bureau

in 1659 and to the British in 1667. Cape Coast was the capital of the British Gold Coast possessions until 1876, when the capital was transferred to Accra. The city was chartered in 1905. Pop. (1970) 71,594.

**CAPE COD,** peninsula of Massachusetts, co-extensive with Barnstable Co., comprising the s.e. extremity of the State, from which it is separated by the Cape Cod Canal (q.v.). The cape is surrounded by Cape Cod Bay to the N.; the Atlantic Ocean to the E.; Nantucket Sound to the s.; and Buzzards Bay to the s.w. The cape is deeply indented; in shape it resembles a flexed arm. It extends eastward about 35 mi. and then northward about 30 mi. The width varies from about 20 mi. between the towns of Sandwich and Woods Hole at the neck to a few hundred yards at the tip near the town of Provincetown (q.v.). The cape is sandy, hilly, and thickly forested in spots, and contains many lakes and ponds. Cape Cod is well known as a summer resort, and has excellent facilities for swimming, fishing, and boating. Fishing is a leading industry, notably in Provincetown, which has one of the largest and safest harbors on the Atlantic seaboard. Cranberries are the chief crop. Other towns on Cape Cod are Barnstable (q.v.), Yarmouth, Orleans, Falmouth, Bourne, and Hyan-

nis. The cape has a number of lighthouses, including Chatham Light at Chatham, and Cape Cod Light at Truro. Cape Cod was discovered and named in 1602 by the English explorer Bartholomew Gosnold (q.v.), who was impressed by the abundance of codfish in the surrounding waters. In 1620 the Pilgrim Fathers (q.v.) dropped anchor in Provincetown Harbor. In 1961 the Cape Cod National Seashore was established. It contains an area of 44,600 acres and extends about 40 mi. along the E. shore from the Long Point Lighthouse to the tip of Nauset Beach.

**CAPE COD CANAL,** sea-level ship canal built between 1909 and 1914 in s.e. Massachusetts, separating the peninsula of Cape Cod from the mainland. It connects Cape Cod Bay on the N. to Buzzards Bay on the s., a distance of 7.7 mi. The maximum width is 540 ft. and the depth is 32 ft. The approach channels at the extremities are each almost 5 mi. long. A breakwater protects the Cape Cod Bay entrance. Except for one turn, the canal is straight. It shortens the water route from New York City to Boston and eliminates the hazardous alternative route around Cape Cod. The Federal government purchased the canal from private interests in 1928, and since that time has operated it as a toll-free waterway.

**CAPE COD NATIONAL SEASHORE,** area administered by the National Park Service (q.v.), located on the outer part of Cape Cod, Barnstable County, Mass. Covering 12,000 Federally owned acres and 32,600 acres of private land, the national seashore extends for about 35 mi. from the tip of Cape Cod, near Provincetown, s. to beaches near Chatham. The area includes the entire Atlantic beach front, and also extends to Cape Cod Bay on the western side of Wellfleet Harbor. Beaches, sand dunes, marshes, ponds, and woodlands are included in the area, which was authorized in August, 1961. Facilities for bathing, picnicking, camping, and hiking are available. Headquarters are near South Wellfleet, Mass.

**CAPE COLONY.** See CAPE OF GOOD HOPE, PROVINCE OF THE.

**CAPE FEAR,** promontory in North Carolina, on the s. tip of Smith Island, jutting into the Atlantic Ocean, near the mouth of the Cape Fear R. It was so named because of the treacherous waters surrounding it. A lighthouse stands on Cape Fear.

**CAPE FEAR,** river of North Carolina, rising in the N.-central part of the State, flowing S.E. for about 200 mi. before emptying into the Atlantic Ocean. The river is formed by the junction of the Haw and Deep rivers. The largest tributaries are the South R. from the E., and the North East Cape Fear R. from the N.E. It is the longest river wholly within the State, and is navigable to Fayetteville, 150 mi. inland. Rice growing is an important industry along the lower region of the river.

**CAPE FINISTERRE** (Lat., "Land's End"), promontory in Spain, N.W. extremity of the Iberian Peninsula, extending into the Atlantic Ocean. It is noted as the scene of two British naval victories over France, on May 3, 1747 in the War of the Austrian Succession (see SUCCESSION WARS: War of the Austrian Succession) and on July 22, 1805 in the Napoleonic Wars (q.v.).

**CAPE FLATTERY,** high promontory in Washington State, extending into the Pacific Ocean, at the s. side of the entrance to Juan de Fuca Strait. It was discovered by the British explorer and navigator Captain James Cook (q.v.) in 1778, on his last voyage. When the American explorers Meriwether Lewis and William Clark (qq.v.) arrived at the cape in 1806, it was inhabited by the Makah Indians. In 1855 the tribe ceded all their lands to the Federal government, except for the cape and a small area adjacent; a Makah reservation still occupies this land.

**CAPE GIRARDEAU,** city of Missouri, in Cape Girardeau Co., on the Mississippi R., about 100 miles S.E. of Saint Louis. Cape Girardeau is in a fertile region producing general farm crops, fruits, livestock, dairy products, and timber. Industries in the city are the manufacture of shoes, lumber and lumber products, cement, tobacco, foundry products, electrical appliances, and surgical cotton goods. Cape Girardeau is the site of the Southeast Missouri State College and of Saint Vincent's Academy, founded in 1843 and one of the oldest Catholic schools w. of the Mississippi. Cape Girardeau was founded about 1793 by a French-Canadian trader as an Indian trading post, in what was then Spanish territory; it was chartered as a city in 1843. Pop. (1960) 24,947; (1970) 31,282.

**CAPE GUARDAFUI** (Anc. *Aromata*), promontory in the Somali Republic, and most easterly point of the African continent. Cape Guardafui is situated on a promontory between the Gulf of Aden and the Indian Ocean. The cape forms the tip of the so-called horn of Africa.

**CAPE HATTERAS,** promontory of North Carolina, projecting into the Atlantic Ocean from Hatteras Island, a long, narrow, sandy beach separated from the mainland of North Carolina by Pamlico Sound. Shoals and frequent gales and storms make the surrounding waters dangerous for navigation. Southbound coasting vessels are apt to be crowded toward the cape by the E. and W. vibrations of the Gulf Stream, which is about 20 mi. to the E. Cape Hatteras National Seashore (28,500 acres) is noted for points of historical interest, including the Cape Hatteras Lighthouse, built in 1870.

**CAPE HORN** (Sp. *Cabo de Hornos*), promontory in Chile, in the Terra del Fuego archipelago, on Horn Island. It marks the southernmost point of South America and extends into Drake Passage, the antarctic strait connecting the South Atlantic and South Pacific oceans. The rocky terrain of the cape rises to a height of 1391 ft. Storms, strong currents, and icebergs make passage around the cape extremely hazardous. During the time of sailing ships, hundreds of vessels were wrecked while "rounding the horn". The Dutch navigator Willem Cornelis Schouten (1567?–1625), the first to sail around the cape (1616), named it for his birthplace, Hoorn, Netherlands.

**ČAPEK,** name of two Czech brothers, who were prominent in the arts.

**Josef Čapek** (1887–1945), painter and writer, born in Hronov. Čapek studied painting in Prague and Paris. Although his earliest paintings were done in the cubist style, Čapek later developed an original primitive style; *see* CUBISM. He illustrated some of the books of his younger brother, Karel Čapek (see below) and collaborated with him in the writing of short stories and a play. As an art critic Josef defended his painting style in *The Art of Primitive Nations* (1938). He also wrote the play, *The Land of Many Names* (1923; Eng. trans., 1926); many short stories; and two short novels. His prose was influenced by surrealism (q.v.). Čapek was taken prisoner by the Germans when they invaded Czechoslovakia in 1939, and died in the concentration camp (q.v.) at Belsen, Germany.

**Karel Čapek** (1890–1938), novelist, playwright, and theatrical producer, born in Malé Svatoňovice, and educated at the University of Prague. Čapek was a close friend of the first Czech president, Tomáš Garrigue Masaryk (*see under* MASARYK), and together they worked to preserve the Czech nation after World War I; *see* CZECHOSLOVAKIA: *History*. Simultaneously Čapek was an editor for a Prague newspaper, founder and director of the Vinohradsky Art Theater in Prague, political essayist, playwright, and novelist.

Čapek is best known for his plays, the most famous of which is *R.U.R.* (1921; Eng. trans., 1923), a dramatic fantasy in which man is dehumanized by the machine age. *R.U.R.* stands for "Rossum's Universal Robots", and is the source of the English word "robot". Čapek is also well known for two other dramas: *The Insect Play* (1921; Eng. trans., 1923), known in the United States as *The World We Live In,* a satire that foretells the evils of totalitarianism; and *Power and Glory* (1937; Eng. trans., 1938), an attack on dictatorship. His novels include fanciful romances, science fiction, and a philosophical trilogy. Among his other writings are short stories, some of which he wrote with Josef, travel sketches, and impassioned political essays.

**CAPE KENNEDY.** *See* CAPE CANAVERAL.

**CAPELIN** *or* **CAPLIN,** common name for two species of small, slender, saltwater fish of the Smelt family (Osmeridae): the Atlantic capelin, *Mallotus villosus,* found in the north Atlantic and Arctic oceans, and the Pacific capelin, *Mallotus catervarius,* found in the north Pacific Ocean. Capelin are silvery in appearance, averaging about 8 in. long. They spawn on gravelly beaches by riding the breakers to the shore. Important as food fish, capelin are also used as bait for cod fishing, and as fertilizer. *See* SMELT.

**CAPELLA,** first-magnitude star in the northern constellation Auriga. It is also known as Aurigae. A giant yellow star with a spectrum much like that of the sun, it is one of the brightest stars visible in the sky. Capella is a spectroscopic binary (double star) with a rotation period of 104 days; *see* STARS: *Double Stars.* Capella is approximately 40 light-years from earth and is much larger and brighter than the sun. In Roman mythology Capella was the she-goat that suckled the infant god Jupiter (q.v.).

**CAPELLA, Martianus.** *See* ENCYCLOPEDIA.

**CAPE MAY,** city in New Jersey, at the S. tip of Cape May Co., about 40 miles S.W. of Atlantic City. It is one of the oldest seashore resorts on the New Jersey coast. The harbor of about 500 acres, with an average depth of 35 ft., is the only port of refuge on the State's coast S. of Sandy Hook. The Cape May Naval Air Base and the Witmer Stone Sanctuary for migratory wild fowl are near the city. The history of Cape May as a fashionable summer resort dates back to the beginning of the 19th century. It was first incorporated in 1848 as the Borough of Cape Island. In 1851 it became the City of Cape Island and in 1875, the City of Cape May. Pop. (1970) 4392.

**CAPE MAY,** southernmost point of New Jersey, on the N. side of the entrance to Delaware Bay. It has a revolving light 160 ft. above sea level.

**CAPE OF GOOD HOPE,** name of two promontories. **1.** Northern extremity of Vogelkop Peninsula, West Irian (West New Guinea), Republic of Indonesia, lying about 20 miles S. of the equator. **2.** Headland on the S.W. coast of the Province of the Cape of Good Hope, Republic of South Africa, about 30 miles S. of Cape Town. Rising 840 ft. above sea level, the headland marks the turning point for vessels plying between the South Atlantic and Indian oceans. It is erroneously regarded as the extremity of the continent; Cape Agulhas (q.v.), about 92 mi. to the S.E., is the southernmost point of Africa. The Cape of Good Hope was discovered by the Portuguese navigator Bartholomeu Dias (q.v.) in 1488 and named by him *Cabo Tormentoso* (Port. "Cape of Storms"). It was renamed *Cabo da Bõa Esperança* (Port. "Cape of Good Hope") by John II (q.v.), King of Portugal, because of the commercial importance of the new route to the East. The cape was not rounded again by a European until 1497, when the Portuguese navigator Vasco da Gama (q.v.) made the first voyage from Europe to India.

**CAPE OF GOOD HOPE, PROVINCE OF THE,** *or* CAPE PROVINCE, formerly CAPE COLONY, largest province of the Republic of South Africa, occupying the S. extremity of Africa, and bordered on the N. by Botswana, on the N.E. and E. by the provinces of Natal, Transvaal, and Orange Free State, as well as Lesotho (formerly Basuto-

*A beach scene at Hout Bay in the Cape of Good Hope Province.*  South African Tourist Office

land), and on the N.W. South-West Africa. The province includes British Bechuanaland, Griqualand West, and Transkei Province. Cape Town is the provincial capital and the largest city. Other cities in Cape Province are Port Elizabeth, East London, Kimberley, Uitenhage, and Paarl. Area of province, 278,380 sq.mi.

**Physical Features.** Physiographically, the north-central interior forms part of the Southern Plateau of Africa. Averaging about 3000 ft. in height and consisting chiefly of rolling veld, this region is demarcated on the S. by a series of steep ranges, including the Drakensberg and Stormberg mountains. Mont aux Sources, highest peak in the Drakensberg Mts., has an elevation of 10,822 ft. The region adjacent to these ranges on the S. is a vast, barren tableland, known as the Karoo (q.v.), which varies between 1000 and 3000 ft. in elevation. Two parallel mountain chains, with numerous peaks over 6000 ft., occupy most of the region S. of the

Karoo. An upland plain fringes the coast, which is about 1300 mi. in length. The E. coast is singularly regular, but the S. and W. coasts have many indentations, notably Saint Francis, Walker, and Saint Helena bays. Cape Agulhas, about 92 miles S.E. of the Cape of Good Hope, is the southernmost extremity of Africa. Among the principal rivers are the Orange, which rises in Lesotho and flows in a generally westerly direction partly along the N.W. boundary, and the Olifants; both empty into the Atlantic Ocean.

**Climate.** Climatic conditions are marked by wide seasonal and regional variations. Although in the vicinity of Cape Town the annual average temperature is about 62° F., generally lower temperatures prevail in the upland areas, particularly during the winter season. Summer temperatures in these areas average about 90° F. Precipitation in the Karoo and along most of the W. coastal region is negligible, averaging under 10 in. annually. Average annual rainfall throughout the remainder of the province, however, ranges from about 20 to 40 in.

**People.** The Bantu (q.v.), one of the principal Negroid peoples of Africa, comprise a bare majority of the population. Persons of European origin number more than 1,100,000. This section of the population consists predominantly of descendants of early Dutch settlers and of later English, French, German, and Scandinavian immigrants. Mixed Negroid and Negroid European peoples make up the remainder of the population. Pop. (1970) 7,110,896.

**Economy.** The principal industry is the raising of livestock, extensive areas being highly suitable for pasturage and grazing. The most important pastoral enterprises are the raising of cattle, sheep, goats, ostriches, horses, and donkeys. Crop cultivation is limited largely to areas in the E., S., and S.E. Among the chief crops of the province are wine grapes, olives, citrus and other fruits, oats, barley, wheat, and tobacco. Apiculture (beekeeping) is another important enterprise.

Diamond mining is a major source of wealth; the diamond mines in the vicinity of Kimberley are the most productive in the world. Blue asbestos and tin are mined also. Among other leading industries are wine and brandy making, fruit canning, food processing, brewing, fishing, lumbering, and the manufacture of textiles, building materials, furniture, shoes, and metal products.

**History.** European colonization of the region comprising present-day Cape Province began in 1652, when the Dutch East India Company (q.v.) established a settlement on Table Bay, near the site of modern Cape Town. Growing numbers of Dutch emigrants arrived in the colony during the 18th century. In 1795, during the French Revolution, British military forces seized the colony in the name of the Dutch stadtholder William V, Prince of Orange (1748–1806), who had fled to Great Britain after French troops occupied the Netherlands. The region was returned to Dutch control in 1803, under terms of the Treaty of Amiens; see AMIENS, TREATY OF. Hostilities were renewed, and the British again seized the colony, which was formally ceded to Great Britain in 1814.

Various reforms, including the abolition (1833) of slavery, were instituted by the British, but the first few decades of their rule were marked by a series of wars with the Kaffirs (q.v.) and other Bantu tribes, and by growing antagonisms between the Dutch, or Boers (q.v.), and the British sections of the population. A mass withdrawal from the Cape Province by angered Dutch farmers led to the establishment of Transvaal and the Orange Free State (qq.v.).

In 1865 Kaffraria, now Transkei Province, homeland of the Kaffirs, was annexed. The discovery (1867) of diamonds in Griqualand West, a part of Transvaal, tremendously stimulated the industrial and population growth of the colony. Cape Colony annexed Griqualand West in 1871 and Transvaal in 1877, provoking profound hostility among the Boers.

During the premiership (1890–96) of the British financier and political leader Cecil John Rhodes (q.v.), native uprisings were suppressed in several frontier areas and British Bechuanaland was annexed. The climactic development of the period was an abortive British attempt, in 1895, to overthrow the Transvaal republic; see JAMESON, SIR LEANDER STARR. As a result of the attack on Transvaal, relations between the British and Boers deteriorated steadily during the next three years, finally culminating in 1899 in war; see SOUTH AFRICAN WAR. British annexation in 1900 of Transvaal and Orange Free State and the subsequent collapse of the Boers created conditions favorable to the establishment of a federal dominion in South Africa. Cape Colony figured prominently in the ensuing movement for such a dominion. On May 31, 1910, the British colonies in South Africa were confederated as the Union of South Africa (now the Republic of South Africa), Cape Colony becoming the Province of the Cape of Good Hope.

See SOUTH AFRICA, REPUBLIC OF: *History.*

**CAPE PRINCE OF WALES,** westernmost point of the mainland of Alaska and of the North American continent, separated by the Bering Strait from Cape Dezhnev, Siberia, which is 55 mi. to the N.W. Cape Prince of Wales is 100 miles N. of the city of Nome, Alaska.

*Caper,* Capparis spinosa                    Edith A. Schmitz

**CAPER,** common name for a low, spiny shrub of the Mediterranean area, *Capparis spinosa,*

123

belonging to the family Capparidaceae. A round-leaved bush with white flowers, it grows to a height of about 3 ft. Although not native to the United States, it is sometimes grown in southern gardens. The unopened buds of the flowers, known also as capers, are pickled in vinegar and used as a condiment and an ingredient of sauces. They are gray-green in color and have a pungent taste.

**CAPERCAILLIE** *or* **CAPERCAILZIE,** common names for a grouse of Europe and western Asia, *Tetrao urogallus,* also known as the wood grouse or cock of the wood. The male, which is the largest of old-world grouse, grows to a length of about 3 ft. and may weigh 12 lb. or more. It has black plumage with metallic green on the breast and is distinguished from other grouse by a red circle around each eye. The female, which grows only to 1 or 2 ft. in length, is mottled brown above and has a reddish-brown breast. The birds live in pine forests where they subsist on berries, seeds, worms, and insects in the summer and on pine shoots in the winter. Like most grouse, the male capercaillie is polygamous and may have as many as twelve mates. The female makes a nest on the ground and in it lays from six to twelve yellow eggs. *See also* GROUSE.

**CAPERNAUM,** town in ancient Palestine, on the N.W. shore of the Sea of Galilee (now Lake Tiberias), about 6 miles N.E. of the modern town of Tiberias, Israel. Excavations begun at the village of Tell Hum in 1905 identified it with Capernaum, the home of Jesus Christ during much of his ministry. It was also the home of his first disciples Saint Andrew, Saint Matthew, and Saint Peter (qq.v.). A hill nearby is thought to have been the site of the Sermon on the Mount (q.v.). Today only a few ruins of the ancient town remain, among them a synagogue built

*The ruins of the synagogue in Capernaum where Jesus supposedly taught.* **Trans World Airlines**

between the 2nd and 4th centuries A.D. In the late 19th century Franciscan monks restored part of the synagogue and built a monastery, which they still maintain. *See* JESUS CHRIST.

**CAPE SABLE. 1.** The southernmost point of the mainland of the United States and of the State of Florida, extending into Florida Bay. **2.** The southernmost point of Nova Scotia, at the s. end of Cape Sable Island, extending into the Atlantic Ocean.

**CAPET,** family name of the dynasty of kings that ruled France from 987 to 1328. In 987, upon the death of Louis V, the last of the Carolingian (q.v.) kings of France (*see under* LOUIS), Hugh Capet, Duke of France and Count of Paris (*see* HUGH CAPET), was elected king by the nobility with the aid of the clergy. The feudal domain of the Capet family was Île de France (q.v.). The kings of the Capetian dynasty greatly strengthened the royal power in France by insisting on the principles of heredity, primogeniture, and indivisibility of crown lands. Shortly after Hugh became king, he had his son Robert crowned as Robert II (q.v.), known as the Pious. Hugh appointed Robert as his associate, and this practice of the father having his eldest son rule with him was followed until the reign of Philip II (q.v.), known as Philip Augustus. The Capetian dynasty secured direct overlordship of almost all of France by the process of incorporating additional fiefs, large and small, with their own territories. In 1328 Charles IV (*see under* CHARLES: *France*) died without male heirs; the Capetians were succeeded by the Valois, a younger branch of the Capet family which ruled France until 1589; *see* VALOIS, HOUSE OF. *See also* FRANCE: *History: The Capetian Dynasty.*

**CAPE TOWN,** city and legislative capital of the Republic of South Africa, and capital of Cape of Good Hope Province, on the s.w. side of Table Bay, along the base of Table Mt. (3563 ft.), about 30 miles N. of the Cape of Good Hope. The principal port of South Africa, Cape Town has an extensive artificial harbor, well equipped with modern cargo-handling facilities. It is a regular port of call for freight and passenger vessels operating from all parts of the world and is served by several railroad lines and by domestic and international air lines. Gold, diamonds, and citrus fruits are among the chief exports. Shipbuilding, diamond cutting, printing, food processing, and the manufacture of clothing, plastics, and leather goods are important industries. In addition to being the second-largest industrial area in South Africa, Cape Town is also a popular vacation resort, noted for natural scenic beauty and fine beaches.

A view of Cape Town from a cable station on Table Mt.
South African Tourist Corp.

Cultural attractions in Cape Town include theater, opera, ballet, and a symphony orchestra. Points of interest include the Castle, the oldest structure in the city, begun in 1666; the South African Museum, founded in 1855; and the Michaelis Collection, which houses Dutch and Flemish paintings of the 16th–18th centuries. On the southern outskirts of the city is the official residence of the premier of the republic. Nearby are the University of Cape Town, founded in 1873, and the South African Astronomical Observatory, founded in 1972.

The oldest city of European origin in South Africa, Cape Town was settled in 1652 by the Dutch. The British held it from 1795 to 1803, during the Napoleonic Wars (q.v.), and obtained permanent possession in 1806. In 1910, when the British Cape of Good Hope colony was made a province of the Union of South Africa, Cape Town, capital of the colony, became also the seat of the Union legislative body. Pop. (greater city; 1970 prelim.) 825,752.

**CAPE TRAFALGAR,** low promontory on the s. coast of Spain, about 29 miles N.W. of Tarifa, at the w. entrance to the Strait of Gibraltar. It is memorable for the great naval victory obtained off its shores by the British fleet under Admiral Horatio Nelson (q.v.) over the combined fleets of France and Spain under French Vice-Admiral Pierre Villeneuve (1763–1806), on Oct. 21, 1805. Nelson was mortally wounded at this battle.

**CAPE VERDE,** republic, made up of an island group in the Atlantic Ocean. The ten islands and five islets that constitute the group are about 320 mi. due w. of Cape Verde, w. Africa. The principal islands are São Tiago (or Santiago), Maio, Brava, Fogo, São Vicente, Santo Antão, São Nicolau, Santa Luzia, Sal, and Boa Vista. Volcanic in origin, the group is generally mountainous. Pico do Cano (9281 ft.), an active volcano on Fogo, is the highest point in the islands.

Fishing and farming are the chief industries. Other industries include sugar refining, fish processing, and the manufacture of cotton goods, distilled liquors, and straw hats. Among the leading exports are coffee, sugar, millet, fish, livestock, and hides. Coal, petroleum, wine, tobacco, textiles, machinery, and foodstuffs are important imports. A large majority of the population is made up of Negroes and persons of Negroid-European ancestry. The capital and largest town is Praia (pop. 1970, 4054) on São Tiago. Porto Grande, on São Vicente, is an important fueling station for ocean vessels.

**History.** The islands were discovered in the 1450's, possibly by Alvise da Ca Da Mosto (1432?–1511), in the service of Henry (q.v.), called Henry the Navigator, Prince of Portugal. The islands were made crown property of Portugal by King Emanuel (q.v.) in 1495. The Portuguese brought large numbers of black African slaves to the islands, which were uninhabited when discovered, and rapidly developed their resources. Slavery was abolished between 1857 and 1876. Cape Verde became independent on July 5, 1975. Area, 1557 sq.mi.; pop. (1974 est.) 290,000.

**CAPE WRATH,** promontory on the N.W. extremity of Scotland, 368 ft. high, extending into the Atlantic Ocean. It is noted for its wildness and grandeur. The lighthouse on the cape is visible for 27 mi.

**CAP-HAÏTIEN,** known as LE CAP, city and seaport in Haiti, and capital of Nord Department, on the Bahia de Manzanillo, an inlet of the Atlantic Ocean, about 80 miles N.N.E. of Port-au-Prince. Cap-Haïtien has a spacious harbor and is an export center for coffee, cocoa, hides, honey, and logwood. In the 17th century the Spaniards built on the site of Cap-Haïtien a settlement that became a French possession in 1697. Under the French, who made it the capital of their colony of Saint-Domingue, it was a flourishing town, referred to as Little Paris. From 1811 to 1820 Cap-Haïtien was the capital of Henri Christophe (q.v.), King of Haiti, when he ruled northern Haiti. The town was almost destroyed by an earthquake in 1842. Pop. (1971) 43,559.

**CAPILLARIES,** minute blood vessels that form the connection between the arteries and the veins. These tiny vessels vary in diameter from 0.0005 in. to about 0.008 in., and are present in great numbers throughout the entire body. The walls of capillaries are exceedingly thin and readily permeable. They are surrounded by lymph, and there is a constant interchange between the substances in the blood within the capillaries and the waste products in the body tissues and lymph (q.v.) outside. It is thus that the processes of nutrition and elimination are carried on, and the exchange of oxygen and carbon dioxide takes place. Lymph capillaries assist the blood capillaries in this process.

**CAPILLARITY,** elevation or depression of the surface of a liquid where it is in contact with a solid, such as the sides of a tube. This phenomenon is an exception to the hydrostatic law that a liquid seeks its own level; see FLUID MECHANICS: *Fluid Statics or Hydrostatics.* It is most marked in capillary tubes (Lat. *capillus,* "hair"), that is, tubes of very small diameter. Capillarity depends upon the forces created by surface tension and by wetting of the sides of the tube. If the forces of adhesion of the liquid to the solid (wetting) exceed the forces of cohesion within the liquid (surface tension), the surface of the liquid will be concave, and the liquid will rise up the sides of the tube; that is, it will rise above the hydrostatic level. This action is typified by water in clean glass tubes. If the forces of cohesion exceed the forces of adhesion, the surface of the liquid will be convex, and the liquid will be repelled from the sides of the tube; that is, it will fall below the hydrostatic level. This action is typified by water in greasy glass (in which the adhesion is small) and by mercury in clean glass (in which the cohesion is great). The absorption of water in a sponge and the rise of molten wax in a wick are familiar examples of capillary rise. Water rises in soil partly by capillarity.

**CAPITAL,** in architecture, crown of a column (q.v.) above the shaft and below the entablature.

**CAPITAL,** accumulation of wealth (q.v.) used to create additional wealth. In ordinary usage, the term capital denotes goods and money devoted to business purposes as distinguished from goods consumed and money spent for personal satisfaction. Thus a businessman regards the land, buildings, equipment, inventory, and raw materials used in his business, as well as the holdings of securities and bank balances available for business, as capital. His home and its furnishings, or the other goods that he and his family may consume for their personal enjoyment, or the money set aside for purchasing such goods, are not considered by him as capital.

In the more precise usage of accounting (q.v.), capital is defined as the stock of property owned by an individual or corporation at a given time, as distinguished from the income derived from that property during a given period. A business firm accordingly has a capital account (frequently called a balance sheet), which is a report of the assets of the firm at a specified time, and an income account, which is a reckoning of the flow of goods and of claims against goods during a specified period.

Among 19th-century economists capital designated only that segment of business wealth that was the product of past industry. Wealth that is not produced, such as land or ore deposits, was excluded from the definition. Income from capital (so defined) was called profit, or interest, whereas the income from natural resources was called rent. Among contemporary economists, for whom capital means simply the aggregate of goods used in the production of other goods, this distinction is no longer made.

The forms of capital can be distinguished in various ways. One common distinction is between fixed and circulating capital. Fixed capital consists of all the more or less durable means of production, such as land, buildings, and machinery. Circulating capital comprises production goods capable of only a single service, such as raw materials and fuel, and the funds required to pay wages and other claims against the enterprise.

Businessmen frequently categorize all of a firm's assets that can be converted readily into cash, such as inventories of finished goods and negotiable securities, as liquid capital. By contrast, all the relatively inconvertible assets, such as plant and equipment, are considered frozen capital. See ACCOUNTING: Assets.

Another important distinction is between productive capital, or capital goods, and financial capital. Machines, raw materials, and other physical goods constitute productive capital; claims against these goods, such as corporate securities and accounts receivable, are financial capital. Although destruction of productive capital reduces productive capacity, destruction of financial capital merely changes the distribution of income.

**Theories of Capital.** The 18th-century French economists known as physiocrats were the first to attempt a serious analysis of capital (see ECONOMICS). Their work was developed by the British economist Adam Smith (q.v.) and

emerged as the classic theory of capital after further refinements by the British economist David Ricardo (q.v.). According to the classic theory, capital is a store of values created by labor. Part of capital consists of consumers' goods used to sustain the workers engaged in producing items for future consumption. Part comprises producers' goods channeled into further production for the sake of expected future returns. The use of capital goods raises labor productivity, making it possible to create a surplus above the requirements for sustaining the labor force. This surplus constitutes the interest or profit paid to capital. Interest and profits become additions to capital when they are plowed back into production.

The German revolutionist Karl Marx (q.v.) and other socialist writers accepted the classic view of capital with one major qualification. They regarded as capital only the productive goods that yield income independently of the exertions of the owner. An artisan's tools and a small farmer's land holding are not capital in this sense. The socialists held that capital comes into being as a determining force in society when a small body of men, the capitalists, own most of the means of production and a much larger body of men, the workers, receive only bare subsistence as their reward for operating the means of production for the benefit of the owners.

In the mid-19th century the British economists Nassau William Senior and John Stuart Mill (qq.v.) and others, became dissatisfied with the classic theory, especially because it lent itself so readily to socialist purposes. To replace it, they advanced a psychological theory of capital based on a systematic inquiry into the motives for frugality or abstinence. Starting with the assumption that satisfactions from present consumption are psychologically preferable to delayed satisfactions, they argued that capital originates in abstinence from consumption by persons hopeful of a future return to reward their abstinence. Because such people are willing to forgo present consumption, productive power can be diverted from making consumers' goods to making the means of further production, consequently, the productive capacity of the nation is enlarged. Therefore, just as physical labor justifies wages, abstinence justifies interest and profit.

Inasmuch as the abstinence theory rested on subjective considerations, it did not provide an adequate basis for objective economic analysis. It could not explain, in particular, why a rate of interest or profit should be what it actually was at any given time.

To remedy the deficiencies of the abstinence theory, the Austrian economist Eugen Böhm-Bawerk (1851–1914), the British economist Alfred Marshall (q.v.), and others, attempted to fuse that theory with the classic theory of capital. They agreed with the abstinence theorists that the prospect of future returns motivates individuals to abstain from consumption and to use part of their income to promote production, but they added, in line with classic theory, that the amount of returns depends on the gains in productivity resulting from accretions of capital to the productive process. Accretions of capital make production more roundabout, thus causing greater delays before returns are realized. The amount of income saved, and therefore the amount of capital formed, would accordingly depend, it was held, on the balance struck between the desire for present satisfaction from consumption and the desire for the future gains expected from a more roundabout production process. The American economist Irving Fisher (q.v.) was among those who contributed to refining this eclectic theory of capital.

The British economist John Maynard Keynes (q.v.) rejected the theory because it failed to explain the discrepancy between money saved and capital formed. Although, according to the eclectic theory and, indeed, all previous theories of capital, savings should always equal investments, Keynes showed that the decision to invest in capital goods is a quite separate decision from the one to save. If investment appears unpromising of profit, saving still may continue at about the same rate, but a strong "liquidity preference" will appear that will cause individuals, business firms, and banks to hoard their savings instead of investing them. The prevalence of a liquidity preference causes unemployment of capital, which, in turn, results in unemployment of labor.

**History of Capital.** Although theories of capital are of relatively recent origin, capital itself has existed in civilized communities since antiquity. In the ancient empires of the Middle East and to a larger degree in the Greco-Roman world, a considerable amount of capital, in the form of simple tools and equipment, was employed to produce textiles, pottery, glassware, metal objects, and many other products that were sold in international markets. The decline of trade after the fall of the Roman Empire led to less specialization in the division of labor and a reduced use of capital in production. Medieval economies engaged almost wholly in subsistence agriculture and were therefore essentially noncapitalist. Trade began to revive during the time of the Crusades (q.v.). The revival was accelerated throughout the period of exploration and colonization that began late in the 15th century. Expanding trade fostered greater division of labor and mechanization of production and therefore a growth of capital. The flow of gold and silver from the New World facilitated the transfer and accumulation of capital, laying the groundwork for the Industrial Revolution (q.v.). With the Industrial Revolution, production became increasingly roundabout and dependent on the use of large amounts of capital. The role of capital in the economies of western Europe and North America was so crucial that the socioeconomic organization prevailing in these areas from the 18th century through the first half of the 20th century became known as the capitalist system or capitalism.

In the early stages of the evolution of capitalism, investments in plant and equipment were relatively small, and merchant or circulating capital, that is, goods in transit, was the preponderant form of capital. As industry developed, industrial or fixed capital, for example, capital frozen in mills, factories, railroads, and other industrial and transportation facilities, became dominant. Late in the 19th and early in the 20th centuries financial capital in the form of claims to the ownership of capital goods of all sorts became increasingly important. By creating, acquiring, and controlling such claims, financiers and bankers exercised great influence on production and distribution. After the Great Depression of the 1930's, financial control of most capitalist economies was superseded in part by state control. A large segment of the national income (q.v.) of the United States, Great Britain, and various other countries flows through government, which exerts a great influence in regulating that flow, thereby determining the amounts and kinds of capital formed.

Also, as capital has become more plentiful, the influence of those who control it has declined. When land is plentiful, as in early America, the power of the landholder is less, and when labor is plentiful, as in the late 19th century, its relative power is less, unless it is somehow monopolized. Today, in this country, there is more capital than the world has ever known. Therefore, like the other factors of production when they were plentiful, it is treated with less respect. The importance of the factors of production to one another keeps changing. Government supervision, of course, affects the relationship. *See* CAPITALISM; LABOR. D.L.K.

**CAPITALISM,** in economics, the order prevailing since the 17th century in western Europe, North America, and, to a varying extent, in numerous other regions into which western European culture has penetrated. Capitalism, known also popularly as the "free-enterprise system", is distinguished from other past and contemporary economic orders by certain specific characteristics; its most distinctive single feature is private ownership of most capital (q.v.), particularly the factories and other industrial production facilities.

The term "capitalism" has come into general use only since the beginning of the 20th century. The word was not known to such 18th-century pioneers of economics as the British economists David Ricardo and Adam Smith (qq.v.), who were among the first to analyze the order systematically. The term was introduced about the middle of the 19th century by the German socialist and economist Karl Marx (q.v.), a revolutionary opponent of the existing order. Nineteenth-century nonsocialists were slow to adopt Marx's designation, but most contemporary economists accept it as valid and useful.

**Characteristics of Capitalism.** Certain features of capitalism originated in remote antiquity and still prevail in various primitive economies. The modern capitalist economy, however, invariably exhibits a distinctive combination of characteristics. Besides the private ownership of production facilities, these characteristics include a developed system of markets, in which purchase and sale by private persons and business firms are the chief means of distributing goods and services. Capitalism employs the universal use of money as a medium of exchange and as a measure of value, the private accumulation of money by saving and the practice of lending and borrowing money at interest. It also makes use of the sale of labor power for monetary compensation by workers who are legally free to accept or decline any offer of employment, the legal freedom of anyone who will risk his money in an enterprise, or who can persuade others to do so, to undertake most kinds of production or distribution, the rapid advance of technology, and the wide use of these advances by business enterprises.

These traits distinguish a modern capitalist economy from a primitive economy, such as that of certain tribes of South American Indians who sustain themselves by hunting, and from the economy of simple agricultural communities in which households derive most of their material necessities from their own land and labor.

On a larger scale, modern capitalism may be distinguished from the more static medieval economy in which the principal form of productive property was land in the possession of hereditary landlords, and in which membership in hereditary social classes determined the status and occupations of most persons. During the feudal era the dominant economic unit was the nearly self-sustaining manor, with its serfs bound to the land. Products were distributed within the manor predominantly on the basis of right and custom rather than by purchase and sale. Persons who accumulated money were likely either to hoard it or to spend it for luxuries instead of investing it in productive enterprises. The lending of money at interest was contrary to the prevailing ethical code. Even guilds of craftsmen or merchants, with their rigid system of masters, journeymen, and apprentices, with their monopolies (see MONOPOLY AND COMPETITION), and with their tradition-bound regulation of prices and qualities, were scarcely capitalistic in the modern sense. See FEUDALISM; GUILD. Nonetheless, private merchants existed and prospered in medieval Europe, as did professional moneylenders.

Capitalism is not a system in the sense that someone invented it as a complete whole and obtained its adoption by appeals to self-interest or reason; rather, it is the outcome of a long process of growth, more rapid during some periods than in others. Having changed radically since it replaced the feudal system of society, capitalism is in some respects still changing, and is not in exactly the same form in all capitalistic countries.

**Development of Capitalism.** Economic historians usually distinguish six stages of capitalism, namely, ancient, early-modern, mercantilist, industrial, finance, and welfare, or state, capitalism. Ancient capitalism originated during the 5th millennium B.C. in Mesopotamia and Egypt and spread to the rest of the ancient Middle East, to the Greek city-states, and to the Roman Empire. Early-modern capitalism arose in western Europe about the 13th century and, after centuries of slow development, evolved into the European mercantilist capitalism which reached its height in the 16th and 17th centuries. Industrial capitalism matured in Great Britain during the 18th century (see GREAT BRITAIN: Economy) and became dominant throughout the Western world in the 19th century, but it was partly superseded toward the end of that century by finance capitalism, which remained ascendant through the first third of the 20th century. After the Depression of the 1930's (see BUSINESS CYCLE), finance capitalism was in part replaced by welfare capitalism, the form that has prevailed since the late 1950's in the countries of Western Europe, the United States, and some members of the Commonwealth of Nations (q.v.).

**Early-Modern Capitalism.** The origins of modern capitalism may be traced to the 13th century, when a revival of international trade, initiated in part by the Crusades (q.v.), began to foreshadow the overthrow of the subsistence economies of feudal Europe. In time social and economic forces transformed the medieval world from a static, rigid agricultural society into a culture hospitable to capitalistic enterprise.

Fully as influential as economic forces in preparing the ground for modern capitalism were the concurrent revolutions in ideas known as the Renaissance and the Reformation (qq.v.). The humanist outlook that characterized the Renaissance grew out of the rediscovery of ancient Greek philosophy and literature, in which life was regarded as an end in itself. The revival and diffusion of humanist thought eroded the medieval belief that life was but a short testing period determining whether the individual soul would be saved or damned after death. The new outlook affirmed instead the desirability of material advancement and the possibility of improving conditions among the populace. The revival of secular thought and classical learning during the Renaissance led to the establishment of universities, encouraged original thought, and animated the spirit of scientific discovery. The art of navigation was advanced by the rise of modern astronomy and the development of the mariner's compass. Diffusion of knowledge was aided by the invention of printing presses with movable type; see TYPE-SETTING. For reliable knowledge of man's natural environment, men turned from reliance on authority to direct observation and experiment, and so began the rapid advance in science and technology essential to the rise of modern industry. Political philosophers stressed the rights of individuals, thus laying the basis of a social order which recognized freedom of contract between individuals, as opposed to the fixed hereditary relationships characteristic of feudalism. These and other related developments helped to prepare the way for private enterprise and for free wage labor (q.v.). See also POLITICAL THEORY.

Through its emphasis on individual conscience, the Protestant Reformation undermined the authority not only of the medieval Church but of the feudal lords as well. Although Protestantism retained otherworldliness in its theology, it did stimulate the materialistic drive necessary for the growth of capitalism, especially through the influence of the French Protestant religious reformer John Calvin (q.v.). This stimulus was provided by recognition of the legitimacy of collecting interest on borrowed money, by emphasis on the virtues of hard work and of thrift, and by interpreting the doctrine of predestination in terms that made business success appear to be a mark of God's favor.

The upsurge of trade and business activity which followed the discovery of the New World and of new trade routes to Asia was another of the forces which gave rise to modern capitalism. The ensuing vast extension of trade, called the Commercial Revolution, brought eminence to Spain, Portugal, France, England, and the other European nations bordering on the Atlantic Ocean and held out to them promises of material riches and power. The Spanish conquerors of Mexico and Peru brought to Europe large quantities of gold and silver, providing a more than ample supply of internationally accepted currency at a time when additional money was needed to further the expansion of markets and the growth of business enterprise. Rising prices swelled the profits of merchants and stimulated new business ventures. Banks and other financial institutions flourished.

**Mercantilist Capitalism.** The combination of dynamic forces engendered by the Renaissance, the Reformation, and the Commercial Revolution eventually led to the creation of relatively centralized states and to the rise of mercantilist capitalism, or the mercantile system (q.v.), which was characterized by governmental promotion and regulation of commerce in the interest of national aggrandizement. With power centralized in his hands, the national monarch created more stable conditions for the expansion of trade, improved transportation, and validated coins by putting the royal stamp on them. Because he needed large funds with which to pay his standing army and to meet his other governmental expenses, the reigning monarch became a natural ally of merchants and bankers. In addition, the growing business enterprises could be taxed lucratively. National rivalries for power and trade led the sovereign to grant royal monopolies to trading companies, to subsidize new industries, and to protect and regulate certain economic activities; as a result, mercantile capitalism became the dominant form of economic organization in western Europe. The mercantilists took it for granted that the chief economic aim of a nation, like that of a merchant, was to accumulate monetary wealth in the form of gold and silver; this accumulative process consisted in selling more goods abroad than the nation bought from abroad, as measured in terms of value. The mercantilist view of economic policy later was attacked by Adam Smith and others. *See* FOREIGN TRADE.

**Industrial Capitalism.** The gradual maturation of the mercantile system prepared the way for a stage of capitalism closer to Smith's ideal. This stage, in which the principal forms of economic activity were concentrated in the hands of independent factory owners, developed into industrial capitalism.

The main influences contributing to the development of industrial capitalism were the widening of markets and the consequent growth of trade; the increasing specialization of production among regions; the increasing availability of propertyless laborers; and the invention of the steam engine and of mechanically powered machinery. All four influences were closely connected.

The growth of trade between the 14th and 18th centuries made it profitable for certain towns and regions to specialize in the mass production of certain commodities for international markets. One of the most momentous examples of this phenomenon was the expansion, beginning in the 14th century, of the Flemish woolen-textile industry. This boom, in turn, stimulated Flemish demand for wool, in the production of which England had begun to specialize. The growing demand for wool encouraged powerful English landlords to drive small farmers from their holdings and to consolidate these small holdings into large, enclosed tracts of land suitable for pasturing sheep. Known in history as the Enclosure Movement, this process also facilitated the introduction of new and more efficient methods of farming and enabled rural areas to supply the growing towns with food. Meanwhile refugees from the enclosed lands, searching desperately for some means of livelihood, poured into the towns, forming a reservoir of cheap labor for manufacturing establishments.

Until the 18th century most industrial production was in small workshops. Because the tools were simple and human energy was the main source of power, many craftsmen found it feasible to own and operate small establishments with a few apprentices and journeymen. The invention of the steam engine and of powered textile machinery drastically changed this situation. Few craftsmen could afford to buy the new equipment, which became progressively bulkier and more expensive. Production in many in-

*A major means of raising capital for the modern corporation is the sale of interest-bearing bonds, like the ones shown here.*   Edward C. Topple

dustries accordingly became increasingly concentrated in a diminishing number of ever-larger factories which were owned by capitalists and staffed by considerable numbers of propertyless laborers. This process, called the Industrial Revolution (q.v.), of increasing mechanization, specialization, concentration, and expansion of industrial production spread to western Europe, to the U.S., and eventually throughout the world. *See* FACTORIES AND THE FACTORY SYSTEM.

The new system eliminated almost all of the vestiges of feudalism which had persisted during the growth of commercial capitalism and greatly increased output per manhour in numerous lines of industry. The increase was accomplished by division of labor (q.v.), a technique characterized by the concentration of large numbers of wage earners in a single work place and the assignment of each worker to a single repetitive operation which was but a small part of the process required to turn out a finished product. According to Adam Smith, division of labor not only made possible the use of machinery but stimulated its invention; often the workers themselves devised efficient machines as a means of lightening their tasks. As factories became larger and more efficient, independent craftsmen lost the capacity to compete with factory owners. In most cases the craftsmen had no choice but to become factory hands. Thus they sacrificed not only their independence but also whatever security they might have enjoyed under the more stable conditions of the guild system. In return they gained the freedom to

131

take better jobs when such were available and to strive for improved living conditions.

A rapid increase in the volume of sales was made possible by the cheapness and abundance of factory-made goods. The profits earned by successful firms, in turn, induced the formation of new plants and industries and provided money for expansion of established concerns. Advances in technology reduced unit costs and stimulated the growth of industry. In the U.S., Great Britain, Germany, and some other nations, the manufacturing industry was deliberately encouraged by governmental action, which on one hand kept the internal market free of obstructions and on the other hampered foreign competition by imposing protective tariffs on imports or by granting subsidies to domestic businesses.

Once the Industrial Revolution had secured a foothold, it spread rapidly wherever conditions for it were favorable. In Great Britain, where the new system first established itself, governmental policy eventually was based on the doctrines of Smith and other classical economists, such as Ricardo and John Stuart Mill (q.v.), who argued that the best interests of all would be served by unobstructed competition among independent and unsubsidized firms. This doctrine, known as *laissez faire,* held that unimpeded competition would enable consumers to seek out the best goods in the cheapest markets, would bring success to the more efficient producers, and would effectuate a division of labor on an international scale. During the latter part of the 19th century Great Britain achieved wealth and power in world markets without protective customs duties (q.v.), although at considerable sacrifice of its domestic agriculture, which could not compete with that of certain newly developed countries, particularly the U.S., in growing staple crops.

Major facilities, such as canals and railroads (qq.v.), which were necessary to the development of internal markets, involved the investment of vast sums and a long wait for profitable operation. Because individual entrepreneurs were unable to finance such facilities, canals and railroads were built generally either by governments or by companies with governmental charters granting special inducements and privileges, e.g., limited liability and the right of eminent domain (q.v.). In addition, such investment companies frequently received subsidies in the form of land, of loans on very easy terms, or even of monopolies in a given territory. The prototypes of the chartered firms were the great trading companies of the commercial revolu-

tion, such as in Great Britain the East India Company (q.v.). Eventually the corporate form of organization, under a charter assuring individuals of only limited liability, was commonly employed by manufacturing enterprises and other business firms as a means of raising sums of capital greater than that which single entrepreneurs possessed or would be willing to risk in any one venture. *See* CORPORATION.

**Finance Capitalism.** Finance capitalism developed during the 19th century in response to the need for large amounts of capital by governments and business corporations. Investment bankers, who specialized in the sale of securities for concerns seeking to raise capital, gradually achieved great power over the firms whose capital needs they supplied. They often initiated and organized mergers of competing concerns, especially in the fields of railroading, manufacturing, and public utilities. Although such mergers and other combinations and agreements designed to limit competition were countered by antitrust legislation in the U.S. and certain other countries (*see* TRUST), the merger movement continued, however. Bankers, with their international affiliations, also played an important role in the rise of imperialism (q.v.). In the U.S. financial institutions began to dominate the economy shortly after the Civil War. This development reached its apex in the period from about 1890 to 1930, which is often called the era of finance capitalism.

**Welfare Capitalism.** The so-called great depression of the 1930's focused attention on some of the inequities of the capitalist system, such as the high level of unemployment. It also ushered in a significant shift of capitalism toward what became known as welfare capitalism. This modified type of capitalism, sometimes referred to as "enlightened capitalism", is a system aimed at improving poor living and working conditions among industrial workers, raising minimum wage levels, and at continuous government involvement, by providing increasing social services.

Criticism of the capitalist system dates almost from its inception, but grew in density after the beginning of the Industrial Revolution (q.v.). The capitalist system often tended to ignore the welfare of workers, who suffered particularly during periods of depression and unemployment. Child labor and long hours of labor (qq.v.) for subsistence wages provoked widespread criticism from social historians. Living conditions in overcrowded and industrial centers frequently were squalid and unhealthful. The competitive race for profits and concentration on rapid accumulation of wealth were often thought to lead to unethical business practices. Inevitably, many proposals were made for a more cooperative or socially oriented order that would emphasize production for use rather than for profit.

In virtually all industrialized countries a trade-union movement arose which sought to increase the workers' wages, improve working conditions, and shorten hours of work by both collective bargaining and legislation (see TRADE UNION; SYNDICALISM). Socialist parties gradually became a significant political force in almost every country except the U.S.; in a number of instances Socialists achieved governmental power (see SOCIALISM). Co-operative societies, especially in retail and wholesale trade, attempted to replace profit-seeking businesses in the distribution of common necessities (see CO-OPERATIVE MOVEMENT.

However, in all capitalist countries which had developed modern industries the national product grew over the long term more rapidly than did the population; living standards progressively improved and the working day was shortened. For this reason movements for the destruction of the capitalist order frequently were transformed into movements for its reform. During the first half of the 20th century many of the advanced industrial countries allowed public ownership of a few basic industries, established maximum working hours and minimum wages, and enacted comprehensive systems of social insurance (q.v.) against unemployment, old age, sickness, and other common hazards. In the U.S. modifications of the capitalist system were enacted piecemeal, and many forms of regulation were applied to businesses affecting the public interest. Popular demand for reforms broke through traditional resistance to change, especially during the Depression of the 1930's.

Economic thought after the 1930's has been strongly influenced by the British economist, John Maynard Keynes (q.v.) whose theories seemed to offer solutions to severe business fluctuations that caused depressions. Keynes maintained that cyclical unemployment (q.v.) was caused by a decline in the total income circulating through the economy and that in a capitalist economy the flow of income depended on decisions by consumers to spend money and on the level of business investment. Neither of these two factors was amenable to governmental regulation. Keynes suggested, therefore, that the government was the only agency in a position to regulate the flow of income. Through its taxing and spending policies, it could compen-

sate for any drop in the flow of income by reducing taxes and increasing spending. In turn, in times of inflation taxes could be increased and spending reduced in order to put brakes on the economy; see INFLATION AND DEFLATION. The role played by government in the various capitalist economies was enlarged after the depression of the 1930's and also as a result of Keynes' theories, as well as by the economic, social, and political consequences of the two World Wars. The volume of governmental spending and revenue increased so markedly after World War II that governmental fiscal policy became perhaps the most dominating influence in the economy of a nation. In passing the Employment Act of 1946, the U.S. government committed itself to maintaining a high level of employment and production. By the late 1960's about a quarter of the U.S. Gross National Product represented governmental expenditures as compared to about 5 percent at the turn of the century; in Canada, the percentage was about a third, and in the countries of Europe it was even higher.

The widespread growth of government participation in the economy of many capitalist countries since 1945 gave rise to the term "mixed economy", meaning a combination of government and private activity that was responsible for the economic growth of a country. The term, "welfare capitalism", also gained wide acceptance, particularly in the U.S., where the government continues to increase the level of its social services and where private industry has been increasing the fringe benefits it offers the employees in addition to steadily increasing wages. The emergence of the new form of capitalism has not brought, however, a decline in the activity of private business. The tendency within the new form of capitalism was rather to buttress private investment and render it even more profitable. Nonetheless, by the middle of the century capitalistic enterprises had changed drastically in structure and character. Personally managed and highly competitive small firms were no longer characteristic of the economic order. Although most capitalist countries had more small firms than ever before, production and employment increasingly were concentrated in the plants of great corporations, most of which had a widely distributed ownership and were managed by professional executives rather than by owners. (See BUSINESS EDUCATION). Such corporations were particularly prevalent in heavy industry, e.g., the steel and automobile industries. These gigantic institutions developed their own bureaucracies and characteristic ethical codes. They are widely acknowledged to bear a public character and to have public responsibilities in addition to their profit-making function. In the U.S., corporations increasingly accept their public responsibility, particularly since it has become apparent that social and environmental problems are becoming too complex for governments at all levels to cope with them adequately without the cooperation of industry. Some environmental problems, such as pollution, are directly related to the primary industrial activity of many corporations. The public, at the same time, has become increasingly concerned and tends to hold industry accountable for environmental problems.

**Challenge of Communism.** The critics of the capitalistic system in the U.S., Great Britain, and other advanced capitalist countries had been placated on the whole by mid-20th century, but new and formidable threats to the system had developed in Soviet Russia and in many backward countries. Communism (q.v.), a movement dedicated to the destruction of capitalism, had seized power in 1917 in Russia. *See* BOLSHEVISM; THIRD INTERNATIONAL. Besides abolishing private capitalism and obstructing the development of democracy in Russia, now the Union of Soviet Socialist Republics (q.v.), the Soviet Communists promoted the formation and growth of similarly oriented movements in practically all other countries. After World War II international Communism began to extend its domain in Europe and Asia, gaining control over more than one third of mankind. Communism tends to prohibit private trade, investment, and economic initiative. The rate of industrial development was at times impressive, particularly in the Union of Soviet Socialist Republics and China (q.v.), and capitalist countries became concerned that the rise of nationalist leaders in economically backward countries of Asia, Africa, and Latin America would be attracted to the Communist system. Some countries, such as Cuba (q.v.), did regard Communism as the more effective means of rapid economic development and altered their economy to conform to that pattern.

Communist countries have, however, experienced many economic setbacks. Both the Soviet Union and China have had serious problems of maintaining suitable economic growth, and other Communist countries have withdrawn, in some cases, from pure socialism and have reintroduced a modified profit-making system into their economies. A few Communist governments have signed contracts with companies from capitalist countries to assist them in expanding certain industries. Even the Soviet

Union has reintroduced, to a limited degree, the profit motive in some of its industries and by 1970 was attempting to improve economic performance by trying so-called capitalist measures. All means of production, however, remain state-owned.

Both economic systems, capitalism and Communism, seek to persuade the uncommitted countries of the world of the attractiveness of their respective systems, means of increasing production, and improving living standards. Many uncommitted countries are, however, not selecting either system but are evolving other "mixed" economic systems of combined public and private enterprise.

Despite the threats to which modern capitalism has been subjected, and indeed largely because of them, appreciation has grown in the Western world of the special merits of the capitalist system. Even the heavy hardships suffered by workers during the first decades of the Industrial Revolution were, in fact, less severe than those suffered by the workers of Communist countries undergoing rapid industrialization. The inhuman sufferings brought on by forced industrialization are exemplified by the programs of industrialization and collectivization of agriculture decreed by the Soviet dictator Joseph Stalin (q.v.) in the early 1930's that cut the lives of millions of people and uncounted livestock. Because power in a private-enterprise economy is fragmented instead of concentrated as in a Communist economy, capitalism affords more freedom, more room for enterprise, more opportunity for individuals to make the most of their capabilities.

A wider degree of redistribution of the income produced by the capitalist system has silenced much of the criticism leveled against the system. Collective bargaining and the continued growth of the trade union (q.v.) movement, have brought labor higher wages that keep pace with, and often surpass, the rise in productivity.

**The Free Market.** To the present, mankind has devised no more efficient regulator of the allocation of resources according to the desires of industrial consumers than the free market. In seeking to maximize profit, the competitive businessman tries to cut his costs; to find and develop the most efficient modes of production and distribution; to install the most advanced equipment; to take steps to improve his employees' productivity and, especially, their morale, upon which productivity so greatly depends; to improve his product and his service to the consumer. Most enterprises survive and prosper depending on their ability to satisfy the consumer. Certain enterprises prosper and others fail by virtue of the buying decisions of the public.

Critics of the contemporary capitalist economy argue that large concerns, which have the power to set the prices at which they will sell, bias the behavior of the free market as it was supposed to operate by classical and neo-classical theorists; that by intensive publicity and advertising they create demands for products which consumers might not otherwise want. It is argued also that social needs which cannot be satisfied through search for profit in commercial markets often are inadequately served, e.g., conservation of natural resources, education, or research in pure science. This is becoming less true as industry assumes more social responsibility and actively seeks solutions to contemporary problems. Although serious depressions may be avoided in the future, no responsible authority holds that the business cycle has been conquered, and the question remains whether, in a full-employment economy, inflation can be checked.

Despite some shortcomings of the system, the rapid advance of productivity characteristic of Western capitalism nevertheless has facilitated the highest average material levels of living that the world has ever known. Continuing advances in output per man hour and increased automation of many production functions could make possible a high level of productivity which would reduce the work week allowing more leisure time. In such a higher stage of western industrial culture (as hinted more than a century ago by the English economist and philosopher John Stuart Mill) an opportunity exists for unprecedented cultural achievements shared widely by a democratic society.  G.So. & J.T.M.

**CAPITAL PUNISHMENT,** legal penalty of death, in modern law the severest sentence a court may pronounce. It has been exacted in all parts of the world from earliest times to the present day.

**Great Britain.**  In medieval England death was the usual punishment for practically all felonies. In the 18th century 160 offenses were punishable by death, mostly offenses against property. Early in the 19th century more humane measures were introduced, and the Statute of 1861 provided that only four crimes remain punishable by death, those of murder, treason, piracy with violence, and setting fire to royal dockyards or arsenals. In 1965 the death penalty was provisionally abolished; an effort to reinstate it failed in 1969.

**United States.**  In colonial North America a large number of felonies were punishable by death. The Quaker proprietor of Philadelphia, William Penn (q.v.), allowed only murder and treason to be so punished, but following his death the English penal code was reinstated, with fourteen offenses designated as capital crimes. In 1794 Pennsylvania again abolished the death sentence for all offenses except first-degree murder. The other former colonies followed the lead of Pennsylvania by curtailing use of the ultimate penalty.

By the late 1960's fourteen States were generally regarded as having no death penalty, although a few of them retained the sanction for certain crimes, such as treason, the murder of a police officer on duty, or murder committed by a prisoner serving a life sentence for murder. In practice, many governors in the thirty-six remaining capital-punishment States exercised executive clemency.

In June, 1972, the Supreme Court of the United States (q.v.), in a 5-to-4 decision, outlawed the death penalty. The court did, however, leave the way open for reinstatement, provided new Federal or State statutes could be formulated so that the death penalty would not be imposed "wantonly and freakishly", as two justices described previous impositions. The three other justices in the majority believed the penalty to be inherently "cruel and unusual" and therefore violative of the Constitution of the United States (q.v.).

In response to this challenge fifteen States enacted new capital punishment laws, restoring the death penalty for a limited, specified list of crimes (usually murder). Several of these laws make the penalty mandatory in cases with one or more aggravating factors (including prior conviction for a crime of violence, or the murder of a policeman) and with no mitigating factors (such as the age of a young offender). Other States have retained a measure of discretion in the courts but require a two-part trial, one to determine guilt and the other to determine the presence of aggravating or mitigating factors not made evident in the first trial. If the jury finds only aggravating factors the judge is empowered to impose the death penalty. But at the end of the 1972–73 term none of these statutes had been tested to determine its acceptability to the majority of the Supreme Court.

**U.S. Statistics.**  During the period from 1930 through 1967 (the most recent year in which executions took place), 3859 executions were carried out under civil authority in the U.S. Of these, 3334 were for murder, 455 for rape, 25 for armed robbery, 20 for kidnaping, 11 for burglary, 6 for aggravated assault, and 8 for espionage. Thus, although there were thirty-one categories of capital crime among the civil jurisdictions, only these seven resulted in actual executions.

In addition to the 3859 civil executions, the United States Army and Air Force executed 160 military personnel during this thirty-eight-year period, most of them during World War II. Of these, 106 were for murder, 53 for rape, and 1 for desertion. The navy has not executed anyone since 1849.

The average number of executions per year in the U.S. for murder was 151 in the 1930's and 60 during the 1950's. During the period 1960 to 1965 the annual average of executions was 42.

**Other Nations.** The imposition of capital punishment has been abolished by many countries; as the 1970's began more than seventy nations had laws against capital punishment. Many countries, however, have wavered regarding abolition of the death penalty. A few have reinstated it for crimes of treason, espionage, and sabotage; premeditated murder; and embezzlement, forgery, and fraud; as well as certain crimes against the public peace.

**Types of Execution.** Methods are less harsh today than in primitive and medieval times; burning at the stake, crucifixion, drawing and quartering, strangulation, pressing with stones, and boiling in oil were common. Today, outside the U.S., hanging (q.v.) is the most prevalent form of capital punishment. The Soviet Union employs shooting as well as hanging; Spain and a few South American countries use execution by strangling with an iron collar, or garrote; and France continues to use the guillotine (q.v.). In the U.S., hanging as a method of execution was supplanted by other means in all but seven capital-punishment States, including Utah, which gave the condemned prisoner the option of shooting or hanging. Electrocution (q.v.), introduced into the U.S. in 1888, became the prescribed method in twenty-three of the thirty-six capital-punishment States and the District of Columbia. Lethal gas was used in ten States. The Federal government used the facilities and methods of the States in which its prisoners were sentenced by U.S. district courts.

In earlier times executions were occasions for public amusement and were conducted before crowds. Today the public is usually excluded from the place of execution; access is then permitted only to the few witnesses required by law.                                        J.V.B.

**CAPITALS OF THE UNITED STATES.** Since 1800 Washington, D.C., has been the capital of the United States. Before 1800, however, the seat of government was located at various times in eight different cities. These were:

Philadelphia, Pa., July 4, 1776, to Dec. 12, 1776.

Baltimore, Md., Dec. 20, 1776, to March 4, 1777.

Philadelphia, March 5, 1777, to Sept. 18, 1777.

Lancaster, Pa., Sept. 27, 1777 (one day only).

York, Pa., Sept. 30, 1777, to June 27, 1778.

Philadelphia, July 2, 1778, to June 21, 1783.

Princeton, N.J., June 30, 1783, to Nov. 4, 1783.

Annapolis, Md., Nov. 26, 1783, to June 3, 1784.

Trenton, N.J., Nov. 1, 1784, to Dec. 24, 1784.

New York City, N.Y., Jan. 11, 1785, to Aug. 12, 1790.

During the following ten-year period, while the permanent capital, Washington, D.C., was being built, the seat of government was again in Philadelphia. Congress (Sixth; second session) met for the first time in Washington, D.C., on Nov. 17, 1800. *See* DISTRICT OF COLUMBIA; WASHINGTON (CAPITOL OF THE U.S.).

**CAPITOLINE HILL,** highest of the Seven Hills of Rome, Italy, above the Roman Forum (q.v.). *See* ROME.

**CAPITOL OF THE UNITED STATES,** seat of the Congress of the United States (q.v.) in Washington, D.C. Built on a hill popularly called Capitol Hill, the Capitol contains floor space equivalent to four acres; its grounds cover 155 acres. The Capitol is constructed of white marble, except for the center part of the west front, which is Virginia sandstone painted white. The iron dome, also white, is surmounted by a 19½-ft.-high statue of Freedom by the American sculptor Thomas Crawford (q.v.). The height of the Capitol from the base line on the east front to the top of the statue is 287½ ft. The overall length of the building is 751 ft., and its greatest width, including approaches, is 350 ft. The three main entrances on the east front contain massive bronze doors depicting scenes of American history and the life of Columbus. Other historical events are portrayed on a 9-ft.-high fresco circling the Rotunda, directly under the dome. Four of the eight large canvases are the work of the American painter John Trumbull (q.v.). In the center of the dome a fresco, the "Apotheosis of Washington", is surrounded by allegorical figures of great men of the arts, science, and industry. Other important parts of the Capitol include the Senate Chamber in the north wing, the House Chamber in the south wing, the National Statuary Hall (which contains statues of famous Americans from each State), and the President's Room. Until 1935, the Supreme

*The central dome of the Capitol building was completed in 1863. Crowning the cupola is a great bronze statue of a woman, representing Freedom, designed by the American sculptor Thomas Crawford. Wearing classical robes and a crested helmet, she holds a sword in one hand, a wreath in the other. The dome is modeled after the one designed by Michelangelo for Saint Peter's Basilica in Rome.* UPI

Court of the United States (q.v.) met in the Old Senate Chamber, which was located in the original north wing.

The original plans of the Capitol were drawn by William Thornton (1759–1828), an American physician, in 1792. Work on the area that is now the north wing of the central building was begun on Aug. 1, 1793, and President George Washington (q.v.) laid the cornerstone on Sept. 18 of that year. Despite difficulties in financing and in obtaining supplies and workmen, the original wing was occupied by Congress in November, 1800. The House and Senate, the Library of Congress (q.v.), and the Supreme Court were accommodated in this 126-ft.-long wing for seven years. In 1803 the British-American architect and engineer Benjamin Henry Latrobe (q.v.) was placed in charge of construction by President Thomas Jefferson (q.v.). Latrobe completed

his addition of the matching south wing in 1807 and remodeled the original north wing interior. During the War of 1812 (q.v.), invading British troops set fire to the still incomplete Capitol on Aug. 24, 1814, gutting the interior. Latrobe supervised the reconstruction for two years following the war. In January, 1818, Charles Bulfinch (*see under* BULFINCH) became the first American-born architect of the Capitol. Bulfinch is credited with the center building (the Rotunda area), the original low copper dome, and the west central portico. He also planned the gates, fences, and landscaping of the Capitol grounds. The new wings extending from the central building were drafted by Thomas Ustick Walter (1804–87), who became architect of the Capitol in 1851. His new south wing was occupied by the House in 1857, and the Senate occupied its new north wing in 1859. The new cast-iron dome was completed in 1863. The present landscaping and terraces were designed by Frederick Law Olmsted (q.v.), the first landscape architect in America. In 1962, under J. George Stewart (1890–    ), then architect of the Capitol, the east front was extended 32½ ft. with marble to match the extension wings and to protect the deteriorating sandstone. Plans for the renovation of the west front were later considered.

**CAPITOL REEF NATIONAL PARK,**    area of natural and historic interest in Wayne County, south-central Utah. Formerly a national monument. *See* NATIONAL PARK SERVICE.

**CAPO D'ISTRIA, Count Giovanni Antonio** *or* **KAPODISTRIAS, Count Ioannes Antonios.** *See* GREECE: *History: The War of Independence.*

**CAPORETTO, BATTLE OF,** engagement of World War I, fought between October and December, 1917, that resulted in a disastrous defeat of the armed forces of Italy by the armies of the Central Powers (q.v.). On Oct. 24, German and Austrian troops launched a sudden attack on Italian positions near the Austrian town of Caporetto (now Kobarid, Yugoslavia). Within twenty-four hours units of the Italian army, under the command of General Luigi Cadorna (q.v.), collapsed along the entire Isonzo R. front, precipitating a retreat that continued until Nov. 12. During this period the forces of the Central Powers occupied Italy south to the Piave R., captured vast quantities of material, and inflicted casualties totaling about 320,000 killed, wounded, and missing. British and French troops that had arrived early in November saved Italy from total destruction. General Armando Díaz (q.v.) replaced Cadorna as Italian commander in chief. *See* WORLD WAR I: *The Campaigns and Other Events of 1917.*

**CAPOTE, Truman**    (1924–    ), American writer, born in New Orleans, La. He was educated chiefly at Trinity School and Saint John's Academy, both in New York City. His first novel, *Other Voices, Other Rooms,* was published in 1948. Some of his other works include *A Tree of Night, and Other Stories* (1949), *Local Color* (1950), *The Grass Harp* (1951), *The Muses Are Heard* (1956), *Breakfast at Tiffany's* (1958), *Observations* (1959), *Selected Writings* (1963), *In Cold Blood* (1966), an account of the murder of four members of a family in Garden City, Kans., which was made into a motion picture in 1967, and *The Thanksgiving Visitor* (1968).

Capote also was the author of the script for the musical stage play *House of Flowers* (1954) and he collaborated on the scenario of the motion picture *Beat the Devil* (1954). He has been

*Truman Capote*    Rudy Valenzuela

praised by critics for his technical virtuosity and powers of observation.

**CAPP, Al,**    real name ALFRED GERALD CAPLIN (1909–    ), American cartoonist, born in New Haven, Conn. After leaving high school, he studied at several art schools, including the Pennsylvania Academy of Fine Arts. In 1932 he was hired as a cartoonist by the Associated Press; he later worked for the Boston *Sunday Post* and for Hammond Edward "Ham" Fisher (1900–55), creator of the comic strip *Joe Palooka.* Capp launched his own comic strip, *L'il Abner,* in 1934. The strip concerns itself with the imaginary hillbilly community of Dogpatch and the Yokum family. By 1941 *L'il Abner* was appearing in some 400 newspapers. Capp's fanciful characters, including L'il Abner, Daisy Mae, Lena the Hyena, Fearless Fosdick, and Marryin' Sam, became household names. Many of their expressions have become part of the American idiom, and their misadventures often constitute pointed social satire. *L'il Abner* was the subject of a musical comedy in 1957 that was made into a motion picture in 1959.

**CAPPADOCIA,**    ancient name for eastern Asia Minor, from the Pontus Euxinus (now the Black Sea) to the Taurus Mts., in present-day E.-central Turkey. As early as 1900 B.C. merchants of Assyria (q.v.) established a colony in Cappadocia. From about 1750 B.C. to the formation of the Persian Empire of the Achaemenid dynasty (*see* PERSIA) in the 7th century B.C., this region was the center of power of the Hittites (q.v.). Later the Persians controlled the area that then comprised two satrapies, or provinces: the northern province became known as Cappadocia near the Pontus or merely Pontus (q.v.); the southern area retained the name Cappadocia, by which it was known in classical times. After the conquest of Persia by Alexander III (q.v.), known as the Great, early in the 4th century B.C., Cappadocia became independent. The first king of the Cappadocian dynasty, Ariarathes I (d. 322 B.C.), paid tribute to Alexander, but the successors of Alexander were unable to conquer the country. Later the kings of Cappadocia sided with the rising power of Rome against the Seleucids and against Pontus; see SELEUCIDAE. Cappadocia frequently alternated in its support of the various factions during the Roman civil wars of the 1st century B.C.; see ROME, HISTORY OF. The independence of the country ended in fact, when the Romans supplanted the Cappadocian dynasty with a puppet king about 40 B.C. In 17 A.D. the Roman Emperor Tiberius (q.v.), incorporated Cappadocia into the Roman Empire as a province. Thereafter, the importance of Cappadocia as a separate political unit declined. For the subsequent history of the region, see ASIA MINOR; TURKEY: History. Among the important towns of Cappadocia were the capital of the kingdom, Mazaca (now Kayşeri, Turkey), known in Roman times as Caesarea Mazaca; Tyana; and Melitene (now Malatya). The modern town of Boğazkale is on the site of the Cappadocian town of Pteria, which in turn occupied the site of the city of Hatti, capital of the Hittite Empire.

**CAPPER, Arthur** (1865–1951), American political leader and publisher, born in Garnett, Kans., where he was educated. Starting his journalistic career as a compositor with the Topeka *Daily Capital* in 1884, he later became reporter, city editor, Washington correspondent, and finally, in 1892, publisher and owner of the paper. He also acquired two other Kansas daily newspapers and two radio stations, and was one of the largest publishers of agricultural periodicals in the United States. He was governor of Kansas for two terms between 1915 and 1919, and he served in the United States Senate from 1919 until 1949.

**CAPRA, Frank** (1897–    ), American motion-picture director and producer, born in Palermo, Italy. Capra was six years old when his family migrated to the United States, settling in Los Angeles, Calif. His first important job in Hollywood was as a writer for the Mack Sennett (q.v.) studios. Capra later joined Columbia Pictures, at which he gained his greatest success as a director of sophisticated comedies having social overtones. Such films include three that won Capra the American Academy of Motion Picture Arts and Sciences award for best director, *It Happened One Night* (1934), *Mr. Deeds Goes to Town* (1936), and *You Can't Take it With You* (1938). During World War II Capra produced military documentaries. Other films he directed or produced include *Lost Horizon* (1937), *Mr. Smith Goes to Washington* (1939), *Arsenic and Old Lace* (1941), *State of the Union* (1948), *A Hole in the Head* (1959), and *A Pocketful of Miracles* (1961). His autobiography, *The Name Above the Title*, was published in 1971.

**CAPRERA,** small rocky island of Italy, in the Tyrrhenian Sea, off the N.E. coast of Sardinia, connected with the island of Maddalena by a causeway and drawbridge. It is famous as the residence of the Italian patriot Giuseppe Garibaldi (q.v.), who died and was buried there in 1882. Area, 6 sq.mi.; pop. (latest census) 171.

**CAPRI** (anc. *Capreae*), island of Italy, at the entrance of the Bay of Naples, Naples Province, about 17 miles S. of the city of Naples. It is about 4 mi. long and 1½ mi. at its widest point. Limestone cliffs, 900 ft. high, rise from the sea in the E.; Monte Solaro, in the W., the highest point on the island, is 1920 ft. above sea level. The town of Capri, 450 ft. high, is an episcopal see. From the town 784 steps, carved in the rock, lead upward to Anacapri. To the W. of the town of Capri is the Grotto Azzurra, or Blue (Blue Grotto), a cavern, entered from the sea by a narrow opening not more than 3 ft. high, but which inside is of magnificent proportions. Elliptical in form, it is 175 ft. long, 100 ft. at the widest part, and 41 ft. high; the water in the cavern is 48 ft. deep. Stalactites hang from the roof and sides. The blue color within the grotto is caused by the light passing through the water. Capri contains relics of prehistoric ages and numerous remains of Roman times, including ruins of the twelve villas built by Emperor Tiberius (q.v.), who resided in Capri for ten years. There are no springs or streams on Capri, but it has abundant rainfall and is fertile, producing olive oil, wine, and fruit. The tourist trade provides the principal source of income for the islanders. Area, 4 sq.mi.; pop. (1971 prelim.) 8025.

**CAPRICORNUS** (Lat. "goat horn"), constellation of stars, the tenth of the twelve constellations of the zodiac (q.v.). Capricornus is situated in the heavens far south of the equator (q.v.), between the constellations Sagittarius, the archer, and Aquarius, the water carrier (qq.v.). The name of the constellation is derived from

*Capuchin,* Cebus capucinus

Greek myths about the god Pan (q.v.), who was often represented as a goatlike figure. Capricornus has no stars brighter than those of the third magnitude; its brightest star, Alpha Capricornus, is a wide multiple of which two separate stars can be distinguished by the naked eye; *see* STARS. In the North Temperate Zone the constellations can be seen near the southern horizon in June. The ancient Greeks named the Tropic of Capricorn (*see* TROPICS) after this constellation because the sun entered Capricornus at the winter solstice (q.v.) about December 22. *See also* ECLIPTIC.

**CAPSELLA,**  genus of plants belonging to the family Cruciferae. *Capsella bursa-pastoris,* commonly known as shepherd's-purse, grows from 4 to 24 in. high. A weed naturalized from Europe, it produces rosette leaves, a raceme of small, white flowers, and seed pods.

**CAPSICUM,**  red pepper plant, ranging from 6 to 8 ft. in height, a genus of the Solanaceae (Nightshade) family. The fruit is a many-seeded berry known variously as pod pepper, red pepper, chili, or capsicum, and is pungently flavored. Some species of the plant are bushy in appearance, and are cultivated in tropical and subtropical countries. Under its Mexican name, chili, the fruit is used in sauces and mixed pickles. Cayenne pepper is made from the dried, ground seeds and pods.

**CAPSTAN.**  *See* WHEEL AND AXLE.

**CAPUA,**  town of Italy, in Caserta Province, on the Volturno R., 18 miles N. of Naples. Notable buildings include the Cathedral of San Stefano, erected in 856; a Roman amphitheater; and the Museo Campano, containing relics of ancient Capua, which was about 3 miles S.E. of the modern town.

Ancient Capua, a flourishing city founded before the 6th century B.C., was the largest city in Italy except for Rome. During the second of the Punic Wars (q.v.) Capua renounced its allegiance to the Romans for the Carthaginian general Hannibal (q.v.), after which the city lost the autonomy it had been granted. Capua continued to be an important city, despite its temporary destruction by the Vandals in 456, until 840 when the Saracens destroyed it. In 856 the Lombards refounded Capua nearby on the site of ancient Casilinum. Pop. (1971) 17,920.

**CAPUCHIN MONKEY,**  *or* CAI, a name often given to *C. capucinus,* and some other species of the genus *Cebus.* These monkeys have the head covered with short hair, resembling the cowl of a Capuchin monk, with the face almost naked. They frequent wooded country in Guiana, Venezuela, and Peru. Some species grow to a length of 24 in. and have tails of from 18 to 20 in. long.

**CAPUCHINS,**  branch of the Roman Catholic order of Franciscans (q.v.), so designated from the *cappuccio* ("cowl") worn by them as their headdress. The Italian monk Matteo da Bascio (about 1495–1552) founded the branch in 1528 at Montefalco in Umbria to restore the literal observance of the Rule of Saint Francis (*see* FRANCIS OF ASSISI, SAINT). An order of Capuchin nuns, properly a branch of the Poor Clare order, was founded in Naples, Italy, in 1538.

**CAPULETS AND MONTAGUES,**  English form of the names of the Capelletti and Montecchi, two noble families of north Italy. According to tradition, they lived in Verona (q.v.) in the 14th century and were bitter enemies. They are chiefly memorable for their legendary feud that William Shakespeare described in his play *Romeo and Juliet.* Juliet was a Capulet; Romeo, a Montague. Literary historians believe that Shakespeare derived the plot for this play from a short story written by the Italian writer Matteo Bandello (q.v.).

**CAPULIN MOUNTAIN NATIONAL MONUMENT,**  site of extinct volcanic craters in Union County, N.E. New Mexico. The monument includes Capulin Mt., an extinct volcanic cinder

cone estimated by some geologists to have been active about 2000 years ago; *see* VOLCANO. The crater of the mountain is about 1500 ft. wide and 400 ft. deep. The mountain itself is 8215 ft. above sea level, and 1347 ft. above the town of Capulin. The monument, covering an area of 775.42 acres, was established in 1916 and is administered by the National Park Service (q.v.).

**CAPYBARA,** common name for *Hydrochoerus capybara,* the largest living rodent, of the Caviidae family. The capybara, also known as the carpincho, grows to a length of about 4 ft., weighs about 100 lb., is semiaquatic in its habits, and is a vegetarian. The rodent runs clumsily because of slightly webbed feet, but swims· well and can remain under water for several minutes. A plump animal, with coarse, thin, brownish hair, it is easily tamed. It lives in pairs or families along the banks of rivers and lakes in South America.

**CAQUETÍO.** *See* ARAWAKAN.

**CARABAO.** *See* BUFFALO; PHILIPPINES, REPUBLIC OF THE: *The Land: Natural Resources.*

**CARABIDAE.** *See* GROUND BEETLE.

**CARABOBO, BATTLE OF,** decisive military engagement in the Venezuelan war of independence against Spain, fought on June 24, 1821. The revolutionary army, under the command of Simón Bolívar and José Antonio Páez (qq.v.), was intercepted during an advance on the city of Caracas (q.v.) by a Spanish force of Royalist troops. The action, which lasted little more than an hour, resulted in complete defeat for the Spanish and assured freedom for Venezuela. The battle took place near Carabobo, a village about 20 miles S.W. of Valencia. *See* VENEZUELA: *History.*

**CARACAL,** *or* PERSIAN LYNX, lynxlike member of the Cat family (Felidae), *Felis caracal,* or *Caracal caracal,* native to Africa and the warmer parts of Asia. Somewhat larger than a fox, it has a reddish-brown coat, white belly, and black-tipped ears tufted with hair (Turk., *caracal,* "black ears"). Caracals live on small deer, hare, and birds. In India they are sometimes tamed and used for hunting because of their speed and agility. *See* LYNX.

**CARACALLA,** nickname of Roman Emperor MARCUS AURELIUS ANTONINUS (188–217 A.D.). He was born BASSIANUS in Lugdunum,

*Marble bust of Caracalla.*

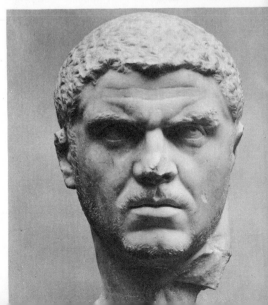

*University City, Caracas.*  Creole Petroleum Corp.

Gaul (now Lyon, France) and was nicknamed Caracalla because he introduced into Roman fashion a long cloak or tunic from Gaul called the caracalla. When his father, Emperor Lucius Septimius Severus (q.v.), died in 211, Caracalla became joint emperor with his younger brother, Publius Septimius Geta (189–212). In 212 Caracalla became sole emperor after causing the murder of Geta and the massacre of several thousand of Geta's followers. The reign of Caracalla was marked by cruelty, extravagance, and treachery, particularly in military campaigns against the Alamanni (q.v.) and the peoples of Gaul and Parthia. During his reign the Baths of Caracalla and the Arch of Septimius were constructed in Rome. Caracalla was assassinated in Mesopotamia by Marcus Opelius Macrinus (164–218), who then succeeded as emperor.

**CARACARA,** popular name of several birds of the Falcon family, especially those of the genus *Polyborus*. The face, bare of feathers, is brightly colored; the legs are long and adapted to walking on the ground. They feed mostly on carrion, but also prey on small living animals. Most species are to be found in South America; only one, Audubon's caracara, *P. cheriway*, ranges as far north as southern United States. The caracara ranges in length from 21 to 24 in. and has a wingspan of about 33 in.

**CARACAS,** capital and chief city of Venezuela, and capital of the Federal District, in the fer-

tile Caracas Valley, about 8 miles s. of La Guaira, which serves as the Caribbean port of the city. The commercial and industrial center of Venezuela, Caracas has a great variety of industries, including auto assembly, sugar refining, meat packing, brewing, leather tanning, and the manufacture of paper, tobacco products, glassware, textiles, rubber goods, and pharmaceuticals. Oil refining has recently become a leading industry. The city is linked by air routes, railroads, and highways with La Guaira, with w. Venezuela, and with Ciudad Bolívar in the s.

The Plaza Bolívar, one of many squares and public gardens in Caracas, contains a bronze equestrian statue of Simón Bolívar (q.v.), South American statesman and revolutionary, who was born in Caracas. Near the plaza are many Caracas landmarks, including the capitol, Central University of Venezuela, and the National Pantheon, where Bolívar is buried. Another notable building is a Roman Catholic cathedral built in 1636; Caracas is the seat of the Roman Catholic archbishop of Venezuela.

The city was founded in 1567 as Santiago de León de Caracas and became one of the most prosperous Spanish colonial communities in South America. It was sacked by English buccaneers under the English navigator Sir Francis Drake (q.v.) in 1595. In 1810, under the leadership of Simón Bolívar, it became the center of the first revolt in the war for independence from Spain (1810–21). Caracas became the capital of the Venezuelan Republic in 1829. The city has suffered several earthquakes; in 1812, 12,000 people were killed and most of the city was destroyed, and in 1967, 277 people were killed and many buildings collapsed. Pop. (1971 prelim.) 1,035,499.

**CARACCI.**  *See* CARRACCI.

**CARAPA,** genus of trees of the Meliaceae (Mahogany) family, native to tropical climates. *Carapa guianensis,* commonly called the crabwood, is a large tree found in South America and the West Indies. The wood is sold as Brazilian mahogany. The fruit, called the carap nut, is about 5 in. in diameter and contains many seeds. A thick, bitter oil obtained from the seeds of the crabwood is used in soapmaking and by South American natives as an insect repellent. The seeds from several other species of Carapa yield a similar oil, which is used in soapmaking.

**CARAT,** term expressing the ratio of precious metal to base metal in an alloy, and also a unit of weight for precious stones. In the first sense, a carat (usually spelled karat) indicates one twenty-fourth part by weight of a precious metal, such as gold, in an alloy. Thus, 18-karat gold is 18/24, or 3/4, gold, and 24-karat gold is pure gold. As a unit of weight for precious stones, the international metric carat, now used by the principal countries of the world, was standardized by the United States government in 1913 at 200 mg, or 0.2 g. This standard carat is divided decimally; 0.01 carat is usually called a point.

**CARAVAGGIO, Michelangelo da,** real name MICHELANGELO MERISI or MICHELANGELO MERISIO (1573–1609), Italian painter, born in Caravaggio, Lombardy. He studied painting in Milan and then went to Rome. His life was a stormy one and included duels and a murder, which forced him to flee from Rome. His temperament was reflected in his paintings, which are full of dramatic action and strong emotion. The originator of a style of painting based on close imitation of nature, Caravaggio depicted ordinary people in ordinary surroundings and used light and shadow with intense, even melodramatic, effect.

Early in his career, Caravaggio painted mainly genre pieces (*see* GENRE PAINTING); in his later period, chiefly religious paintings. Caravaggio's work profoundly influenced his successors, especially the Spanish painter José Ribera and the Flemish painter Peter Paul Rubens (qq.v.). Notable among the numerous paintings by Caravaggio are "The Young Bacchus" (about 1585, Uffizi Gallery, Florence), "Narcissus at the Fountain" (1590–95, National Gallery of Ancient Art, Rome), "The Supper at Emmaus" (1598, National

*"Boy with a Basket of Fruit" (about 1589), an oil painting by Michelangelo da Caravaggio in the Borghese Gallery, Rome*  Alinari

Gallery, London), and "Beheading of Saint John the Baptist" (about 1608, Cathedral of Saint John, Valletta, Malta).

**CARAVAGGIO, Polidoro da,** real name POLIDORO CALDARA (about 1495–1543), Italian painter, born in Caravaggio. As a youth Caravaggio worked as a laborer in the Vatican. He studied under the Italian painter Raphael (q.v.) and under his guidance executed several friezes in the Vatican galleries. After Raphael died in 1520, Caravaggio became well known as a decorator of house facades with classical scenes done in the chiaroscuro (q.v.) style. These earlier works, most of which have been destroyed, are known in copies by various etchers. After the sack of Rome in 1527 he settled in Naples. The painting most typical of the second phase of his career is "Christ Bearing the Cross" (1534), in the Naples Gallery.

**CARAVAN,** name applied to groups of pilgrims or merchants organized for mutual help and protection against the hazards of travel, particularly on the deserts of Asia and Africa. On these journeys, many of which cover long distances, the beasts of burden most frequently used are the camel, the llama (qq.v.), and the donkey (*see* ASS). The animals are traditionally arranged in a single file that in larger caravans may extend for a distance of 5 mi. Pilgrims en route to the holy city of Islam, Mecca (q.v.), particularly the groups that assemble annually in Cairo, Egypt, and in Damascus, Syria, form the most celebrated caravans. These groups sometimes consist of several thousand people, and the number of camels used for the journey may be more than 10,000.

Trade caravans figured prominently in the ancient history of Asia and Africa. Wars were

A camel caravan plods its way to a remote area of Niger, in western Africa. Camels can travel over tracks impassable even for four-wheel-drive trucks.　UPI

fought for control of caravan routes, many of which, for centuries, were the only arteries of communication and trade between parts of the various empires. Although trade caravans are still used in parts of Africa, China, and the Soviet Union, in recent times camels and donkeys have been replaced by specially equipped motor vehicles and, to a certain extent, by the airplane.

**CARAVEL** *or* **CARVEL.** *See* Ships and Shipbuilding.

**CARAWAY,** common name for a plant, *Carum carvi*, of the Parsley family (Umbelliferae), that has long been cultivated in temperate zones for its aromatic fruit, called caraway seeds. These seeds are used in cookery, confectionery, and medicine. The caraway plant is a biennial herb 1 to 2 ft. high, with finely divided leaves and clusters of white flowers. The large oil glands of the seed contain caraway oil, which is used in the preparation of a liqueur, and also in perfumery and in pharmacy, as an aromatic stimulant and flavoring ingredient.

**CARBAMIDE.** *See* Urea.

**CARBERRY, John Joseph, Cardinal** (1904– ), American Roman Catholic prelate, born in Brooklyn, N.Y., and educated at Cathedral College of the Immaculate Conception in Brooklyn, North American College in Rome, Italy, and Catholic University of America, Washington, D.C. He was ordained a priest in 1929. Carberry taught at Immaculate Conception in 1935 and again from 1941 to 1945; he then served eleven years on the tribunal of the Brooklyn diocese. In 1956, while serving as president of the Canon Law Society of America, he was consecrated a bishop. Carberry was bishop of Lafayette, Ind., from 1957 until 1965, when he was named bishop of Columbus, Ohio. In 1968 he was appointed archbishop of Saint Louis, Mo. Pope Paul VI (*see under* Paul) elevated Carberry to the cardinalate in 1969.

**CARBIDES,** compounds of carbon with various metals and metalloids. These compounds have very high melting points, and are not readily volatilized. They are produced by heating appropriate mixtures to high temperatures in electric furnaces. The carbides are divided into four categories, according to the manner in which they react with water or acids. The largest of these is the Acetyledic group, including the carbides of beryllium, calcium, strontium, sodium, potassium, copper, silver, gold, and nickel. The acetylides, the most important of which is calcium carbide, are formed by a reaction with

*Caraway*, Carum carvi

water or acids. A second group, consisting of aluminum, beryllium, and manganese carbides, is termed the Methanides. These carbides yield methane (q.v.) on reaction with water or acids.

Important metallic carbides include iron carbide, or cementite, the hardening constituent in steel; tungsten carbide, from which are made very hard tools for the machining of tough metals; and boron carbide, a material almost as hard as diamond. An important nonmetallic carbide is silicon carbide, or carborundum, used for grinding wheels and electrical heating elements.

**CARBINE,** light, short-barreled rifle. The carbine is essentially the same as the rifle (q.v.), but has a shorter barrel, a generally smaller caliber, and a more limited range. The carbine was formerly carried only by mounted cavalry troops, but during World War II the M2 carbine was substituted for the .45-caliber pistol as the personal weapon of artillerymen and service troops. Carbines were also modified for semiautomatic firing, but they were replaced officially by the M14 rifle in the early 1960's. See SMALL ARMS.

**CARBOHYDRATE,** any of a large group of compounds in which hydrogen and oxygen, in the proportions in which they exist in water, are combined with carbon; the formula of any of these compounds may be expressed as $C_m(H_2O)_n$. However, these compounds are not, structurally, hydrates of carbon. Carbohydrates are made by living plants in a process known as photosynthesis (q.v.). The group consists principally of sugars, starch, dextrin, cellulose (qq.v.), and glycogen, substances which constitute an important part of the diet of man and of many animals.

The simplest carbohydrates are the monosaccharides, of which the most important is glucose (q.v.). Two monosaccharide molecules joined together by an oxygen atom with the elimination of a molecule of water yield a disaccharide, of which the most important are sucrose (ordinary cane sugar), lactose, and maltose (qq.v.). The polysaccharides have enormous molecules made up of one or more monosaccharide units: about 10 for glycogen, 25 for starch, and 100 to 200 for cellulose. Polysaccharides, in living organisms, are considered protective materials. Hemicellulose, a plant-cell polysaccharide, is a source of sugar as well as a substance used to modify paper during its manufacture. The carbohydrate dextran is a polysaccharide used in medicine as a blood-plasma-volume expander to counteract acute shock; another carbohydrate, heparin sulfate, is a blood anticoagulant.

Carbohydrates are used in the manufacture of fabrics, photographic film, plastics and other products. Cellulose, a carbohydrate, can be converted into viscose rayon, acetate rayon, and paper products. Nitrocellulose (cellulose nitrate) is used in the production of motion-picture film, cement, guncotton, Celluloid, and similar kinds of plastics. Forms in which carbohydrates occur are starch, employed in the preparation of foods for livestock and humans; pectin (see PECTINS), a jelling agent; gum arabic (see GUM); and agar (see BACTERIOLOGY: *Culture*), used in the production of adhesive (q.v.) materials, sizing materials, and emulsions. Gum arabic is also used in demulcent medicines. Agar, a constituent of some laxatives, is also used as a thickening agent in food and as a medium for bacterial culture.

**CARBOLIC ACID.** Former name of phenol (q.v.).

**CARBON,** element with at.no. 6, at.wt. 12.010, b.p. over 4500° C. (8132°F.), m.p. sublimes above 3500° C. (6332° F.), sp.gr. of diamond 3.15–3.53, sp.gr. of graphite 2.3, and symbol C. In 1961 carbon-12, the most common isotope of carbon, was assigned the atomic weight of exactly 12 and was chosen to replace oxygen-16 as the standard for atomic weights; see ATOM AND ATOMIC THEORY: *Atomic Weight*.

Pure carbon occurs in three forms: diamond, graphite, and amorphous carbon. All forms are solids of extremely high melting point, and are insoluble in all solvents at ordinary temperatures. Carbon burns in air at high temperatures, and it dissolves in some molten metals, notably molten iron.

Graphite and diamond are discussed in separate articles. Amorphous carbon is found in varying degrees of purity in charcoal, coal, coke, carbon black, and lampblack. Absolutely pure amorphous carbon may be made by heating purified sugar at 900° C. (1652° F.) without access of air. Lampblack, sometimes incorrectly called carbon black, is made by burning natural gas with an insufficient quantity of air, producing a smoky flame. The smoke or soot is collected in a separate chamber. Lampblack was long used as a black pigment in inks and paints, but it has been almost entirely displaced by carbon black. This latter product, also called gas black, is made by the incomplete combustion of natural gas in contact with moving, cold, metallic surfaces. It is finer than lampblack, with particle sizes ranging from 0.0001 to 0.0002 in. United States production of carbon black averages about 2,500,000,000 lb. a year; Texas and Louisiana are the leading producers. About 75 percent of this production is absorbed by the rubber industry, which uses carbon black as a filler and reinforcing agent. The remainder is used as a pigment in the manufacture of such substances as inks, polishes, paints, and carbon paper.

Bone black, or animal charcoal, which absorbs many kinds of coloring substances, is used as a decolorizing agent in the refining of sugar, glycerine, and fats. Activated carbon, prepared from coconut husks, fruit pits, or other organic matter, is a form of charcoal from which foreign substances such as hydrocarbons have been removed by distillation and steam treatment. It is used in gas masks, as a clarifying and decolorizing agent, in removing fusel oil from alcohol, and in absorbing vapors in various chemical processes; it can be reactivated by reheating.

Carbon reacts directly with most metals to form compounds called carbides (q.v.). It forms three oxides: carbon monoxide, $CO$; carbon dioxide, $CO_2$ (qq.v.); and carbon suboxide, $C_3O_2$. Carbon dioxide combines with metallic oxides to form an important group of compounds called carbonates (q.v.). Carbon also forms compounds with most of the nonmetallic elements, although some of these, such as carbon tetrachloride, $CCl_4$, must be formed indirectly. See CHEMISTRY: *Organic Chemistry*.

Carbon is not a common element, making up only about 1/4000th of the crust of the earth, mostly in the form of carbonates. It is, however, vital to life, because it is an essential constituent of almost all biologically important chemicals, including protoplasm itself. Carbon atoms have the unusual ability to attach themselves to one another, forming complex chains and rings. This characteristic leads to an almost infinite variety of carbon compounds and justifies setting up a separate branch of chemistry for these compounds alone. The combination of carbon plus hydrogen, the most common of carbon compounds, is involved in over 1,000,000 known organic compounds. The number of inorganic compounds is much smaller. See CHEMISTRY, ORGANIC.

In biochemical research carbon is used extensively as a tracer element (see TRACERS). The artificially prepared radioisotope carbon-14 is suitable for most organic tracer studies because of its slow rate of decay. This radioisotope is utilized also in the technique called radiocarbon dating, which provides a means of determining the approximate age of fossils and other organic materials. The radiocarbon technique is possible because carbon-14 is produced in the atmosphere by cosmic rays and is incorporated into all living matter: as carbon-14 decays with a half-life (q.v.) of 5570 years, the radiocarbon activity of an organic specimen is a measure of its approximate age. See RADIOACTIVITY.

**CARBONADO.** See DIAMOND.

**CARBONARI** (It., "charcoal burners"), early 19th-century secret political society active in Italy and France. The group originated in Naples during the reign of Joachim Murat (q.v.) as a nationalist and anticlerical movement seeking the political independence of the Italian states from foreign and papal rule. Later the society adopted antimonarchical aims and spread to France. After 1820 Paris became the international headquarters of the Carbonari, which at its height numbered about 700,000 members. Although the membership was drawn from all social classes, young men of the bourgeoisie (q.v.) and armed forces were the most numerous. The secret ritual of the Carbonari used terminology borrowed from the Italian charcoal burners of the mountains where the Carbonari held their first secret meetings. The members were organized in a hierarchy of lodges in two parallel structures, one in the civil population and the other in the armed forces.

Attempting to overthrow tyranny by rebellions, principally in the armed forces, the Carbonari led several unsuccessful uprisings in Italy in the 1820's. They participated in the French revolution of 1830, after which date most French Carbonari supported Louis Philippe (q.v.), King of France. About 1831 Giuseppe Mazzini (q.v.), an active member of the Carbonari, founded a new secret society called Young Italy. This group absorbed most of the membership of the Carbonari, which then ceased to be an effective political movement.

**CARBONATES,** compounds containing the carbonate radical, $CO_3$. Carbonates may be considered as derivatives of carbonic acid, $H_2CO_3$, formed when carbon dioxide, $CO_2$, dissolves in water. If the hydrogen atoms in carbonic acid are replaced by metal atoms, an inorganic carbonate is formed, exemplified by sodium carbonate, $Na_2CO_3$. If the hydrogen atoms are replaced by organic radicals, organic carbonates, or carbonic acid, esters are formed. An example is ethyl carbonate, $(C_2H_5)_2CO_3$.

Several inorganic carbonates occur in nature and are important minerals or ores; these include calcite (q.v.), $CaCO_3$; magnesite (q.v.), $MgCO_3$; siderite, $FeCO_3$; and smithsonite, $ZnCO_3$. As a class, they can be recognized by their effervescence when treated with hydrochloric acid. All these carbonates decompose when heated, yielding carbon-dioxide gas and usually a solid metal oxide.

Only the alkali-metal carbonates dissolve readily in water, and the resulting solutions are alkaline. Because of their alkalinity, solutions of sodium carbonate, known as washing soda, are used as cleaning agents and water softeners. Although sodium carbonate occurs to some extent in nature, most of this substance is made commercially by the Solvay process (*see* SODA).

Replacement of only half the hydrogen of carbonic acid produces bicarbonates, or hydrogen carbonates, which contain the bicarbonate radical, $HCO_3$. Only the alkali-metal bicarbonates are stable enough to be isolated. Among the bicarbonates, sodium bicarbonate, $NaHCO_3$, or baking soda (*see* SODA), is the best known and the most useful.

**CARBON BLACK.** *See* CARBON.

**CARBON COMPOUNDS.** *See* CHEMISTRY: *Organic Chemistry.*

**CARBONDALE,** city of Illinois, in Jackson Co., about 19 miles S.W. of West Frankfort. Carbondale is in an agricultural and bituminous coal-mining region. The city is a trade and rail center for the area. Clothing is manufactured. It is the site of Southern Illinois University (q.v.). A United States Army ordnance plant, a wildlife refuge, Giant City State Park, and Crab Orchard Lake are nearby. Pop. (1960) 14,670; (1970) 22,816.

**CARBONDALE,** city of Pennsylvania, in Lackawanna Co., on the Lackawanna R., about 14 miles N.E. of Scranton. Carbondale is in an anthracite coal-mining area. Manufactures include metal products, textiles, and plastics. Pop. (1960) 13,595; (1970) 12,808.

**CARBON DIOXIDE,** colorless, odorless, and slightly acid-tasting gas, sometimes called carbonic acid gas, the molecule of which consists of one atom of carbon joined to two atoms of oxygen ($CO_2$). It was called "fixed air" by the Scottish chemist Joseph Black (q.v.), who obtained it by the decomposition of chalk and limestone and recognized that it entered into the chemical composition of these substances. The French chemist Antoine Laurent Lavoisier (q.v.) proved that it is an oxide of carbon by showing that the gas obtained by the combustion of charcoal is identical in its properties with the "fixed air" obtained by Black. Carbon dioxide is about 1.5 times as dense as air. It is soluble in water, 0.9 volume of the gas dissolving in 1 volume of water at 20° C. (68° F.).

Carbon dioxide is produced in a variety of ways: (1) by combustion, or oxidation (q.v.), of materials containing carbon, such as coal, wood, oil, or foods; (2) by fermentation of sugars; and (3) by decomposition of carbonates under the influence of heat or acids. Commercially, carbon dioxide is recovered from furnace or kiln gases; from fermentation (q.v.) processes; from reaction of carbonates with acids; and from reaction of steam with natural gas, a step in the commercial production of ammonia (q.v.). The carbon dioxide is purified by dissolving it in a concentrated solution of alkali carbonate (*see* ALKALIES) or ethanolamine, and then heating the solution with steam. The gas is evolved and is compressed into steel cylinders.

The atmosphere (q.v.) contains carbon dioxide in variable amounts, usually 3 to 4 parts per 10,000. It is used by green plants in the process known as photosynthesis (q.v.), by which carbohydrates are manufactured.

Carbon dioxide is used in the manufacture of sodium carbonate, $Na_2CO_3 \cdot 10H_2O$ (washing soda); sodium bicarbonate, $NaHCO_3$ (baking soda); and basic carbonate of lead, $Pb_3(OH)_2(CO_3)_2$ (white lead). Dissolved under a pressure of 2 to 5 atmospheres, carbon dioxide causes the effervescence in carbonated beverages. Carbon dioxide does not burn and does not support ordinary combustion, and because of these properties it is used for extinguishing fires. The $CO_2$ extinguisher is a steel cylinder filled with liquid carbon dioxide, which, when released, expands suddenly and causes so great a lowering of temperature that it solidifies into powdery "snow". This snow volatilizes upon

*A fossilized crinoid or sea lily from the Carboniferous Period imbedded in limestone. Its stalk held the sea lily to the ocean floor.*  American Museum of Natural History

contact with the burning substance, producing a blanket of gas that cools and smothers the flame. Solid carbon dioxide, known as dry ice, is widely used as a refrigerant. Its cooling effect is almost twice that of water ice; its special advantages are that it does not melt as a liquid but turns into gas, and that it produces an inert atmosphere that reduces bacterial growth.

The presence of carbon dioxide in the blood stimulates breathing (see RESPIRATION). For this reason, carbon dioxide is added to oxygen or ordinary air in artificial respiration, and to the gases used in anesthesia (q.v.).

**CARBON DISULFIDE,** colorless, extremely volatile and flammable compound, $CS_2$, with a disagreeable, fetid odor, freezing point −111.53° C., b.p. 46.25° C., and density of 1.256 g per milliliter at 25° C. It is made by heating carbon and sulfur together, or by the reaction between methane and sulfur vapor. It is used as a solvent (q.v.) for oils, fats, and waxes; as a reagent in the manufacture of regenerated cellulose (q.v.); as the starting material in the manufacture of carbon tetrachloride (q.v.); and in the vulcanization of rubber (q.v.). About 1,000,-

000,000 lb. of carbon disulfide were produced annually in the United States in the late 1960's; about 65 percent of this was used for rayon and cellophane (qq.v.) production, and 15 percent was used for the manufacture of carbon tetrachloride. See CHEMICAL COMPOUNDS, SYNTHETIC.

**CARBONIFEROUS PERIOD,** a division of geologic time in the Paleozoic Era, following the Devonian Period and preceding the Permian Period (qq.v.). It is subdivided into two closely related periods with an indeterminate time boundary between them; the earlier is the Mississippian Period, the later, the Pennsylvanian Period. Together they span about 80,000,000 years, beginning about 350,000,000 years ago. The name Carboniferous (Lat. *carbo,* "coal"; *ferre,* "to bear") was first used in England, because of the coal seams contained in the strata; see COAL. The rocks of the Carboniferous systems include a vast series of sandstones, shales, conglomerates, limestones, and beds of coal, which are of variable thickness and more or less interbedded. The Carboniferous and underlying Devonian rocks in both Europe and North America are similar. The rocks often show a basin-shaped arrangement, and in some areas intense folding; but thousands of square miles of nearly horizontal Carboniferous strata are found in China, the U.S.S.R., and western North America.

The Carboniferous rock strata are classified into an upper, Pennsylvanian system, and a lower, Mississippian system. These systems are found in a number of areas in North America. In Rhode Island is a small system of highly metamorphosed rocks, in which the coal beds are partly anthracitic. A large area of Carboniferous strata extends from Pennsylvania southward to Alabama and westward to Missouri and Arkansas and Texas. Along the Appalachians the prevailing rocks of this period are sandstones and shales, which contain many coal seams and are much folded; but westward the folds die out and limestones begin to predominate. Workable beds of coal are found in all the States of this area. In the Mississippi valley the crinoidal limestones are important members. The Carboniferous sections show a variable thickness, having a maximum of nearly 8000 ft. in Pennsylvania and only 1200 ft. to 1500 ft. in Illinois; the beds thicken again in the States west of the Rocky Mts. (Utah, Nevada, and Arizona), where they are represented mainly by limestones and sandstones that contain no coal. Where coal occurs, it usually rests on beds of clay, representing the ancient soils, in which are sometimes found the upright trunks of trees, still rooted, that grew in the many stretches of Carboniferous swampland.

**Flora and Fauna.** Animal and vegetable remains are abundant in the Carboniferous Period and, in many cases, are well preserved. Great uniformity is observed in the character of plant life, the same genera and often the same species being found in widely separated regions. About 2000 species are known, most of which belong to the flowerless cryptogams. In addition to numerous ferns, early club mosses, horsetails, and forest trees (*Cordaites*) were common. The contemporary land fauna has left few traces, but the fauna of seas and lagoons is much better represented. The first true reptiles began to appear, developing from the earlier amphibians. Corals, crinoids, and minute foraminifers were abundant. A few trilobites and eurypterids were to be found. Snails and mollusks, including cephalopods and nautiloids, were widespread. Insects were frequent, particularly a giant form of dragonfly. Polyzoa and brachiopods were common, and ganoid and placoid fishes and sharks were well represented. See GEOLOGY, HISTORICAL; PALEONTOLOGY.

**CARBON MONOXIDE,** chemical compound of carbon and oxygen with the formula CO. At ordinary temperatures it is a gas; when cooled below $-139°$ C. ($-218°$ F.) it can be liquefied; the liquid boils at $-192°$ C. ($-314°$ F.) at ordinary pressure and freezes at $-207°$ C. ($-341°$ F.). Carbon monoxide is a colorless, odorless gas, about 3 percent lighter than air, and is violently poisonous to man and all warm-blooded animals and to many other forms of life. When inhaled it combines with hemoglobin (q.v.) in the blood, preventing absorption of oxygen.

Carbon monoxide is formed whenever carbon or substances containing carbon are burned with an insufficient air supply. Even when the amount of air supplied is theoretically sufficient, the reaction is not always complete, so that the combustion gases contain some free oxygen and some carbon monoxide.

An incomplete reaction is especially probable when it takes place quickly, as in an automobile engine; for this reason, automobile-exhaust gases contain harmful quantities of carbon monoxide, sometimes several percent, although antipollution devices are intended to keep the level below 1 percent. As little as $\frac{1}{1000}$ of 1 percent of carbon monoxide in air may produce symptoms of poisoning, and as little as $\frac{1}{5}$ of 1 percent may prove fatal in less than 30 min. It is a major ingredient of urban air pollution (q.v.).

Because of its odorless nature, carbon monoxide is an insidious poison. It produces only mild symptoms of headache, nausea, or fatigue, followed by unconsciousness. An automobile engine running in a closed garage can make the air noxious within a few minutes; a leaking furnace flue may fill a house with unsuspected poison. Fuel gas, which may contain as much as 50 percent carbon monoxide, often has small quantities of unpleasant-smelling sulfur compounds purposely added to render leaks noticeable.

Carbon monoxide is an important industrial fuel because it contains more than two thirds of the heating value of the carbon from which it was formed. It is a constituent of water gas, producer gas, blast furnace gas, and coal gas; see GAS. In the smelting of iron ore, carbon monoxide formed from coke used in the process acts as a reducing agent, that is, it removes oxygen from the ore. Carbon monoxide is an unsaturated compound and will combine with other substances as well as with oxygen. Thus it combines actively with chlorine to form carbonyl chloride, or phosgene (q.v.), and it combines with hydrogen, when heated in the presence of a catalyst (see CATALYSIS), to form methyl alcohol. The direct combination of carbon monoxide with certain metals, forming gaseous compounds, is used in refining those metals, particularly nickel.

**CARBON TETRACHLORIDE,** heavy, colorless liquid, $CCl_4$, with a characteristic non-irritant odor, freezing point $-22.92°$ C., b.p. $76.72°$ C., and density of 1.5947 g per milliliter at 20° C. It is made by treating carbon disulfide (q.v.), $CS_2$, with sulfur monochloride, $S_2Cl_2$, or by the chlorination (see CHLORINE) of hydrocarbons (q.v.). About 500,000,000 lb. of carbon tetrachloride are produced annually in the United States, nearly all of which is used to make compounds such as chlorofluoromethanes, used as refrigerants, and as aerosol-spray propellants; see AEROSOL; REFRIGERATION.

**CARBORUNDUM.** See ABRASIVE.

**CARBUNCLE,** in gemology, common name for almandite, a variety of the gemstone garnet (q.v.), formerly used for jewelry and carved with a convex face. In the early Christian Era, the term was applied indiscriminately to rubies and most other red, fiery stones. See GEM; RUBY.

**CARBUNCLE,** in medicine, localized inflammation of tissue under the skin caused by infection. A carbuncle is caused usually by the bacteria staphylococcus, and is larger and more serious than a boil that results from an inflammation beginning in an infected hair-sac. As the carbuncle develops, the area affected becomes red and swells slightly. The subcutaneous tissue becomes hard, the color darkens, and several heads may develop and discharge pus. Tissue is destroyed and sloughs off, leaving a scar upon healing. Building up the general health and resistance of the patient is the principal treatment. Local treatment usually includes surgery and the use of antibiotics and antiseptics.

**CARBURETOR,** device used in gasoline-powered internal-combustion engines to meter and inject the fuel into the engine inlet airstream in correct amounts to assure proper combustion; *see* INTERNAL-COMBUSTION ENGINE. Gasoline-powered land vehicles and boats usually have a float carburetor in which a float controls the level of the fuel by opening or closing the fuel-inlet valve. The fuel is sucked through jets into the air-inlet manifold, which has a restriction or venturi tube at the jet exits so that the air is speeded up and its pressure reduced by Bernoulli's principle (q.v.) to provide the necessary suction. The fuel is then vaporized and mixed with air before entering the cylinders, where combustion takes place.

Efficient engine operation depends on the correct mixture of air and fuel, with about 15 lb. of air for 1 lb. of gasoline for normal steady-speed running. The fuel droplets must also be completely vaporized in the air-inlet manifold, which is sufficiently hot to achieve this after the engine has been running for a while. To start a cold engine, in which vaporization would be in-

complete, however, the air inlet to the carburetor is partially blocked by a choke valve to create an additional vacuum at the location of the jet, and to permit additional fuel to be sucked in. A starting engine thus runs at a rich mixture of about 10 to 12 lb. of air for 1 lb. of fuel. The power output of the engine is controlled by a butterfly throttle valve at the outlet of the carburetor which controls the air, and with it the fuel flow. Modern carburetors also utilize additional valves and jets to permit idling of the engine if the throttle is closed, and to assure proper engine operation over the full speed and power range. An injection pump is sometimes added, providing additional fuel for fast acceleration when the engine needs a rich mixture for quick spurts.

In gasoline-powered, piston-driven aircraft engines, the float is replaced with a spring-loaded diaphragm to meter the fuel evenly under maneuvering conditions in which a float valve would not work. In addition, the fuel is usually injected through a spray nozzle to avoid vapor lock or carburetor icing which can occur at high altitudes. Injectors are also used for high-performance or racing-car engines with the fuel for each cylinder metered and injected separately. Diesel engines, which operate at higher cylinder pressures and temperatures than gasoline engines, do not depend on a premixed air-fuel mixture. Instead, a fuel pump meters and injects the fuel directly into the cylinders

*Diagram of a carburetor.*     American Motors Corp.

Bowl Vent Valve     Air Horn Assembly

Code Tag     Main Body Assembly

Heat Shield

Power Valve     Accelerator Pump Assembly

Idle Limiter Cap

The crenellated walls of the Cité (restored in 1855–79) once protected Carcassone against the siege (1355) of the Black Prince, Edward of England.

French Cultural Services

through a properly-timed intermittent high-pressure atomizing spray.                    F.La.

**CARCAJOU.**  *See* WOLVERINE.

**CARCASSONNE,**  town in France, and capital of Aude Department, on the Aude R., about 50 miles S.E. of Toulouse. Carcassonne is divided into two sections: the modern town of Ville Basse; and the medieval walled town known as the Cité. The business of the town is concentrated in Ville Basse which is an important center of trade in wine, grain, and fruit produced in the surrounding region. The town has an important clothing industry; other industries include tanning, distilling, and the manufacture of agricultural implements, preserved fruits, and jam. Ville Basse contains the 13th-century Cathedral of Saint Michael and the 14th-century Church of Saint Vincent. The Cité contains some of the finest remains of medieval fortifications in Europe, and is an important tourist attraction. Set atop a hill on the left bank of the Aude R., the Cité contains ancient ramparts and towers, some parts dating from the time of the Visigoths (*see* GOTHS), and others from the 11th to the 13th centuries. A 12th-century castle and the Romanesque and Gothic Church of Saint-Nazaire (11th to 14th centuries) is located in the old town.

The Cité was the site of a Roman town which fell to the Visigoths (*see* GOTHS: *Visigoths*) in the 5th century. In the 8th century, it came under Frankish rule; *see* FRANKS. During the crusade against the Albigenses (q.v.) in the 13th century, the town was captured and the inhabitants massacred by the English general Simon de Montfort (q.v.). Carcassonne became a possession of the French crown in 1247. The Cité was restored in the 19th century by the French architect Eugène Emmanuel Viollet-le-Duc (q.v.). Pop. (1968 est.) 43,709.

**CARCHARODON,** genus of sharks of the family Lamnidae. The man-eater or great white shark, *C. carcharias,* is the most formidable of all sharks and one of the largest, swiftest, and most voracious of fish. The thick, rounded body of the white shark attains a length of up to 40 ft., with jaws about 2 ft. wide. This species has a pointed snout and teeth that are large, triangular, and sharp, with serrated edges. Found along both coasts of the United States and in almost all tropical and temperate seas, the man-eater is carnivorous, feeding on large fishes, seals, and other marine animals. The great white shark is extremely dangerous. It has been known to maim or kill bathers and attack small boats without provocation. Fossil remains indicate that extinct forms of *Carcharodon* attained a length of about 90 ft. *See* SHARK.

**CARCINOMA.** *See* CANCER.

**CARDAMINE.** *See* CRESS.

**CARDAMOM** *or* **CARDAMON,** aromatic seed of certain species of Zingiberaceae (Ginger) family, particularly *Elettaria cardamomum,* native to India and southeastern Asia. The plant has large leaves and white flowers with blue stripes and yellow borders; it grows to about 10 ft. in height. The fruit is a small capsule containing eight to sixteen brown seeds, which are used as a spice for foods and beverages.

**CÁRDENAS, Lázaro** (1895–1970), Mexican soldier and statesman, born in Jiquilpán de Juárez, Michoacán State. Leaving school at eleven, he was apprenticed to a printer and at the age of seventeen organized a cooperative printing establishment. Following the overthrow of President Porfirio Díaz (q.v.) in 1911, intermittent revolution plagued Mexico, and in 1913 Cárdenas joined the local revolutionary forces. During the next sixteen years he took part in many revolutionary campaigns and in 1925 was made a brigadier general in the Mexican revolutionary army. He served as governor of Michoacán State from 1928 to 1932 and in the meantime was chosen (1930) president of the National Revolutionary Party. He became minister of the interior of Mexico in 1931 and minister of war and marine in 1933. Cárdenas was president of Mexico from 1934 to 1940. During his administration the six-year plan for economic and social reform formulated by his party was put into action. Large tracts of privately owned land were divided and distributed among the peasants, and many industries were converted to worker cooperatives. In 1938 foreign-owned oil properties were nationalized. Although a conciliatory attitude was taken toward the Roman Catholic Church, education was secularized. Cárdenas was one of the most popular presidents of Mexico, but under Mexican law he could not run for a second term. In 1942 he was made commander of all Mexican forces on the Pacific coast, and he also served as minister of defense (1942–45). In 1955 he was awarded the Stalin Peace Prize, which he accepted. He refused the money that accompanied it, however, and in his acceptance speech denounced dictatorships, saying that promises of peace lack meaning when individual liberty is not respected.

*See also* MEXICO: *History.*

**CARD GAMES.** *See* CARDS, PLAYING; see also separate articles on many popular games.

**CARDIAC.** *See* HEART.

**CARDIFF,** Great Britain, county borough of Glamorganshire, Wales, near the N. coast of Bristol Channel about 1 mi. above the mouth of the Taff R., and about 130 miles W. of London. Cardiff is the largest city in Wales and one of the most important seaports of Great Britain with extensive docking and shipping facilities. The chief export is coal. Among the principal industries are fishing, shipbuilding, flour milling, and the manufacture of metal products, chemicals, and paper. Cardiff is the site of the University of Wales and of its constituent University College of South Wales and Monmouthshire. Points of historic interest in the city include Cardiff Castle, built in the 11th century, and the Church of Saint John the Baptist, the tower of which was constructed in the 15th century. The history of Cardiff dates from the 1st century, when the Romans established a camp in the area. After the Roman withdrawal, the area was settled by Welsh natives. Occupied by the Normans in the 11th century, Cardiff was for several centuries thereafter a possession of feudal lords. In the first part of the 19th century it became an outlet for the mineral wealth of the surrounding region and, for a time, chief coal-export center of the world. It was chartered as a city in 1905. Pop. (1971) 278,221.

**CARDIGAN, 7th Earl of, James Thomas Brudenell** (1797–1868), British army officer, born in Hambleden, England, and educated at the University of Oxford. Cardigan was a member of the House of Commons from 1818 to 1829, and entered the army in 1824. He was forced to give up his first command in 1834, however, because of his dictatorial behavior with a subordinate officer. In 1836 he was able to secure command of a unit later known as the 11th Hussars. As commander of a light cavalry brigade in the Crimean War (q.v.), he led the famous Charge of the Six Hundred at Balaklava (q.v.), Oct. 25, 1854. The British brigade was virtually annihilated. Cardigan survived the battle, was acclaimed a hero, and became a lieutenant general in 1861. The cardigan, a buttoned sweater, is named for him.

**CARDIGAN BAY,** semicircular bend of Saint George's Channel in the Irish Sea, on the w. coast of Wales. The bay is about 65 mi. long and 35 mi. wide.

**CARDIGANSHIRE,** Great Britain, a county in Wales, on Cardigan Bay, an inlet of Saint George's Channel. The eastern section of the county is mountainous, with an extreme elevation of about 2450 ft. The coastal terrain consists of a low plateau, broken by a series of valleys with generally poor soil. Stock farming, mainly the raising of cattle, sheep, and horses, is the chief activity, but dairying is gradually becoming an important industry. A small fishing industry exists in the coastal towns, a number of which are summer resorts. The leading manufacturing industry is woolen weaving. For centuries, Cardiganshire was noted for lead mines, and from 1830 to 1880 it was a leading lead-producing region. Partly because of inadequate railway facilities, the industry subsequently declined in importance. Both rail and highway communications are still poorly developed, making the county one of the most inaccessible in Great Britain. Many traditional Welsh customs are retained by the people, who use the Welsh language (q.v.) more extensively than do the inhabitants of other sections of Wales. Various relics dating from the Bronze Age and ancient Roman ruins, including the remnants of a highway, have been found in the county. Most of the population lives on scattered farms. The principal towns are Aberystwyth and the county town of Cardigan. Area, 693 sq.mi.; pop. (1971) 54,882.

**CARDINAL** (Lat. *cardinalis*, "pivotal", "principal", from *cardo*, "hinge"), highest dignitary in the Roman Catholic Church after the pope (q.v.), whose elector and councillor he is. Applied in the period following the councils of Nicaea (*see* NICAEA, COUNCILS OF) to the clergy who were permanently attached to a cathedral church anywhere, the title was later restricted to particular members of the clergy in Rome. Gradually the priests permanently ruling the parish churches in Rome were called cardinal priests; the deacons permanently administering the charities of a particular region of the city were called cardinal deacons; and the bishops in charge of the suburban sees of Rome were called cardinal bishops. Until the late Middle Ages the term "cardinal" was used to designate prominent priests in important churches, such as those of Constantinople (now İstanbul, Turkey), Naples, and Milan.

The cardinals are appointed by the pope and constitute the Sacred College. The pope is not obliged to consult them, but does so as a matter of fact. Their number has varied at different times; in 1586 it was fixed by Pope Sixtus V (*see under* SIXTUS) at seventy, that is, six cardinal bishops, fifty cardinal priests, and fourteen cardinal deacons. The pope, however, was not obliged to maintain this number, and there were generally from ten to fifteen vacancies. The cardinal bishops take their ecclesiastical names from the suburban sees mentioned above; the cardinal priests, the majority of whom are bishops throughout the world, are given titles taken from the churches of Rome; and the cardinal deacons are usually priests associated with the administrative offices of the Vatican. In 1958 Pope John XXIII (*see under* JOHN) abrogated the legislation that limited the number of cardinals to seventy; Pope Paul VI (*see under* PAUL) followed John's tradition, so that, by the late 1960's, no limit was set to the number of cardinals at any given time. As a result of the consistory announced in 1973, the college included 145 cardinals (twelve of them American).

Precedence in the Sacred College is determined by the see held and by the date of consecration of the individual cardinal. Those consecrated earlier rank higher in the college. The dean of the Sacred College, a cardinal bishop, is elected to the post of dean, according to a ruling by Pope Paul VI in 1965. The first cardinal bishop has the right to consecrate the pope if the pope is not a bishop at the time of his enthronement; *see* CONSECRATION. The first cardinal deacon is first deacon of the college and has the right to proclaim and crown the new pope. The cardinal camerlengo (chamberlain) takes care of the temporal good of the Holy See and rules the church during a papal vacancy.

The cardinals are chief members of the Sacred Congregations of the papal government. They meet in consistory (q.v.), or assembly, over which the pope presides. Cardinals are limited in their duties according to age; like other high prelates, they are expected to retire at 75 from administrative duties. At 80 they are no longer permitted to serve as papal electors. These restrictions were announced by Paul VI in 1970. As electors of the pope, they usually choose one of their own number for that honor; *see* CONCLAVE. They enjoy extraordinary privileges and honors,

*Cardinal bird,* Richmondena cardinalis
Maslowski and Goodpaster—National Audubon Society

and are addressed as "Eminence", usually either "His Eminence" or "Your Eminence", or "lord cardinal". They wear a distinctive scarlet dress and a red cap, or biretta, that is placed on their heads by the pope. The use of the galero, or large, tasseled, red hat that was given to them in a public consistory, was discarded by decree of the pope in 1969. Cardinals in charge of Sacred Congregations, Tribunals, or Offices enjoy an income from the papal treasury. Cardinals frequently act as the pope's representatives upon delicate missions; for the duration of such missions they are called *legati a latere.*

See also ROMAN CATHOLIC CHURCH; VESTMENTS, ECCLESIASTICAL.

**CARDINAL BIRD,** or REDBIRD, a large and brilliant bird, *Richmondena cardinalis,* of the Finch family. It is one of the finest song birds of America, and is common throughout the southern part of the United States. The cardinal grows to a length of 8 in. The general color of the male is red, the head being vermilion, with a small black portion around the base of the bill. The female cardinal is much less brightly colored than the male. The feathers of the crown are long, and erected into a conical crest. The cardinal bird migrates northward in spring, but never farther than Massachusetts. Its loud, clear, sweet, and varied song is heard chiefly in the mornings and evenings. It is a popular cage bird. The nest is built in bushes, and consists of twigs, rootlets, and strips of bark, lined with grasses and other finer material. The eggs are usually

four in number, white or bluish, speckled and spotted with brown. Geographical races of this species extend its range westward to southern California and Mexico, and related species are found in Mexico and Central America.

**CARDINAL FLOWER,** common name for a perennial herb plant, *Lobelia cardinalis,* of the family Lobeliaceae. It is a narrow-leaved plant about 4 ft. high with a cluster of brilliant red flowers. Common in marshy places throughout the eastern United States and Canada, the cardinal flower is found growing in the slack water of shallow streams. See LOBELIA.

**CARDOZO, Benjamin Nathan** (1870–1938), American jurist, born in New York City, and educated at Columbia University. In 1891 Cardozo was admitted to the bar and began to practice law in New York City. In 1914 he was elected justice of the supreme court of the State of New York. The following year he became associate justice of the court of appeals of the State of New York, and in 1927 he was made chief justice of that court. Five years later Cardozo succeeded Oliver Wendell Holmes (q.v.) as Associate Justice of the United States Supreme Court. Recognized as one of the most influential liberal judges of his time, Cardozo was famous for his scholarly opinions written with exceptional clarity, and for his liberal interpretation of legal questions, particularly those dealing with public welfare. Cardozo upheld most of the New Deal (q.v.) measures advocated by the administration of President Franklin Delano Roosevelt (q.v.) that came before the U.S. Supreme Court, notably the Social Security Act, for which he wrote the majority opinion. The writings of Cardozo include *The Nature of the Judicial Process* (1921), *The Growth of the Law* (1924), and *The Paradoxes of Legal Science* (1928).

**CARDS, PLAYING,** set of flat pieces of thin pasteboard or cardboard used in playing various games of skill and chance. Cards are ornamented with figures and numbers and are usually rectangular in shape, usually with rounded corners. Some scholars believe that man began making cards soon after he learned to draw pictures, at first perhaps for magical purposes and later to serve as markers in intellectual contests simulating maneuver and battle. According to one theory, cards originated in India as a derivative of chess (q.v.), for the purpose of providing young nobles with a bloodless equivalent for war. Other theories credit the invention of cards to the Egyptians, Babylonians, or Chinese of ancient times.

Reference to playing cards did not appear in

The earliest existing printed European playing cards were made from wood blocks in 15th-century France.

European writings until the 13th century; this fact suggests that cards were brought back from the Middle East by the crusaders. By the 14th century playing games with cards had become a fashionable pastime throughout the Continent, particularly in Italy, where the tarrocchi or tarot, deck was developed. This deck consisted of seventy-eight cards, organized into four plain suits and a triumph, or trump, suit. Each plain suit had ten cards, numbered from one through ten, and four court cards representing a king, queen, chevalier, and valet. The trumps, or *atouts,* were picture cards, numbered from one to twenty-one with one unnumbered card, the fool, from which the modern joker was derived. The trumps stood for the physical and spiritual forces affecting man. Plain suits represented social positions and occupations, the aristocracy being symbolized by swords (later spades), the merchant class by coins (later diamonds), the clergy by cups (later hearts), and the peasantry by staves (later clubs).

Shorter decks were later developed without trump suits and with the valet and knave combined into one card, known today as the jack in the United States, knave in England, and cavalier in Italy. Packs of from thirty-two to forty-eight cards are used in several countries, among them Spain, Italy, and Germany. In England, the U.S., France, and certain other countries, the pack became generally standardized at fifty-two cards, though sets of denominations are deleted for such short-deck games as piquet and euchre. A later development was a special deck for games of the pinochle family consisting of doubles of denominations from seven or nine up, but containing no cards of lower rank. To lend flexibility to certain games, the mistigris, or joker, representing the court jester who could assume any role he chose, was added to the standard deck.

A wide variety of pictures, symbols, and designs have been imprinted on cards. Suits have been indicated by acorns, bells, birds, crowns, eagles, elephants, flowers, hawks, horsemen, leaves, or simply numbers. Attempts have been made in France, the U.S., and the Soviet Union to replace permanently the monarchs of the playing deck with national heroes and legendary figures. From time to time manufacturers have tried to supplant the traditional red and black suits with suits of four distinct colors, such as black, yellow, red, and green. None of these changes, however, was well received by card players.

As early as the 15th century, decks of cards that told stories, satirized politics, lampooned famous personalities, or recorded historical events were published widely throughout Europe. Humorous proverbs and love mottoes, as well as the words and music of songs, have been printed on playing cards.

**Card Games.** Hundreds of card games have been devised, but few have had lasting appeal. Such once-popular games as swabbers, ombre,

*Two atout cards representing the sun (left) and the moon (right), from a tarot pack of the late 17th century.*

quadrille, triomphe, and noddy survive only through their influence on modern games. Poker, for example, is based on the forgotten games of poque, primero, and brag.

Although no precise classification is possible, card games may be divided, for convenience, into five broad categories. The first group includes the trick-winning games, in which certain cards or an entire suit are trumps. Among these are the various forms of whist, bridge, euchre, five hundred, and skat. A second group comprises games in which bidding and trumps also figure but in which the object is to own or win certain valuable counting cards, and sometimes to show specific scoring combinations known as melds. Among such games are pinochle, klaberjass, bezique, piquet, sixty-six, and solo. The all-fours family of games may also be included in this category, along with the nontrump game of casino and the game of hearts, in which the aim is to avoid the capture of counting cards.

The object of another group of games is to obtain a given score by matching, assembling, or discarding cards. Of these the rummy games are the most widely played. Two of the most popular forms are gin and canasta. Related to rummy are the so-called stop games, such as fan-tan or crazy eights, in which a player may either match off eligible cards to a table layout according to denomination, suit, or sequence, or pass his turn if unable to do so. A similar idea of card disposal by matching plus rearranging underlies the varied forms of solitaire, as well as such children's games as authors and old maid.

Comprising a fourth category are the showdown games, in which players wager that they can show cards, or combinations of cards, outranking those of their opponents. Poker is the best known of the showdown games; among others are red dog and stuss. A final group, based on adding or matching numbers, includes such betting games as blackjack or twenty-one, baccarat and chemin de fer, and cribbage.

Most of the games mentioned above are played either with the full, standard fifty-two card deck; with decks from which cards have been stripped out to form a short deck; or with two or more standard decks combined to form a single playing pack, as in canasta. In many games one or more jokers may be added. For pinochle, a double-denomination pack is used.

Card play has a conventional terminology. Some of the most commonly used special words are defined as follows: call, a declaration or pass in bidding; color, a suit; cut, to divide the deck into two sections with the bottom portion going atop the other; deal, to distribute the cards, or the turn to distribute cards, or the active period from one distribution of cards to the next; deck, the cards used for the game, either the full pack or some portion of it; discard, to get rid of an undesired card (in rummy) or to play the card of a suit other than trump or the suit led (in trump games); follow suit, to play a card of the same suit as that led; hand, the cards dealt a player or held by him, or the player himself; meld, a valuable combination of cards, or to announce or show such a combination; shuffle, to mix the cards of a deck before dealing; trick, cards played collectively by all the players in one round; trump, a card or suit having greater power or value than other cards or suits; stock, the undealt portion of the deck, which may also be used for play in the same deal; wild card, or joker, a card that may be given any rank or suit, or both, by its holder.

The procedure for dealing the deck is standard throughout the world. The first turn to deal is usually decided by a turn of cards, the deal going to the high card when dealing is an advantage, to the low card when it is not. The deck, shuffled by the dealer or an opponent, is cut by the player to the right of the dealer, and cards are then distributed beginning with the player to the left. The same number of cards, as called for by the game, are dealt to the players in clockwise rotation. These cards are usually given face down, but some may be exposed, as in stud poker. Subsequent turns to deal generally pass around the table in clockwise rotation, alternate in two-handed games, or may go to the winner or loser of the preceding game.

Popular card games are described in this encyclopedia under individual entries.

**CARDUCCI, Giosuè,** pen name ENOTRIO ROMANO (1835–1907), Italian poet, critic, and teacher, born in Val di Castello, Tuscany, and educated at the University of Pisa. From 1860 to 1904 he was professor of Italian literature at the University of Bologna. Carducci was opposed to the papacy, the monarchy, and the romantic sentimentalism that dominated Italian literature at the time. He advocated a return to the pagan spirit in religion and a revival of the classical spirit and forms in literature. As a young man he frequently expressed his radical ideas in his poetry, but in his later years his writing became much less polemical. He was the first to adapt successfully classical Latin meters to modern Italian verse.

In 1906 Carducci became the first Italian to receive the Nobel Prize for literature. He is generally considered to be the greatest Italian poet of the late 19th century. Among his best works are *Rime Nuove* (1861–87; Eng. trans., *New Rhymes,* 1916), *Odi Barbari* (1877–89; Eng. trans., *Pagan Odes,* 1950), and *Rime e Ritmi* (1899; Eng. trans., *Lyrics and Rhythms,* 1942); see ITALIAN LITERATURE: *19th Century.*

**CAREW, Thomas** (1595?–1645?), English poet, born probably in West Wickham, Kent, and educated at the University of Oxford and Middle Temple. After a brief diplomatic career, Carew in 1630 became a court official to Charles I (q.v.), King of England, who considered him a favorite and presented him with an estate. Carew was the first of the so-called Cavalier poets (q.v.). He was strongly influenced by both the English poet Ben Jonson and the English metaphysical poet John Donne (qq.v.). Carew wrote numerous short songs and light love lyrics, many of which were set to music by composers. The poems are notable for their sensuous imagery and polished beauty. Carew is also well known for a longer love poem, "The Rapture", a masque (q.v.), and the poem "Elegy on the Death of Dr. Donne".

**CAREX,** widely distributed genus of grasslike plants called sedges, of the family Cyperaceae, including many hundreds of species found throughout temperate and arctic climates. Very few species are cultivated or have any agricultural use, although carex is sometimes of use in converting swamps into dry ground. *Carex morrowi* is sometimes cultivated as a pot or border plant for its white-striped, grasslike evergreen leaves.

**CAREY, Henry** (1687?–1743), British poet and composer, born in London, England. Carey is believed to have been an illegitimate son of the English statesman, the Marquis of Halifax, Sir George Savile (q.v.). He wrote a number of musical dramas, burlesques, and ballad operas, but he is most famous for his songs, particularly the ballad "Sally in Our Alley". Carey also wrote two volumes of poetry, one of which he set to music. Many years after his death, his son claimed that Carey wrote the British national anthem, "God Save the King". The claim, however, has been discounted by musical scholars.

**CARIA,** ancient country of S.W. Asia Minor (now part of Turkey), south of the Maeander (now Menderes) R., bordered on the S. by the Aegean Sea. The Taurus Mts. extend into the interior region, and the irregular coastline has numerous deep inlets. The islands of Rhodes and Kos (qq.v.) lie off the coast.

Ancient Greek and Roman historians recorded that the native people of this region were pushed inland by an influx of people called Carians. The Carians, who were notable as mercenary soldiers, had been driven from their native islands in the Aegean Sea by invading Greeks. The Greeks established colonies along the coast of Caria, notably Cnidus and Halicarnassus (qq.v.). In the 6th century B.C. Caria was incorporated into the kingdom of Lydia (q.v.), and then was made a Persian dominion, ruled by Carian kings who were subject to Cyrus the Great (q.v.). Mausolus (d. about 353 B.C.) was the best known of these monarchs; his widow built the Mausoleum (q.v.) at Halicarnassus, one of the Seven Wonders of the World (q.v.). In the 4th century B.C. the Macedonian conqueror Alexander III (q.v.), called The Great, seized Caria. In later years Caria became a part of the empire of Syria (q.v.) and then of the kingdom of Pergamum (q.v.), which in the 2nd century B.C. became the ancient Roman province of Asia.

**CARIB,** tribe of native American Indians of the Cariban linguistic stock, occupying various regions of South and Central America. During the late 15th century the Caribs occupied most of the islands of the Lesser Antilles and the coast of what is now Venezuela, territories from which they had expelled the Arawakan (q.v.) Indians. The Caribs, who probably originated in the valley of the Orinoco R. (q.v.), were noted for their ferocity and practiced cannibalism (q.v.); the word cannibal is derived from the Spanish term for these indians, *Caribales*. The Caribs were expert canoeists and their fleets sometimes included 100 canoes. They lived in small settlements and practiced fishing and agriculture. In the 17th century, when several European countries struggled for control of the Lesser Antilles, the Caribs were scattered. Large groups remained only on Saint Vincent Island and Dominica Island. In 1796 the British government deported almost all the remaining members of the tribe, numbering about 5000, from the island of St. Vincent to Roatan Island off the coast of Honduras. They spread over the neighboring mainland, and today they survive in Guatemala and in a reservation on Dominica.

*See* AMERICAN INDIAN LANGUAGES; AMERICAN INDIANS: *Indians of Mexico, Central America, and the West Indies.*

**CARIBBEAN SEA,** arm of the North Atlantic Ocean, partially enclosed on the N. and E. by the islands of the West Indies, and bounded on the S. by South America and Panama, and on the W. by Central America. The sea derives its name from the Carib (q.v.) Indians, who inhabited the area when Spanish explorers arrived there in the 15th century. The Caribbean is approximately 1500 mi. long E. and W. and between about 400 and 900 mi. wide. It has an area of about 750,000 sq.mi. At the N.W. extremity it is connected with the Gulf of Mexico by the Yucatán Channel, a passage about 120 mi. wide between Cuba and the Yucatán Peninsula (q.v.). The Windward Passage between Cuba and Haiti is a major shipping route between the United States and the Panama Canal. Many gulfs and bays indent the coastline of South America, notably the Gulf of Venezuela, which carries tidal waters to Lake Maracaibo in Venezuela, the largest lake of the continent. With a few exceptions the entire Caribbean basin is more than 6000 ft. deep. Large areas of the sea exceed 12,000 ft. in depth; the greatest depth measured thus far is Cayman Trench (24,720 ft.) between Jamaica and the Cayman Islands (q.v.). Navigation is open and clear, making the Caribbean a major trade route for Latin American countries. The major oceanic current in the Caribbean Sea is an extension of the North Equatorial and South Equatorial currents, which enter the sea at the S.E. extremity and flow in a generally N.W. direction. A popular resort area, the Caribbean Sea is noted for its mild tropical climate. *See* NEGROES IN LATIN AMERICA AND THE CARIBBEAN AREA.

**CARIBE.** *See* PIRANHA.

**CARIBOU,** common name for undomesticated reindeer (q.v.) of North America. Caribou, also called New World Caribou, range in height from 40 to 60 in. at the shoulder and weigh from 200 to 700 lb. They are divided into two principal groups: Barren Ground or Arctic caribou and woodland caribou. The Barren Ground caribou, which are named for the so-called Barren Grounds of northern Canada, are native to the tundra regions of northern Canada from Greenland to Alaska, as far north as the Arctic islands. The natives who live in the Arctic region (*see* ESKIMO) depend on these caribou for survival; they utilize every part of the body for food, implements, and clothing. The best-known species is *Rangifer arcticus*, noted for a white winter coat that the caribou sheds in the summer, growing a new summer coat of gray or light brown hair. This species is also well known for its migrations in winter from the tundra regions south to the warm Canadian forest areas, migrating back to the tundra in the spring. Of less economic importance is the woodland caribou, *R. caribou*,

*Barren Ground bull caribou,* Rangifer arcticus
Charles J. Ott–National Audubon Society

native to Newfoundland and southeastern Canada. This species is darker and stockier and has heavier antlers than the Arctic species. At one time woodland caribou were common from Maine to Montana, but they have been exterminated in most parts of the United States. *See* DEER.

**CARICATURE** (It. *caricare,* "to overload", "exaggerate"), picture or other representation that exaggerates the particular physical or facial features, dress, or manners of an individual to produce a ludicrous effect. Caricature may also be used to ridicule political, social, or religious situations and institutions, or actions by various groups or classes of a society. The latter types of caricature are usually done with satirical rather than humorous intent in order to effect a change in the element that is being ridiculed. The most common form of these political and social caricatures is the cartoon (q.v.).

Although, by extension, the term "caricature" also applies to exaggerations by means of verbal description (*see* BURLESQUE; PARODY; SATIRE), its use is generally restricted to pictorial representations.

Caricature in its modern sense originated at the close of the 16th century in the art school founded by a family of Italian painters, the Carraci (q.v.), in Bologna. For diversion, the students at this academy often drew pictures of visitors in the likeness of various animals or in-animate objects. The engraver Pier-Leone Ghezzi (1674–1775), working in Rome, continued the Carraci tradition, making caricatures for tourists at a small fee. The caricatures done by these Italian artists were humorous portraits intended for private circulation, and were rarely satirical or malicious.

**Caricature in England.** Political caricatures intended for wide distribution originated in England about the middle of the 18th century. One of the originators of the art of caricaturing well-known persons was George Townshend (*see under* TOWNSHEND), who had his caricatures printed on cards and distributed as handbills. The painter and engraver William Hogarth (q.v.), perhaps the greatest of all British pictorial satirists, caricatured the absurdities of social customs and the corruption of morals in his contemporary Londoners. Between 1761 and 1770 publications such as the *Town and Country Magazine,* the *Political Register,* and the *Universal Museum* offered artists a new vehicle for satirizing prominent personalities and political issues. Three of the most important of these caricaturists were the engraver Thomas Rowlandson (q.v.), who ridiculed the ludicrous behavior of types such as the old maid, the aristocrat, and the pedant; the illustrator James Gillray (1757–1815), who comically pictured the public characters of his day with fantastic costumes and enormous heads; and the etcher George Cruikshank (*see under* CRUIKSHANK), who spread his satire among all classes and all institutions of British life.

In 1841 the humorous weekly magazine *Punch, or the London Charivari* was founded. *Punch* became one of the best-known publications in the world for caricature, and was especially noted for its satirical thrusts at the royal family. Among the caricaturists who contributed to the magazine were George Louis Palmella Busson du Maurier (*see under* DU MAURIER), who satirized the fashionable social life of the middle and upper classes; John Leech, who dwelt on the careers of prominent, contemporary statesmen; and Sir John Tenniel (qq.v.), whose cartoons chronicled the international events of the times. After 1868 the magazine *Vanity Fair* featured colored lithographic caricatures of prominent personalities, chiefly the work of Sir Leslie Ward (1851–1922), known as "Spy". In the late 19th and early part of the 20th centuries, outstanding caricaturists were Sir Max Beerbohm, who specialized in caricatures of social and literary personages, and David Low (qq.v.), who through his caricatures became one of the most influential political commentators of his time.

*Caricature of a British lord by William Hogarth (1697–1764).*  Newark Public Library

Low created many political symbols, the most famous being Colonel Blimp, a symbol for British conservatism. Gerald Scarfe (1936–  ) is a leading political cartoonist in England today.

**The Art Form Spreads to the Continent.**  In France the art of political caricaturing also began to flourish in the early 18th century. Numerous books and magazines containing caricatures were published from the late 18th century through the 19th century, particularly during the Revolutionary period. The French journalist Charles Philipon (1800–62) made the caricature an important part of French political life through his satirical magazines, *La Caricature* (founded 1830), *Le Charivari* (1832), and *Le Journal pour Rire* (1848). The principal contributors were the artists Honoré Daumier, Gustave Doré, and Gavarni (qq.v.). Daumier, the most famous of the group, was thrown into prison for his scathing caricature of King Louis Philippe (q.v.). Later influential French caricaturists were the artists Henri Toulouse-Lautrec (q.v.), who caricatured theater and music hall habitués, and Jean Louis Forain (1852–1931), who was particularly noted for his attacks on the French legal system.

Elsewhere on the continent artists used the caricature as a vehicle for social criticism. The Spanish painter Francisco José de Goya y Lu-

cientes (q.v.) bitterly satirized the religious, political, and social injustices of his age in a series of eighty etchings called *Caprichos* (published 1799). These caricatures, among the most powerful in the history of art, were thinly veiled caricatures of well-known personages and were confiscated by the government. A later German painter, George Grosz (q.v.), was another vehement social critic. His most famous collection of cartoons and caricaturists, *Ecce Homo* (1922), was a fierce attack on the growing militarism and national socialism in Germany following World War I.

**Caricature in America.**  Perhaps the most important 19th-century American caricaturist was Thomas Nast (q.v.). His work, the best of which appeared in *Harper's Weekly*, was a powerful weapon on the side of the North during the Civil War, and in the overthrow of the corrupt political group known as the Tweed Ring, which controlled the government of New York City from about 1869 to 1872 (*see* TWEED, WILLIAM MARCY). Nast also created the symbols for the Republican and Democratic parties, the elephant and the donkey. Other important American cartoonists of the century were Joseph Keppler (1838–94), who founded (1876) and edited the humorous weekly *Puck*, and his associate Bernhard Gillam (1856–96), both of whom attacked the corrupt practices of political bosses and wealthy industrialists.

In the 20th century cartoonists and caricaturists have continued to have a profound effect on American life. Some of the more effective cartoon campaigns were conducted by Rollin Kirby (1875–1952), who focused anti-Prohibitionist sentiment in his Mr. Bluenose figure; Bill Mauldin, who, in his Army cartoons, focused on the drudgery, rather than the glory, of war; and Clarence Daniel Batchelor (qq.v.), who used his cartoons to promote nationwide concern for public health and automobile safety. Influential political cartoonists include Arthur Henry Young (1866–1943), Daniel Robert Fitzpatrick (1891–1969), Herbert Lawrence Block, or "Herblock", and Tom Little (qq.v.).

One of the most powerful outlets of American social satire in recent times has been *The New Yorker* magazine. Regular contributors have included the critics of café society and the idle rich, Peter Arno (1904–68) and Whitney Darrow, Jr. (1909–  ), and the satirists of suburbia, Helen Hokinson (d. 1949) and Gluyas Williams (1888–    ). Jules Feiffer (1929–  ) and Walt Kelly (1913–73) are caricaturists who work in the comic strip (q.v.) form. The theatrical caricatures of Al Hirschfeld (1903–  ) are also well known. Many have been republished in book form. In Canada, current political caricaturists of note include Len Norris, Duncan Macpherson, Edward Franklin, and Andrew Donato.

**CARILLON,** group of cast bells (twenty-three or more) tuned to a chromatic musical scale of more than two octaves. The carillon is hung in a fixed position in a tower. It is played manually by a keyboard called a clavier, or automatically by a clockwork mechanism or by means of air pressure from an electropneumatic mechanism. The lowest tones are produced by the largest bells, some of which weigh several tons; the highest tones are made by bells weighing as little as 10 to 20 lb. When the carillon is played manually, the clapper of each bell is wired to the clavier keys; the bellmaster, or carillonneur, depresses the clavier keys with a closed hand and the clapper strikes the inside of the bell. The essential differences between a chime and a carillon, both of which are constructed in the same way, are the number of bells and the method of tuning; the chime is tuned to a different scale, the diatonic, and has fewer than twenty-three bells. See BELL TOWER; SCALE.

Music written for the carillon may be a simple melody or a complex composition of several parts in harmony. The art of carillon playing is called campanology, and the best-known school teaching the subject is in Malines, Belgium; the school was founded by Jef Denijn (1862–1941), the famous carillonneur.

Although small carillons were used as early as ancient times, the art of casting bells and making large carillons was perfected in Europe between the 15th and 18th centuries, particularly in Belgium, the Netherlands, and France. Before the two world wars, which destroyed many of the carillons of Europe, carillonneurs were often municipal employees. North America has more than sixty cast-bell carillons, notably the carillon in the Peace Tower in Ottawa, Canada; the Bok Singing Tower Carillon near Lake Wales, Fla.; the carillon of the University of Chicago Chapel; and the largest carillon in the world, the Rockefeller Memorial Carillon in Riverside Church, New York City. The Rockefeller carillon contains seventy-four bells and the world's heaviest tuned bell, weighing 20½ tons.

In the 20th century the art of carillon making has been revolutionized by the introduction in the United States of so-called electromechanical carillons. These electronic devices are made of tiny bars of bell metal that are struck by hammers operated by keyboards; see BELL. The Bok Singing Tower uses a carillon of this type as a companion instrument to the cast-bell carillon.

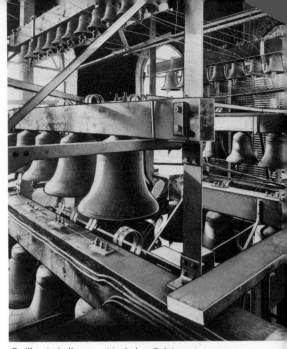

*Carillon in bell tower, Mechelen, Belgium.*
Belgian Information Center

**CARINTHIA,** province of Austria, bordered by the provinces of Tirol on the N.W. and E., Salzburg and Styria on the N., and by Yugoslavia on the S.E., and Italy on the S.W. The principal rivers are the Drau, which flows in a generally W. to E. direction, and the Gail, which flows generally E. and then N. to join the Drau near the town of Villach. The area W. of the confluence of the rivers, known as Upper Carinthia, is in a mountainous section of the Alps and is the site of the Grossglockner (12,457 ft.), the highest peak in Austria. Mining of lead, zinc, iron, and lignite are important in the region, as are lumbering and the raising of cattle and sheep. The area E. of the confluence of the Drau and the Gail is known as Lower Carinthia. This region is also mountainous, but it contains the fertile Drau basin in which wheat, rye, corn, and fruit are grown. The Wörthersee is a resort lake that attracts many tourists. The capital city of Klagenfurt and the town of Villach are the chief industrial centers with plants for the manufacture of metals, chemicals, and textiles. Carinthia, originally a Roman possession, was made an independent duchy in 976. It fell to the Hapsburg (q.v.) family in the 13th century and became an Austrian crown land in the 14th century. After World War I (q.v.) Carinthia lost some of its territory to Italy and Yugoslavia. The present province is sparsely populated. Slovenes predominate in the southern section. Area, 3681 sq.mi.; pop. (1971) 526,075.

**CARISSIMI, Giacomo** (1604?–74), Italian composer, born in Marino, near Rome. Carissimi began his career as a singer and organist. In 1627 he was appointed choirmaster in Assisi, and from about 1628 to 1674 he held that office in the Church of Sant' Apollinare in Rome. He was a pioneer in the development of the chamber cantata and was one of the originators of the oratorio (qq.v.). Carissimi deviated from the polyphonic musical style of the Renaissance period to emphasize arias for solo voice and the use of chords to support melody. He thus anticipated the later development of opera. His masterpiece was the oratorio *Jephtha*. As a teacher Carissimi influenced many Italian composers, notably Alessandro Scarlatti (q.v.).

**CARITAT.** *See* CONDORCET, MARQUIS DE, MARIE JEAN ANTOINE NICHOLAS DE CARITAT.

**CARLETON, Sir Guy, 1st Baron Dorchester** (1724–1808), British soldier and administrator, born in Strabane, Ireland. Carleton entered the British army in 1742, and went to Canada in 1758 to serve as an officer in the French and Indian War (q.v.). After the war ended, Carleton was appointed lieutenant governor of Lower Canada (now Québec Province) in 1766, then governor in 1768. He was also placed in command of all British troops in Canada during the American Revolution (q.v.). Carleton defended Québec successfully against the American attack in December, 1775. The next year he drove the Americans out of Canada and defeated the American general Benedict Arnold (q.v.) in a battle on Lake Champlain. In 1777 Carleton was succeeded as commander in Canada by General John Burgoyne (q.v.), but five years later Carleton became commander in chief of British forces in America during the period of their evacuation. For his services he was created Baron Dorchester and was commissioned governor of all British possessions in Canada in 1786. *See* QUÉBEC: *History*.

**CARLISLE,** borough in Pennsylvania, and county seat of Cumberland Co., in a fertile farming district, about 18 miles S.W. of Harrisburg. Carlisle was founded in 1751 and incorporated in 1872. Among the buildings of historic interest in the borough are the First Presbyterian Church, constructed between 1757 and 1770; the Old Guard House, erected during the American Revolution by Hessian prisoners of war; and Dickinson College, founded in 1783. At various times Carlisle was the residence of James Wilson (q.v.) as well as other signers of the Declaration of Independence, and also of Molly Pitcher (q.v.), heroine of the American Revolution. During the Whiskey Rebellion (q.v.) in 1794, President George Washington (q.v.) established his headquarters here. Carlisle Indian School, the first off-reservation school for Indians, was in the town from 1879 until 1918. Among the principal manufactures of Carlisle are textiles, clothing, shoes, rugs, and carpets. Pop. (1960) 16,623; (1970) 18,079.

**CARLISLE,** Great Britain, county borough of Cumberland, England, on the Eden R., about 9 miles S. of the border with Scotland, about 270 miles N.W. of London. The city is a major railway and industrial center with plants for metalworking and for the manufacture of textiles and biscuits. It also serves as a market center for the surrounding agricultural region and is the site of important livestock auctions. Places of historical interest include remains dating from Roman times, and a well-preserved medieval castle. Among the principal buildings are the cathedral, begun in Norman times but never completed, a museum, an art gallery, and the city hall.

Carlisle is on the site of the ancient Roman town of Luguvallum, about 1 mile S. of Hadrian's Wall (q.v.). Carlisle Castle built in 1092 became an English bulwark during the wars with the Scots in the following centuries. During the rise of the guilds in the later Middle Ages, Carlisle was a thriving commercial and handicraft-manufacturing center. The city was frequently besieged during the English civil wars; *see* GREAT REBELLION. The growth of Carlisle was stimulated by the development of railroads in England during the 19th century. Pop. (1971) 71,820.

**CARLISLE, Earls of.** *See* HOWARD.

**CARLISTS,** members of a Spanish political movement that originated in 1831 during a controversy over the succession to the Spanish throne. The Carlists originally comprised various political conservatives who supported the claims of Don Carlos, Carlos María Isidro de Borbón (*see under* CARLOS, DON) against those of the young queen Isabella II (q.v.). After several unsuccessful insurrections throughout the 19th century, the group became part of the fascist government organized by the dictator Francisco Franco (q.v.) in 1937. When the latter failed to restore a descendant of Don Carlos to the throne of Spain, however, the Carlists began a continuing agitation against the Spanish government. In the early 1970's they numbered between 500,000 and 700,000. *See* SPAIN: *History*.

**CARLOMAN.** *See* CHARLEMAGNE.

**CARLOS, Don,** name of several Spanish princes (listed chronologically), of whom some were pretenders to the throne.

**Carlos, Don** (1421–61). *See under* CHARLES: *Navarre: Charles IV.*

**Carlos de Austria, Don** (1545–68), son of Philip II (q.v.), King of Spain. His father betrothed him to Princess Elizabeth of France (1545–68), but married her himself in 1559. During the revolt of the Netherlands against Spanish rule in 1567 Carlos apparently conspired against his father. Philip imprisoned Carlos in 1568 and may have ordered his death later that year. The fate of Carlos has inspired several dramas, including the tragedy *Don Carlos* (1787) by the German dramatist Johann Christoph Friedrich von Schiller (q.v.), and operas, including *Don Carlos* (1867), by the Italian composer Giuseppe Verdi (q.v.).

**Carlos, Don,** in full CARLOS MARÍA ISIDRO DE BORBÓN, CONDE DE MOLINA (1788–1855), son of Charles IV, King of Spain (*see under* CHARLES), and brother of Ferdinand VII (q.v.), King of Spain. Carlos was the heir of his brother until Ferdinand abrogated the laws restricting the royal succession to males and in 1830 made his infant daughter crown princess (*see* ISABELLA II). Carlos refused to recognize this act but did not encourage resistance to it until after Ferdinand's death. In 1833 Carlos's adherents, who recognized him as Charles V, began the so-called Carlist Wars; *see* CARLISTS. When they were finally defeated in 1839, Carlos fled to France. In 1845 he transferred his claim to the throne in favor of his son Carlos.

**Carlos, Don,** in full CARLOS LUIS FERNANDO DE BORBÓN, CONDE DE MONTEMOLÍN (1818–61), son of Don Carlos (1788–1855). Claiming to be Charles VI, he entered Spain in 1860 and attempted to organize a revolt. He was captured, however, and resigned his pretended rights in favor of his brother Juan (1822–87). The latter subsequently transmitted his claims to his son Carlos.

**Carlos, Don,** in full CARLOS MARÍA DE LOS DOLORES DE BORBÓN, DUQUE DE MADRID (1848–1909), nephew of Don Carlos (1818–61). When he claimed the throne as Charles VII in 1872, the Carlists rose in revolt and captured many provinces, but were subdued during the next four years. Carlos lived thereafter in various European countries but he did not abandon his claims.

**CARLOS I** (1863–1908), King of Portugal (1889–1908), born in Lisbon. A member of the Braganza (q.v.) royal house, he succeeded his father King Louis; *see under* LOUIS: *Portugal.* In 1891 Carlos concluded a treaty with Great Britain ending a long-standing border dispute over the Portuguese colony of Mozambique (q.v.). The treaty, however, was strongly opposed in Portugal. To curb the growing dissent, in 1906 Carlos gave the Portuguese statesman João Franco (1855–1929) virtual dictatorial powers. The harsh measures of Franco increased the unrest, and resulted in the assassinations of the king and of his eldest son. A younger son succeeded Carlos as Manuel II (q.v.). *See* PORTUGAL: *History.*

**CARLOVINGIAN.** *See* CAROLINGIAN.

**CARLOW,** county of the Republic of Ireland, in Leinster Province. The surface is mostly level, but in the S.E. are barren mountains, the highest peak of which is Mt. Leinster (2611 ft.). The great coal field of Leinster is in the western part of the county. The chief rivers are the Barrow and the Slaney. Among the principal towns are the county seat of Carlow, Tullow, and Muinebeag. The most important industry is the raising of dairy cattle, sheep, and poultry. Chief articles of trade produced in the county are grains, beet sugar, flour, and dairy products. Area, 346 sq.mi.; pop. (1971) 34,237.

**CARLSBAD,** city in New Mexico, and county seat of Eddy Co., on the Pecos R., about 230 miles S.E. of Albuquerque. About 20 mi. to the S.W. is the Carlsbad Caverns National Park (q.v.). The city is the headquarters of large irrigation projects supervised by the United States Bureau of Reclamation. The most important industry is the mining and refining of potash. Carlsbad was founded in 1888 and incorporated as a city in 1918. Pop. (1960) 25,541; (1970) 21,297.

**CARLSBAD CAVERNS NATIONAL PARK,** area of scenic interest in S.E. New Mexico, in the foothills of the Guadalupe Mts. The park is the site of Carlsbad Caverns, largest known subterranean labyrinth in the world. The caverns, first explored in 1924 by a party of the National Geographic Society (q.v.), are believed to have been formed about 60,000,000 years ago by the erosive action of water on limestone. The full extent of Carlsbad Caverns is not yet known, although more than 37 mi. of connecting corridors and chambers have been explored. The deepest known level is the third, at 1100 ft. below the surface of the earth. On the first level, 750 ft. down, is the principal cavern, the Big Room, which is about 4000 ft. long and 625 ft. wide and reaches a height of 285 ft. It contains a variety of stalactites and stalagmites, the most notable being Crystal Spring Dome and Rock of Ages; *see* STALACTITE. Chambers on the second level 829 ft. down include King's Palace, Green Lake Room, Papoose Room, and Queen's Chamber. Several million bats inhabit the caverns and emerge nightly. The caverns area, covering 46,753.07 acres, was declared a national monument in 1925 and a national park in 1930.

**CARLSBAD DECREES.** *See* KARLOVY VARY.

**CARLSON, Evans Fordyce** (1896–1947), American general, born in Sidney, N.Y., and educated at George Washington University. He entered the United States Army in 1912 and served in Europe during World War I. In 1922 he joined the United States Marine Corps. Until 1936 he was stationed at various times in China, Nicaragua, and Japan. As a U.S. military observer, he traveled from 1937 to 1938 with Chinese guerrilla forces behind enemy Japanese lines. He resigned his commission in 1939 to lecture and write about his experiences. Recommissioned in the Marine Corps in 1941, during World War II he organized under his command a special task force known as Carlson's Raiders that in 1942 fought the Japanese army on Little Makin Island in the Gilbert Islands (q.v.) and on Guadalcanal (q.v.). He retired with the rank of brigadier general in 1946.

**CARLYLE,** name of a British family, of which two members were distinguished writers and scholars.

**Thomas Carlyle** (1795–1881), essayist and historian, born in Ecclefechan, Scotland, and educated as a divinity student at the University of Edinburgh. After five years of study he abandoned the clergy in 1814, and spent the next four years teaching mathematics. Dissatisfied with teaching, Carlyle moved to Edinburgh in 1818 where, after studying law briefly, he became a tutor and wrote articles for the *Edin-*

*Thomas Carlyle*             Granger Collection

*burgh Encyclopedia.* He also made an intensive study of German literature, publishing *Wilhelm Meister's Apprenticeship* (1824), a translation of the novel *Wilhelm Meisters Lehrjahre* (1796) by the German writer Johann Wolfgang von Goethe (q.v.). Carlyle also wrote *Life of Schiller* (1825), which appeared first in serial form in 1823 and 1824 in the *London Magazine.* After a trip to Paris and London, he returned to Scotland and supported himself by writing for the *Edinburgh Review,* a literary periodical.

In 1826 Carlyle married Jane Baillie Welsh (1801–66), a writer, whom he met in 1821. The marriage was frequently disturbed by his domineering disposition and outbursts of temper. After 1828 the Carlyles lived on a farm in Craigenputtock, Scotland, where Carlyle wrote a philosophical satire, *Sartor Resartus* ("The Tailor Retailored"). The work, first published between 1833 and 1834 in *Fraser's Magazine,* is partly autobiographical. In the guise of a "philosophy of clothes", Carlyle comments on the falseness of material wealth; and in the form of a philosophical romance, he details the crises in his life and affirms his spiritual idealism. In the satire, Carlyle emerged as a social critic deeply concerned with the living conditions of British workers. At the farm he also wrote some of his most distinguished essays, and established a lifelong friendship with the American essayist Ralph Waldo Emerson (q.v.). In 1834 Carlyle moved to the Chelsea section of London, England, where he soon became known as the "Sage of Chelsea" and belonged to a literary circle that included the British essayists Leigh Hunt and John Stuart Mill (qq.v.).

In London Carlyle wrote *The French Revolution, A History* (2 vol., 1837), a historical study concentrating on the oppression of the poor, which was immediately successful. This was followed by a series of lectures, in one of which, published as *On Heroes, Hero-Worship, and the Heroic in History* (1841), he contended that world civilization had developed because of the activities of heroes. His hatred and fear of democracy and praise of feudal society was reflected in much of his subsequent writing, especially in *Chartism* (1839) and *Past and Present* (1843). His concept of history appeared in a number of his later works, notably in *Oliver Cromwell's Letters and Speeches, With Elucidations* (1845) and *History of Frederick II of Prussia, Called Frederick the Great* (10 vol., 1858–65), his most extensive work. After the death of his wife, he edited her letters; his autobiography, *Reminiscences,* was published in 1881.

**John Aitken Carlyle** (1801–79), physician and scholar, younger brother of Thomas Carlyle, born in Ecclefechan, Scotland, and educated in medicine at the University of Edinburgh. After 1831 he was personal physician to several members of European royalty. In 1849 he published a prose translation of *The Inferno* from *The Divine Comedy* by the Italian poet Dante Alighieri (q.v.). Carlyle also did extensive research in Icelandic literature.

**CARMAGNOLE,** an anonymous song and street dance popular during the Reign of Terror of the French Revolution (q.v.). Reportedly brought into Paris from Marseille, the song became well known after the storming of the Tuileries (q.v.) palace on Aug. 10, 1792. The carmagnole, consisting originally of thirteen two-line stanzas, began ridiculing Marie Antoinette (q.v.), Queen of France, and ended with a refrain praising the revolution. New stanzas were added from time to time and a street dance was improvised. The carmagnole was sung and danced at revolutionary gatherings, including festivals and executions. Carmagnole was also the name of a jacket worn by the French Revolutionists.

**CARMAN, William Bliss** (1861–1929), Canadian poet, born in Fredericton, New Brunswick, and educated at the universities of New Brunswick and Edinburgh and at Harvard University. After 1890 he did editorial work on the New York City periodical *The Independent* and on the Boston magazines the *Atlantic Monthly* and the *Chap-Book*. He also edited several poetry anthologies. Carman was a lyric poet; his poems were in praise of joy, love, and nature. His first book of poetry was *Low Tide on Grand Pré* (1893), and his last was *Wild Garden* (1929). His most famous poems were published in *Vagabondia* (3 vol., 1894–1901). In 1928 he was awarded the Lorne Pierce Gold Medal of the Royal Society of Canada, the highest literary distinction in that country.

**CARMARTHENSHIRE,** Great Britain, county in Wales, on Carmarthen Bay, an inlet of Bristol Channel. The Towy is the principal river. The chief towns include Carmarthen, the county town, Llanelly, and Ammanford. The largest county, in Wales, it contains numerous relics of prehistoric ages, and of Roman and Norman times. The principal industries are coal mining, stock raising, and the manufacture of metals and textiles. Area, 919 sq.mi.; pop. (1971) 162,313.

**CARMEL** *or* **CARMEL-BY-THE-SEA,** city of California, in Monterey Co., s. of Monterey Bay, about 90 miles s.e. of San Francisco. The city is a residential community, with good facilities for swimming, fishing, and boating. Carmel was established in 1904 as a retreat for artists and writers. Pop. (1960) 4580; (1970) 4525.

**CARMELITES,** *or* BROTHERS OF THE BLESSED VIRGIN MARY OF MOUNT CARMEL, monastic order probably founded in the 12th century. The earliest proof of a Carmelite order is their rule, written between 1206 and 1214 by Saint Albert (1149?–1214), Patriarch of Jerusalem. The Carmelite rule was approved by Pope Honorius III (r. 1216–27) in 1226. In 1238 the Carmelites began to found offshoot communities in Cyprus, Messina, Marseille, and parts of England, where they were known as "White Friars". Their settlement on Mt. Carmel (*see* CARMEL, MOUNT) was abandoned in 1291 when the nearby port of Acre was captured by the Muslims. In 1247 the change from hermit to community life was sanctioned by Pope Innocent IV (r. 1243–54) and the Carmelites were ranked with the mendicant orders (*see* MENDICANT FRIARS). During the French siege of Acre (1799), the monastery was used as a hospital by the forces of Napoléon Bonaparte, later Napoleon I (q.v.), Emperor of France. After Napoleon's withdrawal the monastery was destroyed by the Arabs; it was later rebuilt. The Carmelites have been active in mission work and in the spread of mystical theology. According to the most recent statistics, the order numbered about 3600 monks in 13 countries, including the United States.

Among the several orders of Carmelite nuns, the best known and most widely spread is the order of Discalced Carmelites, founded in Spain in the 16th century by Saint Theresa (q.v.). The first convent of the order to be established in the U.S. was founded in Port Tobacco, Md., in 1790. The order has about 725 convents throughout the world. This includes more than 60 in the U.S. (with about 850 members), and a total membership of more than 15,000 nuns.

**CARMEL, MOUNT,** short mountain ridge of N.W. Israel, and peak in the ridge, 1791 ft. above sea level. Mount Carmel is famous for connections with Biblical characters and events. The ridge is 13 mi. long and 3 to 8 mi. wide; it extends in a northwesterly direction from the Plain of Jezreel, or Esdraelon, to the Mediterranean Sea, near the port of Haifa. There, the ridge ends in a promontory that marks the southern limit of the Bay of Acre. The highest point of the ridge is about 1800 ft. above sea level.

From early times Mt. Carmel was a holy place, containing an altar of Jehovah long before the contest for the allegiance of the children of Israel was fought out there (1 Kings 18) between the Hebrew prophet Elijah (q.v.) and the prophets of the divinity Baal (q.v.). Mount Carmel also was famed in literary composition for natural beauty (Song of Sol. 7:5, Isa. 35:2). It is one of the points of Palestine that especially demonstrates God's favor to the Israelites in bestowing upon them such a beautiful country (Jer. 50:19, Mic. 7:14). The devastation of Mt. Carmel is, therefore, a sign of God's decided displeasure (Isa. 33:9, Jer. 4:26, Amos 1:2, Nah. 1:4). In post-Biblical times Carmel continued to be a holy site among both heathens and Christians, serving finally as the site of a renowned monastery (see CARMELITES).

**CARMICHAEL,** unincorporated area of California, in Sacramento Co., on the American R., 10 miles E. of Sacramento. Dairying and livestock raising are important in the area. Pop. (1960) 20,455; (1970) 37,625.

**CARMICHAEL, Hoagy,** in full HOAGLAND HOWARD CARMICHAEL (1899–    ), American composer of popular music, born in Bloomington, Indiana, and educated at the University of Indiana. While a student, he supported himself by playing piano in a dance band. He earned a law degree and practiced law before turning to writing songs full-time. Carmichael's most famous song, "Stardust" (1931), quickly became a standard among popular songs. His music is marked by relaxed rhythms and enchanting melodies. Among his other well-known compositions are "Lazy Bones", "Georgia on My Mind", "Two Sleepy People", and "I Get Along Without You Very Well". Carmichael appeared as an actor in several motion pictures, including *To Have and Have Not* (1945) and *The Best Years of Our Lives* (1946).

**CARMINA BURANA.** *See* GERMAN MUSIC: *Recent Trends*; GOLIARD.

**CARMINE** *or* **CARMINE LAKE,** red pigment obtained from the red dyestuff cochineal. The coloring principle of cochineal is carminic acid, $C_{22}H_{20}O_{13}$, which with alum (q.v.) and either zinc oxide or cream of tartar forms the pigment. Formerly much used in inks, paints, and dyes, carmine has largely been replaced by synthetic pigments, which are cheaper and more permanent in color. Because it is a natural pigment, carmine is still used as a food coloring and in cosmetics, drug preparations, and biological stains.

**CARMONA, Antonio Oscar de Fragoso** (1869–1951), Portuguese general and statesman, born in Lisbon. He was one of three generals who overthrew the provisional government of

Portugal in May, 1926. By the end of the year he assumed full leadership as prime minister and provisional president of Portugal. With the support of monarchist political groups he established a dictatorship and in 1927 he suppressed popular revolts in Oporto and Lisbon. He outlawed the party system in Portugal, and in 1928, as the sole candidate, he was elected president. He was reelected in 1935, 1942, and 1949, but after 1932 the country was actually controlled by his prime minister, Antonio de Oliveira Salazar (q.v.). *See* PORTUGAL: *History*.

**CARNAC,** village of N.W. France, in Morbihan Department, on the southern coast of Brittany. Within the village and the surrounding area are thousands of megalithic monuments (q.v.) consisting of menhirs, dolmens, and tumuli. The monuments were arranged in three groups which archeologists believe were joined at one time. The principal group lies N.W. of the village and has 1099 rude monoliths of granite. They are arranged in eleven roughly parallel rows more than ½ mi. long and end in an arc, the extremities of which touch the outer horizontal rows. Although their origin and object remain a mystery, they are generally considered to have been associated with Druidism (q.v.). The Bossenno, about 1 mile E. of Carnac, is the site of numerous burial mounds and the remains of a Gallo-Roman villa. Pop. of village (latest census) 1044.

**CARNALLITE,** greasy, milk-white or reddish mineral, an important source of potash compounds used in fertilizers. It is found in massive form in extensive deposits near Stassfurt, Germany; smaller deposits occur in Alsace, Poland, and Persia. Small amounts of carnallite are also found in the potassium deposits in Texas and New Mexico. This hydrous potassium-magnesium chloride, $KMgCl_3 \cdot 6H_2O$, crystallizes in the orthorhombic system. It is brittle and very soluble in water.

**CARNARVON, Earls of.** *See* HERBERT.

**CARNARVONSHIRE.** *See* CAERNARVONSHIRE.

**CARNATIC** *or* **KARNATIC,** historic region of S.E. India, between the Coromandel Coast and the Eastern Ghats mountains. In the middle of the 18th century Carnatic figured prominently in the struggle between the French and British for supremacy in India. Annexed by the British in 1801, the region is now included in Tamil Nadu State, India. The principal city in Carnatic is Madras (q.v.).

**CARNATION,** common name for any of the numerous varieties of a species of herbs, *Dianthus caryophyllus* of the Pink (q.v.) family (Caryophyllaceae).

The species, usually a perennial, is native to

southern Europe, where it has been cultivated outdoors for more than 2000 years. In the United States the most common varieties are grown in greenhouses. The carnation grows to between 2 and 3 ft. high, with a branching stem and opposite leaves. It has terminal double flowers, usually ruffled or toothed. Carnations (Fr. *carne*, "flesh") were at one time only flesh colored, but through cultivation they are often red, white, or pink, and less commonly yellow or purple. The flowers may also be variegated; they are called flaked when striped with one color; bizarre when striped or flecked with more than one color; and picotee when fringed with a different color.

**CARNAUBA PALM,** or CARANAIBA PALM, common name for a species of palm tree, *Copernicia cerifera*. This graceful tree grows to a height of about 20 to 40 ft. and has a trunk diameter of about 8 in. It is indigenous to South America, where it is found from Brazil to Argentina. Growing best in slightly saline soil, the tree withstands drought but not frost. The wood of the tree is hard and valuable as timber, making excellent veneers. The tree bears a black fruit that is about the size of an olive and is sweet and edible either raw or cooked. Starch is obtained from the stems of the tree and sugar from the sap. The leaves are fibrous, and the leaf fibers are made into cordage, mats, hats, and other articles.

A wax, also called carnauba, forms in scales on the lower surfaces of the leaves and is removed by shaking the dried harvested leaves. The wax particles are then boiled in water and strained. The raw wax is yellowish green, with an agreeable odor. It is soluble in ether, hot alcohol, and alkalines. The hardest and most important vegetable wax of commerce, it is used for making lubricants, polishes, floor wax, plastics, and carbon paper.

**CARNEADES** (214?–129 B.C.), Greek philosopher, born in Cyrene (now Shahat, Libya). He studied Stoicism (q.v.) in Athens and later founded the New or Third Academy. The Academy was an extension of the Old Academy begun by the Greek philosopher Plato (q.v.). In 155 B.C. Carneades was sent as a member of an embassy to Rome. While there he lectured on skepticism (q.v.), asserting that knowledge is impossible and truth has no criterion. The Roman statesman Marcus Porcius Cato, known as Cato the Elder (*see under* CATO), however, believed the philosophy was dangerous to the youth of Rome and he forced the Roman Senate to banish Carneades. See PHILOSOPHY: *Hellenistic and Roman Philosophy: Skepticism.*

*Carnation,* Dianthus caryophyllus       W. Atlee Burpee Co.

**CARNEGIE,** borough of Pennsylvania, in Allegheny Co., about 5 miles s.w. of central Pittsburgh. The city manufactures steel, diesel engines, beverages, metal products, chemicals, bedding, and lubricants. Bituminous coal is mined. The borough was named for the American industrialist and philanthropist Andrew Carnegie (q.v.). Pop. (1960) 11,887; (1970) 10,864.

**CARNEGIE, Andrew** (1835–1919), American industrialist and philanthropist, born in Dunfermline, Scotland. He came to the United States in 1848 and soon began work as a bobbin boy in a cotton mill in Allegheny, Pa., for $1.20 per week. The following year he became a messenger boy in a Pittsburgh telegraph office and learned telegraphy. He was then employed by the Pennsylvania Railroad as the private secretary and telegrapher to the railroad official Thomas Alexander Scott (1823–81). Carnegie advanced by successive promotions until he was superintendent of the Pittsburgh division of the railroad. His financial interest in what is now the Pullman Company laid the foundation of his fortune, and investments in oil lands near Oil City, Pa., increased his means. During the American Civil War he served in the War Department under Scott, who was in charge of military transportation and government telegraph service. After the war Carnegie left the railroad and formed a company to produce iron railroad

*Andrew Carnegie*

bridges. He later founded a steel mill and was one of the earliest users of the Bessemer process of making steel in the U.S.; *see* IRON AND STEEL MANUFACTURE. Carnegie was extremely successful, acquiring a controlling interest in other large steel plants. By 1899, when he consolidated his interests in the Carnegie Steel Company, he controlled about 25 percent of the American iron and steel production. In 1901 he sold his company to the United States Steel Corporation for $250,000,000 and retired.

Carnegie did not have a formal education, but as a youth working in Pennsylvania he developed a life-long interest in books and education. At the age of thirty-three, when he had an annual income of $50,000, he said, "Beyond this never earn, make no effort to increase fortune, but spend the surplus each year for benevolent purposes". During his lifetime he gave more than $350,000,000 to various cultural, educational, and peace institutions, many of which bear his name. His first public gift was in 1873 for baths in the town of his birth; his largest single gift was in 1911 for $125,000,000 to establish the Carnegie Corporation of New York (q.v.). He was a benefactor of Tuskegee Institute (q.v.). He also endowed nearly 1700 libraries in the U.S. and Great Britain, and he donated funds for the construction of the Palace of Peace at The Hague, the Netherlands, for what is now the International Court of Justice (q.v.) of the United Nations. Carnegie was honored throughout the world during his lifetime.

**CARNEGIE CORPORATION OF NEW YORK,** American public trust, the largest of the philanthropic agencies founded by American industrialist and philanthropist Andrew Carnegie (q.v.). The corporation, established in 1911 and chartered under the laws of the State of New York, received $135,000,000 from Carnegie, including about $10,000,000 provided under the terms of his will. It promotes the advancement and diffusion of knowledge and understanding among the peoples of the United States and certain British Commonwealth countries.

The corporation is primarily interested in education. Grants are made to colleges and universities, professional associations, and other educational organizations for specific programs in higher education, early childhood education, certain aspects of elementary and secondary education, and research and the dissemination of information in regard to the functioning of government at all levels. The corporation's Commonwealth program is focused on university activities in the field of education in developing countries, embracing teacher training, curriculum development, and educational research. Activities of the Carnegie Corporation in the 1960's included grants for improvement of Negro education in the American South; grants to African universities for teacher training and improvement of education in Africa; the financing of a study of the future structure of American higher education; and grants to finance educational television. During the first sixty-one years of its existence grants of all kinds awarded by the corporation amounted to $440,547,815. In 1973, assets of the corporation totaled about $350,000,000. *See also* CARNEGIE FOUNDATION FOR THE ADVANCEMENT OF TEACHING.

**CARNEGIE ENDOWMENT FOR INTERNATIONAL PEACE,** private operating foundation, established in 1910 by the American industrialist and philanthropist Andrew Carnegie (q.v.), with an endowment of $10,000,000, for the purpose of hastening the abolition of war. Since World War II, the Carnegie Endowment has concentrated on the development of international institutions, particularly the United Nations (q.v.) and its agencies. It sponsors study groups, publications, and scholarship programs in furtherance of that goal and supports the training in international law of foreign-service officers of developing countries. The Carnegie Endowment is also concerned with the problem of arms control and the proliferation of nuclear weapons. It publishes many valuable histories and surveys in its field of concern, as well as an annual report. In the year ending in June, 1972, the Carnegie

Endowment's assets amounted to $55,665,250; gifts received totaled $222,230; and expenditures were $2,481,735. Its headquarters are located in the Carnegie International Center in New York City, which houses some twenty organizations devoted to research in international affairs. A European office is maintained in Geneva, Switzerland.

**CARNEGIE FOUNDATION FOR THE ADVANCEMENT OF TEACHING,** private operating foundation, established in 1905 by American industrialist and philanthropist Andrew Carnegie (q.v.). The initial endowment of $10,000,000 was subsequently increased to $15,000,000 by gifts from Carnegie and from the Carnegie Corporation of New York (q.v.). The foundation was created primarily to provide free pensions for American and Canadian college and university teachers, and for their widows. In 1918 the foundation and the Carnegie Corporation established the Teachers Insurance and Annuity Association, a nonprofit, life-insurance company specifically designed to provide the academic profession with retirement allowances and other forms of insurance. Research and studies in the field of higher education are also conducted as monies formerly allocated to pensioners become available. By 1973 the foundation had disbursed about $82,878,000 in retirement allowances and pensions. The foundation is located in New York City.

**CARNEGIE HALL,** concert hall in New York City. When erected in 1891 it was known as the Music Hall and was the largest concert hall in the city. In 1898 the name was changed to Carnegie Hall to honor the American industrialist and philanthropist Andrew Carnegie (q.v.), the chief contributor of the funds for construction. The building was designed by the American architect William Burnet Tuthill (1855–1929). Carnegie Hall, notable for excellent acoustics, has a seating capacity of 2800; the adjacent Carnegie Recital Hall seats about 300 persons. Carnegie Hall opened on May 5, 1891, with a five-day music festival given by the New York Symphony Orchestra (which later merged with the New York Philharmonic) and the New York Oratorio Society. The Russian composer Pëtr Ilich Tchaikovsky (q.v.) was guest conductor. Since that time many renowned musicians have given their first American performances in Carnegie Hall. When the Philharmonic announced plans to move from Carnegie Hall to Lincoln Center for the Performing Arts (q.v.), Carnegie Hall was to be demolished. Through the efforts of the American violinist Isaac Stern (q.v.) and others, the hall was saved. In 1960 New York City acquired ownership of the building through State legislation, which also created the Carnegie Hall Corporation, a nonprofit organization, to operate the hall. The corporation also presents important concert events each year, notably the International Festival of Visiting Orchestras, which brings major symphony orchestras from the United States and other countries to New York. In 1964 Carnegie Hall was registered as a national historic landmark.

**CARNEGIE HERO FUND COMMISSION,** American institution, formed in 1904 to administer a fund of $5,000,000 given by American industrialist and philanthropist Andrew Carnegie (q.v.). The commission honors those persons who under certain conditions have performed heroic deeds in the United States, Canada, and the waters thereof. A medal that recites the heroic deed is given, and monetary grants are made if the deed causes injury, death, or exposure to the possibility of death to the hero. In the event of death, the grants are given to the widow or next of kin.

Carnegie established similar funds in Belgium, Denmark, France, Germany, Great Britain, Italy, the Netherlands, Norway, Sweden, and Switzerland. The American commission, with headquarters in Pittsburgh, Pa., has awarded more than $12,000,000 to heroes and their families since it was founded.

**CARNEGIE INSTITUTE OF PITTSBURGH,** cultural institution in Pennsylvania, founded and endowed by the American industrialist and philanthropist Andrew Carnegie (q.v.) in 1896. It comprises a Museum of Art, exhibiting painting, sculpture, and decorative arts; the Carnegie Museum of Natural History, with exhibits in the natural sciences; and the Carnegie Music Hall, used for music recitals by many distinguished performers. The Sarah M. Scaife Gallery, scheduled to open in the fall of 1974, was expected to add extensive new space for art exhibitions.

**CARNEGIE INSTITUTE OF TECHNOLOGY.** *See* CARNEGIE-MELLON UNIVERSITY.

**CARNEGIE INSTITUTION OF WASHINGTON,** nonprofit educational and research organization founded and endowed by the American industrialist and philanthropist Andrew Carnegie (q.v.) in 1902 with an original endowment of $10,000,000, later increased to $22,000,000. The institution supports research and education for research in the physical and biological sciences. It maintains six research centers: the Geophysical Laboratory and the Department of Terrestrial Magnetism in Washington, D.C.; the Department of Embryology, Baltimore, Md.; the Department of Plant Biology, Stanford, Calif.; the Hale Observatories (formerly Mount Wilson and Mount Palomar observatories), operated jointly with the California Institute of Technology, in Pasadena, Calif.; and the Las Campanas Observatory, Las Campanas, Chile. The results of the research projects are published in the *Carnegie Institution Year Book* and in a series of monographs. Headquarters is in Washington, D.C.

**CARNEGIE-MELLON UNIVERSITY,** coeducational privately controlled institution of higher learning, located in Pittsburgh, Pa., founded in 1900 by the American industrialist and philanthropist Andrew Carnegie (q.v.). The university was originally named the Carnegie Technical Schools and became Carnegie Institute of Technology in 1912, when the institution received a State charter. The institute merged with Mellon Institute (founded 1913) on July 1, 1967. Among the main divisions of the university are Carnegie Institute of Technology, which offers programs of undergraduate and graduate study in chemical, civil, electrical, mechanical, and metallurgical engineering; Mellon Institute of Science, offering undergraduate and graduate programs in biological sciences, chemistry, computer science, mathematics, and physics; the college of fine arts, with courses in drama, music, painting, design, sculpture, and architecture; the college of humanities and social sciences, with courses in English, history, modern languages, psychology, and social studies; a school of urban and public affairs; and a graduate school of industrial administration. Other divisions include a computation center, a metals research laboratory, a radiation chemistry laboratory, and institutes of environmental studies, processing research, and transportation research. The degrees

*The leopard, a carnivore of Asia and Africa, uses its sharp pointed teeth to tear the flesh of its prey.*
South African Tourist Corp.

of bachelor, master, and doctor are conferred. In 1972 the university library housed more than 365,000 volumes. Student enrollment in 1972 totaled 4400, the faculty numbered 480, and the endowment of the university was about $120,-000,000.

**CARNELIAN** *or* **CORNELIAN,** clear variety of the mineral chalcedony (q.v.), varying in color from a pale to a deep red. The finest specimens come from Brazil, India, and Arabia. The carnelian, a fibrous variety of quartz (q.v.), is cut and polished and used in jewelry. The blood-red varieties were greatly valued by the ancients, who executed beautiful engravings in carnelian and frequently used them for seals.

**CARNIC ALPS,** range of the Eastern Alps of Europe. Forming a part of the border between Italy and Austria, they extend from the frontiers of the Austrian province of Tirol and the Italian region of Venetia to the frontier of Carinthia. Hohewarte, the highest peak of the Carnic Alps, rises 9121 ft. above sea level.

**CARNIOLA** (Ger. *Krain*), region of N.W. Yugoslavia, in Slovenia, formerly a crownland and duchy of Austria. The mountainous region, with an area of about 3842 sq.mi., was settled by the Slovenes (q.v.) during the 6th century A.D. and was an Austrian duchy from the 14th century until 1849, when it became a crownland. In 1918 Carniola was partitioned between Yugoslavia and Italy. Nearly 80 percent was given to Yugoslavia. In 1947 the Italian portion passed to Yugoslavia. *See* SLOVENIA.

**CARNIVORA,** order of mammals including most of the forms popularly known as beasts of prey. The Carnivora are found in all parts of the world except the Antarctic and some oceanic islands.

**General Characters.** The dentition of most Carnivora is usually characteristic. Each jaw contains six pointed cutting teeth; two strong,

sharp, recurved canines; and molar teeth often adapted for cutting. The skull is short and dense. The lower jaw moves up and down in a deep, transverse, semicylindrical groove, and the skull includes deep hollows on the sides and prominent crests on the roof, to which the powerful jaw muscles are attached. The stomach is simple and the caecum is either absent or small.

Vagrant, predatory habits, a flesh diet, fierce disposition, and high intelligence are characteristic of most members of this order, although exceptions to these generalizations are common. Some forms are omnivorous and a few are almost completely herbivorous. Most of the families are more abundant in the tropics than elsewhere, but some are more generally inhabitants of temperate regions, and a few are especially common in the far north.

**Classification.**   The order Carnivora is generally divided into three suborders: Creodonta, which are extinct forms, Pinnipedia, with paddlelike feet, and Fissipedia, with pawlike feet. Creodonta are primitive carnivores which are believed to have given rise to the carnivores of today. Pinnipedia contains three families: Otariidae, the sea lions and fur seals, animals with four feet and external ears; Phocidae, the true seals, animals with two feet and a tail fin and no external ears; and Odobaenidae, the walruses. The suborder Fissipedia is separated into many families: Canidae, the dogs, wolves, and foxes; Ursidae, the bears; Ailuropodidae and Ailuridae, the pandas; Procyonidae, the raccoons; Mustelidae, the badgers, skunks, minks, martens, sables, weasels, polecats, and others; Viverridae and Nandiniidae, the civets; Herpestidae, the mongooses; Hyenidae, the hyenas; Protelidae, the aardwolves; and Felidae, the cats, including lions, tigers, cheetahs, leopards, and similar animals.

**CARNIVOROUS PLANTS,**   known also as INSECTIVOROUS PLANTS, part of whose food consists of animals, especially insects, captured by the plants themselves. Most of these plants live in bogs where the soil is acid and poor in available nitrogen, and the capture of insects is one way of getting nitrogenous compounds without manufacturing them. At the same time the green leaves of these plants manufacture carbohydrate.

The pitcher plants, such as those of the genera *Sarracenia* and *Nepenthes* (q.v.), are so named because of their tubular leaves which contain water; and to these so-called pitchers insects are attracted and then drowned. In some cases nectar (q.v.) is secreted around the mouth of the pitcher, which attracts insects. Inside the

The *Venus's-flytrap,* Dionaea muscipula, *grows wild only near Wilmington, N.C.*          Hugh Morton

pitcher, just below the rim, is a glazed zone, and below this another zone with thickly set downward-pointing hairs; when a fly slips upon the glazed zone and plunges into the liquid at the bottom of the pitcher, the zone of downward-pointing hairs effectually prevents any escape.

The sundews, of the genus *Drosera,* are among the most common of the insectivorous plants, the leaves forming small rosettes upon the ground in bog areas. The upper surface of the leaf is covered with prominent glandular hairs. All of these glands excrete a clear sticky fluid, which clings to them like dewdrops, and which, not being dried up by the sunlight, gave rise to the name sundew. If a small insect alights on the leaf, or even brushes past it, it is held fast by the sticky hairs, which slowly curve inward and press the victim down upon the surface of the blade, where it is digested.

The Venus's-flytrap, *Dionaea muscipula,* is one of the rarest insect-trapping plants, growing wild only in sandy bogs near Wilmington, N.C. The leaf blade resembles a steel trap in its action, the two halves snapping together and the marginal bristles interlocking like the teeth of a trap. Three pairs of trigger hairs are located on the upper leaf surface. When one of these is touched by a small flying or hovering insect, the trap snaps shut, and the insect is caught. Fluids are then secreted and the insect is digested. *See also* BLADDERWORT.

The trapping mechanism of all carnivorous plants is relatively small, the largest being that of an Australian pitcher plant, *Cephalotus follicularis,* with a capacity of about one liter. Prey is therefore almost invariably limited to small insects.

Certain species of fungus are known to be carnivorous.

**CARNOT,** name of a French family prominent both in the fields of physics and politics.

**Lazare Nicolas Marguerite Carnot** (1753–1823), statesman and military engineer, born in Nolay. He became a member of the Legislative Assembly in 1791, of the National Convention in 1792, and of the Committee of Public Safety in 1793. Although never in full command, Carnot was the principal strategist of the victories of French troops in the battles of 1792–95 (*see* FRENCH REVOLUTION). His knowledge of and aptitude for military tactics caused Carnot to become known as the "Organizer of Victory".

During the complex events that followed the Reign of Terror and continued through the accession of Napoleon I (q.v.), Emperor of France, Carnot moved in and out of France several times. Finally he died in exile in Magdeburg, Germany, then part of Prussia.

The books written by Carnot include several on mathematical theory, but more important are his works on military tactics. *De la Défense des Places Fortes* ("On the Defense of Fortresses", 1810) is a classic study of fortification.

**Nicolas Léonard Sadi Carnot** (1796–1832), physicist and military engineer, son of Lazare Nicolas Marguerite Carnot, born in Paris, and educated at the École Polythechnique. In *Thoughts on the Motive Power of Heat* (1824), he described his conception of the perfect engine, the so-called Carnot engine, in which all available energy is utilized. He discovered that heat cannot pass from a colder to a warmer body, and that the efficiency of an engine depends upon the amount of heat it is able to utilize. This discovery, called Carnot's cycle, is the basis of the second law of thermodynamics. *See* THERMODYNAMICS.

**Marie François Sadi Carnot,** known as SADI (1837–94), statesman, nephew of Nicolas Léonard Sadi Carnot, born in Limoges, and educated at the École Polytechnique. He entered the civil service and later gained renown as an organizer of French resistance to the Germans in 1870 during the Franco-German War (q.v.). In 1871 he was made prefect of what is now Seine–Maritime Department and was elected to the National Assembly. He served as minister of public works in 1880 and again in 1885, and was minister of finance in 1885 and 1886. The following year he was elected the fourth president of the Third Republic. His tenure was marred by the scandal over construction of the Panama Canal (q.v.) and by the conspiracy trial of General Georges Boulanger (1837–91). Carnot was assassinated by an Italian anarchist.

**CARNOTITE.** *See* URANIUM; VANADIUM.

**CARNOVSKY, Morris** (1897–    ), American actor, born in Saint Louis, Mo., and educated at Washington University. One of the most versatile character actors in the American theater, Carnovsky started his career with the Henry Jewitt Players in Boston, and first appeared on the New York stage in *God of Vengeance* (1922). From 1924 to 1930 he appeared in many plays produced by the Theatre Guild, among which were *Saint Joan* (1923), *Marco Millions* (1927), and *Hotel Universe* (1930). In 1930 he became one of the founding members of the Group Theatre, for which he appeared in *Men in White* (1933), *Awake and Sing* (1935), *Waiting for Lefty* (1935), *Johnny Johnson* (1936), and *Golden Boy* (1937). His other Broadway appearances include *An Enemy of the People* (1950), *Tiger at the Gates* (1955), *Rhinoceros* (1961), and *A Family Affair* (1962). Between 1956 and 1963 he appeared with the American Shakespeare Festival Company at Stratford, Conn., in such roles as Shylock in *The Merchant of Venice,* Prospero in *The Tempest,* Feste in *Twelfth Night,* and the title role in *King Lear.*

**CARO, Joseph ben Ephraim** or **KARO, Joseph ben Ephraim** (1488–1575), Talmudic scholar (*see* TALMUD) and codifier of Jewish law, born in Toledo, Spain. To escape religious persecution, his family fled in 1492 to Portugal and later to Turkey and Palestine. His notable works are *Bet Yoseph* ("House of Joseph", 1550–59), a commentary on religious law, and the *Shulhan Arukh* ("The Prepared Table", 1564–65), a compilation, mainly from Talmudic and later sources, of Jewish civil and religious law. The code of the *Shulhan Arukh* was praised by many scholars and opposed by others. Orthodox Jews, however, accepted it as authoritative in religious matters. Caro belonged to the cabalistic circle at Safed, Palestine.                    N.N.G.

**CAROB,** or ALGARROBA or SAINT-JOHN'S-BREAD or LOCUST BEAN, common names for a tree, *Ceratonia siliqua,* of the Leguminosae (Pea) family. It grows to about 50 ft. in height and has dark, evergreen, pinnate leaves. The small, red flowers have no petals. The fruit is a brown, leathery pod about 4 to 12 in. long and about an inch wide, a little curved, and containing gummy pulp of an agreeable sweet taste, in which lie a number of seeds. The pods are edible and are often used for livestock feed. The seeds, which are remarkably uniform in size and weight, are thought to have been the original standard karat weight used by jewelers and goldsmiths. The carob is native to countries around the Mediterranean Sea and is cultivated in other warm climates.

"The Christmas Carol" (from an English woodcut, 1847).
Granger Collection

**CAROL,** popular religious song usually associated with the great Christian festivals, especially Christmas. The first carol was sung by the angel heralding the birth of Christ (Luke 2:9–14). As popular religious songs carols may have first appeared in the 12th century. They were important in England in the 15th century. One of the earliest extant English carols is "Boar's Head Carol", printed in 1521 and still sung at the University of Oxford. The singing of carols was banned in England and Scotland by the Puritans (q.v.) and came into use again at the time of the Restoration (q.v.) in 1660.

Carols, called *noëls* in France and *Weihnachtslieder* in Germany, were also popular in continental Europe. Many of the familiar carols of today have been translated from foreign languages. They include "Silent Night" (1818) from German, and "O Come, All Ye Faithful" from Latin. One of the earliest American carols was "We Three Kings of Orient Are", written about 1857.

**CAROL,** name of two kings of Rumania.

**Carol I,** originally KARL EITEL FRIEDRICH (1839–1914), King (1881–1914) of the house of Hohenzollern-Sigmaringen, born in Sigmaringen (now in West Germany), and educated in Dresden and Bonn. He served in the Prussian army, and in 1866 he was elected prince of Rumania, then a Turkish principality; see TURKEY: *History*. In 1877, during the Russo-Turkish War (*see* RUSSO-TURKISH WARS), Carol supported Russia and proclaimed the independence of Rumania. Rumania was recognized as a sovereign state by the Treaty of Berlin (*see* BERLIN, CONGRESS OF). Carol was crowned as the first king of Rumania in 1881. He established a parliamentary form of government for the nation. During his reign Rumania took part in the Balkan Wars (q.v.). Carol was succeeded by his nephew Ferdinand I (q.v.). See RUMANIA: *History*.

**Carol II** (1893–1953), King (1930–40), grandnephew of Carol I, born in Sinaia, and educated in Potsdam, now in East Germany. Carol became crown prince in 1914 on the death of his uncle. In 1918 he contracted a morganatic marriage, subsequently dissolved, and in 1921 he married Helen, Princess of Greece (1896–    ). Their son

Michael was born in 1921. In the same year Carol renounced his right to the throne and moved to Paris with his mistress Magda Lupescu (1904?– ). He divorced Princess Helen in 1928. In 1930 he returned to Rumania and was crowned king, supplanting Michael, who had become king under a council of regency in 1927. In the period before World War II Carol tried to achieve a balance between the conflicting interests of Germany and the Soviet Union. During the same period Rumania was beset by the worldwide economic crisis and by the rise of Fascism and anti-Semitism. In 1938 the political situation had become so critical that Carol suspended the constitution and assumed dictatorial powers. His efforts to remain neutral in the war failed, and in 1939 he concluded a commercial agreement giving the Germans control of Rumanian industry and almost guaranteeing their domination of Rumanian policy. In 1940 Carol yielded about 40,000 sq.mi. of Rumanian territory to the Soviet Union, Hungary, and Bulgaria. He then abdicated and spent the remainder of his life in exile. In 1947 he married Madame Lupescu.

**CAROL CITY,** unincorporated suburban area of Florida, in Dade Co., 6 miles N.W. of Miami. Pop. (1960) 21,749; (1970) 27,361.

**CAROLINA,** English proprietary colony in North America established by grant of Charles II (q.v.), King of England, in 1663, and soon afterward divided into the royal colonies of North Carolina and South Carolina. The Carolinas were two of the original thirteen States of the United States. *See* NORTH CAROLINA; SOUTH CAROLINA.

*CAROLINE,* privately owned American ship, seized and destroyed by Canadian troops on the American side of the Niagara R. off Grand Island, N.Y. on Dec. 29, 1837. The incident, in which one American was killed, occurred during a rebellion in Upper Canada (now Ontario Province), and threatened to cause war between the United States and Great Britain; *see* CANADA: *History: British Rule to Confederation.* The steamer had been used by American sympathizers to carry supplies to a party of Canadian rebels on Navy Island, above Niagara Falls. In 1840 Great Britain asserted that the destruction of the *Caroline* was a legitimate act of war. The U.S., however, repeatedly demanded redress on the grounds that the Canadians had invaded U.S. territory in time of peace. The matter came to a crisis in the course of the same year when a Canadian deputy sheriff visiting the U.S. boasted of participating in the affair, and was tried for murder in a New York State court. In spite of the demand of the British ministry for his release, the trial continued; war between the two nations was prevented only by his acquittal. Peaceful relations between Great Britain and the U.S. were finally restored in 1842 with the signing of the Webster-Ashburton Treaty; *see* NORTHEAST BOUNDARY DISPUTE. In the treaty Great Britain expressed regret for failing to have made an immediate apology for the *Caroline* affair.

**CAROLINE ISLANDS,** archipelago in the N. Pacific Ocean consisting of forty-eight islands, together with a number of reefs and shoals. The archipelago is between the Philippine and Marshall islands. The largest islands are Kusaie and Ponape, and the largest island groups are Yap, Truk, and Palau. The population consists mainly of Polynesians (q.v.) and Micronesians. Among the leading exports are copra, tapioca, and dried bonito. Some of the islands yield crops of coconuts and sugarcane. The Portuguese discovered the islands in 1527. In 1666 the group was annexed by the Spaniards, but the Spanish authorities neglected the islands until 1885, when German colonization efforts resulted in a dispute between Spain and Germany. The Spanish government sold the group to Germany in 1899 and following the defeat of Germany in World War I (q.v.), it was placed under a Japanese mandate. During World War II (q.v.) American airplanes and naval forces intensively bombed and shelled several of the Caroline Islands, notably Truk, which the Japanese had strongly fortified. In 1947 the islands were placed under the trusteeship of the United Nations, to be administered by the United States in the Trust Territory of the Pacific Islands. Area, 550 sq.mi.; pop. (1973) 77,016.

**CAROLINE MATILDA** (1751–75), Queen Consort of Denmark (1766–71) as wife of King Christian VII (1749–1808), whom she married in 1766, and sister of George III (q.v.), King of Great Britain, born in London, England. Christian was her cousin. She later formed a liaison with Count Johann Friedrich von Struensee (1737–72), the court physician and a brilliant statesman. Through her influence Struensee was named minister of state. About 1771 their affair became known. Struensee was dismissed from office and eventually beheaded, and the queen was divorced from her husband. Imprisoned at first, she was later freed and spent her last years in Celle (now in West Germany). Her son ruled later as King Frederick VI (q.v.).

**CAROLINE OF ANSPACH** (1683–1737), Queen Consort of Great Britain and Ireland (1727–37) as wife of King George II (q.v.) whom she married in 1705, and daughter of John Frederick, Margrave of Brandenberg-Ansbach (d. 1687). In London Caroline made her home the meeting place of the noted literary figures of the day. She acted as regent on several occasions during absences of her husband from England and aided the career of the British statesman Sir Robert Walpole (see under WALPOLE).

**CAROLINE OF BRUNSWICK** (1768–1821), Queen Consort of Great Britain (1821) as wife of King George IV (q.v.), whom she married in 1795, and daughter of Charles William Ferdinand, Duke of Brunswick (1735–1806). George III (q.v.), King of Great Britain, her uncle, arranged her marriage to the dissolute and reluctant George IV, then Prince of Wales, who dis-

liked her and whose mistresses persecuted her. After the birth of her daughter, Charlotte Augusta (1796–1817), she was deserted by her husband. After 1813 Caroline lived much of the time on the European continent, returning to England in 1820, when her husband became king. Although she was tried by the House of Lords on the ground of adultery, the trial was abandoned, and she was permitted to assume the title of queen consort. She was forcibly prevented from attending the coronation of George IV in 1821 and died soon afterward.

**CAROLINGIAN,** or CARLOVINGIAN, second dynasty of Frankish kings. The family is traced to Arnulf, Bishop of Metz (d. 640). His son Anseg-

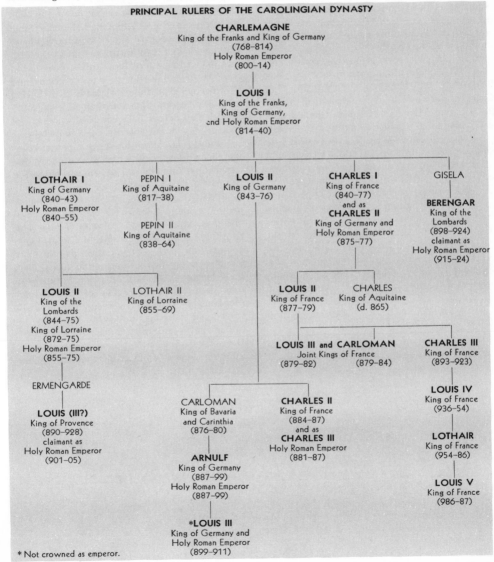

PRINCIPAL RULERS OF THE CAROLINGIAN DYNASTY

isel (r. 632–38) married Begga, a daughter of Pepin the Elder, mayor of the palace of Austrasia, the eastern portion of the Frankish kingdom. The grandson of Pepin, Pepin of Herstal, later succeeded as mayor; *see under* PEPIN. By 687 he had brought Carolingian control to most of the Frankish kingdom, although the first dynasty of Frankish kings, the Merovingians, retained nominal rule; *see* MEROVINGIAN. Pepin of Herstal was succeeded in turn by his natural son Charles Martel (q.v.) and by two grandsons, Carloman (d. 754) and Pepin the Short; *see under* PEPIN. Carloman later abdicated, and in 751 Pepin the Short was crowned as the first Carolingian king of the Franks. This date is generally regarded as the beginning of the Carolingian dynasty. It is historically significant that Pepin was the first French king whose coronation was sanctified by the Church.

Pepin was succeeded by his two sons Carloman (751–71) and Charlemagne (q.v.), who at first ruled the kingdom jointly. After 771 Charlemagne was sole ruler and vastly increased the kingdom. On Dec. 25, 800, Charlemagne was crowned as the first emperor of the Western Roman Empire; *see* HOLY ROMAN EMPIRE. The kingdom was inherited by Louis I (q.v.), and upon his death was divided among his three surviving sons. The kingdom was disturbed by civil war rising from questions of inheritance and in 843 the kingdom was formally divided by the treaty of Verdun; *see* VERDUN. Thereafter the power of the dynasty further declined. In 911 the line became extinct in Germany and the Holy Roman Empire and was replaced by the Saxons (q.v.), and in France in 987 the line was succeeded by the Capetians; *see* CAPET, HOUSE OF.

*See* FRANCE: *History;* FRANKS; GERMANY: *History;* HOLY ROMAN EMPIRE.

*Carp,* Cyprinus carpio      **U.S. Fish & Wildlife Service**

**CAROM BILLIARDS.** *See* BILLIARDS.

**CARON.** *See* BEAUMARCHAIS, PIERRE AUGUSTIN CARON DE.

**CAROTHERS, Wallace Hume.** *See* NYLON.

**CAROTID ARTERIES,** two main arteries supplying blood to the head. The arteries rise from the arch of the aorta (q.v.) as the right common carotid and as the left common carotid. At the upper margin of the larynx each carotid separates into two divisions, the external and the internal, and within the head the two divisions branch out into many capillaries. *See* CIRCULATORY SYSTEM.

**CARP,** common name for a freshwater fish, *Cyprinus carpio,* of the family Cyprinidae. It is a large fish having a long dorsal fin and a small toothless mouth with four barbels, or sensory organs. Carp weigh about 25 lb.; one specimen weighed 73 lb. Exceptionally long lived, the carp was native to eastern Asia, and is now found throughout the world. It lives in ponds and slowly moving streams, particularly those having a muddy bottom and a growth of weeds. Although carp occasionally eat insects, their chief food is vegetation, and the fish often destroys valuable aquatic plant life. Carp hibernate during the winter months and are so hardy that they can be kept alive for days in wet moss. The fish is widely used as food.

**CARPACCIO, Vittore** (1455?–1526?), Italian painter, born in Venice. He was greatly influenced by the Venetian painters Gentile and Giovanni Bellini; *see under* BELLINI. Carpaccio executed four cycles of narrative paintings, of which only the first two are notable. The first, done between 1490 and 1495, was the cycle of nine large paintings, "Legend of Saint Ursula" (Academy of Fine Arts, Venice). This series is considered to be his finest work. Especially important is the painting "Dream of St. Ursula". The second cycle, nine scenes that are mainly from the lives of Saint George and Saint Jerome

(qq.v.), is in Scuola San Giorgio degli Schiavoni in Venice. The two best-known paintings of this cycle are "St. George Slaying the Dragon" and "St. Jerome in his Study". Among his other paintings are "A Saint Reading" and "Virgin and Child", both in the National Gallery of Art, Washington, D.C. Carpaccio was one of the most able and attractive painters of the early Renaissance in Venice. His pageant paintings illustrate in an incomparable manner the Venetian life of his day. The drawing is sometimes faulty, but the color is clear and harmonious, and light and atmosphere are handled with masterly effect.

**CARPATHIAN MOUNTAINS,** major forested mountain system of central and eastern Europe extending about 900 mi. in a great semicircle from Bratislava, Czechoslovakia, to the Iron Gate near Orşova, Rumania. Both ends of the arc rest upon the Danube R. The Carpathians, varying between 20 and 160 mi. wide, are divided into smaller ranges, including the Little Carpathians, the White Carpathians, the High Tatra Range, the East Carpathians, and the Transylvanian Alps. The system, although extensive, is not high; the highest point, Gerlachovka Peak in Czechoslovakia, is 8711 ft. above sea level. The system is broken by numerous passes that were used frequently by invading armies. Several major rivers, including the Dniester and the Vistula, are formed in the Carpathians. Rich deposits of gold, silver, lead, iron, mercury, copper, oil, coal, and salt are found. Forests of oak, beech, fir, and pine cover the slopes from about 1500 ft. to 6000 ft., and bears, lynx, and wolves still inhabit remote forest areas.

**CARPATHO-UKRAINE.** *See* RUTHENIA; UKRAINIAN SOVIET SOCIALIST REPUBLIC.

**CARPENTARIA, GULF OF,** arm of the Arafura Sea, on the N. coast of Australia. The gulf is more than 400 mi. wide and nearly 500 mi. long. It contains many islands, and the shores are generally low with extensive indentations on the w. coast.

**CARPENTER, John Alden** (1876–1951), American composer, born in Park Ridge, Ill., and educated at Harvard University. He later studied composition with the British composer Sir Edward Elgar (q.v.). Carpenter is best known for his ballet *Skyscrapers* (1926) and for his Concertino for Piano and Orchestra (1916).

**CARPENTER BEES.** *See* BEE: *Bumblebees.*

**CARPENTER'S HALL.** *See* PHILADELPHIA: *Historic Sites.*

**CARPENTERSVILLE,** village of Illinois, in Kane Co., on the Fox R., about 37 miles N.W. of Chicago. Carpentersville is in a livestock, dairy, and agricultural region. Manufactures include pumps, valves, and iron and steel products. Pop. (1960) 17,424; (1970) 24,059.

**CARPETBAGGERS,** term of contempt applied by the people of the Southern States mainly to Northerners who came to the South during the Reconstruction (q.v.) period following the American Civil War (q.v.). They were called carpetbaggers because they often carried their belongings in satchels made of carpet. Some were representatives of the Freedmen's Bureau (q.v.)

Caricature of carpetbagger, 1872, by the American cartoonist Thomas Nast
Granger Collection

and other Reconstruction agencies; some were humanitarians intent on aiding the Negro; and some were adventurers who hoped to benefit themselves by questionable means. Those carpetbaggers, who were unscrupulous, came to control the Negro vote and in some instances to establish dishonest governments. The carpetbaggers did serve to broaden Negro voting activity, to improve education, and to aid in the restoration of Southern cities and roads. The carpetbaggers generally cooperated with their Southern counterparts, called scalawags, and both groups were bitterly resented by the white Southerners. Secret terrorist societies such as the Ku Klux Klan (q.v.) were formed to terrorize the Negroes and drive the carpetbaggers out. Today the term carpetbagger refers to roving opportunists or politicians.

**CARPET BEETLE,** common name for a beetle, *Anthrenus scrophulariae,* of the family Dermes-

The tufting machine sews the pile yarns to a broad pre-woven fabric backing, using thousands of fast-moving needles.

tidae, the larvae of which feed on carpets and various other materials of animal origin. The adult beetle, also called the buffalo carpet beetle, is oval in form, with black, red, and white markings on the back and white scales on the underside. The spindle-shaped larva has tufts of stiff bristles along the sides and at the ends of the body. The beetle eggs are deposited in cracks in the floor under the carpet; the developing larvae then feed on the carpet, often following the cracks and cutting long slits. A related species of the same family is *Attagenus piceus*, a black beetle, the larvae of which are more cylindrical and not so destructive.

**CARPETS AND RUGS,** heavy fabrics made of various materials and used traditionally for indoor floor coverings and in recent developments on walls and other special surfaces. The distinction between carpets and rugs is indefinite and largely a matter of size and method of attachment. Rugs are usually smaller than carpets and not secured to the floor; commonly, they cover only a portion of the floor area. Carpets are generally tacked or cemented to the floor, often with an underlay of cushion. The carpet and rug industry in the United States further divides its products into broadloom, which is defined as wall-to-wall carpeting and rugs larger than 4 ft. by 6 ft., and scatter rugs and miscellaneous, a category that includes smaller rugs, such as bath mats, and transportation carpets.

### HISTORY OF RUG MAKING

The use of floor coverings is almost as old as recorded history. At first animal skins, and subsequently coarse fabrics of ordinary weave, were used. Gradual improvements in weaving and design produced the more elaborate tapestry (q.v.) weave. Eventually pile fabrics, materials consisting of a strong backing of ordinary weave but with extra threads added to form a somewhat raised surface, were introduced. The weaving of pile carpets developed in India before the 12th century A.D. and spread to the rest of the East. In the Orient rugs are usually made out of pile fabrics knotted by hand, although other weaves are employed; *see* RUGS, ORIENTAL.

In the West until the 19th century, the most common floor coverings were flat-woven fabrics, as few families could afford the more costly Oriental and domestic hand-knotted pile rugs. Hand-knotted rugs were made in Europe by the Saracens (q.v.) of southern Spain as early as the 13th century. Tapestry rugs were crafted in Aubusson, a small town in central France, which has since become the trade name for this type of carpet. Hand-knotted pile rugs called Savonnerie carpets similarly took their distinctive name from the original factory, established in the 17th century at the site of an ancient soap works (Fr. *savonnerie*) at Chaillot, France. In 1825 the factory was transferred to the Gobelin (q.v.) family and is still active. The same name is given also to rugs of this type made at Aubusson and elsewhere in France. Brussels became an important center of tapestry weaving in the 16th century and by the 18th century had become one of the principal sources of floor tapestries. A similar type of floor covering was developed in the town of Wilton in England. Wilton also produced an important development in the hand-knotting technique, known today as Wilton carpeting.

In the U.S. the first factory for woven yarn carpeting was started in Philadelphia in 1791. In 1841 a steam engine was harnessed to an ingrain loom, raising daily production more than threefold. The first carpet looms produced carpets ¾ yd. wide, which were cut into lengths and sewn together. Today carpet looms range up to 30 ft. in width of carpet produced.

### MANUFACTURING TECHNIQUES

In the early 1950's the U.S. carpet and rug industry underwent a technological revolution when the technique of making carpets and rugs on relatively low-cost, high-speed tufting machines was developed. As a result, many inventive entrepreneurs were attracted to the growing carpet and rug industry.

Concurrently, several petrochemical companies in the U.S. were developing synthetic fibers in deniers suitable for carpet and rug use. Rayon appeared in the mid-1950's and was later replaced by nylon. In rapid order the acrylics were then introduced and were soon joined by the modacrylics, olefins (polypropylenes), and polyesters. The price and delivery fluctuations that had plagued carpet manufacturers in the worldwide wool market were finally relieved.

With pile fibers plentiful and carpet production expanding rapidly, carpets and rugs became two of the fastest-growing consumer products in the nation. As the industry grew, new tufting and dyeing techniques were perfected, and quality continued to improve. With increased competition and reduced costs, prices reached popular levels, and new carpet and rug markets were found, particularly in public and commercial buildings. Because of this revolution, the carpet and rug products in the mid-1970's were of superior quality to those of the early 1950's and generally cost about half as much money.

**Tufted Carpets.** A tufting machine is similar in principle to an ordinary sewing machine (q.v.).

In Axminster carpet weaving, the loom allows an almost unlimited combination of colors.　James Lees

A researcher tests a carpet sample during the manufacturing process to assure that it meets all the necessary performance standards.　Armstrong Carpet

The difference is that a sewing machine stitches a single row at a time, while a tufting machine sews any number of rows at a time, with hundreds of individual needles stitching simultaneously through a backing material as much as 15 ft. wide.

A secondary backing material is usually adhered to the carpet for added strength and dimensional stability, and to hold the individual tufts in place. In some instances, a high-density foam rubber, sponge, or vinyl cushion is used instead of a secondary backing material. Tufted carpet is commonly made in 12-ft. and 15-ft. widths for wall-to-wall installation or is cut into rugs of any size. Tufted carpet tiles with a variety of backings are also made.

Carpet manufactured on a tufting machine can be styled in many different patterns, such as tweeds, solids, or stripes; various pattern attachments used with the machine produce high-low sculptured and embossed effects. Colorful designs are printed over the pile, or randomly placed, and multicolor effects are achieved either on the machine, or during the dyeing process. The pile can be cut (plush), selectively sheared (cut-and-loop), or left totally uncut (loop).

In 1951 tufting accounted for 9 percent of the total broadloom-carpet production, but by 1973 it had increased to 96 percent. The center of the U.S. carpet and rug industry is Dalton, Ga., around which is concentrated about 65 percent of the floor-covering industry.

**Woven Carpets.** Weaving encompasses three basic machine techniques—Wilton, Axminster, and velvet looms. Variations of these machines have their own different capabilities.

The Wilton carpet derives its name from the town in England where the Wilton loom was developed. The loom is distinguished by its specialized Jacquard system—a series of pattern cards perforated like player piano rolls. The cards regulate the feeding of different colored yarns onto the pile surface. Although the number of colors possible on a Wilton loom is not unlimited, the Jacquard mechanism ensures accurate reproduction of intricate patterns, with great clarity and definition. As weaving proceeds, one color at a time is drawn into the pile, and the colors not required are buried beneath the surface. These buried yarns give additional body, resilience, and strength to the Wilton carpet, which is available in a wide range of textures and multicolor patterns as well as solid colors.

The Axminster carpet, which is also named for a town in England, is distinguished by an almost limitless choice of designs and colors. The patterns can be stylized, geometric, classic, modern, or floral. Changing the pattern on an Axminster loom is a slow and demanding process requiring great skill. Separate lengths or ends of different colored yarns must be set with absolute accuracy to ensure faithful pattern reproduction. Axminster looms are thus nearly as versatile as handweaving. The pile is cut, with few exceptions, and almost all the yarn appears on the surface. Another distinguishing feature of the Axminster carpet is its heavily ribbed back.

The velvet carpet employs the simplest of all carpet-weaving techniques and is commonly available in solid colors. However, the range of color and texture variations possible on a velvet loom are almost limitless. Included in the possible texture effects are cut pile plushes, cut pile twist (frieze), pebbly uncut loop pile, and multilevel sculptured effects. Pile yarns can also be selectively cut and uncut for still other attractive surface-texture combinations. *See* LOOM.

**Knitted Carpets.** Knitted carpet, like woven carpet, is fabricated in one operation—face and back simultaneously. Backing yarns, stitching yarns, and pile yarns are looped together with three sets of needles, much the way hand knitting is done. To give the carpet additional body, a coat of latex foam is applied to the backing. A secondary backing material similar to that used on tufted carpet is often added in the finishing process. Because only a single pile yarn is used, knitted carpet is usually solid in color or tweed. Machine modifications make some pattern effects possible. Loop pile effects are most common, though cut pile plushes can also be made with further machine modifications.

**Needlepunch Carpets.** Needlepunch carpet is a flat, abrasion-resistant sandwich of unspun fibers normally covering a prewoven fabric core. The face and back are formed by hundreds of barbed needles punching through webs, or blankets of fiber, to mesh them permanently together. The result is an extremely dense sheet, without pile, of considerable weight and thickness. Needlepunch carpet can be printed with colorful designs, and a high-density rubber cushion may also be bonded to it. Needlepunch carpet, made of weather-resistant olefin (polypropylene) fiber, is the dominant product in the so-called indoor-outdoor market. Other primary applications of this manufacturing technique include kitchen, bath, wall, and patio carpets.

## RECENT TRENDS

Until the early 1960's, wool was the dominant fiber used in the manufacture of carpets and rugs. In 1960, 64 percent of the surface fiber used in broadloom carpets was wool. Since then this percentage has fallen consistently, declining to 2.6 percent in 1973. In 1973 the dominant fiber used in the production of carpets and rugs was nylon (65.7 percent), followed by polyester (12.3 percent), acrylics (9.3 percent), polypropylene (5.4 percent), and cotton and rayon (4.4 percent). In the production of scatter rugs, bath mats, and transportation carpets, cotton and rayon still retain a position that is quite dominant.

The most rapidly growing sector of the carpet and rug industry in the U.S. is the commercial, or contract, market, estimated in 1973 to account for about half of the total shipments. The definition is somewhat vague, but contract is usually regarded as referring to carpet purchased in quantity for residential developments such as apartment buildings, and commercial is regarded as referring to nonresidential applications such as offices, hotels, schools, hospitals, supermarkets, restaurants, theaters, and libraries. Another important but still developing application is the use of such carpeting on the surface of playing fields as a replacement for natural turf.

The carpet and rug industry in the U.S. has grown from gross sales of $1,000,000,000 in 1964 to $2,000,000,000 in 1969. The 1973 figures show that the mill dollar value of all carpets and rugs reached $3,378,490,000, based on a record production of 1,028,985,000 sq.yd. R.D.

ALLEN M. SALE, JR.

**CARPINI, Giovanni de Piano** (1182?–1252), Franciscan monk, historian, and the first European to record a visit to China, born near Perugia, Italy. He served for several years in minor clerical offices in Germany and Spain. In 1245 he was summoned by Pope Innocent IV (d. 1254) to establish an embassy among the Mongols, who had invaded Europe several years before; *see* MONGOL DYNASTIES. The pope hoped to dissuade the Mongols from further attack by a personal appeal and to secure information about them. Carpini led the mission from Lyon, France, to Kiev (now in the U.S.S.R.), then the outpost of Christianity, and to the imperial capital, Karakorum, Mongolia. There the legates witnessed the enthronement of Kuyuk (r. 1246–48). Several months later the legation began the arduous journey back to Lyon. The mission failed to halt the Mongol invasions but is memorable for the account set down by Carpini. *Liber Tatarorum* ("Travels in Tatary") related the customs, geography, history, and leading personalities of the Mongols and the country between Kiev and Mongolia.

**CARR, Emily.** *See* CANADIAN ART: *English Period.*

**CARRÀ, Carlo.** *See* FUTURISM.

**CARRACCI** *or* **CARACCI,** family of Bolognese painters.

**Lodovico Carracci** (1555–1619), studied in Bologna with the Italian painter Prospero Fontana (1512–97), and with other masters in Venice, Padua, and Parma. Lodovico worked during the Mannerist period, the period of transition between Renaissance and Baroque styles (*see* ART: *History: Mannerist Art*), but he represented a return to the pure Classicism of the early Renaissance. His most important contribution was the founding in 1585 and subsequent direction of an academy for artists in Bologna. This school attempted to revive the natural simplicity of the early masters; academy pupils sketched from nature and live models. A new development was the emphasis placed on landscape for its own sake, not merely as background. The movement that grew up around the academy, known as the Bolognese school, has been characterized as eclectic. Among the prominent artists who studied at the academy were Il Domenichino and Guido Reni (qq.v.). Carracci was a prolific painter as well as an influential teacher. His works are found in many Bolognese churches; especially notable is his "Sermon of Saint John the Baptist" in the Pinacoteca. His "Vision of

*"Madonna Appears to Saint Luke and Saint Catherine",
an oil painting by Annibale Carracci.* Alinari

Saint Hyacinth" is in the Louvre, Paris. With his cousins Annibale and Agostino Carracci, Lodovico decorated the friezes of the Fava and Magnani palaces in Bologna.

**Agostino Carracci** (1557–1602), cousin of Lodovico Carracci, joined in the direction of the academy in Bologna, following his studies in Bologna and Venice. Agostino devoted much of his career to engraving. His painting "The Last Communion of Saint Jerome" is in the Pinacoteca, Bologna. With his brother Annibale he decorated the gallery of the Farnese Palace in Rome.

**Annibale Carracci** (1560–1609), brother of Agostino Carracci, studied in Parma and Venice. He was a director of the Bolognese academy. In addition to his joint works with the other Carracci, Annibale decorated the study of the Farnese Palace, Rome. His "The Dead Christ" and "Madonna with Saint Luke" are in the Louvre, Paris, and his "The Temptation of Saint Anthony" is located in the National Gallery, London.

181

**CARRAGEEN,** *or* IRISH MOSS, common names for two species of red algae (q.v.), of the family Gigartinaceae, found on the rocky seashores of northern Europe and on the eastern shores of North America. The species of commercial importance is *Chondrus crispus.* It is a dark purple, branching, cartilaginous plant that yields carrageenin, a colloidal extract, used as a thickening agent, or demulcent, in foods, cosmetics, and pharmaceuticals. It is often mixed with other algae species, most notably *Gigartina mammillosa.* Carrageen is prepared for use by washing and bleaching in the sun.

**CARRANZA, Venustiano** (1859–1920), Mexican statesman, born in Cuatrociénagas de Carranza, Coahuila State, and educated in Mexico City. He held a number of public offices and in 1910 was elected governor of the State of Coahuila. When the Mexican president Porfirio Díaz (q.v.) tried to prevent him from taking office, Carranza joined the revolution that overthrew Díaz and installed Francesco Indalecio Madero (q.v.) as president of Mexico. In 1913, following the overthrow of Madero by General Victoriano Huerta (q.v.) and the assassination of Madero, Carranza led the Constitutionalist, or revolutionary, forces seeking the ouster of Huerta. In the ensuing civil war Huerta was defeated by the Constitutionalist army, under General Álvaro Obregón (q.v.). Carranza was installed as provisional head of the new government in August, 1914. He failed, however, to institute agrarian reform. Two contenders for the presidency, Emiliano Zapata (q.v.) and Pancho Villa (*see* VILLA, FRANCISCO), mounted a mass movement against Carranza and he was driven from Mexico City. In 1915 Carranza won popular support by projecting far-reaching programs of social and agrarian reform. Two years later he was elected president of Mexico following the adoption of a new constitution that embodied the land reform previously decreed and a liberal code of labor law.

His regime was marked by a series of conflicts with foreign investors over attempts by the Mexican government to restrict foreign ownership of agricultural and other property and to establish national ownership of oil and mineral deposits. Carranza, however, did not fulfill his promises for reform and Obregón led a popular revolt. Carranza fled to the State of Puebla, where he was captured and killed. *See* MEXICO: *History.*

**CARREL, Alexis** (1873–1944), French surgeon, born in Lyon and educated at the University of Lyon. In 1905 Carrel came to the United States. With the exception of several years during World War I when he served in the French army, Carrel remained in the U.S. until 1939. From 1906 until 1939 he worked at the Rockefeller Institute for Medical Research (now Rockefeller University) in New York City. He was awarded the 1912 Nobel Prize in medicine and physiology for his development as early as 1902 of a technique for suturing blood vessels. During World War I, Carrel and the British chemist Henry D. Dakin (1880–1952) invented the Carrel-Dakin solution, an antiseptic used on wounds as a gangrene preventive. Carrel performed extensive research on the prolongation of the life of animal tissue outside the body. In the early 1930's he and the American aviator and engineer Charles A. Lindbergh (q.v.) invented a perfusion pump or mechanical heart capable of passing vital fluids through excised organs. Various animal tissues were kept alive for many years in this fashion. After his return to France in 1939, Carrel worked during World War II for the pro-German French government at Vichy. He wrote *Man the Unknown* (1935), expounding his elitist philosophy, and collaborated with Lindbergh on *The Culture of Organs* (1938).

**CARRERA, Rafael** (1814–65), Guatemalan revolutionist and politician, born in Guatemala City. In 1837 he participated in the armed struggle against the regime of Francisco Morazán (1799–1842), president of the Central American Federation, which included what are now Guatemala, Honduras, El Salvador, Nicaragua, and Costa Rica. As leader of the insurgent forces, which included many Indians, he helped to destroy the union in 1839 and proclaimed Guatemalan independence the same year. Becoming virtual dictator of the nation, he ruled, with the support of conservative and clerical political groups, until his death. During this period he served as president on two occasions, from 1844 to 1848 and from 1854 until his death. He was involved in two wars with El Salvador (1850–53 and 1863), in the last of which he deposed the president of that country and installed a regime sympathetic to his own policies.

**CARRERA ANDRADE, Jorgé** (1903– ), Ecuadorian poet and diplomat, born in Quito and educated at the Central University of Ecuador and at the University of Barcelona. He was secretary general of the Socialist Party of Ecuador in 1927–28. Subsequently he held diplomatic posts in Europe, South America, and Japan and served as Ecuadorian minister of foreign affairs. His travels had a marked influence on his poetry, which abounds in place-names and descriptions. Although some of his poems reflect his identification with social revolution, most of his poetry consists of metaphorical descriptions of places and objects. Famed for sensitive, original imagery, Carrera Andrade is considered the greatest Ecuadorian writer and one of the foremost Spanish-language poets of the 20th century. He published his first book, *El Estanque Inefable* (1922; Eng. trans., *Secret Country*, 1946), and won acclaim eight years later with the publication of *Boletines de Mar y Tierra* ("Bulletins of Sea and Land", 1930). Among his other works are *Rol de la Manzana* ("Catalogue of the Apple", 1935), *La Hora de las Ventanas Iluminadas* ("Hour of the Lighted Windows", 1937), and the anthology *Registro del Mundo* ("Census of the World", 1942).

**CARRÈRE, John Merven** (1858–1911), American architect, born in Rio de Janeiro, Brazil, of American parents. He studied architecture at the École des Beaux-Arts in Paris. In 1886 he formed a partnership in New York City with the American architect Thomas Hastings (q.v.), and the two worked together until Carrère's death. With Hastings, Carrère designed a number of notable public buildings mostly in classic Greek, Roman, and Italian Renaissance styles. Among them were the New York Public Library in New York City, the Carnegie Institution of Washington (qq.v.), the United States Senate and House of Representatives office buildings in Washington, D.C., and the Royal Bank of Canada in Montréal. The partners employed Spanish-Moorish styles for the Alcázar and Ponce de León hotels in Saint Augustine, Fla.

**CARRIAGE,** wheeled vehicle; specifically, a vehicle for carrying persons, designed to be drawn by one or more draft animals. Dating from earliest history, it is a development of the sledge, a platform on runners frequently depicted on ancient Egyptian monuments. The first wheels, solid disks cut from tree trunks, doubtless evolved from rollers that were placed under sledges to lessen friction. Originally the axles to which these rude wheels were attached revolved with the wheels. In the next stage of development the wheels were mounted so as to rotate about the axles. Lighter wheels made with spokes were developed later. By 1500 B.C. horse-drawn, two-wheeled chariots for hunting and military purposes was being used by the Egyptians. The Assyrians, Greeks, and Romans also used this kind of chariot. The chariot of antiquity was the prototype of the cart.

The bodies of chariots were small, usually holding only two persons. They were open for entrance at the back and had no seat. At first the wheels were very low, from 3 to 4 ft. in diameter. The primitive form of the chariot was changed as it was adopted by different nations. The wheels were enlarged, it was made to hold many persons, and finally four wheels were used. Little remained of the original chariot but the name. According to the Greek historian Herodotus (q.v.), the Scythians used a four-wheeled vehicle, consisting of a platform on which a covering of basketwork and hides was placed.

During the Middle Ages carriages fell into disuse, mainly because of the ruinous condition of

*Carriage of the 18th century.*

the old Roman roads. Travelers moved from place to place, chiefly on horseback, on mule, or were carried on litters. Goods were conveyed in huge panniers hung on the sides of strong draft animals. The use of carriages was revived gradually, however, at first by the nobility and later by wealthy burghers. One of the earliest vehicles to appear in medieval times was the whirlicote, a form of horse-drawn litter on wheels. Also developed in the Middle Ages was the carretta, a highly ornamented two-wheeled cart. The most important development of carriage making occurred possibly before the 16th century, when the first coach (q.v.) was made, probably in Hungary. Later leather springs and small front wheels were introduced, a modification that made turns in a narrow space possible.

Carriages were not generally in use in England until long after they had become popular on the Continent. Although stagecoaches were first built during the reign of Elizabeth I (q.v.), Queen of England, and other changes in the art of carriage making occurred during the 17th and 18th centuries, the most significant developments in the field did not begin, in the British Isles, until the early part of the 19th century. Then, as a result of the work of the British engineer John Loudon McAdam (q.v.) and others, the highways of Great Britain were put into a condition that made vehicular travel pleasant. In 1804 a device was patented in Great Britain by which vehicles were hung upon elliptic springs, thus eliminating the heavy perch, or longitudinal wood or iron pole, that had always been used to connect the front and back wheels of four-wheeled carriages. With this invention modern methods of carriage construction began. The best known of the many types of carriages invented in the course of the next century include the phaeton, the brougham, the barouche, the chaise, the omnibus, and the hansom cab.

In the United States the manufacture of carriages and wagons was an important industry throughout the 18th and 19th centuries. Among the many types of horse-drawn vehicles produced during this period were the buckboard, the surrey, and the Conestoga wagon (q.v.), the forerunner of the famed prairie schooner (q.v.). The buggy, mass produced between 1865 and 1910 in the U.S., became very important as a family conveyance before the introduction of the bicycle and the horseless carriage in the 1890's.

**CARRIER, Willis Haviland** (1876–1950), American engineer, born in Angola, N.Y., and educated at Cornell University. In 1902 as an engineer with the Buffalo Forge Company, Buffalo, N.Y., he invented and installed a system that supplied moisture-controlled air throughout a printing plant in Brooklyn, N.Y. Carrier called his invention "air conditioning". In 1911 he wrote a paper, "Rational Psychrometric Formulae", that formulated the scientific principles of air conditioning. In 1915 he founded The Carrier Corporation in order to produce air conditioning equipment.

**CARRIER CURRENT,** high frequency alternating current (50,000 cycles per sec. or higher) that can be used to carry modulated signals; see MODULATION; SOUND. Radio broadcast signals are impressed on the carrier by frequency modulation (FM) or amplitude modulation (AM); see FREQUENCY MODULATION; RADIO.

The carrier current is usually kept at a fixed frequency by the transmitter and is detected in the receiver by a resonant circuit at the carrier frequency; see RESONANCE. A message is sent by changing the carrier amplitude or phase proportional to the desired transmission signal. If the amplitude is changed, amplitude modulation results, and a change of phase results in phase modulation, a form of frequency modulation.

*See also* RADIO AND TELEVISION BROADCASTING.

J.J.Ke.

**CARRION FLOWER,** common name for any plant of the genus *Stapelia* of the Milkweed family (Asclepiadaceae). *Stapelia* are cactuslike desert herbs with flowers that have a putrid odor. The term is also used for *Smilax herbacea* of the Lily family (Liliaceae), a greenbrier climbing vine with flowers that smell like carrion.

**CARROLL, Charles,** known as CHARLES CARROLL OF CARROLLTON (1737–1832), American patriot, born in Annapolis, Md., and educated in Paris and London. Upon his return to America in 1764 his father presented him with the large estate known subsequently as Carrollton Manor. In 1775 he was elected to the Continental Congress and, in the following year, he signed the Declaration of Independence (qq.v.). He was also a member of the commission, appointed by the Continental Congress, that visited Canada in 1776 in a vain effort to induce the Canadians to join the war against Great Britain. He resigned from the Congress in 1778 to serve in the Maryland State Senate. He was one of the first United States Senators from Maryland, serving from 1789 to 1792. Carroll was the last survivor of the group of fifty-six men who signed the Declaration of Independence.

**CARROLL, James** (1854–1907), American bacteriologist, born in Woolwich (now part of London), England. Carroll emigrated to Canada at the age of fifteen, and later joined the United States Army. He received his medical degree from the University of Maryland in 1891. From 1902 until his death he was professor of bacteriology and pathology at George Washington University and at the Army Medical School. He is best known for his work in collaboration with the American bacteriologist Walter Reed (q.v.) on the Yellow Fever Commission in Cuba. The commission ascertained the exact mode of transmission of yellow fever (q.v.); Carroll was one of the four men who permitted themselves to be bitten by yellow-fever-bearing mosquitoes so that the disease might be studied and preventive methods developed. Carroll proved that a filterable virus is the infectious agent of the disease.

**CARROLL, John** (1735–1815), American Roman Catholic prelate, born in Upper Marlboro, Md., and educated at Saint Omer's College and at Liège. In 1771 he joined the Society of Jesus, or Jesuits (q.v.), and taught at the College of Bruges, maintained by the order. He returned to America in 1774, following the suppression of the Society of Jesus by Pope Clement XIV (see under CLEMENT). In 1776 he joined the American statesmen Benjamin Franklin, his cousin Charles Carroll, and Samuel Chase (qq.v.) in a delegation to Montréal, unsuccessfully attempting to bring Canada into the American Revolution on the side of the colonists. In 1784 he was confirmed as head of the Roman Catholic missions in the United States by Pope Pius VI (see under Pius). In 1790 Carroll was consecrated bishop, the first American to hold that position. He founded Georgetown Academy (now Georgetown University) in 1789, and established several other colleges and seminaries. In 1808, when the diocese of Baltimore became an archdiocese, he was made archbishop.

**CARROLL, Lewis,** pen name of Charles Lutwidge Dodgson (q.v.).

**CARROLLTON,** city in Georgia, and county seat of Carroll Co., about 41 miles S.W. of Atlanta. Carrollton is in a rich agricultural area. Manufactures include textiles, lumber, monuments, fertilizer, and shoes. The city is the site of West Georgia College, founded in 1933. Pop. (1960) 10,973; (1970) 13,520.

**CARROT,** plant, Daucus carota, in the Parsley family (Umbelliferae), native to Eurasia and northern Africa and widely distributed throughout the North Temperate Zone; the name is also applied to the root of this plant. The wild variety, popularly known as Queen Anne's Lace, has a tough, woody root, unsuitable for food. The cultivated variety (var. sativa), is the popular table vegetable. It is a biennial. During the first season of its growth it forms a rosette of finely divided leaves and stores a surplus of food in its root, which thus becomes large and fleshy. First-season carrots are harvested for food. If left in the ground for a second season, a terminal bud in the center lengthens, at the expense of the food stored in the root, into a bristly branched stem 3 to 5 ft. high; this stem bears a nestlike umbel of white or pinkish flowers, the central flower of each umbelet often being purple in color. The fruit consists of two one-seeded nutlets, each of which has four rows of radiating spines, which cause the ripe seeds to cling to animals and thus to be dispersed to new locations.

Popular varieties among cultivated carrots are the Oxheart, the Chantenay, the Danvers Half-Long, and the Danvers Long. Large-rooted late types are used for stock feeding, and are relished by farm animals. Carotene is the orange coloring matter of the root, a prolific source of provitamin A; see VITAMIN: Vitamin A.

In recent years, annual carrot production in the United States has been about 900,000 tons, and an average of about 6 million 24-can cases have been packed annually. California and Texas are the foremost carrot-producing states.

**CARSON,** city in California, in Los Angeles Co., 15 miles S. of downtown Los Angeles. Pop. (1960) 38,059; (1970) 71,150.

**CARSON, Christopher,** better known as KIT CARSON (1809–68), American hunter, trapper,

Kit Carson Brown Brothers

*A view of the marketplace in Cartagena, Colombia, with a portion of the city's skyline in the background.*
Luis Villota

and scout, born in Madison County, Ky. When he was an infant his parents moved to Howard County, Mo., where he later became an apprentice to a saddler. He ran away from home in 1826 to accompany a party of hunters to Santa Fe, N.Mex., and thereafter devoted himself almost entirely to hunting and trapping, making trips to California in 1829 and to the Rocky Mts. the following year. From 1832 to 1840 he was employed as hunter for the garrison at Bent's Fort, Colo. Between 1842 and 1846 he accompanied the American explorer John Charles Frémont (q.v.) on expeditions, serving as a guide in Frémont's expedition to California. Carson served in the Mexican War in 1846 and 1847, playing an important part in the conquest of California. In 1854 he was appointed Indian agent for the Ute and Apache (qq.v.) at Taos, N.Mex. During the American Civil War he helped organize New Mexican infantry volunteers and in 1865 he was brevetted brigadier general. The Kit Carson legend developed in the 1860's and 1870's when Carson was popularized as a Western hero in dime novels.

**CARSON, Rachel Louise** (1907–64), American author and marine biologist, born in Springdale, Pa., and educated at the former Pennsylvania College for Women and Johns Hopkins University. She taught zoology at the University of Maryland from 1931 to 1936. She was aquatic biologist with the United States Bureau of Fisheries and its successor, the United States Fish and Wildlife Service, from 1936 to 1952. Her books on the sea, *Under the Sea Wind* (1941); *The Sea Around Us* (1951), for which she was awarded the 1952 National Book Award in nonfiction; and *The Edge of the Sea* (1955), are praised for beauty of language as well as scientific accuracy. In *Silent Spring* (1962) she questioned the use of chemical pesticides and was responsible for arousing worldwide concern for the preservation of the environment.

**CARSON CITY,** city and capital of Nevada, independent, and coextensive with the former Ormsby Co., 12 miles E. of Lake Tahoe, about 30 miles S. of Reno. Stock raising, farming, and mining are the most important industries of the surrounding region. Named for the American trapper and scout Kit Carson (*see* CARSON, CHRISTOPHER), Carson City was founded in 1858; it became the capital of Nevada Territory in 1861 and the State capital in 1864. It was chartered as a city in 1875. Pop. (1970) 15,468.

**CARTAGENA,** city and seaport in Colombia, and capital of Bolivar Department, on the Caribbean Sea, about 65 miles S.W. of Barranquilla. The city is on an island formed by a shallow extension of the harbor, one of the best of N. South America. Cartagena is connected by a causeway with the mainland. The older part of the city contains two old forts and is surrounded by a wall 40 ft. thick in places, constructed in Spanish colonial times. Among the notable buildings of the city are the cathedral, the Jesuit church of San Juan de Dios, and the palace that was the headquarters of the Spanish Inquisition in South America. The site of the University of Bolívar, Cartagena also is the terminus of an oil pipeline extending about 375 mi. into the interior of Colombia. The principal exports are oil and petroleum products and coffee. Other exports include tobacco, cattle and cattle products, fine woods, and precious stones. Chocolate and candles are among the products manufactured there.

Founded in 1533 by the Spanish, the city rapidly became a thriving commercial port, later referred to as the Queen of the Indies. Pirates sacked the city in 1544. In the first half of the early 17th century the city was second to Mexico City in commercial importance in the New World. Nationalist revolutionists, led by Simón Bolívar (q.v.), in 1815 took the city from the Spanish, lost it the same year, and recaptured it in 1821. Pop. (1973) 347,600.

**CARTAGENA** (anc. *Carthago Nova*), city and seaport of Spain, in Murcia Province, on the Mediterranean Sea, about 30 miles S.E. of the city of Murcia. Lead, iron, copper, zinc, and sulfur are mined in the surrounding region. The principal exports of Cartagena are metallic ores, hydraulically compressed esparto grass, olive oil, wine, and dried fruits; imports include machinery, coal, coke, lumber, and codfish. Smelters are the principal industrial establishments in the city. Other establishments include glass works and factories for the manufacture of esparto-grass fabrics. Cartagena is encircled by mountains and is the principal naval base of Spain. Its fortifications include forts and other military and naval installations. The city contains the remains of old walls, a castle probably constructed in Carthaginian times, and a church that was formerly a 13th-century cathedral. Cartagena is on a site selected, about 243 B.C., by the Carthaginian general Hasdrubal (*see under* HASDRUBAL). When captured by the Roman general Publius Cornelius Scipio Africanus (*see under* SCIPIO) in 210 B.C., the city was a flourishing port exporting gold and silver mined in the surrounding region. Sacked by the Goths in 425 A.D., Cartagena was restored and improved by the Moors during their occupation of Spain. In 1269 it became a possession of the kings of Aragón and subsequently was included in the kingdom of Spain. It served as a naval base for the Republicans in the Spanish Civil War of 1936–39. Pop. (1972) 146,904.

Howard Carter precedes an assistant carrying a statue found in 1922 in the tomb of the pharaoh Tutankhamen and said to be a likeness of his young queen, Ankhes-en-Amen.　　　　　　　　　　　　　UPI

**CARTAGO,** city in Costa Rica, and capital of Cartago Province, about 10 miles S.E. of San José. It is on the plateau of San José, 4930 ft. above sea level, at the base of Irazú, a volcano 10,525 ft. above sea level. Hot mineral springs are in the suburb of Bella Vista. Cartago is a center for trade in coffee produced in the volcanic soil of the surrounding region. Founded in 1522 by the Spanish conquistador Juan Vásquez de Coronado (q.v.), the town subsequently became an important commercial center with an estimated population of more than 35,000. Until 1823 Cartago was the seat of government in Costa Rica. The town was several times severely damaged by earthquakes, the most destructive of which was that of 1841. Pop. (1970) 203,809.

**CARTE, Richard D'Oyly.** *See* D'OYLY CARTE, RICHARD.

**CARTEL.** *See* BUSINESS; MONOPOLY AND COMPETITION.

**CARTER, Howard** (1873–1939), British archeologist and Egyptologist, born in London, England. From 1891 to 1899 he served in Egypt on the staff of the Archeological Survey of Egypt. In 1892 he assisted the British Egyptologist Sir William Matthew Flinders Petrie (q.v.) in the excavation at Tel el 'Amarna, Egypt. Carter also served as inspector in chief of the antiquities department of the Egyptian government. Among the discoveries he made in Egypt were the tombs of the pharaoh Thutmose IV (*see under* THUTMOSE) and Queen Hatshepsut (q.v.). In 1922 Carter and the British Egyptologist George Herbert, 5th Earl of Carnarvon (*see under* HERBERT), made one of the greatest archeological finds of the 20th century. In the Valley of the Tombs of the Kings in Luxor, Egypt, they discovered the tomb of Tutankhamen (q.v.), a pharaoh who reigned in the 14th century B.C. The tomb, which was virtually untouched, held a great collection of treasures, which are now on display in the Egyptian Museum in Cairo, Arab Republic of Egypt. The treasures of Tutankhamen were exhibited during 1972 at the British Museum in London; from 1976 to 1979 a similar exhibition was shown at six museums in the United States.

**CARTER, Jimmy,** in full JAMES EARL CARTER, JR. (1924– ), thirty-ninth President of the United States.

Carter was born on Oct. 1, 1924, in Plains, Ga., where he spent his youth and attended high school. His family had lived in Georgia since the late 18th century. Carter was graduated from the United States Naval Academy in Annapolis, Md., in 1946, the same year he married Rosalynn Smith (1927– ), the daughter of a Plains mechanic. He then spent seven years in the United States Navy, serving mostly in the submarine program and rising to the rank of lieutenant. After his father died in 1953, he returned to Plains in order to manage the family farm and peanut warehouse, which prospered under his guidance.

Entering Georgia politics as a Democrat, Carter served two terms in the State senate (1963–67). In 1966 he unsuccessfully sought the Democratic nomination for governor. Soon after this setback, he had a profound religious ex-

perience and thereafter devoted much time to prayer and to activities in the Southern Baptist church. In 1970 he was elected governor of Georgia; during his term of office (1971–75) he reorganized the State's bureaucracy and worked to improve its judicial, educational, and health systems.

In December, 1974, while still virtually unknown nationally, Carter announced his candidacy for President. After many personal appearances around the country, he emerged in early 1976 as the leading contender for the Democratic Presidential nomination. He was chosen as the party's candidate in July, and Senator Walter F. Mondale (q.v.) became his Vice-Presidential running mate. In the ensuing campaign, highlighted by three nationally televised debates, Carter claimed that the Republican nominee, Gerald R. Ford (q.v.), the incumbent President, had dealt inadequately with the nation's economic and social problems. Carter was elected by a narrow margin on Nov. 2.

In his first months in office Carter proposed a program to stimulate the economy, called for a reshaping of the Federal bureaucracy, and asked for stringent measures to conserve the nation's energy supply. He adopted a vigorous policy on human rights, urging a number of foreign governments—notably that of the Soviet Union—to respect the civil rights of their citizens. He also pressed for further arms-control agreements between the U.S. and the U.S.S.R.

**CARTERET,** residential and industrial borough of New Jersey, in Middlesex Co., on the Arthur Kill, at the mouth of the Rahway R., opposite Staten Island, N.Y., 5 miles s.w. of Elizabeth. The section of Carteret bordering the Arthur Kill is important industrially. Copper and oil are refined, and chemicals, machinery, textiles, cigars, and wood, paper, and metal products are manufactured. The borough was incorporated in 1922. Pop. (1960) 20,502; (1970) 23,137.

**CARTERET,** name of a family of English statesmen prominent in government affairs and closely associated with the founding and the early history of New Jersey. Among the more important members of the family were the following.

**Sir George Carteret** (1610?–80), naval officer and colonial proprietor, born on the island of Jersey, in the Channel Islands. He joined the navy as a boy, and rose through the ranks, becoming comptroller of the English navy in 1639. During the civil war, known as the Great Rebellion (q.v.), he fought for the Royalists and was rewarded for his services by being made lieutenant governor of Jersey. In 1651 he was forced

*President Jimmy Carter.*　　　The White House

to surrender the island to the Commonwealth, and later joined other English exiles in the French navy. Returning to England after the Restoration in 1660 of Charles II (q.v.), King of England, Carteret held several important offices, including that of treasurer of the navy (1661–67). He took an active interest in the colonization of America. In 1663 he became one of the original proprietors of Carolina, and in 1664 he and Lord John Berkeley (d. 1678) were made Lords Proprietors and granted the territory that is now the State of New Jersey. The name New Jersey was given to the colony in honor of Carteret's administration of the island of Jersey. In 1676 the colony was divided into West Jersey and East Jersey; Carteret became sole proprietor of East Jersey and upon his death the territory passed to his widow and several trustees. See NEW JERSEY: *History.*

**Philip Carteret** (1639–82), colonial governor in America, born on Jersey, Channel Islands. He was the first English colonial governor of New Jersey, having been appointed in 1664 by the Lords Proprietors, one of whom was his fourth cousin Sir George Carteret. Philip Carteret arrived at New Jersey in 1665 and founded Elizabethtown (now Elizabeth). Philip attempted to secure emigrants from the New England colonies by publicizing among them the liberal concessions granted by the proprietors of New Jersey. Except in 1673 and 1674, when the western part of New Jersey was held by the Dutch, he was governor of the entire colony until it was divided into East Jersey and West Jersey in 1676. Thereafter until his death, he was governor of East Jersey. The early part of his administration was marked by conflicts with Sir Edmund Andros (q.v.), governor of New York, who claimed that New Jersey belonged under his jurisdiction.

**John Carteret, Earl Granville** (1690–1763), statesman and diplomat, great-grandson of Sir George Carteret, born in Bath, England, and educated at the University of Oxford. He succeeded to the title of Baron Carteret in 1695 and took his seat in the House of Lords in 1711. Carteret was appointed ambassador to Sweden in 1719, secretary of state in 1721, and lord lieutenant of Ireland in 1724. From 1730 to 1742 he led the opposition in the House of Lords to the government of the British statesman Sir Robert Walpole (*see under* WALPOLE). When Walpole's government fell in 1742, Carteret again became secretary of state. In this office, which he held for two years, he was the most influential member of the cabinet. From 1751 to 1763 Carteret served as lord president of the privy council.

**CARTESIANISM.** *See* DESCARTES, RENÉ: *Science.*

**CARTHAGE,** city in Missouri, and county seat of Jasper Co., about 13 miles N.E. of Joplin. Carthage is a region that has lead and zinc mines and marble quarries. The city is an industrial and shipping center and has resort facilities. Nearby, in Diamond Grove, is the George Washington Carver National Monument. Pop. (1960) 11,264; (1970) 11,035.

**CARTHAGE** (Lat. *Carthago*), great city of antiquity, on the northern coast of Africa, near modern Tunis, Tunisia. Dido (q.v.) was the legendary founder and queen of Carthage; the city was probably established as a trading post toward the end of the 9th century B.C. by Phoenicians (*see* PHOENICIA). The earliest artifacts unearthed by archeologists at the site date from 800 B.C. The city was known to its Punic or Phoenician inhabitants as the "new city", probably to distinguish it from Utica (q.v.), the "old city". Built on a peninsula jutting into the Gulf of Tunis, Carthage had two splendid harbors, connected by a canal. Above the harbors on a hill was the Byrsa, a walled fortress.

**Extension of Empire.** By the subjugation of the Libyan tribes and by the annexation of older Phoenician colonies, Carthage in the 6th century B.C. controlled the entire North African coast from the Atlantic Ocean to the western border of Egypt, as well as Sardinia, Malta, the Balearic Islands, and part of Sicily. A Carthaginian admiral, Hanno (q.v.), made a voyage along the Atlantic coast of North Africa. The maritime power of the Carthaginians enabled them to extend their settlements and conquests, forming a scattered empire devoted to commerce. Among the commercial enterprises were the mining of silver and lead; the manufacture of beds and bedding; a lumber industry in the Atlas Mts.; the production of simple cheap pottery, jewelry, and glassware for trade; and the export of wild animals from African jungles, of fruits and nuts, and ivory and gold.

Carthage produced little art. Most of the work of the Carthaginians was imitative of Egyptian, Greek, and Phoenician originals. In literature only a few technical works appeared. Thus little is known of the everyday life of Carthage, its government, or its language. Religion in Carthage involved human sacrifice to the two principal gods, Baal (q.v.) and Tanit, the equivalent of the Phoenician goddess Astarte (q.v.). The Greek gods Demeter and Persephone and the Roman goddess Juno were adapted to later religious patterns of the Carthaginians.

Carthage engaged in war almost continually, with Greece and with Rome, for 150 years. Wars with Greece, beginning in 409 B.C., concerned

*Ruins of public baths on the site of ancient Carthage.*
TWA

the control of Sicily, which lay only 100 mi. from Carthage and formed a natural bridge between North Africa and Italy. Carthage first encountered defeat in Sicily in 480 B.C., when the Carthaginian general Hamilcar (fl. 5th cent. B.C.) commanded a force that hoped to expand Carthaginian influence throughout Sicily, but was defeated by the tyrant (ruler) of Syracuse, Gelon (q.v.). Further Carthaginian attempts to conquer Sicily were thwarted by armies under the command of the Syracusan tyrants Dionysius the younger, Dionysius the elder (*see under* DIONYSIUS), Agathocles (q.v.), and Pyrrhus (q.v.), King of Epirus. After their final defeat in 276 B.C., the Carthaginians continued to hold territory on Sicily; twelve years later the first of the Punic Wars (q.v.) against Rome began.

**Punic Wars.** The First Punic War (264–241 B.C.) brought to the fore the Carthaginian general Hamilcar Barca (q.v.). Defeated in Sicily, Hamilcar invaded Spain. His conquests in southern Spain were completed by his son-in-law Hasdrubal (*see under* HASDRUBAL) and by his son Hannibal (q.v.). Carthage ceded its holdings in Sicily to Rome after the final Roman victory at the Aegates Islands. During the Second Punic War (218–201 B.C.), Hannibal marched eastward along the northern shore of the Mediterranean from Spain and finally crossed the Alps into Italy. Hannibal's final defeat, however, resulted in the loss of Spain and various island possessions of Carthage. In the Third Punic War (149–146 B.C.), the Romans under Publius Cornelius Scipio Aemelianus Africanus Numantinus (*see under* SCIPIO) destroyed the city of Carthage. In a final gesture of contempt, the Romans spread salt over the ruins. The victors thus fulfilled the wish of the Roman statesman Marcus Porcius Cato, known as the Elder (*see under* CATO).

Occupancy of the site was forbidden for twenty-five years. In 122 B.C. a new city, Colonia Junonia, was founded; it lasted only thirty years. In 46 B.C. the Roman general and statesman Gaius Julius Caesar (q.v.) visited the site and proclaimed that a city should be built there. His wishes were fulfilled by the Roman emperor

Augustus (q.v.) when in 29 B.C. a city called Colonia Julia Carthago was founded. This new city flourished until, according to some historians, it was second only to Rome in prosperity and administrative importance. Roman Carthage also became a center of Christianity, being the seat of a bishop from late in the 2nd century. Saint Cyprian (q.v.) was bishop there in 248; Tertullian (q.v.), a Christian ecclesiastical writer, lived and worked in Carthage in the 3rd century; and Saint Augustine (q.v.) was bishop of nearby Hippo in the early 5th century.

Carthage was fortified against barbarian attack in 425. In 439 the Vandal king Genseric (q.v.) subjugated the city. It remained the Vandal capital until 533, when the Byzantine general Belisarius (q.v.) captured the city, renaming it Colonia Justiniana Carthago in honor of the Byzantine emperor Justinian I (q.v.). In 697 the city was seized by the Arabs, and in 698 it was again destroyed. Much archeological activity was carried on at the site, particularly in the late 19th century, uncovering early Punic artifacts and Roman, Byzantine, and Vandal buildings. Today Carthage is a wealthy suburb of Tunis.

**CARTHUSIANS,** monastic order founded by Saint Bruno (q.v.), who in 1084 retired with six companions to the solitude of La Chartreuse near Grenoble. There they lived as hermits, wearing rude clothing and eating vegetables and coarse bread.

After 1170, when the order received papal approbation, it extended rapidly. It dates from 1180 in England, where the name Chartreuse Houses was corrupted into Charter Houses. The order is now conducted under the rules approved in 1682 by Pope Innocent XI (*see under* INNOCENT). The Carthusians were divided into two classes, fathers (*patres*) and lay brothers (*conversi*). Each father occupied a separate cell, with a bed of straw, a pillow, a woolen coverlet, and the tools for manual labor or for writing. They left their cells, even for meals, only on festivals and on days of the funeral of a brother of the order. Three times a week they fasted on bread, water, and salt, and observed several lengthened fasts during the year. Meat was forbidden at all times, as was wine, unless mixed with water. Unbroken silence was enforced except on rare occasions.

These austerities were continued, with little modification, by the modern Carthusians. The order at one time counted sixteen provinces and boasted of the most magnificent convents in the world, including La Grande Chartreuse, now a museum consisting for the most part of 17th-century buildings, in France, and the Certosa di Pavia, in Italy, 18 miles S. of Milan. The latter, the church of which was begun in 1396 and expanded during the 15th and 16th centuries, is an Italian national monument.

The order of Carthusian nuns was founded at Salette, on the Rhône, in France, about 1229. They followed the rules of the Carthusian monks. When the monasteries in England were suppressed under King Henry VIII (q.v.) in the 16th century, nine Carthusian monasteries were active in the country. Today one remains, near Steyning, 8 mi. from Brighton. One Carthusian monastery is located in the United States, in Arlington, Vt.

**CARTIER, Sir George Étienne**  (1814–73), Canadian statesman, born in Saint Antoine, Lower Canada (now Québec Province). After practicing law for a short time, Cartier took part in the rebellion of 1837–38 and fled the country to avoid arrest, but, after public feeling began to subside, he returned and resumed his law practice. In 1848 he was elected to the Canadian legislative assembly and he soon became a leader of the French Canadians. He was secretary of Lower Canada from 1855 to 1857, when he became provincial attorney general. Between 1858 and 1862 he shared the office of prime minister with Sir John Alexander Macdonald (q.v.). In this office Cartier favored the plan to federate Lower Canada and Upper Canada (now Ontario Province) with the other British colonies in North America; the plan resulted in the establishment of the Dominion of Canada in 1867. Cartier joined Macdonald's first dominion cabinet as minister of militia and defense (1867–73). He was influential in getting approval from the Canadian parliament for the initial charter of the Canadian Pacific Railway.

**CARTIER, Jacques**  (1491–1557), French explorer and mariner, discoverer of the Saint Lawrence R., born in Saint-Malo. Selected by Francis I (q.v.), King of France, to lead an expedition to discover the Northwest Passage to China, he departed from St.-Malo with two ships in April, 1534; *see* NORTHWEST PASSAGE. He sighted Newfoundland after twenty days, and sailing through Belle Isle Strait, between Newfoundland and Labrador, he proceeded southward along the western coast of Newfoundland and rounded the entire Gulf of Saint Lawrence. On this voyage he saw Prince Edward Island and the New Brunswick mainland, sailed into Chaleur Bay, which he named, landed on the Gaspé Peninsula, and crossed the St. Lawrence R. estuary. Much of the French claim to Canada rests upon Cartier's explorations.

*Jacques Cartier*

Again sailing on orders from King Francis in 1535, Cartier crossed Belle Isle for the second time and then sailed up the St. Lawrence R., which he named on this occasion, as far as the Indian village of Stadacona, where modern Québec stands. He later proceeded up the river to the Indian village of Hochelaga and climbed the hill behind the village to observe the Ottawa R. and Lachine Rapids. Cartier called the hill Mont Réal ("Mount Royal"), from which the city of Montréal derived its name. After wintering in Stadacona, Cartier sailed for France on a course south of Newfoundland, and for the first time passed through what is now called Cabot Strait.

Beginning his third voyage in 1541, Cartier again sailed up the St. Lawrence R., this time as far as Lachine Rapids. His purpose was to establish a colony in Canada, but the mission was not successful. He returned to France the following year. He spent the rest of his life in St.-Malo and wrote an account of his expeditions that was published in 1545.

**CARTIER-BRESSON, Henri** (1908– ), French photographer, born in Chanteloup, and educated at the Lycée Condorcet in Paris. Originally interested in painting, he took up photography in 1930. Since 1931 Cartier-Bresson has traveled widely and the many photographs made on his trips have been published and frequently exhibited. During World War II he spent 35 months in German prison camps and, after the third attempt, escaped and made his way to Paris, where he joined the underground. In 1945 Cartier-Bresson directed the documentary film *Le Retour,* which was produced for the United States Office of War Information. Two years later he had a one-man exhibit of his photographs at the Museum of Modern Art in New York City. In 1955 he was invited to become the first photographer to exhibit at the Louvre (q.v.). Among the published collections of his photographs are *The Decisive Moment* (1952), *The World of Henri Cartier-Bresson* (1968), and *Cartier-Bresson's France* (1971).

**CARTILAGE,** or GRISTLE, fibrous connective tissue found in man and animals that have backbones. *See* BONE; CONNECTIVE TISSUE; SKELETON.

**CARTOGRAPHY,** the science of map making. *See* MAP.

**CARTOON** (It. *cartone,* "pasteboard"), in the fine arts, design drawn on thick paper or pasteboard and used as a model for a work to be executed in fresco, mosaic, tapestry, or other media. The cartoon is prepared to give the artist an opportunity to make whatever alterations he desires in his projected work before he actually executes it. Cartoons are generally composed of a number of sheets of stout paper pasted together at the edges and stretched on a frame. When finished, charcoal is rubbed on the back of the drawings. The cartoon is then transferred to the plaster or other medium on which the work is to be executed, either by tracing with a hard point or by pricking with pins (a process called "pouncing"). In fresco painting, the plaster on which the work is executed must be kept wet in order for it to absorb the color, and consequently only a small portion can be executed at a time. For this reason the cartoon must be traced in small sections that the artist can finish without stopping. In weaving superior tapestries, such as the Gobelins (*see* GOBELIN), or the celebrated tapestries in the Vatican by the Italian painter Raphael (q.v.), it is the practice to cut out all the figures represented, which are always in color, and place them behind or under the wool.

The chiaroscuro (q.v.) studies used by the great masters of the Renaissance as guides in almost all their decorative works are often as interesting artistically as fresco and oil work. The nine cartoons of the series "The Triumph of

*The photographic originality of Henri Cartier-Bresson is epitomized in this picture of the Swiss-born artist Alberto Giacometti, taken in Paris in 1963.*

*"The Virgin and Child with Saint John the Baptist and Saint Anne"*, a cartoon or preliminary drawing made by the Renaissance master Leonardo da Vinci. The final version did not include the figure of John.      UPI

Caesar", by the Italian painter Andrea Mantegna (q.v.), long used as hangings in the ducal palace in Mantua, Italy, and now at Hampton Court, England, are the most celebrated surviving examples of chiaroscuro studies from the 15th century. *See* FRESCO.

A pictorial sketch, usually of a humorous or satiric nature, published in a magazine or newspaper, is also called a cartoon. In this meaning the expression is especially applied to a pictorial caricature. *See* CARICATURE; COMIC STRIP.

The first American cartoon, published by Benjamin Franklin in his Pennsylvania Gazette, 1754.
Granger Collection

**CARTWRIGHT,** name of two brothers who were prominent in Great Britain at the end of the 18th century.

**John Cartwright** (1740–1824), politician and pamphleteer, born in Nottinghamshire, England. He entered the navy at the age of eighteen and rose rapidly as an officer. At the outbreak of the American Revolution, however, he espoused the cause of the colonies and declined to fight against them. He devoted himself instead to political writing, urging reforms such as universal male suffrage, the secret ballot, annual parliaments, the improvement of national defenses, the freedom of Spain and Greece from foreign rule, and other causes. In 1820 he was indicted for sedition and fined £100. He became known as "The Father of Reform".

**Edmund Cartwright** (1743–1823), inventor, born in Nottinghamshire, England, and educated at the University of Oxford. After spending several years as a country clergyman, he visited the cotton-spinning mills of the British inventor Sir Richard Arkwright (q.v.) in Derbyshire and became interested in new methods of weaving. The result in 1785 was Cartwright's invention of a power loom, upon which he subsequently effected major improvements. The introduction of the power loom was vehemently opposed by those whose jobs were replaced, and a mill at Manchester equipped with his looms was burned down. Cartwright in 1789 took out a patent for a wool-combing machine, and he secured patents for various other machines. In 1797 he patented a steam engine in which alcohol was the fuel employed. He also assisted the American inventor Robert Fulton (q.v.) in his steamboat experiments. But his patents yielded him little return, and in 1809 the British government, in consideration of his inventions, granted him £10,000. Cartwright retired to a farm in Kent and invented improvements on farm machinery in the later years of his life. Meanwhile the power loom became one of the machines that made the industrial revolution (q.v.) of the 19th century possible. *See* FACTORIES AND THE FACTORY SYSTEM.

**CARUSO, Enrico** (1873–1921), Italian dramatic tenor, born in Naples. He made his debut in Naples in 1894. His first great success was in Milan in 1899 when he created the role of Loris in *Fedora*, by the Italian composer Umberto Giordano (1867–1948). Engagements followed in Saint Petersburg (now Leningrad), Monte Carlo, London, Rome, and Lisbon. In 1903 he made his debut at the Metropolitan Opera House in New York City in *Rigoletto* by the Italian composer Giuseppi Verdi (q.v.). His repertoire included

*George Washington Carver in his laboratory.*

more than forty operas (chiefly Italian). He created roles in *Adriana Lecouvreur,* by the Italian composer Francesco Cilea (1866–1950), and *The Girl of the Golden West,* by the Italian composer Giacomo Puccini (q.v.). He is best remembered, however, for the role of Canio in *I Pagliacci,* by the Italian composer Ruggiero Leoncavallo (q.v.). From his first appearance in 1903 Caruso became the chief attraction of the Metropolitan Opera House, his voice being one of extraordinary beauty and power. His position as the greatest living dramatic tenor was unchallenged during the last decade of his life. Caruso's last appearance was at the Metropolitan Opera House on Dec. 24, 1920.

**CARVER, George Washington** (1864–1943), Negro American educator and scientist, born of slave parents near Diamond, Mo. He left the farm where he was born when he was about ten years old and eventually settled in Minneapolis, Kans., where he worked his way through high school.

Following his graduation in 1894 from Iowa State College of Agriculture and Mechanic Arts (now Iowa State University), he joined the college faculty and continued his studies, specializing in bacteriological laboratory work in systematic botany. In 1896 he became director of the Department of Agricultural Research at Tuskegee Normal and Industrial Institute, now Tuskegee Institute (q.v.), where he began an exhaustive series of experiments with peanuts.

Carver developed several hundred industrial uses for peanuts, sweet potatoes, and soybeans, and developed a new type of cotton known as Carver's hybrid. His discoveries induced Southern farmers to raise other crops in addition to cotton. He also taught methods of soil improvement. In recognition of his accomplishments he was awarded the Spingarn Medal in 1923 by the National Association for the Advancement of Colored People. In 1935 he was appointed collaborator in the Division of Plant Mycology and Disease Survey of the Bureau of Plant Industry of the United States Department of Agriculture. In 1940 he donated all his savings to the establishment of the George Washington Carver Foundation at Tuskegee for research in natural science. His birthplace in Diamond Grove was established as the George Washington Carver National Monument in 1951.

**CARVER, John** (1576?–1621), leader of the Pilgrim Fathers (q.v.) and the first governor of Plymouth Colony (q.v.), born probably in Nottinghamshire, England. Carver was a wealthy London merchant, but he left England and went to Leiden, the Netherlands, in 1607 or 1608, because of religious persecution. In 1617 he became the agent for the Pilgrims in securing a charter and financial support for the establishment of a colony in America. He chartered the *Mayflower* (q.v.), and with 101 other colonists

*Joyce Cary*                                    Harper & Row

set sail from Plymouth, England, in September, 1620. He signed the Mayflower Compact on Nov. 11, 1620, and on the same day was elected to a one-year term as governor. He was probably instrumental in picking Plymouth (q.v.) as the site for settlement. During the hardships and privations of the next few months he encouraged his associates and promoted the success of Plymouth Colony. Shortly after being re-elected governor he died of a stroke.

**CARY, Alice** (1820–71) and **CARY, Phoebe** (1824–71), two American poets, sisters, born near Cincinnati, Ohio, and self-educated. They gained their first recognition with the publication of *Peoms of Alice and Phoebe Cary* (1849). Subsequently they moved to New York City, where they achieved a literary and social success that lasted for nearly two decades. They were popular with the American journalist Horace Greeley (q.v.) and his friends. Alice Cary's writings, both poetry and prose, were published in the leading magazines of the day. Her novels of domestic life and tales of life in the Midwest were very popular. Phoebe Cary was best known as a religious poet and hymn writer. She is most remembered as the author of the hymn "Nearer Home", with the opening line: "One

sweetly solemn thought comes to me o'er and o'er".

**CARY, (Arthur) Joyce (Lunel)** (1888–1957), British novelist and poet, born in Londonderry, Northern Ireland, and educated at Trinity College, University of Oxford. After serving in a Nigerian regiment during World War I, he was a British public administrator in Africa for two years. Ill health and injuries forced Cary to retire in 1920 to Oxford, where he began his writing career. His first published work, *Aissa Saved* (1932), concerned the conversion of a Negro girl to Christianity. Cary is best known for a trilogy which includes *Herself Surprised* (1941), *To Be a Pilgrim* (1942), and *The Horse's Mouth* (1944), later made into a motion picture. These three works were acclaimed for their well-developed plots and credible characterizations. Literary critics have noted Cary's superb skill in delineating character and producing high comic effect.

**CARYOTA,** genus of lofty plants of the Palm family (Palmaceae), native from Asia to Australia, also known as fish-tail palms. They are easily recognized by their unusual bipinnate leaves. One species, *C. urens*, called the wine palm, is cultivated in India. It is remarkable for the acridity of its fruit and valuable for the great quantity of sap (toddy) that flows from its wounded spathes. Sometimes, in the hot season, 100 pints of sap is obtained from a single tree in twenty-four hours. Because jaggery, an unrefined brown sugar, is made from this juice by boiling it down, the tree is sometimes called the jaggery palm. Other species of *Caryota* yield sago, rope fiber, and hardwood.

**CASABIANCA, Louis de** (1755?–98), French naval officer, born in Bastia, Corsica. He fought against the British in the American Revolution, serving under the French admiral Comte François de Grasse (q.v.) at the siege of Yorktown, Va. In 1792 he was a member of the National Convention in France. He commanded the *Orient*, flagship of the fleet that transported Napoleon I (q.v.), Emperor of France, and his army to Egypt. In the Battle of the Nile in Abukir (now Abu Qir) Bay, the commanding officer of the fleet was killed, and Casabianca assumed command. Although he was seriously wounded and the *Orient* was in flames, he remained at his post. His son, ten years of age, refused to leave him and both were lost with the vessel. The story of their death is recounted in the poem *Casabianca* (1829) by the British poet Felicia Hemans (1739–1835).

**CASABLANCA,** largest city and chief seaport of the Kingdom of Morocco, on the Atlantic

Ocean, about 50 miles s.w. of Rabat. Casablanca is one of the leading commercial cities of North Africa. It is served by railroads, highways, and an international airport and has one of the largest artificial harbors in the world. Almost all of Moroccan industry is located in Casablanca, and two thirds of the foreign trade of Morocco passes through the city. Cereals, leather, wool, and phosphates are the chief exports. The leading industries are fishing, fish canning, sawmilling, and the manufacture of furniture. Also in the city are plants manufacturing bricks, glass, cement, and tobacco products.

In medieval times Casablanca was a prosperous town known as Anfa. It was destroyed by the Portuguese in 1468 and rebuilt by them in 1515. Following a severe earthquake in 1755, the city was again rebuilt. In 1907 Casablanca was occupied by the French. Under French administration it grew rapidly, and the modern city was built around the old Moorish city.

During World War II, Casablanca was one of the three major landing places in the invasion of North Africa by Allied forces. From Jan. 14 to Jan. 26, 1943, the city was the site of the Casablanca Conference between United States President Franklin Delano Roosevelt and British Prime Minister Winston Churchill (qq.v.), at which both leaders pledged that their countries would fight until the Axis powers surrendered unconditionally; *see* WORLD WAR II: *Conclusion of the War in Europe: The Casablanca Conference.*

The withdrawal of the French when Morocco became independent in 1956 caused Casablanca severe economic hardship. A thriving tourist trade and increased industry have, however, restored prosperity. Pop. (1971) 1,371,330.

**CASADESUS, Robert Marcel** (1899–1972), French pianist and composer, born in Paris. He studied with Louis Diémer (1843–1919) at the Conservatoire de Musique in Paris and won the Prix Diémer in 1920. In 1946 he became head of the American Conservatory at Fontainebleau, France. In 1935 he performed in New York City as soloist with the New York Philharmonic Orchestra and appeared thereafter in recitals and as soloist with leading orchestras throughout the United States. With his wife Gaby Casadesus (1901– ), and occasionally with his son Jean Casadesus (1927–72), he gave many duo-piano concerts. His compositions include a concerto and other works for the piano.

**CASA GRANDE RUINS NATIONAL MONUMENT,** area of prehistoric interest in Pinal County, Ariz., at the edge of the Gila River Indian Reservation, established as a national mon-

ument in 1918. It is the site of prehistoric ruins of an Indian people, known today as the Hohokam, who came to the Gila Valley about 700 A.D. and built settlements and an extensive irrigation system for farming there. They were joined in the 14th century by the Pueblo (q.v.) Indians. Among the most noteworthy prehistoric relics in the United States, the ruins were first discovered in 1694, at which time they had been abandoned for more than two centuries. The principal building, Casa Grande, was erected as a watchtower, and is the best preserved medieval Indian structure of its type in the U.S. Its walls, of caliche blocks (a cement composed of lime, earth, and pebbles), are still standing at their original height of four stories. In addition to Casa Grande there are ruins of several Hohokam Indian villages. The monument, covering 472.5 acres, was established in 1918. It is administered by the National Park Service (q.v.).

**CASALS, Pablo,** original name PAU CARLOS SALVADOR DEFILLO DE CASALS (1876–1973), Spanish cellist, conductor, composer, pianist, and humanitarian, one of the most influential musicians of the 20th century. He was born in Vendrell, Dec. 29, 1876. He received his first musical instruction from his father; later he studied at the Madrid Conservatory. After mak-

*Pablo Casals with his wife Marta.*

ing his debut as a cello soloist at the Concerts Lamoureux in Paris in 1898, he toured Europe, the United States, and South America. He revolutionized the role of the cello by the virtuosity of his technique and his indisputable musicality. He was particularly noted for his interpretation of the suites for unaccompanied cello of the German composer Johann Sebastian Bach (*see under* BACH). With the French pianist Alfred Cortot (1877–1962) and the French violinist Jacques Thibaud (1880–1953) Casals formed a noted chamber-music trio. In 1919 he founded the Orquesta Pau Casals in Barcelona which, with Casals as conductor, became an important cultural organization in Catalonia until 1936, when the Spanish civil war interrupted its activities. After the overthrow of the Republican government in Spain, Casals took up residence in France. He gave what was reported to be his last public performance in 1947. Three years later, however, he organized and conducted a music festival in Prades, France, commemorating Johann Sebastian Bach. Thereafter, Casals participated regularly in the annual Prades Festival. In 1956 he moved to San Juan, Puerto Rico; the Casals Festival, an annual musical event, originated there in 1957. He died at Rio Piedras, Puerto Rico, Oct. 22, 1973.

As a personal contribution to the advancement of world peace, he composed the oratorio *El Pesebre* ("The Manger", 1960), which he conducted throughout the world. His reminiscences and opinions on music and musicians are contained in *Conversations with Casals* (recorded by Jose Maria Corredor, 1955). His reflections on his life were published as *Joys and Sorrows* (1970).

**CASANOVA, Giovanni Jacopo** or **CASANOVA DE SEINGALT, Giovanni Jacopo** (1725–98), Italian adventurer, born in Venice. His parents, who were actors, intended him for the priesthood, but when he was sixteen he was expelled from a seminary because of misconduct. Thereafter Casanova was in turn a secretary, a soldier in the Venetian army, a preacher, an alchemist, a gambler, a violinist, a lottery director, and a spy. In addition, he was constantly involved in political or amatory intrigues. In 1755 the Venetian authorities imprisoned him for impiety and practicing magic, but he made a sensational escape the following year. He traveled throughout Europe, winning the confidence or friendship of many important people and gaining a reputation for his wit and charm with women. He was a favorite in the court of Louis XV (q.v.), King of France, and took as his mistress the Marquise de Pompadour (q.v.). In 1785

Casanova retired to the castle of a friend to write his *Mémoirs*, which were published posthumously (12 vol., abridged version, 1826–38; unabridged edition, 1960). The work recounts his adventures and love affairs, and has considerable historical value because it gives an account of the personalities and customs of the period.

**CASAUBON, Isaac** (1559–1614), French classical scholar and theologian, born in Geneva, Switzerland. His parents were French Huguenot refugees; see HUGUENOTS. Casaubon studied at the University of Geneva, at which he became professor of Greek in 1582. In 1596 he was appointed to a similar position at the university in Montpellier, France. Although Henry IV (q.v.), King of France, summoned him to Paris in 1599, powerful Catholic opposition prevented his receiving a professorship. Instead, Casaubon was appointed royal librarian. After the murder of the king in 1610, Casaubon left France for England, where King James I (q.v.) received him with favor, appointing him prebendary of Canterbury Cathedral. He was buried in Westminster Abbey.

Casaubon was the first scholar to systematically treat an important field of literary history. His chief effort was preparing commentaries on classical writers. The most important commentary was his masterpiece (1600) on the Greek scholar Athenaeus (fl. early 3rd cent. A.D.), on which he worked for ten years. In addition to many other commentaries on both Greek and Roman scholars, Casaubon left a diary which was published in 1850.

**CASBAH** (Ar. *qasabah*, "fortress"), in northern Africa, the historic native section of a town. Originally designating a Moorish fortress in such a quarter, the term is now suggestive of old and narrow streets, nightlife, and mystery. The best-known casbah is that in Algiers (q.v.).

**CASCA, Publius Servilius** (d. about 42 B.C.), Roman politician, and one of the assassins of the Roman statesman Gaius Julius Caesar (q.v.). Casca struck the first blow, stabbing Caesar in the back, according to the Greek biographer Plutarch (q.v.).

**CASCADE RANGE,** mountain range about 700 mi. long, forming the N. extension of the Sierra Nevada (q.v.). The range begins in California, near the Oregon border, and passes through Oregon and Washington into British Columbia, where it connects with the structurally related Coast Mts. In the United States the course is nearly parallel to the Pacific coast, and from 100 to 150 mi. distant from it. Throughout most of its course the W. part of the range is

*Mount Hood, in the Cascade Range, is the highest point in Oregon.*

Oregon State Highway Travel Division

heavily wooded, chiefly by firs, pines, and other conifers; along the E. section grass and semiarid scrub plants grow. The range receives its name from the great cascades of the Columbia R., which cuts through the mountains E. of Portland, Oreg. The Klamath R. passes through the S. part of the Cascades, and the Fraser R. divides it from the Coast Mts.

In California are Mt. Shasta, 14,162 ft. high, and several other peaks more than 10,000 ft. in height. In Oregon the Cascades include Mt. Hood, 11,235 ft. high, the highest elevation in the State, and Mt. Jefferson, 10,495 ft. high. Washington has Mt. Rainier, which at 14,410 ft. has the highest elevation of the State and the highest of the range; Mt. Adams, 12,307 ft.; and Mt. Baker, 10,778 ft. The British Columbia section is very rugged, with ridges rising to between 8000 and 10,000 ft.; the highest peak, Mt. Waddington, is 13,260 ft.

The Cascade Range is about the same age, geologically, as the Sierra Nevada. It was formed about the close of the Pliocene Epoch, although the volcanic products seen along the range are of much later date.

**CASCARA SAGRADA,** or CHITTAM BARK, aromatic bark of *Rhamnus purshiana,* a tall shrub also called bearberry or California buckthorn (q.v.), in the family Rhamnaceae. Various organic ingredients in the bark give it therapeutic properties. Fluid extracts of cascara sagrada, used as mild purgatives and intestinal tonics, are present in several proprietary laxatives.

**CASCO BAY,** inlet of the Atlantic Ocean, on the S.E. coast of Maine, extending about 12 mi inland. The city of Portland is on the edge of Casco Bay. Many of the more than 200 small islands in the bay are popular as summer resorts.

**CASE,** in grammar, inflectional form of a noun or pronoun, that serves to indicate the relationship (such as that of subject, object, and attribute) between it and other words. In a broader sense, especially in modern English, the term case indicates such relationships whether or not they are designated by an inflectional form. In modern English the recognized cases are the nominative, possessive, and objective. *See* GRAMMAR.

**CASE HARDENING,** any of several processes for hardening the outer surface of steel products in order to make it more resistant to abrasion and wear, while leaving the interior soft and therefore more resistant to strain and impact. Case hardening is important in the manufacture of gears, axles, and other machine parts subject to much mechanical wear. The hardening may be accomplished by dissolving carbon into the surface, called carburizing, or by adding nitrogen, called cyaniding or nitriding. Steel may be carburized by being embedded in glowing charcoal, from which it absorbs carbon, in a furnace at a temperature of 800°–900° C. (1470°–1652° F.) for periods varying from several hours to several days. The steel is then suddenly immersed in cold water. In another process articles are case hardened by being heated to redness in powdered potassium cyanide, which decomposes and liberates carbon. The carbon dissolves into the steel to a depth usually of .01 in. to .10 in., depending on the length of time of the treatment.

**CASEIN,** group of proteins precipitated when milk is mildly acidified. Casein comprises about 80 percent of the total proteins in cow's milk and about 3 percent of its weight. It is the chief ingredient in cheese. The composition and properties of casein vary somewhat from sample to sample, but it is, when dried, a white, amorphous powder without taste or odor. Casein dissolves very slightly in water but more extensively in alkalies or strong acids.

The enzyme rennin, when added to unacidified milk, produces a precipitate of proteins different from the material precipitated by acids, and the resulting product is known by a modified name, paracasein. This variety of casein is preferred for making a plastic, through the reaction of the casein with formaldehyde, which goes into the manufacture of buttons and other small objects. Casein is also used as a food supplement and as an adhesive, a constituent of water paints, and a finishing material for paper and textiles.

**CASE INSTITUTE OF TECHNOLOGY.** *See* CASE WESTERN RESERVE UNIVERSITY.

**CASEMENT, Sir Roger David** (1864–1916), British consular agent and Irish revolutionist, born near Dublin, Ireland. After holding consular posts in the British foreign service in several parts of Africa betwen 1892 and 1903, Casement returned to England to present to the foreign office the results of his two-year study of the inhuman treatment of the natives in the Congo Free State, then the personal holding of Leopold II, King of Belgium (*see under* LEOPOLD). World opinion was aroused by Casement's report with its detailed, eyewitness accounts of atrocities, and the Belgian king was eventually forced to relinquish his personal sovereignty over the Congo. *See* ZAIRE, REPUBLIC OF: *History.*

Plagued by ill health, and disdaining the posts offered to him by the foreign office, Casement remained in the British Isles for almost three years. During this time he seriously considered resigning but could not afford to do so. Finally, in 1906, he accepted a post in Brazil, where he served as consul in various cities for the next five years.

In 1910–11 he again investigated and exposed conditions of brutal exploitation, this time of the Indians of Brazil. For these services he was knighted in 1911. As a result of his findings (published by Parliament in 1912) the British company he accused was dissolved in 1913.

Casement retired from consular service and in 1913 returned to Ireland. A dedicated Irish nationalist, he took active part in the movement for Irish independence. He sought help for the Irish cause first in America and then, after World War I broke out, in Germany, where he remained until 1916. In March, 1916, the Germans agreed to send 20,000 rifles to Ireland to help the Easter rebellion, an uprising of Irish patriots. The British intercepted the arms and captured Casement after he landed from a German submarine in Ireland, three days before the Easter rebellion on April 24. Imprisoned in the Tower of London, he was convicted of high treason and hanged. The Irish consider Casement a martyr patriot.

**CASERTA,** city in Italy, in Campania Region, capital of Caserta Province, about 22 miles N.E. of Naples. Located at a railway junction, the city is a center for trade in cereals, citrus fruit, tobacco, and hemp. Explosives, soap, and tobacco products are manufactured. Among the notable buildings in the city is a magnificent palace constructed between 1752 and 1754; adjoining it are large gardens. The modern town, Caserta, grew up around the palace in the 18th century. The old town, Caserta Vecchia, founded by the Lombards (q.v.) in the 9th century and containing a 12th-century cathedral, is about 3 miles N.E. of Caserta. During World War II, Caserta served as the Mediterranean headquarters of the Allied forces, and the surrender of the German forces in Italy was signed there on April 29, 1945. Pop. (1971 prelim.) 67,298.

**CASE WESTERN RESERVE UNIVERSITY,** coeducational privately controlled nonsectarian institution of higher learning, located in Cleveland, Ohio. The university comprises two formerly separate institutions, Western Reserve University and Case Institute of Technology. The latter was founded in Cleveland in 1880 and named for its endower, Leonard Case (1820–80). Until 1947 its name was Case School of Applied Science. Western Reserve University was founded in 1826 in Hudson, Ohio, 20 miles S.E. of Cleveland, as Western Reserve College for

men. In 1882 it was renamed Adelbert College of Western Reserve University and moved to Cleveland. It was incorporated as Western Reserve University in 1884. Women were admitted in 1888, with the founding of Flora Stone Mather College.

In July, 1967, Case Institute of Technology and Western Reserve University federated to become Case Western Reserve University. The university has two undergraduate colleges: Western Reserve College, offering programs in the arts and sciences, and the Undergraduate College of Case Institute of Technology, offering programs in engineering, the sciences, and management. Other divisions of the university are the schools of medicine (1843), dentistry (1892), law (1892), library science (1904), applied social sciences (1916), management (1952), the Frances Payne Bolton School of Nursing (1923), and the School of Graduate Studies (1926). The bachelor's, master's, doctor's, and initial and advanced professional degrees are conferred.

The university libraries contain about 1,300,000 volumes and include several noted collections, among them the Scherer collection in Germanic literature and philology and the Kirtland collection in natural history. Student enrollment in 1972–73 was 9209, the faculty numbered about 1200, and the endowment was about $150,000,000.

**CASEWORM.** *See* CADDIS FLY.

**CASGRAIN, Henri Raymond** (1831–1904), French Canadian historian, born in Rivière-Ouelle, Québec Province. Casgrain was ordained a Roman Catholic priest in 1856. During his early career he founded two literary periodicals and was an influential member of a group of intellectuals known as the École de Québec. Compelled to give up his parochial duties in 1870 because of ill health, Casgrain devoted himself to writing. His main interest was French Canadian history, and he wrote prolifically about the life and customs of Canadian pioneers. His master work was *Montcalm and Lévis* (2 vol., 1891). In 1889 he was elected president of the Royal Society of Canada, of which he was a charter member.

**CASHEW NUT,** bean-shaped fruit of *Anacardium occidentale,* a large, spreading evergreen tree in the Cashew family (Anacardiaceae). The tree, native to tropical America, is cultivated in all tropical countries. The nutmeats are enclosed in a double shell. An oil between the two shells can produce a skin rash similar to poison ivy. The oil is removed by roasting the nuts until the outer shells split. The roasted nut has a pleasant

*Twig of the cashew-nut tree,* Anacardium occidentale.

flavor and is used in many parts of the world as a food and as the source of an oil much like olive oil. The swollen, pear-shaped stalks bearing the nut are called cashew apples. They have a pleasant, acid taste, and are eaten in the countries in which the cashew tree grows. The milky juice from the stem of the tree yields a gum, similar to gum arabic, used to make a type of varnish.

**CASHMERE,** fine, soft, light wool from the undercoat of the Kashmir goat, originally raised in central and s.w. Asia, especially in Kashmir (q.v.); also the fabric made from the wool of the Kashmir goat. The term is sometimes applied to fabrics which contain other fibers in addition to cashmere wool. Cashmere yarns spun in Scotland, among the softest and most luxurious of all woolens, are used primarily for knitting sweaters and shawls and for weaving paisley shawls.

**CASH REGISTER,** machine that records the amount of a sale as the sale is made. Payment for the sale is placed in a cash drawer that is part of the machine and which opens only when the sale is registered. The first practical cash register was invented by James Ritty (1836–1918), of

Dayton, Ohio, who secured his patent in 1879. When a sale was registered on his machine, the amount of the sale appeared on a large dial on the front of the machine. The sale was also recorded within the cash register as a series of holes punched on a roll of paper tape. At the end of the day the merchant totaled his sales by adding up the rows of punched holes.

Today, a cash register not only performs these functions, but it (1) calculates the total sale when a customer purchases several items; (2) maintains a printed record of every sale, and the department in which it was made; (3) records whether the sale was paid for by cash or is to be charged; and (4) prints the details of the sale on a sales check which is given to the customer as his receipt. Running totals of sales by each department are also printed on the paper tape. Cash registers can also record automatically the information embossed on charge-account plates as part of the sales information. Cash registers used in supermarkets not only perform the functions described above, but they also automatically calculate the sales tax on taxable items as they are recorded and add the tax to the sales total; some models can also calculate change.

Special printed numbers have been developed for the cash-register tape that can be "read" by a computer. The tape is placed on an optical device that converts the printed numbers into electrical impulses that are read into the computer. The computer then processes the sales information automatically.

**CASILINUM.** *See* CAPUA.

**CASIMIR III,** known as CASIMIR THE GREAT (1309–70), King of Poland (1333–70). He was the

*Cash register invented by James Ritty.*

*Modern cash registers speed checkout procedures by itemizing and totaling purchases automatically.*

son of Władysław I Łokietek (1260–1333), whom he succeeded. Although his possessions were threatened by the Teutonic Knights (q.v.) and the king of Bohemia, Casimir succeeded in winning the friendship of both, and brought peace to Poland. He developed commerce, protected German and Jewish refugees, who made many settlements in his domains, and so improved the condition of the peasants that he was called the "Peasants' King". In 1364 he founded the University of Cracow. He reconstructed the entire administration and made Poland a power in Europe. Casimir was the last ruler of the Piast dynasty, the first dynasty in Poland. *See* POLAND: *History.*

**CASINO** *or* **CASSINO,** popular family card game, which originated in Italy in the 19th century. Casino is played with a fifty-two card deck by two, three, or four participants, but is best played with two hands or four in partnerships. The object is to take in the 10 of diamonds, called "big casino", counted as 2 points; the 2 of spades, called "little casino", 1 point; aces, 1 each; the majority of cards, 3; the majority of spades, 1. A variation called "sweeps" may also be played by agreement, 1 point going to a player any time he takes all the exposed table cards in a single play. The winner is either the player or side scoring highest after all cards in the deck have been played once, or the player or side scoring 21 points.

The dealer in casino is the player with the low cut. In the two-handed game four cards are given first to the dealer's opponent, four are exposed on the table, and four are taken by the dealer. A second round is dealt in similar fashion. In the four-handed game each player is dealt four cards in clockwise rotation, four cards are faced, and the process is repeated.

Play begins with the nondealer in the two-handed game, or the player to the left of the dealer in a partnership contest. A player in his turn may make one of the following plays. (*a*) *Take in.* If he has a card matching one or more on the table he may show it and take in such cards. An alternate play is to take in table cards whose spot values add up to the value of a card shown from the hand. (*b*) *Build.* A build is made by adding one hand card to one or more on the table, putting them into a single pile face up, and announcing their total point value. A player must have a card in his hand to match this total, except that in the partnership game he can add to a build initiated by his partner. Picture cards, which have no numerical value, may not be built. (*c*) *Continue building.* A player may form new builds and add them to any already made. (*d*) *Change the point value of a single build.* This is done by adding a card from the hand and announcing the new point value of the build. (*e*) *Trail.* A player may place a card face up on the table instead of taking in or building.

A player may take in any build, whether

203

formed by him or not. He must take in his own build in his next turn unless he chooses to make further builds, take in a card or combination of cards, or take in the build of an opponent. He may not trail with his own build waiting. In the final deal of a deck any cards remaining on the table go to the last player to take in cards.

**CASINO, MONTE.** *See* MONTE CASSINO.

**CASLON, William** (1692–1766), British type-founder, born in Cradley, Worcestershire, England. He began his career in London as an engraver of firearms, and later became a tool cutter in a book bindery. Subsequently he established a typefoundry and developed a remarkably legible type, notable for the simplicity of its design and for its readability.

## This is a sample of Caslon type.

The outstanding printers of the period in both Europe and America were supplied by Caslon's foundry. In 1776 the American Declaration of Independence was printed in Caslon type. The type diminished in popularity in the early 19th century but about 1845 printers began to use it widely again. Before long a standard maxim in the trade was, "When in doubt, use Caslon". His eldest son William Caslon (1720–78) continued the business after his death.

**CASPER,** second largest city in Wyoming, and county seat of Natrona Co., 5101 ft. above sea level, on the North Platte R., and about 150 miles N.W. of Cheyenne. Founded in 1888, on the site of Fort Caspar, it was previously known as the Upper Crossing of the Platte (until 1847) the Mormon Crossing and Ferry (1847–58), and Platte Bridge Crossing (1858–65). It was incorporated as a city in 1889. About 40 mi. to the N. are the Teapot Dome (*see* FALL, ALBERT BACON) and Salt Creek oil fields; about 20 mi. to the E. is the Big Muddy Field. An important oil-refining center, Casper is also a center of trade in wool, sheep, and livestock. Pop. (1960) 38,930; (1970) 39,361.

**CASPIAN SEA** (anc. *Caspium Mare* or *Hyrcanium Mare*), landlocked saltwater lake, and the largest inland body of water in the world, located on the boundary between Europe and Asia. Except for the S. and S.W. extremities, which are contiguous to Iranian territory, the Caspian Sea is bounded on all sides by the Soviet Union. It extends about 750 mi. in a N. and S. direction and from about 130 to 271 mi. in an E. and W. direction. It has an area of 143,243 sq.mi. Because of variations in the amount of water from its tributaries and in the extent of evaporation, the level of the Caspian Sea differs considerably

from year to year. It averages about 92 ft. below sea level. The Caspian Sea has a mean depth of approximately 550 ft. with extremes ranging from about 26 ft. in the N. to about 3200 ft. in the S. In recent years the water level has fallen, isolating villages on the shoreline and hampering navigation by large ships.

The coastline is irregular, particularly on the E., where several large gulfs are located, including Krasnovodsk Gulf and Kara-Bogaz-Gol. The S. and S.W. shorelines of the sea are bordered by the Elburz and Greater Caucasus mountain ranges. The sea has numerous tributaries, notably the Volga, Ural, and Emba rivers, all of which flow into it from the N. Other tributaries include the Gurgan and Atrek rivers, flowing from the E., and the Kura R., flowing from the W. The sea has no outlet. The Caspian Sea is linked to the Baltic, White, and Black seas by an extensive network of inland waterways, the chief of which is the Volga R. These waterways provide an outlet to N. Europe for the oil fields of Baku on the Apsheron Peninsula. The Caspian Sea also contains highly productive fisheries, yielding valuable catches of sturgeon (chief source of caviar), salmon, perch, herring, and carp. Animal life in the Caspian Sea includes tortoises, porpoises, and seals.

Navigation is frequently dangerous because of violent S.E. storms, and during the winter months the N. parts of the Caspian Sea are closed by ice. The chief ports are Krasnovodsk, Baku (q.v.), and Makhachkala, all in the Soviet Union. The sea has no major Iranian ports.

**CASS, Lewis** (1782–1866), American statesman, born in Exeter, N.H., and educated at Phillips Exeter Academy. Lewis studied law privately in Ohio and was admitted to the bar in 1802. He was elected to the Ohio legislature in 1806. When the War of 1812 with Great Britain broke out, he entered the United States Army and rose rapidly to the rank of brigadier general. From 1813 to 1831 he was governor of the Michigan Territory, and in 1831 he became secretary of war in the cabinet of President Andrew Jackson (q.v.). He resigned the post in 1836 to serve as the United States minister to France. Cass was elected to the United States Senate, serving from 1845 to 1848 when he was the unsuccessful Democratic Presidential candidate; he was defeated by the Whig Party nominee General Zachary Taylor (q.v.). He again served in the Senate from 1845 to 1857, when he was appointed secretary of state under President James Buchanan (q.v.). Cass resigned from the cabinet in 1860 when the President refused to reinforce Fort Sumter (q.v.) in Charleston, S.C.

*"Portrait of a Young Girl", oil painting by Mary Cassatt.*

**CASSANDRA,** in Greek mythology, daughter of King Priam and Queen Hecuba (qq.v.) of Troy. The god Apollo (q.v.), who loved Cassandra, granted her the gift of prophecy, but when she refused to return his love, Apollo made the gift useless by decreeing that no one would believe her predictions. Cassandra warned the Trojans of many dangers, including the wooden horse by which the Greeks entered the city (*see* TROJAN HORSE), but she was dismissed as a madwoman. After the fall of Troy, she was dragged from her sanctuary in the temple of the goddess Athena by Ajax (qq.v.) the Lesser, and brought to the Greek camp. When the spoils were divided Cassandra was awarded to King Agamemnon (q.v.) as his slave and mistress. Cassandra warned him that he would be killed if he returned to Greece; again she was not believed. Upon their arrival in Mycenae she and Agamemnon were murdered by Clytemnestra (q.v.), Queen of Mycenae and wife of Agamemnon.

**CASSATION, COURT OF.** *See* COURTS.

**CASSATT, Mary** (1845–1926), American painter and etcher, born in Allegheny City, now part of Pittsburgh, Pa. She studied painting at the

Pennsylvania Academy of Fine Arts and in Europe. About 1874 she moved permanently to Paris, where she met the French painter Edgar Degas (q.v.). He invited her to exhibit with the group of painters known as impressionists (*see* IMPRESSIONISM), whose style she adopted. Noted for her pictures of mothers and children, and also for her pastels and tinted etchings, Mary Cassatt was one of the first women in history to establish a reputation as an important artist. She was awarded the Legion of Honor in 1904. Unfortunately she began to go blind in 1912 and was no longer able to paint. Notable examples of her work, which is well represented in both European and American museums, include "Mother and Child" (1905, Metropolitan Museum of Art, New York City), and "The Boating Party" (1893–94) and "The Loge" (about 1882), both in the National Gallery of Art, Washington, D.C.

**CASSAVA,** *or* MANDIOC *or* MANIOC, common names for plants of the genus *Manihot* of the Spurge family (Euphorbiaceae), native to tropical regions in the Americas. Cassava is the West Indian name and is used in the United States; manioc, or mandioc, is the Brazilian name; and juca, or yuca, is used in other parts of South America. The plant grows in a bushy form, usually about 6 to 8 ft. high, with greenish-yellow flowers. The roots are about 1 to 3 in. thick and about 1 to 3 ft. long.

Two varieties of cassava are of economic value, the poisonous and the nonpoisonous, or sweet. Because the volatile poison can be destroyed by heat in the process of preparation, both varieties yield a wholesome food. Cassava is the chief source of tapioca, and in South America a sauce and an intoxicating beverage are prepared from the juice. The root, in powder form, is used to prepare farinha, a meal used to make thin cakes sometimes called cassava bread. The starch of cassava yields a product

*Cassava,* Manihot esculenta
American Museum of Natural History

called Brazilian arrowroot. In Florida, where sweet cassava is grown, the roots are eaten as food, fed to stock, or used in the manufacture of starch and glucose.

**CASSEL.** *See* KASSEL.

**CASSIA,** large genus of herbs, shrubs, and trees of the Pea family (Leguminosae), native to tropical and temperate regions. Although some species, particularly *C. marylandica,* are cultivated in the United States for their graceful foliage and handsome yellow flowers, their chief importance is medical; the leaves of several of these species furnish senna (q.v.). The drug known as Cassia fistula, or purging cassia, is derived from the pod of *C. fistula,* native to India. The bark of the pod is used in tanning leather and is also the source of a yellow dye. In Europe cassia bark, the aromatic bark of the plant *Cinnamomum cassia* of the Laurel family (Lauraceae), is used in the preparation of a spice that is a substitute for cinnamon.

**CASSIANUS, Johannes,** also called JOHANNES EREMITA or JOHANNES MASSILIENSIS (360?–435?), early Christian monk and theologian. After spending perhaps fifteen years among the ascetics of the Egyptian deserts, he studied in Constantinople (now İstanbul, Turkey) with Saint John Chrysostom (*see* CHRYSOSTOM, SAINT JOHN), by whom he was ordained a deacon. About 415, by now a priest, he settled in Marseille (in what is now southern France), where he founded the monasteries of Saints Peter and Victor, for men, and Saint Savior, for women, and brought eastern monasticism to the West. Cassianus was one of the first of the Semi-Pelagians (*see* PELAGIANISM), who rejected the view of the Latin Father Saint Augustine (q.v.) that mankind generally is damned by the sin of Adam (*see* ADAM AND EVE) and that some souls are saved purely through the grace (q.v.) of God, which cannot be earned. He opposed the Augustinian view, the concept of moral choice in attaining salvation.

**CASSIN, René** (1887-1976), French jurist, born in Bayonne, and educated at the universities of

Aix-en-Provence and Paris. Cassin has combined three careers for more than forty years, as jurist, diplomat, and educator. He was a member of the French delegation to the League of Nations from 1921 to 1938, served in the cabinet of the Free French government-in-exile during World War II, joined the French Constitutional Council in 1960, and became a member in 1959 and president in 1965 of the European Court of Human Rights. Cassin was the principal author of the Universal Declaration of Human Rights (q.v.), which was adopted by the United Nations General Assembly in 1948; he also served as president of the U.N. Human Rights Commission from 1954 to 1956. He was a founder of the U.N. Educational, Scientific, and Cultural Organization (UNESCO). Cassin was awarded the Grand Cross of the French Legion of Honor. He won the 1968 Nobel Peace Prize for his role in fostering the UN declaration on human rights.

**CASSINO,** a game of cards; *see* CASINO.

**CASSINO,** city of Italy, in Frosinone Province, on the Rapido R., about 85 miles S.E. of Rome. It lies at the foot of a hill crowned by the Benedictine monastery of Monte Cassino (q.v.). In 1943 during World War II (q.v.) the Germans attempted to block the Allied advance to Rome by using both the town and the abbey as key defense points. When the Allied attempt to divert the German troops by landing at Anzio failed, a concentrated ground attack on the German position was begun. By the time the Germans surrendered in the spring of 1944, the air and artillery bombing had reduced the town and the abbey to rubble. The abbey has since been reconstructed and the town has been rebuilt. Pop. (1971 prelim.) 26,287.

**CASSIODORUS, Flavius Magnus Aurelius** (about 490–about 583 A.D.), Roman historian, born in southern Italy of a noble family. During the reign of the Ostrogoths in Italy (*see* GOTHS: *Ostrogoths*), Cassiodorus became secretary to the Ostrogothic king, Theodoric (q.v.), and held several other important offices. After the death of Theodoric in 526 he acted as chief minister to Theodoric's daughter, Amalasontha (498–535?), who succeeded to the throne.

Cassiodorus wrote a *History of the Goths,* which is extant only in the form of an abridgment made by the medieval historian Jordanes (fl. 6th cent.). His other major work is a collection of the letters that he wrote while serving the Gothic sovereigns. Cassiodorus is remembered principally for founding the monastery of Vivarium in Bruttium (q.v.) about 550 for the purpose of translating and preserving both ancient and Christian manuscripts.

**CASSIOPEIA,** in astronomy, constellation of the northern heavens, near the celestial pole. It is distinguished by a group of five stars, of second to fourth magnitude, in the form of a straggling letter W. The brightest supernova on record appeared in the constellation in 1572, and was observed and recorded by the Danish astronomer Tycho Brahe (q.v.). Brighter than the planet Venus, for about sixteen months it was visible to the naked eye even at noon. The constellation is named for the mythological Ethiopian queen Cassiopeia, the mother of Andromeda (q.v.).

**CASSIOPEIA,** in Greek mythology, the wife of Cepheus, King of Ethiopia. When Cassiopeia boasted that she was more beautiful than the Nereids, these water nymphs complained to Poseidon (qq.v.), the god of the sea, who sent a sea monster to ravage the land. The god demanded that Cassiopeia's daughter Andromeda (q.v.) be punished for her mother's vanity by being sacrificed to the monster, but the girl was rescued by the hero Perseus (q.v.). According to tradition, at death Cassiopeia was changed into the constellation that bears her name.

**CASSIRER, Ernst** (1874–1945), German philosopher and educator, born in Breslau (now Wrocław, Poland), and educated at the universities of Berlin, Leipzig, Munich, Heidelberg, and Marburg. Cassirer became professor of philosophy at Hamburg University in 1919, and taught there until he was ousted in 1933, when the German dictator Adolf Hitler (q.v.) came to power. Subsequently Cassirer lectured at the universities of Oxford and Göteborg, became visiting professor at Yale University in 1941, and joined the staff of Columbia University in 1944. A great admirer of the philosophy of the German philosopher Immanuel Kant (q.v.), Cassirer was a leader of the so-called Marburg Neo-Kantian school of philosophy. His works deal mainly with the theory of knowledge, the history of epistemology, and the philosophy of science. He also revised and annotated Kant's writings. Cassirer's works include *The Problem of Knowledge* (3 vol., 1906–20) and *The Philosophy of Symbolic Forms* (3 vol., 1923–29).

**CASSITERITE,** or TINSTONE, mineral consisting of tin dioxide. It forms crystals in the tetragonal system, and has hardness 6 and sp.gr. 7. Usually dark brown to black, it has a dull adamantine luster. Cassiterite is the only commercially important ore of tin. It has been mined in Cornwall, England, since ancient times, but the principal sources today are Bolivia, the Malay Peninsula, Indonesia, Nigeria, and the Republic of the Congo.

Cassowary, Casuarius casuarius

**CASSIUS, Dio.** *See* Dio Cassius.

**CASSIUS LONGINUS, Gaius** (d. 42 B.C.), Roman general and one of the assassins of the Roman statesman and general Gaius Julius Caesar (q.v.). Cassius distinguished himself in the war against the Parthians (53–51 B.C.) and served as fleet commander under Pompey the Great (q.v.) against Caesar in 49 B.C. Although pardoned by Caesar, who made him a legate, Cassius was one of the leaders of the conspiracy against Caesar and participated in the assassination. Subsequently he raised an army to fight against Caesar's commander in chief Marcus Antonius (q.v.), and later against the Triumvirate, the three men who ruled Rome after Caesar's assassination. With the Roman politician Marcus Junius Brutus (q.v.) Cassius besieged his foes at Philippi in Macedonia, but was defeated in battle. Cassius ordered his freedmen to kill him so that he would not be captured. His life is recounted in the play *Julius Caesar* by William Shakespeare (q.v.).

**CASSIVELAUNUS or CASSIVELLAUNUS** (fl. 1st cent. B.C.), ancient British tribal chieftain. He ruled the Catuvellauni in the region now included in Berkshire, Buckinghamshire, and Hertfordshire. In 54 B.C. he opposed the second invasion of Britain by the Roman statesman and general Gaius Julius Caesar (q.v.), but was compelled to pay tribute and give hostages to his Roman conqueror.

**CASSOCK.** *See* Vestments, Ecclesiastical: *Vestments in the Roman Catholic Church.*

**CASSOWARY,** common name for a genus, *Casuarius,* of flightless, running birds closely related to the true ostrich, and more closely to the emu (qq.v.), of the family Casuariidae. Cassowaries are found mainly in Queensland, Australia, in New Guinea, and in Ceram, Indonesia. About 5 ft. high, it resembles the ostrich but has a shorter neck. The loose hairlike feathers are brownish black. The head and neck are bare and brilliantly colored in red, blue, and yellow. On top of the head is a large, bony, helmetlike crest. Two species have wattles hanging from the chin. When attacked, the cassowary can run up to thirty m.p.h., or kick forward with sharp claws or strike with the rigid barbs of its degenerate wings. Cassowaries live in pairs in wooded districts. The three to six eggs are incubated mainly by the male cassowary, and are of greenish color and thinner in shell than those of the ostrich.

**CASTAGNO, Andrea Del** (1423–57), Italian Renaissance painter, born in Castagno (now Il Castagno d'Andrea), near Florence, of peasant stock. His talent attracted the attention of a member of the powerful Medici (q.v.) family, who placed him with a competent teacher in Florence, probably the painter Paolo Uccello (q.v.). Influenced also by the work of the Florentine sculptor Donatello (q.v.), Castagno translated Donatello's style of sculpture into his paintings. Of the realists who followed the great Florentine painter Masaccio (q.v.), Castagno was the most gifted and influential. His drawing is bold and firm, his color bright and crude, and the impression gained from his works is one of rugged strength. Castagno's principal works are "The Last Supper", several scenes of Christ's Passion, and a series of larger than life-size figures called "Famous Men and Women", all frescoes in the Sant' Apollonia Castagno Museum, Florence. Other works by Castagno are the equestrian portrait "Niccolò da Tolentino" (1456) in the cathedral of Florence, and "The Youthful David" (National Gallery of Art, Washington, D.C.).

**CASTANETS,** in music, percussion instruments consisting of a pair of hollow shells of hard wood, ivory, or composition material loosely bound together by a cord. The cord is generally fastened about the first finger and thumb of the hand of the performer. When the other fingers strike the two castanet halves together, a hollow, clicking sound is produced. Used chiefly with Spanish music to accent the rhythm of the piece being performed, castanets are used also by performers of Spanish dances, who play them as they dance, usually holding one instrument in each hand. An instrument similar to the castanet was used in ancient times, but the modern term is derived from the Spanish word for chestnut (castaño), from which castanets were commonly made.

**CASTE,** term applied to one of the many hereditary classes established among the Hindus on the Indian subcontinent; *see* HINDUISM. Sometimes the term is also used in a general sense, to refer to any society that has a rigid class structure. The word caste was first used by 16th-century Portuguese traders, and is derived from the Portuguese *casta,* denoting family strain, breed, or race. The Sanskrit word is *jati.* The Sanskrit term *varna* denotes a group of jati, or the system of caste.

The traditional caste system of India developed over 3000 years ago when Aryan-speaking nomadic groups migrated from the north to India about 1500 B.C. The Aryan priests (*see* BRAHMAN), according to the ancient sacred literature of India (*see* VEDA), divided society into a basic caste system. Sometime between 200 B.C. and 100 A.D., the Code of Manu (q.v.) was written. In it the Aryan priest-lawmakers created the four great hereditary divisions of society still surviving today, placing their own priestly class at the head of this caste system with the title of earthly gods, or Brahmans. Next in order of rank were the warriors, the Kshatriyas. Then came the Vaisyas, the farmers and merchants. The fourth of the original castes was the Sudras, the laborers, born to be servants to the other three castes, especially the Brahman. Far lower than the Sudras (in fact, entirely outside of the social order, and limited to doing the most menial tasks) were those persons of no caste, the untouchables. These were the Dravidians (q.v.), the original aboriginal inhabitants of India, to whose ranks from time to time were added the pariahs, or outcasts, persons expelled for religiosocial sins from the classes into which they had been born. Thus created by the priests, the caste system was made a part of Hindu religious law, rendered secure by the claim of divine revelation.

The characteristics of an Indian caste include rigid, hereditary membership in the caste into which one is born; the practice of marrying only members of the same caste; restrictions on the choice of occupation and on personal contact with members of other castes; and the acceptance of each individual of a fixed place in society. The caste system has been perpetuated by the Hindu idea of *karma.* According to this religious belief, each person has a reincarnation on earth, at which time he has a chance to be born

into another, higher caste, but only if he is obedient to the rules of his caste in his life on earth. In this way karma has discouraged people from attempting to rise to a higher caste or to cross caste lines for social relations of any kind.

The four original castes have been subdivided again and again over many centuries, until today it is impossible to tell their exact number. Estimates range from 2000 to 3000 different castes established by Brahmanical law in different parts of India, each region having its own more or less distinct groups defined by craft and fixed by custom.

The complexities of the system have constituted a serious obstacle to civil progress in India. The trend today is toward the dissolution of the artificial barriers between the castes. The stringency of the caste system of the Hindus was broken down greatly during the period of British rule in India. The obligation of the son to follow the calling of his father is no longer binding as it once was; men of low castes have risen to high ranks and positions of power; and excommunication, or the loss of caste, is not so serious as it may once have been. In addition, the caste system was from time to time burst from within by ecclesiastical schisms, most notably by the rise of Buddhism (q.v.), itself a reaction from, and protest against, the intolerable bondage of the caste system. *See* BRAHMO SAMAJ.

In recent years considerable strides toward eradicating unjust social and economic aspects of the caste system as practiced in India have been made through educational and reform movements. The great leader in this endeavor was the Indian nationalist Mohandas Karamchand Gandhi (q.v.). The drafted constitution of the Dominion of India, which was published not many days after the assassination of Gandhi in January, 1948, stated in a special clause under the heading "human rights": "Untouchability is abolished and its practice in any form is forbidden".

**CASTEL.** *See* CHÂTEAU.

**CASTEL GANDOLFO,** town of Italy, in Rome Province on Lake Albano, about 14 miles S.E. of the city of Rome. The town is the site of the papal residence, Castel Gandolfo, a palace constructed in the 17th century, and of the Church of Saint Thomas of Villanova designed by the Italian architect and sculptor Giovanni Lorenzo Bernini (q.v.). Politically the town is part of the independent papal state of Vatican City (q.v.). Pop. (1971 prelim.) 4814.

**CASTELLO-BRANCO, Camillo, Visconde de Correia-Botelho** (1826–90), Portuguese writer, born in Lisbon. Orphaned when very young, he led a dissolute life for a number of years. He took minor orders, but, tiring of religious life, resumed his secular existence and devoted himself to writing. In 1885 he was made a viscount in recognition of his work. A few years later, after his health failed and he became blind, Castello-Branco committed suicide.

Although Castello-Branco wrote about 100 volumes of poetry, plays, critical writing, and novels, his significance as a writer rests almost entirely on his fifty-eight novels. These portrayed the social and domestic life of his time, in which idealization of some of his characters was intermingled with savage ridicule of such characters as members of the commercial middle class. His style was remarkable for the brilliant use of Portuguese.

His novels include *Where Is Happiness?* (1856), *What Women Do* (1858), *Love of Perdition* (written in 1862 and accounted his most beautiful work), and *The Brazilian Girl from Prazins* (1882).

**CASTIGLIONE, Conte Baldassare** (1478–1529), Italian writer and diplomat, born near Mantua.

*Conte Baldassare Castiglione*    New York Public Library

He served numerous eminent Italian nobles on diplomatic missions, and in 1524 he was appointed mediator of a dispute between Pope Clement VII (*see under* CLEMENT) and Charles V (q.v.), Holy Roman Emperor. Castiglione was honored by the emperor and made bishop of Ávila. He is best known as author of one of the great prose dialogues of the 16th century, *Il Cortegiano* ("The Courtier", 1528), a discussion of the qualities of the ideal courtier or gentleman of the Renaissance. In addition to being a literary masterpiece, the work is an important historical document.

**CASTILE,** former kingdom of Spain, comprising Old Castile and New Castile. It extended from the Bay of Biscay on the N. to Andalusia on the S., and included most of the central portion of the Spanish peninsula. In 1833 Old Castile, which made up the N. half of the kingdom, was divided into the provinces of Palencia, Valladolid, Ávila, Segovia, Soria, Burgos, Logroño, and Santander. New Castile was divided into the provinces of Madrid, Toledo, Guadalajara, Ciudad Real, and Cuenca. Receiving its name because of the large number of its frontier castles, Castile was under the suzerainty of the kings of Asturias and León from the 8th century to 1035, when Ferdinand I (q.v.) established a unified kingdom. In 1058 Ferdinand initiated the first of a long series of wars against the Moors (q.v.), expelling them from numerous regions. Despite internal strife, the kingdom was further expanded in the following centuries, and in 1479, as a result of the marriage of Ferdinand V (q.v.) of Castile and Isabella I (q.v.), it was united with Aragón (q.v.). The united kingdom subsequently became the kingdom of Spain. *See* SPAIN: *History.*

**CASTILLA, Ramón** (1797–1867), Peruvian general and statesman, born in Tarapacá Province (now in Chile). He entered the Spanish army in 1816, and joined the revolt against Spanish rule in 1821. After independence had been secured he was appointed prefect of his native province in 1824 and chief of staff in 1830. In 1837 he joined the Peruvians who marched against Santa Cruz, and was made minister of war under President Agustín Gamarra (1785–1841). In 1841 Castilla was one of the leaders of the Peruvian force that invaded Bolivia, and in 1845 he was elected president of Peru. When his successor, José Rufino Echenique (1808–79), became unpopular, Castilla started a revolution, overcame Echenique, and became, in 1855, sole ruler of the country. One of his most important reforms was the abolition of slavery; another was the abolition of tribute paid by the Indians to the great

*Sargans Castle in northern Switzerland, formerly a Swiss fortress. Built in the 12th century, the fortress became a museum in 1899.*   Photo Floreani

landed proprietors. In 1858 he was reelected president, and in 1860 he proclaimed a new constitution. In 1862 he resigned, and he lived in retirement until he became president of the Senate in 1865.

**CASTILLO ARMAS, Carlos.** *See* GUATEMALA: *History.*

**CASTILLO DE SAN MARCOS NATIONAL MONUMENT,** historic area in Saint Johns County, Fla. It is administered by the National Park Service (q.v.).

**CASTING.** *See* FOUNDING.

**CAST IRON.** *See* IRON; IRON AND STEEL MANUFACTURE.

**CASTLE** (Lat. *castellum,* "small fortified place"), fortified residence of a feudal lord or monarch; *see* FEUDALISM. Derived from the walled cities of ancient Rome and the fortified

palaces of Byzantium, the castle became virtually ubiquitous in western Europe during the continuous wars of the late Middle Ages. At first the castle consisted of a simple wooden structure on top of a mound, surrounded by a ditch. If a lord's domains were flat, he constructed an artificial mound, or motte. As medieval siegecraft developed, a wall or series of walls was raised to separate the motte from the wooden structure; the open area within these walls became known as the bailey. By the 11th century the motte-and-bailey form of castle was widely prevalent. Outer walls gradually became thicker and were topped with wide battlemented parapets. The next step in the development of the

Castle of Saint Leo in the province of Pesaro e Urbino, Italy, amidst the Apennine Mts., was probably built in the 13th century. UPI

Cochem Castle, (built in the 14th century) in the Mosel River valley of Germany was destroyed in 1689 and rebuilt in the 19th century. German Tourist Information Office

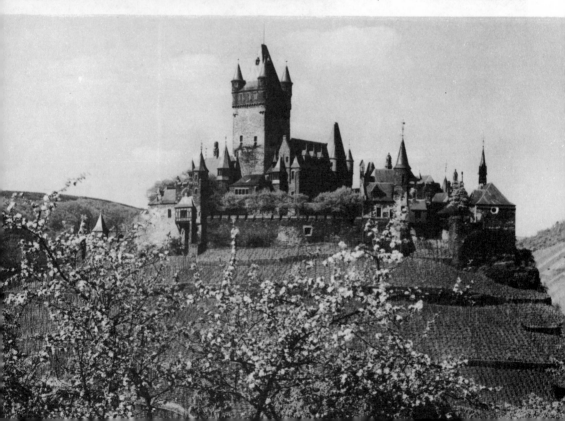

Château de Chenonceaux in the Loire River valley of France. The château, which bridges the Cher River, was built in the 16th century. French Government Tourist Office

castle was the addition by the Normans (*see* NORMANDY) of a towering masonry keep or donjon within the bailey. The keep, often 40 to 50 ft. high, had thick walls and small windows. The White Tower within the Tower of London (q.v.) is an example of a Norman keep. Wide, deep moats replaced the crude ditches; ideally filled with water but often dry, these moats were crossed by drawbridges that could be raised from within the castle. At the castle end of the drawbridge was an opening in the wall, containing a portcullis, a thick, iron-plated wooden door that could be raised to clear the entrance. Within the Norman keep were private apartments, a well for water, and everything else necessary to sustain the inhabitants of the castle through a long siege. At first the keep was rectangular. Later, when it was learned that a round keep was easier to defend, the keep was constructed without outside angles. In the 13th century the castle became increasingly sophisticated. Living and administrative quarters were moved from the keep into new buildings raised within the bailey. The keep, made smaller and stronger, became the final defensive position within a series of battlements. A castle was often built on the edge of an impregnable cliff, ideally at a bend in the river where it could command a veiw of the surrounding countryside. The Château Gaillard, built by Richard I (q.v.), King of England in Les Andelys, France, is an example of a well-situated castle. The use of gunpowder in projectiles brought to an end the impregnability of the medieval castle. After 1500 the construction of castles to serve both military and domestic purposes was no longer feasible,

and the castle became merely an imposing residence. *See also* FORTIFICATION AND SIEGECRAFT.

**CASTLE,** name of husband and wife team of exhibition ballroom dancers: **Vernon Blythe Castle** (1887–1918) and **Irene Foote Castle** (1893–1969).

He was born Vernon Blythe in Norwich, England; she was born in New Rochelle, N.Y. After their marriage in 1911 they helped to develop and popularize a new style of social dancing; they were immensely popular performers until his death in World War I. Among the dances they performed were the turkey trot, the maxixe, the one-step, and the Castle walk. Together they wrote *Modern Dancing* (1914); Irene Castle wrote *My Memories of Vernon Castle* (1918) and collaborated with the American writers Bob and Wanda Duncan on *Castles in the Air* (1958).

**CASTLE CLINTON NATIONAL MONUMENT,** circular red sandstone fort in Battery Park at the southern end of Manhattan Island, New York City. It was built by the Federal government in 1811 to protect New York harbor against possible enemy attack. The British did not attempt to attack the city during the War of 1812 (q.v.), and at the end of the war the fort became headquarters for the Third Military District. In 1823 it was ceded to New York City. The following year the fort was reopened as Castle Garden, a place of public entertainment. From 1855 to 1890, when it served as an immigrant depot, more than 7,000,000 immigrants passed through Castle Garden. The structure was again completely remodeled and opened in 1896 as the New York City Aquarium. In 1941 the aquarium was closed and the building was scheduled for demolition. It was saved, however, when it was established as a national monument in 1946. The one-acre site has since been partially restored to its original condition. The monument is administered by the National Park Service (q.v.).

**CASTLEREAGH, Viscount, Robert Stewart** (1769–1822), British statesman, born in County Down, Ireland, and educated at the University of Cambridge. In 1790 he entered the Irish parliament as a Whig, but joined the Tory Party in 1795 when he entered the British House of Commons. In 1796 he was created Viscount Castlereagh, a courtesy title. As chief secretary for Ireland from 1799, he bent his energies towards supporting the measure of the British prime minister, William Pitt, known as the Younger (*see under* PITT), to bring about the political union of Ireland with Great Britain. The measure, known as the Act of Union, was carried in the Irish parliament in 1800, largely through Castlereagh's skill in bribing parliamentary members. Soon after the measure became law on Jan. 1, 1801, Castlereagh resigned from office because of the opposition of George III (q.v.), King of Great Britain to the passing of a Catholic Emancipation Act, which Castlereagh had hoped would follow the Act of Union.

Castlereagh was a member of the House of Commons from 1801 until his death, serving as leader from 1812. As secretary of state for the war and colonial department during most of the period from 1805 to 1809, he helped plan British campaigns in the Napoleonic Wars (q.v.).

From 1812, as foreign secretary in the cabinet of the British Tory statesman Robert Banks Jenkinson (1770–1828), 2nd Earl of Liverpool, Castlereagh became the leader of the coalition of nations against Napoleon I (q.v.), Emperor of France, keeping it united during the critical campaigns of 1813–14. He represented Great Britain at the Congress of Vienna (*see* VIENNA, CONGRESS OF) in 1814–15 and at the signing of the Treaty of Paris in 1815, ending the wars. Just before a conference of the great powers in Verona, Italy, in 1822, which he was to have attended, Castlereagh, oppressed by overwork and heavy responsibilities committed suicide.

**CASTOR,** star, α Geminorum, of magnitude 1.6, the fainter star of the zodiacal constellation Gemini (q.v.), or the Twins. In 1719 it was discovered to be a visual binary star, with components of magnitudes 2.8 and 2.0 separated by 6 sec. of an arc and revolving around each other in about 350 years. Each of these components

has been found to be a spectroscopic binary. In addition, a faint companion, separated from the other two by 72 sec. of an arc, has been discovered. This star is also a spectroscopic binary, the two components of which revolve around each other in about 1 day. Hence, the entire system of the star Castor contains at least six stars. Its distance is about 16 light-years from the earth. *See also* POLLUX; ZODIAC.

**CASTOR AND POLLUX,** in Greek and Roman mythology, the twin sons of Leda (q.v.), wife of the Spartan king Tyndareus. They were the brothers of Clytemnestra, Queen of Mycenae, and Helen of Troy (qq.v.). Although both boys were known as the *Dioscuri,* or sons of Zeus, in most accounts only Pollux was held to be immortal, having been conceived when Zeus appeared to Leda in the form of a swan; Castor, although his fraternal twin, was considered to be the mortal son of Tyndareus. Both were worshipped as deities in the Roman world, however, and were regarded as the special protectors of sailors and warriors. Living just before the Trojan War (q.v.), the brothers took part in many of the famous events of the day, including the Calydonian boar hunt (*see* MELEAGER), the expedition of the Argonauts (q.v.), and the rescue of their sister Helen when she was carried off by the Greek hero Theseus (q.v.). Throughout all their adventures the brothers were inseparable, and when Castor was slain by Idas, a cattle owner, in a dispute about his oxen, Pollux was inconsolable. In response to his prayers for death for himself or immortality for his brother, Zeus reunited the brothers, allowing them to be always together, half the time in the underworld and half with the gods on Mount Olympus. According to a later legend, they were transformed by Zeus into the constellation Gemini (q.v.), or the Twins.

**CASTOR-BEAN PLANT** *or* **CASTOR-OIL PLANT,** *or* PALMA CHRISTI, common names for a plant, *Ricinus communis,* of the Spurge family (Euphorbiaceae). Native to India, the plant has been introduced into most tropical countries. In the tropics the plant is treelike, growing as high as 40 ft. In temperate climates it is easily grown from seed as an annual, sometimes reaching a height of 12 ft. during a summer, and it is often planted where rapidly growing, dense foliage is required to provide landscaping or a screen. The leaves are ornamental, often 2 to 3 ft. wide, divided into from five to eleven lobes. The flowers are without petals and are borne in panicles covered with dark brown spines. The fruit is a three-lobed capsule, containing three large, bean-shaped seeds that are grayish-brown and

*Castor bean,* Ricinus communis

are covered with a fine, dark brown or black pattern, different on each seed. The seeds and leaves are poisonous, because of the presence of a nitrogenous substance, ricine. Three seeds are enough to kill a man. The seeds are sometimes placed in mole runs to kill moles. The endosperm, or fleshy interior of the seed, is the source of the castor oil (q.v.) of commerce.

**CASTOR OIL,** colorless or yellow to yellowish-brown, thick, oily liquid obtained from the seeds of the castor-bean plant (q.v.). Although it has a nauseating taste, it is practically odorless. It is insoluble in water, but soluble in organic solvents. The medicinal oil is prepared from husked seeds. Unhusked seeds, the source of industrial castor oil, yield from 45 to 55 percent oil. The oil is pressed from the seeds, purified, and bleached.

In addition to use as a simple purgative, castor oil is used as a plasticizer in nitrocellulose compositions, in hair dressings and other cosmetics, in electrical insulating compositions, and in rubber substitutes. It is a nondrying oil, but dehydrated castor oil, from which about 5 percent of the chemically combined water has been removed, oxidizes in air, forming a solid, and is used as a substitute for tung oil in the manufacture of waterproof lacquers and paints.

**CASTRATION,** in surgery, removal of the gonads in the human male or female for the purpose of family planning (*see* PLANNED PARENTHOOD), sterilization (*see* STERILITY: *Sterilization*), eugenics (q.v.), or to combat the spread of a malignant tumor (q.v.); *see* CANCER; REPRODUCTIVE SYSTEM: *Gonads. See also* EUNUCH.

In animal husbandry, a similar surgical procedure, known as gelding in male animals and spaying in the female, is used for various purposes, such as selective breeding of horses, to make an ox docile, or a cat sterile. *See* AGRICULTURE: *Animal Husbandry.*

**CASTRIES.** *See* SAINT LUCIA.

**CASTRO, Cipriano** (1858?–1924), Venezuelan military leader and statesman, born near San Antonio, Táchira State. In 1899 Castro led an insurrection, captured Caracas, and became president of Venezuela. One of the most corrupt dictators in Venezuelan history, Castro was also a libertine. His administration was marked by insurrections and by disputes with foreign countries over Venezuelan debts and his attempts to confiscate foreign property. These quarrels with European creditor nations took place between 1902 and 1907, and Venezuela was brought close to bankruptcy; *see* VENEZUELA: *History.* In 1908, during Castro's absence in Europe, a revolution broke out in Venezuela. Castro was deposed, his friend Vice-President Juan Vincente Gómez (q.v.) had himself elected president, and Castro was exiled.

**CASTRO, Fidel.** *See* CASTRO (RUZ), FIDEL.

**CASTRO, Inés de** (about 1320–55), Spanish noblewoman, descended from the Castilian line, whose unhappy fate has been the subject of tragedies and poems. After 1340, Inés lived with her cousin Constantia (d. 1345), who was later the wife of Dom Pedro (1320–67), son of Alfonso IV, King of Portugal (*see under* ALFONSO). After the death of Constantia, Dom Pedro secretly married Inés. Alfonso feared that this union might affect the claim to the throne of his grandson, son of Constantia. Thereupon, Inés was condemned to die and was executed. Dom Pedro declared civil war against Alfonso, but they were soon reconciled. According to legend, when Pedro became king he established the legality of his marriage with Inés and had her body exhumed and placed upon the throne.

**CASTRO, João de** (1500–48), Portuguese naval officer and explorer, born in Lisbon. As a youth he distinguished himself in a number of campaigns against the Moors of Tangier and Tunis. In 1543, when he returned from an expedition to the Red Sea, he was appointed commander of a fleet to clear the European seas of pirates. Castro was sent in 1545 to Portuguese India, where he overthrew the king of Gujarat and relieved the beleaguered town of Diu. Castro subsequently completed the subjugation of Malacca and prepared the way for the invasion of Ceylon. In 1547 he was made viceroy of Portuguese India.

*Fidel Castro*                                    UPI

**CASTRO (RUZ), Fidel** (1927– ), Cuban lawyer and revolutionary leader, born in Mayarí. He
received a degree in law from the University of
Havana in 1950. After the Cuban soldier and
politician Fulgencio Batista y Zaldívar (q.v.)
seized control of the Cuban government in
1952, Castro became the leader of an underground, antigovernment faction. In 1953 he was
jailed for having led the July 26th uprising
against Batista. Released in 1955, he went into
exile. In 1956 he returned to Cuba and led a rebellion from the Sierra Maestra region of
Oriente Province. The rebellion, known as the
26th of July movement commemorating the
abortive uprising of 1953, won steadily increasing popular support. Batista fled from the country on Jan. 1, 1959, and Castro assumed power.
He became premier of Cuba on Feb. 16. On July
17 Castro, as an expression of opposition to the
president, Lleo Manuel Urrutia (1901– ), resigned as premier. He resumed office on July 26,
following the resignation of Urrutia and the appointment of the Cuban jurist Osvaldo Dorticos
Torrado (1919– ) as puppet president. Castro's
regime moved more and more openly into the
Soviet orbit and in 1965 Castro dissolved his
United Party of the Social Revolution and announced the establishment of the Communist
Party of Cuba. In 1961, Castro was awarded the
Lenin Peace Prize by the Soviet government.
In the early 1970's, Castro continued his efforts
to improve relations between Cuba and the
other Western Hemisphere nations, which had
deteriorated because of his aggressive policies.
He also reinforced the ties between his country
and the U.S.S.R., gaining extension of previously reached economic-aid agreements. *See
also* CUBA: *History: Cuba Under Castro.*

**CASTRO VALLEY,** unincorporated suburban
area of California, in Alameda Co., on Cull
Creek, 15 miles S.E. of downtown Oakland and 2
mi. N.E. of Hayward. It was named for Guillermo
Castro, an early 19th-century property owner.
Poultry-raising and fruit-growing are important
occupations of the village. Pop. (1960) 37,120;
(1970) 44,760.

**CASTRO Y BELLVIS, Guillén de** (1569–1631),
Spanish dramatist, born in Valencia of a distinguished family. He enjoyed the friendship of
many celebrated and powerful personages in
society, letters, and government. In 1593 he was
a captain in the military forces of Valencia, a position that he seems to have held at least
throughout the rest of the century. He won first
prize in a literary tournament held in Valencia in
1602. Like his friend the renowned Spanish
dramatist Lope de Vega (q.v.), Castro was a well-
known playwright of the so-called golden age
of Spanish literature. Castro's most celebrated
play is *Las Mocedades del Cid* (1618; Eng. trans.,
*The Youthful Deeds of the Cid,* 1969), from
which the French dramatist Pierre Corneille
(q.v.) derived his masterpiece *Le Cid* (1636 or
1637); *see* CID, THE. Most of the approximately

fifty dramas written by Castro deal with the legendary deeds of the Cid. *See also* SPANISH LITERATURE: *Renaissance and Golden Age.*

**CAT.** *See* CAT, DOMESTIC; FELIDAE.

**CATACOMBS,** network of subterranean chambers and galleries excavated in soft rock, used for burial purposes by the early Christians, and, in times when they were persecuted, for refuge and for religious services. These underground chambers were called *coemeteria* ("sleeping chambers") or *crypta* ("hidden places"). Although exactly how they came to be called catacombs is unknown, some archeologists believe that it was by way of applying to all such burial places a part of the name of one of them—the Coemeterium Catacumbas.

Greeks and Romans were usually cremated, but because Christian custom forbade incineration, catacombs were constructed outside city limits on property belonging to wealthy converts or purchased by groups of Christians. Such catacombs have been found in various parts of what was the early Christian world: the Crimea, Asia Minor, Syria, Egypt (Alexandria), Cyrenaica, Tunisia (Sousse), Malta, Sicily (Syracuse), and Italy (Rome, Naples).

By far the most important group of catacombs is near Rome. These catacombs are all outside the city walls, within a radius of 3 mi. The larger ones are a confusing maze of galleries, the result of gradual evolution. During the 1st and 2nd centuries A.D., a Christian landowner would establish a small catacomb for the burial of his family, freedmen, and slaves, and would set aside for the purpose a small rectangular patch of ground, which was registered as a family burying ground. Under the common law of Rome this became inviolable.

A single gallery ran within the outer edge of this rectangle, about 8 ft. high by 3 ft. wide, in the sides of which were cut loculi, one above another, to receive the bodies. The loculus was as long as the body, and the depth varied to contain from one to three or four members of the same family. Persons of distinction were buried in chambers that opened out of these galleries, and carved sarcophagi, placed in arched niches, were used for such burials. Usually some martyr was buried in such a chamber, his tomb serving as an altar. As Christianity gathered more converts and burials multiplied, the plot of ground was honeycombed with galleries, parallel and at right angles to one another, and when one story of them was no longer sufficient, staircases were made and a second line of galleries excavated beneath. If necessary, a third, fourth, or even fifth story of galleries was added.

As persecutions increased in virulence, the catacombs became places where Christians could avoid arrest, because burial places, under the law, were sacrosanct. When churches above ground were confiscated and destroyed by imperial orders, it was always possible to use the chapels in the catacombs for services. There-

*The Crypt of the Five Virgins in the Catacombs of Saint Callistus in Rome. This crypt is named after the five original paintings on the wall.* Ewing Galloway

fore, the catacombs assumed such importance that in the 3rd century their administration was no longer left in the hands of private persons, but was taken over by the church.

A new period began, however, in the middle of the 3rd century, when the violence of popular hatred refused any longer to recognize the inviolability of the Christian places of burial and persecuting mobs and officials invaded them. Christians then destroyed the entrances, with their oratories, feasting halls, and open staircases, filled up the front galleries, and made secret entrances, usually from neighboring sand-pits. Since there was no longer any need to restrict the catacomb limits, as there was no longer any legal protection, all the spaces between the various small catacombs were honeycombed with passages, and one immense catacomb was made out of many.

The persecution of the Christians came to an end with the conversion to Christianity of the Roman emperor Constantine I (q.v.), known as the Great. Soon afterward Bishop Damasus, later Pope Damasus I (see under DAMASUS), began his monumental restoration of the catacombs, restoring passages, identifying the tombs of martyrs and marking them with commemorating inscriptions in verse, and building or decorating underground chapels and basilicas at the entrances. During the whole of the 4th century, and until about 410 A.D., burials continued to be numerous in the catacombs, through the desire of the faithful to rest near the martyrs, and then, finally, all burials were transferred to the surface cemeteries connected with churches.

Provided with small basilicas and chapels at their new entrances, the catacombs, however, remained objects of sacred pilgrimages and anniversary services, not only for Romans, but for pilgrims from the whole Christian world. During the invasions of Rome in the following centuries, by the Goths, Vandals, Lombards, and Saracens, the galleries of the catacombs were filled with earth to prevent their desecration, the entrances were sealed, and the bones of the martyrs were transported to places of safety. From the 9th to the 16th centuries the catacombs were entirely abandoned. After that they were gradually reopened and restored by the Roman Catholic Church.

Several of the catacombs contain magnificent works of art, such as highly decorative ceilings, frescoes, sculpture, and glassware. Some of the catacomb inscriptions are fine bits of engraving representing every variety of technique. The catacombs found near Rome in 1956 and 1959 also contain magnificent frescoes.

**CATALAN LANGUAGE AND LITERATURE,** language and literature that originated in Catalonia (q.v.), a region in N.E. Spain. Catalan is spoken by more than 3,500,000 people, in Spain in the provinces of Gerona, Lérida, Barcelona, Tarragona, Castellón, Valencia, Alicante, and the Balearic Islands; in France in nearly the whole of the present department of Pyrénées-Orientales; in the town of Alghero in Sardinia; and in some parts of Cuba and Argentina.

**Language.** The Catalan language is a Romance language. For years some philologists held that it was merely a dialectal offshoot of Provençal (see PROVENÇAL LANGUAGE AND LITERATURE) and that during the Middle Ages it raised itself for a time to the dignity of a literary language. Subsequent research led other scholars to claim the complete independence of Catalan as a language. Ranged in the group of Hispanic languages, Catalan has a character as distinctive as that of Castilian, Portuguese, and Galician. Among the characteristics of Catalan are the following: a number of perfect participles are formed from the perfect stem instead of from the infinitive stem; the pronunciation of b and v has not merged; the voiced sound of intervocalic s has persisted; in unaccented final vowels, a is retained and other vowels are dropped; the Latin au is changed to o as in Castilian; final dentals are vocalized, which is held to be the essential characteristic of classic Catalan; noun declensions are totally absent; and the original pronunciation of the Latin ū is retained in cases in which French and Provençal use ü.

**Literature.** Under the influence of the splendor of the literary courts of independent Provençal potentates, Catalan poets adopted the verse forms of the troubadours of Provence and Toulouse. The 15th century was the golden age of Catalan poetry. During this period the language used in poetry as well as prose showed an increasing devotion to purely Catalan forms until it became an entirely native product. The greatest among the brilliant poets of this period was Ausías March (about 1397–1460), a Valencian. The subsequent decline of Catalan poetry was caused not by a lessening of the genius of Catalan poets, but by the loss of independence of Aragon to Castile and the triumphant rise and spread of Castilian. A Catalan, Juan Boscán Almogáver (1493?–1542), inaugurated in Castilian the use of Italian poetic forms.

Few important prose works were produced in Catalan before the end of the 13th century. In the 15th century Catalan translators and historians flourished. After the 15th century, aside from several romances of chivalry and adventure, Catalan writers produced very little memorable literature until the 19th-century renaissance. A major writer during the early years of this period was Buenaventura Carlos Ariba (1798–1862) whose *Oda a la Patria,* written in 1833, is one of the best poems in modern Catalan. Other Catalan writers attained celebrity, including Mosén Jacinto Verdaguer (1845–1902), author of two epics; and Ángel Guimerá (1847–1924), poet and dramatist. Among important Catalan writers of the 20th century are the novelists Narcis Oller (1846–1930), Joaquim Ruyra (1858–1939), and Prudenci Bertrana (1867–1941), and the poets Joan Maragall (1860–1911) and Carles Riba (1893–1959). Under the regime established in 1938 by the Spanish dictator Francisco Franco (q.v.), all traces of Catalan autonomy were abolished, and the use of the Catalan language was discouraged in Spain.    J.F.S.

**CATALEPSY,** nervous condition characterized by loss of voluntary motion and by a plastic rigidity of the muscles, usually accompanied by loss of consciousness. The muscles of the cataleptic will retain any position they are placed in for an indefinite time period. The cataleptic state may continue for several minutes or several days. It commonly occurs in the catatonic form of schizophrenia, and occasionally in hysteria (q.v.); *see* MENTAL DISORDERS. The patient may assume the attitude of attention, with hand and forefinger raised, or may raise his arm as if to protect himself. In all instances the facial expression comports with the gesture, and the whole body remains rigid till the arm falls slowly by gravity and relaxation. Although circulation, respiration, digestion, and similar organic functions continue, they may be so reduced as to be almost imperceptible. In such cases catalepsy may resemble death, but ordinary tests are sufficient to distinguish it, even though sensibility to pain or heat may be lost. Close scrutiny is necessary to detect simulated cases of catalepsy, because even in genuine cases patients may respond to suggestion.

**CATALINA.** *See* SANTA CATALINA.

**CATALONIA** (Sp. *Cataluña*), region of N.E. Spain, comprising the provinces of Tarragona, Lérida, Barcelona (qq.v.), and Gerona. Having the shape of an inverted triangle, it is bounded on the N. by the Pyrenees Mts., on the w. by the region of Aragón, and on the E. by the Mediterranean Sea. Catalonia is bisected by the Sierra Llena mountain range, which extends from the s.w. to the N.E. Most of the territory is wooded and contains few meadows and little pasture land. Among the principal rivers are the Ebro, the Llobregat, and the Ter, which drain into the

The village of Salardu in the mountainous province of Lérida in Catalonia.    Spanish National Tourist Office

Mediterranean. The principal cities include the ports of Tarragona and Barcelona.

Corn, wheat, rye, flax, and licorice are cultivated; pigs, goats, and sheep are raised; and almonds, chestnuts, walnuts, figs, oranges, and grapes are grown in Catalonia. Among the principal industries are fishing, wine making, the manufacture of cotton textiles, and potash mining.

Catalonia was an early possession of the Romans, who lost it to the Goths and Alans (qq.v.) about 470 B.C. The Moors (q.v.) conquered the region in 712 A.D., but were expelled seventy-six years later by Spaniards allied with Charlemagne (q.v.), King of the Franks. Frankish counts subsequently ruled Catalonia and constituted it an independent domain. In 1137 it was united with the kingdom of Aragón, and later was included in the kingdom of Spain. The French held it as a possession from 1640 to 1659, from 1694 to 1697, and again from 1808 to 1813.

French influence in Catalonia contributed to the development of a distinct Catalan culture. In the 19th century, a movement for cultural and governmental autonomy developed in Catalonia. Following the overthrow of King Alfonso XIII (q.v.) in the Spanish revolution of 1930–31, Catalonia, in 1932, acquired the right to have its own president and parliament, within the framework of the Spanish republic. In the Spanish Civil War (1936–39), Catalonia supported the

*Cloisters of the Cathedral Museum in Barcelona, one of the provinces in Catalonia.* Air France

Republican cause against the counterrevolution led by General Francisco Franco (q.v.). Franco ended the autonomy of Catalonia after his victory in 1939.

Area, 19,852 sq.mi.; pop. (1970) 5,122,567.

*See* CATALAN LANGUAGE AND LITERATURE; SPAIN: *History.*

**CATALPA,** name of a genus of trees of the family Bignoniaceae. *Catalpa bignonioides,* native to the s. United States, is cultivated there and in cities of the N. States as an ornamental shade tree, growing to 40 ft. tall. It has silver-gray bark, widely spread but few branches, and large, pale green, heart-shaped leaves. The flowers are white, tinged and dotted with violet or purple. They are succeeded by long, beanlike pods, called Indian beans, that sometimes hang on the limbs all winter. The seeds are winged; the wings cut into a fringe. The wood is light and fine and useful in cabinetwork. A second species, *C. speciosa*, the catawba tree, is a larger and more hardy tree, indigenous from Indiana to Tennessee, and west through Arkansas and Missouri. It is readily distinguished from the former species by thicker bark, and in that the flowers are inconspicuously tinged or spotted. In rich lowlands this latter tree grows quickly, reaching a height of 60 ft. It has been successfully planted in Kansas and Oklahoma for its timber, the wood being valuable for railroad ties and posts. Other species are native to Japan and China.

**CATALYSIS,** alteration of the speed of a chemical reaction through the presence of an additional substance, known as a catalyst, which is chemically unchanged by the reaction. A catalyst in a solution with, or in the same phase as the reactants is called a homogeneous catalyst. An example is sulfuric acid, which promotes the formation of esters (q.v.) in solutions of sulfuric acid, alcohol, and an organic acid. A catalyst that is in a separate phase is said to be a heterogeneous or contact catalyst. An example is solid manganese dioxide, which promotes decomposition of molten potassium chlorate. Sometimes a substance that does not have catalytic ability by itself increases or promotes the effectiveness of a catalyst. A substance that acts in this way is called a promoter. Thus, when alumina, which by itself is ineffective, is added to finely divided iron, it increases the ability of the iron to bring about the formation of ammonia in a gas composed of nitrogen and hydrogen.

Materials that reduce the effectiveness of a catalyst are referred to as poisons. Arsenic compounds reduce the ability of finely divided platinum to catalyze formation of sulfur trioxide in a gas containing oxygen and sulfur dioxide. Negative catalysts or inhibitors act by "poisoning" positive catalysts or sometimes by preventing chain reactions. Thus acetanilide inhibits decomposition of hydrogen peroxide. Enzymes (q.v.) are a class of naturally occurring catalysts that catalyze biochemical reactions essential to life.

**CATAMARAN,** name applied to any craft having twin hulls. Originally it denoted a form of sailing and paddling raft employed on the coasts of India. In a catamaran two similar or identical hulls are joined parallel to each other at some distance apart by beams or a platform. Such craft were rather highly developed by the native peoples of the Hawaiian, Marquesas, and

*Southern catalpa,* Catalpa bignonioides
U.S. Forest Service

Tuamotu islands, and Tahiti. Some of these double-hull craft had hulls of equal length and others had hulls of unequal length.

The double hull probably was employed occasionally in ancient and medieval Europe to transport cargoes too heavy for the capacity of a single small hull. At least four sailing double-hull craft were built in England during the reign of Charles II (q.v.), King of England. A few double-hull gunboats were built in England at the end of the 18th century, and during the next century many double-hull pleasure craft, gunboats, and steamers were constructed and tested. The catamaran design was employed also in the early American animal-treadmill-propelled ferryboats prior to the application of steam propulsion to ferries. The first United States Navy steam-propelled man-of-war, the U.S.S. *Demologos,* which was designed by the American inventor Robert Fulton (q.v.), appears to have been a double-hull vessel. In both the U.S. and Europe during the 19th century experiments were made with double-hull or catamaran steamers up to 300 ft. in length. Power catamarans were found useful as ferries, dumping scows, research vessels, river snag boats, and for salvage work.

After 1860 numerous experiments were made

*A three-bowed catamaran, built for Johns Hopkins University as an oceanographic research vessel.* UPI

with sailing catamarans in the U.S. and in Europe, especially in France. In 1876 the American marine architect Nathanael Greene Herreshoff (1848–1938), of Bristol, R.I., built and patented a sailing catamaran in which the hulls could pitch independently of one another by use of ball-and-socket joints at the ends of the joining beams and by other means. This type of catamaran proved very fast under certain conditions, and Herreshoff built a number of them. One of the boats is said to have reached a speed of 18 knots running with wind astern (*see* SAILING). A copy of the original boat with some modifications reached a speed of 19.8 knots in 1933. Neither the Herreshoff craft nor later versions of the type were allowed to compete in conventional yacht racing.

In recent years the sailing catamaran again has become popular. Attempts to improve upon the Herreshoff design have produced some very fast boats, some of which can plane, or skim on top of the water, running free. In general, modern catamarans have returned to the original rigid platform connection of the hulls. A variation of the catamaran produced in Canada in 1898 was a combination racing scow and catamaran in which the bilges were nearly cigar-shaped below the water line and were joined by a platform above the water line; the general appearance was that of a racing scow with a tunnel running the length of the bottom along the

center of the hull longitudinally. This boat was very successful, but was not further developed.

The advantage of the catamaran is that great stability can be combined with lightness and low water resistance. These characteristics have prompted the U.S. Navy to construct large catamaran ships as submarine rescue vessels. In general, all catamarans require large turning circles for their size. The sailing catamaran is, therefore, often slow in tacking. Although it is very fast on some points of sailing, usually the sailing catamaran does not show the all-around speed of the racing scow. Structurally, large catamarans of the rigid-platform type are subject to very great strains in rough water, and some of the craft have broken up in heavy seas. The planing catamaran has been developed to a limited degree recently in both power and sailing forms. The planing type requires rather large power to be effective; the sailing catamaran, in particular, requires a large sail area to obtain the speed inherent in the planing type.

In recent years a triple-hull craft, called a trimaran (q.v.), was developed. H.I.C.

**CATANIA,** city in Italy, and capital of Catania Province, on the island of Sicily, at the base of Mt. Etna (q.v.), an active volcano. It is a major seaport and a commercial and manufacturing center. Refined sugar and sulfur are the chief exports. The city has flour mills, sugar refineries, sulfur refineries, and asphalt factories. Catania contains numerous architectural remains of ancient times, including the ruins of Greek and Roman theaters and Roman aqueducts and baths. Among the notable buildings of the city are a cathedral, built in the 12th century and rebuilt in the 18th century; Ursino Castle, originally built in the 13th century and later restored; and the University of Catania (1443), the first university founded in Sicily.

Catania was founded as a Greek colony in the 8th century B.C. and captured by the Romans in 263 B.C., during the First Punic War (*see* PUNIC WARS). In 1169 it was plundered by the Normans. It has suffered many earthquakes and volcanic eruptions, and was severely damaged by bombing in World War II. Pop. (1971) 401,670.

**CATANZARO,** city in Italy, and capital of Catanzaro Province, about 4 mi. from the Gulf of Squillace, an arm of the Ionian Sea, and about 300 miles S.E. of Rome. The city is an important rail junction and a center of trade in wheat, oil, and wine. It was famous in the 17th century for the silks, velvet, and damask it produced. Pop. (1971) 86,070.

**CATAPULT,** any of various engines of war used in ancient and medieval times to discharge javelins, darts, rocks, and other missiles. The larger kind were mounted on a strong wooden platform; the trigger or projector of a gigantic crossbow was drawn back by ropes and held by a catch. Another type of catapult employed the principle of torsion to hurl heavy stones or objects over walls and across moats, cords being twisted by winches to pull back the propelling mechanism. Smaller hand-carried catapults were also used. *See* FORTIFICATIONS AND SIEGE-CRAFT.

In modern naval warfare, airplanes are catapulted from the decks of aircraft carriers, along a runner or track. The plane is propelled off the runner at flying speed by means of an explosive charge, by hydraulic pressure, or by steam pressure.

**CATARACT,** in medicine, opaque condition of the lens of the eye or of its capsule. Its position behind the pupil readily distinguishes it from opacities of the cornea. Cataract is called spontaneous when independent of other diseases of the eye, and complicated when the reverse is true. The opacity of the capsule of the lens or of the lens itself, following operations for cataract, is known as secondary cataract. Cataract may affect the lens alone (lenticular), or the front or back of the capsule of the lens (capsular), or both lens and capsule (capsuloenticular cataract). A cataract is partial when limited to a portion of the lens; complete when involving the whole; stationary if it remains partial; progressive if it tends to include the entire lens. Cataracts may also be characterized as senile, congenital, juvenile, or traumatic.

Cataract is painless and unaccompanied by inflammation. Although it causes blindness simply by obstructing passage of light, even in complete cataract the patient can distinguish light from darkness.

Traumatic cataract results from a perforating wound of the capsule of the lens. The entire lens becomes opaque, and a portion usually remains so; but at times, unless inflammation of other portions follows, the cloudiness entirely disappears. Congenital cataract is due to imperfect development or to inflammation. Juvenile cataract may be hereditary. The lens is soft and white in both congenital and juvenile cataracts. Both are treated by "needling", an operation in which a needlelike knife is used to cut and break up the lens in several successive operations. The injured lens is then absorbed by the body.

Senile cataract, the most important form, usually occurs in persons over fifty and generally involves both eyes. Its period of development may be a few months or many years. Beginning in the form of dark streaks extending from the periphery toward the center of the lens, or as spots in any portion, it eventually makes the entire lens opaque. As the fluid of the lens is absorbed, it becomes easily separated from its capsule and is considered mature, or "ripe" for operation. Later, if not extracted, the lens undergoes degenerative changes, or liquefies, and the capsule becomes thickened and opaque, making results of operation less satisfactory. The only method of relieving senile cataract is extraction of the lens. After removal of the cataract special glasses must be worn to compensate for the loss of the lens.

**CATASETUM,** genus of about forty species of terrestrial American plants of the Orchid family (Orchidaceae), natives of the Tropics. Male and female flowers, which are yellow, brown, or red, are borne on separate plants and are so different in appearance that the plants have often been mistaken for separate species. The anthers eject the ripe pollen with surprising force. For this reason the plants are often called jumping orchids. These orchids differ from most terrestrial orchids in requiring little water. They are cultivated by florists and other professional growers.

**CATASTROPHISM.** *See* GEOLOGY: *History.*

**CATBIRD,** common name for an American songbird, *Dumetella carolinensis,* of the Mockingbird family (Mimidae). The catbird is about 10 in. long and is slate gray except for a black crown and tail and a chestnut-colored region under the tail. The name refers to the mewing call of the bird, but like its relatives, the catbird can engage in ornate song and mimicry of other birds, so that it is often called the gray mockingbird. Ranging as far north as southern Canada in the summer, the catbird winters in the Gulf States and in Mexico.

**CATCHFLY,** common name for any one of several plants having a viscid fluid to which insects adhere on the stems, especially plants belonging to the genera *Lychnis* and *Silene* of the Pink family (Caryophyllaceae). The stem and calyx exude a viscid secretion that holds fast small insects that alight on it. The pollen is thus preserved for the bees or other flying insects by which cross-fertilization is effected. The alpine catchfly, *Silene alpestris,* is an ornamental perennial species from the Austrian Alps, with tufted forked stems about 6 in. high, mostly radical leaves, and loose clusters of white flowers. The German catchfly, *Lychnis viscaria,* is a perennial herb with red or purple flowers and long, tapering leaves.

A domestic short-haired cat.　　　　A.F.P. from Pictorial

**CAT, DOMESTIC,** small, carnivorous animal, *Felis catus,* belonging to the family Felidae (q.v.), popular as a household pet, and valuable for killing mice and rats. Like other members of the family, the domestic cat has retractile claws, a keen sense of hearing, remarkable night vision, and a compact, muscular, and highly supple body. More than thirty breeds of *F. catus* exist, with no subspecies. The breeds are generally classified as long-haired and short-haired.

Cats were domesticated in prehistoric times, but the origin of the species is obscure. Most authorities believe that the short-haired breeds are derived from the Caffre cat, *F. libyca,* a species of African wildcat domesticated by the ancient Egyptians. According to some authorities, the long-haired breeds may have sprung from the Asian wildcat, *F. manul.* Ancestors of the cats common in the United States were imported from foreign countries.

The cat figured significantly in the civilizations of ancient India, Egypt, Syria, and China; it was deified by the Egyptians as the goddess Bast. Priestly decrees protected the animal against harm, and on death it was embalmed and entombed in elaborate mummy cases, along with mummified mice intended as food for its journey to the kingdom of the dead. *See* Bubastis. The exalted status of the cat probably arose from its value as a ratter and mouser in the granaries of Egypt. In modern times many countries have afforded legal protection to cats in recognition of their role in rodent control.

As a household pet the cat is second in popularity only to the dog. Affectionate but reserved, the cat is more independent than the dog and possesses a high order of intelligence. It has an excellent memory and exhibits considerable aptitude for establishing associations and for learning by observation and experience. Its homing instinct is proverbial, as is its cleanliness. The lifespan of the cat is about fifteen years, although some have been known to live for over twenty years. The gestation period is about sixty-three days, and the litter averages from two to five offspring. The cat population of the U.S. is about 21,000,000, of which about 10,500,000 belong to homes.

Cats are divided into two main groups, the short-haired and the long-haired. All but a very small percentage of domestic cats are in the short-haired group, including the familiar tabbies, so called because the pattern of their coats resembles watered, or tabby, silk. A tabby has a ground color of brown, gray, silver, or blue, and the stripes, swirls, or blotches are darker, usually black. The domestic short-haired cats include also the black cat, which is associated superstitiously with bad luck; the gentle Russian blue or Maltese cat; the orange or red and cream cats, sometimes called marmalade cats; the rarer white cats, gray cats, and tortoise-

224

**Cat. Plate 1.** *Siamese cats are prized for their beauty, their intelligence, and their practicality as house pets.*

**Cat. Plate 2.** *Among the many breeds of domestic cats, the Persian is one of the most popular.*

shell cats; and various combinations of the above.

The Siamese cat, often called the Royal Siamese, is the common cat of Thailand (formerly Siam). It is not large, but is firmly muscled. The Siamese has blue eyes, sometimes crossed, and, when mature, a coat of creamy beige running to either dark brown or blue-gray at the feet, muzzle, ears, and tail. Siamese cats are born white. Their hind legs are longer than their front legs, giving the Siamese somewhat the look and gait of a panther. First brought to America about 1895, Siamese cats became a popular breed because of their appearance, disposition, intelligence, and ability as mousers.

The Manx cat was probably indigenous to the Isle of Man. It is believed that the progenitor of the breed swam ashore in 1588 from a sinking ship of the Spanish Armada. This hypothesis is based on an assumption that Spanish sailors may have adopted some of the bobtail cats which are common in parts of the Soviet Union, China, Japan, and the Malay Peninsula. The true Manx has no tail at all and is found in a number of colors. Their long hind legs give Manx cats great speed, and they are proficient ratters, fishers, and snake hunters. Lively, muscular, and fearless, the Manx cat is not friendly to strange humans and will repel strange dogs.

Other foreign short-haired cats are the Abyssinian cat, believed to be a descendant of the sacred cat of ancient Egypt, and the Burmese cat, similar to, but darker than, the Siamese cat.

The Persian cat has a luxurious coat of long hair and a shorter, wider body than the short-haired cats. These cats have a magnificent ruff around the neck and a deep frill between the forelegs. The nose is short, and the face broad. The breed originated in central Asia. Persian cats are found in many colors: silver, red, black, white, and with mixtures in tabby and tortoise patterns.

The Angora cat has a coat like that of the Persian. Its distinguishing characteristics are a tail with the longest hairs at the base and a nose that is longer than that of the usually snub-nosed Persian. The Angora is named for Angora (now Ankara), Turkey.

**Diseases in Cats.** Diseases contracted by cats include pneumonia, distemper, rabies (q.v.), or hydrophobia, mange, ringworm, and tapeworm. Pneumonia is characterized by loss of appetite, fever, coughing, and strained breathing. Signs of distemper include runny eyes and nose, vomiting, and fever. Cats may suffer from either of two forms of rabies: furious rabies, marked by extreme excitability, and dumb rabies, charac-terized by extreme sluggishness. Mange can be identified by reddish spots surrounded by broken hairs. Symptoms of tapeworm are vomiting, diarrhea, change in appetite, potbelly, and emaciation.

**CATEAU-CAMBRÉSIS, TREATY OF,** treaty signed in the town of Cateau-Cambrésis (now Le Cateau), France, on April 3, 1559, by Henry II, King of France, and Philip II (qq.v.), King of Spain, terminating a state of war between their countries. By the terms of the treaty, France returned most of the territories in the Low Countries and Italy which it had taken from Spain but retained the bishoprics of Toul, Verdun, and Metz. The treaty reaffirmed control by Spain over the greater part of the Italian Peninsula.

**CATECHISM,** any compendious system of teaching drawn up in the form of question and answer, especially one for religious instruction. The first such manual was compiled by the English scholar Alcuin (q.v.) in the 8th century and was followed in the next hundred years by many others, among them those of Notker Labeo (952?–1022), monk of the Abbey of Saint Gall, in Switzerland, and of the German monk Otfried of Weissenburg (800?–880?) in Alsace. At an early period in the history of the Reformation (q.v.), catechisms became important. After the German religious reformer Martin Luther (q.v.) published his primer of religion, entitled *A Brief Explanation of the Ten Commandments, the Creed, and the Lord's Prayer* (1520), several catechisms were prepared by leading Protestant theologians. Luther's visitation of the Saxon churches in 1528 led to preparation of his Larger and Smaller Catechisms (1529). The Reformed churches also published catechisms. The most noteworthy are the Geneva and Heidelberg catechisms, and those of the German theologian Johannes Oecolampadius (1482–1531), in Basel in 1526, and of the Swiss reformer Heinrich Bullinger (q.v.), in Zürich in 1555. The Geneva Catechisms, Larger and Smaller, were the work of the French Protestant theologian John Calvin (q.v.). The latter was published in French in 1536; the former appeared in French in 1541 or 1542, was translated into various languages, and became an acknowledged standard of the Reformed churches.

The Heidelberg, or Palatinate, Catechism was compiled in Heidelberg by the German theologians Caspar Olevianus (1536–87) and Zacharias Ursinus (1534–83), at the request of the Elector Frederick III (1515–76), of the Palatinate. It was published in 1563 and has been translated into all the languages of Europe. It is the standard of the Dutch and German Reformed churches of America. The Protestant religious doctrines of the Socinians (*see* SOCINUS) are embodied in the greater and smaller Racovian Catechisms (Raków, Poland, 1605). Besides a catechism of 1660, in the form of a conversation between father and son, said to have been written by the English founder of the Society of Friends, George Fox (q.v.), the Quakers have that of the Scottish writer Robert Barclay (1648–90), which appeared in 1673.

In the Roman Catholic Church, the first official catechism, prepared by the Council of Trent (*see* TRENT, COUNCIL OF) and published in 1566, was known as the *Roman Catechism,* or the *Catechism of Pius V.* It was not a textbook, but a compendium of doctrine for the guidance of pastors and teachers. Catechisms for popular use were prepared by the German Jesuit Peter Canisius (q.v.), published 1555–58. In the United States a committee of American bishops of the Third Plenary Council of Baltimore, Md., published the Baltimore Catechism in 1885.

The catechism of the Church of England in the smaller form, published in the *Book of Common Prayer* (q.v.) is in two parts: the first contains and explains the Baptismal Covenant, the Creed, the Ten Commandments (*see* DECALOGUE), and the Lord's Prayer; and the second explains the two sacraments, baptism, and the Lord's Supper (qq.v.). It was originally published in the reign of King Edward VI (q.v.), was condemned as heretical in the reign of Queen Mary I (q.v.), and underwent several modifications from 1549 to 1661. This first part of the church catechism was formerly spoken of as the Shorter Catechism. At the Hampton Court Conference (1604), it was considered too short. Accordingly, at the suggestion of King James I (q.v.), that explanation of the two sacraments which now forms the second part of the church catechism was added.

The Larger and Shorter Catechisms, which, with the Westminister Confession of Faith, constitute the standards of the Presbyterian churches throughout the countries of the former British Empire and the United States of America, were compiled by the Assembly of Divines at Westminster (1645–52). In July, 1648, the General Assembly of the Church of Scotland sanctioned both the Larger and Shorter Catechisms.

Emphasis on the use of a catechism, particularly its memorization by rote, has diminished in recent years. For further information regarding confessions of faith, *see* CREEDS and the individual entries under the names of various church denominations. *See also* LUTHERANISM; PRESBYTERIANISM.

**CATEGORICAL IMPERATIVE,** term coined by the German philosopher Immanuel Kant (q.v.) to designate what he considered an absolute moral law in which reason was inherent. "So act", he wrote, "that the moral of thy doing shall, at thy will, become universal law". In Kant's view the categorical imperative was the injunction, to be obeyed by the individual as a moral duty, regardless of his impulses, to produce a humanitarian society based on reason, and thus created by the free will of man.

**CATERPILLAR,** larval stage of butterflies and moths, members of the order Lepidoptera (q.v.),

*Resemblance of royal-moth caterpillar to fir tree twig helps conceal it from predators.*   **Walt Disney Productions**

and corresponding in this special order to the grub, maggot, or larva phase in the life history of other insects. The caterpillar develops like any other larva from the segmented egg and differentiating embryo, and undergoes several moltings, or ecdyses. It then begins to develop some of the adult structures, later falling into a quiescent pupa stage. The pupa is usually sheathed in a silken cocoon. It may be fixed or free, suspended by one thread or more to leaf or branch, or hidden underground. See BUTTERFLY; MOTH.

Comparatively few caterpillars reach maturity. Many are destroyed by weather, by hungry birds, reptiles, and other animals, and by insect pests of the families Ichneumonidae, such as the ichneumon fly (q.v.); Tachinariae, such as the tachina fly; and Carabidae, such as the caterpillar hunter (q.v.). The ichneumon flies pierce the caterpillars, and make them receptacles for their eggs and the edible cradles of their larvae.

**CATERPILLAR HUNTER,** common name for a predatory beetle of the genus Calosoma in the family Carabidae. It is a large, brightly colored, nocturnal beetle. Several species prey upon caterworms and earthworms. Calosoma scrutator is a common American species, and C. sycophanta was imported into the United States in large numbers to combat the brown-tail moth (q.v.). See ENTOMOLOGY, ECONOMIC; GROUND BEETLE.

**CATFISH,** common name for a fish of the suborder Siluroidea of the order Ostariophysi, comprising from 25 to 31 families and about 2000 species.

Two families, the Ariidae and the Plotosidae, are marine. All other families inhabit fresh water. Their name is derived from the feelers, or barbels, that extend from each side of the upper jaw and, in some species, from the lower jaw also, suggesting the whiskers of a cat. The dorsal and pectoral fins are often edged with sharp spines, in some cases poisonous, which are used as weapons and which inflict severe wounds. Catfishes are mostly nocturnal scavengers, living near the bottom in shallow waters.

Of the numerous species of North American catfish, which belong to the family Ictaluridae, the bullhead, Ictalurus nebulosus, is a common panfish. Of greatest commercial importance are catfish of the genus Ictalurus in the Mississippi R. valley and Gulf States, some of which weigh up to 150 lb. The species I. furcatus, the blue catfish, or chucklehead, and I. punctatus, the channel cat, the flesh of which is esteemed as equal to that of black bass, form the major part of the catch. Another genus, Ameiurus, abounds in the fresh waters of North America. A Euro-

Common freshwater catfish, the bullhead, Ictalurus nebulosus. UPI

pean species, the Sheatfish or wels, Silurus glanis, of the family Siluridae, reportedly reaches a weight of 650 lb. and a length of almost 13 ft. The blind catfish, Gronias nigrilabris, found in caverns in eastern Pennsylvania, has atrophied eyes, and the electric catfish of the Nile R. and tropical central Africa, Malapterurus electricus, is capable of giving an electric shock; see ELECTRIC FISH. In 1968 the so-called "walking catfish" Clarias batrachus was discovered near Boca Raton in Florida. This species was originally imported from eastern India and Southeast Asia by tropical-fish dealers. Maximum size is 22 in. In "walking" this catfish moves by a slithering motion combined with a thrashing of its tail. In addition, a stout spine in each pectoral fin is dug into the ground to help balance and propel it. In order to breathe air the rear part of each gill has evolved into a form of lung.     K.A.C.

**CATGUT** or **GUT,** tough, membranous cord made from the intestines of certain animals and manufactured chiefly in France and Italy. It is used primarily for surgical sutures, strings of musical instruments, and tennis racket strings. Because the intestines of hogs, horses, and sheep are used for the cord, the name catgut is a misnomer of uncertain origin. The intestines are first cleaned, scraped, and cured, and are then dried and polished before being woven into cords.

**CATHARI** or **CATHARISTS** (Gr. katharos, "pure"), name assumed by many widely diffused heretical Christian sects of the Middle Ages. The Cathari were characterized by a rigid asceticism and by a dualistic theology based on the belief that the universe was comprised of two conflicting worlds, the spiritual world created by God and the material world created by Satan; see DUALISM. Their views were based on the religious doctrine of Manichaeism (q.v.). Under the general name of Cathari were included the Novatians, a sect originating in the 3rd century that advocated the denial of church membership to "fallen" Christians. The Paulicians (q.v.) were a kindred sect; they had been transported to the region of Thrace (q.v.) in southeastern Europe in the 9th century and were known there as Bogomili (*see* BOGOMILS). In the second half of the 12th century the Cathari were in great strength in Bulgaria, Albania, and Slavonia. They divided into two branches, distinguished as the Albanenses (absolute dualists) and the Garatenses (moderate dualists). In Italy the heresy appeared in the 11th and 12th centuries. The Milanese adherents of the heresy were known as Patarini (or Patarines), from Pataria, a street in Milan frequented by rag-gatherers. The Patarine movement assumed some importance in the 11th century as a reform movement, emphasizing action by lay people against a corrupt clergy. The Cathari reached their greatest numbers in southern France; here they were called Albigenses (q.v.) or Poblicants, the latter term being a corruption of Paulicians, with whom they were confused. By the late 14th century, however, the Cathari had all but disappeared. Their decline was caused, for the most part, by a rise in the popularity of mendicant orders (*see* MENDICANT FRIARS). The only extant Catharist writing is a short ritual in the Romance language of the 13th-century troubadours.

**CATHEDRAL**   (Gr. *kathedra*, "seat"), principal church of a diocese (q.v.), the administrative territory over which the bishop (q.v.) has authority, and containing the cathedra or throne of the bishop. Originally, the residence of the bishop was a cathedral city, and a formal decision of the bishop was an ex cathedra utterance. All churches within the diocese except for the one episcopal church, the cathedral, were called parish churches. The power of the bishop over monastic churches varied greatly in different countries and at different times; *see* MONASTICISM. Cathedrals were important in the 4th and 5th centuries, but later, from the 7th to the 11th century, monks occupied the cathedral thrones, and episcopal churches could not vie with monasteries. Then a hybrid class of monastic cathedrals arose.

With the rise of the semiautonomous town or commune (q.v.), often supported by kings and emperors, the cathedral became both a symbol of civic autonomy and the center of religious life. Construction of cathedrals was begun in the 10th and 11th centuries in the Rhenish cities, such as Speyer, Worms, and Mainz (qq.v.), and spread to towns throughout Europe, including England. In the 13th century many of the great Gothic cathedrals were built with voluntary contributions from all classes; *see* GOTHIC ART. The cathedral served, except in England, also as a town hall for political meetings and as the hall in which the mystery play (q.v.) was presented. In England, with no large cities, many of the great monastic churches were at the same time cathedrals, and the abbot also served as the bishop of the diocese. These included the regular or monastic cathedrals in Canterbury, Durham, and Winchester, and the secular cathedrals in Salisbury and Wells.

No particular style or plan was used to make the cathedral distinct from other churches; however, in continental Europe the cathedral remained the center of civic life. In Italy the cathedral, the bell tower, and the baptistery (qq.v.) frequently formed a group of three in the great square, and to them the episcopal palace was often added. Sometimes, as in France and England, dependent buildings, such as cloister (q.v.), chapter house, and refectory, were attached to the cathedral in monastic fashion, but usually the cathedral stood clear, on the most conspicuous side of the city. In England the entire group, usually with an open space in front, was sometimes enclosed within a wall with several gates. Rome occupied a unique position. Saint John Lateran, a basilica (q.v.), was more than the Cathedral of Rome; it was the mother of all Roman Catholic churches, being the seat of the pope, but it was not called a cathedral. Saint Peter's Basilica (q.v.) succeeded it in the

*Burgos Cathedral, Spain*                    Embassy of Spain

**Cathedral. Plate 1.** *Interior of the Gothic Cathedral of Notre Dame, in Reims, France, built in the 13th century.*

The 11th-century Gothic Cathedral of Basel, Switzerland, known as the Münster, was rebuilt in the 14th century. It is the burial place of the 16th-century Dutch scholar and humanist Desiderius Erasmus.          Swiss National Tourist Office

*Cathedral. Plate 2.*

Below. The Romanesque cathedral in Pisa, Italy. Built of marble, the cathedral was begun in 1063, but construction continued for several centuries.

15th century. The other great basilicas of Rome, Saint Paul's Outside the Walls, Santa Maria Maggiore, and Santa Croce in Gerusalemme, also had a rank superior to that of the ordinary cathedral.

Architecturally, the most important cathedrals are in the following cities (see also separate articles on the individual cities):

ITALY. Bari, Bologna, Como, Ferrara, Florence, Lucca, Milan, Modena, Orvieto, Piacenza, Pisa, Rome, Siena, and Venice.

GERMANY. Bonn, Cologne, Freiburg, Mainz, Regensburg, Speyer, and Worms.

SWITZERLAND. Basel and Zürich.

AUSTRIA. Vienna.

FRANCE. Amiens, Beauvais, Bourges, Chartres, Laon, Le Puy, Lyon, Noyon, Orléans, Paris, Poitiers, Reims, Rouen, Strasbourg, Tours, and Troyes.

ENGLAND. Canterbury, Coventry, Durham, Ely, Exeter, Lichfield, Lincoln, London, Salisbury, Truro, Wells, Westminster, Winchester, Worcester, and York.

SPAIN. Barcelona, Burgos, Granada, León, Salamanca, Seville, and Toledo.

BELGIUM. Antwerp, Brussels, Ghent, Louvain, Mechelen, Tournai, and Ypres.

At present, all dioceses of the Roman Catholic Church (q.v.) in the United States and many dioceses of the Protestant Episcopal Church (q.v.) have cathedrals. Two outstanding American examples are the Roman Catholic Saint Patrick's Cathedral and the Protestant Episcopal Cathedral of Saint John the Divine (qq.v.), both in New York City.

**CATHER, Willa Sibert** (1873–1947), American novelist, born near Winchester, Va. She was taken to Nebraska as a child and was educated

*Willa Cather (extreme left) in 1933 on the occasion of receiving the first Prix Femina Americana for her novel Shadows on the Rock. Left to right: Edna St. Vincent Millay, poet; Mrs. Dwight Morrow, author; Mme. Jeanne Dauban of France.* UPI

at the University of Nebraska. She worked first as a journalist, teacher, and magazine editor before devoting herself to writing. Her early novels *O Pioneers!* (1913), *The Song of the Lark* (1915), and *My Ántonia* (1918) depict the life of the immigrant farmer on the Midwestern prairies in a simple, straightforward manner. The characters in these novels are notable for their calm resolution and quiet dignity. Miss Cather also used the prairie setting in her next three novels, *One of Ours* (1922), *A Lost Lady* (1923), and *The Professor's House* (1925). In these works, most notably in *One of Ours,* which won a Pulitzer Prize in 1923, she depicts the conflict between the encroaching urban life and the rural Midwestern environment. In *Death Comes for the Archbishop* (1927) she deals with the missionary experiences of a Roman Catholic bishop among the Indians of New Mexico, and in *Shadows on the Rock* (1931) she describes French Catholic life in 17th-century Québec.

Characterized by restraint, lucidity, and economy of construction, the writing of Willa Cather amply validates her belief that fiction should serve as a vehicle for "the full play of emotions".

**CATHERINE,** name of two empresses of Russia. **Catherine I,** original name MARFA SKAVRONSKAYA (1682?–1727), Empress (1724–27), wife of Emperor Peter I (q.v.), known as Peter the Great, born in Jakobstadt, Livonia (now Jekabpils, U.S.S.R.). Of peasant parentage, she was orphaned as a child and raised by a pastor in Marienburg (now Malbork, Poland). At the capture of Marienburg by the Russians in 1702 Catherine was taken prisoner by the Russian commander, who kept her with him when the other captives were sent to Moscow. A few months later she became the mistress of the Russian statesman Prince Aleksandr Danilovich Menshikov (1627–1729), a companion of Czar Peter I. Attracting the attention of Peter, she soon became his mistress and most influential adviser and confidante. In 1712 Peter married Catherine after setting aside his first wife. By a ukase, or imperial order, of 1721 the emperor proclaimed his right to designate his successor. In 1724 Catherine was crowned empress, and, after the death of Peter in 1725 she became ruler of Russia. Her accession was established with the aid of Menshikov; the claims of Peter, later Peter II (*see under* PETER: *Russia*), a grandson of Peter I, were set aside. During her brief reign Catherine was counseled by Menshikov. She had eight children by Peter, only two of whom, Anna and Elizabeth Petrovna (q.v.), survived infancy.

**Catherine II,** known as CATHERINE THE GREAT (1729–96), Empress (1762–96), wife of

*Catherine II, Empress of Russia*

Emperor Peter III (*see under* PETER: *Russia*), born in Stettin, Prussia (now Szczecin, Poland). She was originally named Sophia Augusta Frederica of Anhalt-Zerbst, and was the daughter of a minor German prince. She was chosen by the Russian empress Elizabeth Petrovna (q.v.) to be the wife of Elizabeth's nephew, Grand Duke Peter. Sophia was rebaptized in the Russian Orthodox Church under the name of Catherine and was married in 1745. Catherine, a German by birth, became a Russian of the Russians and carefully cultivated her political power. Peter openly maintained a mistress, and Catherine was equally adulterous.

When Peter became emperor as Peter III in January, 1762, he threatened to divorce Catherine, to declare their son Paul (1754–1801) illegitimate, and to marry his mistress. In June, 1762, Catherine, assisted by a group of conspirators, seized power and was declared empress of Russia. Within a month Peter died, probably assassinated by the Russian count Aleksei Grigorievich Orlov (1737–1809), a lover of Catherine.

The gross immorality of her private life was as notable as her administrative energy. The rule of all the sovereigns was notorious for the influence possessed by favorites, but Catherine engaged in wholesale methods that are almost unique in history. She had a succession of recognized lovers, including the brother of Aleksei Orlov, the

Russian general Count Grigori Grigorievich Orlov (1734–83) and the Russian statesman Grigori Aleksandrovich Potëmkin (q.v.).

**The Sovereign.** Catherine gave close personal attention to governmental affairs. In regard to foreign affairs, she was her own minister. Her policy simply was to expand Russian territory, and in this she succeeded. She led Russia into war with the Ottoman Turks in 1768, from which the Russians acquired part of the Crimea (q.v.); *see* RUSSO–TURKISH WARS. She had formed an alliance with Prussia and Austria that led to the three partitions of Poland in 1772, 1793, and 1795; *see* AUSTRIA: *History*; POLAND: *History*; PRUSSIA: *History*. Russia benefited the most from the partitions, gaining a broad corridor extending from the Baltic Sea nearly to the Black Sea. A second war with the Turks in 1787 led to Russian acquisition of the land between the Bug, or Western Bug, and the Dniester rivers. By the end of her reign, Catherine had given Russia control of the Black Sea, access to the Mediterranean Sea, and ports on the Baltic Sea. *See* RUSSIA: *History*.

In internal affairs Catherine strove to reform and Westernize Russia. She convoked representatives of all the provinces in Moscow to reform the government, but the commission failed to accomplish any reforms. She encouraged immigration; introduced inoculation for smallpox and other sanitary measures; established elementary schools in all the cities and many small towns; founded institutions of learning, military and naval schools, and hospitals; built canals and fortresses; and sent Russian scholars and artists abroad to study. By liberal expenditure and patronage of the arts, Catherine made her court one of the most brilliant in Europe. She turned to French thinkers as her source of inspiration and was flattered by their applause. Among those who frequented her court were the French philosopher Voltaire and the French encyclopedist Denis Diderot (qq.v.). The German-born critic Baron Melchior von Grimm (q.v.) was her literary agent.

During the early part of her reign Catherine frustrated many plots against her authority and suppressed the formidable peasant revolt in southeastern Russia. Toward the end of her reign her extravagance and the corruption of her court brought her into discredit in Russia as well as among the sovereigns of Europe. The outbreak of the French Revolution checked her ardor for reform according to French models, and she finally prohibited the publication of French works in Russia. She was succeeded by her son Paul I (r. 1796–1801).

**CATHERINE DE MÉDICIS** (1519–89), Queen of France (1547–59), born in Florence, Italy, the daughter of the ruler of Florence, Lorenzo de' Medici, known as Lorenzo the Magnificent (*see under* MEDICI), and mother of the last three Valois kings of France; *see* VALOIS (family). In 1533 she married the Duc d'Orléans, who became king of France in 1547 as Henry II (q.v.). She had little power during the reign of her husgand and that of her first son Francis II (q.v.), but with the death of Francis in 1560 the government fell entirely into her hands. She ruled as regent for her second son Charles IX (q.v.) until he reached his majority in 1563, and she continued to dominate him for the duration of his reign.

**Political Role.** In her determination to preserve royal power at any cost, Catherine devoted her energies to maintaining a balance between the Protestant group known as the Huguenots (q.v.), led by the French military leader Gaspard de Coligny (q.v.), and the Roman Catholics, led by the powerful house of Guise (q.v.). During the religious civil wars which began in 1562 Catherine, a Roman Catholic, usually supported the Catholics; sometimes, however, political expediency led her to switch her support to the Huguenots. Her political manipulations also affected the personal affairs of her family. In 1560 Catherine arranged for her daughter Elizabeth of Valois (1545–68) to become the third wife of the powerful

*Catherine de Médicis, in an 18th-century French copper engraving.*                    Granger Collection

Roman Catholic king of Spain, Philip II (q.v.). In 1572 Catherine found it propitious to marry another daughter, Margaret of Valois (q.v.), to the Protestant king Henry of Navarre, who later became Henry IV (q.v.), King of France. Later in 1572 she found the growing Huguenot influence over her son Charles, the French king, frightening; and accordingly she supported both the attempted assassination of the Protestant leader Coligny and the death of 50,000 Huguenots in the Saint Bartholomew's Day Massacre (*see* SAINT BARTHOLOMEW'S DAY, MASSACRE OF). After the death of Charles in 1574 and the accession to the throne of her third son as Henry III (q.v.), Catherine's power declined.

**Art Patron.** Apart from her political role, Catherine was a patron of the arts. Her interest in architecture was demonstrated in the building of a new wing of the Louvre Museum, in initiating construction of the Tuileries (qq.v.) gardens, and in building the château of Monceau. Her personal library containing rare manuscripts was renowned in Renaissance France.

**CATHERINE OF ALEXANDRIA, Saint** (d. 307?), Christian virgin and martyr, of whom little is known. According to Roman Catholic tradition, although but a girl, she was extremely learned. In Alexandria she rebuked the Roman emperor Galerius Valerius Maximinus (*see under* MAXIMINUS) by converting the philosophers he had ordered to debate with her. Maximinus condemned her to be broken on the wheel, but, by a miracle, the wheel collapsed. She was subsequently beheaded. Her traditional feast day, Nov. 25, is no longer included in the Roman Catholic calendar; *see* SAINT.

**CATHERINE OF ARAGÓN** (1485–1536), Queen Consort of England (1509–33), the first wife of King Henry VIII (q.v.) and the daughter of Ferdinand V and Isabella I (qq.v.), King and Queen of Aragón and Castille. Catherine was born in Alcalá de Henares (now in Spain). She occupies a prominent place in history because the question of her marriage to Henry was a factor in the Reformation (q.v.) in England. Henry VII (q.v.), King of England, hoped to form a binding alliance with Spain when he negotiated the marriage of Catherine and his son Arthur, Prince of Wales (1486–1502). She went to England in 1501 and was married in November, but Arthur died in April, 1502. A few months later Henry VII arranged a second marriage for Catherine with his second son Henry, then twelve years old. A papal dispensation enabling Henry to marry the widow of his brother was obtained in 1503. Henry succeeded to the throne in April, 1509, and in June he married Catherine.

Although the marriage was, on the whole, fairly successful, the pro-Spanish sympathies of Catherine brought some difficulties during the periods of French alliance. Catherine bore Henry six children, only one of whom, a daughter, later queen as Mary I (q.v.) survived.

In 1527 Henry tried to annul his marriage to Catherine so that he could marry Anne Boleyn (q.v.), who he hoped would give him an heir to the throne. The pope refused to make a decision on the proposed annulment, and in 1533 Henry was married to Anne by the Archbishop of Canterbury. In 1534 the pope finally declared that the first marriage was valid, thus bringing about the alienation of Henry VIII from the Roman Catholic Church. Catherine did not quit the kingdom, but was thereafter closely guarded. During this time Catherine displayed heroic courage and steadfastly refused to sign away her rights and those of Mary.

**CATHERINE OF SIENA, Saint** (1347–80), Italian mystic and patron saint of Italy. Born in Siena, as a child she experienced mystical visions that later led her to join the order of the Dominicans (q.v.). She became quite influential. In 1377 she persuaded Pope Gregory XI (1331–78) to leave Avignon and reestablish the papal authority in Rome, and she was also instrumental in gaining support for Pope Urban VI (*see under* URBAN) at the start of the Western Schism; *see* SCHISM, WESTERN. Catherine wrote devotional pieces, letters, and poems. She was canonized in 1461; in 1970 Pope Paul VI (*see under* PAUL) proclaimed her a doctor of the Church. Her feast day is April 29.

**CATHERINE OF VALOIS** (1401–37), Queen Consort of England (1420–22), wife of Henry V (q.v.), King of England, and daughter of Charles VI, King of France (*see under* CHARLES), born in Paris. When she was twelve years old, Henry V renewed the negotiations begun by his father for a marriage with Catherine. Henry demanded a large dowry and the French regions of Aquitaine and Normandy (qq.v.). The proposition was rejected, and in 1415 Henry invaded France and forced compliance with his terms. When he married Catherine in Troyes, France, in June, 1420, he received the provinces claimed, the regency of France during the life of Charles, and the reversion of the sovereignty after the death of Charles. In February, 1421, Catherine was crowned at Westminster Abbey, and in December she bore a son, later King Henry VI (q.v.). After the death of Henry V in 1422, little is known of Catherine except that her union with the Welsh squire Owen Tudor produced four children; *see* TUDOR. One of her sons, Edmund

Tudor, Earl of Richmond (1430?–56), married Margaret Beaufort (q.v.); their son became Henry VII (q.v.), the first Tudor King of England.

**CATHERINE THE GREAT.** *See under* CATHERINE: *Catherine II.*

**CATHODE.** *See* ELECTRONICS: *Diode.*

**CATHODE RAYS,** high-speed electrons emitted by the negative electrode of a vacuum tube when an electric current is passed through it. Cathode rays were first generated by means of the Crookes tube (q.v.), an invention of the British physicist Sir William Crookes (q.v.). While conducting research, the German physicist Wilhelm Konrad Röntgen (q.v.) in 1895 discovered accidentally that cathode rays striking a metal target produce X rays (*see* X RAY). Cathode rays can be deflected and focused by electrical and magnetic fields. These properties are utilized in the electron microscope, in the cathode-ray oscillograph, in the image tube of the television receiver, and in the electrostatic storage tube, sometimes used as a memory device in electronic computers. *See* COMPUTER; ELECTRON; ELECTRONICS.

**CATHODE RAY TUBE.** *See* ELECTRONICS.

**CATHOLIC CHURCH.** The term "catholic" (Gr. *katholikos*, "universal", from *katholou*, "in general") was first used in the letter of Saint Ignatius of Antioch (q.v.) to the Smyrnaeans (about 110 A.D.). The term was later used by Clement of Alexandria (q.v.) in his *Stromata* ("Miscellanies"). The technical use of the word seems to have been established by the beginning of the 3rd century. The formal principle of the Catholic Church was expressed by a French priest and writer, Vincent of Lerins (d. 450?), as follows: "That which has been believed everywhere, always, and by all. This is what is truly and properly catholic". *See* ROMAN CATHOLIC CHURCH.

**CATHOLIC EMANCIPATION ACT,** statute of the British Parliament, passed in 1829, enabling Roman Catholics in Great Britain and Ireland to vote and hold many public offices. The act superseded earlier anti-Catholic laws, some of which dated from the time of Henry VIII (q.v.), King of England. The gradual granting of British liberties to Catholics began in 1778 when Catholics were permitted to buy and inherit land if they swore loyalty to the king. A second relief measure, sponsored by the British statesman William Pitt, known as the younger (*see under* PITT), was passed in 1791. This law granted Catholics the right to serve in the military, practice law, worship, and organize religious schools. Irish Catholics, previously enjoying widespread freedoms, were subjected to the British restrictions when Ireland was united with Great Britain in 1801. Catholic agitation led to the formation of the Roman Catholic Association in 1823 by the Irish statesman Daniel O'Connell (q.v.) and finally to passage of the Roman Catholic Relief Bill, better known as the Catholic Emancipation Act, in 1829. The act, introduced by the British statesman Sir Robert Peel (q.v.) through the efforts of O'Connell, provided that Catholics could be admitted to Parliament. Although certain disabilities still existed, most of them were gradually eliminated by 1926. In 1910 language offensive to Catholics was removed from the British coronation ceremonies.

**CATHOLICS, OLD.** *See* OLD CATHOLICS.

**CATHOLIC UNIVERSITY OF AMERICA, THE,** coeducational institution of higher learning, located in Washington, D.C., and affiliated with the Roman Catholic Church in the United States. The university was chartered by Congress and opened for instruction in 1889. The board of trustees comprises thirty members of whom at least fifteen must be lay, together with some U.S. cardinals in an ex-officio capacity. Among the various divisions of the university are the college of arts and sciences, the schools of education, engineering and architecture, law, music, philosophy, religious studies, social service, nursing, and the graduate school of arts and sciences. The degrees of bachelor, master, and doctor are conferred. Numerous residence and study halls are maintained by various Roman Catholic religious orders for their student members. In 1972 the library housed more than 881,800 bound volumes. In 1972 student enrollment totaled 6654, the faculty numbered 531, and the endowment of the university was about $8,226,000.

**CATILINE,** in full LUCIUS SERGIUS CATILINA (108?–62 B.C.), Roman political leader and conspirator. He was a partisan of the Roman statesman Lucius Cornelius Sulla (q.v.), whom he succeeded as quaestor, or judge, in 77 B.C. Catiline was also praetor, or magistrate, in 68 and governor of the province of Africa in the following year. Shortly thereafter he was falsely accused of misconduct and was prevented from becoming a candidate for consul, or chief magistrate. He hoped to avenge himself and capture power by assassinating the consuls but the plot failed. Catiline was acquitted of the earlier charges, and in 63 he ran for consul against the Roman statesman and orator Marcus Tullius Cicero (q.v.). Cicero became consul and exposed the assassination plot, driving Catiline to open insurrection. Cicero then delivered his famous first oration against Catiline: *Quousque tandem*

*Painting of the buffalo dance of the Mandan Indians by George Catlin (about 1832).*     Smithsonian Institution

*abutere, Catilina, patientia nostra?* ("How long now, Catiline, will you abuse our patience?") After a second oration Catiline and his coconspirators were proclaimed public enemies. He was killed in battle near Pistoia in central Italy.

**CATLIN, George** (1796–1872), American painter and writer, born in Wilkes-Barre, Pa. He studied and practiced law, but abandoned it to study art. Keenly interested in the various types and customs of the American Indian, about 1832 Catlin began a series of travels extending over many years among the Indian tribes of North America and South America. In the course of his travels he painted about 500 Indian portraits and scenes and made hundreds of sketches. He stimulated popular interest in Indian culture by publicly exhibiting his paintings and by presenting groups of Indians to audiences in the United States and Europe. Most of his Indian paintings constitute the Catlin Gallery of the National Museum, Washington, D.C. The American Museum of Natural History in New York City owns about 700 of the sketches.

Catlin also wrote and illustrated several books. They include *Manners, Customs, and Conditions of the North American Indians* (2 vol., 1841), *Catlin's North American Indian Portfolio* (1844), *My Life Among the Indians* (1867), and *Last Rambles Amongst the Indians of the Rocky Mountains and the Andes* (1868).

**CATNIP** *or* **CATMINT,** common names for a hardy perennial herb, *Nepeta cataria*, of the family Labiatae or Mint (q.v.). Native to Europe, it is a common weed in North America. The sharp fragrance of the plant is attractive and exciting to cats, who enjoy eating it.

**CATO,** name of two ancient Roman statesmen.

**Marcus Porcius Cato,** known as CATO THE ELDER *or* CATO THE CENSOR (234–149 B.C.), statesman and writer, born in Tusculum (now Frascati, Italy). Born on a farm, he remained interested in agriculture and the simple life typical of Roman landholders of the early Roman Republic. He distinguished himself at an early age as an enemy of Greek culture, which he believed enervated the Romans. Cato served as a quaestor in 204 B.C., as aedile in 199, as praetor in 198, and as consul in 195. He also served in the army, winning the honor of a triumph for his victories in Spain. His chief renown came from his activities as censor in 184. He campaigned against the immorality and luxury of Roman life, and used the privileges of his office to weed out of the Senate all whom he considered unworthy, either because of their extravagance or of their departure from Cato's conception of virtuous Roman character. In 157 he was sent to Africa on a mission of arbitration between the Carthaginians and the Numidian tribesmen. During this visit he became obsessed with the idea that the city of Carthage (q.v.), which repelled him because of the luxury and wealth he saw there, was a menace to Rome. Until his death he concluded every speech, regardless of the subject, with the words: *Delenda est Carthago* ("Carthage must be destroyed.") In the year of his death, largely due to his influence, war between Carthage and Rome, the Third Punic War, began, resulting three years later in the complete destruction of Carthage; *see* PUNIC WARS. Cato is also remembered as the first to write a prose history of Rome, *Origines*. Only small portions of the work are extant. His *De Agri Cultura,* a treatise on farming, is the oldest surviving prose work in Latin.

**Marcus Porcius Cato,** known as CATO THE YOUNGER (95–46 B.C.), statesman, great-grandson of Cato the Elder, born in Rome. His conduct in his first important public office, that of quaestor in 65 B.C., gave him a reputation for frugality and honesty. An ardent opponent of the Triumvirate (q.v.), Cato opposed the Roman general Pompey the Great (q.v.) when Pompey returned from his victories in the East to demand land for his veterans, a step that had become the means of building a personal following. In 60 Cato opposed the candidacy of the Roman general and statesman Gaius Julius Caesar (q.v.) for the consulship. Cato's influence was so great that the leaders comprising the First Triumvirate, Pompey, Caesar, and the Roman politician Marcus Licinus Crassus (q.v.), sent him on a two-year mission to Cyprus to remove him from active politics. During the civil war between Caesar and Pompey in 49, Cato sided with Pompey. Cato attempted unsuccessfully to defend Sicily against Caesar's forces and maintained a hopeless defense in the city of Utica, in Africa, after which he committed suicide rather than surrender to Caesar. His writings, except for a letter to the Roman statesman and orator Marcus Tullius Cicero (q.v.), have not survived; however, his reputation as an incorruptible citizen became legendary in the writings of contemporaneous and later Romans.

**CATONSVILLE,** unincorporated suburban area of Maryland, in Baltimore Co., adjoining the city of Baltimore on the s.w. Industries include plant nurseries and bottling plants. Catonsville Community College and Saint Charles College, which is a branch of Saint Mary's Seminary and University, are in Catonsville Patapsco State Park, along the Patapsco R., lies to the s.w. Founded in 1720 as Johnnycake, the area was renamed about 1800. Pop. (1970) 54,812.

**CATS, Jakob,** known as FATHER CATS (1577–1660), Dutch poet and statesman, born in Brouwershaven, Zeeland, and educated as a lawyer. In 1602 he married a woman of wealth and was able to retire to a farm in Zeeland, where he spent his time in farming and writing poetry. In 1627 and 1631 he was sent by the government of Holland on missions to England. He served from 1636 to 1651 as grand pensionary of Holland, the highest office of the province. He is the author of many books of poetry that were very popular in the Netherlands for about 200 years, but were relatively unknown elsewhere. His autobiography, *Eighty-Two Years of My Life,* was published in 1734.

**CAT'S-EYE,** semiprecious stone, usually either chrysoberyl or quartz (qq.v.), that when cut *en cabochon,* or in a convex form, shows a line of light across the dome. The position of the line changes as the gem is turned, giving the stone a

*Catnip,* Nepeta cataria

resemblance to the eye of a cat. This property, known as chatoyance, is related to asterism, and is caused by a parallel arrangement of fine fibers of some foreign substance, such as amianthus, or of minute hollow tubules similarly arranged.

**CATSKILL MOUNTAINS,** low mountain group in S.E. New York State forming part of the Appalachian Mts., located w. of the Hudson R., chiefly in Delaware, Greene, and Ulster counties. The highest peak is Slide Mt., 4204 ft. above sea level. The region is drained by the headstreams of the Delaware R. and has several reservoirs owned by New York City. The Catskills are well wooded and contain many lakes and streams for fishing and swimming. Picturesque features of the area include many deep gorges and waterfalls. The summer climate is cool, and the area is noted as a vacation ground. About 236,000 acres in the Catskill Mts. are in the Catskill Forest Preserve. The American writer Washington Irving (q.v.) used the region as the locale of his novel *Rip Van Winkle.*

**CATT, Carrie Chapman** (1859–1947), American woman-suffrage leader and lecturer, born in Ripon, Wis., and educated at the State College of Iowa. After serving as teacher and principal in the schools of Mason City, Iowa, for three years, she was an organizer and lecturer for the Iowa State Woman Suffrage Association from 1890 to 1892. In 1892 she joined the staff of the National American Woman Suffrage Association. She was president of this organization from 1900 to 1904, and of the International Woman Suffrage Alli-

*Carrie Chapman Catt*                                    UPI

ance, which she helped to organize, from 1904 to 1923. She was reelected president of the national association in 1915, retaining this post until her death. She lectured in nearly every State during the campaign to obtain a suffrage amendment to the Constitution of the United States, achieving success in 1920, when the 19th Amendment was ratified. In addition to her work in the U.S., she lectured in behalf of woman suffrage in many countries of Europe. She became honorary president of the International Woman Suffrage Alliance in 1923. Subsequently she helped to organize the National Committee on the Cause and Cure of War, serving as chairman from 1925 to 1932 and as honorary chairman thereafter. She was also a founder and honorary chairman of the National League of Women Voters. *See* WOMEN VOTERS OF THE UNITED STATES, LEAGUE OF.

**CATTAIL,** common name for a tall monocotyledonous, perennial herb of the genus *Typha,* of the Cattail family (Typhaceae). It is characterized by a creeping rootstock, long, flat leaves, flowers in dense cylindrical terminal spikes, and brown, cylindrical fruit with a velvety surface. The plant grows in freshwater swamps, in both temperate and tropical climates, and is occasionally cultivated along pond borders and in bog gardens. It grows and spreads rapidly when sufficient water is present in the soil. The most common species, *T. latifolia,* grows to about 5 to 9 ft. high. Another species widely distributed throughout the Northern Hemisphere, *T. augustifolia,* grows to a height of 10 ft., and *T. domingensis,* of California, Texas, Mexico, and Argentina, attains a height of about 18 ft. and an inflorescence of 3 ft. The leaves are often used for making chair seats, mats, and baskets.

**CATTEGAT.** *See* KATTEGAT.

**CATTELL, James McKeen** (1860–1944), American psychologist, born in Easton, Pa., and educated at Lafayette College and the universities of Paris, Geneva, and Göttingen. He was a lecturer at the University of Cambridge in 1888 and professor of psychology at the University of Pennsylvania from 1888 to 1891. In the latter year he joined the staff of Columbia University, teaching anthropology, philosophy, and experimental psychology. He retired from active teaching in 1917. He was editor of the periodicals *The Psychological Review* (1894–1904), *Science* (1894–1944), *The Scientific Monthly* (1900–44), *American Men of Science* (1906–44), *The American Naturalist* (1907–44), and *School and Society* (1915–39). He was president of the American Association for the Advancement of Science in 1924, and in 1929 was president of the first American International Psychological Congress, at New Haven, Conn. He was the recipient of many awards for his work.

**CATTLE,** term restricted to animals of the genus *Bos,* of the family Bovidae, especially *B. taurus,* the domestic species of Europe and the Americas, and *B. indicus,* the humped species of India and Africa. Young cattle are called calves; females are known as heifers until they give birth, at which time they become cows; and males are called bulls at any age. Castrated males are called steers when raised particularly for beef; *see* MEAT. Some castrated males are raised as draft animals in various parts of the world and are called oxen.

Cattle have been domesticated since prehistoric times. No members of the genus are native to the Western Hemisphere; the Genoese navigator Christopher Columbus (q.v.) brought cattle to the New World on his second voyage. By colonial times, draft oxen were valued quite highly in America but the beef of oxen was of little importance.

Anatomically, cattle are characterized by straightness of the spine; a membranous pad instead of incisor teeth at the extremity of the upper jaw; a four-compartmental stomach, from which the so-called cud, or regurgitated food, is forced back to the mouth for rechewing; and horns, although hornless varieties exist.

Among the important products made from the carcasses of cattle are leather, glue, gelatin, and fertilizer (qq.v.), but cattle are raised primarily for milk (q.v.) and meat. As a result, two principal types have been developed, dairy breeds and beef breeds. A third type, a dual-purpose breed that yields both milk and meat, has gained favor in some parts of the world. The more specialized types predominate in the United States. *See* ANIMAL HUSBANDRY.

Dairy cows have large udders and can produce milk far in excess of that required for nursing calves. In the commercial dairy herds of the U.S. calves are seldom allowed to stay with the mothers for longer than three days after birth; *see* DAIRYING. The calves are raised for the most part on diluted whole milk, skim milk, or milk replacers. Most females are kept as replacement stock. The males, except for the occasional superior individual sold for breeding, are butchered for meat while still calves.

**Breeds.** Several breeds of dairy cattle are raised, including Jersey, Guernsey, Holstein-Friesian, Ayrshire, and Brown Swiss. The Jersey is fawn or brown, usually without white markings, though some American strains may have white markings. Jersey cows produce milk of high but-

Holstein-Friesian cow.          Strohmeyer & Carpenter

Hereford cow.          U.S. Dept. of Agriculture

terfat content but do not often yield the volume of other breeds. Guernsey cattle, brown and white, are larger than the Jerseys, and on the average produce a higher annual quantity of milk and butterfat. Holstein-Friesian cattle are black and white, are larger than either the Jerseys or Guernseys, and on the average give more milk but with a lower percentage of butterfat. Holstein-Friesian constitute the major proportion of milk-producing cattle in the U.S. Red-and-white Holstein-Friesian have evolved from the black-and-white variety.

Ayrshire cattle are predominantly red, brown, and white; a few individuals have some black color. The Ayrshire breed produces more milk than the Guernseys and less than the Holstein-Friesian, but their milk has a slightly greater fat content than that of the Holstein-Friesians. Brown Swiss cows are brown, sometimes with a gray stripe down the back, and are larger than other breeds except the Holstein-Friesians. Brown Swiss produce more milk than do Ayrshires, but the butterfat content is about the same.

Beef cattle are larger than dairy cattle. Heavily covered with flesh, they are somewhat rectangular in profile and have shorter legs. Beef breeds include the Shorthorn, Hereford, Aber-

*Brahman bulls or zebu.*     Florida State News Bureau

deen Angus, Brahman, Longhorn, Santa Gertrudis, Charolais, and Charbray.

Shorthorn beef cattle have the greatest distribution of all beef breeds throughout the world. The breed is reddish brown, sometimes mixed with white. In the U.S. the Hereford beef breed is most common. Herefords are distinguished by white faces and reddish-brown bodies; they are hardy, attain full size quickly, and yield excellent meat. The common variety of Hereford is horned, but the polled or hornless variety is increasing in numbers in the U.S. The Aberdeen Angus, a hornless breed, is black, smaller than either the Shorthorn or the Hereford, and produces excellent beef.

In the U.S. the names Brahman, Brahma, or zebu are applied interchangeably to the many breeds that have been imported from India. Brahman cattle are characterized by prominent humps over the shoulders and loose, pendulous skin under the throat. The breed has been crossed with other beef varieties in the U.S. in attempts to secure animals suited to unfavorable environmental conditions. Because Brahman cattle stand heat so well and are not bothered greatly by insects, the animals are favored in the southeastern and Gulf States. The Longhorn, once the mainstay of western herds, has practically disappeared except for rodeo and show animals.

The Santa Gertrudis, the only cattle breed of American origin, was created by crossing the Brahman with the Shorthorn; it is named after a section of the King Ranch in Kingsville, Texas. The Santa Gertrudis is large, cherry in color, and produces high-quality beef. The Charolais is a white breed that was introduced into the U.S. from France in 1936. This breed is sometimes crossed with the Brahman to produce a white

breed called Charbray. Many of the cattle produced for beef purposes are the result of crossing between breeds. The white-faced black cattle often seen are the result of crossing the Angus and Herefords. Recently, there has been a trend toward crossing beef breeds with Holsteins, the dairy breed, for beef purposes.

The so-called dual-purpose breeds combine fair milk production with fair meat production. Examples of such breeds are the Milking Shorthorn, usually red, white, or roan; the Red Poll, a hornless red type; and the Devon, a horned, dark-red animal.

**Statistics.** In the mid-1970's, the cattle population of the U.S. totaled over 128,000,000, including about 11,300,000 dairy cows and heifers of breeding age. Over 50 percent of the milk-producing cattle are artificially bred. Over 36,400,000 beef-type animals, including calves, were sold for slaughter or were slaughtered in the U.S. in 1973.

*See also* separate articles under the names of the various breeds of cattle.          R.R.St.

**CATTLE TICK.** *See* TEXAS FEVER.

**CATTLEYA,** genus of about fifty species of epiphytic orchids of the Orchid family (Orchidaceae), native to tropical America; *see* EPIPHYTES. Favored for use in corsages, many species of these orchids are cultivated. The various species and hybrids of *cattleya* show a wide range of colors in their blossoms, including purple, lavender, yellow-brown, green, and pure white. *See* ORCHID.

**CATTON, Bruce** (1899–    ), American historian, born in Petoskey, Mich. He attended Oberlin College. Early in his career as a newspaperman, he worked in Cleveland, Ohio; Boston, Mass.; and Washington, D.C. From 1942 to 1948 he held various posts with the World War II War Production Board and the Department of Commerce. In 1954 he became an editor of *American*

*Heritage,* a magazine on Americana, and in 1959 was named senior editor of the American Heritage Publishing Co. He wrote more than a dozen evocative, scholarly books on the American Civil War, including *Mr. Lincoln's Army* (1951), *Glory Road* (1952), and *Grant Takes Command* (1969). For *A Stillness at Appomattox* (1953), Catton was awarded both the 1954 Pulitzer Prize in history and the 1954 National Book Award in history and biography.

**CATULLUS, Gaius Valerius** (84?–54 B.C.), Roman poet, born in Verona of a respected and well-to-do family. Few facts are known about his life. When he was about twenty years old he settled in Rome, where he was on terms of familiarity with many of the leading men of his day. He formed a passionate attachment for a beautiful Roman woman, whom he celebrated in his poetry under the name Lesbia. She has been identified as Clodia (fl. 1st cent. B.C.), sister of the politician Publius Clodius Pulcher (93?–52 B.C.) and wife of the statesman Quintus Metellus Celer (d. 59 B.C.). The love Catullus had for Lesbia became the theme of many of his finest lyrics. In them he records his hopes, joys, jealousy, quarrels, reconciliations, and final despair when he discovers her open infidelity. His poetry, of which he left more than 100 examples, is intensely personal and utterly without reserve. His lyrics are often passionately sensual, and are distinguished also for their rich imagery. In many of them he expressed deep affection for his friends and wrote stinging invective for his enemies. The longer poems are based largely on Alexandrian Greek models; *see* ALEXANDRIAN AGE. The most notable are two marriage songs, one concerning the legendary characters Peleus and Thetis and the other, the Phrygian god of fertility Attis. Catullus is also famous for his epigrams. He was a master of poetic diction and one of the great lyric poets of all time.

**CATULUS,** name of an ancient Roman family of soldiers and statesmen, of the Lutatian gens, that flourished from the 3rd to the 1st centuries B.C.

**Gaius Lutatius Catulus** (fl. 3rd cent. B.C.). He became a consul in 242 B.C., and the following year he commanded the Roman fleet that defeated a Carthaginian armada off the Aegates Islands (now Egadi Islands) near Sicily, thus ending the first of the Punic Wars (q.v.).

**Quintus Lutatius Catulus** (152?–87 B.C.). In 102 B.C. he became a consul with Gaius Marius (q.v.); together, the following year, they conquered and destroyed the Cimbri (q.v.), a Teutonic people. In 88 B.C. Catulus supported Lucius Cornelius Sulla (q.v.) in the civil war against Marius. Catulus was proscribed by the latter in 87, and committed suicide or was killed.

**Quintus Lutatius Catulus** (about 120–61 B.C.), son of Quintus Lutatius Catulus. He became a consul in 78 B.C. and the following year supported Pompey the Great (q.v.) in suppressing the armed uprising of Marcus Aemilius Lepidus (d. about 77). In 63 he accused the Roman soldier and statesman Gaius Julius Caesar (q.v.) of sharing in Catiline's conspiracy to assassinate the heads of the Roman state and plunder the city; *see* CATILINE. Catulus, in turn, was accused by Caesar of having embezzled state funds. Caesar later dropped his charges, and the charges against Caesar were not pressed.

**CAUCA,** river of Colombia, chief tributary of the Magdalena R. Rising in W. Colombia, it flows in a northerly direction through the Andes Mts., forming many waterfalls, and becoming navigable at Cácereso. The Cauca R. joins the Magdalena N. of Mompós, about 150 mi. from the Caribbean Sea, after a course of about 600 mi.

**CAUCASIA,** region of the Soviet Union, in the extreme S.E. part of Europe, between the Black and Caspian seas, and divided into two parts by the Caucasus (q.v.) mountains. The portion to the N., known as the Caucasus (formerly Ciscaucasia), is characterized physically by gently sloping plains ending in low, marshy steppes. Lying within the Russian S.F.S.R., it contains the autonomous republics of Chechen-Ingush, Kabardin-Balkar, North Ossetian, and Dagestan, and the autonomous oblasts of Karachay-Cherkess and Adygey. From the late 1920's until World War II, the Karachay-Cherkess Oblast was divided into separate Karachay and Cherkess autonomous regions. The present autonomous region was established in 1957. The S. and larger portion of Caucasia (Transcaucasia) is physically characterized by a rugged terrain, with chains of mountains (the Little Caucasus) running parallel to the central range of the Caucasus Mts. This region consists of the Georgian S.S.R., Armenian S.S.R., and Azerbaidzhan S.S.R.

Caucasia is noted for fertile lands, mineral deposits, and, in modern times, oil fields. Although Russian attempts to conquer the rich region, containing independent tribes ruled by their own princes, began early in the 18th century, the warlike Georgians, Circassians, and other Caucasian mountaineer peoples withstood Russian domination until 1865. Russian rule was marked by great severity and the repression of the native peoples. After the collapse of czarist Russia in World War I, the southern sections of Caucasia became independent republics. In 1921 they became the

Mount Kazbek, one of the many lofty peaks in the Caucasus Mts.
Ewing Galloway

Transcaucasian S.F.S.R., one of the four original union republics of the U.S.S.R. They separated again in 1936, however, becoming union republics in their own right. Caucasia was subjected to mass purges and executions under the Soviets; in 1943 the Chechen-Ingush, Karachay, and Balkar peoples were almost all deported in large groups to Siberia.

The people of Caucasia are largely Muslim in religion, with the exception of the Georgians and Armenians, who are Christian. The predominant ethnic strains are, in the north, Japhetic, Turco-Tatar, and Iranian, and, in the south, Japhetic and Turco-Tatar. Because some anthropologists have maintained that the Caucasus was the cradle of the white race, the word Caucasian has come to designate the white peoples (see CAUCASIAN RACE).

Farming, livestock raising, and mining are the principal industries in Caucasia. Azerbaidzhan, Chechen-Ingush, and Adygey are noted particularly for the production of oil (in Baku, Groznyy, and Maykop, respectively). For further information on Caucasia see the various political units and divisions under separate headings. Total area of Caucasia, about 154,250 sq.mi. Pop. about 15,000,000.

**CAUCASIAN RACE,** term formerly widely used by anthropologists to differentiate men with white skins from those whose skins are yel-

low, brown, red, or black. It was supposed that men having white skins came from the Caucasus region; see CAUCASIA. The modern concept of the Caucasian race is far more complex than this simple division. The racial characteristics as presently defined include such factors as the size of the teeth and the shape of the head, and little account is taken of skin color. The term Caucasian race is entirely rejected by some anthropologists. See RACES OF MANKIND: *Racial Classification: Caucasoid Race.*

**CAUCASUS** (Russ. *Kavkaz*), mountain range in the s.w. Soviet Union considered a boundary between Europe and Asia. The range extends for about 750 mi. from the peninsula of Apsheron on the s.w. shore of the Caspian Sea to the mouth of the Kuban' R. on the N.E. shore of the Black Sea. The w. region is drained by the Kuban' R. and the E. portion by the Kura R. Of the two principal chains within the Caucasus mountains, the most northerly range has a number of peaks higher than 15,000 ft. above sea level. Mount El'brus, which has an altitude of 18,481 ft., is the highest peak in Europe. Other notable peaks include Dykh-Tau, 17,085 ft.; Koshtan-Tau, 16,880 ft.; and Kazbek, 16,558 ft. The highest peaks of the w. chain are about 12,000 ft. above sea level. Geologically, the Caucasus mountains belong to a system that extends from s.E. Europe into Asia. The mountains are composed of granite and crystalline rock. Some volcanic formations and many glaciers are found throughout the range. The uplifting of the N. chain was begun during the Jurassic Period. The W. chain dates from the Tertiary Period; *see* GEOLOGY, HISTORICAL. Of the few practicable routes through the range, one of the most important is a Georgian military highway from Ordzhonikidze, in the North Ossetian A.S.S.R., on the N. side, to Tbilisi, in the Georgian S.S.R., on the S. side. The chief minerals of the Caucasus mountains are coal, copper, lead, manganese, and oil. *See* CAUCASIA.

**CAUCHY, Augustin Louis** (1789–1857), French mathematician, born in Paris, and educated at the École Polytechnique. After working for several years as an engineer, Cauchy was appointed professor simultaneously at the École Polytechnique, the University of Paris, and the Collège de France. Refusing to take the oath of allegiance required by Louis Philippe (q.v.), King of France, Cauchy went into voluntary exile in 1830. He returned to France in 1837, but his political views barred him from the higher professorships until the establishment of the Second Republic in 1848, when he was made professor of mathematical astronomy at the University of Paris, a chair he held except for a brief interruption until his death.

Cauchy made major contributions in all fields of pure and applied mathematics. He verified the periodicity of elliptic functions, gave the first impetus to the general theory of functions, contributed to determinants, and laid the foundation for the modern treatment of the convergence of infinite series. He emphasized the imaginary as a fundamental, not subsidiary, quantity; perfected the method of integration of linear differential equations (*see* CALCULUS); advanced the theory of substitutions; invented the calculus of residues; and, in general, was one of the leaders of the 19th century in infusing vigor into analysis. He also gave his attention to the propagation of light and the theory of elasticity.

**CAUCUS,** closed meeting of members of a political party or faction for the purpose of making decisions expected to be binding on the party or faction as a whole. The word is of uncertain origin. Its first significant usage was in connection with an 18th-century political organization in Boston, Mass., the Caucus Club, which was influential in local elections. Between 1800 and 1824 candidates for the Presidency of the United States were regularly chosen by meetings, or caucuses, of the members of Congress belonging to the respective political parties. Subsequently these candidates were selected by conventions, but Congressional caucuses have continued to function for the purpose of deciding the official party position on matters of importance before the legislature. Similar political caucuses in many State and local legislative bodies have continued to meet, although their function of selecting candidates has been superseded by conventions or by direct primaries. In other organizations in which factions may exist, such as clubs or trade unions, a meeting of the members of a faction to formulate policy or choose candidates for office is often called a caucus. In Great Britain the term designates a partisan organization that would be termed a "political machine" in the U.S., or to the system of forming or maintaining such an organization.

**CAULFIELD,** residential city of Australia, in Victoria State, in the Melbourne metropolitan area, 7 miles S.E. of Melbourne. It is the site of Caulfield Race Course. Pop. (1971) 81,865.

**CAULIFLOWER,** plant related to the common cabbage, *Brassica oleracea* var. *capitata,* of the Mustard family (Cruciferae). Only the deformed inflorescence or heads of the cauliflower are used for food. It is much less hardy than broccoli (q.v.), another related plant, and the cauliflowers that are reared in August for the purpose of supplying the first crop of the following summer need to be protected in cold frames during winter. To produce cauliflower of first-rate quality the ground must be rich and well cultivated. *See* CABBAGE.

**CAUSALITY,** in philosophy, relationship of a cause to its effect. The Greek philosopher Aristotle (q.v.) enumerated four different kinds of causes: the material, the formal, the efficient, and the final. The material cause is what anything is made of, for example, brass or marble is the material cause of a given statue. The formal cause is the form, type, or pattern according to which anything is made, that is, the style of architecture would be the formal cause of a house. The efficient cause is the immediate power acting to produce the work, such as the manual energy of the workmen. The final cause is the end or motive for the sake of which the work is produced, that is, the pleasure of the owner. The principles that Aristotle outlined formed the basis of the modern scientific concept that specific stimuli will produce standard results under controlled conditions. Other Greek philosophers, particularly the skeptic Sextus Empiricus (fl. 3rd century B.C.), attacked the principles of causality; *see* SKEPTICISM.

In early modern philosophy Aristotle's laws of causality were also challenged, resulting in two rival notions of cause. The French philosopher and mathematician René Descartes (q.v.) and his school made cause identical with substance. The physical scientists often had a mechanical view of causality, reducing cause to a motion or change followed by other motion or change with a mathematical equality between measures of motion. The British philosopher David Hume (q.v.) carried to a logical conclusion the contention of Sextus Empiricus that causality is not a real relation, but a fiction of the mind. To account for the origin of this fiction Hume used the doctrine of association.

Hume's explanation of cause led the German philosopher Immanuel Kant (q.v.) to the position that the only knowable objective world is, so far as all the relations obtaining within it go, the product of a synthetic activity of the mind. Kant accepted Hume's skeptical result as far as it concerned itself with the world of things-in-themselves. Dissatisfied, however, with the concept that experience is only a succession of perceptions without any discoverable relationship or coherence, Kant decided that causality is one of the principles of coherence obtaining in the world of phenomena, and that it is universally present there because thought, as part of its contribution to the nature of that world, always puts it there. The British philosopher John Stuart Mill (q.v.) took up the problem at this point. He denied the fundamental postulate of Kant's transcendentalism, namely, that thought is responsible for the order of this world. Mill sought to justify belief in universal causation by tracing it back to an induction that rests upon a larger experience than any other induction can have.

Along with this account of the origin of knowledge of cause goes a definition of cause that is widely accepted today. The cause of any event is a preceding event without which the event in question would not have occurred. This is a mechanistic view of causality popular in scientific circles. All the indispensable previous events would constitute the complete cause.

Many philosophers deny the ultimate reality, or at least the fundamental validity, of the causal relation. Thus the American philosopher Josiah Royce (q.v.) maintains that the category of serial order, of which the category of cause is a particular case, is itself subordinate to the ultimate category of purpose. To the French philosopher Henri Louis Bergson (q.v.), ultimate reality or life is not bound by exact causal sequences. It is a process of growth in which the unpredictable, and therefore the uncaused, constantly occurs. There is no exact repetition in real time; and where there is no repetition

there is no cause, for cause means the antecedent that repeatedly is followed by the same consequence. *See also* METAPHYSICS.

**CAUSSES,** region of limestone plateaus, called *causses* (Fr. *chaux*, "lime, limestone"), in S.-central France, comprising part of the Lot, Aveyron, Lozère, and Tarn-et-Garonne departments. The plateaus are separated by deeply eroded river valleys. Causses is sparsely populated and is principally a sheep-raising area. Geologically the region dates from the Jurassic Period (q.v.), with underground streams, stalactite caverns, and sinkholes.

**CAUSTIC ALKALIES.** *See* ALKALIES; POTASSIUM; SODIUM.

**CAUTO,** longest river of Cuba. It rises in the Sierra Maestra and flows N.W. and then W. into the gulf of Guacanayabo. Nearly 150 mi. long, it is navigable for about 75 mi.

**CAUVERY,** river in the Republic of India. *See* KAVERI.

**CAVALCANTI, Guido** (1250?–1300), Italian poet, born in Florence. During the civil war in Florence between the political parties known as the Guelphs and Ghibellines (q.v.), Cavalcanti became the head of the Ghibellines. In 1266 the Ghibellines were exiled to Sarzana, in northwestern Italy; Cavalcanti contracted malaria there and died soon after his return to Florence. The author of many sonnets expressing idealistic love, Cavalcanti was the most important Florentine poet before Dante Alighieri (q.v.), his friend and admirer. Translations of many of Cavalcanti's sonnets, originally published as *Canzone d'amore* ("Song of Love"), were included in *Dante and His Circle* (1874) by the British poet and painter Dante Gabriel Rossetti (*see under* ROSSETTI).

**CAVALIER** (Fr., from Lat. *caballus*, "a nag"), term meaning originally a horseman and later a mounted knight. By extension the word acquired the meaning of "gallant" and "haughty". During the Great Rebellion (q.v.) the term "Cavaliers" was applied as a nickname to the partisans of Charles I (q.v.), King of England, in opposition to the "Roundheads" or Parliamentarians.

**CAVALIER, Jean** (1681–1740), French soldier and leader of the Camisards (q.v.) born near Anduze, and brought up in the Huguenot faith. When threatened with persecution for his religious beliefs he fled to Geneva, Switzerland, where in 1701 he worked as a baker. He returned to France the following year and became the leader of the Camisard revolt in the Cévennes (q.v.), defeating the forces of King Louis XIV (q.v.), King of France, in a number of engagements. In 1704 Cavalier abandoned the struggle for religious freedom in exchange for a commission as a colonel in the French army and a yearly pension from the king. He was disavowed by all but a handful of his followers, found no favor at the French court, and went to England. In 1706 he fought for the English in Spain and later settled in Dublin. After gaining military promotion in England, he was given a pension and, in 1738, was appointed lieutenant governor of the island of Jersey. He wrote *Memoirs of the Wars of the Cévennes under Col. Cavalier* (1726).

**CAVALIER POETS,** group of 17th-century English lyric poets, associated with the Royalists, who were the followers of Charles I (q.v.), King of England, at the time of the Great Rebellion (q.v.). Three of them, Thomas Carew, Sir John Suckling, and Richard Lovelace (qq.v.), were attached to the court of Charles, and one, Robert Herrick (q.v.), was a clergyman. The term Cavalier lyrics is often applied to the poetry of these authors and to that of some of their contemporaries, such as John Cleveland (1613–58). Generally marked by brevity, correct and polished form, and restrained emotion, these poems dealt with the subjects of loyalty, beauty, and love. The Cavalier poets' philosophy is often cynical and hedonistic.

**CAVALLINI, Pietro** (about 1250–about 1330), Italian artist, born in Rome. Cavallini was one of the most important Italian painters of the 13th century. His work showed the formalism of Byzantine art (q.v.), but he was one of the first Italian painters to break away from the medieval Byzantine tradition by a more natural and less one-dimensional use of space in his works. He influenced the style of the great Florentine painter Giotto (q.v.), and through him played a part in the inauguration of the Renaissance (*see* RENAISSANCE ART AND ARCHITECTURE) in Italy. Important among the works ascribed to Cavallini are such mosaics as "Birth of the Virgin" in the Church of Santa Maria in Trastevere, Rome and fragments of frescoes in the Church of Santa Cecilia, Rome.

**CAVALRY,** mounted soldiers trained to fight on horseback, as distinguished from mounted infantrymen, who use horses for rapid transportation between engagements, but fight on foot. Throughout history cavalry troops were valued for their speed and mobility, and were used for reconnaissance, delaying actions, raiding parties, and pursuit and harassment of enemy troops. In modern armies cavalry and mounted infantry have been largely replaced by so-called armored cavalry, comprising soldiers using tanks, armored cars, helicopters, and other mechanized equipment.

*Persian cavalry of the period of the Mogul Emperor Akbar, late 16th and early 17th century.*
Metropolitan Museum of Art—Gift of Alexander Smith Cochran

*"Cavalry Charge on the Southern Plains", an oil painting by the American artist Frederic Remington (1861–1909).* Metropolitan Museum of Art—Gift of several gentlemen

The origins of cavalry are lost in antiquity. The earliest known cavalry consisted mainly of horse-drawn chariots, which seemingly antedated mounted soldiery. The wheels of some war chariots were fitted with sharp scythe blades designed to cut a wide swathe through enemy ranks. Although cavalry units were employed by the Assyrians, Babylonians, and other ancient peoples, the first regular cavalry, consisting of trained mounted troops, was probably created by the Egyptian king Ramses II (*see under* RAMSES). With the rise of the Persian Empire in the 6th century B.C., cavalry developed into a fully effective operational force.

Among the ancient Greeks the development of cavalry was hindered for centuries by a lack of horses. In Macedonia, however, where horses were plentiful, the military leader Philip II of Macedon and his son, Alexander III (qq.v.), known as the Great, developed a formidable striking force by adding cavalry wings to the heavy infantry formation known as the phalanx. Later the Carthaginians, the Romans, and the Gothic barbarians who conquered Rome in the 5th century A.D. used similar cavalry wings with devastating effect.

The earliest cavalry weapons were the lance, the javelin, and other weapons thrown by hand; the sword; and the bow and arrow. Until about 300 A.D. the troops rode without saddles, but they often enjoyed the protection of leather armor and helmets of metal or leather. During the Middle Ages warfare was dominated by mounted knights wearing metal armor and wielding the iron-tipped lance and the two-edged sword. Probably the greatest cavalry genius in history was the Mongol warrior Genghis Khan (q.v.), whose mounted hordes conquered much of Asia and Russia during the 13th century. Tightly coordinated and disciplined in battle, his armies used the smoke screen and such novel devices as signal flags and signal lanterns.

With the advent of gunpowder and armor-piercing bullets early in the 14th century, cavalry organization and strategy were profoundly modified. The era of disorganized clashes between heavily armored knights came to an end. Mounted troops gradually were forged into disciplined units armed with swords and hand-held firearms. Firearms also enhanced the importance of the infantry. Under Napoleon I (q.v.), Emperor of France, mounted troops became an elite military force, although the infantry did most of the fighting. Napoleon was the first general to employ cavalry simultaneously to conceal his main troop movements and to reconnoiter the front. In Russia the Cossacks (q.v.) became famous for their daring and skill as cavalrymen.

The emergence of the repeating rifle in the latter half of the 19th century was the most serious blow to the importance of cavalry. Charging cavalrymen were easy prey to infantry troops armed with automatic weapons. Among the last major conflicts in which horse cavalry figured prominently were the American Civil War (1861–65), the Austro-Prussian War (1866), and the South African War (1899–1902). Horse cavalry was used only to a limited extent during World War I. Between World Wars I and II the cavalry was transformed into armored cavalry units. The few horse cavalry units remaining in the United States Army after World War II were absorbed in 1946 into the armored forces. *See* ARMY.

**CAVAN,** county of the Republic of Ireland, in the Province of Ulster, bordering on Northern Ireland, about midway between the Atlantic Ocean and the Irish Sea. Except for the mountainous N.W. section, the terrain is generally undulating, with many bogs and lakes. The principal river is the Erne. Small-scale farming is the chief activity in the county, which yields mainly crops of oats, potatoes, and flax. Stock farming is conducted in the highlands. Industrial activity consists of whisky distilling and linen bleaching. The administrative center of the county is Cavan, a town about 65 miles N.W. of Dublin. Area, 730 sq.mi.; pop. (1971) 52,618.

**CAVE or CAVERN,** chamber of varying size and shape beneath the surface of the earth or in the side of a hill, cliff, or mountain. Many caves have large openings to the surface.

**Formation of Caves.** Naturally formed caves evolve in various ways, mainly as a result of the solvent action of water and compounds in it. Known technically as caves of solution, such chambers are most common in limestone formations, particularly in regions that have ample rainfall. The surface water in such regions contains carbon dioxide and humid acids derived from the organic constituents of the soil. Attacking the soluble limestone, this acidic water dissolves it and carries it away in solution. Over long periods of time, such action results in the formation of subterranean chambers. The solvent action of the water may be assisted by the abrasive action of undissolved particles carried along in the water. Underground rivers erode and transport sediments and rock fragments in a manner analogous to that of surface streams. If such action has been predominant, the cave is said to have been formed by mechanical abrasion; *see* GEOLOGY: *Geomorphology.*

Other types of caves include the sea cave, which is formed by wave action against seaside cliffs; lava caves, which form under lava flows; and ice caves, which form in glaciers and icebergs. River action forms still another type of cave, commonly with a very large opening that gives it the appearance of a natural amphitheater. A river entrenched in a steep-walled canyon most actively erodes that portion of the canyon wall against which the current is strongest, as at a bend or in a meander. By erosion (q.v.), solution, and quarrying, the river excavates a large quantity of rock, forming a large undercut area in the side of the canyon. With the passage of time the river bed is lowered, and eventually the cave is left high in the side of the canyon. Such rock shelters were used extensively in what is now the southwestern United States by the prehistoric American Indians known as cliff dwellers (*see* CLIFF DWELLERS), who built their homes within them.

Finally, aeolian, or wind, action is partially responsible for the formation of small caves that are confined mostly to desert or semidesert regions. The action of windblown sand is one of several factors involved in the formation of these grottoes and caves in rock ledges and cliffs.

**Cave Detection.** The presence of caves in limestone regions may be detected by means of clues provided by the topography of the land. In such a region the roofs of large caverns may collapse and leave depressions and troughs at the surface of the ground. Natural bridges, another phenomenon of cave regions, may remain after the collapse of a tunnel bearing an underground stream. The Natural Bridge in Virginia is a classic example of this type of formation. In the phenomenon known as disappearing streams, which is a common feature in areas underlain by caves, whole watercourses may vanish down sinks, or sinkholes, leading to the underground caverns. The sinks are indicative of caves below. Because of the capture of the surface waters by the subterranean drainage system, some cave

*Limestone formation in Boyden Caves, Fresno, Calif.*
Fresno County Chamber of Commerce

regions have a rather dry, dusty, poorly vegetated appearance. Such regions are said to have a karst topography, a name derived from a famous cave region along the Adriatic Sea in Italy and Yugoslavia. Steep-walled sinks called cenotes, found in Yucatán, Mexico, constituted the chief source of water for the Mayan Indians in areas lacking surface streams.

**Interesting Features.** Caves range in size from small hillside openings to vast interconnected subterranean systems of many chambers and galleries. Some cave systems extend for miles beneath the surface of the earth and may have many outlets. As a result of water action during the time of formation, the features in major caves may be distributed along various levels. Typical of such caves in the U.S. are those in the Carlsbad Caverns National Park (q.v.) in New

Mexico, and Mammoth Cave National Park (q.v.) in Kentucky.

Natural air conditioning is characteristic of some large caverns in which the temperature varies only a few degrees throughout the year, and the caves are more or less constantly ventilated with fresh air. These conditions are, in part, the result of complex meteorological phenomena, primarily variations in barometric pressure.

Caves formed by abrasion commonly consist of myriads of winding tunnels and former underground waterways that show many features analogous to those of surface streams, such as deposits of sand and gravel. Abrasion-formed caves normally lack the weird formations found in caves of solution.

In caves of solution, the dissolved lime carbonate is often precipitated in such a fashion as to form grotesque deposits. The best-known structures are the stalactites, which hang like icicles from the roofs of caves, and the stalagmites, which extend upward from the cavern floors; see STALACTITE. If the two growths meet and join, a pillar forms, helping to support the roof. Less well-known forms of carbonate deposition include flowstone and dripstone. Depending on dissolved mineral impurities brought into the cave by the ground waters, the formations vary in color from alabaster white to hues of dusky red and brown. The dripstone formations may be exceedingly thin and translucent. Among rare formations is the helictite, a twisted, flowerlike variety of stalactite. Many cave formations are rather delicate and easily broken, and some of the best examples have been damaged or removed by unscrupulous cave explorers and visitors to public caves.

Many formations in commercial caves have been given fanciful names, such as "Rock of Ages" and "Temple of the Sun" in Carlsbad Caverns and "Martha Washington's Statue" and "Fatman's Misery" in Mammoth Cave. Frequently recurring names include "Japanese Temple", "Frozen Waterfall", "King's Bed Chamber", and "Great Hall".

A practice in many large caves, particularly those administered by the U.S. National Park Service (q.v.), is to backlight the more spectacular formations for the benefit of sightseers. Many public caverns have miles of lighted trails, with stairways and adequate safety guards near areas considered dangerous. In some caves visitors can take all-day hiking tours.

**Cave Life.** Through evolutionary processes some plants and animals have become specially adapted to living in caves. As a rule, these organisms are confined to the area near the entrance, but some species penetrate to the darkest reaches of the cave. Properly, cave life may be divided into those forms living exclusively in caves and those that live in caves part of the time but forage in the open. The cave cricket and some cave fish are examples of animals modified for continuous life in caves. Although such species are blind, as is usual among animal forms completely adapted to cave life, their organs of touch are highly developed. Animals that live completely in caves commonly have as their diet the edible matter carried into the caves by streams.

Bats exemplify animals that utilize caves for resting and hibernating purposes but forage in the open for their food. Rich deposits of guano (q.v.), or bat droppings, have accumulated over the centuries in caves where bats congregate. The guano is sometimes marketed as fertilizer. The number of bats inhabiting a large cave may be astoundingly large. For example, hundreds of thousands of the animals can be observed in the evening flight of bats from Carlsbad Caverns. See BAT.

Because lack of sunlight precludes green-plant growth, fungi is the only form of plant life that can grow in caves. Ground waters containing dissolved organic substances frequently provide nutrients for the fungi.

In past ages man often took shelter in caves, notably in western Europe, the Mediterranean regions, China, South Africa, and Chile. These early cave inhabitants popularly have been called cavemen, but the term is misleading, for it implies that a race of men at one time dwelt exclusively in caves. Actually, during the Ice Age man, like other animals, sought refuge in caves from time to time. Many artifacts of Paleolithic and Neolithic men have been found in refuge heaps near the entrances of caves. Primitive paintings have been found on the walls of some caves, notably in France and Spain. Modern critics acclaim the artistic beauty of these paintings, attributed to the Cro-Magnon (q.v.), a race of the late Paleolithic period. See CAVE DWELLERS.

**Speleology.** The science of cave study is properly termed speleology. A subdivision of geology, speleology has furthered knowledge in mineralogy, hydrodynamics, archeology, biology, and many other formal disciplines. Speleologists use many special contrivances and methods in exploring caves. One technique is the use of dye stains to reveal the outlets of complicated underground-stream systems. Use of special shoes, safety helmets, flexible ladders and cables, and dependable lamps enables present-day speleologists to explore the recesses of large caves much more thoroughly than was formerly possible. Cave explorers occasionally stay underground for a number of days, mapping and studying an extensive area.                    C.C.

**CAVEAT EMPTOR** (Lat., "let the buyer beware"), principle applied in early common law that the buyer of defective goods could not hold the seller legally responsible. The theory of the early common law was based on the assumption that the buyer was able to examine the goods for any obvious defects, and that if there were latent defects of which the seller was unaware the buyer should bear the loss. Under modern law, however, the rule of caveat emptor does not apply to the sale of goods. The rule instead is that the seller is deemed to make an implied warranty that the goods are reasonably fit for the purpose intended by the buyer (*see* SALE). Goods that are defective may be sold without legal liability if the fact is brought to the attention of the buyer. The rule of caveat emptor is sometimes used in modern law in reference to a real-estate sale in which the seller does not specifically state that he has a clear title. In such sales, which usually are conducted under supervision of a court in bankruptcy or mortgage foreclosure, or in other judicial proceedings, the buyer takes the risk of acquiring a defective title.

*Cro-Magnon cave dwellers left impressive paintings on the walls of caves in southern France (mural by American artist Charles Robert Knight, 1874–1953).*
American Museum of Natural History

**CAVE DWELLERS,** groups of prehistoric men who dwelt in caves in various parts of the world. Although the terms "cave dwellers" and "cavemen" often are misunderstood to mean all very ancient men or are equated with an overall stage in the evolution of man, a more restricted meaning is assigned these terms in archeology.
**Cave Localities.** Some of the best evidences of human occupancy in caves in the remote past are preserved in western Europe. Artifacts, refuse layers, and human burials occur in caves in France, Belgium, Germany, Italy, southern Spain, and the British Isles. The association of these remains with the bones of extinct animals, such as the cave bear and the saber-tooth tiger, indicates the great antiquity of many of the deposits. During the long span of the Pleistocene Period, or Ice Age (*see* QUARTERNARY PERIOD), these caves were inhabited at repeated intervals, and the stratified layers of trash and artifacts mark the successive progression of many cave cultures. *See* ARCHEOLOGY.

Such caves often are called bone caves. Among the more famous bone caves are those of Kirkdale and Kent's Hole in England; Muggendorf in Germany; Spy in Belgium; and the caves in the valleys of the Dordogne, Vézère, and Ain rivers in southern France. Kirkdale Cavern is notable as one of the first caves excavated according to scientific principles. The excavation was the work of the British geologist William Buckland (1784–1856), who explored the cave and recovered the material therein about 1820. Kent's Hole is notable as the site of

one of the first authentic discoveries of human relics associated with the bones of Pleistocene mammals. Although at the time of the discovery evidences for contemporaneous burial of all the material were hotly contested, they have since gained scientific acceptance.

Other caves that have yielded relics of early man include the Cro-Magnon, Comberelles, La Madeleine, Le Moustier, and La Solutre caves of France. In the cave of La Colombière, beside the Ain R. in France, a remarkable series of sketches engraved by cave dwellers on bone and on smoothed stones was unearthed in 1913. Similarly decorated caves were found in many of the lands bordering the Mediterranean Sea, and also in South Africa. Other such caves are known in the Far East, for example, in China. One of the most important, and most recently excavated, caves is Shanidar Cave in northern Iraq. There, in 1957, the American archeologist Ralph Solecki (1917–  ) uncovered the skeleton of a Neanderthal man dating back perhaps 50,000 years. Similar caves have been studied in South America, notably in Chile and in Patagonia in Argentina. Radiocarbon dating (see CHRONOLOGY) indicates that man was living in the southern parts of South America more than 9000 years ago. Generally, however, the term "cave dwellers" is inapplicable in the Western Hemisphere because of strictly limited use of caves by the Paleo-Indians (early men) anywhere in the Americas. Even in those regions of the world that harbor caves with unmistakable signs of human habitation, early men did not live exclusively in this manner, according to authoritative opinion. Recent research tends to show that prehistoric men were primarily forest rangers and shore dwellers. Probably dictated by local conditions, cave life was secondary. See ANTHROPOLOGY.

**Periods of Occupation.** Cave dwellers date generally from the Stone Age, a term derived from the fact that these peoples used stone for the manufacture of implements. The Stone Age is divided into the Eolithic (Early Stone), Paleolithic (Old Stone), and Neolithic (New Stone) periods. The Eolithic period, which is shrouded in obscurity, dates from the very earliest times; it was followed by the Paleolithic which started, according to some authorities, about 600,000 years ago. The Paleolithic merges gradually into the Neolithic, which, though ending in western Europe about 2500 B.C., continued elsewhere in the world down to modern times. For example, some American Indians had a Neolithic culture at the time of their discovery by Europeans. The various lithic periods are further subdivided into

Prehistoric painting in Altamira Cave, near Santillana, Spain.

epochs or culture stages, mainly of interest to specialists.

**Types of Cave Dwellers.** The various cave-dwelling men include a variety of races and types. Neanderthal man dwelt in caves, as did also various members of *Homo sapiens; see* MAN, ANCIENT. The Heidelberg man, Peking man, and the Cro-Magnons were other Paleolithic men; of these, the Cro-Magnons certainly lived in caves for some time.

Cave dwellers ordinarily inhabited only the outer parts of caves, chiefly because they needed light. The remains of cave dwellers often are found, therefore, just inside the mouths of caves or in the immediate recesses or passageways opening off cave entrances. The Cro-Magnons, however, cave dwellers noted for their artistic talent, apparently lived well inside their caverns. Many of their paintings have been found deep in the interior recesses of caves. Religious notions and details of the hunt appear to be the basis for much cave art. One technique of these early artists was based on use of dry colors obtained by grinding bits of colored earthstuffs and charcoal into fine powders. These powders were blown through hollow bones and bone tubes onto the walls of the caves, with a high degree of artistic expression and balance of tone.

**Preservation in Caves.** In dry caves, preservation is often excellent, due to dry air and limited bacterial activity. Organic remains such as charred wood, nutshells, plant fibers, and bones often are found intact. In wet caves, artifacts and other remains often are found encrusted with, or buried beneath, calcareous deposits of cavestone. The collected evidences of human habitation on the cave floor were often buried under rock falls from the ceilings of caverns. Intentional burials have also been found in a number of cave sites.

Because of the unusual preservative nature of caves and the great antiquity of many remains found in them, the fallacious belief that there was a race of cavemen has been fostered. Actually, the cultural remains of peoples who lived outside caves were subject to greater decay than were the protected remains in caves. Hence, the archeological record of remote times is sometimes better seen in cave deposits.

Some of the Old World caves continued to be inhabited even following the close of the Stone Age. Relics from the Bronze and Iron ages have been found in cave deposits; on occasion, material assigned to the time of the Roman Empire has been recovered. The famous Dead Sea Scrolls (q.v.), discovered in 1947, were preserved in caves. These Biblical documents are chiefly from Caves 1Q and 3Q on the Qumran Wady (watercourse) near ancient Khirbet, Palestine.

M.R.

**CAVELL, Edith Louisa** (1865–1915), British nurse, born in Swardeston, Norfolk, England. After studying nursing in London, she was invited in 1907 to become matron of a large training center for nurses in Brussels, Belgium. In 1914, at the outbreak of World War I, this school became a Red Cross hospital and she attended many wounded German and Allied soldiers there. On Aug. 5, 1915, during the German occupation of Brussels, she was arrested by the Germans for having sheltered 200 British, French, and Belgian soldiers in her house and for having helped them to escape from Belgium. Unsuccessful appeals for postponement of her execution were made by the American and Spanish ministers to Germany, and she was shot by a firing squad on Oct. 12, 1915. The execution aroused widespread indignation. Vast multitudes attended her memorial service at Westminster Abbey, and a commemorative statue to her was erected in Saint Martin's Place, Trafalgar Square, London.

**CAVENDISH, Henry** (1731–1810), British physicist and chemist, born of British parents in Nice, France, and educated at Peterhouse College, University of Cambridge. His earliest experiments were concerned with heat and included the study of the evolution of heat when a liquid is solidified or a gas condensed, as well as an investigation into the specific heats of substances. In 1766 Cavendish discovered the properties of the element hydrogen (q.v.) and determined its specific gravity. His most celebrated work was the discovery of the composition of water; he stated that "water consists of dephlogisticated air [oxygen] united with phlogiston [hydrogen]". By what is now known as the Cavendish experiment, he determined that the density of the earth was 5.45 times as great as the density of water, a calculation very close to the 5.5268 established by modern techniques. For his calculations he improved the torsion bal-

ance (q.v.), a measuring device. Cavendish also determined the density of the atmosphere and made important investigations of electrical currents. The Cavendish Physical Laboratory at the University of Cambridge was named in his memory.

**CAVENDISH, William, Duke of Newcastle** (1592–1676), English soldier and statesman, educated at the University of Cambridge. Cavendish inherited an immense fortune, and on his estates in Welbeck, Nottinghamshire, he lavishly entertained James I, King of England, and his successor King Charles I (qq.v.). In 1638 Charles appointed Cavendish to the Privy Council. During the Great Rebellion (q.v.) Cavendish raised and commanded a volunteer army to aid Charles and donated nearly £1,000,000 to the Royalist cause. After Cavendish was defeated at Marston Moor (q.v.) in July, 1644, he retired to the Continent. In 1650 he was appointed to the Privy Council of Charles II (q.v.), King of England, then in exile. Ten years later, when the monarchy was restored (*see* RESTORATION), Cavendish returned to England. In 1665 he was created Duke of Newcastle (*see* NEWCASTLE), and shortly thereafter withdrew from public life. He spent much of his time restoring his estates and writing plays and books about horsemanship. Cavendish was also a patron of several English writers, including Ben Jonson and John Dryden (qq.v.).

**CAVE OF THE WINDS.** *See* NIAGARA FALLS.

**CAVIAR.** *See* STURGEON.

**CAVITATION,** process of formation of local cavities in a liquid as a result of the reduction of pressure below a critical value, known as the vapor pressure. On cavitation, bubbles of vapor begin to appear in the liquid; in pumps, these bubbles reduce the desired flow of a liquid, and in the case of ship propellers, reduce the propulsive force. If the pressure in the liquid rises again, the bubbles implode, or collapse very suddenly, and the liquid rushes into the cavities generating large, concentrated forces. If the cavities are located close to a metal part in the liquid, small particles may be dislodged from the surface of the part, as in the case of a ship's propeller that has suffered severe cavitation and has had to be replaced after a single transatlantic trip. Similar erosion can occur in pumps, hydraulic turbines, or marine structures in contact with water; *see* PUMPS AND PUMPING MACHINERY; TURBINE.

**CAVITE,** city and seaport in the Republic of the Philippines, in Cavite Province, on Luzon Island, on Manila Bay, about 9 miles s.w. of Manila. The city has a fine harbor and is encircled by walls. The principal articles of trade include corn, rice, sugar, coffee, cacao, copra, and Manila hemp. On a narrow neck of land extending eastward into the bay are the remains of fortifications dating from Spanish colonial times, and an American naval arsenal. Under Spanish rule Cavite was a naval base and following its capture by the American admiral George Dewey (q.v.) in 1898, in the Spanish-American War, it became the principal base of the United States Asian fleet. The Japanese captured Cavite in December, 1941, in World War II, and held it until 1945. Pop. (1970) 63,000.

**CAVITY.** *See* TEETH: *Tooth Decay.*

**CAVOUR, Conte Camillo Benso di** (1810–61), Italian statesman, born in Turin, Piedmont, then part of the Kingdom of Sardinia (q.v.). He was educated at the military academy in Turin, and from 1826 to 1831 was a lieutenant of engineers in the Sardinian army. After resigning his commission, he became interested in politics and in 1847 he helped to found the newspaper *Il Risorgimento* ("The Rebirth"), a nationalist journal that advocated expelling the Austrians from Sardinia and unifying all of Italy under a Sardinian constitutional monarchy. In 1848 Cavour became a member of the Sardinian chamber of deputies. During the ministry of the Marchese d'Azeglio (q.v.), Cavour served in important cabinet positions and in 1852 he became premier. In this office he improved internal conditions in Sardinia and conducted the foreign affairs of the country with the aim of unifying the Italian peninsula. He allied Sardinia with Great Britain and France in the Crimean War (1854–56) against Russia. In 1858 Cavour made an alliance with Napoleon III (q.v.), Emperor of France, against Austria. The following year Cavour maneuvered Austria into a war against Sardinia and France, expecting by a victory to drive the Austrians from Lombardy and Venetia, which they controlled. Although France and Sardinia were victorious, Napoleon III made peace with Austria in July, 1859, without consulting Cavour. By the terms of the Treaty of Zürich in November, 1859, Austria retained Venetia and ceded most of Lombardy to France. France in turn transferred the Lombardy cities of Peschiera and Mantua to Sardinia. When Victor Emmanuel II, King of Sardinia (*see under* VICTOR EMMANUEL), accepted the peace terms that left Austria powerful in northern Italy, Cavour resigned as premier.

In August and September, 1859, the people of Parma, Modena, Romagna, and Tuscany voted for annexation to Sardinia. Cavour became premier again in January, 1860, and, as the price of Napoleon III's consent to the annexations, ceded Nice and Savoy to France (Treaty of Turin, March, 1860). In September, 1860, Cavour sent Sardinian troops to aid the Italian patriot Giuseppe Garibaldi (q.v.) in the conquest of the Kingdom of Two Sicilies (*see* SICILY: *History*). As a result of Cavour's intervention, on Oct. 21 and 22, 1860, Sicily voted for union with Sardinia. Cavour was also instrumental in bringing about the proclamation of the Kingdom of Italy on March 17, 1861, and the proclamation of Victor Emmanuel II as the first king. Cavour's diplomacy, which prepared the way for the unification of Italy, when Rome became the capital in 1870, earned Cavour the reputation of being one of the most skillful European statesmen of the 19th century. *See* ITALY: *History*.

**CAVY,** common name for a genus of rodents, *Cavia,* in the family Caviidae, which is native to South and Central America. The genus includes the guinea pig, the agouti, the capybara (qq.v.) and the paca.

**CAWDOR,** Great Britain, parish in Nairn County (q.v.) in Scotland, situated 5 miles s.w. of Nairn. Located nearby is Cawdor Castle, seat of the Earl of Cawdor and the traditional scene of the murder of King Duncan I by Macbeth in 1040. Pop. (1971) 530.

**CAWNPORE.** *See* KANPUR.

**CAXTON, William** (1422?–91), first English printer, born probably in Tenterden, Kent. In 1438 Caxton was apprenticed to a wealthy London textile merchant. After the death of his master in 1441 Caxton moved to Bruges, Flanders (now part of Belgium), where he later opened his own textile business, and became the governor of English merchants in the Low Countries. About 1471 he moved to Cologne, Germany, where he learned the art of printing. At this time Caxton was also translating into English a popular French romance, which he printed in Bruges as *The Recuyell of the Historyes of Troye* (about 1474 or 1475). The circumstances of the printing have been a matter of some dispute, but some scholars believe that Caxton financed the printing press that published the book, which is famous as the first book printed in English. His *Game and Playe of the Chesse,* published in Bruges in 1475, was the second book printed in English. Returning to England in 1476, Caxton set up a printing press at Westminster Abbey. His first publication was of an indulgence by Abbot Sant, which was distributed in December, 1476. This was followed by *The Dictes and Sayengs of the Phylosophers* on Nov. 18, 1477, the first dated book printed in England. During his career Caxton printed

*William Caxton (from a woodcut); under the portrait are his initials and trademark.*  Granger Collection

nearly 100 publications, about twenty of which he also translated from French and Dutch. Among the more notable books from his press are Volume 8 of *Polychronicon,* an updating of a general history by the English Benedictine monk Ranulf Higden (d. 1364); *The Canterbury Tales* and *Troilus and Criseyde* by the English poet Geoffrey Chaucer; and *Confessio Amantis* by the English poet John Gower (qq.v.). Caxton also wrote prefaces and epilogues to many of the works he published, notably the preface to the prose epic *Le Morte d'Arthur* by Sir Thomas Malory (q.v.). In this, as in all his original writing, he displayed a lively, humorous style that considerably influenced 15th-century English literature. Fewer than forty of his publications are extant, and these exist only in single copies or in fragments. Caxton's type faces were close facsimiles of the Gothic character. One of his type faces is the original type known as Old English. Caxton's assistant and successor was Wynkyn de Worde (d. 1534?).

**CAYAMBE,** extinct volcano of the Andes Mts., in Ecuador, about 60 miles N.E. of Quito and almost directly at the equator. Covered with perpetual snow, it is about 19,200 ft. above sea level.

**CAYENNE,** city, seaport, and capital of French Guiana, South America, a department of France since 1947, on Cayenne Island at the mouth of the Cayenne R. The leading port of Guiana, it has steamboat service to other coastal points and is included in the itinerary of an air-transport system. The harbor is navigable to vessels with drafts under 14 ft. Larger vessels receive and discharge cargo 6 mi. from the city. The chief exports include bananas, gold, rum, hides, spices, fish glue, and various kinds of timber. Among the imports are grain, flour, wines, clothing, glass, hardware, cotton and silk goods, and tobacco. The first French settlement at Cayenne was established early in the 17th century. It was occupied by the Dutch from 1654 to 1664, when the French reestablished their control. Following another period of Dutch occupation, beginning in 1667, the French acquired permanent control of the town early in the 18th century. A French penal colony, established in 1854, is in Cayenne. The French government abandoned, in April, 1946, the practice of transporting prisoners to the colony. Devil's Island (q.v.), another French penal colony, is located about 30 miles N.W. of Cayenne. Pop. (1967) 24,581.

**CAYENNE PEPPER.** *See* CAPSICUM.

**CAYES.** *See* LES CAYES.

**CAYLEY, Arthur** (1821–95), British mathematician, born in Richmond, Surrey, England, and educated at King's College, and Trinity College, University of Cambridge. Devoting much time in his early life to the study and practice of law, he made some of his most brilliant mathematical discoveries during this period. In 1863 he became professor of pure mathematics at Cambridge. Cayley's most important contribution to mathematics is the theory of algebraic invariants. He also discovered a higher curve, known as the Cayleyan, and the principal proposition of matrices, called Cayley's theorem. A collected edition of his writings was published at Cambridge between 1889 and 1898.

**CAYMAN ISLANDS,** three British islands of the West Indies, in the Caribbean Sea, forming a crown colony. Grand Cayman, 22 mi. long and 4 to 8 mi. wide, is about 200 miles N.W. of the W. end of Jamaica. The others, located approximately 80 miles N.E. of Grand Cayman, are Little Cayman, 10 mi. long and 2 mi. wide, and Cayman Brac, 12 mi. long and 1¼ mi. wide. The islands are of coral formation, and the soil on them is fertile. Fishing, shipbuilding, and stock raising are the chief industries, and the leading exports include thatch rope, mahogany, logwood, turtle shells, green turtles, shark skins, cattle, and ponies. The capital is Georgetown, on Grand Cayman. Discovered in 1503 by the

Genoese-born navigator Christopher Columbus (q.v.), who named them Tortugas (Sp., "turtles"), the Cayman Islands were colonized about 1734 by the British. Before becoming a separate colony in 1959, they were a dependency of Jamaica (q.v.). They were part of the Federation of the West Indies until 1962. Area, 100 sq.mi.; pop. (1971 est.) 11,300.

**CAYUGA,** North American Indian word meaning "the place where locusts were taken out", and the name of one of the original five tribes of the Iroquois (q.v.), or Five Nations. Although their home in colonial times was on Cayuga Lake, in New York State, when the American Revolution broke out many members of the tribe took the side of the British and moved to Canada. The Cayuga who remained in America were absorbed into other Iroquois tribes. They now live chiefly in the Six Nations Reserve in Ontario.

**CAYUSE,** North American Indian tribe belonging to the Waiilatpuan linguistic stock. The Cayuse Indians formerly occupied the Blue Mt. region of northeastern Oregon and sections of Washington. During a severe smallpox epidemic in 1847 many members of the tribe died. The remnants of the tribe now live on the Umatilla Reservation, Oregon, where they have largely intermarried with other Indian tribes. The Cayuse were probably the first North American Indians to domesticate the bronco (q.v.). In the northwestern United States this breed of horse is often called the Indian pony, or cayuse.

**CEANOTHUS,** large genus of American shrubs, vines, and small trees of the family Rhamnaceae. The genus comprises more than fifty species, most of which are found in the Pacific coast States. Only a few of the species are cultivated as ornaments. A hardy species, *C. americanus,* found from Canada to Texas, is a deciduous shrub attaining a height of about 3 ft. It has ovate, irregularly serrate, bright green leaves and abundant, short-lived, ornamental white flowers in large clusters. The leaves of the plant, commonly called New Jersey tea, were said to have been used as a substitute for tea during the American Revolution.

**CEBU,** third-largest city of the Philippines, and capital of Cebu Province, on the E. coast of Cebu Island, about 350 miles S.E. of Manila. The city is connected with other E. coast points by rail and has an excellent harbor. Shipping is the chief industry and consists mainly of trade with other Philippine ports. The leading exports include sugar, copra, and hemp. Among other industries of the city are manufacture of salt, sugar sacks, fabrics, and pottery. Cebu is the seat of a Roman Catholic bishop and has an 18th-century cathedral. One of the oldest settlements in the Philippines, Cebu was first visited by a European on April 7, 1521, when the Portuguese navigator Ferdinand Magellan landed there. The Spanish conquerors made it their capital from 1565 to 1571. Pop. (1970) 347,116.

**CEBU,** island and province of the Philippines, between Bohol and Leyte islands on the E. and the island of Negros on the W. The province includes also several small islands adjacent to Cebu, which is about 135 mi. long and about 20 mi. across at its greatest width. The terrain of Cebu is mountainous, with an extreme elevation of 2200 ft. Its fertile soil yields valuable crops of tobacco, sugar, cotton, coffee, hemp, and rice. Among its principal industries are coal mining and the manufacture of wines, cloth, pottery, and refined sugar. The administrative center of the province is the city of Cebu (q.v.). Area of island, 1707 sq.mi.; of province, 1878 sq.mi. Pop. of province (1970) 1,634,182.

**ČECH, Svatopluk.** See CZECH LITERATURE: *Fourth Period or National Revival (from 1774).*

**CECIL,** name of a distinguished English family that has been traced back to David Cecil (d. 1541), high sheriff of Northamptonshire. His son Richard Cecil (d. 1552), held the offices of constable of Warwick Castle and high sheriff of Rutland. The two extant branches of the Cecil family comprise the earls and marquises of Exeter and the earls and marquises of Salisbury. Important members of the Cecil family include the following.

**William Cecil, 1st Baron Burghley** *or* **Burleigh** (1520–98), statesman, born in Bourne, and educated at Saint John's College, University of Cambridge. Cecil first served in the Court of Common Pleas, then as a member of Parliament, and eventually, through the patronage of the protector Somerset, became a secretary to King Edward VI (q.v.). During the reign of Mary I (q.v.), though invited to participate in the government, he chose to withdraw from court.

Upon the accession in 1558 of Elizabeth I (q.v.), whose favor he had carefully cultivated, Cecil became Principal Secretary to the Queen. At a time when great turmoil troubled the country's internal and foreign affairs, Cecil's abilities as a shrewd politician and masterful administrator, and his devotion to Elizabeth, made him a potent asset to the new Queen.

Together with the strong-willed and politically astute Elizabeth, Cecil set about improving the economic footing of England, among other measures adopting a new coinage in 1561. To

*William Cecil, 1st Baron Burghley*

National Portrait Gallery, London

heal the religious division in the country, he and the Queen prepared a compromise settlement, acceptable to the majority of Englishmen, that resulted in the establishment of the Anglican Church (1559). Striving for a speedy end to the costly war with France, he secured the Queen's intervention in Scotland, forcing the removal of French forces from that land.

Their most immediate problems solved, at least temporarily, Cecil and the Queen began to develop the long-term policies of moderation and compromise that were to guide England for the next forty years: measures aimed at building up prosperity at home and dealing prudently with threats from foreign powers. Despite his distaste for the military, Cecil strengthened the army and navy, and because the government periodically was menaced by subversion, he organized an efficient secret service. Cecil's own position was threatened at times by men who sought to supplant him in the Queen's confidence. One such rival was the powerful favorite Robert Dudley, Earl of Leicester, with whom he carried on a lengthy power struggle. Cecil managed, however, to survive the many challenges to his relationship with the Queen, and his triumph over all his enemies was manifest when he was made 1st Baron Burghley in 1571 and lord high treasurer in 1572.

During the 1570's and 1580's, Cecil's attention

was occupied chiefly in keeping careful watch over the safety of England and its sovereign against the many plots and invasion schemes hatched by Catholic nations to unseat the Protestant Queen. His close scrutiny of the machinations of Elizabeth's cousin, Mary Stuart of Scotland, led ultimately to her trial for treason and her execution. His insight into the intentions of Spain and his preparations for resistance, especially by sea, culminated in the defeat of the Armada in 1588, bringing relative security at last.

William Cecil's enormous contribution to the success of the Elizabethan state was perhaps best recognized by Elizabeth herself, who said of him: "No prince in Europe hath such a counselor as I have in mine".

**Thomas Cecil, 1st Earl of Exeter, 2nd Baron Burghley** (1542–1623), soldier, son of William Cecil, born in Cambridge, and educated privately. He distinguished himself in 1585 while fighting under Robert Dudley, 1st Earl of Leicester (*see under* DUDLEY) in the Low Countries. Three years later he fought against the Spanish Armada, and in 1601, he helped quell the revolt led by Robert Devereux, 2nd Earl of Essex (*see under* DEVEREUX). Cecil was made a Knight of the Garter in 1601 and was created Earl of Exeter in 1605.

**Robert Cecil, 1st Earl of Salisbury** (1563–1612), statesman, son of William Cecil, born in London, and educated at Saint John's College, University of Cambridge. Groomed for government service by his father, he entered the House of Commons in 1584. He was appointed secretary of state in 1596, having acted unofficially in that capacity for nearly six years. In 1589 he succeeded William Cecil as Principal Secretary to Queen Elizabeth.

Blessed with his father's prudence and administrative skill, he dedicated his efforts to continuing the policies of moderation established by the elder Cecil and the Queen. Upon becoming Elizabeth's chief adviser, Cecil, a rather frail man with a spinal deformity, found himself among a group of young and highly aggressive competitors for power. His main rival was Robert Devereux, 2nd Earl of Essex, a favorite of the Queen. Essex's pride overreached itself, however, and his ill-conceived rebellion against the Queen brought him to the block in 1601.

This threat removed, Cecil turned his attention to paving the way for a proper successor to Elizabeth. Secretly, he prepared for the accession of James VI of Scotland as James I of England and Scotland, thus uniting the two crowns. When James succeeded Elizabeth upon her death in 1603, Cecil was retained as chief minister to the new King. Honors followed, as he was made Baron Cecil of Essendine in 1603, 1st Viscount Cranborne in 1604, 1st Earl of Salisbury in 1605, and Knight of the Garter in 1606.

When Cecil became lord high treasurer in 1608, he found that the King was more than £1,000,000 in debt. He managed to reduce this amount, but failed to convince the King that he could halt the country's deepening economic crisis by adopting the Great Contract of 1610, a plan that would have limited the spending of the Crown to a fixed annual sum. In his last years Cecil lost his influence with the King to the favorite Robert Carr.

**Robert Arthur Talbot Gascoyne-Cecil, 3rd Marquis of Salisbury** (1830–1903), statesman, a lineal descendant of the 1st Earl of Salisbury, born at Hatfield and educated at Christ Church College, University of Oxford. Gascoyne was his mother's maiden name. He entered the House of Commons as a Conservative in 1853 and was soon noted for his writings on public questions, especially the articles he wrote, after 1860, for the *Quarterly Review.* He served briefly in 1866–67 as secretary of state for India, resigning the post in protest over the Reform Bill of 1867; *see* REFORM BILLS. In 1868, upon the death of his father, Cecil became the Marquis of Salisbury and a member of the House of Lords. Six years later he was again Indian secretary, and in 1878, he became foreign secretary in the government of Benjamin Disraeli (q.v.). Salisbury was made a Knight of the Garter in honor of his efforts at the Congress of Berlin; *see* BERLIN, CONGRESS OF. In 1881 he succeeded Disraeli as Conservative leader and in June, 1885, he became prime minister and secretary of state for foreign affairs, a portfolio he held in each of his three ministries. The Salisbury government fell in January, 1886, but he was returned to power the following July. He followed an imperialist but conciliatory foreign policy, and soon after taking office, he secured the eastern frontier of India by annexing Burma. His most important achievements, however, were in African affairs. In 1888 he increased British influence in the Upper Nile R. region by granting a charter to the British East Africa Company; the following year he granted a charter to the British South Africa Company to colonize what is now Rhodesia; and in 1890 he arranged a British protectorate over Zanzibar, now part of the United Republic of Tanzania. The Conservatives failed to gain a majority in the general elections of 1892, and Salisbury resigned. He formed his third ministry in 1895.

Following the Anglo-Egyptian victory at Omdurman (q.v.) in 1898, he forced France to relinquish claims in the Sudan. He negotiated the Anglo-Japanese Treaty of 1902 by which Chinese and Korean independence were recognized, and the treaty of the same year that ended the South African War (q.v.). His only major foreign policy failure occurred in 1897, when he sought an open-door trade policy in China; *see* OPEN DOOR. Important domestic legislation passed during his ministries included the Workmen's Compensation Act in 1897 and the Criminal Evidence Act of 1898. He relinquished the foreign ministry in 1900 and was succeeded as prime minister in 1902 by his nephew Arthur James Balfour (q.v.).

**Edgar Algernon Robert Cecil, 1st Viscount Cecil of Chelwood** (1864–1958), statesman, son of the 3rd Marquis of Salisbury, born in London, and educated at University College, University of Oxford. He was elected to Parliament in 1906, as a Conservative, and during World War I he held several ministerial positions. At the 1919 Paris Peace Conference, he helped draft the Covenant of the League of Nations; *see* LEAGUE OF NATIONS. An ardent believer in disarmament, he resigned as Lord Privy Seal from the cabinet of Prime Minister Stanley Baldwin in 1927, when the government failed to support compromise measures of the Geneva Naval Conference. Cecil was awarded the Nobel Peace Prize in 1937.

**Lord Edward Christian David Cecil** (1902– ), writer, educated at Christ Church, University of Oxford. His first important work was the biography *Life of Cowper* (1929). This was followed by other biographies, including *Sir Walter Scott* (1933), *Jane Austen* (1935), and *The Young Melbourne* (1939). Cecil edited the *Oxford Book of Christian Verse* (1940), and wrote *Reading As One of the Fine Arts* (1949) and *Victorian Novelist* (1958). In 1948 he became Goldsmiths' professor of English literature at Oxford.

**David George Brownlow Cecil, 6th Marquis of Exeter** (1905– ), sportsman and statesman, a lineal descendant of the 1st Earl of Exeter, educated at Magdalene College, University of Cambridge. He won eight British field championships and the 400-meter hurdles in the 1928 Olympic games (q.v.). He served in Parliament from 1931 to 1943, and during World War II, he had a government position as controller of aircraft repairs and overseas supplies. Exeter was the governor of Bermuda from 1943 to 1945.

**CECILIA, Saint** (d. 230 or 176 A.D.), Christian martyr. According to tradition she was be-

*Cedar of Lebanon,* Cedrus libani    **Brooklyn Botanic Garden**

trothed to a youth named Valerian, whom she converted to Christianity, and the two were martyred for refusing to honor the Roman gods. She is said to have been thrown into a boiling bath but to have escaped unharmed. The executioner attempted to behead her in three strokes, but he failed and she lived three days longer. In 821 her remains were interred in a crypt in the Basilica of Saint Cecilia in Rome. Since legend speaks of her singing to God in her heart, she came to be regarded as the patroness of music. The English poets Geoffrey Chaucer, John Dryden, and Alexander Pope have celebrated St. Cecilia in literature, and she has been the subject of many paintings. Her feast day is Nov. 22.

**CECROPIA MOTH,** common name for a large American silkworm moth, *Samia cecropia,* of the family Saturniidae. Cecropia, the largest moth native to the eastern United States, has a wingspread of about 6 or 7 in. The reddish-brown wings are bordered with red, white, and gray markings with an outlined white crescent-shaped mark in the center. In the larva stage, the moth is about 4 in. long. The body is bluish green and covered with rows of blue, yellow, and coral-red tubercles, or knoblike projections. The larvae feed on, and eventually destroy, the foliage of many forest and fruit trees. *See also* SILKWORM.

**CECROPS,** in Greek mythology, the founder of Athens and of Greek civilization. Reputed to have sprung half man and half serpent from the soil, he became the first king of Attica and established or abolished many marital, burial, property, and sacrificial customs. During his fifty-year rule he arbited a dispute over possession of Athens between Athena and Poseidon (qq.v.), awarding the city to Athena.

**CEDAR,** common name of four species of coniferous evergreen trees native to Africa and Asia, constituting the genus *Cedrus* of the Pine (q.v.) family (Pinaceae). Generally only three species are recognized: *C. libani,* the cedar of Lebanon, native to Asia Minor; *C. deodara,* the deodar cedar of India; and *C. atlantica,* the Atlas cedar of the mountains of northern Africa. All grow to about 100 ft. and are characterized by their fragrant, light red, durable wood. The cones of the three species are brownish, vary in size from 2 to 5 in. in length, and are about 2 in. wide. The cedars of Lebanon have been famous from early times, being mentioned in the Bible (Isa. 35:2). The original groves, greatly reduced in size, contain specimens that are of great age. The cedars of Lebanon are distinguished from most conifers by their wide-spreading branches, which split off from a single trunk. The needles, or leaves, are dark green and at least 1 in. long. The tree grows at elevations of about 6000 ft. in the mountainous regions. The deodar cedar, *C. deodar,* called the Tree of God by Hindus, often grows in a pyramidal shape to a height of about 150 ft. The needles, about 1 in. long, vary in color from bluish green to silver. The deodar forms extensive forests in the Himalayas at elevations of from about 6000 to 12,000 ft. The wood takes a high polish and is in demand for cabinet work. The Atlas cedar, *C. atlantica,* also pyramidal in shape, has the same foliage variations as the deodar, but the foliage is shorter and denser. It grows at elevations of between 4000 and 6000 ft.

Although the true cedar is not native to the United States, the name cedar is given to many other American species of coniferous trees, especially in the Cypress (q.v.) family. Particularly notable is the white cedar, *Chamaecyparis thyoides,* which is about 80 ft. high, and grows in swampy areas from Maine to Mississippi. Another cypress, *Thuja occidentalis,* is also sometimes called white cedar or arborvite. Trees other than conifers to which the name cedar is given include species of the genus *Cedrela,* such as *C. odorata,* the West Indian or Spanish cedar.

**CEDAR,** river rising in s.e. Minnesota and flowing s.e. across Iowa from the N. to the s.e. boundary. It empties into the Iowa R. at Columbus Junction, about 30 mi. above the point at which the Iowa R. joins the Mississippi. The Cedar R. is about 300 mi. long and drains a beautiful and fertile region. The chief cities along its course are Cedar Rapids, Vinton, and Waterloo, all in Iowa.

**CEDAR BIRD.** See Waxwing.

**CEDAR BREAKS NATIONAL MONUMENT,** area of natural interest in Iron County, Utah. It is administered by the National Park Service (q.v.).

**CEDAR CREEK, BATTLE OF,** important military engagement of the American Civil War, fought on Oct. 19, 1864, near Cedar Creek, a tributary of the Shenandoah R., in Shenandoah County, Va.; see CIVIL WAR, THE AMERICAN. The action began when a Confederate force of about 18,000 men, under General Jubal Anderson Early (q.v.), made a surprise attack on contingents, totaling about 31,000 troops, of the Army of the Shenandoah, commanded by Union General Philip Henry Sheridan (q.v.). Early's forces struck at dawn under the cover of fog and darkness, overrunning the Union positions, and by midday they had succeeded in advancing as far as Middletown, Va. Meanwhile Sheridan, who had been absent from the front on official business, rejoined his army after a fast ride from Winchester, Va., and assumed command. Late in the afternoon he ordered a general counteroffensive, which broke through the Confederate lines. Early's army retreated in panic, pursued by Sheridan's cavalry across Cedar Creek to Woodstock, Va. Union casualties were 644 killed, 3430 wounded, and 1591 missing; Confederate losses were about 320 killed, 1540 wounded, and 1050 missing. As a result of their defeat at Cedar Creek, the Confederates made no further attempts to strike the North through the Shenandoah Valley. Sheridan's famous ride from Winchester and its aftermath, one of the most dramatic episodes of the Civil War, are the theme of "Sheridan's Ride", by the American poet Thomas Buchanan Read (1822–72).

**CEDAR FALLS,** city of Iowa, in Black Hawk Co., on the Cedar R., 6 miles N.W. of Waterloo and 85 miles N.E. of Des Moines. Manufactures include agricultural equipment, tool and die products, furniture, processed feed, and canned vegetables. The city is the site of the State College of Iowa (1897), formerly Iowa State Teachers College. Settled about 1845, laid out in 1851, and incorporated as a village in 1857, Cedar Falls was chartered as a city in 1865. Pop. (1960) 21,195; (1970) 29,597.

**CEDAR MOUNTAIN, BATTLE OF or CEDAR RUN, BATTLE OF,** indecisive military engagement of the American Civil War, fought on Aug. 9, 1862, near a hill called Cedar Mt., in Culpeper County, Va.; see CIVIL WAR, THE AMERICAN.

A Union force, under the command of General John Pope (1822–92), commander of the Army of Virginia, met an advancing Confederate army of about 24,000, commanded by General Thomas Jonathan (Stonewall) Jackson (q.v.). Pope sent General Nathaniel Prentiss Banks (1816–94) to meet Jackson with a force of about 8000, about half the size of the Confederate force that was engaged in the battle. After furious fighting, Banks' troops pursued by Jackson's forces, withdrew toward the town of Culpeper. The Union army received reinforcements, however, and counterattacked, checking Jackson's advance. On Aug. 11 the Confederate army fell back toward Gordonsville, Va. Jackson's losses were 1338 killed and wounded, and Union casualties included 1759 killed and wounded and 594 missing.

**CEDAR RAPIDS,** city in Iowa, and county seat of Linn Co., 733 ft. above sea level, on the Cedar R., about 105 miles N.E. of Des Moines.

The city is a center of wholesale trade in the agricultural produce of the surrounding region. The principal industrial establishments in Cedar

*White cedar,* Chamaecyparis thyoides

*View of the carved ceiling in the Doge's Palace, Venice.*

Rapids include factories for the processing of grain, chiefly oats, to produce oatmeal, and sorghum and corn syrups. Among other establishments are railway shops and plants for the manufacture of road-building machines, snow plows, furnaces, oil burners, pumps, radio equipment, ice-cream-making machinery, creamery and dairy-farm equipment, and office machines.

The city was settled between 1838 and 1839, named Rapids City in 1841, and incorporated as the town of Cedar Rapids in 1849; it became a city in 1856. Cedar Rapids is the site of Coe College, a Presbyterian institution chartered in 1881, and of the Iowa Masonic Library, which contains a large collection of works on Freemasonry. The Cedar Rapids Art Association has a collection of contemporary American art. Pop. (1960) 92,035; (1970) 110,642.

**CEIBA,** or ERIODENDRON, large genus of trees of the Bombax family (Bombacaceae), which attain a height of 130 ft. or more. They have palmate leaves and large flowers shaped like bells. Their thick, woody seed capsules contain a kind of fiber that resembles cotton.

The ceiba tree, God tree, or silk-cotton tree, *C. pentandra,* is widely cultivated in the tropics for its fiber, known as kapok. Because of its shortness, elasticity, and brittleness, the fiber cannot be spun like cotton but is used in various ways in upholstery and in making floss. Because of its lightness and water-repellent properties, kapok is used in large quantities as the buoyant material in life preservers. The principal supplies come from Java. The seeds of the tree also yield kapok oil, used in making soap. The soft spongy wood of the African variety, which is called bentang, is used for making canoes. The round seeds, the size of peas, are eaten on the Indonesian island of Celebes.

**CEILING** (Fr. *ciel;* Lat. *caelum,* "sky"), in architecture, inner horizontal surface, or overhead covering, of a room, opposite the floor. The principal types of ceilings include flat, curved, beamed, and vaulted.

In ancient Egyptian temples the underside of the flat stone roofs formed the ceiling and was generally painted blue, with yellow stars, bands of hieroglyphs, and emblems of the heavens. The ceilings of Babylon and Assyria were stuccoed and painted, and apparently gilding was used in the sanctuaries. The horizontal ceilings of Greece were deeply paneled (coffered), and the flat surfaces of the panels were painted with ornaments. Arched ceilings among the Romans were known as *camerae.* However, the ceilings most commonly in use among the Romans were flat. In early times the beams were visible; later they were covered with planks and plaster.

Ceilings of churches in the Middle Ages were

often painted and gilded in the most brilliant manner. The older ceilings generally follow the line of the timbers of the roof, which, in the Early English and Decorated styles, are often arranged to give the shape of a barrel vault. These ceilings often have only a single rib along the top. In the Perpendicular style, the ceiling often consists of a series of slanted flat surfaces, or cants, formed on the timbers of the roof. The timbers are frequently enriched with ribs that divide the cants into square panels, with bosses or flowers at the intersections. Wooden ceilings are sometimes formed like stone groining, with ribs and bosses, examples of which are found in York, Winchester, and Lincoln, in England. Although in the Elizabethan age ceilings were generally of plaster, they were ornamented with ribs that had bosses or small pendants at the intersections.

During the Renaissance the ribbed vault was abandoned. In Italy three principal types of ceiling developed: the smooth vaulted ceiling with or without penetrations plastered and painted in fresco or tempera, as in the Sistine Chapel in Rome; the coved ceiling with penetrations, having a flat central field and curves (coving) along the sides and ends penetrated by lunettes, the whole richly painted; and the flat paneled ceiling of wood or plaster, in an endless variety of decoration which reached its highest splendor in Venice (Doge's Palace), with sumptuously carved panels framing paintings by the Italian painters Titian, Tintoretto, and Paolo Veronese (qq.v.). Plaster and stucco came into general use throughout Europe, and in England a type of flat ceiling was developed with all-over decorations modeled in low relief in the plaster. Modern ceilings are usually flat, made of plaster or wood.

*See also* ARCHITECTURE; DOME; VAULT.

**CELANDINE** *or* **CELANDINE POPPY,** common names for the plant *Chelidonium majus,* of the Poppy family (Papaveraceae). Celandine is a biennial herb, native to Europe, but now naturalized in eastern North America and found in hedgerows, barnyards, and thickets, often in rich soils. It grows to about 4 ft. in height and bears pinnately cleft or divided, dark green leaves. The flowers, grouped in sparsely flowered clusters, are buttercuplike, but with only four bright yellow petals. Leaves and stems usually display a conspicuous orange-yellow sap when broken. Poppy alkaloids have been isolated from celandine and may account in part for its potent acridity. The sap causes intense irritation and digestive upset if ingested. Although frequently found in barnyards, celandine is normally avoided by livestock.      J.M.K.

**CELANESE,** trademark of the Celanese Corporation of America, used to designate the synthetic fiber manufactured by this company, which is made from cellulose acetate and used in the manufacture of yarn and fabric. The term is also applied to a cellulose acetate plastic manufactured by the same company. By extension, the term celanese is now commonly used to designate a cellulose acetate fabric made by any manufacturer. The yarn of such fabric is made by forcing cellulose acetate (a flaky solid) dissolved in a volatile solvent through fine nozzles into a heated atmosphere in which the solvent evaporates, leaving a filament of solid cellulose acetate. A dinstinctive property of cellulose acetate is that it is thermoplastic; that is, the threads can be fused together by heat. Because the fibers are cylindrical and absorb little moisture, garments made from them wash easily and dry quickly. *See* CELLULOSE; PLASTICS.

**CELEBES** *or* **SULAWESI,** island of the Republic of Indonesia, and one of the larger islands of the Malay Archipelago, situated E. of Borneo and W. of the Moluccas. It consists mainly of four

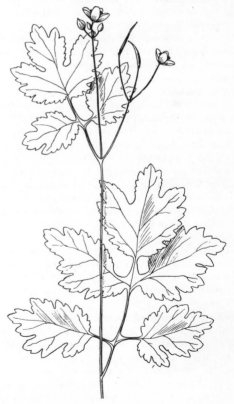

*Celandine,* Chelidonium majus

peninsulas, separated by deep gulfs, two of the peninsulas extending southward, and two northeastward. This singular conformation gives the island a coastline of about 3500 mi. The surface reaches one of its highest elevations in Mt. Lompobatang, an extinct volcano in the southern part of the island, 9419 ft. high. There are also a number of active volcanoes in the E. end of the N. peninsula, but most of the volcanoes have reached the solfataric stage. The largest river is the Sadang, which is navigable by small boats.

The climate is tropical, but somewhat modified by the elevation and the proximity of the sea. Among the animals peculiar to the island are the tailless baboon; the babiroussa, with upper canines curved backward and nearly touching the forehead; the marsupial cuscus; and the sapiutan or wild cow. The forests include oak, teak, palm, cedar, upas trees, and bamboo. Cloves, nutmeg, spices, tropical fruits, corn, rice, tobacco, and sugar are raised. The coffee crop is not large, but is of superior quality. The minerals of the Celebes include gold, copper, tin, sulfur, salt, and diamonds and other precious stones. Among the chief items of trade are coffee, spice, copra, coconuts, and trepang, an edible sea slug.

The Portuguese first discovered and named the island in 1512, but from about 1607 the Dutch gradually obtained supremacy, though it was not until well into the 19th century that every district was under their control. Under the Dutch the island formed an important province of the Netherlands East Indies, consisting of the Celebes Government in the S. part of the island, and the Manado Residency in the N. The capital of the Celebes Government and chief port of the island was Makassar (q.v.), situated on Makassar Peninsula, on the Strait of Makassar. The seat of the Residency was in Manado, at the end of the Manado Peninsula on the Celebes Sea. During World War II, the Japanese held the island from 1942 until the fall of 1945. In 1946 Celebes Island was included in the autonomous state of East Indonesia, a part of the new United States of Indonesia (now Republic of Indonesia). Area, about 73,000 sq.mi.; pop. (1968 est.) 7,200,000.

**CELERY,** common name for biennial herb, *Apium graveolens,* of the Parsley family, a native of Europe but now widely grown throughout the world. The stalks, about 12 to 30 in. high in cultivated varieties are eaten, raw or cooked, as a vegetable or salad. When allowed to grow naturally, the stalks are greenish in color and slightly bitter in taste. They are often "blanched" during the last stages of their growth by preventing access of sunlight except to the leaves; this process removes the color and the bitter taste, but also some of the vitamins. If allowed to grow a second year, celery sends up flower stalks about 2 to 3 ft. tall with small white flowers in umbels. The dried fruit of celery is used as a condiment alone under the name of celery seed or ground and mixed with salt under the name of celery salt. Celery seed is also used in pharmacy, as a sedative or to disguise the flavor of other drugs. Since the celery stalks themselves contain a small amount of apiol (*see* PARSLEY), they have been recommended for various medical purposes.

The culture of celery requires moist and heavily fertilized soil. To harvest the celery within a single year it must either be planted indoors in late winter, or brought indoors in late autumn, except in tropical climates. In any case it must be transplanted one or more times while young. In addition, to blanch the celery the stems must be covered by soil, boards, or paper cylinders. Celery is subject to attack by several blights, by the tarnished plant bug (*Lygus pratensis*), and by the larva of the black swallowtail butterfly. The production of celery has increased steadily in the United States, and after World War II, passed 21,000,000 crates (of 65 lb.) per year, produced principally in California and Florida.

**CELESTA.** *See* MUSICAL INSTRUMENTS: *Percussion Instruments.*

**CELESTIAL MECHANICS,** branch of astronomy and applied mathematics that deals with the development of the laws of motion of heavenly bodies and the calculation of such motion in specific cases. This branch of astronomy, in its classical form, is based on the three laws of planetary motion of the German astronomer Johannes Kepler (q.v.) and the law of gravitation and three laws of motion of the English mathematician and astronomer Sir Isaac Newton (q.v.). Kepler proved that the orbits of planets are ellipses, with the sun at one focus; that the speed of a planet varies in such a way that the line connecting it with the sun, known as its radius vector, passes over equal areas in equal times; and that the square of the planetary period is proportional to the cube of its mean distance from the sun; *see* KEPLER'S LAWS. Newton proved that the only force required to keep a planet in its orbit is one acting between the earth and the sun, and therefore the same force that causes unsupported objects to fall to the surface of the earth must also act between the sun and the planets, and in fact, between all particles of matter in the universe; *see* NEWTON'S

LAWS OF MOTION. Newton derived the mathematical expression of the law of gravity from Kepler's third law. On the basis of this law of gravitation, the British physicist Henry Cavendish (q.v.) determined the mass of the earth, and from this the masses of the moon, the sun, and the other planets were calculated. The gravitational action of the planets upon one another, in causing perturbations of one another's orbits, may also be calculated. The position of any body in the heavens at any past or future day, hour, or second may now be calculated with great accuracy. Certain corrections, however, are necessary when mass, speed, or distance are great; these corrections are made in accordance with the Einstein theory of relativity (q.v.). *See also* EINSTEIN, ALBERT; GRAVITATION.

**CELESTIAL NAVIGATION.** *See* NAVIGATION: *Celestial Navigation.*

**CELESTINA, LA.** *See* SPANISH LITERATURE: *The Middle Ages.*

**CELESTINE,** name of five popes.

**Saint Celestine 1** (d. 432), pope from 422 to 432. He devoted himself to the spreading of Christianity. He excommunicated Nestorius (*see* NESTORIANS) after the Council of Ephesus in 431; see EPHESUS, COUNCILS OF. He sent Saint Germain (378?–448) to Britain to convert the adherents of Pelagianism (q.v.) and is said to have sent Palladius (368?–431) and Saint Patrick as missionaries to Ireland. His traditional feast day is April 6.

**Celestine II** (d. 1144), original name GUIDO DEL CASTELLIS, pope in 1143–44. Although he was pope for less than six months, he restored peaceful relations between the church and France by removing an earlier papal interdict placed on Louis VII (q.v.), King of France.

**Celestine III** (1106?–98), original name GIACINTO BOBONE, pope from 1191 to 1198, born in Rome. He crowned Henry VI (q.v.) as Holy Roman Emperor in 1191 only after Henry threatened to overrun the Italian peninsula.

**Celestine IV** (d. 1241), original name GEOFREDO CASTIGLIONI, pope in 1241, born in Milan. He was a Cistercian monk and cardinal bishop of Sabina before his election as pope. Celestine died within a month of his election, possibly of poisoning.

**Saint Celestine V** (1215?–96), original name PIETRO DI MURRONE, pope in 1294, born in Isernia. He was a monk of the Benedictine order when, about 1254, he formed the monastic order of Celestines (q.v.). He was living as a hermit when he was elected pope in 1294. He allowed Charles II, King of Naples (*see under* CHARLES), to dictate church policies, and within six months he resigned. Celestine was held

prisoner until he died by his successor Boniface VIII (*see under* BONIFACE). He was canonized in 1313. His traditional feast day, May 19, is no longer in the Roman Catholic calendar; see SAINT.

**CELESTINES,** order of Benedictine monks (*see* BENEDICTINES), founded about 1254 by Pietro di Murrone, later Pope Celestine V (*see under* CELESTINE). The Celestines were confirmed as a monastic order by Pope Urban IV (*see under* URBAN) in 1264 and by Pope Gregory X (r. 1271–76) in 1274. The order spread rapidly through France, Italy, and Germany but subsequently decayed and became extinct in the late 18th century.

**CELESTITE** *or* **CELESTINE,** mineral variety of strontium sulfate, $SrSO_4$, which is one of the principal sources of the element strontium. Widely distributed, it is found in whitish orthorhombic crystals with hardness of from 3 to 3.5 and sp.gr. 3.96. Although it is found in several localities in the United States, there has been little domestic production. *See* STRONTIUM.

**CELIBACY,** in ecclesiastical history, abstention from the married state by clergy and by those who have entered upon the monastic life. The Roman Catholic Church (q.v.) requires celibacy and the practice of perfect chastity on the part of its clergy of the Latin rite. The church holds that this practice is sanctioned, though not required, by the New Testament, basing this claim upon what it avers to have been the constant tradition of the church and upon several biblical texts (notably, 1 Cor. 7:6–7, 25, Matt. 19: 12). The principles upon which the law of celibacy is founded are: (1) that the clergy may serve God with more freedom and with undivided heart, and (2) that, being called to serve Jesus Christ, they may embrace the holier life of self-restraint. This statement does not imply, it is said, that matrimony is not a holy state, but simply that celibacy is a state of greater perfection.

Having no doctrinal bearing in the Roman Catholic Church, celibacy is regarded as a purely disciplinary law, though as of prime importance in maintaining the dignity and character of the priesthood (*see* PRIEST). A dispensation from the obligation of celibacy has occasionally been granted to ecclesiastics under exceptional circumstances, for instance, to provide an heir for a noble family in danger of extinction.

The celibacy of the clergy was rejected by the Protestant reformers (*see* REFORMATION), the German religious reformer Martin Luther (q.v.) setting the example to his followers by marrying a former nun. Both the marriage of ministers and the abolition of monastic vows became a common feature of those bodies that withdrew their allegiance from the Roman Catholic Church.

According to the articles of religion of the Church of England (q.v.), "bishops, priests, and deacons are not commanded by God's law, either to vow the estate of single life, or to abstain from marriage; therefore it is lawful for them, as for all other Christian men, to marry at their own discretion, as they shall judge the same to serve better to godliness".

The history of priestly celibacy has been a stormy one since it became law for the clergy of the Latin rite in the 6th century. Although Pope Paul VI (*see under* PAUL), in his encyclical of June 24, 1967, reaffirmed the traditional position, the requirement of priestly celibacy remains a much disputed ecclesiastical question.

**CÉLINE, Louis-Ferdinand,** pen name of LOUIS-FERDINAND DESTOUCHES (1894–1961), French novelist whose attempts to depict the absurdity of human existence through the breakdown of conventional literary language helped create a stylistic revolution in modern French literature.

Céline was born in Courbevoie, a Paris suburb, on May 27, 1894. After distinguished service in World War I, he studied medicine, and from 1924 to 1928 traveled widely, working as a physician and medical researcher. Back in France, he joined the staff of a state clinic in Clichy.

His nightmarish first novel, *Voyage au Bout de la Nuit* (1932; Eng. trans., *Journey to the End of Night*, 1934), soon recognized as a perverse but brilliant innovation, was followed by a second major work, also nihilistic and grotesque: *Mort à Crédit* (1936; Eng. trans., *Death on the Installment Plan*, 1938).

Céline's savagely misanthropic outlook —especially as expressed in his anti-French and anti-Semitic writings of the late 1930's—caused him to be regarded as pro-fascist even before World War II. Nonetheless, he remained aloof from the war and, when France fell to the Nazis in 1940, refused to leave his practice. In 1944, fearing reprisal by the returning Free French, he fled to Germany, then to Denmark (1945). Traced there by the French and imprisoned for a time at their request, he remained an exile until 1951, when he was pardoned by the French government. He spent his last years, broken in health and a near-recluse, as a physician to the poor in Meudon, where he died on July 3, 1961.

His later works, ever more tortured in style, include *D'un Château de l'Autre* (1957; Eng. trans., *Castle to Castle*, 1968) and *Rigodon* (1969; Eng. trans., *Rigadoon*, 1969).

**CELL,** basic structural unit of a plant or animal. Cells may be removed from complex plants or animals and grown in an artificial environment, called a culture, such as a test tube containing nutrients. In living organisms, cell multiplication and function are correlated in a complex way. Hormones (q.v.), chemicals that regulate life processes such as growth and reproduction, direct some phases and interrelationships of cells, as may the toxins of infecting organisms. The shape of a cell is determined by the tissue in which it occurs. When free of other cells, it may be round; when compressed, in a tissuelike pith, it may be polyhedral. Most cells vary in diameter between 1/1000 in. and 1/50,000 in.

**Composition.** The main parts of a living cell are the plasma or cell membrane; the nucleus, which is surrounded by its own membrane; and the cytoplasm, a complex liquid filling the space between the nucleus and the cell membrane. More than a protective barrier, the cell membrane keeps some substances out of the cell and keeps others in. Substances involved in the functioning of cell life may pass through tiny pores in the cell membrane.

The cell membrane of most plant cells is surrounded by a cell wall composed basically of numerous, ultramicroscopic threads of cellulose (q.v.). Some cell walls contain other or additional chemicals, such as lignin, present in the walls of wood cells; pectic compounds, important in cell elasticity; or suberin, a fatty substance found in cork cell walls. The endoplasmic reticulum, a network of hollow sheets running through the cytoplasm, is believed to be connected to both the nuclear and cell membranes, perhaps serving as a transport system within the cell. The reticulum may have a smooth or rough appearance. Roughness is attributed to ribosomes, tiny bumps on the outside of the reticulum, which are involved in the manufacture of proteins and contain ribonucleic acid and protein.

The nucleus of each cell is a discrete structure

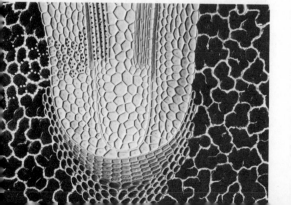

*Enlarged model of root tip of a plant, cut lengthwise to show arrangement of cells.* Buffalo Museum of Science

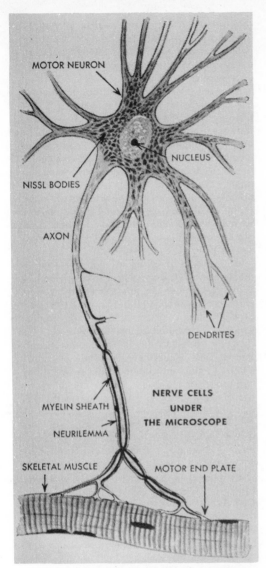

MOTOR NEURON

NUCLEUS

NISSL BODIES

AXON

DENDRITES

**NERVE CELLS UNDER THE MICROSCOPE**

MYELIN SHEATH

NEURILEMMA

SKELETAL MUSCLE

MOTOR END PLATE

*Typical neuron, or nerve cell, has fibers connecting with other nerve cells and organs.* TODAY'S HEALTH, published by the AMERICAN MEDICAL ASSOCIATION

A definite number of chromosomes is characteristic of each species of animal and plant. Particular chromosomes may be identified at the point of maximum contraction during cell division. Sex chromosomes, for example, occur in unlike pairs in some plants and in most animals having male and female individuals. These chromosomes determine the sex of an individual, depending on which of the pair is passed on to the next generation; *see* HEREDITY. Chromosomes are composed mostly of nucleic acids (q.v.), which are also found in the nucleolus, a small, globular body within the nucleus. One or more nucleoli may appear in each nucleus. Tiny parts of the chromosomes, called genes, are the units of heredity. Heavier than cytoplasm, the components of the nucleus can be separated from the rest of the cell with a centrifuge (q.v.).

Cytoplasm is a fluid material containing organelles (little organs), which are involved in the manufacture and transport of substances important to cell life. Energy for the cell is provided by granular material called mitochondria in the cytoplasm. The inner and outer membranes of mitochondria contain enzymes (q.v.), protein substances that control the chemical reactions within the cell. Nutrients for cell use are broken down by enzymes in the mitochondria, thus providing energy and such by-products as water and carbon dioxide. Lysosomes, tiny structures within the cell, contain digestive enzymes that break up large molecules into smaller ones, which are more easily digested by the mitochondria. Lysosomes also contain powerful enzymes that can protect the cell against bacteria and viruses. Near the nucleus but in the cytoplasm is the centrosome, a small body containing still smaller units, the centrioles, which play a part in cell division. A complex system called the Golgi apparatus, used for storage of proteins, is found in the cytoplasm, which also contains salts, food materials, oil droplets, bits of pigmented chemicals, and free molecules, such as proteins. The cytoplasm of plant cells contains bodies called plastids (*see* HEREDITY: *Cytological Inheritance*). The plastids include chloroplasts, which contain chlorophyll and are responsible for starch manufacture and photosynthesis (q.v.); chromoplasts, within which are formed pigments; and leucoplasts, or colorless plastids, which change sugar into starch or oil. Colorless plastids may develop into chromoplasts. As a result of chemical activities of the plant, waste products are formed in the cytoplasm. In unicellular organisms, waste products are simply excreted through the cell membranes; in higher plants, excretion takes place

surrounded by its own membrane, which is porous enough to permit the transfer of material between the surrounding cytoplasm and the nucleus. Nuclei appear to vary in shape from globular to elongate. The nucleus contains globules of a substance known as chromatin, which has an affinity for certain dyes. Thus a nucleus stained with such a dye has a granular appearance. The chromatin is believed to be located on fine threads, called chromosomes, which contain almost all of the hereditary material of an individual; *see* CHROMOSOME.

through the roots or openings in the leaves. *See* PROTOPLASM.

**Cell Division.** The usual type of cell division is called mitosis, which proceeds according to the following pattern: prophase, metaphase, anaphase, telophase, and interphase. In prophase, the chromosomes contract and the nuclear membrane and the nucleolus disappear. The centrioles travel to opposite sides of the nucleus, where they form spindle fibers (rays). The chromosomes become attached to the fibers. In metaphase, the chromosomes divide into two identical sets. In anaphase, the new chromosomes migrate to their respective "poles", the opposing centrioles. In telophase, the new chromosomes begin to resemble thin threads and a new nuclear membrane forms around them. Mitosis is complete when two new cells have sprung from their parent cell. Interphase is the interval during which the new cells carry on their normal activities and prepare for mitosis. The appearance and function of structures within the cell may vary at different stages of mitosis or during interphase, the time between successive cell divisions.

After cell division in plants, the formation of a wall usually takes place by means of a cell plate, a disk of wall material which advances outward from the center of the cell until it meets the original cell wall. In animals the cell membrane typically pushes inward to the center of the cell, forming two new cells by means of a ringlike contraction. Mitosis results in duplication of chromosomes and the distribution of the resulting pairs to daughter cells. In this manner each of the daughter cells contains the same number of chromosomes as the cell which gave rise to them.

Another type of nuclear division, occurring in the formation of sex cells (eggs or sperms), is known as meiosis. In this process the paired chromosomes separate but do not split. Instead of duplicating, one of each pair of chromosomes is distributed to the daughter cells or daughter nuclei. In this manner are produced the sex cells, which have half the number of chromosomes. Fertilization (q.v.), in which the egg and sperm are joined, restores the full number of chromosomes characteristic of the somatic cells of the species. This process, in which cells with the half number of chromosomes, known as haploid cells, occur in reproductive phases, whereas the remainder of the plant or animal body has the double, or diploid number, is a condition of the alternation of generations (q.v.).

**Cell Types.** Cells may be distinguished by their contents, walls, shapes, and functions. For example, wood cells, which are dead at maturity, contain sap, are elongated in shape, and have specially thickened and pitted walls to aid in water conduction and transfer. Other cells in plants are specialized for conduction and storage of food materials, mechanical strengthening, protection (such as hairs which cover a plant), and photosynthesis. The nerve cells, bone cells, cartilage cells, and several types of blood cells in animals are easily recognized by their appearance and function. The science of histology (q.v.) deals with the characteristics of tissues and of various cells and their origins. *See* ANATOMY.

Both plants and animals usually have two types of sex cells. The egg is large and nonmotile, whereas the sperm is small and provided with one or more cilia which enable it to swim to the egg. The fusion of egg and sperm in fertil-

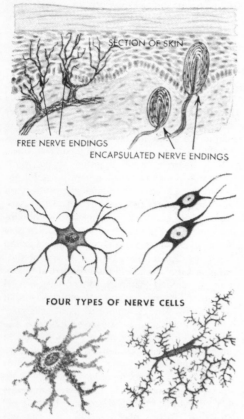

SECTION OF SKIN

FREE NERVE ENDINGS

ENCAPSULATED NERVE ENDINGS

**FOUR TYPES OF NERVE CELLS**

*Six kinds of nerve cells. Top: Section of skin has cells with free nerve endings (left) for sensing pain or touch; encapsulated nerve endings (right) are sensitive to pressure or cold. Middle: Cells from white matter of brain. Bottom: Gray matter cell (left); microglia cell (right) is a scavenger of damaged nervous tissue.*

TODAY'S HEALTH, published by the AMERICAN MEDICAL ASSOCIATION

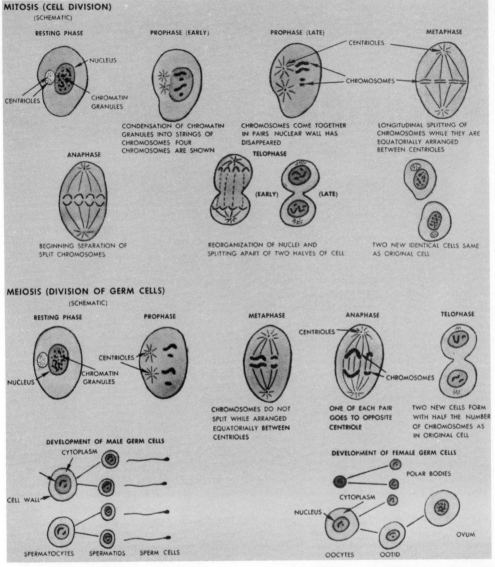

MITOSIS (CELL DIVISION)
(SCHEMATIC)

RESTING PHASE
NUCLEUS
CENTRIOLES
CHROMATIN GRANULES

PROPHASE (EARLY)
CONDENSATION OF CHROMATIN GRANULES INTO STRINGS OF CHROMOSOMES FOUR CHROMOSOMES ARE SHOWN

PROPHASE (LATE)
CENTRIOLES
CHROMOSOMES
CHROMOSOMES COME TOGETHER IN PAIRS NUCLEAR WALL HAS DISAPPEARED

METAPHASE
LONGITUDINAL SPLITTING OF CHROMOSOMES WHILE THEY ARE EQUATORIALLY ARRANGED BETWEEN CENTRIOLES

ANAPHASE
BEGINNING SEPARATION OF SPLIT CHROMOSOMES

TELOPHASE
(EARLY)   (LATE)
REORGANIZATION OF NUCLEI AND SPLITTING APART OF TWO HALVES OF CELL

TWO NEW IDENTICAL CELLS SAME AS ORIGINAL CELL

MEIOSIS (DIVISION OF GERM CELLS)
(SCHEMATIC)

RESTING PHASE
NUCLEUS
CHROMATIN GRANULES

PROPHASE
CENTRIOLES

METAPHASE
CHROMOSOMES DO NOT SPLIT WHILE ARRANGED EQUATORIALLY BETWEEN CENTRIOLES

ANAPHASE
CENTRIOLES
CHROMOSOMES
ONE OF EACH PAIR GOES TO OPPOSITE CENTRIOLE

TELOPHASE
TWO NEW CELLS FORM WITH HALF THE NUMBER OF CHROMOSOMES AS IN ORIGINAL CELL

DEVELOPMENT OF MALE GERM CELLS
CYTOPLASM
CELL WALL
SPERMATOCYTES   SPERMATIDS   SPERM CELLS

DEVELOPMENT OF FEMALE GERM CELLS
POLAR BODIES
CYTOPLASM
NUCLEUS
OVUM
OOCYTES   OOTID

ization assures hereditary contributions from both the male and the female parent. *See* REPRODUCTION.

**Specialized Animal Cells.** Animal cells vary in size from 1/1,905,000 in. in diameter to the size of neurons, several feet long but ultramicroscopically thin, which transmit nerve impulses. Brain cells may be pyramidal, with one very long dendrite (or fiber); or star-shaped, with many dendrites extending in various directions. Other cells have tiny hairs that help circulate cerebrospinal fluid. In the eye, rod cells, which differentiate between light and dark, are cylindrical. Cone cells in the eye usually are forked and

*Two types of cell division. Mitosis (top) is the process by which cells increase in size and weight through division. Cell parts organize themselves in a pattern that distributes chromosomes and other material equally so that each new cell is identical to the other and to the original cell. Meiosis (above), the process by which germ cells divide, differs from mitosis in that each new cell contains only half the chromosomes from the original cell. The normal number of chromosomes is restored when the female cell is fertilized by the male germ cell.* TODAY'S HEALTH, published by the AMERICAN MEDICAL ASSOCIATION

contain pigments for color vision. Smooth muscle cells are spindle-shaped, with a nucleus near the central part, but skeletal muscles are composed of cylindrical or prismatic fibers contain-

A plastic model of a human cell, magnified more than one million times so that its smallest working parts can be seen. *Wide World*

ing many nuclei. The red blood cells of mammals lose their nuclei and become biconcave as they mature. The concavities improve their function in transporting oxygen. Some white blood cells make amoeboid movements that enable them to pass through cell walls. Cells of endocrine glands may be specialized for hormone secretion. The acidophiles of the pituitary, for example, contain specific secretion granules. *See* CYTOLOGY; EMBRYOLOGY.

**History.** The science of cytology, the study of the cell, began with the description of cork cells in 1665 by the English physicist Robert Hooke (q.v.). As the quality of microscopes improved, knowledge of the cell increased rapidly. In 1838 the German botanist Matthias Jakob Schleiden (q.v.) developed the cell theory that living organisms are composed of cells and that the nucleus is essential to the formation of new cells.

In the 20th century special microscopes, such as the X-ray microscope, the phase-contrast microscope, and the electron microscope have greatly expanded knowledge of the cell. These tools permit investigation of the molecular structure of the cell. As knowledge of the cell extends to increasingly finer structural details, the cell has proved to be an intricately organized and exceedingly complicated system of chemical compounds and chemical reactions.

In 1970 scientists at the New York University School of Medicine achieved the first synthesis of a particle of the human cell when they created an artificial lysosome. Major advances have also been made toward the laboratory creation of ribosomes. In 1974 scientists at the University of Colorado at Boulder took the nucleus and cytoplasm in mammalian cells apart and then reconstructed the cells by putting the nuclei in new bodies of cytoplasm. The new "hybrid" cells continued to grow for many generations, and it was hoped that this method might make it possible to substitute healthy nuclei for those in cancerous cells in order to check malignant growth.

*See also* MICROSCOPE; PLANT MORPHOLOGY. S.C.

**CELL, ELECTRIC,** device that converts chemical energy into electricity; *see* ELECTROCHEMISTRY. All electric cells consist of a liquid or moistened electrolyte and an external electric circuit connected between a positive and a negative electrode (q.v.). The electrolyte, a liquid in which a dissolved chemical will dissociate into negative and positive ions (*see* IONIZATION) may be a solution of salts, acids, or bases; a weak acid solution is commonly used because it conducts electricity for a longer time. The electrodes are made of substances that will also dissociate in the electrolyte. In one of the simplest examples of an electric cell the electrolyte is a dilute solution of sulfuric acid, which dissociates into positive hydrogen ions and negative sulfate ions. The positive electrode is copper; the negative electrode is zinc, which when submerged in the electrolyte dissociates into positive zinc ions and free electrons. The electrons travel from the electrode through the external electric circuit, producing an electric current, and reenter the cell at the positive, copper electrode. There the electrons combine with the positive hydrogen ions in the electrolyte to form molecules of hydrogen gas, which bubble to the surface.

Cells in which the chemicals cannot be reconstituted into their original form once the energy has been converted, that is, they cannot be recharged, are called primary cells or voltaic cells. Cells in which the chemicals can be reconstituted (by passing an electric current through the electrolyte in a direction the reverse of normal cell operation) are called secondary cells, storage cells, or accumulators. A battery usually consists of two or more connected cells.

**Primary Cells.** The most common form of primary cell is the Leclanché cell, invented by Georges Leclanché (1839–82), a French chemist, in the 1860's. It is popularly called a dry cell or flashlight battery. The Leclanché cell in use today is very similar to his original invention. The electrolyte consists of a mixture of ammonium chloride and zinc chloride made up into a paste. The negative electrode consists of zinc, which also forms the outside shell of the cell, and the positive electrode is a thin carbon rod surrounded by a mixture of carbon and manganese dioxide. The Leclanché cell produces about 1.5 volts.

Another widely used primary cell is the zinc-mercuric-oxide cell, more commonly called a mercury battery. It can be made in the shape of a small flat disk and is used in this form in hearing aids, photoelectric cells, and electric wristwatches. The negative electrode consists of zinc, the positive electrode is of mercuric oxide, and the electrolyte is a solution of potassium hydroxide. The mercury battery produces about 1.34 volts.

The fuel cell is another type of primary cell. It is unique in that the chemicals are not contained within the cell but are supplied from outside; see Fuel Cell.

**Secondary Cells.** Secondary cells can be recharged by connecting them in reverse to a source of direct current, which reverses the chemical reaction. The lead-acid battery, which consists of three or six cells connected in series, is the most common type, used in automobiles, trucks, aircraft, and other vehicles. Its chief advantage is that it can deliver a strong current of electricity for starting an engine; however, it runs down quickly. The electrolyte is a dilute solution of sulfuric acid, the negative electrode consists of lead, and the positive electrode of lead dioxide. In operation, the negative lead electrode dissociates into free electrons and positive lead ions. The electrons travel through the external electric circuit, and the positive lead ions combine with the sulfate ions in the electrolyte to form lead sulfate. When the electrons reenter the cell at the positive lead-dioxide electrode, another chemical reaction occurs. The lead dioxide combines with the positive hydrogen ions in the electrolyte and the returning electrons to form water, releasing lead ions, which combine with negative sulfate ions in the electrolyte to form additional lead sulfate.

A lead-acid storage cell runs down as the sulfuric acid gradually is converted into water and lead sulfate. The amount of charge remaining in the cell can be measured with a hydrometer, because water is less dense than sulfuric acid. When the cell is being recharged, the chemical reactions described above are reversed until the chemicals have been restored to their original condition. A lead-acid battery has a useful life of about four years. It produces about 2 volts per cell.

Another widely used secondary cell is the alkaline cell, or Edison battery, developed by the American inventor Thomas Alva Edison (q.v.) in the 1900's. The principle of operation is the same as in the lead-acid cell except that the negative electrode consists of iron, the positive electrode of nickelic oxide, and the electrolyte is a solution of potassium hydroxide. This battery is used principally in heavy industry, because it can stand rough treatment better than a lead-acid battery, which tends to leak acid. The Edison battery has a useful life of about ten years and produces about 1.15 volts.

Another alkaline cell similar to the Edison battery is the nickel-cadmium cell, or cadmium battery, in which the iron electrode is replaced by one consisting of cadmium. It also produces about 1.15 volts, and its useful lifetime is about twenty-five years.

**Solar Battery.** Solar batteries produce electricity by a photoelectric conversion process. The source of electricity is a photosensitive semiconducting substance (see Transistor: *N-Type and P-Type Semiconductors*), such as a silicon crystal to which impurities have been added. When the crystal is struck by light, electrons are dislodged from the surface of the crystal and migrate toward the opposite surface. There they are collected as a current of electricity. Solar batteries can last forever and are used chiefly in spacecraft as a source of electricity to operate the equipment aboard.

**CELLINI, Benvenuto** (1500–71), Italian sculptor, engraver, and goldsmith, born in Florence. Apprenticed to a goldsmith at the age of fifteen, Cellini became one of the foremost goldsmiths of the Italian Renaissance, executing exquisitely crafted gold and silver coins, jewelry, vases, and ornaments. His stormy passions drove him into continual duels and brawls, which several times compelled him to flee from Florence to various other Italian cities. In Rome he was for a time a pupil of the Italian artist Michelangelo (q.v.). He was present at the siege of Rome by the army of Charles V (q.v.), Holy Roman Emperor, in 1527 and participated in the fighting. He numbered among his patrons many of the rich and great, including Pope Clement VII (*see under* Cle-

MENT), Pope Paul III (q.v.), Francis I (q.v.), King of France, and the Florentine nobleman Cosimo I de' Medici (*see under* MEDICI). Francis I invited him in 1540 to Paris, where he remained for five years. During this time he modeled the bronze reliefs of the Nymph of Fontainebleau (now in the Louvre). He also executed an elaborate gold saltcellar for Francis I (now in the Kunsthistorisches Museum, Vienna). Compelled to leave France because of his quarrels and eccentricities, he returned to Florence, where, under the patronage of Cosimo de' Medici, he executed many fine works in metal, among them a bronze portrait bust of Cosimo and the colossal bronze statue "Perseus with the Head of Medusa" (now in the National Museum, Florence). The qualities and training that made him unequaled in delicate work in gold and silver impaired his powers as a sculptor. Although his statues are perfect in finish they lack the loftiness of conception and breadth of treatment of the great masters. In an apparently impulsive moment of religious fervor, Cellini decided to become a priest in 1558; he secured a release from his vows in 1560 in order to marry.

Cellini is especially noted for his *Autobiography,* written between 1558 and 1562 (published 1728) and considered a literary masterpiece. A frank account of the escapades, adventures, and intrigues in which he engaged, this work is a valuable portrait of a typical personality of the Italian Renaissance. The *Autobiography* is important also as a mirror of the political, social, and ecclesiastical life that flourished during Cellini's period.

**CELLO,** abbreviation for violoncello (q.v.).

**CELLOPHANE,** originally a trade name for a flexible, transparent film made of regenerated cellulose and used principally as a wrapping material. Cellophane is produced by dissolving wood pulp or other cellulose material in an alkali with carbon disulfide, neutralizing the alkaline solvent with an acid, impregnating the precipitated sheet with glycerine, and drying and cutting the film into sheets. Cellophane was invented about 1910 by the Swiss chemist Jacques Edwin Brandenberger (1873?–1954), who in 1912 invented the first machines for large-scale production and established a factory near Paris. In 1923 he sold the North American rights to the production of cellophane and the use of the trade name to a subsidiary of E.I. du Pont de Nemours and Company, which produces it in the United States today. The word cellophane is commonly used to refer to this product, regardless of the manufacturer. *See* CELLULOSE.

**CELLULAR TISSUE.** *See* HISTOLOGY.

**CELLULOID,** originally the trade name and now the common name of a synthetic plastic made by mixing pyroxylin, or cellulose (q.v.) nitrate, with pigments and fillers in a solution of camphor in alcohol. When heated, the substance is pliable or plastic, and can be molded into a variety of shapes. Upon drying and cooling, the material becomes hard. In the United States celluloid was invented by John Wesley Hyatt (1837–1920), who was trying to win a $10,000 award for finding a substitute for ivory in making billiard balls. Hyatt failed to win the prize, but he received a patent for his discovery in 1870. The patent was disputed by the British inventor of a similar product, Xylonite.

Celluloid is transparent and colorless and in paste form can be colored or rolled or molded into specific shapes. Some of the advantages of celluloid are that it is cheap and durable, takes a high polish, does not warp or discolor, and is not affected by moisture. It is, however, highly flammable, and although modifications in manufacture have reduced the dangers of fire, it has been largely superseded by other materials. Celluloid is used in making combs as well as brushes.

**CELLULOSE** (Lat. *cellula,* "little cell"), chief constituent of the cell wall of all vegetable cells. These walls constitute the plant skeleton and also form a protective covering for the sensitive, living protoplasm. The term cellulose covers a number of bodies of similar chemical nature, the relative composition of which may be represented by the formula $C_6H_{10}O_5$; their molecular structures are, however, extremely complex. In plants, cellulose is normally combined with woody, fatty, or gummy substances. A typical form, from which pure cellulose can be easily isolated by chemical methods, exists in cotton and flax fibers. Certain plants, such as peas, beans, and Arabian coffee, store reserve food in the walls of their seeds as a hemicellulose, which in this form undergoes hydrolysis more readily than other celluloses.

With some exceptions in the insect world, true cellulose is not found in animal tissues. Much of it is digested and absorbed by the herbivora, but the amount that man assimilates is relatively small. No digestive enzyme that acts specifically on cellulose has been observed in the animal body. Microorganisms in the digestive tracts of hoofed animals break down the cellulose into products which can then be absorbed by these animals.

Cellulose makes up more than one third of all vegetable matter. It is manufactured on a large scale from wood, cotton, linen rags, hemp, flax, and similar materials. Insoluble in all ordinary solvents, it may be readily separated from the other constituents, which are soluble in water, alcohol, ether, dilute alkalies, or acids. Cellulose is soluble in an ammoniacal solution of cupric hydroxide (Schweitzer's reagent), from which it separates out in a pure state on addition of acid and is obtained in the form of a white, amorphous powder.

Sulfuric acid acts upon cellulose to produce, depending upon concentration, glucose, soluble starch, or amyloid; the last is a form of starch used for the coating of parchment paper.

When cellulose is treated with an alkali and then exposed to the fumes of carbon disulfide, it goes into solution as cellulose xanthate. Further treatment of this solution yields viscose films and threads. Rayon and cellophane are cellulose regenerated from such solutions. Cellulose acetates are obtained by the action of acetic anhydride on cellulose in the presence of sulfuric acid. They are spun into fine filaments for the manufacture of such fabrics as Celanese (q.v.), and are also used for photographic safety film, as a substitute for glass, for the manufacture of safety glass, and as a molding material in the manufacture of many plastic objects. Cellulose ethers, such as ethyl cellulose and methyl cellulose, are used in paper sizings, adhesives, soaps, and synthetic resins. They are stable, inexpensive, and soluble in a wide variety of solvents.

With mixtures of nitric and sulfuric acids, cellulose forms a series of inflammable and explosive compounds known as cellulose nitrates, or nitrocelluloses, the compositions of which depend on the strength of the acids and the duration of the treatment. Pyroxylin, also called collodion cotton, is a cellulose nitrate used in various lacquers and plastics. When pyroxylin is dissolved in a mixture of alcohol and ether, it yields collodion, a cellulose nitrate used in medicine and photography, and in the manufacture of artificial leather and some lacquers. Guncotton is cellulose nitrate of more than 12 percent nitration. It is a high explosive, used in blasting gelatin, demolition blocks, and various other explosives (q.v.).

The most important use of cellulose is in the manufacture of paper. For the cheaper grades of paper, the impure cellulose of wood pulp is employed; better grades are manufactured from cotton and linen rags. See PAPER; PLASTICS; WOOD: *Chemical Wood Products.*        H.A.N.

**CELLULOSE ACETATE.** *See* CELANESE; CELLULOSE; PLASTICS.

**CELLULOSE NITRATE.** *See* CELLULOID; CELLULOSE; PLASTICS.

**CELSIUS, Anders** (1701–44), Swedish astronomer, born at Uppsala. From 1730 to 1744 he was professor of astronomy at Uppsala University, built the observatory there in 1740, and was appointed its director. In 1733 his collection of 316 observations of the Aurora Borealis was published. In 1737 he took part in the French expedition sent to measure one degree of meridian in the polar regions. In his monograph *On the Measurement of Heat* (1742) he presented the first idea of the Celsius, or centigrade, thermometer, which has a scale separating the boiling and freezing points of water by 100 degrees. He wrote, among other scientific treatises, *De Observationibus pro Figura Telluris Determinanda in Gallia Habitis Disquisitio* ("An Examination into Observations Concerning the Determination of the Shape of the Earth as Conducted in France", 1738). *See* TEMPERATURE: *Temperature Scales.*

**CELSUS, Aulus Cornelius** (fl. 1st cent. A.D.), Roman writer. He wrote an encyclopedia on the subjects of medicine, rhetoric, history, philosophy, warfare, and agriculture. Part of this work, the eight books on medicine, *De Medicina* ("Of Medicine"), were translated into English in 1756; three are still in print. The books were largely based on the opinions and observations of the Greek physician Hippocrates (q.v.).

**CELT.** *See* CELTIC PEOPLES AND LANGUAGES.

**CELTIC ART,** works of art produced in pre-Christian and early Christian times by Celts (*see* CELTIC PEOPLES AND LANGUAGES) inhabiting the British Isles and the European continent. Celtic art is considered by several authorities to be the first great contribution made to European art by peoples other than those living in the Mediterranean regions. Among the outstanding characteristics of Celtic art is the skillful ornamentation of bronze, gold, and silver objects, as in the characteristic neck ring known as the *torc.* Celtic art is also characterized by a distinctive preference for motifs showing plants and animals, with human elements playing a secondary, occasional role. The two open ends of a torc, for example, are usually depictions of the heads of animals; Celtic pottery shows bands of repeated designs of water birds or horses. Stylized treatment of such plants as leaves and ferns is also a characteristic practice in Celtic art.

The earliest Celtic art was created late in the Iron Age (q.v.) by Celtic tribesmen living on or near the Lake of Neuchâtel, in present-day Switzerland. The products of this era, known as the La Tène period, include pottery, metal, and woodwork ornamented with spiral and S-shaped figures, as well as other geometric de-

*Symbol of Saint Matthew, detail of a page containing symbols of the four evangelists, from the Book of Kells, the masterpiece of Celtic manuscript illumination.*

signs. Celtic art is also preserved in Greece and in other parts of Europe.

The early, or pagan, period of Celtic art in Britain dates from about three centuries before the beginning of the Roman occupation (55 B.C.). Notable remains from the period include rude but impressive stone monuments that apparently played an important role in fertility rites and other folk practices. Such monuments are found in many parts of Scotland, Ireland, Brittany, Wales, and Cornwall. Other pre-Christian artifacts include shields, swords, sheaths, helmets, and armlets. The basic material was generally bronze, but occasionally silver and gold were used. The principal motifs were elliptical curves, divergent spirals, and chevrons; they were formed in high or low relief by the use of chased or engraved lines and dots on plates and of champlevé enamels of red, yellow, blue, and green. The patterns were highly intricate. Many articles found throughout England, Scotland, and Ireland, are in the national museums of London, Edinburgh, and Dublin. Pottery took the form of cinerary urns, food vessels, drinking cups, and incense cups, turned by hand and imperfectly baked but of fine workmanship. Such outstanding workmanship is also a notable feature of Celtic jewelry.

With the introduction of Christianity into the British Isles, Celtic art became religious in character. Craftsmen of this period produced illuminated pages of manuscript copies of the Gospels, the most famous of which are the *Book of Kells* in Trinity College, Dublin, and the *Lindisfarne Gospels* in the British Museum, London. Specimens of metalwork include chalices, crosiers, bells, and shrines. Examples of stone sculpture are the incised cross slabs and monumental stones of Scotland and Ireland, which are similar in decorative characteristics to the metalwork and manuscripts.

**CELTIC PEOPLES AND LANGUAGES,** peoples belonging to an ensemble of different racial groups predominant in central and western Europe in antiquity, and the languages spoken by those peoples.

**History.** The geographical and ethnological origins of the Celts are obscure. Their name is derived from *Keltoi,* the Greek form of a Celtic word meaning, possibly, "heroes" or "lofty ones". They first appeared in central Europe during the 2nd millennium B.C. and eventually became the dominant military and cultural force in north-central Europe, giving their language, customs, religion, and traditions to the peoples they subjugated. More than 150 distinct Celtic-speaking tribes, of whom the Britons and the tribes of Gaul (qq.v.) were the most prominent, ultimately emerged in Europe.

Late in the 2nd millennium B.C. the Goidels, or Gaels, moved westward from the Continent and occupied the islands known later as Ireland (q.v.) and the Isle of Man (*see* MAN, ISLE OF). The Goidels were the ancestors of the modern Irish, Manx, and Scottish Gaels, many of whom still speak a Celtic language; *see* GAELIC LANGUAGE; MANX LANGUAGE AND LITERATURE. In the 5th or 4th century B.C., Britain (q.v.) was settled by a Celtic tribe known as the Brythons. During the Roman occupation of Britain the Brythons retained their language and their culture, both of which were modified extensively by Roman influences.

Toward the close of the 2nd millennium B.C., or at some time early in the 1st millennium B.C., the Gauls, the largest grouping of Celtic tribes on the Continent, became dominant in the territory to which they gave their name; see GAUL. By the end of the 5th century B.C., they swept over most of Europe, invading the Iberian peninsula, northern Italy, Macedonia, and Thessaly. They plundered Rome in 390 B.C., sacked Delphi in 279 B.C., and penetrated Asia Minor, where they founded Galatia (q.v.). As a result of these far-flung deployments, their positions in central Europe became increasingly vulnerable to the Germanic tribes east of the Rhine. About the end of the 2nd century B.C., the Romans inflicted two disastrous defeats on the Gauls in northern Italy. The Roman statesman and soldier Gaius Julius Caesar (q.v.) subjugated the remainder of the Gallic tribes, notably the Belgae (q.v.), between 58 and 50 B.C., concluding the era of Celtic supremacy in western Europe. Celtic continued to be the universal language of Gaul until the end of the 2nd century A.D., but thereafter Latin became the predominant tongue. Celtic languages had virtually ceased to exist on the European continent by the 4th century A.D.

**Celtic Culture.** The Celtic tribes of the Continent were bound together by common speech, customs, and religion, rather than by any well-defined central government. The absence of political unity contributed substantially to the extinction of their civilization, which, in many respects, was considerably more advanced than that of the Teutonic tribes in the east. Their social system was dominated by fiducial and religious factors, as illustrated by the hierarchic power of the Druids (see DRUIDISM), an order of priests who performed sylvan and magical ceremonies, and by the deep-rooted tribal or clan system, still clearly traceable in the Scottish clans. Their mythology, which included earth gods, various sylvan genii, and sun deities, was peculiarly rich in elfin demons and tutelaries, beings that still pervade the lore of peoples of Celtic ancestry. The art of the Continental Celts attained a remarkable degree of perfection, notably in the early phase (about 550 to 420 B.C.) of the period known in archeology as the La Tène Period. Their craftsmen excelled in technique and ornamentation, as revealed in excavated specimens of their pottery and horse harness, and bronze swords, helmets, and jewelry.

Because their tradition was purely oral, the most ancient Celtic-speaking peoples left no literature. The few examples of Gaulish in existence consist mostly of inscriptions on monuments and coins, which yield proper names as well as scattered clues to the nature of Gaulish grammar and phonology. References to Gaulish proper names are also found in the works of

Greek and Roman historians. The germ of Celtic literature appeared in the oghamic inscriptions of Ireland, simple records of men and events carved in stone and wood. Before the development of a formal alphabet the Goidelic tribes employed a symbolic system of writing that utilized the cross, the fylfot or swastika, the trefoil or trivet, and other figures. To some extent the symbolism included the use of colors and weaves, later exemplified by the Scottish tartans. The music and poetry of the insular Celtic-speaking peoples of ancient times were preserved by bards and other entertainers, who chanted tribal traditions, sang patriotic songs, and recited folktales. The literary talent and heritage developed in this fashion eventually found expression in the literatures of the various insular Celtic peoples, particularly during the Middle Ages.

**Celtic Languages.** The characteristic of Celtic languages that most conspicuously distinguishes them from other Indo-European linguistic groups is their loss of the original Indo-European sound p; see INDO-EUROPEAN LANGUAGES. In most other Indo-European linguistic groups the sound was preserved. Thus, a Latin, Greek, or Sanskrit word containing an initial or medial p will appear in the Celtic family without that consonant (for example, Latin porcus, Goidelic orc; Latin plenus, Breton leun). In relation to the other members of the Indo-European family of languages, the Celtic group is closest, linguistically as well as geographically, to the Italic and Germanic, although this relationship is not very close.

The Brythonic variation of the Celtic languages survives in Welsh, the most thriving Celtic language; see WELSH LANGUAGE; WELSH LITERATURE. Cornish, a variation of Brythonic spoken in Cornwall, became practically extinct about the end of the 18th century; see CORNISH LANGUAGE AND LITERATURE. A form of Brythonic, known as Breton, is also spoken in Brittany, the Amorican peninsula of western France settled in the 5th and 6th centuries A.D. by refugees escaping from the Germanic invaders of Britain; see BRETON LANGUAGE AND LITERATURE.

The Goidelic and Brythonic groups of Celtic languages differ in that Goidelic preserves the velar element of the Indo-European labiovelar qu sound (later written c), whereas Brythonic renders this sound as p. Thus Irish mac (son) corresponds to the Middle Welsh map (mab in modern Welsh); Irish coic (five) corresponds to Welsh pump. The Brythonic p is not, however, identical in origin with the original Indo-European sound p, which dropped out of Celtic long

Steps in the manufacture of portland cement. Above: In huge kilns, rotating at about one turn per min., raw materials are burned into clinkers. Below: After cooling, the clinkers are conveyed to grinders, where they are ground into fine powder. Bottom: Finished cement is stored in silos, from which it can be loaded into trucks or railroad cars.                Portland Cement Assn.

before the differentiation of that tongue into separate languages. For convenience, the Goidelic family is known as Q-Celtic and the Brythonic as P-Celtic. Most Gaulish dialects were probably closely related to Brythonic. A striking characteristic of all Celtic languages is the mutation of initial consonants, as in the Welsh *tad* ("a father"), *fy nhad* ("my father"), *ei thad* ("her father"), *ei dad* ("his father").

**CEMENT,** any material that hardens and becomes strongly adhesive after application in plastic form. The term "cement" is often used interchangeably with glue and adhesive (qq.v.); in engineering the term is usually applied to a finely powdered substance consisting of gypsum plaster, lime or portland cement, which hardens and adheres after being mixed with water; see CEMENT, PORTLAND.

Cements are used for various purposes, such as binding sand and gravel together with portland cement to form concrete (q.v.), for uniting the surfaces of various materials, or for coating surfaces to protect them from chemical attack. Cements are made in a wide variety of compositions for a wide variety of uses. They may be named for the principal constituents, such as calcareous cement, which contains calcium, siliceous cement, which contains silica, and rubber cement; for the materials they join, such as glass or vinyl cement; for the object to which they are applied, such as boiler cement, or for their characteristic property, such as acid-resisting cement or quick-setting cement. Cements used in construction are sometimes named for their reputed place of origin, like Roman cement, or for their resemblance to other materials, such as portland cement, which produces a concrete resembling the Portland stone used widely for building in England. Cements which resist high temperatures are called refractory cements.

Cements set by the evaporation of the plasticizing liquid such as water, alcohol, or oil, by internal chemical change, by hydration, or by the growth of interlacing sets of crystals. Other cements harden as a result of chemical reaction with the oxygen or carbon dioxide in the atmosphere.

**CEMENT, PORTLAND,** substance composed of silicates and aluminates, which hardens after being mixed with water. It is a hydraulic cement, that is, it will harden under water, and is almost universally used for structural concrete. Typical portland cements are mixtures of tricalcium silicate ($3CaO \cdot SiO_2$), tricalcium aluminate ($3CaO \cdot AL_2O_3$), and dicalcium silicate ($2CaO \cdot SiO_2$), in varying proportions, together with small amounts of magnesium and iron compounds. Gypsum is often added to slow the hardening process.

These active compounds in cement are unstable, and when water is added they rearrange their structure. The initial set or hardening of the cement is caused by hydration of tricalcium silicate, which forms jellylike hydrated silica and calcium hydroxide. These substances ultimately crystallize and bind together the particles of sand or stone, which are always included in a mortar or concrete mixture, into a hard mass. Tricalcium aluminate acts in the same way to produce the initial set, but does not contribute to the ultimate hardening of the mixture. The hydration of dicalcium silicate proceeds similarly, but far more slowly, hardening gradually over a period of years. The process of hydration and setting of a cement mixture is known as curing; during this period heat is evolved.

Portland cement is manufactured from lime-bearing materials, usually limestone, together with clays, shales, or blast-furnace slag containing alumina and silica, in the approximate proportions of 60 percent lime, 19 percent silica, and 8 percent alumina, 5 percent iron, 5 percent magnesia, and 3 percent sulfur trioxide. Some rocks, called cement rocks, are naturally composed of these elements in approximately suitable proportions and can be made into cement without the use of large quantities of other raw materials. In general, however, cement plants rely on mixed materials.

In the manufacture of cement the raw materials are ground together, the mixture is heated until it fuses into a clinker, and the clinker is ground into a fine powder. The heating is usually accomplished in rotary kilns more than 500 ft. long and 12 or more feet in diameter. The kilns are slightly tilted from the horizontal, and the raw material is introduced at the upper end, either in the form of a dry rock powder or as a wet paste composed of ground-up rock and water. As the charge progresses down through the kiln, it is dried and heated by the hot gases from a flame at the lower end. As it comes nearer the flame, carbon dioxide is driven off, and in the area of the flame itself the charge is fused at temperatures between 2800° F. (1538° C.) and 2900° F. (1593° C.). The material takes approximately 6 hr. to pass from one end of the kiln to the other. After it leaves the kiln, the clinker is cooled quickly and ground, and then conveyed by a blower to packing machinery or storage silos.

In a modern kiln, 100 lb. of raw material will make 60 to 65 lb. of cement. The weight lost is largely carbon dioxide and water. Kilns usually burn coal in the form of powder and consume about 1 lb. of coal for every 2 lb. of cement produced. Oil and gas are also used.

Cement is a grayish-green powder so fine in texture that 90 percent or more of its particles will pass through a sieve with 200 openings per inch. It is packed in bags containing 94 lb., or in barrels of 376 lb.

A number of tests are used to check the quality of the cement. A common one is to use a mortar specimen of one part of cement and three parts of sand and measure its tensile strength after a week in air and under water. A good cement will show a tensile strength of 275 lb. per sq.in. under these conditions.

**Special Cements.** By varying the percentage of its normal components or adding others, portland cement can be given various desirable characteristics, such as rapid hardening, low heat during hydration, and resistance to alkalis. Rapid-hardening cements, sometimes called high-early-strength cements, are made by increasing the proportion of tricalcium silicate or by finer grinding: up to 99½ percent through a 325-mesh screen. Some of these cements will harden as much in a day as ordinary cement does in a month. They have the disadvantage, however, of producing much heat during hydration, which makes them unsuitable for large structures where such heat may cause cracks. Special low-heat cements, which usually have a large proportion of dicalcium silicate, are generally used for massive pourings. Where concrete work must be exposed to alkaline conditions, which attack concretes made with ordinary portland cement, resistant cements with a low aluminum content are generally employed. Cements for use under salt water may contain as much as 5 percent iron oxide, and those with as much as 40 percent aluminum oxide are used to resist the action of sulfate-bearing waters.

**Production.** It was not until the 20th century that the United States produced portland cement in any great quantity. In 1910, 76,550,000 bl. were manufactured. After 1910 production rose steadily until 1928, when 176,300,000 bl. were made. There was a sharp drop in the early 1930's, then production began to rise again. In the late 1960's the cement industry annually produced about 390,000,000 bl., including shipments from Puerto Rico, and imports. California ranks first among the States of the U.S. in the production of cement; other leading producers are Pennsylvania, Texas, Michigan, and New York. *See* CONCRETE.

**History.** Hydraulic cements made from lime and clay have been used since the middle of the 18th century. The name portland cement was first used in 1824 by Joseph Aspdin, a British cement maker, because of the resemblance between concrete made from his cement and Portland stone, which was much used in building in England. The first modern portland cement, made from lime and clay or shale materials calcined to a clinker and then ground, was produced in England in 1845. At that time cements were usually made in upright kilns where the raw materials were spread between layers of coke, which was then burned. The first rotary kilns were introduced about 1880.     A.G.H.D.

**CENCI, Beatrice** (1577–99), Italian noblewoman, called "the beautiful parricide". She was the daughter of Francesco Cenci (1549–98), a wealthy but cruel and vicious Roman nobleman. According to legend, after his second marriage he imprisoned her and made incestuous advances until circumstances enabled him to gratify his lust. She sought the help of her relatives, and, with her stepmother and her brother, conspired to murder Francesco on Sept. 9, 1598. During a lengthy trial, in which the conspirators were charged with murder, Beatrice persisted in declaring her innocence. All three, however, were condemned and beheaded in 1599. The story has been the theme of numerous literary works, notably a tragedy by the British poet Percy Bysshe Shelley (*see under* SHELLEY), *The Cenci* (1819), and of a portrait painting attributed to the Italian artist Guido Reni (q.v.).

**CENIS, MONT** (It. *Moncenisio*), pass in the Alps, on the border between France and Italy. The pass reaches an elevation of about 6850 ft. above sea level. A road was constructed between 1803 and 1810 by order of the French emperor Napoleon I (q.v.). A tunnel, completed in 1871, is about 8 mi. long and connects Turin, Italy, with Chambéry, France. *See* TUNNEL.

**CENOZOIC ERA,** last great division of geologic time, beginning about 70,000,000 years ago and extending through the present. It follows the Cretaceous Period of the Mesozoic Era (qq.v.) and is subdivided into the Tertiary Period and the Quaternary Period. Features of Tertiary times are considered in articles under the names of the various shorter time periods (epochs) making up the Tertiary Period: in order, from earliest to latest, these are the Paleocene, Eocene, Oligocene, Miocene, and Pliocene. The last two, the Pleistocene, and the Recent epochs are discussed under QUATERNARY PERIOD.

The Cenozoic, shortest of the geologic eras, is that period during which the modern world, with its characteristic geographical features and its animals and plants came into being. *See* GEOLOGY, HISTORICAL; MAN, ANCIENT; PALEONTOLOGY.

**CENSORSHIP,** supervision and control of the content in periodicals, books, theatrical productions, motion pictures, and other media of communication before or after they are produced and for the purpose of preventing the publication or production of material deemed by the censoring group to be immoral or against the interest of the public. In a broader sense, censorship denotes the attempt to limit the circulation of ideas in any setting.

The word "censorship" derives from censor, the title of ancient Roman magistrates whose original function, when the office was instituted in 443 B.C., was to supervise the enumeration of the population for the purpose of levying taxes. Those censors later became responsible for the supervision of citizens in their performance of public obligations and eventually became also the guardians of public morals. The agencies of censorship are usually the state, the church (as an established or state church), and private groups (including religious organizations in countries that do not have an established church).

## HISTORY

From earliest times censorship has existed wherever the rule of a church or a state has been powerful enough to impose its authority upon society. Perhaps the first distinct form of censorship can be seen in the taboo (q.v.), commonly found among primitive peoples. The taboo is an interdiction originating in custom and imposed by tribal priests or rulers upon such things as specified foods, forms of intermarriage, clothes, and names whose use was believed to be either forbidden by the gods or spirits or threatening of mortal danger.

**Antiquity.** In all ancient civilizations, such as the Egyptian, Babylonian, Persian, Hindu, and Chinese, different forms of religious and social censorship often may be traced to their origin in taboos. At the same time, however, the autocratic rulers of those civilized nations imposed their own types of political censorship in order to restrain the expression of opposition to their power. The principle of free and uncontrolled expression of ideas or communication of information was generally alien to the ancient world.

**Church Censorship.** During the Middle Ages the most powerful source of censorship was the Roman Catholic Church. In the Papal States (q.v.) and in localities where the bishop was the feudal lord, church censorship was official and absolute. Elsewhere it was more limited in application. Censorship in this period was concerned primarily with suppressing heresy (q.v.). For the purpose of punishing all such manifestations, Pope Gregory IX (1147?–1241) instituted the Inquisition (q.v.) about 1230. For almost five hundred years the Inquisition remained an influential agency of religious censorship. In 1600 the Italian philosopher Giordano Bruno (q.v.) was burned at the stake by the Inquisition for questioning certain dogmas of the church and expressing a belief in pantheism (q.v.). In 1633 the Italian scientist and father of modern astronomy, Galileo Galilei (q.v.), was forced to recant the Copernican theory, confirmed by his telescopic observations, that the earth revolves around the sun; *see* COPERNICAN SYSTEM. Perhaps the best-known example of church censorship has been the Index of Forbidden Books (q.v.).

During the 16th and 17th centuries the authorities of the Protestant churches of Europe and America suppressed everything they considered heretical with a fervor equal to that prevailing during the Inquisition. Men and women were burned at the stake in many countries where Calvinists or Lutherans were in power. Under the rule of Lord Protector Oliver Cromwell (q.v.), severe censorship was instituted in England, and it was extended to the American colony of Massachusetts. In particular, theaters were closed and other forms of popular entertainment were outlawed. Dissenters to the general use of censorship in the colonies included the clergyman Roger Williams and the English-American Quaker, William Penn (qq.v.). *See also* LEVELLERS; RELIGIOUS LIBERTY.

In the 20th century, fewer European nations have established churches; however, churches as private groups that participate in or control decisions affecting public education and other social and cultural services still have influence over the circulation of ideas.

**The Influence of Printing.** The innovation of printing (q.v.) with movable type in the 15th century was followed by a more scrupulous censorship of books and pamphlets than had ever before been exercised. Laws were enacted throughout most of Europe prohibiting all printing except by governmental license. For almost two centuries these laws encountered little opposition. One of the first and most famous denunciations of such laws was made by the English poet John Milton (q.v.). In 1644, without a license from the crown, he issued *Areopagitica,* an influential pamphlet in favor of freedom of the press. In it he protested that "he who destroys a good Booke, kills reason itself . . .". Although the statutes to which he objected expired in 1695, forms of censorship of the press remained in force throughout the rest of Europe. *See* PRESS, FREEDOM OF THE.

## MODERN POLITICAL CENSORSHIP

The right of the state to censor was not generally questioned in Europe until the latter half of the 18th century, when the political philosophy of the Enlightenment gained currency among European thinkers; *see* ENLIGHTENMENT, AGE OF. Except for a brief period in France after the Revolution of 1789, however, political censorship continued to flourish until after 1850 and the rise of republican governments. Coincident with the ebb of political censorship was a widespread increase in the censorship of obscenity, particularly in Great Britain under the rule of Queen Victoria (q.v.).

In the 1930's, a new wave of political censorship swept the West in the totalitarian states of Italy under fascism and Germany under National Socialism (qq.v.). Since the defeat of these regimes in World War II, censorship has been minimal in Germany and Italy. State censorship remains severe in the Soviet Union and other one-party states; in nations governed by multiparty systems, censorship by private groups resulting from specific local pressures is often the chief bar to the free expression and dissemination of ideas.

**State Censorship.** The usual justifications for state censorship include the necessity of maintaining political stability, national security, or public morality. Although voluntary censorship and censorship by private groups have been powerful social forces, state censorship is at present the most far-reaching and effective type of censorship because of its extensive enforcement powers. The state censors military information in peace as well as in war; it may also censor political ideas and information or social expressions, attitudes, and manners ranging from dress to sexual matters, and even religious beliefs.

Both totalitarian and relatively democratic governments exercise censorship according to the nature and degree of threat perceived; they limit personal freedoms in the interest of maintaining either power or a particular version of government. Totalitarian governments, however, tend to do so more consistently, usually in the name of an overall governmental objective requiring the subordination of individual liberty for the defined good of the society; such governments also tend to suppress opposition by permitting the existence of only one party.

One-party nations determine directly the ideas and information to be published, circulated, and taught. When publishers, authors, or broadcasters in such nations are adjudged to have trespassed the political or moral boundaries set by law or by administrative edict, they may be arbitrarily punished by fines, prison or labor-camp sentences, house arrest, confiscation of the offending publication, prohibition of future publications, or closing of the publishing house or other medium of communication.

In those nations in which the electorate chooses the government from two or more parties for a limited term and limited power, such as the United States and Great Britain, state censorship is generally designed to prevent the publication or dissemination only of material considered obscene or politically dangerous in the sense of being seditious. Legal definitions of obscenity and of sedition vary from country to country and alter with time and with the definition of threat to the nation. In Great Britain, where traffic in ideas has been almost entirely free of state control for a century, the lord chamberlain's office nevertheless until 1968 had the authority to refuse to license a play for public performance on the grounds of obscenity and bad taste, which included expressions of disrespect for the royal family or for public figures. When the lord chamberlain denied a license to a play for public performance, the play could still be produced for a so-called private showing in a club.

The U.S. has also restricted ideas in certain areas at different periods in its history; see *Censorship in the United States*, below.

All nations censor military information to some extent at all times, but during certain periods of emergency, as in time of war, the extent and intensity of censorship increases. The purpose of wartime censorship is to keep data concerning military preparations and movements from the enemy, to safeguard the public order and morale from agitation that may foster defeatism or subversion, and to prevent news of adverse military developments from affecting the public morale. For these reasons, both the

mail proceeding to and from fields of military training and operations and the news dispatches about military or political subjects are carefully scrutinized, and the dissemination of ideas considered obstructive to the pursuit of the war or dangerous to the stability of the government is often forbidden or restricted.

In general, proponents of state censorship maintain that the national or public welfare should be protected against sedition, breaches of military security, and immorality even at some expense to individual liberty. Advocates of church and private censorship maintain that the average person is less able to recognize harmful material in information, doctrine, or entertainment than are church authorities or trained and well-informed individuals.

Opponents of censorship generally do not advocate outright abolition of all censorship. They are concerned rather with the difficult questions of when, where, and how to apply censorship. Few would deny, for example, that some degree of military censorship is necessary in time of war or that some degree of censorship is necessary to keep obscene material out of general circulation, particularly among the young. Nevertheless, the opponents of censorship maintain that, carried beyond certain minimal limits, the infringement on freedom of expression is harmful and more grave in its consequences than the damage that might ensue from the unlimited circulation of ideas and information. Some argue for the abolition of all censorship, even of obscene or pornographic material, on the ground that no single definition, by law or otherwise, of material that constitutes obscenity or pornography can satisfactorily be drawn.

### CENSORSHIP IN THE UNITED STATES

The tradition of a free exchange of ideas and of religious liberty had taken root before the American Revolution (q.v.); *see* ZENGER, JOHN PETER. The press in the American colonies was subject to licensing laws administered by the British and similar to those in Great Britain. After the revolution and the adoption of the Constitution of the United States (q.v.), freedom of speech and of the press were guaranteed in the Bill of Rights (q.v.) by the First Amendment to the Constitution that declares that Congress shall make no law abridging freedom of religion, assembly, petition, speech, or press.

Within seven years of ratification of the Bill of Rights, Congress, however, passed the Alien and Sedition Acts (q.v.) of 1798. The acts were designed to keep out of circulation in the U.S. the ideas of the French Revolution (q.v.) and, with respect to the Alien Act, the advocates of such ideas. Under the Sedition Act editors were sentenced to jail for printing articles critical of President John Adams (q.v.) and his administration. Three of the laws expired in 1800–01, and the last was repealed in 1802.

At various times many States have passed laws in contradiction to the freedoms guaranteed in the First Amendment of the Federal Constitution. In the pre-Civil War period abolitionist literature against slavery (q.v.) was outlawed in the South. In the postwar period the extent to which the First Amendment applied to the States long remained unclear. Decisions rendered by the Supreme Court of the United States (q.v.) in 1927 and 1931 finally held that the Fourteenth Amendment applied the Bill of Rights to the States as well as to the Federal government and therefore Constitutionally required the individual States to refrain from abridging freedom of speech.

**Political Censorship.** Perhaps the most controversial political censorship in the U.S. in recent years was the direct and indirect result of the accusations of United States Senator Joseph Raymond McCarthy (q.v.) of Wisconsin in regard to the Communist Party and its effect on the security of the nation. One result of his efforts was the passage of the Internal Security Act by the Congress in 1950 over the veto of President Harry S. Truman (q.v.). The act was designed to control subversive activities in the U.S., and especially to exclude Communists from Federal employment in sensitive positions and to disallow their naturalization; parts of this law have subsequently been rescinded. In 1967 the Supreme Court ruled that Communists could not be banned from jobs in defense plants under the 1950 act. The requirement of loyalty oaths for State employees was another result of McCarthy's efforts; however, many such oaths have been declared unconstitutional. Still another result was the removal from the United States Information Service libraries abroad of thousands of books written by alleged Communists and similar acts of censorship at home. The atmosphere of suspicion prevailing during that period subsided substantially after the Senate formally censured McCarthy in December, 1954.

A major battle in the history of censorship in the U.S. arose in 1971 as a result of the publication in newspapers of secret documents belonging to the Department of Defense. These documents were derived from a 47-volume study, titled "History of the United States Decision-Making Process on Vietnam Policy", ordered in

XCIII.

THE

New-York Weekly JOURNAL

*Containing the freſheſt Adviſes, Foreign, and Domeſtick.*

*MUNDAY August 18th. 1735.*

*The tradition of a free press in America dates from the trial of colonial newspaperman John Peter Zenger on charges of libeling public officials. His acquittal is celebrated in the Aug. 18, 1735, issue of the New-York Weekly Journal, of which Zenger was editor. Zenger based his defense on his right to print the truth no matter how unflattering it might be.* Granger Collection

1967 by Robert S. McNamara (q.v.), then secretary of defense. The documents, later known as the Pentagon papers, came into the possession of two newspapers, the New York *Times* and the Washington *Post*, from a former civilian aide of the Defense Department, Daniel Ellsberg (1931– ). When the newspapers began publication of the documents, the Department of Justice attempted to block them with injunctions. The newspapers appealed the injunctions to the Supreme Court of the United States (q.v.). Within a few days the Court decided by a 6-3 vote that the government failed to prove that national security was endangered by the publication of the documents and therefore "prior restraint" in the dissemination of information could not apply.

**Censorship by Private Groups.** In the U.S. many different private groups bring to government agencies, publishers, and the communications industries their views on material they consider objectionable not only to their own members but also to the public in general.

These groups include religious denominations, as well as such ethnic and racial organizations as Americans of Italian Descent, the Anti-Defamation League, the Polish-American Guardian Society, and the National Association for the Advancement of Colored People (q.v.). Such groups as the National Office for Decent Literature of the Roman Catholic Church in the U.S. specifically advise their members not to read, watch, or listen to certain material, and they try to prevent or to restrict the circulation of material. One private group, the American Civil Liberties Union (q.v.), promotes the open flow of all types of information in the belief that individuals should have free access and opportunities for the exercise of their personal discretion and that no group should limit the availability of the resources from which such choices are made.

**Censorship of Books.** American censorship of printed material has generally been concerned with works alleged to be obscene or pornographic. The first American case involving such a work was brought to court in Philadelphia in 1815 and concerned the importation of the novel *Fanny Hill* by the British author John Cleland (1709–89). This case, and a similar one tried in Massachusetts six years later, resulted in convictions for the offending parties. Also in 1821, Vermont passed the first American statute against indecent literature; Connecticut passed a similar law in 1834 and Massachusetts in the following year. At the Federal level, Congress simultaneously passed a customs law against the importation of pictorial obscenity; it made no attempt, however, to regulate the interstate movement of obscene materials. A subsequent statute, passed in 1865, made the mailing of obscene material a criminal offense. In 1873 Congress passed the Comstock Law, named for the American reformer Anthony Comstock (q.v.), which enacted more stringent prohibitions against the sending or receiving of indecent matter through the mails.

A major problem in the enforcement of regulations against obscenity has been the difficulty of defining the term. Judicial definitions were rarely attempted until 1896, when the Supreme Court ruled that a political article in a Kansas newspaper contained no "sexual impurity" and was therefore not obscene. In 1915 a Federal court indicated some initial judicial regard for changing community tastes and standards in deciding the nature of obscenity. In 1933, a Federal judge ruled that the novel *Ulysses,* by the Irish novelist James Joyce (q.v.), was not pornographic because of the absence of the author's

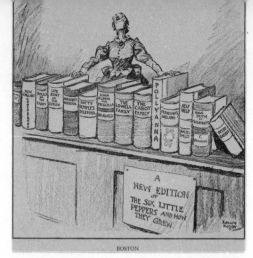

A 1929 cartoon by American cartoonist Rollin Kirby satirized the reading material acceptable to those censors who had made the phrase "banned in Boston" famous throughout the country.　Granger Collection

intent to exploit the sensual and his positive effort to forge a new literary technique, and the failure of the book, when read in its entirety, to rouse sexual excitement; it could therefore be admitted into the U.S.

Although the Supreme Court has consistently held that obscene publication is not Constitutionally protected, it has not left such publication outside the protection given free speech and free press. In the leading case of *Roth vs. U.S.* (1957) the Court held that sex and obscenity are not synonymous; the portrayal of sex in literature and art is not itself sufficient reason to deny material Constitutional protection. The Court held that a book cannot be condemned on the basis of selected passages; the proper test is whether "the dominant theme of the material taken as a whole appeals to prurient interest". Nor may a book be judged obscene by its effect on the most susceptible persons, but rather by its effect on the normal adult. And finally the Court held in this case that the publication must be judged by present-day standards of the community. In subsequent cases, until 1973, the Court interpreted its decision in the Roth case as also standing for the proposition that a publication can be condemned as obscene only if it is found to be "utterly without redeeming social importance".

Under these guidelines, lower Federal courts in 1960 cleared the publication of *Lady Chatterley's Lover* by D.H. Lawrence (q.v.), the unexpurgated version of which had not been legally available since it was written in 1928. In 1964 the Supreme Court upheld the publication of *Tropic of Cancer* by Henry Miller (q.v.), and in 1966 it upheld the right to publish *Fanny Hill.* These decisions affecting famous books that had long been under bans of postal, customs, and police authorities were far-reaching in their effects on literature and public mores.

In 1969 the Supreme Court held that the possession of obscene materials in the privacy of one's home, for one's private entertainment or interest, cannot be punished as a criminal offense. In *Ginzburg vs. U.S.* (1966) the Court held, however, that in a case involving the charge of obscenity, the trial court may take into consideration the manner in which the publication was advertised, and in a case decided in 1968 the Court held that a State may have a law that prohibits the sale to minors of publications which could not Constitutionally be banned for adults.

In a series of cases decided in 1973, the Supreme Court redefined some of the propositions and tests that had been used by the Court since its decision in the Roth case about sixteen years before. The Court now said that the First Amendment standards by which obscenity was to be tested were: (a) whether the average person, applying contemporary community standards—not national standards, as had been the case up to then—would find that the work, taken as a whole, appealed to prurient interest; (b) whether the work depicted or described in a patently offensive way sexual conduct specifically defined by the State law; and (c) whether the work, taken as a whole, lacked serious literary, artistic, political, or scientific value, and not whether the material was "utterly without redeeming social value". These decisions, especially the substitution of a State or local community standard for the previous test of a national standard, had been widely interpreted as more restrictive or less liberal than the precedent of the Roth case.

It should be noted that a minority of two of the Supreme Court justices consistently argued that obscenity is no exception to the guarantee of the First Amendment and so should be as fully protected as is any other type of publication; and another minority group of three justices have contended since 1973 that the First Amendment warrants State interference with obscenity only in two instances, namely, when it involves exposure of such publication to juveniles or when it involves danger of offending unwilling recipients. Because of this basic division, decisions of the Court in obscenity cases are often made by a bare majority.

**Censorship of Motion Pictures and the Theater.** In 1915 the Supreme Court held that motion pictures were mere "spectacles" and therefore not protected by the First Amendment guarantees of free speech and free press; this decision was, however, overruled in 1952. But obscenity, regardless of the medium used for its expression, is, as noted in the above discussion, outside Constitutional protection. Motion pictures, however, like books, are entitled to certain Constitutional safeguards mandated by the First Amendment. These safeguards are mainly of a procedural nature. Thus, the Court has held that the decision of the censoring authority against the showing of a film cannot be final; there must be judicial review, which must be afforded through a speedy procedure, and the burden of proof rests on the State. In part because of these Constitutional safeguards, official censorship of movies has virtually ended in the U.S. and been replaced by a voluntary system formulated by the Motion Picture Association of America (M.P.A.A.), under which theaters show the rating of a film as determined by the M.P.A.A. rating board. The films are classified with an eye chiefly to what is considered appropriate or inappropriate for persons under seventeen or eighteen years of age.

In a case decided in 1975, the Supreme Court extended to theatrical productions the same Constitutional safeguards against advance censorship and prohibition that are enjoyed by books and motion pictures. A city had refused to rent a municipally owned theater to a stock company that proposed to present the musical *Hair* on the ground that it was obscene. This action, the Court held, accomplished "a prior restraint under a system lacking the Constitutionally required minimal procedural safeguards". Because of the Constitutional shield offered to the stage and motion pictures, even under the more restrictive decisions of the Supreme Court in the 1970's, the theater in the U.S. enjoys a larger measure of freedom than can be seen anywhere else in the Western world with the possible exception of Great Britain and the Scandinavian countries.

**Censorship in Radio and Television.** Broadcasting stations may operate only by license from the Federal Communications Commission (q.v.), known as the F.C.C., an independent agency of the U.S. government that assigns radio wavelengths and television channels to private stations "in the public interest"; it requires that the programs presented be above a certain minimum cultural standard. The stations are obliged to present both sides of current issues in news and discussion programs and to provide equal time to all candidates for President and Vice-President of the U.S.; Congress suspended this rule, by law, for the 1960 Presidential campaign.

In 1970 the F.C.C. ordered that, beginning Sept. 1, 1971, network-affiliated television stations had to originate at least one hour of programming between 7 and 11 P.M. In 1973 the rule was modified and eased by the F.C.C. The many challenges to license renewal that are filed with the F.C.C. are instances of increased pressures on television networks and stations. The National Association of Broadcasters, whose Television Code is subscribed to by two thirds of the U.S. stations, adopted a self-regulatory provision, effective in September, 1975: "Entertainment programs inappropriate for viewing by general family audiences" will not be broadcast between the hours of 7 and 9 P.M.

**Current Concerns of Censorship.** At the base of all censorship is the objective of protecting particular interests, interpretations, or ideas by excluding those which contradict the views of the censoring group, whether it is a government, church, or private body. Historically, before the expansion of the media of communications, the roots of censorship were primarily religious and social. Today, censorship focuses on the attempt to control thought and learning. Censorship, today, must examine questions of academic freedom (q.v.), the behavior of dissenters, and advertising, especially of products damaging to health.

**CENSUS** (Lat. *censere,* "to assess"), term meaning primarily the official and periodical counting of the people of a country, or section of a country; also the printed record of the counting. In actual usage the term is applied to the collection of information on the size and characteristics of population, as well as information on the numbers and characteristics of dwelling units, various business enterprises, and governmental agencies.

References to counting the population are found in accounts of ancient peoples, such as the Hebrews and the Romans. The early form of census differed from the modern, however, in that it involved a count of the people solely for purposes of taxation or military conscription. As a result census taking was widely resented. In Western Europe, however, as autocratic government changed to constitutional, the census became a statistical review for information on populations. This development, which took place in Sweden in 1749, in the United States in 1790, and in Great Britain, the Netherlands, Norway, and France in 1801, marked the beginning of the modern census.

During the 19th century and the first half of the 20th, the practice of census taking spread throughout the world. International organizations, such as the United Nations (q.v.) and the International Statistical Institute, have encouraged all countries to adopt uniform standards in taking their censuses. Decennial censuses are taken presently by a considerable number of countries throughout the world. Between 1955 and 1964 ninety-nine countries took national censuses. According to the U.N., between 180 and 190 countries planned to conduct a census between 1965 and 1974.

## UNITED STATES CENSUS

The first census of the U.S. was taken to provide, in accordance with Article I, Section 2, of the Constitution, an enumeration of the "respective numbers" of people in the several States. This census served as a basis for the apportionment of representation in Congress and of direct taxes. The Constitution provides that the first actual enumeration should be made within three years of the last meeting of the Constitutional Convention and within every subsequent term of ten years.

**Procedure.** The first nationwide U.S. census recorded by name only the heads of families and grouped the members of the family into the following classes: free Whites, males sixteen years and over, males under sixteen years, females, other free persons, and slaves. Until 1850 no essential change was made in the manner of enumeration, though the classes were enlarged to embrace age, occupation, physical infirmity, and other data.

In this early period no combinations of statistics other than those given in the original schedule were made, and facts given under one head, for example, age, were not correlated with those given under another, for example, illiteracy. By 1850, however, for the first time, every inhabitant was recorded by name, the questions being answered for each person specifically, and not for the family group of which he was a part. This change in the manner of asking the questions and the establishment of a central office in Washington brought about greater uniformity of reports, and made numerous cross-tabulations possible. The 1850 census is regarded as the first scientific census in the U.S.

The census of 1880 marked the next major improvement in the census procedure. Previously, U.S. marshals, and a temporary force of assistants appointed by the marshals, had conducted the census. In 1880, the work was placed in charge of the Census Office at Washington. In 1902, after it had been recognized that the nature and importance of the modern census was

A 19th-century census taker gathers information from a farm family.                    Bettmann Archive

such as to require constant investigation, not merely decennial work, the Census Office, now known as Bureau of the Census, was made a permanent bureau of what is now the Department of Commerce. Until 1950, however, the field organization for carrying out the decennial censuses was recruited especially for each census and completely disbanded at the end of the undertaking. In 1950, for the first time, the field organization was based upon a small permanent field staff created to carry out the continuing work needed for the various monthly, quarterly, and annual surveys of the Bureau of the Census.

In most cases, answers to census questions are legally compulsory, but the bureau has traditionally stressed voluntary cooperation, making it clear that the answers to questions are held in strictest confidence and cannot be used to the detriment of any individual or organization. All Bureau of the Census employees are sworn to secrecy with respect to such information when they enter upon their duties, and no material is published except in such combinations of statistics as can be useful without revealing confidential material.

**Scope.** The decennial census has from the beginning been utilized to secure information beyond the mere number of inhabitants. As early as 1810, additional inquiries were introduced in an attempt to gather statistics on industry. Information was first collected on dependent and delinquent persons in 1830. Agriculture, mines, commerce, manufactures, and schools appeared as subjects of inquiry in 1840. A separate schedule for manufacturing and mechanical industries was adopted in 1850, and in that year the census first included such vital statistics as those relating to birth, mar-

riage, and mortality. Because of the unwieldy complexity of the censuses of 1880 and 1890, the 1900 census was limited in subject matter to population, mortality, agriculture, and manufactures; provision was made, however, for extensive investigations in other fields after the completion of the decennial work. Since 1902 supplemental decennial censuses of the wealth, public debt, and taxation of State and local governments have been taken; financial reports of States, and of cities with a population of 100,000 or more, have been issued annually by the Bureau of the Census.

The published results of the Fifteenth Census of the United States (1930) contained statistics of population, occupations, unemployment, agriculture, irrigation and drainage, manufactures, mines and quarries, and, for the first time on a national scale, statistics of wholesale and retail distribution, of construction, and of hotels and other service establishments. The population schedule reported the sex, color, age, marital status (whether single, married, widowed, or divorced), place of birth, and occupation of each person. It also carried questions as to school attendance, and ability to read, write, and speak English; and in the case of the foreign-born it asked whether naturalized or alien, and the year of immigration to the U.S.; it also included questions concerning unemployment.

In addition to new information on the types of material gathered in previous censuses, the 1940 compilation included a special census of housing which covered the continental U.S. and all outlying possessions. Many of the phases of census taking were based upon the principles of modern sampling. For example, one person in twenty was asked several additional questions, covering matters of interest only to the Federal government, States, and large cities.

**Electronic Compilation.** In the Eighteenth Census of the United States (1960) compilation and cross-tabulation of the data were carried out with the aid of electronic equipment. In the fields of population, housing, and agriculture, it was the most comprehensive survey yet taken.

The scope of the supplemental inquiries of the Bureau of the Census has been enlarged in recent years to cover industry and commerce. At the beginning of the 20th century the only industrial statistics collected were those on manufactures and mines and quarries, gathered every ten years. To satisfy modern statistical requirements, the Bureau of the Census began to conduct a dozen censuses each decade on a variety of subjects. These included the census of population and of housing, conducted in the 0 years; the census of governments, covering the 2 and 7 years; the census of business, manufactures, and mineral industries for the years ending in 3 and 8; and the census of agriculture, for the 4 and 9 years.

The application of electronic equipment to large-scale processing of figures has greatly improved the handling of mass data. The 1954 censuses of manufactures and business were the first to be carried out almost entirely with the aid of electronic equipment.

The 1970 census was intended to provide the basis for reapportionment of representation in the United States Congress and most State legislatures. Information requested were facts about education, income, occupation, race, and other characteristics of population needed by local governments for planning community services.

Innovations in methodology were the mailing of the forms to be completed and returned by the urban recipients, and the making of house calls by census personnel only in rural and specially selected regions.

The results of the various censuses in the U.S. are widely used by government, business, and the general public. At all levels of government, many decisions regarding legislation, the building of schools, roads, and other facilities, and the allocation of funds are based upon the results of one or more of the censuses of the nation. In rapidly growing areas, many special censuses are taken to provide more up-to-date population totals for the distribution of State revenues. Census statistics have been used increasingly for many kinds of business decisions.

Such statistics provide a measure of potential markets for consumer goods and industrial goods, give a sound basis for advertising and marketing programs, and help in the making of decisions regarding the location of new plants and facilities of various kinds.

The Bureau of the Census also publishes projections of future levels and characteristics of the population, based on estimates of current population and of components of change such as births, deaths, and net immigration.

**Bureau Publications.** Among the publications of the Bureau are *Current Population Survey*, issued monthly, the *Monthly Survey of Current Business*, and the annual *Statistical Abstract of the United States* with its supplements, the *County and City Data Book* and the *Historical Statistics of the United States.* The *Statistical Abstract*, in one volume, presents the more important statistical studies prepared by the bureau and by other public and private agencies.

For statistical information, *see* UNITED STATES and separate articles on individual States, cities, and towns.

**CENTAURS,** in Greek mythology, a race of monsters believed to have inhabited the mountain regions of Thessaly and Arcadia. They were usually represented as human down to the waist, with the lower torso and legs of a horse. The centaurs were characterized by savageness and violence; they were known for their drunkenness and lust, and were often portrayed as followers of Dionysus (q.v.), the god of wine. The centaurs were driven from Thessaly when, in a drunken frenzy, they attempted to abduct the bride of the king of the Lapiths from her wedding feast. An exception to their bestial behavior was the centaur Chiron, who was noted for his goodness and wisdom. Several Greek heroes, including Achilles and Jason (qq.v.), were educated by him.

**CENTAURUS,** constellation of stars, the centaur, located in the southern celestial hemisphere, and visible chiefly south of the equator. The brightest star in this constellation, Alpha Centauri, is also the third brightest star in the sky. It is about 4.3 light-years from the earth and possibly the closest visible star to our solar system. The star is actually a double star, with a third star, Proxima Centauri, revolving around the other two. *See* DOUBLE STARS; STARS.

**CENTIGRADE.** *See* CELSIUS, ANDERS; THERMOMETER.

**CENTIMETER-GRAM-SECOND SYSTEM.** *See* C.G.S. SYSTEM.

**CENTIPEDE,** general name for the members of the class Chilopoda of the phylum Arthropoda. The centipedes are segmented animals bearing jointed appendages, having a head furnished with feelers and jaws, and breathing by means of air tubes or tracheae.

**Structure.** The centipede is like a primitive insect in its general structure. The body is divided into well-marked rings, but the region behind the distinct head is not divisible into thorax and abdomen. The number of rings varies from twelve to more than a hundred. The head, which is covered by a flat shield above, bears a pair of antennae, usually of considerable length, and consisting of from twelve to over one hundred joints; a pair of small, strong, toothed, and bristly mandibles; and a pair of under jaws, usually with palps. The next appendages are limblike and are followed by a modified pair of legs, the basal pieces of which generally meet in the middle line, while the strong joints terminate in a sharp claw, at which a poison gland opens. These appendages are used for seizing and killing prey. The legs of the other segments are usually seven-jointed, sometimes bearing spurs and glands, and are generally clawed. The class Chilopoda is distinguished from the Diplopoda, or millipedes, by having only one pair of legs on each segment.

The large brain is connected with a ventral chain of ganglia. Compound eyes occur in one family, and simple eyes in many, although many forms have no eyes at all. The feelers, certain bristles, and portions of the skin are also sensory. The alimentary canal is straight, and has associated with it salivary and digestive glands and excretory (Malpighian) tubules. The heart is represented by a chambered dorsal vessel. Tracheae or air tubes open on the sides of the body and are connected to one another on each side by a longitudinal stem. Most centipedes measure 1 to 2 in. in length, but some tropical species grow to 12 in.

**Life and Habits.** Centipedes are nocturnal in their food hunting, and remain under stones or wood during the day. They are all carnivorous and not vegetarian like the millipedes. They kill their prey by poisoning it.

**Development.** In some cases the males are said to deposit their reproductive elements in packets (spermatophores) fixed by a web to the ground. In most cases copulation probably occurs. *Scolopendra* is viviparous; the others lay eggs.

**Classification and Forms of Interest.** The principal families of centipedes are Scutigeridae, Lithobiidae, Scolopendridae, and Geophilidae. The family Scutigeridae, to which the common house centipede belongs, includes forms with compound eyes, long feelers, eight

*A mockingbird stalks a centipede,* Scolopendra cingulata.                                    UPI

shields along the back, and fifteen pairs of very long legs. The feelers and the last pair of legs are longer than the body; generative appendages are external. Lithobiidae have simple eyes, fifteen pairs of legs, antennae measuring a third or more of the body length, and fifteen dorsal shields. The genus *Lithobius* includes over one hundred species; *L. forficatus* (of a reddish-brown color, and about 1 in. long) is common throughout America and Europe. *L. mutabilis,* also common, has the habit of feigning death. The Scolopendridae have over a score of legs; short, many-jointed antennae, not more than one fifth of the total length of the body; and simple eyes, not over four pairs in number, or altogether absent. The poisonous bite of some of the larger forms is dangerous to man. *Scolopendra* is the most important genus. The Geophilidae are long, wormlike centipedes, of sluggish habit, with 31 to 173 pairs of legs, short feelers, and no eyes. Well-developed spinning glands are seen in this family, and their secretion cements together ova and spermatozoa.

**Distribution.** Centipedes are worldwide, but abound especially in warm regions. Unsatisfactory fossil remains have been obtained from the American carboniferous strata; better-preserved centipedes have been obtained from the Solenhofen strata, but it is not certain that centipedes existed before Tertiary times.

**CENTRAL AFRICAN REPUBLIC,** independent nation in the French Community (see COMMUNITY), bounded on the N. by Chad, on the E. by Sudan, on the S. by Zaire (formerly the Democratic Republic of the Congo) and the People's Republic of Congo, and on the W. by Cameroon. It is situated between about lat. 2°16′ N. and lat. 11°20′ N. and long. 14°20′ E. and long. 27°45′ E. The area of the Central African Republic is about 240,000 sq.mi. The country is a member of the United Nations, the Organization of African Unity, and the African-Malagasy-Mauritius Common Organization (OCAM).

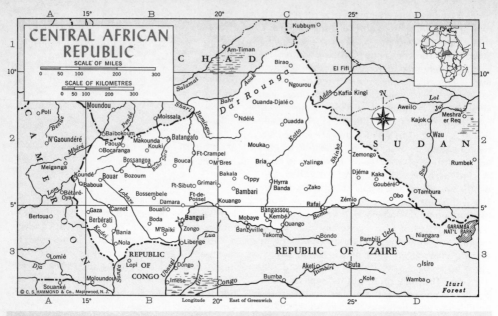

## INDEX TO MAP OF CENTRAL AFRICAN REPUBLIC

### THE LAND

The republic is situated on the N. edge of the Congo basin. Most of the land is a plateau that ranges in elevation from 2000 to 2500 ft. Two ranges of hills in the N. and N.E. rise to heights of 3750 ft. and 4200 ft. Most of the country is open grassland, especially in the N.; a dense rain forest covers the major part of the S. area. The country is drained by two river systems, the Shari in the N. and the Ubangi in the S.

**Climate.** The climate is hot and humid. Tornadoes and floods are common at the onset of the rainy season, which lasts from June to November. Annual rainfall varies from about 70 in. in the Ubangi R. valley to 31 in. in the semiarid N.E. and E.

**Natural Resources.** The mineral resources of this primarily agricultural country are relatively undeveloped, although gold and diamonds are mined. Deposits of uranium exist, as well as iron ore, zinc, copper, and tin. Commercially valuable trees include the sapele mahogany and the

obeche. Almost every animal of the African tropics is found in the Republic, including the gorilla and chimpanzee, which inhabit the rain forest.

About 42,000,000 kw hours of hydroelectric power are produced annually.

### THE PEOPLE

The four main ethnic groups are the Mandjia-Baya, the Banda, the Mbaka, and the Azande. About nine-tenths of the people inhabit small villages, living and working according to traditional customs. The cultural influence of French colonialism is most noticeable in urban centers and among government workers.

**Population.** The population of the Central African Republic (official census 1960) was 1,202,910; the United Nations estimated (1970) 1,612,000. The overall population density is 8 per sq.mi. (U.N. est. 1970). The capital and most important city is Bangui (pop., 1971 est., 187,000).

**Religion and Language.** About 70 percent of the population follows traditional animist beliefs. Christians (mainly Roman Catholic) comprise about 12 percent of the total population and Muslims about 4 percent. French is the official language. Many African languages and dialects are spoken, but the trade language *Sango* is used as the lingua franca. *See also* AFRICAN LANGUAGES: *The Niger-Kordofanian Family*.

**Education.** The educational system, patterned after that of France, is gradually being changed to suit local needs and traditions. Schools that conform to the officially prescribed education programs are aided by the government. Less than 10 percent of the population is literate. In the late 1960's about 15 secondary, 15 technical, and 10 teacher-training institutions were in operation. Adult education in rural areas is undertaken by mobile crews using audio-visual aids.

## THE ECONOMY

The republic is one of the most remote and underdeveloped areas in Africa. About 90 percent of the population earns its livelihood by farming. The agricultural output is fairly evenly balanced between subsistence and export crops. The principal source of revenue comes from diamond exports. A recent budget showed revenues and expenditures balanced at approximately $49,500,000.

**Agriculture and Forestry.** About 9 percent of the total land area is arable. Cassava, the basic food crop, is raised on about 3 percent of the arable land. In order to increase the wage-earning power of the peasant farmer the government has organized agricultural cooperatives, placing primary emphasis on introducing new crops that are expected to produce a higher income. The cultivation of rubber, sesame, tobacco, peanuts, and rice is encouraged by the government. The first commercial production of cotton, the most important cash crop, began in 1924. The second most important cash crop is coffee, which is grown mostly on European-owned plantations.

Exploitation of the forest reserves was slow to develop, but by the late 1960's some 2,500,000 cubic yards of roundwood were being produced annually.

**Mining.** Diamonds are the most important mineral. Production was about 494,000 carats a year in the early 1970's. Some gold is mined, and plans have been made to work the iron deposits at Danera. Uranium was discovered in the E. part of the country in 1966.

**Currency, Commerce, and Trade.** The unit of currency is the C.F.A. franc, consisting of 100 centimes (204 C.F.A. francs equal U.S.$1; 1973).

Diamonds, cotton, and coffee account for about 95 percent of the total value of exports, diamonds alone constituting more than half. Most trade is carried on with the other members of the West African Economic-Customs Union (Cameroon, People's Republic of Congo, and Gabon).

**Transportation and Communications.** The Ubangi R. and the Shari and Logone river systems are extensively used for transportation. The Republic has about 12,000 mi. of roads, 3600 mi. of which are passable throughout the year. Principal airports are at Bangui, Barberati, and Bouar.

One daily newspaper and a weekly are published in Bangui. The single radio broadcasting station is government-owned. Telephone and telegraph services are available between Bangui and major towns in the interior.

## GOVERNMENT

Following the military coup of January, 1966, the National Assembly was dissolved and power was given to the ten-member Revolutionary Council. The council controls the national government as well as the appointment of officials in local government and the judiciary.

## HISTORY

Most of the tribes inhabiting the Republic are not indigenous to the area, but entered the region in the 19th century to escape slave traders operating in the Sudan. The area was first visited by French explorers in the 1880's. In 1910 Ubangi-Shari, as the region was known, and Chad were merged into a single colony and incorporated into French Equatorial Africa. In 1946 Ubangi-Shari was made an overseas territory of France. On Dec. 1, 1958, the territory was proclaimed a semiautonomous republic within the French Community, adopting the name Central African Republic. On Aug. 13, 1960, the republic gained full autonomy, with David Dacko (1930– ) as president. In November, 1962, the government dissolved all opposition parties and established a one-party government. Charging corruption in the existing system, the army under its commander in chief, Colonel Jean-Bedel Bokassa (1921– ) staged a coup in January, 1966. After a period of diplomatic isolation, the regime gradually gained recognition from other governments. In April, 1969, an armed attempt to overthrow the military government of President Bokassa was crushed. A contingent of French soldiers was dispatched to the republic to assist in preventing any further moves against the Bokassa government. In 1972 Bokassa was proclaimed president for life.

As the 1970's began, the extension of the trans-Cameroon railroad into the Central Afri-

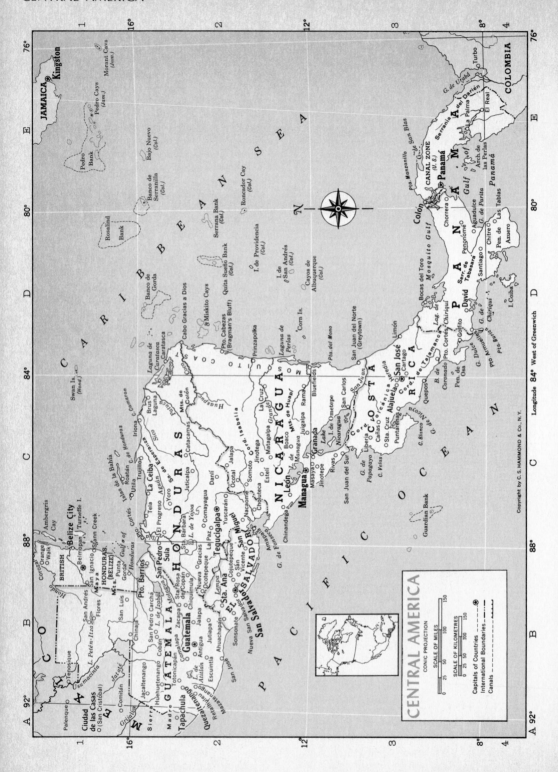

CENTRAL AMERICA

CONIC PROJECTION

SCALE OF MILES
0  25  50  100  150

SCALE OF KILOMETRES
0  25  50  100  150

Capitals of Countries ........... ✪
International Boundaries ......... -----
Canals .......................... -----

can Republic was expected to contribute greatly to the expansion of trade.

**CENTRAL AMERICA,** term commonly applied to the long, narrow isthmus of North America (q.v.), lying N. of Colombia, South America, S. of Mexico, and between the Atlantic and the Pacific oceans. The seven countries of Central America are: Costa Rica, Guatemala, Honduras, Nicaragua, Panama, El Salvador, and the self-governing British colony of British Honduras (qq.v.).

**CENTRAL AMERICAN COMMON MARKET.** See INTER-AMERICAN COOPERATION.

**CENTRAL BANK.** See BANKS AND BANKING.

**CENTRAL CITY,** town in Colorado, and county seat of Gilpin Co., in the Rocky Mts., 8515 ft. above sea level about 30 miles N.W. of Denver. It was founded in 1859 after the first important gold discovery in Colorado was made in the Central City area. Gold and silver are still mined in the surrounding region. The town is the site of the Central City Historical Museum, the Opera House Museum, and the Teller House, built in 1872, at a cost of $107,000, to house miners during the gold rush. Pop. (1970) 228.

**CENTRAL FALLS,** city of Rhode Island, in Providence Co., on the Blackstone R., about 4 miles N. of Providence. The city manufactures clothing, plastics, chemicals, glass, paper and wood products, and machinery. Pop. (1960) 19,858; (1970) 18,716.

**CENTRALIA,** city of Illinois, on the border between Marion and Clinton counties, about 57 miles E. of East Saint Louis. The city is in an area that produces oil, bituminous coal, grain, poultry, livestock, fruit, and dairy products.

Centralia is the trade and shipping point for the area. Metal products, candy, clothing, and shoes are manufactured. The city has oil refineries, meat-packing plants, and railroad shops. It is the site of Kaskaskia College, established in 1965, as a replacement for Centralia Junior College. Pop. (1960) 13,904; (1970) 15,217.

**CENTRAL INTELLIGENCE AGENCY,** agency of the Executive Office of the President of the United States, created in 1947, together with the National Security Council (q.v.), to supersede the National Intelligence Authority and the Central Intelligence Group, formed in 1946. The Agency, known as the C.I.A., is responsible for coordinating the foreign intelligence activities of the various government departments and agencies. It is headed by the director of central intelligence, who is appointed by the President and confirmed by the Senate.

The director is principal adviser to the President and the National Security Council on all matters of intelligence related to the national security and provides estimates of specific foreign situations affecting that security. The director himself is advised by the United States Intelligence Board, made up of the deputy director of central intelligence, the heads of the State and Defense Department intelligence organizations, and representatives of the Atomic Energy Commission and the Federal Bureau of Investigation.

**CENTRAL POWERS,** name of a coalition during World War I comprising the German Empire and Austria-Hungary, and, by extension, their allies, Bulgaria and Turkey. Originally, the term referred to the geographical position of Germany and Austria-Hungary in Europe.

**CENTRAL PROVINCES AND BERAR.** See BRITISH INDIA.

**CENTRAL TREATY ORGANIZATION** (abbr. CENTO), mutual defense and security organization that evolved in 1959 from the earlier Middle East Treaty Organization (METO), which emerged from the Baghdad Pact of 1955. The purpose of the organization is to provide joint defense against possible aggressors and to encourage the economic and scientific development of the member nations: Iran, Pakistan, Turkey, and Great Britain. The name CENTO was adopted in 1959 after Iraq, originally a cosigner, withdrew from the Baghdad Pact; CENTO refers to a central area between regions included in the North Atlantic Treaty Organization (q.v.), to which Turkey belongs, and the Southeast Asia Treaty Organization (q.v.), of which Pakistan is a member. Although not an official member of CENTO, the United States has actively sup-

ported the organization. The U.S. participates in the economic, military, and scientific committees of the organization and has signed bilateral agreements with the member nations and contributed more than $1,000,000,000 in economic aid. CENTO has been instrumental in promoting such programs as the construction of roads and railways, the improvement of harbor facilities, and the establishment of a telecommunications network. Headquarters, originally established at Baghdad, were moved to Ankara, Turkey, after the pro-Western Iraqi government was overthrown in 1958.

**CENTRAL VALLEY** or **GREAT VALLEY.** See CALIFORNIA: The Land.

**CENTREVILLE,** city of Illinois, in Saint Clair Co., about 3 miles S.E. of East Saint Louis. Centreville is a residential community. Nearby is Scott Air Force Base. Pop. (1960) 12,769; (1970) 11,378.

**CENTRIFUGAL FORCE.** See GRAVITATION.

**CENTRIFUGE,** mechanical device using the principle of centrifugal force to separate substances of different densities. A common centrifuge is a container that is spun rapidly. The only limit to the centrifugal force is the strength of the metal of which the device is made. Centrifugal forces may be thousands of times as great as the force of gravity; see GRAVITATION.

Centrifuges may be used for rapid separation of substances that would normally separate slowly under the influence of gravity. The draining of water from a wet solid, for example, may be accelerated by spinning the solid. This principle is used in the spin cycle of an ordinary automatic washing machine. The first successful centrifuge, a cream separator, was invented in 1883 by the Swedish engineer Carl Gustav Patrik de Laval (1845–1913). The operation of this device may be continuous, with cream constantly withdrawn from the center and skim milk from the periphery. Since then numerous other applications of centrifugation have been made. For the separation of isotopes, see ISOTOPE; for the separation of blood cells from whole blood, see BLOOD; and for the separation of sugar from syrup, see SUGAR.

**Ultracentrifuge.** The smaller the diameter of a centrifuge, the greater the forces and accelerations exerted on the contents and the more rapidly it may be spun without breaking. The most powerful centrifuges, known as ultracentrifuges, are long, narrow tubes rotated at enormous speeds. The ultracentrifuge was developed about 1920 by the Swedish chemist The(odor) Svedberg (q.v.), and improved by the American physicist Jesse Wakefield Beams (1898–    ).

The rotor, the spinning part of the centrifuge, in the Beams ultracentrifuge is magnetically suspended in a vacuum and electrically driven. Friction is thus reduced to a negligible amount; for example, if a $\frac{1}{16}$-in. rotor is spinning in a vacuum of 1/400,000,000 atmospheric pressure at 100,000 revolutions per second and the driving force is turned off, it will lose only 100 revolutions per second in an hour. The greatest forces thus far achieved, 428,000,000 times as great as those of gravity, were obtained with a $\frac{1}{50}$-in. rotor spinning at 38,000,000 revolutions per minute. *See* COLLOIDAL DISPERSION.

**CENTURION,** in the army of ancient Rome, officer commanding a century, or one hundred men, sixty of which constituted a legion. Within each Roman legion, centurions held degrees of rank with the senior centurion taking part in councils of war. Centurions were chosen from among veteran soldiers by the six tribunes in command of a legion; *see* TRIBUNE. Although they were of plebeian origin, their military counterpart today would more accurately be commissioned than noncommissioned officers.

**CENTURY PLANT.** *See* AGAVE.

**CEPHAËLIS.** *See* IPECAC.

**CEPHALIC INDEX.** *See* INDEX, CEPHALIC.

**CEPHALONIA.** *See* KEFALLINÍA.

**CEPHALOPODA** (Gr. *kephalē*, "head", *pous*, "foot"), highest class of marine animals of the phylum Mollusca (q.v.), divided into the orders Tetrabranchiata and Dibranchiata. Both orders are comprised of usually large animals, with well-developed heads, with the foot or ventral surface grown around the mouth and split up into arms or tentacles bearing hooks or suckers. The arms capture prey. Another part of the foot forms a funnel through which water is jetted to provide propulsion. Two or four gills are present in the usual mantle cavity. In most forms a second funnel or siphon is attached to an ink sac. A dark fluid is ejected for camouflage in times of danger. Because the eyes are peculiarly large and have a ferocious appearance, several forms have been given the name "devilfish". The mouth, in the midst of the arms, has powerful horny jaws. The central nervous system, with closely associated ganglia, is surrounded by a protective cartilaginous covering. The sexes are separate.

Tetrabranchiata is represented at present only by the genus *Nautilus*, a spiral-shaped, shelled animal, having no hooks, suckers, or ink sac. Numerous fossil animals of this order are known. The Dibranchiata differ from other mollusks by having only a rudimentary shell or no shell. They are further subdivided into the Octopoda or eight-footed animals, such as the octopus (q.v.), and the Decapoda or ten-footed animals, such as the squid and the cuttlefish (qq.v.).

**CEPHEUS,** northern constellation, located near the north celestial pole. Alderamin, the brightest star of the constellation, is of the third magnitude. More important, however, is the fainter Delta Cephei, which is a star of the class known as Cepheid variables. *See* STARS: *Variable Stars.*

**CEPHISODOTUS,** name of two Greek sculptors who flourished during the 4th century B.C.

**Cephisodotus the Elder,** elder brother, or possibly the father, of the Greek sculptor Praxiteles (q.v.). Little is known of his life and his art is known only through an extant ancient copy of his group "Irene and Plutus".

**Cephisodotus the Younger,** son of Praxiteles. Of his works only scanty mention has been preserved. He is believed to have made portrait sculptures, but none has survived. The base of a statue has been found bearing the signature of Cephisodotus.

**CERAM,** island of the Republic of Indonesia, one of the Molucca Islands, in the province of Maluku, between the Ceram Sea on the N. and the Banda Sea on the S. It lies between New Guinea on the E. and Buru on the W. Ceram is about 216 mi. long from W. to E., is mountainous, and has jungles containing ironwood trees and sago palms. Many rivers of the island drain to the Ceram Sea and are dry part of the year. The climate is tropical, hot and humid, with heavy rains in the wet season. Earthquakes sometimes occur. The greater part of the interior is unexplored. A majority of the population live along the coasts. The principal towns, Amahai and Tehoru on the S. coast, Bula on the E. coast, Wahai on the N. coast, and Piru on the W. coast, are ports of call.

The people along the coast are principally Malay immigrants from the islands of Makassar, Java, and Ternate, and are engaged chiefly in fishing and as workers on plantations devoted to the cultivation of coconuts, spices, rice, corn, sugarcane, and tobacco. They are also employed in the production of sago flour and cajuput oil. Trade is dominated by Chinese, Arab, and Makassarese merchants; copra is the principal export. The prevailing religions of Ceram are Malayan, Christian, and Mohammedan. The people of the interior, descendants of intermarriages between Malayans and Papuans, live chiefly by hunting and fishing and observe pagan religious rites. Under Dutch rule, which began in the middle of the 17th century, Ceram was included, for administrative purposes, in the Resi-

*Ceramic plate made in Pennsylvania in the 19th century.*
National Gallery of Art

dency of Amboina. In 1946, following the uprising of the Indonesians against Dutch rule, Ceram became a part of the self-governing state of East Indonesia. Area, 6621 sq.mi.; pop. (latest est.) 96,797.

**CERAMICS** (Gr. *keramos,* "potter's clay"), originally the art of making pottery, now a general term for the science of manufacturing articles prepared from plastic earthy materials and then made rigid by high-temperature treatment. Ceramics now thus includes the manufacture of earthenware, porcelain, bricks, and some kinds of tile and stoneware. Ceramic products are used not only for artistic objects and tableware, but also for such utilitarian purposes as sewer pipe and the walls of buildings. Ceramic insulators with a wide range of electrical properties have increasingly replaced conventional manufacturing materials. In space technology, ceramic materials and cermets (strong, highly heat-resistant alloys, typically made by mixing, pressing, and then baking an oxide or carbide with a powdered metal) are used in the manufacture of nose cones, heat shields, and many other components.

In nuclear reactors, ceramic materials are frequently combined with such materials as oxides of uranium for use as a fuel element. Control rods, inserted into and withdrawn from the reactor, are typically made of cadmium or boron and ceramic materials. *See* BRICK; CLAY; POTTERY.

**CERASTIUM.** *See* CHICKWEED.

**CERBERUS,** in Greek mythology, a three-headed, dragon-tailed dog that guarded the entrance to the lower world. The monster permitted all spirits to enter Hades, but would allow none to leave. Only a few heroes ever escaped Cerberus' guard; the great musician Orpheus (q.v.) charmed it with his lyre and the Greek hero Hercules (q.v.) captured it bare-handed and brought it for a short time from the underworld to the regions above. In Roman mythology both the beautiful maiden Psyche and the Trojan prince Aeneas (qq.v.) were able to pacify Cerberus with a honey cake and thus continue their journey through the underworld. Cerberus is sometimes pictured with a mane of snakes wrapped around its body.

*Five of the most widely grown cereals. Left to right, wheat, oats, rye, barley, rice.*

**CEREALS** or **CEREAL PLANTS,** various species of the Grass family (Gramineae) cultivated for their seed, which is used as an article of food. The name is derived from Ceres (q.v.), the Roman goddess of grains and agriculture. Although the cereals proper do not belong to any particular tribe of the grasses, the use of particular species as bread plants seems to have been determined chiefly by the superior size of the seed or by the ease of procuring it in sufficient quantity and of freeing it from its inedible covering. The most extensively cultivated grains are wheat (*Triticum*), barley (*Hordeum*), rye (*Secale*), oats (*Avena*), rice (*Oryza*), corn or maize (*Zea*), different kinds of millet (*Setatia, Eleusine, Panicum,* and *Pennisetum*), and the grain sorghums known as durra or Guinea corn (*Sorghum* or *Andropogon*). These have all been cultivated since ancient times in Europe, Asia, and Africa. Maize is the only grain that originated in America. Barley, oats, and rye are the grains of the coldest regions. The cultivation of barley and oats extends even within the Arctic circle. Wheat needs a somewhat warmer climate. In the warmer regions of the temperate zone wheat is grown with corn and rice. The latter two are extensively cultivated in the tropics. The millets belong to warm climates, and durra is tropical or subtropical. See separate articles on plants mentioned.

The seeds of plants of other families, notably buckwheat (q.v.), are sometimes incorrectly called cereals. *See also* GRASSES.

**CEREBELLUM.** *See* BRAIN.

**CEREBRAL HEMISPHERE.** *See* BRAIN.

**CEREBRAL HEMORRHAGE.** *See* STROKE.

**CEREBRAL PALSY,** inclusive term for various nonprogressive disorders, resulting from brain damage, of motor function in young chilren. Damage to the brain may occur *in utero* or prenatally, at birth, or shortly after birth, and may be caused by a number of different circumstances. Prenatal causes or factors include developmental defects, inherited metabolic errors, maternal infections such as rubella (*see* GERMAN MEASLES), irradiation *in utero,* asphyxia *in utero,* administration of drugs, and toxemia (qq.v.) of pregnancy. The natal factors include trauma in delivery, anoxia or oxygen deficiency, and prematurity. In the postnatal period the injurious factors include trauma, anoxia, infections, cerebral vascular lesions, and Rh incompatibility; *see* RH FACTOR. *See also* GESTATION.

The symptoms and signs of cerebral palsy depend upon the distribution and severity of the changes in the brain. On this basis, five groups are recognized: 1) spastic diplegia, with exag-

geration of voluntary movements; 2) hemiplegic cerebral palsy, with half of the body affected; 3) spastic quadriplegia, with choreoathetosis or uncontrollable movement; 4) atheotic cerebral palsy, with uncontrolled movements of the affected muscles; and 5) ataxic cerebral palsy, in which balance is disturbed; *see* PARALYSIS. These categories commonly overlap because of multiple symptoms. Moreover, defects in vision and speech and convulsive seizures (*see* CONVULSION) may be present. About 30 percent or more of children having cerebral palsy are mentally retarded. The variable manifestations and the lack of specific clinical classification make it difficult to obtain definitive data on incidence of the disease. Some authorities find the rate to be about 6 per 1000 births, and the prevalence among children aged five to nine years to be 600 per 100,000. In many cases, evidence of brain damage may not be apparent until several months after birth. In instances where defects are less severe, the disorder may not be recognized for some years.

The chief goals in treating cerebral palsy are the improvement of symptoms and the teaching

*A physician gently examines and evaluates the condition of a young cerebral palsy victim.*

United Cerebral Palsy

of the patient to compensate for his disability. Usually the full extent of damage cannot be fully appraised until about the second year. When damage is relatively severe, physical therapy (q.v.), education of movement, speech therapy when indicated, and in some cases, orthopedic surgery may be useful (*see* ORTHOPEDICS; REHABILITATION). Convulsive patients may be treated with appropriate drugs.          A.T.M.

**CEREBROSPINAL MENINGITIS.** *See* MENINGITIS.

**CEREBRUM.** *See* BRAIN: *Anatomy.*

**CERES.** *See* PLANETOID.

**CERES,** in Roman mythology, the goddess of agriculture. She and her daughter Proserpine were the counterparts of the Greek goddesses Demeter and Persephone (qq.v.). The Greek belief that her joy at being reunited with her daughter each spring caused the earth to bring forth an abundance of fruits and grains was introduced into Rome in the 5th century B.C., and her cult became extremely popular, especially with the plebians. Her chief festival, the *Cerealia,* was celebrated from April 12 to 19.

**CEREUS,** genus of plants of the family Cactaceae, including a large but undetermined number of species. Six species are native in the southwestern United States, including one on the coast of California and five in the deserts. Four are native to Florida, and five other species of *Cereus* native to tropical America have been introduced there. The genus is found in the U.S., Mexico, South America, and the West Indies.

Many species are common in cultivation, some of them under the name of night-blooming cereus. Some of the best-known plants are *C. nycticalus, C. triangularis,* and *C. grandiflorus.* The species *C. grandiflorus, C. pteranthus, C. undatus,* and *C. peruvianus* are common in cultivation and have also become sparingly natu-

ralized in Florida and Hawaii. The best-known species in the U.S. is the saguaro, or giant cactus, *C. giganteus,* which occurs commonly in Arizona and adjacent Sonora State, Mexico, and more rarely on the eastern margin of California. This plant attains as much as 50 ft. in height, and the trunk may be up to 2½ ft. in diameter. Young plants consist of a single trunk, but older plants have twenty, or in exceptional cases, up to fifty upturned branches. The night-blooming cereus of the desert, *C. gregaii,* is well known for its very large white, fragrant flowers, nearly all of which bloom at night. Two varieties of this species are found in the deserts of Arizona, New Mexico, and Texas.

In several different recent classifications, *Cereus* is divided into a number of genera, including *Cephalocereus, Pilocereus Harrisia, Carnegiea, Lemaireocereus, Bergerocactus, Lophocereus, Acanthocereus, Hylocereus,* and *Selenicereus.*          L.B.

**CERINTHUS** (fl. about 100 A.D.), Christian heretic considered a Gnostic (*see* GNOSTICISM) by modern scholars. He had a number of followers in Asia Minor. He preached that the world was created by a subordinate deity, called a demiurge, or by angels, one of whom gave the Ten Commandments (*see* DECALOGUE) to Moses (q.v.). Cerinthus also asserted that Jesus Christ (q.v.) was the natural son of Mary and Joseph. He taught that the spirit of God, called Christ (q.v.), descended upon Jesus at his baptism and enabled him to work miracles and to proclaim the unknown Father, but that the spirit of Christ left Jesus before the Passion and the Resurrection (q.v.).

**CERIUM,** metallic element with at.no. 58, at.wt. 140.12, b.p. estimated 3470° C. (6278° F.), m.p. 800° C. (1472° F.), sp.gr. 6.8, and symbol Ce. It has valences of 3 (cerous) and 4 (ceric). Cerium was discovered independently in 1804 by the Swedish chemist Baron Jöns Jakob Berzelius (q.v.) and by the German chemist Martin Heinrich Klaproth (1743–1817); the pure metallic element was not isolated until 1875.

Cerium is the most abundant of the rare-earth elements (*see* RARE EARTHS); it is more abundant in the crust of the earth than the more familiar metals zinc, lead, or tin. It occurs with the other rare-earth metals in monazite sand and samarskite in the Ural Mts. of the U.S.S.R., in Norway, Brazil, and the United States (North Carolina). It also occurs in the minerals cerite, found in Sweden, and allanite, found in Greenland and New York State. Cerium is the only one of the rare-earth metals that can be easily separated from the others.

*Night-blooming cereus,* Hylocereus undulatus.

Metallic cerium is most familiar in the form of an alloy with iron that composes the "flints" used in cigarette lighters. Large quantities of ceric oxide were formerly employed in the manufacture of gas mantles. Compounds of cerium are employed in small quantities in the manufacture of glass, ceramics, arc-lamp electrodes, and photoelectric cells. Cerous nitrate has been used medicinally in the treatment of seasickness and chronic vomiting. Ceric sulfate is employed in analytic chemistry laboratories as an oxidizing agent.

**CERMET.** *See* ALLOY; CERAMICS.

**CERNĂUŢI.** *See* CHERNOVTSY.

**CERRO DE PASCO,** town in Peru, and capital of Pasco Department, about 14,000 ft. above sea level, 138 miles N.E. of Lima, with which it is connected by rail. The town was once noted as one of the world's richest silver-mining centers, but is more important now for the mining of copper, which began there in the early 20th century under the management of the Cerro de Pasco Corporation, a United States-controlled firm. Gold, lead, zinc, and bismuth are also mined at Cerro de Pasco; the valuable silver deposits were exhausted by the Spanish. Smelting of the copper is carried on in one of the largest metallurgical plants in the world, in La Oroya, 81 miles s. of Cerro de Pasco. The city has recently been relocated a short distance from its original site. Pop. (1972 prelim.) 47,178.

**CERRO GORDO.** *See* MEXICAN WAR.

**CERTHIIDAE,** family of birds in the order Passeriformes, with stiff, pointed tail feathers that act as props and assist the birds in climbing. The family includes species of creeper (q.v.).

**CERTIORARI,** in common law, writ or written command issued by a superior court to a lower court, or to a public officer or public board, having judicial authority. The writ of certiorari requires that the record of the proceedings in a lower court be sent to the superior court for review. The higher court studies the record while the case is still pending and decides whether or not the inferior court is acting in accordance with the law. Superior courts may use the writ in either criminal or civil cases in order to ensure speedier justice. They do not judge the proceedings according to their merits; they review only the legal aspects of the case, such as whether or not the lower court has jurisdiction to try the case. On the basis of its findings, the superior court may remove the action or proceedings to a higher court for trial. In the United States, the power to issue writs of certiorari is strictly governed by the constitutions and statutes of each State. It may be used only when there is no other remedy to ensure protection of the rights of the applicant for the writ.

**CERUSSITE,** *or* WHITE LEAD ORE, mineral consisting of lead carbonate. In a pure form cerussite is colorless and transparent, but it is usually yellow or grayish because of various impurities. It has hardness 3 to 3.5 and sp.gr. 6.5, and crystallizes in the orthorhombic system. It is formed by the alteration of galena or lead sulfide, which, as it oxidizes to sulfate, may be changed to a carbonate by action of solutions of calcium bicarbonate. The most famous sources of cerussite are the lead mines of Siberia and the Altay Territory (q.v.), and various places in Sweden and Germany; fine crystals are found in Cornwall, England. In the United States it can be found in Phoenixville, Pa., and in lead deposits in Virginia, North Carolina, Missouri, Wisconsin, Colorado, Idaho, Utah, and Arizona.

**CERVANTES SAAVEDRA, Miguel de** (1547–1616), Spanish novelist, born in Alcalá de Henares. His father was an indigent surgeon with a large family. In 1568, when Cervantes was a student, a number of his poems appeared in a volume published in Madrid to commemorate the death of the Spanish queen, Elizabeth of Valois (1545–68). In 1569 he went to Rome, where in the following year he entered the service of Cardinal Giulio Acquaviva (1546–74). Soon afterward Cervantes joined a Spanish regiment in Naples. He fought in 1571 against the Turks in the naval Battle of Lepanto, in which he lost the use of his left hand; *see* LEPANTO, BATTLE OF. While returning to Spain in 1575 Cervantes was captured by Barbary pirates. He was taken to Algeria as a slave and held there for ransom. During the next five years he made several heroic but unsuccessful attempts to escape, and he was finally ransomed in 1580 by both his family and friends.

Returning to Spain at the age of thirty-three, Cervantes, despite his wartime service and Algerian adventure, was unable to obtain employment with a noble family, the usual reward for veteran soldiers who had distinguished themselves. Deciding to become a writer, he turned out poems and plays at a prodigious rate between 1582 and 1585; very few of these are extant. His pastoral novel *La Galatea* (1585) gained him a reputation, but the proceeds from its sale were insufficient to support him. Cervantes then took government jobs, first furnishing goods to the fleet of the Armada (q.v.) and later as a tax collector. The government imprisoned him several times because he failed to render a satisfactory account of his activities as tax collector.

*Miguel de Cervantes Saavedra*

While in prison Cervantes conceived the idea for a story about an amusing madman who imagines himself a knight-errant performing the splendid feats described in medieval tales of chivalry. The first part was issued under the title *El Ingenioso Hidalgo Don Quijote de la Mancha,* (1605; Eng. trans., *The History of the Valorous and Wittie Knight-Errant Don Quixote of the Mancha,* 1612); see DON QUIXOTE. It became such an immediate success that within two weeks after publication three pirated editions appeared in Madrid. Partly because of the pirating and partly because of his lack of financial acumen, Cervantes never gained any substantial wealth from the enormous success of the work.

His *Novelas Ejemplares* ("Exemplary Novels", 1613), a collection of twelve short stories, includes romances in the Italian style, descriptions of criminal life in Seville, and sketches of unusual events and characters. One of these stories, "El Coloquio de los Perros" ("The Talking Dogs"), is particularly renowned for its satirical prose style. The second part of *Don Quixote* was published in 1615. Cervantes completed the fantastic allegorical novel *Persiles y Sigismunda* (1617) four days before he died.

Generally regarded as the first modern novel and as one of the greatest novels ever written, *Don Quixote* is a brilliant satire, not only of the chivalric romances of the Middle Ages and early Renaissance, but also of the sentimental and pastoral novels popular in Cervantes' own time.

E.F.

**CERVERA Y TOPETE, Pascual, Conde de Jerez, Marqués de Santa Ana.** *See* SPANISH-AMERICAN WAR.

**CÉSAIRE, Aimé Fernand** (1913– ), French poet and political leader, born in Basse-Pointe, Martinique, and educated at the Sorbonne and the École Normale Supérieure, Paris. He taught secondary school in Fort-de-France, Martinique, from 1940 to 1945. In 1946 he was elected a deputy to the French National Assembly and in 1956 he was elected mayor of Fort-de-France. Also in 1956 he resigned from the Communist Party of France.

As a poet, Césaire was discovered by the French poet and critic André Breton (q.v.). Breton provided a preface to the 1942 edition of *Cahier d'un Retour au Pays Natal* (1939; Eng. trans., *Return to My Native Land,* 1968), in which Césaire explores what he calls *négritude,* Negro culture as a valid and independent entity. His verse, although influenced by surrealism (q.v.), remains impassioned and clear. His later books of poetry include *Les Armes Miraculeuses* ("Miraculous Weapons", 1946), *Soleil Coupé* ("Interrupted Sunshine", 1948), *Corps Perdu* ("Lost Body", 1949), and *Ferrements* ("Ironwork", 1959).

**CESALPINO, Andrea,** *or* (Lat.) ANDREAS CAESALPINUS (1519–1603), Italian botanist and physician, born in Arezzo, Tuscany, and educated at the University of Pisa. He became director of the botanical garden and professor of materia medica (the science dealing with the preparation of drugs) at the university in 1555. In 1592 he became physician to Pope Clement VIII (*see under* CLEMENT) in Rome. Cesalpino theorized on the circulation of the blood in the human body, thereby anticipating the discoveries of later scientists, most notably, those of the English physician and anatomist William Harvey (q.v.). Among Cesalpino's written works are sixteen short books entitled *De Plantis* ("Of Plants", 1583), the first classification of plants according to the characteristics of their fruits and seeds. The work formed, in part, the basis of the system of botanical classification established by the Swedish botanist Carolus Linnaeus (q.v.).

**CESAREAN SECTION** *or* **CESARIAN SECTION,** surgical removal of the fetus through incisions in the abdominal wall and the uterus when normal delivery is inadvisable or impossible. This operation has been practiced since ancient times on dead and, probably, on dying mothers, to save the life of the fetus (q.v.). According to tradition the Roman soldier and statesman Gaius Julius Caesar (q.v.) was born by this method. Roman law restricted the operation to cases in which death occurred immediately before childbirth, however, and inasmuch as Caesar's mother lived long after he was born the tradition has no basis in fact. The term cesarean section derives from the fact that under the Roman emperors the law requiring such an operation was known as *lex Caesarea*. The first authenticated case of a cesarean section on a living woman occurred in 1610 but, because of the high mortality, this operation did not become widespread until the end of the 19th century, when increased use of antiseptics and advances in surgical technique rendered it comparatively safe. In present-day obstetrics a cesarean section is scheduled for those cases in which the size of the birth canal is disproportionately small in relation to the size of the fetus; *see* BIRTH. The operation is utilized also as a precautionary measure for mothers with a history of stillbirths and as an emergency procedure in case of abnormal developments during delivery.

**CESARION.** *See under* PTOLEMY: *Ptolemy XIV.*

**CESIUM,** element with at.no. 55, at.wt. 132.90, b.p. 682° C. (1259.6° F.), m.p. 28.6° C. (82.4° F.), sp.gr. $1.89^{20°}$, and symbol Cs. This white, soft alkali metal was discovered in 1860 by Robert Wilhelm Bunsen and Gustav Robert Kirchhoff (qq.v.) in mineral waters by means of the spectroscope, in which it shows two bright blue lines as well as fainter red, yellow, and green ones. The natural source yielding the greatest quantity of cesium is the rare mineral pollux (or pollucite). Ores of this mineral found on the island of Elba contain 34 percent of cesium oxide; American ores of pollux, found in Maine and South Dakota, contain 13 percent of the oxide. Cesium also occurs in lepidolite, carnallite, and certain feldspars. It is extracted by separating the cesium compound from the mineral, transforming the compound thus obtained into the cyanide, and electrolysis of the fused cyanide. Cesium may also be obtained by heating its hydroxides or carbonates with magnesium or aluminum, and by heating its chlorides with calcium. Commercial cesium usually contains rubidium, with which it usually occurs, and which resembles it so closely that no effort is made to separate them. Like potassium, cesium oxidizes readily when exposed to air, and it is on this account used as a "getter" to remove residual oxygen from radio vacuum tubes. Because of its property of emitting electrons when exposed to light, it is used in the photosensitive surface of the cathode of the photoelectric cell. The radioactive isotope cesium-137, which is produced by nuclear fission, is a useful by-product of atomic-energy plants. Cesium-137 emits considerably more energy than radium and is employed in present-day medical and industrial research; *see* TRACERS.

**ČESKÉ BUDĚJOVICE** (Ger. *Budweis*), city and river port of Czechoslovakia, in Jihočeský Region, on the Vltava R., about 77 miles s. of Prague. It is a rail junction and the trade center of s. Bohemia. Among its principal articles of commerce are lignite, iron ore, and other raw materials produced in the surrounding region, and a variety of products manufactured in the city, including beer, porcelain, earthenware, and lead pencils. Founded in the 13th century, the city became an episcopal see in the 18th century. Among the city's notable buildings are the Gothic Church of Saint Mary, the bishop's palace, and the town hall. Pop. (1970) 76,945.

**CESTA,** wicker basket used to catch and maneuver the ball in the game jai alai (q.v.).

**CESTODA,** class of flatworms of the phylum Platyhelminthes, consisting of tapeworms and similar endoparasites. Some zoologists classify Cestoda as a subclass of the class Cestoidea. These flatworms are characterized by the absence of cilia and intestines and by the presence of numerous testes and ovaries with occasional yolk glands. Cestodes are widely distributed, but are especially abundant in warm climates. Although they occur as intestinal parasites in species of all classes of vertebrates, especially mammals, the complete life history is known for comparatively few species. The group contains two subclasses, the Cestodaria or Monozoa, unsegmented individuals (rare), and the Eucestoda or Merozoa, segmented tapeworms. *See* FLATWORM; TAPEWORM.

**CETACEA,** order of aquatic mammals, comprising the whales, dolphins, and porpoises, of the class Mammalia, phylum Chordata. The members of this order, in becoming more perfectly adapted to an aquatic life, have evolved the external structure of fish. The bodies are fishlike, with smooth skins. The forelimbs are reduced to paddles that perform the functions of the pectoral fins of fish; the pelvic or hind limbs have disappeared entirely, and the pelvis itself has become reduced to a pair of horizontal bones that are remnants of the ischia. A posterior dorsal fin is usually present on the back, and the tail has a horizontal caudal fin. There are also important modifications in the vertebral column and skull. Cetaceans bear their young live and suckle them with milk, and they breathe atmospheric air like other mammals (q.v.). The order comprises three suborders: Archaeoceti, all extinct animals, with long snouts, forward nostrils, and two-rooted teeth; Odontoceti, including several families and about sixty species, comprising the toothed whales, including the small porpoises, dolphins, belugas, and killers, and the huge sperm whales; and Mystacoceti (or Mysticeti), with nostrils far back, and jaws bearing whalebone instead of teeth, as in the baleen or whalebone whale.

Fossil forms of the Cetacea are not common, and the evolution of the order cannot be satisfactorily traced. The earliest representative is the genus *Zeuglodon*, the only member of the suborder Archaeoceti. This genus appears in the Eocene rocks of Europe, North Africa, and North America. The skull of the *Zeuglodon* more closely resembles the normal mammalian skull than does that of any other cetacean. *See* DOLPHIN; PORPOISE; WHALE.

**CETUS,** *or* THE WHALE, equatorial constellation lying to the south of Aries (q.v.), the Ram. The two brightest stars are normally Beta Ceti, a second-magnitude star also called Deneb Kaitos (Ar., "the tail of the whale"), and Alpha Ceti, a third-magnitude star also called Menkar (Ar., "nose"). The most remarkable star is Omicron Ceti, called Mira (New Lat., fr. Lat. *Mirus,* "wonderful"), a variable star first discovered in 1596. It usually varies in brightness from the ninth to the third magnitude (q.v.) over a period of about eleven months. Occasionally it reaches a brightness of second magnitude. Mira is one of the largest stars known, with a diameter of about 220,000,000 mi., slightly larger than the diameter of the orbit of the earth. The constellation is named after the sea monster of Greek mythology sent by the god Neptune to destroy Andromeda, but killed by Perseus (qq.v.).

**CEUTA,** city and seaport of Spain, on the N. coast of Morocco, 14 miles S. of the Rock of Gibraltar, from which it is separated by the Strait of Gibraltar, and about 200 miles N.E. of Casablanca. For administrative purposes Ceuta is governed as part of Cádiz Province in Spain. The city is on a headland consisting of seven peaks, at the end of a narrow isthmus. The highest of these peaks, Jebel Musa, thought to be the ancient Abila, is one of the two Pillars of Hercules (q.v.).

A military and penal station, Ceuta is on the site of a Carthaginian settlement on which a Roman colony was later built. The Vandals took it from the Romans and lost it to Byzantium. It later became successively a possession of the Visigoths and of the Arabs. The latter called it Sebta or Cibta, from which the modern name is derived. Ceuta became an important center for the manufacture of brassware and for trade in slaves, gold, and ivory under later Berber and Spanish-Moorish rulers. The Portuguese captured the city in 1415 and the Spaniards in 1580. Moors laid siege to it unsuccessfully several times, one siege lasting from 1694 to 1720. Pop. (1970) 67,187.

**CÉVENNES,** mountain range in S. France, forming an arc from N.E. to S.W., and marking the S.E. limit of the large plateau region of central France called the Massif Central. The Cévennes form the watershed between the river systems of the Rhône and the Saône on the E. and those of the Garonne and the Loire on the W. The Cévennes proper extend for about 40 mi. through the departments of Hérault, Gard, Lozère, and Andèche. The highest peak of the range is Mont Mézenc (elevation 5754 ft.), and the average height is from 3000 to 4000 ft. The chief industries in the mountain area are raising sheep, mining coal, and cultivating olives and fruit. The mountains were the scene of the persecutions of Protestant groups, including the Albigenses and the Waldenses in the Middle Ages and the Camisards (qq.v.) in the 17th century.

**CEYLON** (anc. *Taprobane*), officially REPUBLIC OF SRI LANKA, island and independent state within the Commonwealth of Nations, situated in the Indian Ocean about 50 mi. off the S.E. coast of India, from which it is separated by the Palk Strait and Gulf of Mannar. It is located between about lat. 6° N. and lat. 10° N. and long. 79°30′ E. and long. 82° E. Lying between Ceylon and India is a chain of tiny islands known as Adam's Bridge. Ceylon is somewhat triangular in shape, with its apex in the N. and its base extending from S.W. to N.E. The greatest length from N. to S. is about 272 mi.; the greatest width is about 137 mi. The total area is 25,332 sq.mi.

The Ceylonese coast, particularly the W., S., and S.E., is palm-fringed and indented by lagoons and inlets. The more rugged N.E. coast contains Trincomalee harbor, considered one of the best natural harbors in the world. On the S.W. coast other harbors include the largely artificial one at Colombo, the capital city, and one at Galle.

*THE LAND*

An outstanding feature of the topography of this island state is a mountainous mass in the south-central part of the country, the highest point of which is the peak of Pidurutalagala (8291 ft.). In the upland area are two plateaus, Nuwara Eliya and Horton Plains, which are major centers of commercial tea plantations; the plateaus are noted for their cool, healthful climate. North of the mountains, and extending S.,

is an arid and gently rolling plain known as the dry zone.

Rivers and streams that are broken by rapids are especially numerous in the mountainous south-central region. The longest river is the Mahaweli; it flows E. for about 200 mi. to empty into the Indian Ocean near Trincomalee. Other rivers of the island include the Kelani, the mouth of which is near Colombo; the Kalu, which reaches the sea near Kalutara on the S.W. coast; and the Aruvi Aru, which flows N.W. across the dry zone to a point near Mannar.

**Climate.** Because Ceylon is situated near the equator, the climate throughout the year is generally hot and humid. The hill and mountain areas, however, are cool during all seasons, and the humidity is relatively lower in the dry zone. The average annual temperature is about 90° F. in the lowlands and about 70° F. in the higher mountainous regions.

Precipitation is characterized by wide sea-

sonal and regional variations. The monsoon season in the S.W. is from May to November, when the rainfall is exceptionally heavy. In the northern dry zone the main precipitation of about 40 in. annually occurs during the monsoon season in the N.E., which begins in the first week of November. Most crops in the dry zone, however, require irrigation. The hills and the lowlands of the S.W. section, which is known as the wet zone, normally have some rainfall throughout the year, but peaks occur in May and June and in October and November.

**Natural Resources.** The natural resources of Ceylon are chiefly agricultural, but most of the land is not easily cultivated. The mineral deposits of the country are limited, lacking especially coal and oil resources. In 1970 Ceylon produced approximately 723,000,000 kw hours of hydroelectric power annually.

**Plants and Animals.** Ceylon is noted for the beauty and variety of its vegetation. Dense tropical jungles occupy extensive areas in the S.W., and the upper mountain slopes are thickly forested. Many varieties of palm, including the areca, coconut, and palmyra, flourish in the lowlands along the coast. Mangroves and screw pines abound in coastal areas. Numerous varieties of timber trees, notably mahogany and many species of resin-yielding fruit trees, are indigenous to the wet zone. Among the timber trees that are common in the drier sections of the island are ebony and satinwood. Ferns, water hyacinths, orchids, acacias, eucalypti, and cypresses flourish in various regions.

The animal life of Ceylon, which may be in danger of extinction, is varied and includes the cheetah, leopard, several species of monkey, and elephant. The island contains more than 3000 species of birds and many species of reptiles.

### THE PEOPLE

About 72 percent of the population is composed of Sinhalese Buddhists. The largest minority groups are the Ceylonese and Indian Tamils. These groups account for about 21 percent of the population. The remaining population includes the descendants of the aboriginal Veddas, Malayans, Eurasians, and Europeans. Nonnationals total about 1,000,000. Ceylon is primarily an agrarian society.

**Population.** The population of Ceylon (census 1971) was 12,711,143. The overall population density is 497 per sq.mi. (U.N. est. 1970).

**Political Divisions.** The island is divided into nine provinces. The provinces, with their populations (1971 census), are the Western, 3,404,444; Central, 1,956,755; Southern, 1,666,710; North-

The traditional clock tower in downtown Colombo stands in stark contrast to the modern structure behind it. *Ed Lark*

ern, 877,768; Eastern, 722,883; North-Western, 1,407,894; North-Central, 553,065; Uva, 807,820; Sabaragamuwa, 1,313,804.

**Principal Cities.** Colombo, the capital, had a population of 563,705, according to the 1971 preliminary census figures; it was the only city in Ceylon with a population exceeding 100,000. Eighty-five percent of the freight of the island is routed through Colombo, and the city is an important fueling station for Far Eastern shipping that passes through the Suez Canal. Other important cities are the seaport of Jaffna, with a population (1971 est.) of 99,800; the ancient capital city of Kandy, with a population of 75,900; and the tea-producing village of Galle, with a population of 71,700.

**Religion.** Buddhism, which was introduced into Ceylon in the 3rd century B.C., is the prevailing faith. As practiced in Ceylon, Buddhism also shows elements of Hindu and Islamic traditions. In the early 1970's approximately 67 percent of the population were Buddhists; 18 percent were Hindus; 7 percent were Christians; and 7 percent were Muslims.

**Language.** The official language of Ceylon is Sinhala, or Sinhalese (q.v.). Tamil, a Dravidian language of S. India, is spoken by about 750,000 people and is used for certain purposes. English, the official language of Ceylon until 1957, is still widely used.

**Education.** Free education is provided to the university level; schooling is compulsory for children from six to fourteen years of age. The literacy rate is 65 percent.

ELEMENTARY AND SECONDARY SCHOOLS. In the late 1960's Ceylon had about 9700 primary and secondary schools, with about 2,640,000 pupils. Secondary-level teacher-training schools numbered about 25, with some 6600 undergraduate and graduate students.

UNIVERSITIES AND COLLEGES. The University of Ceylon was founded in 1942. In 1972 that institution was amalgamated with the universities of Peradeniya, Vidyodaya, and Vidyalankara and the Ceylon College of Technology to form a single University of Ceylon, with administrative offices in Colombo. Each campus has its own president and deputy registrar.

**Culture.** Religion plays an important part in Ceylonese life; a revival of Buddhism was associated with the rise of Sinhalese nationalism. The twenty-two public holidays are based on religious festivals. The annual torchlight temple procession, or *Perahara,* in which ornamentally covered elephants and hundreds of dancers participate, draws thousands of devotees. Pilgrimages also play an important role in Ceylonese life. The most important pilgrimage is to the top of Adam's Peak (it is believed by the Muslims that Adam and Eve lived in Ceylon after they left the Garden of Eden). Another important pilgrimage is to the Temple of the Tooth in Kandy, where it is believed that a tooth of Buddha is enshrined.

Sinhalese society, though Buddhist, is stratified along caste lines. Ceylon Tamil society reproduces, although in modified form, the caste features found in India.

LIBRARIES AND MUSEUMS. The Ceylon University Library in Colombo, founded in 1870, is the largest, with about 200,000 volumes. The oldest library is the Department of Government Archives in Gangodavila, which was founded by the Dutch in 1656 and contains about 7000 volumes. The Colombo National Museum, established in 1783, has a library of ancient Oriental texts and Sanskrit manuscripts, as well as exhibits in archeology, zoology, and the arts.

ARCHEOLOGY. Middle Stone Age implements such as bones and grinding stones have been unearthed in the Bandarawela region in the S.; some late Stone Age tools of ground quartz were discovered nearby. Early Buddhist pottery and iron artifacts have been found throughout the country. Hindu burial relics dating from the 3rd century B.C. have been discovered in the North-Western Province.

ART AND MUSIC. The arts are dominated by traditional Sinhalese modes. Renewed interest in

*The skill of making pottery is passed from generation to generation.*

Tamil art forms has resulted from a recent ethnic rivalry between the two groups.

## THE ECONOMY

The economy is based on a mixture of free enterprise and socialism. Although the government owns much of the mining and basic manufacturing industries, private investment is encouraged in consumer industries and other spheres of the economy. The insurance business was nationalized in 1963, and the salt industry is a government-controlled monopoly. In one year the national budget showed revenues of $470,000,000 and expenditures of $662,000,000.

Ceylon receives foreign aid under Colombo Plan arrangements and from Eastern European countries and the United States.

**Agriculture.** The principal economic activity of the island is agriculture. Because of a rapid increase in population, Ceylon is forced to import more than one half of its food supply. About 4,500,000 acres, or 28 percent of the total land area, is under cultivation.

Three crops, tea, rubber, and coconuts, account for about 75 percent of the total agricultural output. Ceylon produces about 30 percent of the world's tea. Although tea occupies only 15 percent of the cultivated acreage, it is the mainstay of the export trade, providing 60 percent of the total export earnings of Ceylon.

The country produces about 5 percent of the world's rubber supply. It is the fourth-largest producer of coconuts in the world, exporting about 50 percent of the crop in the form of copra, the dried kernel of the coconut, coconut oil, fiber, and other products.

Rice is the basic food of the people and the principal crop of the island. More acreage is devoted to the cultivation of rice than to any other crop; but only half of the needs of the country are met by domestic production. Vegetables are grown in small amounts, mostly by farmers for their own consumption.

Animal husbandry is of comparatively little importance to the economy of Ceylon. Cattle, buffalo, and goats are the principal livestock. Pigs and sheep are also raised in some areas.

**Forest and Fishing Industries.** Local timber needs are satisfied by government-owned woodlands. Wood exports, however, are small.

Fishing is restricted to a small coastal fringe and contributes relatively little to the economy; the yield in 1970 amounted to about 100,000 tons annually.

**Mining.** Although mineral resources are generally limited, Ceylon is an important source of high-grade lump amorphous graphite, used in the manufacture of carbon brushes for electric motors. The total graphite production (about 11,500 tons annually in the late 1960's) is exported. Ilmenite is also extracted for commercial

303

uses; about 55,000 tons were exported annually. Limestone is mined for a government-owned cement factory at Jaffna. Other minerals include salt, mica, kaolin, glass sands, and precious and semiprecious stones. Iron-ore deposits are estimated at 6,000,000 tons.

**Manufacturing.** Mechanized industry is relatively limited. The larger industrial enterprises, which are entirely or partly government-owned, produce such products as steel, tires, cement, cotton yarn, sugar, paper and leather goods, chemicals, ceramics, and processed food. Plans for the introduction of heavy industry have recently been announced by the government.

**Currency, Commerce, and Trade.** The Ceylonese rupee, consisting of 100 cents, is the monetary unit (6.06 rupees equal U.S.$1; 1973). The chief exports are tea and rubber, followed by coconut products and graphite. Foodstuffs, mainly rice, fish, and vegetables, make up about 40 percent of imports; others include manufactured goods, petroleum, coal, and minerals.

**Transportation.** A network of about 13,000 mi. of improved roads connects most regions of the island; the best-developed road system is that in the plantation areas. A railroad network totals about 1000 mi.

Ceylon has three international airports. The government-owned airline, Air Ceylon, Ltd., provides domestic and international service.

**Communications.** All electric communications are government-owned, except in some small rural areas. Ceylon has more than a dozen newspapers, and over forty periodicals are published. Some 63,000 telephones and more than 500,000 licensed radio receivers are in use.

**Labor.** Almost 3,000,000 Ceylonese are economically active, mostly unskilled workmen. More than one half of this number is organized in some 1200 trade unions. Progressive labor legislation had been enacted, covering minimum wage, health, and welfare, but enforcement is difficult because of staff shortages.

## GOVERNMENT

Ceylon is an independent member of the Commonwealth of Nations.

**Central Government.** Legislative and executive power is vested in the unicameral National Assembly. The chief of state is the president, who is appointed to a four-year term by the prime minister (chief executive).

**Health and Welfare.** The government provides financial assistance to tuberculosis patients and their dependents and to victims of storms, crop failure, and other natural disasters. Voluntary agencies that provide services for the aged, orphaned, blind, and deaf receive govern-

mental grants-in-aid. A workmen's compensation law became effective in 1948. Family-planning clinics operate on the local level. Because of the elimination of most epidemic diseases, the average life-span has doubled, but a shortage of doctors and medical facilities remains.

**Legislature.** According to the 1972 constitution, the National Assembly is the "supreme instrument of the State". The 157 Assembly members are elected to six-year terms. Among the powers held by the Assembly is the one to amend or replace the constitution.

**Political Parties.** The major parties are the Buddhist-dominated, nationalist, and non-aligned Sri Lanka Freedom Party; the Lanka Sama Samaja Party (L.S.S.P.), or Ceylon Equality Party, a Trotskyite group; the moderate United National Party (U.N.P.); and the nationalist Mahajana Eksath Peramuna (M.E.P.), or People's United Front, which follows the precepts of both Marxism and Buddhism. Two Communist parties exist, one aligned with the U.S.S.R. and the other with Communist China.

**Local Government.** The island is divided into 9 provinces, 22 districts, and 12 municipalities. Members are elected triennially to 34 urban councils, 85 town councils, and 542 village councils.

**Judiciary.** The independent judiciary consists of a Supreme Court, a commissioner of assize, a criminal court of appeals, and a number of subordinate courts. The chief justice of the Supreme Court and ten subordinate justices have appellate and review powers in criminal cases and exclusive powers in the most serious criminal offenses.

**Defense.** In 1957 British military bases were reclaimed by Ceylon. Ceylonese defense was left largely in the hands of the small British-trained Ceylonese army, navy, and air force, totaling fewer than 5000 officers and men.

## HISTORY

According to Hindu legend the greater part of Ceylon was conquered in prehistoric times by Ramachandra, the seventh incarnation of the supreme deity Vishnu. The written history of Ceylon begins with the chronicle known as the *Mahavamsa*. This work was started in the 6th century A.D. and provides a virtually unbroken narrative up to 1815. The *Mahavamsa* was compiled by a succession of Buddhist monks. Because it often aims to glorify or to degrade certain periods or reigns, it is not a wholly reliable source despite the wealth of historical material it contains.

**Ancient Ceylon.** The *Mahavamsa* relates that the island was conquered in 504 B.C. by Vijaya, a

Josephus Daniels–Rapho Guillumette

*Earning a living in Ceylon. Above: Workers picking tea in the Nuwara Eliya district, in the wet highlands. Tea accounts for more than half of the country's export income. Below: Fishermen launch their boat on Mt. Lavinia beach, on the southwestern coast. Fishing, largely limited to the sea, plays a minor role in the country's economy, employing only 40,000 people.*

Bernard Pierre Wolff–Photo Researchers

Hindu prince from northeast India. After subjugating the aboriginal inhabitants, a people now known as Veddas, Vijaya married a native princess, encouraged emigration from the mainland, and made himself ruler of the entire island. The realm (called Sinhala after Vijaya's patrimonial name) inherited by his successors consisted, however, of the arid region lying to the north of the south-central mountain system.

Members of the dynasty founded by Vijaya reigned over Sinhala for several centuries. During this period, and particularly after the adoption in about 307 B.C. of Buddhism as the national religion, the Sinhalese built a highly developed civilization. Extant evidence of their engineering skill and architectural achievements includes remnants of vast irrigation projects; a number of ruined cities, notably the ancient capital Anuradhapura (q.v.); and numerous ruined shrines (dagobas). From the late 3rd century to the middle of the 12th century Sinhala was dominated by Tamil kings and by a succession of invaders from southern India. Native princes regained power briefly in the late 12th century and again in the 13th century. From 1408 to 1438 Chinese forces occupied the island, which had been partitioned into a number of petty kingdoms.

**Portuguese and Dutch Control.** In 1517 the Portuguese, having established friendly relations with one of the native monarchs, founded a fort and trading post at Colombo. Their sphere of influence expanded steadily thereafter, mainly as a result of successful wars of

conquest, and by the end of the 16th century they controlled large sections of the island. Consequently, in 1638 and 1639, when the Dutch launched the first of a series of attacks on Portuguese strongholds in Ceylon, they found numerous allies among the natives. The struggle ended in 1658 with the Dutch gaining control of most of the island, although the kingdom of Kandy remained independent.

**British Rule.** In 1795, following the occupation of the Netherlands by France, the British government dispatched an expeditionary force against Ceylon. The Dutch capitulated early in the next year, and in 1798 the British made all of Ceylon, except the kingdom of Kandy, a crown colony. By the provisions of the 1802 Treaty of Amiens, which terminated the second phase of the Napoleonic Wars, the island was formally ceded to Great Britain. Kandy was occupied in 1803 and annexed to the crown colony in 1815. The British period of rule was marked by abortive native rebellions in 1817, 1843, and 1848. Tea and rubber estates were developed. In this period violent social-religious struggles between the Sinhalese peasants, mostly Buddhists, and the moneylenders and traders, chiefly Muslims, also occurred, and all the native peoples struggled continuously for representative government and national freedom. The first substantial victory in the struggle for self-government came in 1931, when Great Britain promulgated a new constitution that granted the natives semiautonomous control over national affairs.

During World War II Ceylon was an important base of operations in the Allied offensive against the Japanese and a major source of rubber, foodstuffs, and other materials vital to the war effort.

**Self-Rule.** On Feb. 4, 1948, the colony became a self-governing dominion of the Commonwealth of Nations; Sir Henry Moore (1887–1964) and former minister of agriculture and lands and leader of the council of state D. S. Senanayake (1884–1952) of the United National Party (U.N.P.) were installed as governor-general and prime minister, respectively, at ceremonies held

Kandy, one of Ceylon's most populous and commercially important cities, is located on the country's central plateau, about 80 mi. northeast of Colombo.
M. P. Kahl–Photo Researchers

Outside Kandy, elephants are decorated for a Buddhist celebration in which they are paraded through the streets of the city. Kandy contains a shrine where one of Buddha's teeth is reputedly preserved.  Jackie Foryst

in Colombo; and an ancient Sinhalese flag was adopted as the flag of the new state.

The foreign ministers of the Commonwealth of Nations assembled at Colombo in January, 1950, and drafted a tentative plan for the economic development of Southeast Asia. As finally formulated, the Colombo Plan (q.v.) allocated nearly $340,000,000 of Commonwealth funds for a variety of projects designed to advance the Ceylonese economy, notably irrigation works and hydroelectric plants.

D. S. Senanayake died in March, 1952, and his son, former minister of agriculture and lands, Dudley Senanayake (1911–73), who belonged to the same party, was named prime minister. In 1954 Ceylon declined to join the Southeast Asia Treaty Organization, which was formed as a defensive alliance by the United States, Great Britain, and six other nations. However, in April, 1955, the new prime minister, former minister of transport and works Sir John Kotelawala (1897– ), speaking at a conference of Asian and African nations held in Bandung, Indonesia, stated that he regarded Communist expansion as a menace. Later in the year, on Dec. 14, Ceylon was admitted to membership in the United Nations. The U.N.P. lost the elections held in April, 1956, and S. W. R. D. Bandaranaike (1899–1959), leader of the Marxist-oriented People's United Front, became prime minister.

**Recent History.** In the U.N. during 1957 Ceylon adopted a policy of neutrality in the disputes between the Communist and non-Communist countries. The U.S. agreed on Feb. 7,

*Polonnaruwa, an ancient ruined city in northeastern Ceylon, is famed for its 50-ft. reclining statue of Buddha.* Walter S. Clark

1958, to provide Ceylon with technical assistance and a grant of about $780,000 for economic projects. The Soviet Union and Ceylon signed trade and economic agreements in February. On March 4 Ceylon accepted a loan of about $10,500,000 from China.

On Sept. 25, 1959, Prime Minister Bandaranaike was shot by a Buddhist monk and died the following day. His immediate successor was Wijayananda Dahanayake (1902– ), former minister of education. In the general elections of March 19, 1960, the U.N.P. won the greatest number of votes, and two days later Dudley Senanayake again became prime minister in a minority cabinet, which quickly lost parliamentary confidence. New general elections held on July 20 resulted in a near majority of parliamentary seats being won by the Sri Lanka Freedom Party, headed by the widow of the late prime minister and member of the Senate, Mrs. Sirimavo Bandaranaike (1916– ), who was sworn in as prime minister the next day.

On Dec. 31 a bill was passed making Sinhalese the only official language of Ceylon. Spokesmen for the Tamil-speaking minority led mass demonstrations against the measure in early 1961. To cope with the situation, a state of emergency was declared, the Tamil Federal Party was forbidden to operate, and strikes were declared illegal. Sinhalese-Tamil relations continued to be strained until January, 1966, when

Tamil was made the official administrative language in northern and western Ceylon.

During 1962, strikes, unemployment, a continuing population increase, and a drop in the world price of principal Ceylonese exports contributed to a severe financial crisis. Land devoted to the cultivation of rice was increased, and the government appropriated all foreign oil storage and distribution facilities. Regarding compensation for American holdings as inadequate, the U.S. suspended all aid to Ceylon from 1963 until 1966. Severe restrictions were then imposed by Ceylon on most imports.

In 1965 Dudley Senanayake was returned as prime minister, implementing a policy of nonalignment, economic development, and domestic production. In the elections of 1970 a leftist coalition headed by Mrs. Bandaranaike was victorious, and the new government began to move Ceylon toward socialism. In March, 1971, armed revolt broke out, sparked by leaders of the Marxist People's Liberation Front, but the rebellion was largely suppressed by September. In that month the Senate was abolished and the House of Representatives was renamed the National Assembly. The changes were preparatory to the adoption of a new constitution. On May 22, 1972, Ceylon officially became the socialist Republic of Sri Lanka when the Assembly adopted the new constitution. Mrs. Bandaranaike became the first prime minister, and William Gopallawa (1898–      ), the last governor-general, was appointed president.

**CÉZANNE, Paul**  (1839–1906), French painter, born in Aix-en-Provence. In early childhood Cé-

*A self-portrait by Paul Cézanne.*

Bavarian State Gallery, Munich

zanne became friends with his classmate, the French novelist Émile Zola (q.v.), who induced him in 1861 to give up work in his father's bank and to continue his art studies. Cézanne entered the Académie Suisse and became acquainted with the impressionist painter Camille Pissarro (q.v.), who was to exert a strong influence on his work; see IMPRESSIONISM. Later Cézanne became a friend of the French painters Claude Monet (q.v.) and Pierre Auguste Renoir (see under RENOIR), and joined the impressionists, exhibiting with them in 1874 and in 1877. Discouraged by the ridicule of critics and by his various differences with the impressionists, Cézanne retired in 1879 to Aix, where he spent the remainder of his life. Breaking with all his old friends, even Zola, he ultimately seemed to be forgotten by the world.

In this seclusion he developed a style of painting destined to exert a great influence on modern art. Cézanne differed from both impressionists and academicians. Both of these schools were primarily concerned with selective representation of nature, the impressionists emphasizing particularly the scientific study of light and color vibration. In his later period Cézanne tended more and more to accentuate, by subtle variations of color and tone, the geometrical forms found in nature. In all his work, which included still life, portraiture, and landscapes, Cézanne sought to abstract elements of nature and to build them deliberately into three-dimensional compositions that had aesthetic rather than realistic validity. His emphasis on formal values, which had been dissipated by the representational and emotional aims of the realists and the stress on color and atmosphere of the impressionists, led to a new school in painting, postimpressionism (q.v.). Many 20th-century styles of painting, such as cubism, expressionism, and Fauvism (qq.v.), developed from this school.

Cézanne is sometimes called "the father of modernism", but during his lifetime he remained unknown except to a few connoisseurs. It was not until a retrospective exhibition of his work in Paris in 1904 that his reputation as one of the most original modern painters began to be established. His works are in many private collections, and outstanding collections of his work may be seen at the Louvre in Paris, the Museum of Modern Art in New York City, and numerous other museums in Europe and the United States.

**CGS SYSTEM,**  or CENTIMETER-GRAM-SECOND SYSTEM (usually written "cgs system"), is a metric system (q.v.) based on the centime-

***Cézanne. Plate 1.*** *"The Boy with Red Vest" (1890–95) by Paul Cézanne. Sometimes called "the father of modern-ism", the French painter was an important influence on many artists of the 20th century.*

*"Still Life on a Bureau"*, one of the numerous still lifes created by Paul Cézanne that reflect his artistic development and changes of style.

*"The Blue Vase"* (1885–87) by Paul Cézanne. Now considered a towering figure among 19th-century French painters, Cézanne was known to few but his fellow artists until the last years of his life.

**Cézanne. Plate 2.**

ter (c) for length, the gram (g) for mass, and the second (s) for time. It derives from the meter-kilogram-second (or mks) system but uses certain special designations such as the dyne (for force) and the erg (for energy). It has generally been employed where small quantities are encountered, as in physics and chemistry. Both the cgs system and mks system have been supplanted by the International System of Units (q.v.).

See also METRIC SYSTEM; WEIGHTS AND MEASURES.

**CHABRIER, Alexis Emmanuel** (1841–94), French composer, born in Ambert, Puy-de-Dôme. Largely self-educated as a musician, Chabrier was for eighteen years a civil servant in the French government before retiring to devote himself to musical composition. His works are characterized by rich color, vivacity, humor, and strongly marked rhythm. Among his compositions are the operas *Gwendoline* (1886) and *Le Roi Malgré Lui* (1887), and the orchestral pieces *España* (1883) and *Joyeuse Marche* (1888). He also composed choral works and music for piano and for voice and piano. Chabrier's style and unconventional harmonies influenced later French composers, including Maurice Ravel and Erik Satie (qq.v.).

**CHACMA.** See BABOON.

**CHACO.** See GRAN CHACO.

**CHACO CANYON NATIONAL MONUMENT,** site of the archeological remains of the prehistoric Anasazi Indian culture, in N.W. New Mexico, about 60 miles N.E. of the city of Gallup, N. Mex. The monument contains 13 major ruins and more than 300 smaller sites, ranging from the pit houses of the late Basketmakers to the massive structures of the classic Pueblo period. Among the more important sites dating from this later period is Pueblo Bonito, the ruin of a five-story building estimated to have contained 800 rooms with more than 30 large ceremonial chambers (kivas). Originally settled about 700 A.D., the site was abandoned during the 13th century. The monument, covering 21,509.4 acres, was established in 1907. It is administered by the National Park Service (q.v.).

**CHACO WAR.** See BOLIVIA: *History;* PARAGUAY: *History.*

**CHAD, LAKE,** body of fresh water in central Africa, at the junction of the Republic of Chad, Cameroon, Nigeria, and the Republic of the Niger, about 800 ft. above sea level. Lake Chad is fed principally by the Shari and Yobe rivers. Although the lake has no visible outlet, it is steadily decreasing in size because of evaporation and underground seepage. In the rainy season the area of the lake is as great as 10,000 sq.mi., but in the dry season it shrinks to as little as 5000 sq.mi. In open water the depth of the lake varies from 3 ft. in the N.W. to more than 20 ft. in the S. Native tribesmen inhabit the numerous islands lying along the E. shore of the lake. The first Europeans to visit the lake were a party of British explorers in 1823.

**CHAD, REPUBLIC OF** (Fr. *République du Tchad*), republic in N.-central Africa. Chad is bounded on the N. by Libya; on the E. by Sudan; on the S. by the Central African Republic; and

*N'Djamena, the capital of Chad, is at the confluence of the Shari and Logone rivers.*

the w. by Cameroon, Nigeria, and Niger. The country lies between about lat. 7°30′ N. and lat. 23°27′ N. (the Tropic of Cancer) and long. 13°30′ E. and long. 24° E. Chad has an area of 495,755 sq.mi.

## THE LAND

The surface of the country consists mainly of a low plateau sloping from Lake Chad on the s.w. border (about 900 ft.) to heights of 3000 to 4000 ft. in the Ennedi region of the N.E. The greatest elevations are the Tibesti Mts. in the N. which reach a maximum height of 11,204 ft. at Emi Koussi. The N. half of the republic lies in the Sahara Desert.

CLIMATE. The N. portion of Chad is hot and dry. The central section has three seasons. It is hot from March to July; rainy from July to October, rainfall averaging from about 2 to 10 in.; and cool during the remaining months. The s. section has similar seasons, but receives about 47 in. of rain in the same four months.

**Natural Resources.** Although only 5 percent of the land is under cultivation, the agricultural resources are of primary importance. Indigenous crops, as well as those recently introduced, yield important food products. Extensive fish resources in Lake Chad and the Shari R. are also of vital importance. Some mineral deposits have

been discovered but remain largely unexploited.

## THE PEOPLE

The ethnic structure of the population of Chad is the result of the intermingling of indigenous Negroes and invading Arabs.

**Population.** The present-day peoples may be divided into two main population groups: a large Muslim population inhabits the N. and central portions of the country, and the non-Muslims of black African origin live primarily in the s. regions. The largest group among the non-Muslims is the Sara tribe. Chad culture draws most heavily on the ethnic heritage of its Negro peoples, but Islamic and French influences are much in evidence. Chad is 95 percent rural. The population of Chad (census 1964) was 3,254,000; the United Nations estimated (1974) 3,949,000. The overall population density is about 8 per sq.mi. (1974 U.N. est.). Most of the population is concentrated in the south.

**Political Divisions and Principal Cities.** Chad is divided into fourteen prefectures. N'Djamena, formerly Fort-Lamy, with a population (1972 est.) of 166,600, is the capital and largest city. Other cities, with estimated populations (1972), are Sarh, formerly Fort-Archambault (44,000), Moundou (40,000), and Abécher (28,000).

**Language and Religion.** The official language is French, but a wide variety of tribal languages

*A young Buduma tribesman brings a wandering calf back to the herd. The Buduma live along the shore and on the islands of Lake Chad.* Jacques Jangoux

Using a primitive hoe, a Buduma woman prepares the soil for planting. The Buduma cultivate corn, okra, beans, and other crops.

Jacques Jangoux

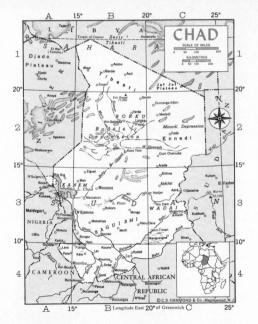

## INDEX TO MAP OF CHAD

are spoken. Chadic languages, especially Hausa (q.v.), are spoken in the Lake Chad area. These languages form a branch of the Afro-Asiatic linguistic family (*see* AFRICAN LANGUAGES; AFRICAN LITERATURE). Muslims comprise 50 percent of the population and animists about 45 percent. About 5 percent are Christians.

**Education.** In the late 1960's Chad had a literacy rate of 5 percent. School attendance was estimated at 172,000 elementary, secondary, and

313

*Fishing is a major occupation of the people who live on Lake Chad. The canoes, known as kadei among the Buduma, are made of papyrus stalks. Paddles, like the one lying across the forward part of this boat, are used to propel the craft out on the lake; poling is more common in shallower waters. Commonest in the catch of this fisherman, who is shown holding his net, is the tilapia, an excellent food fish.* Jacques Jangoux

technical students. During this period nearly 660 public and missionary schools existed and about 330 students were studying abroad.

## THE ECONOMY

The economy of Chad is largely agricultural; 96 percent of the population is engaged in farming and animal husbandry. Only N'Djamena, Sarh, Abécher, and Moundou have electricity. In the mid-1970's annual electric power production reached about 57,000,000 kw hours. In a recent year, budget figures showed revenues of about $46,600,000 and expenditures of approximately $53,300,000.

The currency is the C.F.A. franc, consisting of 100 centimes (224 C.F.A. francs equal U.S.$1; 1976). In the mid-1970's imports totaled more than $92,000,000, exports more than $36,000,000. Chad is a member of the African and Mauritian Common Organization (OCAM), and an associate member of the European Economic Community (E.E.C.).

**Agriculture.** Cotton is the main cash crop; production in the early 1970's was about 42,000 metric tons of ginned cotton annually, approximately 90 percent of exports. The rice crop is becoming increasingly important. Millet, potatoes, squash, beans, peanuts, and other vegetables are grown. Livestock estimates in the early 1970's were about 4,600,000 head of cattle, 4,200,000 sheep and goats, 370,000 camels, 280,000 donkeys, 150,000 horses, and 55,000 pigs. Some 37 percent of the total land area is used for grazing.

**Industries.** The processing of cotton and cottonseed oil and the manufacturing of peanut oil are important industries in Chad. Modern meat-packing plants have been established in N'Djamena and Sarh. The fishing industry supplies fresh, dried, and smoked fish for domestic use and export. Natron (soda) is the only exploited mineral; about 3800 tons are exported annually. Forestry is important in the s.

**Transportation and Communications.** Of a road network of some 17,000 mi., only 4360 mi. are all-weather. Chad has no railroads. The main airport at N'Djamena can accommodate large jets, and thirty-five smaller airports accommodate smaller craft. Domestic and international telephone and telegraph services are available. The one radio station, in N'Djamena, is government-owned.

## GOVERNMENT

Under a constitution approved in 1962, Chad adopted a presidential form of government. The unicameral National Assembly is elected by universal adult suffrage for five-year terms. The president, who is also elected for a seven-year term, has broad powers. The single political party is the Parti Progressiste Tchadien (P.P.T.).

## HISTORY

The African kingdoms of Kanem, Wadai, and Baguirmi were situated in the region occupied by the present-day Republic of Chad when the first European explorers visited it in the 19th century. In 1910 the area was incorporated into the newly formed French Equatorial Africa (q.v.). After 1920 Chad was governed as a separate territory. In 1960 the Republic of Chad became an independent state within the French Community, and former premier François Tombalbaye (1918–75) was appointed president. Elected to a seven-year term in 1962, he abolished all political parties except his own P.P.T. He was reelected to a second term in 1969.

From the mid-1960's Chad was beset by a rebellion, led by Muslims from the north, against the government, dominated by non-Muslims. In 1969 Tombalbaye requested French military intervention against the rebels; in 1972 most of the French troops were withdrawn. In 1973 the cities of Chad were given African names, and the president adopted the given name Ngarta. In April, 1975, Tombalbaye was killed in a military coup d'etat; he was succeeded by Brigadier General Félix Malloum (1932– ).

**CHADWICK, Florence** (1918– ), American swimmer born in San Diego, Calif. On Aug. 8, 1950, she swam the English Channel from France to England in a record 13 hr. 20 min. She swam from England to France on Sept. 11, 1951, in 16 hr. 19 min., becoming the first woman to swim the channel in both directions. On Oct. 12, 1955, she swam from England to France in 13 hr. 55 min., a world record for the southward crossing. In the 1950's she also swam the Bristol Channel from Wales to England and the San Pedro Channel between Santa Catalina Island and Long Beach, Calif.

**CHADWICK, Sir James** (1891–1974), British physicist, born in Manchester, England, and educated at the Victoria University of Manchester. In 1909 he met and began working under the British physicist Lord Ernest Rutherford (q.v.). Chadwick remained at Manchester until 1913, when he went to Germany to study in Berlin. Stranded in Germany at the outbreak of World War I, he was interned there throughout the war. At the end of the war he returned to Manchester and the following year went to the University of Cambridge with Rutherford, with whom he continued fruitful collaboration until 1935. In that year Chadwick became professor at the University of Liverpool. From 1948 to 1958 he was master, and from 1959 a fellow, of Gonville and Caius College, Cambridge.

Chadwick is best known for his discovery in 1932 of one of the fundamental particles of matter, the neutron (q.v.), a discovery that led directly to nuclear fission and the atomic bomb; see ATOM AND ATOMIC THEORY; NUCLEAR POWER. Chadwick was one of the first in Great Britain to stress the possibility of the development of such a bomb and was the chief scientist associated with the British atomic-bomb effort. He spent much of his time from 1943 to 1945 in the United States, principally at the Los Alamos Scientific Laboratory at Los Alamos, N.Mex.; see NUCLEAR ENERGY: *Atomic Bomb.* A fellow of the Royal Society, Chadwick was awarded the Hughes Medal in 1932. He received the Nobel Prize in physics in 1935 and was knighted in 1945.

**CHAERONEA,** town of ancient Boeotia, Greece, now Chaironeia, memorable for the disastrous defeat there of the Athenians and Thebans by Philip II, King of Macedonia, and his son Alexander III (qq.v.), known as the Great, in 338 B.C. This defeat was a prelude to the Macedonian domination of Greece. Archeologists have discovered a well-preserved Greek theater on the site, and the remains of a huge lion statue the Thebans erected to honor soldiers lost in the battle. The Greek essayist and biographer Plutarch (q.v.) was a native of Chaeronea. The modern town of Chaironeia is on the site of Chaeronea.

**CHAFFEE,** name of two American military officers, father and son.

**Adna Romanza Chaffee** (1842–1914), born in Orwell, Ohio, and educated in the public schools of Ohio. He served in the American

Civil War and in the Spanish-American War. As major general of volunteers during the Boxer Rebellion in China in 1900, he commanded the American contingent of the forces that captured Peking. Thereafter he commanded the American forces in the Philippines (1901–02), was commander of the Department of the East (1902–03), and, until his retirement, was lieutenant general and chief of staff of the United States Army (1904–06).

**Adna Romanza Chaffee** (1884–1941), born in Junction City, Kans., and educated at the United States Military Academy. A staff officer in France during World War I, he became a major general in 1940. He was known as the "Father of the Mechanized Forces", principally for his work in organizing the first mechanized brigade of the U.S. Army.

**CHAFFINCH,** common name for a European bird, *Fringilla coelebs,* of the Finch family (Fringillidae). The chaffinch is a small bird, about 5 to 6 in. long. In the male sex the head and neck are blue and gray; the back is chestnut; and the wings are almost black, with conspicuous white bars. The female is a drab olive-brown color. Valued for its song, the chaffinch is one of the most common cage birds, especially in Europe. In the colder northern countries it is migratory, but it spends the winter in flocks in England and in countries around the Mediterranean.

**CHAGALL, Marc** (1889–    ), French painter, born in Vitebsk, Russia, and educated in art in Saint Petersburg (now Leningrad) and Paris, France. He remained in Paris until 1914 and traveled subsequently in Germany. Between 1915 and 1917 he lived in St. Petersburg (then Petrograd); after the Russian Revolution he was director of the Art Academy in Vitebsk in 1918–19 and art director of the Moscow Jewish State Theatre in 1919–22. Chagall painted several murals in the theater lobby and executed the state settings for numerous productions. After 1922 he lived in France, except for a period of residence in the United States from 1941 to 1949.

Chagall's distinctive use of color and form derives partly from Russian expressionism and was influenced decisively by French cubism (*see* CUBISM; EXPRESSIONISM). Crystallizing his style early, as in "Candles in the Dark" (1908; owned by the artist), he later developed subtle variations. His numerous works represent characteristically vivid recollections of Russian-Jewish village scenes as in "I and the Village" (1911; Museum of Modern Art, New York City) and incidents in his private life, as in the series prints "Mein Leben" ("My Life", 1922), in addition to treatments of Jewish genre subjects, of which

"The Praying Jew" (1914; Art Institute of Chicago) is one. A Biblical theme characterizes a series of etchings executed between 1925 and 1939, illustrating the Old Testament, and the twelve stained-glass windows (1962) in the Hadassah Hospital of the Hadassah-Hebrew University Medical Center in Jerusalem, Israel. In 1973 the Biblical Message: Marc Chagall Museum, as it is known, was opened in Nice, France, to house hundreds of his Biblical works.

Chagall's other works include "The Cattle Dealer" (1912; private collection, Switzerland); "Paris Through the Window" (1913) and "The Birthday" (1915–23), both in the Solomon R. Guggenheim Museum, New York City; "The Circus" (1926; private collection, Brussels, Belgium); "Cock and Harlequin" (1928; private collection, Paris); "Time Is a River Without Banks" (1930–39; Museum of Modern Art); and "The Window" (1959; owned by the artist). He has executed many prints illustrating literary classics. A canvas completed in 1964 covers the ceiling of the Opéra in Paris, and two 30 by 36 ft. murals (1966) hang in the lobby of the new Metropolitan Opera House in New York City.

Recognized as one of the most significant contemporary painters and graphic artists, Chagall treats his subjects in a vein of humor and fantasy that draws deeply upon the dreamlike resources of the subconscious and distinguishes him as a master of surrealistic inventiveness; *see* SURREALISM. His personal and circumscribed imagery is often suffused with exquisite poetic inspiration.                                        G.A.

*Marc Chagall*                              Jewish Museum, N.Y.

**Chagall. Plate 1.** *"Self-Portrait with a Glass of Wine" (1917) by Marc Chagall, a painting showing the Cubist influence in the fragmentation of forms and colors.*

"Artist's Portrait with Seven Fingers" (1912–13) by Marc Chagall.

Chagall. Plate 2.

"Maternity" by Marc Chagall. Many of Chagall's works reflect the ways of Jewish life in his native village of Vitebsk, Russia.

**CHAGRES,** river of Panama and the Canal Zone, rising about 45 miles E. of Colón, and flowing into the Caribbean Sea near Nuevo Chagres. The river supplies the water required to operate the locks of the Panama Canal, which follows the bed of the stream from Gamboa to a point just west of Gatún Lake. The great rise of the river from rains or melted snow, up to 32 ft. in 24 hours, presented a formidable problem in connection with construction of the canal. To solve the problem Gatún Dam, which formed Gatún Lake, was built.

**CHAIKOVSKI, Pëtr Ilich.** See TCHAIKOVSKY, PËTR ILICH.

**CHAILLU, Paul Belloni du.** See DU CHAILLU, PAUL BELLONI.

**CHAIN,** any length of connected iron or steel links, used for binding, pulling, and lifting heavy objects. The term also applies to drive-powered belts incorporating sprockets and rollers that are used for conveying materials, as along an assembly line. Since the common coil chains combine strength and flexibility, they are useful for many tasks in industry, construction, and transportation. Some coil chains have twisted links to make the chain lie more flat. For dangerous, large-scale work, high-grade wrought iron chains, called crane chains, are used. Another type of coil chain is the anchor chain, which has a metal stud inside each link to prevent fouling or kinking. Other less flexible chains, such as the pintle chain, have detachable links. On a smaller scale, chains are used in fine mechanisms and for many articles of jewelry.

Conveyor or transmission chains are essentially gearlike belts or beds of chain. One of the most common of these is the roller chain or chain drive, which is also found on bicycles. A fast-moving powered chain is the silent chain, also known as the inverted tooth chain. Composed of steel links joined tightly in rows by pins, it is so called because it operates much more quietly than other automatic chains.

**CHAIN,** in surveying, standard unit of length or measuring band equivalent to 66 ft., subdivided into 100 links of 7.92 in. each. A mile has 80 chains, and an acre has 10 square chains. The surveyor's chain is also known as Gunter's chain, after its inventor, the English mathematician Edmund Gunter (q.v.). In engineering, a chain equals 100 ft., or 100 links of 1 ft. each. *See also* SURVEYING; WEIGHTS AND MEASURES.

**CHAIN, Ernst Boris** (1906– ), German-British biochemist and pathologist, born in Berlin and educated at the University of Berlin. Because he was Jewish, he left Germany after the accession to power in 1933 of the German dictator Adolf Hitler (q.v.). He went to England, where he engaged in research in enzymes at the University of Cambridge. In 1935 he went to the University of Oxford, where he collaborated with the British pathologist Sir Howard Walter Florey (q.v.) on the investigation of antibiotic substances produced by molds. He became a British subject in 1939. By 1941 this investigation had resulted in the production, on a small scale, of penicillin (q.v.), and the demonstration in hundreds of laboratory animals and five human patients of the three important characteristics of penicillin as a germicide: its potency, nontoxicity, and wide effectiveness. After 1950 Chain was professor of biochemistry and scientific director of the International Research Center for Chemical Microbiology at the Higher Institute of Health in Rome, Italy. In 1961 he became professor of biochemistry at the University of London. Chain shared the 1945 Nobel Prize in medicine and physiology with Florey and the British bacteriologist Sir Alexander Fleming (q.v.). In 1949 Chain became a fellow of the Royal Society.

**CHAIN GANG.** See PEONAGE.

**CHAIN MAIL.** See ARMOR; COAT OF MAIL.

**CHAIN REACTION.** See NUCLEAR ENERGY: *Chain Reaction.*

**CHAIN SNAKE,** common name for a harmless king snake, *Lampropeltis getulus,* of North America, so called because of the chainlike yellow or white skin markings. The color and markings vary in chain snakes from different areas. In the moist lowlands of the eastern and southern United States the color is shiny black, crossed by yellow lines. The chain snake is about 4 to 5 ft. long. It is nocturnal, and feeds principally on other snakes and rodents.

**CHAIN STORES,** two or more retail stores dealing in the same general kind of merchandise and operated by the same firm. The outlet is also known as a multiunit, and is generally operated by an employee-manager rather than an individual owner. The manager of a chain store, unlike the independent retailer, does not make policy decisions and is responsible to the individual or company that owns the store where he is employed. Chain stores deal mainly in the general merchandise, food, variety, discount, drug, and shoe store areas. In 1970 chain stores accounted for approximately 14 percent of all the retail outlets in the United States, but were responsible for more than 30 percent of the total retail sales. *See also* MARKETING; RETAILING; SUPERMARKETS.

The American businessmen George F. Gilman and George Huntington Hartford (1833–1917) are generally credited with the development of chain-store retailing; they founded in 1859 what was to become the Great Atlantic & Pacific Tea Company (A&P) in New York City. Although chain-store systems existed prior to this time, and one is said to have been operating in China as early as 200 B.C., the multiunit system as understood today has developed only since the middle of the 19th century. The advantages of the chain-store system, such as lower price structures, are achieved chiefly from buying efficiency that is the result of centralized buying procedures, and because the number of units operated bring the economies related to large-scale buying. This fact was the prime reason for the great increase nationally in the number of stores through merger and acquisition from 1910 to 1931. During this period, for example, the A&P outlets increased from 200 to 15,670 units, and the J. C. Penney Company stores, founded in Wyoming, grew from 14 to 1459 units. Expansion continued until the chains achieved a substantial market share in the major retailing categories including grocery stores, department and general-merchandise stores, drugstores, eating and drinking establishments, men's clothing and furnishing stores, women's apparel and accessories stores, shoe stores, auto-accessory and hardware stores, furniture and house-furnishings stores, and variety stores.

In the early 1920's, however, independent retailers and their suppliers began to organize in opposition to the competition of chain stores. By 1933, a total of 689 anti-chain store bills had been introduced in 28 States. Most of these were tax measures based on a geometric progression, imposing a tax, for example, of $50 on the third store of a chain in the State, $100 on the fourth, $200 on the fifth, and so on. The chain-store system sought to protect itself through direct appeals to consumers, as in California in 1936 when anti-chain legislation was brought before the voters in the form of a referendum; the bill was defeated. Official legislation against chain stores declined after 1933; about 100 such bills have been introduced since then and, of these, only one was actually enacted. On the Federal level, the Robinson-Patman Act of 1936 (see CLAYTON ANTITRUST ACT) was the only notable attempt to regulate chain stores through controlled competition.

Despite attempts to curtail their activities, chain-store systems continued to grow. Today the major chains are diversifying into related fields to broaden the profit base and to expand sales. Expansion has been both horizontal and vertical, food companies acquiring farms and food-processing plants and also drugstores and restaurants. Variety and general-merchandise chains, such as the Sears, Roebuck Company, have launched extensive private-label programs, carrying merchandise with exclusive labels. Because of the scope of their operation, these chains often give the private-label items the merchandising force of a national brand.

C.Cl.

**CHAIR,** a usually movable piece of furniture designed for the use of a single person and consisting of a seat, legs, a backrest, and sometimes arms. Chairs date back to very ancient times. For hundreds of years they were used only by royalty, nobility, the priesthood, and the wealthy nonofficial classes, during which time other persons used stools, chests, and benches for sitting purposes. Chairs did not become a common article of furniture until the 16th century.

## CHAIRS IN ANCIENT AND MEDIEVAL TIMES

The earliest known chairs are Egyptian. They were usually low and sometimes were fitted with curved backs. On the walls of tombs are painted and carved representations of various kinds of Egyptian chairs. The ruling classes of Babylonia used chairs made of palm wood, which was easily worked and strong, light, and soft. The chairs of Assyrian monarchs were elaborate. The massive chair or throne of King Sargon II (722–705 B.C.) had sides on which three representations of the king himself were carved, and below them a figure of his war-horse in harness. The sides of the royal chair of King Sennacherib (705–681 B.C.) consisted of three rows of carved figures, each set bearing supporting crossbars.

**Greek.** Greek chairs were made of bentwood (wood that is bent and not cut into shape) and frequently had sloping backs. The cathedra, a portable Greek and Roman chair originally used only by women, gave its name to a type of chair from which philosophers lectured. In early Christian times the term "cathedra" was applied to the chair in which the bishop sat, and the churches in which this chair stood came to be known as cathedrals.

**Roman.** The chairs used by officials and dignitaries in Rome were known as *sellae,* the most important type of which was the *sella curalis.* At first the *sella curalis* was a prerogative of royalty. When Rome became a republic, only consuls, censors, and magistrates might use a *sella curalis.* During the days of the Empire, it was a seat for the emperors, and during their absence from Rome it was occupied by their statues. The *sella curalis* generally had two pairs of bronze legs, sometimes made to imitate elephants' tusks.

*Egyptian chair of state from the tomb of Tutankhamen (fl. about 1350 B.C.).*
**Ashmolean Museum**

The chairs used in Roman homes or in amphitheaters were named sedilia. The term "sedilia" is now usually restricted to certain seats in a church, most often three in number, used by the officiating clergy. In medieval times sedilia designed for the use of important clerical dignitaries were generally enriched with painting and gilding. The most famous extant chair of Roman times is the portable chair supposedly used by Saint Peter, now in the Vatican, Rome. This wooden chair has ivory carvings that portray the labors of Hercules. The chair is placed on exhibition once a century.

**Medieval.** A famous chair of early medieval times is the "Chair of Dagobert", the throne of a Frankish king of early Merovingian times (7th cent.). It is constructed of cast bronze and has legs in the form of animal heads and feet.

One of the oldest chairs extant in England is the elaborate oak chair used for the coronation of Edward I (13th cent.) and of most of the kings who followed him. Under this chair, which stands in Westminster Abbey, London, is the stone, known variously as the "Stone of Destiny" and "Stone of Scone", on which early Irish and later Scottish kings sat while being crowned; see SCONE.

## CHAIRS IN MODERN TIMES

The change from the conception of the chair as a sign of power to that of an article for common use came about during the Renaissance.

Until the middle of the 17th century, ordinary European chairs were of oak and were not upholstered. Later, leather was used for upholstery, and then velvet and silk were used. The oak chairs were at first massive and heavy; later,

*Above: Coronation chair of Edward I of England. Right: German Renaissance chair.*

cane backs and seats were introduced, as in the Louis XIII chair in France in the first half of the 17th century.

**English.** The earliest chairs for ordinary use in England were low and had heavy, carved backs. Many examples of chairs of this type of the Tudor (q.v.) period are in the Victoria and Albert Museum, London. With the beginning of the 17th century, English chairs, in imitation of French models, were made taller and lighter, and the carving on them was limited to the framework. The English chair of the periods of Charles I (r. 1625–49) and Charles II (r. 1660–85) was characterized by spiral turnings and by seats and backs with cane panels of needlework upholstery. The most elegant English chairs of the 17th century were those made during the Restoration (q.v.). Heavy and inelegant chairs again came into vogue in the reigns of William and Mary (r. 1689–1702) and Queen Anne (r. 1702–14).

In the 18th century several notable English cabinetmakers greatly modified the typical heavy English chair. The first and most famous of these cabinetmakers was Thomas Chippendale. He replaced the solid splat, or backpiece, of the chair with a splat that was pierced and artistically carved, and substituted well-proportioned cabrioles or sometimes square legs for

the massive legs of the chairs of the preceding period. Chippendale chairs are characterized by elegance as well as solidity. George Hepplewhite, Robert Adam, and Thomas Sheraton made chairs less massive than those of Chippendale.

Many new varieties of chairs were made in the 19th and 20th centuries, but these new types were generally derived from the excellent de-

signs made in the second half of the 18th century.

**Early American.** The first chairs made in the American colonies were of oak or pine and were modeled on the chairs of the various countries from which the colonists came, chiefly England, Holland, Sweden, and Germany. In time, variations of these models ap-

Metropolitan Museum of Art

Parke-Bernet Galleries

*Above, left: French chair of the Louis XVI period. Above, right: 18th century Chippendale "cockfighting" chair. Right: Modern steel and canvas armchair by the American architect and furniture designer Marcel Breuer.*

Museum of Modern Art

323

peared. One of the best-known typically American chairs of early Colonial days was the Carver chair, an armchair with turned spindles. The original Carver chair is preserved at Plymouth, Mass. In general, Colonial chairs followed the changing styles of chairs in England. The Windsor chair, a strong rail-back chair, made of oak, ash, or hickory, and patterned on English models, was popular in Colonial days. Important American chairmakers of the 18th century were William Savery (1721–87), Jonathan Gostelowe, Benjamin Randolph, and James Gillingham, all of Philadelphia; and, in the first half of the 19th century, Duncan Phyfe of New York City.

**Contemporary.** At the beginning of the 20th century a new type of chair was developed in various European cities. One of the most important of the centers for this development was the Bauhaus (q.v.), a school for architectural and industrial design located in Weimar and later in Dessau, both in East Germany. In the Bauhaus a number of furniture designers, including Le Corbusier and Mies van der Rohe, designed chairs with simple, functional lines, built for use and comfort and adapted to modern interiors. A great impetus was given to the development of this modern type of chair by its exhibition at the Paris Exposition of Decorative Arts in 1925. In 1927 a number of department stores in New York City imported the new chairs and placed them on sale. Soon many American furniture factories were making such chairs.

Wood is the principal material out of which modern chairs are made. Aluminum, chrome-plated tubular steel, and other metals are also used. Rustproofed wrought iron and cast iron, and other materials are utilized in making modern chairs for outdoor use. *See also* FURNITURE.

See separate biographies for many of the persons mentioned without birth and death dates.

**CHALCEDON** *or* **CALCHEDON,** ancient seaport of Bithynia, Asia Minor, on the Sea of Marmara, at the s. end of the Bosporus strait, opposite Byzantium (later Constantinople). Founded about 685 B.C. by Megarians from Greece, it was ruled by the kings of Bithynia (q.v.), then became a Roman possession in the 1st century B.C. In 451 A.D. Pope Leo I (*see under* LEO) convened the Fourth Ecumenical Council of the Christian Church in Chalcedon, to combat the heretical doctrine of the Monophysites (q.v.). After the capture of the city in 616 by the Persians, the city declined. It was later demolished by the Turks, who used the building stones of Chalcedon for construction in Constantinople (now İstanbul). Kadiköy, a suburb of İstanbul, is on the site of Chalcedon.

**CHALCEDONY,** semiprecious stone, a crypto-crystalline variety of quartz of various shades of white, gray, yellow, brown, green, and blue. Although it is usually transparent or translucent, some of the milk-white varieties are opaque. The color variations occur as the result of the presence of such impurities as iron, aluminum, and nickel. Chalcedony occurs as a lining or filling of cavities in rocks. The principal varieties are agate, which is banded and striped, having alternating layers of chalcedony and opal; jasper, or other forms of quartz; carnelian, which is clear and of various shades of red; chrysoprase, an apple-green variety, in which the color is due to nickel oxide; heliotrope or bloodstone, of a dark-green color, with small spots of jasper; onyx, consisting of bands of opal and chalcedony of different colors, usually black and white; plasma, of a deep-green color; and sardonyx, a red-and-white-banded variety of chalcedony. (See separate articles on most of the above varieties.) The many colors and the high luster that chalcedony takes by polishing render it valuable for brooches, necklaces, and other ornaments, and some varieties are cut as seal stones. Chalcedony is found in may parts of the world; superior varieties prized for gems are mined in Uruguay and in the Lake Superior area of the United States and Canada.

**CHALCID FLIES,** common name for a large group of parasitic insects constituting the super-family Chalcidoidea of the order Hymenoptera (q.v.). They are small, rarely more than 0.1 in. in length, and are characterized by elbowed antennae. Thousands of species make up the group, and their larvae are parasitic on the eggs, larvae, or pupae of other insects. Because so many of these hosts are destructive to plants, the chalcid flies are beneficial economically. They prey upon asparagus beetles, gall wasps, scale insects, cicadas, Hessian flies, cabbage butterflies, and other pests. Many millions of chalcid flies are raised in laboratories and released for the control of such injurious insects.

**CHALCIS** *or* **CHALKIS.** *See* KHALKÍS.

**CHALCOCITE,** *or* COPPER GLANCE, mineral consisting of copper sulfide, having the formula $Cu_2 S$. It crystallizes in the orthorhombic system and has hardness from 2.5 to 3 and sp.gr. from 5.5 to 5.8. An important ore of copper, it is frequently found in granular or compact masses. The luster is metallic and the color lead gray, which tarnishes to dull black on exposure. Chalcocite is usually found in nature in association with other copper minerals, as in the Cornwall mines in England, which have beautiful crystal specimens. It also occurs in southwest Africa,

Mexico, South America, and the United States in Bristol, Conn., and in the Rocky Mountains. *See* COPPER.

**CHALCOPYRITE,** *or* COPPER PYRITES, most widely distributed mineral of copper and one of the principal sources of copper. It consists of a copper-iron sulfide that crystallizes in the tetragonal system, with hardness 3.5 to 4 and sp.gr. 4.1 to 4.3. Possessing a metallic luster, it is of a brass-yellow color and is often tarnished or iridescent. It occurs widely disseminated in metallic veins and in the older rocks, frequently with pyrite or iron sulfide. This mineral occurs in large deposits in Sweden, Germany (in the Harz Mts.), Czechoslovakia, Hungary, Chile, South Africa, and the southwestern United States. When tarnished, it is sometimes called peacock ore because of the iridescent film of brilliant colors with which it becomes coated.

**CHALDEANS.** *See* BABYLONIA: *History.*

**CHALIAPIN, Feodor Ivanovitch** (1873–1938), Russian dramatic bass singer, born in Kazan'. Practically self-taught as a singer, Chaliapin received some training in Tbilisi. He achieved fame in grand opera in 1896 at the Marinsky Theater, Saint Petersburg (now Leningrad). He became world famous for his roles in operas by Russian composers, including *A Life for the Czar* by Mikhail Ivanovich Glinka; *Prince Igor* by Aleksandr Porfirevich Borodin; and *Sadko* by Nikolai Andreevich Rimski-Korsakov (qq.v.). He was noted for his roles in many other operas as well, because of the way in which he blended a rich vocal tone with an outstanding dramatic talent. He first appeared at the Metropolitan Opera House, New York City, in 1907, and scored his most notable success there when he appeared in the title role of the opera *Boris Godunov* by the Russian composer Modest Petrovich Musorgski (q.v.) in 1921. Chaliapin also had many successful seasons with the Chicago Civic Opera Company. Leaving Russia after the Bolshevik Revolution, he settled in France and became a naturalized citizen. His writings include *Pages From My Life* (1927) and *Man and Mask: Forty Years in the Life of a Singer* (1932).

**CHALK,** soft white or whitish form of limestone composed of the remains of small marine organisms such as foraminifera and cocoliths. Chemically it is almost pure calcium carbonate with traces of other minerals. It ranges in hardness and texture from very soft porous varieties to harder close-grained types. Chalk is particularly common in strata of the Cretaceous Period (Lat. *creta*, "chalk"); *see* GEOLOGY, HISTORICAL. Large deposits occur in Iowa, Texas, and Arkansas in the United States, and in the British Isles.

*Feodor Ivanovitch Chaliapin*      Metropolitan Museum of Art

Cretaceous chalk is exposed in the so-called White Cliffs of Dover on either side of the English Channel. *See* CALCITE; LIMESTONE.

**CHALLONER, Richard** (1691–1781), British Roman Catholic churchman, born in Lewes, East Sussex, England. He was educated in Douai, France, and taught philosophy and divinity there from 1713 until 1730, when he settled in London. There he served as a missionary priest and, after 1741, as a bishop. In 1758 he became vicar apostolic of the London district. His works include a popular prayer book, *Garden of the Soul* (1740); *Memoirs of Missionary Priests and Other Catholicks of Both Sexes Who Suffered Death or Imprisonment in England on Account of their Religion* (1741); and an extensively revised edition of the Douai Bible (1749–52). Often called Challoner's Bible, this edition was used by English-speaking Catholics until 1970. *See* BIBLE, ENGLISH TRANSLATIONS OF THE.

**CHALMERS, Thomas** (1780–1847), British theologian and preacher, born in Anstruther, Scotland, and educated at the University of Saint Andrews. In 1803 he was minister of the parish of Kilmany, Fife County, and in 1815 he was called to Tron Church, Glasgow, as pastor. He became one of the most popular preachers in England and Scotland and was noted also for his work in social welfare. In 1819 he became minister of Saint John's parish, where he established schools, revived church attendance, and increased public well-being even while he drastically reduced relief expenditures. He was professor of moral philosophy at Saint Andrews from 1823 to 1828 when he joined the faculty of the University of Edinburgh as professor of theology. He taught there until 1843, when he led a group of 470 Scottish clerics in a movement of secession from the Scottish Church; see SCOTLAND, CHURCH OF. The new organization, the Free Church of Scotland (q.v.), took a position of independence from civil authority in spiritual matters; it was highly successful and within four years had no fewer than 654 churches. The Free Church founded a college in Edinburgh, and Chalmers became its first principal, or vice-chancellor. His chief writings are *Christian and Civic Economy of Large Towns* (1826), *Political Economy* (1832), *On the Adaptation of External Nature to the Moral and Intellectual Constitution of Man* (1833), and *Institutes of Theology* (1843–47).

**CHALMETTE NATIONAL HISTORICAL PARK,** scene of the last decisive engagement of the Battle of New Orleans; see NEW ORLEANS, BATTLE OF. The park is administered by the National Park Service (q.v.).

**CHÂLONS-SUR-MARNE,** city in N.E. France, capital of the department of Marne and the seat of a bishopric. The city is situated on the Marne R., 107 miles E. of Paris by rail. The chief industry of the city is brewing. Other industries are the manufacture of shoes, wallpaper, brushes, and woolen and cotton goods, and the making of champagne. The city has a considerable trade in grain, hemp, and rapeseed oil. On the plain between Troyes and what is now Châlons-sur-Marne, Attila (q.v.) and the Huns were defeated (451 A.D.) by the allied forces of Romans and Visigoths. Notable public buildings in the city are the Cathedral of Notre Dame (12th and 13th cent.) and the Cathedral of Saint Étienne (chiefly 13th cent.). Pop. (1968) 48,729.

**CHALYBITE.** *See* SIDERITE.

**CHAMBAL,** unnavigable river of west-central India, principal tributary of the Jumna R. It rises in the Vindhya Range, a mountain system in Madhya Pradesh State, and flows in a generally N.E. direction for about 650 mi. to the Jumna R., which it joins w. of Kanpur.

**CHAMBERLAIN,** name of a family of prominent British statesmen.

**Joseph Chamberlain** (1836–1914), born in London, England, and educated at University College School. Until he was thirty-eight years old he was a successful manufacturer in Birmingham, retiring with great wealth. Becoming active in the local politics of Birmingham during the later years of his business career, he was elected to the office of lord mayor in 1873. His administration, during which gas and water services were taken over by the city and slums were cleared, was regarded by many as a turning point in the history of Birmingham and a model for other contemporary cities.

Chamberlain's long parliamentary career began in 1876. Four years later, as a representative of the radical wing of the Liberal Party, he was given a seat in the cabinet of Prime Minister William Ewart Gladstone (q.v.), as president of the Board of Trade. Chamberlain's principal interest at this time was in British policy in Ireland. He advocated partial home rule for Ireland, a plan that was not acceptable either to Gladstone or to the Irish nationalists, and that resulted in his resigning from the cabinet in 1885. Chamberlain reentered the cabinet in 1886 as president of the Local Government Board but resigned again the same year because of Gladstone's advocacy of the home-rule bill. In 1887–88 he visited the United States as a member of a commission to settle a fisheries dispute between the U.S. and Canada. He returned to the cabinet in 1895 under Robert Arthur Talbot Gascoyne-Cecil, 3rd Marquis of Salisbury (*see under* CECIL), as secretary of state for the colonies, a post he held for seven years.

During this period Chamberlain maintained his interest in domestic reforms, as evidenced by the Workmen's Compensation Act, which he sponsored and which was passed by Parliament in 1897, but he soon became noted as a champion of imperialism. His conduct in the period immediately preceding the South African War (q.v.), which began in 1899, was bitterly assailed by some and ardently admired by others in England. Most controversial was the question of his complicity in the Jameson Raid of 1896 (*see* JAMESON, SIR LEANDER STARR) and in other aggressive acts that precipitated the South African War. He was acquitted by Parliament of all charges. After the war he set a precedent by visiting the colonies in South Africa in person as secretary of state. After 1902 his chief interest was in colonial policy, which was designed to tighten the economic bonds of the British Commonwealth of Nations (q.v.). His program of so-called imperial preference, which proposed an end to the traditional free-trade policy of England, was unpopular. As a result he resigned and spent three years trying to convince his opposition to give tariff preference to Commonwealth products. He withdrew from public life in 1906 because of illness. His interest in Birmingham, where he founded and became chancellor of the University of Birmingham, continued throughout his life.

**Sir (Joseph) Austen Chamberlain** (1863–1937), eldest son of Joseph Chamberlain, born in

Birmingham, and educated at the University of Cambridge and in Berlin and Paris. During the Irish home-rule controversy he was secretary to his father, becoming a Unionist member of Parliament in 1892. Successively he was chancellor of the exchequer (1903–06, 1919–21), secretary of state for India (1915–17), Conservative leader of the House of Commons and Lord Privy Seal (1921–23), foreign secretary (1924–29), and in 1931, the first lord of the admiralty. During his second term as chancellor he strengthened British credit by imposing heavy income taxes and excess-profit taxes. His 1919 budget reduced by one sixth the duties on articles from British colonies. He thus made the principle of imperial preference, which his father had advocated fifteen years earlier, a regular part of the British financial system. As lord privy seal he advocated and assisted in the establishment in 1922 of the Irish Free State. While foreign secretary he was instrumental in bringing about the signing in 1925 of the Locarno Treaties; see LOCARNO. For this effort toward maintaining peace he was awarded the 1925 Nobel Peace Prize jointly with the American statesman Charles Gates Dawes (q.v.).

Chamberlain was also vitally interested in the League of Nations (q.v.) and attended all meetings of the Assembly and the Council of the league. He was a strong advocate of the Kellogg-Briand Pact (q.v.) and he played an important part in the entrance of Germany into the League of Nations in 1926. His speeches on European and Empire questions were published as *Peace in Our Time* (1928).

**(Arthur) Neville Chamberlain** (1869–1940), son of Joseph Chamberlain and half-brother of Sir Joseph Austen Chamberlain, born in Birmingham, and educated at Rugby College and Mason College (now the University of Birmingham). After managing an estate in the Bahamas and pursuing a successful business career in Birmingham, he became lord mayor of Birmingham in 1915. He established in that city the first municipal bank in England. Becoming a member of Parliament in 1918, Chamberlain served as postmaster general (1922–23), minister of health (1923; 1924–29), and chancellor of the exchequer (1923–24; 1931–37). In 1931 he was successful in balancing the British budget. Succeeding Stanley Baldwin (q.v.) as prime minister in 1937, Chamberlain, with the avowed object of avoiding a European war, followed a policy of appeasement toward the dictators Adolf Hitler of Germany and Benito Mussolini of Italy (qq.v.). This policy culminated in September, 1938, in the Munich Pact (q.v.), which resulted in the

Returning to England after the partition of Czechoslovakia in 1938, Prime Minister Neville Chamberlain announces the Munich Pact, which, he said, would bring "peace in our time".                                      UPI

cession of the Sudetenland (q.v.), a part of Czechoslovakia, to Germany. Chamberlain was also instrumental in establishing a committee for nonintervention on the part of the various powers in the Spanish Civil War (1936–39). In November, 1938, he brought about British recognition of Italian sovereignty over Ethiopia, which Italy had conquered and annexed in 1936, and in 1939 recognition of the government of the Spanish military leader Francisco Franco (q.v.), which had seized power in Spain. His appeasement policy, however, did not prevent additional acts of aggression, and after Germany invaded Poland, Chamberlain announced on Sept. 3, 1939, that Great Britain was declaring war on Germany. After the defeat of the British forces by the Germans in Norway in 1940, Chamberlain was forced to resign as prime minister; he was succeeded by Sir Winston Leonard Spencer Churchill (q.v.). Chamberlain served as lord president of the council under Churchill and was also leader of the Conservative Party until October, 1940, when illness forced his resignation from both offices.

**CHAMBERLAIN, Houston Stewart** (1855–1927), German writer, born in Southsea (now part of Portsmouth), England, and educated in France and Vienna. He immigrated to Germany in 1885. In 1908 he married Eva Wagner (1867–1942), the younger daughter of the German composer Richard Wagner (q.v.). Chamberlain became a naturalized German citizen in 1916. He is noted for his anti-Semitic, racist writings,

327

particularly *Foundations of the Nineteenth Century* (1899; Eng. trans., 1911); *see* ANTI-SEMITISM. In this work he proclaimed the superiority of the German people, who he asserted were descended from so-called superior Teutonic or Aryan stock. Chamberlain's ideas of the racial "purity" of the German people exerted great influence on the racist theories formulated by the German dictator Adolf Hitler (q.v.) and his National Socialist Party. Chamberlain's other writings include several studies of Wagner's music, *Immanuel Kant* (1905), and *Goethe* (1912).

**CHAMBERLAIN, Neville.** *See under* CHAMBERLAIN.

**CHAMBERLAIN, Owen** (1920– ), American physicist, born in San Francisco, Calif. He was graduated from Dartmouth College in 1941 and received a Ph.D. degree from the University of Chicago in 1948. From 1942 to 1948 Chamberlain worked with the Manhattan Engineering District (which built the atomic bomb), and was present in Alamogordo, N. Mex., when the first atomic bomb was tested in 1945. Chamberlain joined the faculty of the University of California in 1948 and was named full professor in 1958. In 1955 Chamberlain and Emilio Segrè (q.v.) first observed the subatomic particle called the antiproton, the existence of which had been postulated by physicists in the 1930's; *see* PROTON: *Antiproton.* For their discovery, Chamberlain and Segrè shared the Nobel Prize in physics in 1959.

**CHAMBERLAIN, Wilt(on)** (1940– ), American basketball player, born in Philadelphia, Pa. After attending the University of Kansas, at which he excelled in basketball and also in track and field, Chamberlain became a professional basketball player. In the National Basketball Association (N.B.A.), he played for the Warriors in Philadelphia, Pa., and San Francisco, Calif., until he was traded in 1965 to the Philadelphia 76ers. Chamberlain, who is 7 ft. $1\frac{1}{16}$ in. tall, became a dominant figure in professional basketball. He won the N.B.A. scoring title seven consecutive years, became the leading lifetime scorer in the league, and in 1962 scored a record 100 points in one game. In 1968 he was traded to the Los Angeles Lakers. In 1973 he joined the San Diego Conquistadors, but was prevented from playing by a contractual dispute. He retired in 1974.

**CHAMBERLIN, Thomas Chrowder** (1843–1928), American geologist and educator, born in Mattoon, Ill., and educated at Beloit College. Chamberlin was professor of geology at Beloit College from 1873 until 1887 and in charge of the glacial division of the United States Geological Survey from 1882 to 1887. He served as president of the University of Wisconsin from 1887 to 1892 and as professor of geology and director of the Walker Museum at the University of Chicago from 1892 to 1919. Chamberlin accompanied the Peary Relief Expedition of 1894 to Greenland to study glaciers. He was one of the originators of the so-called planetesimal hypothesis of the origin of the earth, which postulated the idea that the force of a passing star might have caused eruptions on the sun, which in turn might have thrown off a shower of particles that gravitated together to form the earth (*see* COSMOGONY). In 1892 Chamberlin founded the *Journal of Geology*, of which he was the editor for thirty years. Among his major works are *The Origin of the Earth* (1916) and *The Two Solar Families* (1928).

**CHAMBER MUSIC,** instrumental music for an ensemble, usually ranging from two to about ten players, with one player for each part and all parts of equal importance. Chamber music from about 1750 has been principally for string quartet (two violins, viola, and cello), although string quintets as well as duets, trios, quartets, and quintets of four stringed instruments plus a piano or wind instrument have also been popular. Such music was originally meant for private performance, the term chamber music meaning simply music neither for dance nor for church, theater, or other public performance. Public concerts of chamber music were initiated only in the 19th century.

Secular music in the Middle Ages and the Renaissance (about 1450–about 1600) was typically for small vocal and instrumental ensembles. Most compositions were vocal pieces in three, four, and five parts. Instrumental groups simply played this vocal chamber music using whatever instruments were desired or were available at the time.

In the baroque era (about 1600–about 1750) two instrumental genres became important: the *sonata da chiesa*, or church sonata; and the *sonata da camera*, or chamber sonata. In instrumental music, as in vocal music, the omnipresent musical texture was that of high melody lines supported by a basso continuo—a bass melody played, for example, by cello or bassoon, with harmonies filled in by a lute, harpsichord, or organ. The principal chamber music genres were trio sonatas, which were *sonatas da chiesa* or *da camera* written for two solo violins (or flutes or oboes, often at the players' choice) plus continuo; and solo sonatas, usually for violin and continuo. Trio sonatas, however, might also be played, if desired, by larger ensembles of six or eight players. In addition, chamber cantatas for solo voice and continuo were written, as were vocal duets with continuo, which in fact provided the model for the trio sonata.

The most prominent 17th-century composer of trio and solo sonatas was the Italian Arcangelo Corelli, whose works influenced the chamber music of the English composer Henry Purcell, and, later, of the French composer François Couperin, the German-English composer George Frederick Handel, and the German composer Johann Sebastian Bach. By the time of Handel and Bach, however, the distinction between church and chamber sonata had broken down, and trio sonatas contained elements of both. (*See* MUSIC: *The Baroque Era; Preclassic and Classic Periods.*)

In the classical era (about 1750–about 1820) the Austrian composer Joseph Haydn developed chamber music as a style distinct from other ensemble music. Important as predecessors of the new style were Viennese light music genres such as the divertimento and serenade. Played out-of-doors by groups of stringed and wind instruments, these compositions dispensed with the continuo, using the middle-voiced instruments to fill out the harmony. Haydn established the string quartet as the chamber music ensemble par excellence. The form of his quartets was that which predominated in the classical era, the four-movement sonata (q.v.) form. The classical sonata as it emerged in his quartets was especially marked by finely wrought, complex, intimate interplay between the four instruments. Haydn gave each instrument equal footing, using none merely as harmonic filler. His string quartets influenced and were influenced by those of his countryman Wolfgang Amadeus Mozart. Their successor, Ludwig van Beethoven, greatly expanded the dimensions of the string quartet while preserving its intimate character as well.

Chamber music in the Romantic era (about 1820–about 1900) was developed primarily by composers whose Romantic temperament was mingled with a classical inclination—those such as the Germans Franz Schubert and Johannes Brahms.

Two trends emerged in 20th-century chamber music. Classical genres such as the string quartet were infused with contemporary idioms and techniques in works of the French composers Claude Debussy and Maurice Ravel, the Hungarian Béla Bartók, and the Austrians Arnold Schönberg and Anton von Webern. Chamber ensembles of varied composition—often including voices, harp, guitar, and wind and percussion instruments—became a primary vehicle for new music by composers such as Schönberg, Webern, the Russian-born composer Igor Stravinsky, and the French composer Pierre Boulez.

*See also* biographies of individual composers for further life data.　　　　　　　　G.L.

**CHAMBER OF COMMERCE,** local, national, or international association of businessmen, established to promote commercial enterprises. Chambers of commerce try to attract new industries to their localities by advertising to tourists and businessmen, and they engage in such activities as housing surveys, safety campaigns, and the promotion of laws favorable to trade. Originally, the membership of chambers of commerce was comprised principally of merchants, but these associations later expanded to include bankers and manufacturers. Probably the first trade association to call itself a chamber of commerce was that founded in Marseille, France, in 1599, as a branch of the government of the town, with wide powers, including the appointment and supervision of French consulates in the Near East. In 1700 Louis XIV (q.v.), King of France, decreed the establishment of other chambers of commerce, with more limited powers, in other towns. Since that time they have been an integral part of the French economic and governmental structures. Chambers of commerce in a number of other European countries resemble those in France.

In Great Britain and the United States chambers of commerce have never had governmental functions. The first of these chambers were founded on the British island of Jersey and in New York City, both in 1768. The first chamber in England was the Commercial Society of Manchester, established in 1794. The London chamber was formed in 1881.

The early chambers of commerce were concerned principally with problems of domestic and foreign trade and with governmental policies and political events affecting trade. When large-scale industry and large banks developed in the 19th and 20th centuries, chambers of commerce also became concerned with a wider range of economic and political matters, including labor problems.

In 1919 representatives of manufacturing, banking, and commercial interests in a number of leading countries organized the International Chamber of Commerce, with headquarters in Paris, and provided that a congress be held every second year.

**CHAMBER OF COMMERCE OF THE UNITED STATES,** federation of 2700 local and State chambers of commerce, 1000 trade and professional associations, and 39,000 business firms and individuals, established in 1912, on the recommendation of United States President William Howard Taft. It is supported by more than 5,000,000 business firms, corporations, and individuals, the members of its affiliated organizations. The chamber keeps its members informed about current economic trends and serves as the spokesman for business on national issues. Chamber policy is determined by referendum of the organization membership. The chamber publishes a monthly magazine, *Nation's Business,* a biweekly progress report, *Washington Report,* and many special publications, studies, and reports. *See* CHAMBER OF COMMERCE.

**CHAMBERS, Ephraim.** *See* ENCYCLOPEDIA.

**CHAMBERS, (Jay David) Whittaker.** *See* HISS CASE.

**CHAMBERSBURG,** borough in Pennsylvania, and county seat of Franklin Co., in the Cumberland Valley, about 23 miles N.W. of Gettysburg. The city is noted for its fruit orchards, and is a trading center for this rich agricultural region. Food products and flour are processed. Clothing, metal and paper products, and machinery are manufactured. Chambersburg is the site of Wilson College, established in 1869, and of Penn Hall Junior College, established in 1906. Nearby is the cabin in which President James Buchanan (q.v.) was born in 1791. Pop. (1960) 17,670; (1970) 17,315.

**CHAMBESHI,** *or* CHAMBEZI, river in the Republic of Zambia, central Africa, about 300 mi. long, forming a remote headstream of the Congo R. Rising in a plateau 6000 ft. above sea level in N. Zambia between lakes Tanganyika and Nyasa, it flows S.W., entering Lake Bangweulu in the wet season. During the dry season, however, it skirts the S. border of the shrunken lake, from which it merges directly with the Luapula R.

**CHAMBORD, CHÂTEAU DE,** celebrated château, one of the best examples extant of French Renaissance architecture, located in Loir-et-Cher Department, France, about 9 mi. from Blois. The château contains 440 rooms and stands in the midst of a park of 13,000 acres, which also contains the village of Chambord. Originally a hunting lodge of the counts of Blois, the structure was begun by order of Francis I (q.v.), King of France, and completed in the reign of King Louis XIV (q.v.). Napoleon I (q.v.), Emperor of France, presented the château and its domain to the military leader Louis Alexandre Berthier (q.v.). In 1821 the property was purchased by public subscription and presented to the family of Henri Dieudonné d'Artois, Duc de Bordeaux (1820–1883), who later took the title of Count of Chambord. He bequeathed the castle to a Spanish branch of his family, the dukes of Parma. In 1932 Chambord was purchased by the French government and opened to the public.

**CHAMELEON,** any lizard of the family Chamaeleonidae, consisting of over eighty species, found chiefly in Africa and Madagascar, especially the type species *Chamaeleon vulgaris,* which is also found in Europe and Asia. The body of the chameleon is very compressed and the dorsal line sharp, the skin being rough with granules. The head, elevated into the form of a cone, rests on a very short neck that does not permit the head to turn; to compensate for this handicap, the eyes are large, "turreted", and prominent, and can move independently of each other. In some species, the head is casque-shaped, and as many as three horns may project forward from it. The legs raise the body from the ground; the toes, of both the fore and hind feet, are divided into two sets, one directed forward, the other backward, so that each foot has the power of grasping like a hand. The chameleon's tongue is remarkably extensile and is viscous at the end, enabling the chameleon to easily capture insects, which are its main food. The well-known ability of the animal to change color is due to layers of contractile pigment-bearing cells which can be pressed toward the surface of the skin, and to the inflation of air vessels in connection with the lungs. Other traits of the chameleon are the absence of an external eardrum or tympanic membrane, and

*The three-horned chameleon,* Chamaeleon vulgaris, *an African lizard capable of changing its color to blend with its surroundings.* George Porter — National Audubon Society

of a columella, or epiterygoid skull bone, in which the chameleon differs from all other lizards except the *Amphisbaenae,* a genus and the type of the family Amphisbaenidae.

The name chameleon is popularly given in the United States to several lizards capable of changing color, especially to the genus *Anolis* of the family Iguanidae.

**CHAMISSO, Adelbert von** *or* **CHAMISSO, Louis Charles Adélaïde de** (1781–1838), German poet and naturalist, born in Champagne, France. He fled with his parents to Germany during the French Revolution, settling in Berlin. After a career with the Prussian army from 1798 to 1808, he moved to Switzerland and joined the circle of the exiled French writer known as Madame de Staël (*see* STAËL-HOLSTEIN, ANNE LOUISE GERMAINE). He became interested in both writing and the study of botany. In 1814 he wrote his best-known novel, *Peter Schlemihls Wundersame Geschichte* ("The Remarkable Story of Peter Schlemihl"), a prose fantasy about a man who sells his shadow for ill-gotten wealth. From 1815 to 1818 Chamisso sailed as botanist on the Russian vessel *Rurik* on a scientific circumnavigation of the world. Upon his return he was appointed curator of the botanical gardens in Berlin. Chamisso is also known for his lyrical poetry, especially the cycle *Frauenliebe und Leben* ("Woman's Love and Life", 1830), for which the German composer Robert Schumann (*see under* SCHUMANN) wrote music.

**CHAMOIS,** common name of a goat-antelope, *Rupicapra rupicapra,* in the family Bovidae (q.v.). The chamois is a hoofed, cud-chewing mammal that inhabits the Alps and other high mountains of Central and South Europe. The chamois is about the size of a large goat, but the neck is longer in proportion, and the body shorter. The horns of both sexes, which are seldom more than 6 or 7 in. long, are black and rise nearly straight up from the forehead, bending back at the tip to form a hook. The summer color is reddish brown, with a darker dorsal band and a yellowish ventral surface. The winter color is a darker brown, but white below. A dark brown band runs from the eye along each cheek. The rest of the head is pale yellow. The short tail is black.

The usual summer habitat of the chamois is in the higher regions of mountains, not far from the snow line. In winter it descends to the higher forests. The chamois is an animal of extraordinary agility, and is noted for keen scent, sight, and hearing. When a flock is feeding, one animal is always on watch, and by a sort of whistle announces apprehended danger. The flesh of the chamois is highly esteemed as venison, and chamois hunting has been so popular as sport that the animal is becoming rare. The term chamois is also used to designate a soft pliant leather made from the skin of the animal.

**CHAMOMILE.** *See* CAMOMILE.

**CHAMONIX-MONT-BLANC,** town of S.E. France, in the Alpine valley of the same name, department of Haute-Savoie. The valley, about 3400 ft. above sea level, is 14 mi. long and from 1 to 2½ mi. wide. The Arve R. courses through the entire length of the valley, which runs from N.E. to S.W. In the N.W. part of the valley rise Mont Brévent and the Aiguilles Rouges mountain chain; in the S.W. is Mont Blanc and its glaciers. The principal agricultural products of the valley are potatoes, oats, flax, barley, and honey. Hats and textiles are manufactured, and woodcarving is a principal occupation. The town of Chamonix-Mont-Blanc, lying 39 miles S.E. of Geneva, Switzerland, at an altitude of 3415 ft., is a tourist resort. It attracts many skiers and serves as a starting point for expeditions to explore the glaciers of Mont Blanc or to ascend the mountain. Pop. of the town (latest census) 5907.

**CHAMORRO,** people of mixed stock of the Mariana Islands (q.v.), including Saipan and Guam, in the western Pacific Ocean; *see* MICRONESIA. Believed originally to have been a Mongoloid people, the Chamorro today are a mixture of Micronesian, Filipino, and Spanish peoples, and also include among their descendents American settlers. The faith of the Chamorro is chiefly Roman Catholicism. The term Chamorro is also used for the Malayo-Polynesian language of these people; *see* AUSTRONESIAN LANGUAGES.

**CHAMPAGNE.** *See* WINE: *Foreign Wines: French Wines: Champagne.*

**CHAMPAGNE,** former province of N.E. France, now a region forming the departments of Marne, Haute-Marne, Aube, and Ardennes, and parts of Yonne, Aisne, Seine-et-Marne, and Meuse. Champagne consists mainly of an arid, chalk plateau, and is best known as the home of the sparkling white wine named after the region. Almost all exported French champagne comes from the area around the cities of Reims (q.v.) and Épernay. Other important occupations are the raising of sheep and the manufacture of wool. During the early Middle Ages Champagne was a duchy under Merovingian (q.v.) rulers. About the 10th century it became an hereditary estate known as the county of Champagne. In the 12th and 13th centuries it became famous for commercial fairs attended by merchants from all of Europe. The capital was Troyes. In 1314 Champagne became a province of the royal domain of France when the count of Champagne, who had inherited the area, succeeded as Louis X (q.v.), King of France.

**CHAMPAIGN,** city of Illinois, in Champaign Co., about 127 miles s.w. of Chicago. The city is the trading center for the surrounding agricultural region. Industries in Champaign process food products and manufacture trailers, industrial machinery, forgings, concrete culverts, and sporting goods. The University of Illinois is in the adjoining city of Urbana. Pop. (1960) 49,583; (1970) 56,532.

**CHAMPAIGNE, Philippe de** or **CHAMPAGNE, Philippe de** (1602–74), French painter of Flemish origin, born in Brussels. After studying painting in Brussels, he went to Paris in 1621, and collaborated with the French painter Nicolas Poussin (q.v.) in decorating the gallery of the Luxembourg Palace. Champaigne became official painter to Marie de Médicis, Queen of France, and rector of the Academy of Paris, and at various times served Louis XIII, King of France, and the French statesman and cardinal Duc de Richelieu (qq.v.). The latter commissioned Champaigne to decorate his palace and the dome of the Sorbonne. Champaigne was principally noted for his portraits and religious paintings. Closely associated with the Jansenist movement of the Roman Catholic Church (see JANSEN, CORNELIS), he painted many members of the group. Particularly noteworthy is a portrait of his daughter, a nun at the abbey of Port-Royal, the center of Jansenism. That portrait and his best-known portrait of Richelieu are both in the Louvre, Paris.

**CHAMPLAIN, Samuel de** (1567?–1635), called THE FATHER OF NEW FRANCE, French explorer, born in Hiers Brouage. In 1599 he made his first voyage to the New World, visiting the West Indies and Spanish America. In a report of his observations, which he made to Henry IV (q.v.), King of France, he suggested that a canal across the Isthmus of Panama might "shorten the voyage to the South Sea (Pacific Ocean) by more than 1500 leagues". In 1603 Champlain made his first trip to North America, accompanying an expedition sent to help colonize the New World. On this trip Champlain explored the Saint Lawrence R. to the Lachine Rapids. As geographer and cartographer for the 1604 expedition of the French explorer Pierre du Guast Monts (q.v.), Champlain explored the Bay of Fundy and the New England coast as far south as Massachusetts. His accounts and maps of the territory he explored have been of great value to historians, and are especially interesting for their descriptions of the habits and characteris-

Samuel de Champlain National Film Board of Canada

tics of the Indians. In 1608 he sailed from France for the fourth time, on this occasion as lieutenant governor of New France, and on July 3 he founded the first European settlement on the site of the present city of Québec. He formed alliances with the Indians of Canada and helped them in their wars with the Iroquois of northern New York, thus establishing friendly relations between the French and the Canadian Indians that continued as long as the French held Canada. While on an expedition with the Indians in 1609 he discovered the lake that bears his name. Two years later he built a trading station at Montréal. He also explored the inland waterways of what are now southern Ontario and northern New York State. In 1615 the French explorer Étienne Brulé (q.v.) accompanied Champlain on an exploration of Lake Ontario. In 1629, when an English raiding party captured the settlement of Québec, Champlain was taken prisoner. He was held in England until 1632. Champlain returned to the New World and was governor of New France from 1633 until his death. See also CANADA: History: The French Colonial Period.

**CHAMPLAIN, LAKE,** lake of North America, located along the N. part of the boundary between the States of New York and Vermont, and extending about 6 mi. into Québec Province, Canada. It is about 120 mi. long, varies in width from about ½ mi. to 14 mi., and has a maximum depth of about 400 ft. and an area of about 435 sq.mi. An important link in an extensive waterway, it is connected with the New York State Barge Canal and the Hudson R. by the Champlain Canal and with the Saint Lawrence R. by the Richelieu R. and the Chambly Canal in Québec. Approximately fifty islands are in the lake;

among the larger islands are Grand Isle, Isle La Motte, and Valcour Island. Lake Champlain, which is in a picturesque region between the Adirondack and Green mountains, is the site of numerous summer and winter resorts. Salmon, pike, and shad abound in its waters. Burlington, Vt., and Plattsburgh and Crown Point, N.Y. (qq.v.), are the principal cities on the lake. Lake Champlain was discovered in 1609 by the French explorer Samuel de Champlain (q.v.). During the American Revolution and the French and Indian War the lake was the scene of important battles, particularly those at Ticonderoga (q.v.), N.Y. On Sept. 11, 1814, during the War of 1812, an American fleet won a decisive victory over the British near Plattsburgh.

**CHAMPOLLION, Jean François** (1790–1832), French Egyptologist and founder of modern scientific Egyptology, born in Figeac. After studying Oriental languages in Paris, he became professor of history at the Lyceum of Grenoble at the age of nineteen. In 1821 he began to attempt to decipher the ancient Egyptian writing known as hieroglyphics (q.v.). Three years later Charles X, King of France (see under CHARLES), sent him to Italy to study Egyptian antiquities in the museums of that country. When Champollion returned to France, Charles made him director of the museum of Egyptian antiquities at the Louvre, Paris. In 1828 Champollion and the Italian archeologist Ippolito Rosellini (1800–43), codirected a scientific expedition to Egypt. Upon their return the first chair of Egyptian antiquities at the Collège de France was created for Champollion, and he became a member of the French Academy.

The deciphering of the Egyptian hieroglyphic sacred writing of the Rosetta Stone (q.v.) was Champollion's greatest achievement and enabled him to work out the grammar and compile a dictionary of the ancient Egyptian language. Because of his achievements, Egyptian hieroglyphics, until then a baffling mystery to archeologists, were readily deciphered, and an immense amount of knowledge of ancient Egyptian civilization was acquired.

Champollion's many writings include *Summary of the Hieroglyphic System of the Ancient Egyptians* (1824) and the posthumously published *Egyptian Grammar* (1836–41) and *Egyptian Dictionary* (1842–43).

**CH'AN.** See ZEN.

**CHANCE, Frank Leroy** (1877–1924), American professional baseball player, born in Fresno, Calif. From 1898 to 1912 he was first baseman for the Chicago Cubs, a National League team. From 1905 to 1912 he was the manager of the Chicago club, leading them to four pennant victories (1906–08 and 1910), two World Series victories (1907 and 1908), and a record number of games won in a single season (116 in 1906). With the shortstop Joseph Bert Tinker and the second baseman John Joseph Evers (qq.v.), Chance achieved fame as a member of the "Tinker to Evers to Chance" double-play combination on the Chicago team. In 1946 Chance was elected to the National Baseball Hall of Fame; see BASEBALL HALL OF FAME AND MUSEUM, NATIONAL.

**CHANCELLORSVILLE, BATTLE OF,** important engagement of the American Civil War, fought on May 2–3, 1863, at the village of Chancellorsville (now Chancellor), Spotsylvania Co., Va., about 10 miles W. by S. of Fredericksburg; see CIVIL WAR, THE AMERICAN. The Union forces, the Federal Army of the Potomac, under General Joseph Hooker (q.v.), numbered about 130,000; the Confederate forces, comprising the Army of Northern Virginia under General Robert E. Lee (see under LEE), numbered about 60,000.

Following the Union catastrophe late in 1862 at Fredericksburg (see FREDERICKSBURG, BATTLE OF), Hooker, who superseded General Ambrose Everett Burnside (q.v.) as commander of the Army of the Potomac, had succeeded in thoroughly reorganizing the army, restoring its morale, and preparing it for action. During this period the Federal and Confederate armies were facing one another across the Rappahannock R. at Fredericksburg. Planning to turn the Confederate left flank and to destroy Lee's communications with Richmond, Hooker began operations by sending (April 27) his Ist and VIth Corps, under General John Sedgwick (1813–64) across the Rappahannock below Fredericksburg, with orders to contain the enemy; he then moved the remainder of his army westward about 25 mi. to Kelly's Ford, crossed the Rappahannock and Rapidan rivers, and during the night of April 30 concentrated at Chancellorsville, on Lee's left flank. The Confederate leader, regarding Sedgwick's arrival below Fredericksburg as a diversionary maneuver, had begun meanwhile to marshal the bulk of his forces, notably a corps under General Thomas "Stonewall" Jackson (q.v.), against the main Union force. On the morning of May 1 Hooker started to march on Fredericksburg, but on meeting advance elements of the Confederate army returned to his strongly fortified positions around Chancellorsville.

Early on May 2 Lee ordered Jackson's corps (about 26,000 men) to make a wide detour around the extreme right of Hooker's position and assault his flank. The purpose of this movement was not apparent to the Federals. About 6 P.M., after a march of some 15 mi., Jackson suddenly attacked and stampeded the flank and rear of the XI Corps, constituting the right flank of the Federal army, under General Oliver Otis Howard (q.v.). Jackson, while in advance of his troops, was fired upon and mortally wounded by his own men, who mistook his escort for a detachment of Federals.

During this movement Lee made a series of successfully diversionary attacks on Hooker's frontal positions, thus immobilizing the bulk of the Federal army. On the morning of May 3 Lee vigorously attacked the Federal front and flank, with Jackson's force, commanded by General J. E. B. Stuart (q.v.), figuring prominently in the action. The brunt of the assault fell upon units under General Daniel Edgar Sickles (1825–1914), on the Federal right, and General Henry Warner Slocum (1827–94), at the center. Hooker showed indecision, and the Federal army withdrew to strong defensive positions. Lee was deterred from immediately following up his advantage by the news that his position was threatened on the right by an advance of the Federal force under Sedgwick. Confederate reinforcements checked Sedgwick's advance, and on the night of May 4–5, he was driven across the Rappahannock. Lee then prepared to advance against Hooker on the 5th, but the latter hastily withdrew his army across the river during a heavy storm. The Confederate victory frustrated Federal plans for an assault on Richmond and made possible Lee's subsequent invasion of the North (see GETTYSBURG, BATTLE OF). Union casualties at Chancellorsville totaled about 17,300, including about 1600 killed and 9800 wounded; Confederate losses were about 12,800, including about 1650 killed and 9100 wounded.

Part of the battle area is now included in the Fredericksburg and Spotsylvania County Battlefield Memorial.

**CHANCRE.** See SYPHILIS: *Stages and Symptoms.*

**CHANDELIER** (Lat. *candelabrum*, "candlestick"), frame designed to hold lights, and generally suspended from a ceiling or vault. Originally the light of a chandelier was supplied by candles, which were in time superseded by gas lights, and then by electric lights.

The earliest chandeliers were made of wood, but were so easily damaged by candle grease that the wood was replaced by horn and metal, including copper, wrought iron, brass, and sometimes silver. Some early chandeliers were in the form of a CROSS. In the 12th century chandeliers in the form of a crown became popular. A notable example was the 13-ft. crown chande-

lier presented to the cathedral of Aix-la-Chapelle in 1168 by Frederick I (q.v.), Holy Roman Emperor. In the 17th century the bronze or brass chandelier was popular in northern Europe, notably Flanders and Holland. In the second half of the 17th century rock-crystal (transparent quartz) and cut-glass faceted pendants and other decorations on chandeliers came into vogue. These achieved their greatest popularity in the 18th and the first half of the 19th century. Cut glass from Bohemia (now part of Czechoslovakia) was the principal glass used at first. Many of the most magnificent chandeliers of the 18th century were made in France, where decorations with crystal and with porcelain flowers were popular. In time the decorations of such chandeliers became extremely ornate, with interlaced strings of ornaments suspended from the arms of a central shaft of the fixture. Modern chandeliers tend to be of simple design, and are usually made of metal.

**CHANDIGARH,** city in the Republic of India, and capital of Punjab State, about 150 miles N. of New Delhi. Construction of the city began in 1950 at a 10,000-acre site near the old village of Chandigarh. It was designed by an international team of architects, including Le Corbusier (q.v.), the Swiss-born French architect. Most of the buildings, which are generally residential, were completed in 1956. On Nov. 1, 1966, the city was constituted a union territory. In 1966 Chandigarh became the joint capital of the newly formed States of Punjab (q.v.) and Haryana, but in 1970 the government awarded Chandigarh as the capital to Punjab State. Pop. (1971) 218,743.

**CHANDLER, Albert Benjamin ("Happy").** See BASEBALL: *Professional Baseball Government.*

**CHANDLER, Raymond.** See MYSTERY STORY: *The Realistic Detective Novel.*

**CHANDRAGUPTA** or **CHANDRAGUPTA MAURYA,** or (Gr.) SANDROCOTTUS (d. about 286 B.C.), first king (322?–298 B.C.) of the Maurya dynasty or the ancient kingdom of Magadha (now Bihar State), India. About 325 B.C. Alexander III (q.v.), King of Macedonia, known as the Great, invaded India and established Macedonian rule over the various kingdoms of India, including the largest kingdom, Magadha. After Alexander's death, Chandragupta, a native leader, wrested the Punjab region from the Macedonian forces. Then he conquered Magadha, killed the king, and assumed the royal power. By conquest he extended Magadha until it comprised Afghanistan and all of northern India between the Bay of Bengal and the Arabian Sea. In 305 B.C. Seleucus I, King of Syria (see under SELEUCIDAE) invaded northern India, but was defeated by Chandragupta, who thereupon added to his lands some territory north of the Indus R. According to traditional accounts, Chandragupta abdicated, became a monk, and, while in voluntary exile in the south of India, committed suicide by fasting to death. The Maurya dynasty was extended by his son Bindusara (r. 298–273 B.C.).

*See also* INDIA: *History.*

**CHANEL, Saint Peter** (1803–41), French Roman Catholic missionary priest, born in Cuet. He was sent to Futuna Island, Oceania, in 1837 and in 1841 was clubbed to death by local natives. He thus became the first martyr of Oceania. Other missionaries took up his work, and by 1843 the entire island had become Roman Catholic. Saint Peter Chanel was canonized by Pope Pius XII (*see under* PIUS) in 1954. His feast day is April 28.

**CHANEL, Gabrielle** (1883?–1971), French couturiere, born in the province of Auvergne. In 1914 she settled in Paris and opened a millinery shop. By the mid-1920's she was generally considered to be the most important figure in the world of French fashion. As a designer she usually stressed a comfortable, classic costume consisting of a full-cut skirt, a cardigan with turned-up sleeves, masses of costume-jewelry necklaces, short hair, and a sailor hat. In 1922 she brought out Chanel No. 5, which became a world-famous perfume. *Coco,* a musical based on her life and employing her nickname as its title, opened in New York City in 1969. It was written by the American lyricist Alan Jay Lerner (q.v.) and the German-born American composer Andre Previn (1929–   ).

**CHANEY, Lon** (1883–1930), American motion-picture actor, born in Colorado Springs, Colo. His parents were deaf-mutes, and the pantomimic skill Chaney learned as a child in order to communicate with his parents served him well in his acting career. He first performed in vaudeville and in 1912 appeared in his first motion picture. Chaney is best known for his so-called horror films, in which he appeared in gruesome and grotesque makeups of characters warped by psychological or physical deformities. He played the title roles in *The Hunchback of Notre Dame* (1923) and *The Phantom of the Opera* (1925), two of his most important films, which are often revived. *The Unholy Three* (1930) was his last film.

**CHANGAN.** *See* SIAN.

**CHANGCHIH,** municipality of China, in Shansi Province, 120 miles S.E. of Taiyüan. The surrounding region grows wheat, millet, and grapes, and the nearby Changchih Basin con-

*Georgian cut glass lustre chandelier from the early 19th century is thirty-four inches in diameter and holds fifteen lights.* **Parke-Bernet Galleries**

tains iron and coal deposits. Industries include ironworking, coal processing, silk and wool weaving, and distilling. Ginseng root is processed for medical use. The city was known as Luan until 1912; the present name is also spelled Ch'angchih. Pop. (1970 est.) 300,000.

**CHANGCHOW** *or* **CH'ANG-CHOU,** municipality of China, in Kiangsu Province, on the Grand Canal, about 100 miles N.W. of Shanghai. A manufacturing center, it has plants engaged in the production of combs, textiles, flour, and machinery. From 1912 to 1949 Changchow was known as Wutsin. Pop. (1970 est.) 400,000.

**CHANGCHUN,** city in China, and capital of Kirin Province, in Manchuria, 145 miles S.W. of Harbin. Connected by rail with the U.S.S.R., North Korea, and N. and S. China, Changchun is an important transportation and industrial center. The major industries are the manufacture of railway equipment, automobiles, and electrical equipment; sawmilling; and the processing of soybeans, millet, and flour. The city was founded as Kwancheng in the early 19th century. In 1932 after the Japanese conquest of Manchuria (q.v.), Changchun became the capital of the puppet state of Manchukuo and was renamed Hsinking. Many modern buildings, streets, and parks were constructed at this time. After the defeat of the Japanese in World War II the Chinese recovered possession of the city and restored its former name. Pop. (1970 est.) 1,500,000.

**CHANGE OF LIFE.** *See* MENOPAUSE.

**CHANGKIAKOW.** *See* KALGAN.

**CHANGSHA,** city and river port in China, and capital of Hunan Province, on the Siang R. about 320 miles N. of Canton. Rice, eggs, and coal produced in the surrounding region are exported from the city. In 1911 Changsha was one of the centers of the revolution that resulted in establishment of the Chinese republic. Pop. (1970 est.) 850,000.

**CHANNEL CAT.** *See* CATFISH.

**CHANNEL ISLANDS,** group of small islands belonging to Great Britain, in the English Channel, about 10 to 30 mi. off the N.W. coast of France and 50 to 120 miles S. of England. The principal islands of the group include Jersey (area, 45 sq.mi.; pop. 1971, 69,329), Guernsey (area, 24.5 sq.mi.), Alderney (area, about 3 sq.mi.), and Sark (area, about 2 sq.mi.); Guernsey, Alderney, and Sark have a combined population (1971) of 53,621. The islands are governed by representatives of the British monarch; each island has a constitution and elected government. Since the 16th century, Sark has been ruled as a fief of a hereditary seigneur or dame.

The temperate climate of the Channel Islands (the mean annual temperature is 51.7° F.) and picturesque scenery attract tourists, who play an important role in the economy of the islands. French and English are the official languages, but the people, especially on Guernsey and Jersey, adhere to their traditional speech, a dialect of the old Norman French. In the towns, of which the largest is Saint Helier on Jersey, English is generally spoken.

Agriculture is the principal economic activity, and the islands are famous for cattle. Horticulture and floriculture are successfully pursued, especially in Guernsey, and granite is quarried. German troops occupied the islands from June 30, 1940, until May 9, 1945. Area of Channel Islands, about 75 sq.mi.; pop. (1971) 123,063.

**CHANNEL ISLANDS NATIONAL MONUMENT,** Federal reservation comprising the islands of Anacapa and Santa Barbara, the two smallest of the eight Channel Islands off the coast of S. California, and surrounding waters. Many specimens of unusual plant and animal life are protected here and marine mammals and nesting seabirds find sanctuary. Bounded by cliffs and indented with small bays, the islands shelter sea lions, pelicans, cormorants, and sea fauna. Fossils and indications of volcanism suggest the pattern of the geological history of the earth. The monument, established in 1938, covers 18,166.68 acres, of which 1119.98 acres are land. It is administered by the National Park Service (q.v.).

**CHANNING, Edward** (1856–1931), American historian, born in Dorchester, Mass., and educated at Harvard University. He was a noted professor of history at Harvard from 1883 to 1929. Channing's major work, *A History of the United States* (6 vol., 1905–25), is considered by many to be one of the most comprehensive and accurate histories of the U.S. ever written by one author. The sixth volume, *The War for Southern Independence* (1925), was awarded the Pulitzer Prize for U.S. history in 1926. Among his many other writings are *The Navigation Laws* (1890), *The United States of America, 1765–1865* (1896), and *Guide to the Study and Reading of American History* (with A. B. Hart, 1896), a well-known bibliography.

**CHANNING, William Ellery** (1780–1842), American Unitarian clergyman, known as the "Apostle of Unitarianism", born in Newport, R.I., and educated at Harvard University. Pastor of the Federal Street Congregational Church, in Boston, Mass., from 1803 until his death, Channing was the spokesman of those New England Protestants who were unable to accept the Calvinistic doctrine (*see* CALVINISM) of man's inherent evil. Although at first reluctant to break with orthodox Congregationalism (q.v.), he found his views and those of his followers in such conflict with it that the formation of a new sect became unavoidable. Channing formulated the basic tenets of Unitarianism (q.v.) in a sermon delivered in Baltimore, Md., in 1819 at the ordination of the American historian Jared Sparks (1789–1866), later president of Harvard. In 1820 Channing convoked the Berry Street Conference of liberal ministers that led to the formation (1825) of the American Unitarian Association.

Channing's interest and influence extended beyond the domain of religion. Throughout his career he denounced slavery and war, devoting much of his writing to these subjects. He was an eloquent speaker and a prolific writer whose works are characterized by sincerity and moral fervor. Among his more important writings are the antislavery tract *Slavery* (1835) and the essays "Remarks on the Character and Writings of John Milton" (1826), "Remarks on the Life and Character of Napoleon Bonaparte" (1827), and "Essay on the Character and Writings of Fénelon" (1829). *The Perfect Life,* a collection of his sermons, was published in 1872.

**CHANSON.** *See* MUSIC: *Late Gothic Music;* SONG: *The Renaissance Period.*

**CHANT,** unaccompanied sung melody, the rhythms and melodic contours of which are closely tied to the spoken rhythms and inflections of the text. Chant texts can be either sacred or secular, but the term usually refers to sacred liturgical music.

Chant has been used in religious ceremonies since ancient times. In terms of present-day chant styles in the Western world, the most important of the early repertories is Jewish liturgical chant, or cantillation (*see* JEWISH MUSIC). During its first thousand years, the Christian church borrowed not only the modes, or scales, used in Hebrew cantillation, but also some Hebrew melodies and melodic fragments. Most of the texts in Christian chant are taken from or based on the Psalms, which is one of the Biblical books shared by both Jews and Christians.

Several types of Christian chant, which is often called plainsong, developed during the first thousand years of the Christian era. A repertory called Ambrosian chant developed at Milan, Italy; it is named after Saint Ambrose (q.v.), the Bishop of Milan (374–97), and is still used in some Roman Catholic services in Milan. In Spain, until about the 11th century, there was a chant repertory called Mozarabic chant, named after the Mozarab Christians who lived in Arab-dominated Spain during the Middle Ages. Today Mozarabic chant survives in a few Spanish cathedrals. Until the 9th century, France had its own chant repertory, called Gallican chant; a few traces of it remain today in the Gregorian repertory. In Rome a separate repertory developed, which eventually spread throughout Europe and superseded the others that have been described; it is called Gregorian chant (q.v.) after Pope Gregory I, known as the Great (*see under* GREGORY), who was active in collecting Roman chants, in having them assigned specific places within the liturgy, and in seeing that they were adopted by churches in other cities and countries. Today there are about 3000 different Gregorian melodies.

The Eastern Christian churches developed several types of chant before 1000 A.D., variants of which are still used today. The Armenian, Byzantine, Russian, and Syrian repertories are the most important. Many of the original melodies in these repertories were incorporated into the Gregorian repertory.

Among the Protestant Christian denominations only the Church of England has encouraged an extensive use of chant; its repertory is called Anglican chant.

**CHANTEY** *or* **CHANTY** *or* **SHANTY,** work songs of sailors characterized by a marked rhythm and traditionally sung on large sailing vessels before the appearance of steamships. Such tunes or ballads are commonly led by a leader, or chanteyman, with choruses or refrains being sung by the whole group. Besides lightening the passage of time during hard work, chanteys served the practical purpose of rhythmically coordinating the movements of working seamen, as when they hoisted a sail or heaved a capstan. One of the best known chanteys is "Blow the Man Down". Similar rhythmic songs are also used by loggers and other workmen.

**CHANTILLY,** town of France, in Oise Department, about 25 miles N.E. of Paris. It has two noted châteaux, one of which contains a library and art collection belonging to the Institute of France (q.v.). Noted formerly as a lace-manufacturing center, Chantilly is now a pleasure resort, with a notable park and a well-known racecourse. Pop. (1968) 10,239.

**CHANUKAH.** *See* HANUKKAH.

**CHANUTE,** city of Kansas, in Neosho Co., about 105 miles E. of Wichita. Chanute is in an oil-producing and farming area. Clothing, oil-drilling equipment, chemicals, and electrical supplies are manufactured in the city. Oil and wax refining and cement production are other industries. Chanute is the site of Neosho County Community Junior College, founded in 1936. Pop. (1960) 10,849; (1970) 10,341.

**CHANUTE, Octave** (1832–1910), American engineer and aviation pioneer, born in Paris, France, and educated in the United States. He was a railroad engineer for about twenty years, then became noted as a consulting engineer for bridge construction. Chanute became interested in aviation in about 1889 and made a number of contributions to the field, among them studies of the strength of air currents. He built a biplane glider that was an improvement on the designs of the German engineer Otto Lilienthal (q.v.), and suggested to the Wright brothers (*see under* WRIGHT) the use of movable surfaces to control the direction of flight. He wrote *Progress in Flying Machines* (1894).

**CHAO PHRAYA,** chief river of Thailand. It rises in the N. and flows southward, emptying into the Gulf of Siam, after a course of about 140 mi. The Chao Phraya valley is one of the most important rice-producing regions of Asia.

**CHAOS,** in the ancient Greek theory of creation, the dark, silent abyss from which all things came into existence. Chaos gave birth to the black Night and to Erebus, the dark, fathomless region where death dwells. These two children of the primeval darkness in turn united to produce Love, who brought forth Light and Day. Into this universe of formless natural forces, Chaos generated the solid mass of Earth, from which arose the starry, cloud-filled Heaven. Mother Earth and Father Heaven, personified respectively as Gaea and her husband Uranus (qq.v.), were the parents of the first creatures in the universe. In later mythology Chaos is the formless matter from which the cosmos, or harmonious order, was created. *See* COSMOGONY.

**CHAPALA, LAKE,** largest lake of Mexico, about 50 mi. long and 8 mi. wide, on a high plateau mostly in Jalisco State. The w. end of the lake is about 30 miles s. of Guadalajara. Lake Chapala is encircled by mountains and has a number of islands. The principal source is the Río Lerma; the outlet of the lake is the Río Grande de Santiago. Area, about 415 sq.mi.

**CHAPARRAL,** dense forest growth of stunted trees and hard-leaved shrubs characteristic of warm, arid regions like southern California, Mexico, and certain areas around the Mediterranean Sea. The trees and shrubs are stunted by the short, wet winters followed by long, dry summers. Of the more than 150 species of chaparral, the majority are species of buckthorn, sumac, sagebrush, ceanothus (qq.v.), and scrub oak. These plants are dense and have extensive root systems, and are thus important for conserving water and preventing soil erosion.

**CHAPARRAL COCK.** *See* ROADRUNNER.

**CHAPBOOKS,** tracts written for popular reading, usually in the form of pamphlets of sixteen or thirty-two pages stitched together and bound in paper, widely circulated in England and Scotland from the early 16th century, and later in the American colonies. The pamphlets were sold in small bookshops and by chapmen, or traveling peddlers. Chapbooks contained popular fairy tales, abstracts of popular novels, the lives of heroes and martyrs, ghost stories and tales of witchcraft, stories of murders and executions, historical narratives, travel tales, and religious treatises. The earliest English chapbooks were translations of 15th-century popular French writings circulated in cheap pamphlet form in France. Chapbooks flourished in Great Britain and the United States until the early 19th century, when they were largely supplanted by in-expensive magazines and other publications.

**CHAPEL,** structure, other than a church or cathedral, designed for worship. It may be isolated or within a church or annexed to it, or form part of a group of structures, as in a monastery, college, or palace. Worship in a chapel is usually less elaborate than worship in a church. The term chapel was derived from the Latin *cappella* ("short cloak"), a diminutive of *cappa* ("cloak"), and was the name given to the shrine in which the *cappa* of Saint Martin (q.v.) was transported by the kings of the Franks (q.v.) in early medieval times. Later the term was applied to any sanctuary containing sacred relics, and the priest in charge of the sanctuary was termed the *cappellanus* or "chaplain" (q.v.). By further extension the expression chapel came to have the meaning in use today.

The earliest sanctuaries to which the term chapel may be applied were probably the crypts erected in the catacombs (q.v.) to contain memorials to martyrs. Before the 8th century chapels rarely formed an integral part of any church. (For a description of the main architectural parts of a church, *see* CHURCH: *Architecture and Buildings*.) After that time, because of the multiplication of relics and the increased worship of saints, the practice of building chapels around the periphery of the main apse in cathedrals and churches became widespread. In Greek churches the chapels were placed in apses to the right and left of the main apse; often each was equipped for a separate Mass. In French churches chapels dedicated to various saints were placed between the buttresses off the apse. The chapel devoted to Mary, the Lady Chapel, was sometimes larger than the others. In England the Lady Chapel was usually behind the altar. Examples of French cathedrals with many chapels are the cathedral in Le Mans, which has thirteen chapels, and that of Notre Dame, in Paris, which has a continuous line of chapels opening out of the side aisles. In English churches the apse usually has a straight wall and the chapels are placed in extensions of the transepts.

In medieval times, hospitals, courthouses, and all religious houses usually had chapels annexed to them. Episcopal palaces had chapels, one of the earliest of which was the 5th-century chapel of the episcopal palace in Ravenna, Italy. Palatine chapel was the name given to the chapel in the palace of a civil ruler, or to a chapel for his private use in a religious structure. The popes had a private chapel in the 6th century in the Lateran palace, Rome. One of the most famous royal chapels in the world is La Sainte Chapelle

du Palais in Paris, built from 1245 to 1248 by Louis IX (q.v.), King of France, to house the allegedly true crown of thorns of Jesus Christ. The Sistine Chapel (q.v.), in the Vatican, Rome, was constructed by Pope Sixtus IV (*see under* Sixtus) and was decorated with frescoes by the Italian painters Raphael, Michelangelo (qq.v.), and oth-

ers. Among the royal chapels of England are the chapel of Saint George, at Windsor, and the chapel of Henry VII (q.v.), King of England, at Westminster Abbey, London.

Most universities and colleges have chapels, either detached from or a part of other buildings on the grounds. A notable example of the college chapel is that of King's College, University of Cambridge, England, which approaches cathedral size. The United States has outstanding chapels at Yale, Harvard, Princeton, and Columbia universities, and at the United States Air Force Academy (q.v.).

**CHAPELAIN, Jean** (1595–1674), French man of letters and poet, born in Paris. He became secretary to Louis VIII (q.v.), King of France, in 1632. Through the influence of the king's minister of state, the French statesman and cardinal, Duc de Richelieu (q.v.), Chapelain in 1635 became one of the organizers of the Académie Française; see INSTITUTE OF FRANCE. As a leading member of the academy, he established a code of laws to govern the group and organized the project of having the academy compile a dictionary and grammar of the French language. He gained a reputation as a literary critic and spent twenty years writing La Pucelle, an epic poem about Joan of Arc (q.v.). Twelve cantos were published in 1656; the remaining twelve were published posthumously by 1882.

**CHAPEL HILL,** town of North Carolina, in Orange Co., 28 miles N.W. of Raleigh. The University of North Carolina (q.v.) is located in Chapel Hill. Pop. (1960) 12,573; (1970) 25,537.

**CHAPLAIN,** clergyman attached to a household, society, or public institution. The term apparently derives from cappellanus (M.L. "chaplain", custodian of sacred relics), which in turn comes from cappella (M.L. "chapel", short cloak"). It may first have been applied to the ecclesiastic in charge of the cloak of Saint Martin (q.v.), which was preserved by the kings of France as a sacred relic and carried onto the battlefield in wartime. Later the name "chaplain" was given to any cleric charged with custody over relics or over a chapel (q.v.) where relics might be kept. In modern times it is given to a clergyman in the service of the armed forces; attached to a public or semipublic institution, as a hospital; or employed to minister to a private household, as to a royal or noble family.

**CHAPLIN, Charlie,** in full SIR CHARLES SPENCER CHAPLIN (1889–   ), British motion-picture actor, director, producer, and composer, who achieved worldwide fame through his performances in silent films. Born in London, England, April 16, 1889, he appeared as a child in music halls and pantomime. In 1910 he toured the United States with a pantomime troupe; he decided to remain. Chaplin, often called the most creative individual in motion-picture his-

tory, first appeared on the screen in 1913 with the Keystone Film Company of the American director Mack Sennett (q.v.). In Kid Auto Races at Venice (1914) he originated the role of "Charlie", a little tramp wearing baggy pants, enormous shoes, and a bowler hat, and carrying a bamboo cane; he played this classic role in more than seventy films during his subsequent career. He was associated later with the Essanay Film Company, the First National Film Company, and in 1918 his own studio in Hollywood was completed. During these years Chaplin gradually developed the tramp character from a jaunty, slapstick stereotype into the compassionate human figure beloved by audiences throughout the world. In 1919 he helped found the United Artists Corporation, with which he was associated until 1952. Important pictures Chaplin produced, directed, and starred in include The Kid (1921), The Pilgrim (1923), The Gold Rush (1925), The Circus (1928), City Lights (1931), Modern Times (1936), The Great Dictator (1940), Monsieur Verdoux (1947), Limelight (1952), and A King in New York (1957). The last-named film was not released in the U.S. until 1973. Chaplin wrote, directed, and played a minor role in A Countess from Hong Kong (1967). Chaplin also composed background music for most of his films.

In the late 1940's and early 1950's Chaplin was attacked by various organizations in the United States for his leftist political views. As a result, when he left the U.S. in 1952, his entry permit was rescinded. Chaplin then established permanent residence in Switzerland. In 1972 he briefly returned to the U.S. to receive several tributes, among them a special award from the Academy of Motion Picture Arts and Sciences for his contributions to the film industry. He was knighted in 1975 by Elizabeth II, Queen of Great Britain.

Chaplin perfected an individual style of performing, derived from the circus clown and the mime (see PANTOMIME), combining acrobatic elegance, expressive gesture, facial eloquence, and impeccable timing. His portrayal of the little tramp, a universally recognized symbol of indestructible individuality triumphing over adversity although persecuted by man and machine, won him critical renown as a tragi-comedian. The advent of motion-picture sound recording in the late 1920's, however, imperiled the effectiveness of the pantomime on which much of Chaplin's creative imagination depended; at the same time he became concerned with themes of contemporary significance. In his first two films of the sound era, City Lights and

*Charlie Chaplin as he appeared in the 1916 motion picture* The Vagabond.

*Modern Times,* Chaplin's little tramp remained silent. Subsequently, he abandoned the role of the tramp and relied more upon specific character portrayal in a particular time and setting. *The Great Dictator,* his first film to use all the resources of sound recording, marks this transition. Chaplin's treatment of his subjects in all his films is compounded of satire and pathos and reveals a great love of humanity and of individual freedom. He wrote *My Autobiography* (1964). *See* MOTION PICTURES.          G.A.

**CHAPMAN, Frank Michler** (1864–1945), American ornithologist, born in Englewood, N.J., and educated at Brown University. Chapman was appointed associate curator of ornithology and mammalogy in 1888 at the American Museum of Natural History, in New York City, becoming curator of ornithology in 1898. During his tenure at the museum he inaugurated many of the bird exhibits, donated specimens he had collected in zoological explorations in the Americas, and made outstanding photographic studies of bird life. He is also credited with originating the concept of bird sanctuaries. Among his numerous writings the most well known is *Handbook of Birds of Eastern North America* (1895).

**CHAPMAN, George** (1559?–1634), English dramatist and translator of classical literature, born near Hitchin, Hertfordshire. He is most famous for his translations of *The Iliad* and *The Odyssey* (qq.v.) by the Greek epic poet Homer (q.v.), which were printed together in 1616 and were followed by a collection of Homeric hymns in 1624. Chapman's interest in the classics, particularly the philosophy of stoicism (q.v.), had a great impact on his tragedies, including *Bussy D'Ambois* (1607), *The Conspiracy and Tragedy of Charles, Duke of Byron* (1608), and *Caesar and Pompey* (1631). His comedies, on the other hand, are lively and realistic; the most famous are *May Day* (1611), *The Widow's Tears* (1612), and *Eastward Ho!* (1605), which was written in collaboration with the English dramatists Ben Jonson and John Marston (qq.v.). Chapman also translated the poems of the Italian poet Petrarch (q.v.) in 1612, the *Georgics* of the ancient Greek poet Hesiod (q.v.) in 1618, and a poem by the Roman satirist Juvenal (q.v.) in 1629. His translations of Homer were the inspiration for the poem "On First Looking into Chapman's Homer" by the British poet John Keats (q.v.).

**CHAPMAN, John.** *See* APPLESEED, JOHNNY.

**CHAPULTEPEC,** rocky height surmounted by a historic castle, in Mexico City, Mexico. The

*Chapultepec Castle, a national museum of Mexico.*

terrace of the castle affords a magnificent view of Mexico City. The surrounding area, called Chapultepec Park, contains lakes and fountains, a zoo, an astronomical observatory, stately boulevards, and cypress trees many centuries old.

Chapultepec was known to the early Aztec (q.v.) Indians as Grasshopper Hill, and the Aztec emperors used the park area for recreation. The hilltop was chosen as the site of the residence of the Spanish viceroy in 1783. Construction of the castle began but was stopped after four years. Although still unfinished, the castle was used as a fortress throughout the colonial period. After years of neglect the castle became the home of the National Military Academy in 1842. The fortifications were modernized shortly before the outbreak of the Mexican War in 1847. Chapultepec Castle was captured by United States troops on Sept. 13, 1847, in the final battle of the war. The victory led to the immediate surrender of Mexico City and the opening of negotiations for a peace settlement.

When Maximilian (q.v.), Emperor of Mexico, made the castle his residence in 1864, the building was remodeled, the interior furnished with imperial splendor, and the grounds beautified. After the downfall of Maximilian in 1867 the castle became the summer residence of the presidents of Mexico. In 1937 the property was converted into a national museum and public park. The National Military Academy subsequently was rehoused in part of the castle.

In February and March, 1945, during World War II, delegates to the Inter-American Conference on the Problems of War and Peace met at Chapultepec Castle, where they signed the Act of Chapultepec (*see* CHAPULTEPEC, ACT OF).

**CHAPULTEPEC, ACT OF,** agreement adopted at Chapultepec Castle, in Mexico City, Mexico, by the Inter-American Conference on the Problems of War and Peace (also called the Chapultepec Conference), which met from Feb. 21 to March 8, 1945. The conference was attended by all the nations of North and South America except Argentina. The signatories agreed to a mutual defense of each other in World War II against aggression toward any one of them. Declarations of a similar nature directed against aggression by non-American countries had been adopted at various times by the American republics. The novel feature of the Act of Chapultepec was that it was aimed also at aggressive acts on the part of an American state toward other American states. This feature of the agreement was inspired by fear of the militaristic dictatorship in Argentina that had been sympathetic toward the Axis Powers (q.v.) during the war. Argentina, however, signed the act a few weeks later and declared war on Germany. The Act of Chapultepec also provided for a treaty to be drafted after the end of World War II continuing into the postwar period the guarantees of the act concerning aggressors. The treaty pledge of the act was fulfilled in 1947 by the Treaty of Rio de Janeiro; see RIO TREATY.

**CHAR** or **CHARR,** common name of a fish of the genus *Salvelinus* of the Salmon family related to the trout. The mature char weighs from 2 to 8 lb. The char has smaller scales than the true trout (*Salmo*), differs in the structure of the vomer, and has red instead of black spots, especially during the breeding season. The color is grayish or green above, the lower parts red, especially in the male; the lower fins are anteriorly margined with white. Its sides are marked with round red spots, and its back is not marbled. This species has a wide distribution, occurring in cold lakes and mountain streams of central and northern Europe, of northeastern America, and probably also in Siberia. It is extremely variable, and has consequently received a host of specific names, such as "saibling", "Sälbling", "ombre chevalier", and "Greenland trout". The chars are by far the most active and handsome of the trout, and live in the coldest, clearest, and most secluded waters. They weigh up to 100 lb. The best known of the distinctively American chars is the brook trout, or speckled trout; but trout of the Rangeley Lakes, in Maine, is somewhat nearer the European type. *See* TROUT.

**CHARACTERISTIC.** *See* LOGARITHMS.

**CHARADE,** riddle consisting of a word of two or more syllables, which is to be guessed from the representation, by word of mouth or by pantomime, of a meaning suggested by the separate syllables and then by the entire word. Spoken or written charades may be verse or prose. The British poet Winthrop Mackworth Praed (1802–39) was noted for his witty written charades. The following is an example of the spoken charade.

> "My first is to ramble;
> My next to retreat;
> My whole oft enrages
> In Summer's fierce heat."

Answer: *Gadfly.*

The acted charade consists of a pantomime without words in which the various syllables of a word or the entire word or phrase is acted out. If the answer to the charade is "football", the syllables "foot" and "ball" are pantomimed. Pantomimic charades are a popular game at parties in the United States and Great Britain. The participants are generally divided into two competing groups, each group acting out a number of charades that the other must guess. Charades reputedly originated in France in the 18th century.

**CHARCOT, Jean Martin** (1825–93), French neurologist, considered the father of clinical neurology, born in Paris, and educated at the University of Paris. In 1856 he was appointed physician to the Central Bureau of Hospitals. In 1860 he became professor of pathological anatomy in the faculty of medicine at the University of Paris. Two years later he joined the staff of the Salpêtrière Hospital, and he opened the most highly regarded neurological clinic of his day. He specialized in the study of hysteria, locomotor ataxia, hypnosis, and aphasia. Cerebrospinal sclerosis was named Charcot's disease after him. Achieving international fame, Charcot became an honorary member of the American Neurological Association in 1881. He attracted pupils and scientists from all over the world. His most celebrated pupil was the Austrian physician Sigmund Freud (q.v.).

**CHARD,** or SWISS CHARD, edible plant, *Beta vulgaris* var. *cicla,* of the Beet family (Chenopodiaceae), variety of the common garden beet. The edible portion of chard is the enlarged fleshy stalk and midrib of the leaves. Unlike those of garden beets, the roots of the chard are small and woody. Some varieties, called leaf beet, are grown as ornamental plants. *See* BEET.

**CHARDIN, Jean Baptiste Siméon** (1699–1779), French painter, born in Paris. Chardin received his early training by painting details in the works of other artists and signs for tradesmen. Establishing his reputation as a still-life painter, he gained admission to the Royal Academy of Painting and Sculpture in 1728. After

*"The Young Governess" is typical of Chardin's choice of subject matter from everyday life.*

1733 he did genre paintings as well, excelling in the portrayal of children and scenes of family life. Among the best of his portraits are pastels of himself and his wife. Between 1765 and 1767 he painted a series of decorative panels for the châteaux of Choisy and Bellevue.

Chardin is noted for his genre painting (q.v.), which showed the influence of the Flemish school (see FLEMISH ART AND ARCHITECTURE), and he has been praised for his use of subtle, homogeneous colorings and for his treatment of light. The Louvre, a museum in Paris, has most of his paintings, and some are owned by various American museums, including the Metropolitan Museum of Art, New York City, and the National Gallery, Washington, D.C.

**CHARENTE,** river in w.-central France. It rises 4 miles s.w. of Rochechouart, in Haute-Vienne Department, and then flows N.W. to Civray, where it turns s. into Charente Department to Angoulême. From there it flows w. past Jarnac and Cognac and enters Charente-Maritime Department. Flowing then N.W. past Saintes, it empties into the Bay of Biscay below Rochefort, opposite the Île d'Oléron. The river is about 220 mi. long and is navigable from the mouth to Angoulême. The Charente is important as a transport route for the famous French brandies of the Cognac area.

**CHARGE ACCOUNTS.** See CREDIT: *Credit and the Economy.*

*An Etruscan two-horse chariot for war or racing that dates from the 6th century B.C.*
Metropolitan Museum of Art—Rogers Fund

**CHARGÉ D'AFFAIRES.** *See* DIPLOMACY.

**CHARING CROSS,** square in the metropolitan borough of Westminster, London, England, on the N.W. bank of the Thames R., near Trafalgar Square. It stands on the old site of the 13th-century village of Cherringe, where a Gothic cross was the last of thirteen crosses erected by Edward I (q.v.), King of England, to mark the funeral procession of his wife, Eleanor of Castile (q.v.), from Grantham, Lincolnshire, to Westminster Abbey. In 1647 during the Great Rebellion (q.v.), the cross was demolished by the Roundheads (q.v.), the anti-royalists. The present copy was erected near the original site about 1863. The great cross is within the square that faces Charing Cross railway station.

**CHARIOT,** in ancient times, kind of carriage on two wheels used in both peace and war. The earliest two-wheel chariot, reportedly from Mesopotamia, dates from about 2000 B.C. Thereafter, chariots were used by Egyptians, Assyrians, Persians, Greeks, Romans, and most other ancient peoples. Because of their speed they were important war vehicles in transporting spearmen and archers. The Roman form, the *currus,* was entered from behind and was closed in front and uncovered. It was drawn by two, three, or four horses, and carried either one or two persons, both standing. The word *biga* is often applied to a two-horse chariot for battle or for racing; the *triga* was a chariot drawn by three horses yoked abreast, of which two drew from the pole; the *quadriga* was drawn by four horses abreast. The *currus trium-*

*Allegorical mural, from the Panthéon in Paris, celebrates the coronation of Charlemagne by Pope Leo III.*
Giraudon

*phalis,* in which Roman generals rode during their triumphal entrance into the city, was round, closed on all sides, and had panels richly decorated with carvings in ivory. In Rome chariot racing was one of the most popular sports in circus games. Roman writers recorded the use in Britain and some other foreign nations of war chariots carrying iron blades or scythes fixed to the ends of the pole and axle. The Celtic peo-

ples had introduced the chariot into Britain about the 5th century B.C. British chariots were usually open in the front and were sometimes fitted with seats. *See* CARRIAGE.

**CHARLEMAGNE,** *or* CHARLES THE GREAT *or* CHARLES I (Lat. *Carolus Magnus*) (742–814),

King of the Franks (768–814), King of Germany (768–814), and Emperor of the West, or Holy Roman Emperor (800–814). He was a grandson of the Frankish ruler Charles Martel (q.v.) and the eldest son of the first king of the Franks, Pepin the Short (*see under* PEPIN). He was probably born in Aix-la-Chapelle (now Aachen, West Germany). Upon the death of his father in 768, Charlemagne and his brother Carloman (751–71) jointly succeeded as rulers of the kingdom. When Carloman died in 771, Charlemagne became sole king of the Franks.

At the beginning of his sole reign, Charlemagne, considered the greatest of the Carolingian (q.v.) kings, ruled most of what are now France, West Germany, Belgium, the Netherlands, and Austria. He immediately began to consolidate his control and to extend his kingdom. In 772 he began the thirty-two-year-long conquest of the Saxons (q.v.), a non-Christian Germanic tribe. In 785 he captured the Saxon chief Wittekind (d. 807), introduced Frankish political institutions in Saxony, and made Christianity compulsory. The Saxons continued a fierce resistance against Charlemagne, but by 804 Charlemagne had subdued them.

Although involved in fighting the Saxons, in 773 Charlemagne answered an appeal by Pope Adrian I (*see under* ADRIAN) to aid the papacy in repelling an attack by Desiderius (r. 756–74), King of the Lombards (q.v.). Charlemagne overthrew the king in 774, seized the Lombardy crown, and thus gained control of the northern half of the Italian peninsula. In 778 he invaded Spain in the hopes of driving the Saracens (q.v.) from Europe. The Frankish invasion force was halted at Saragossa (q.v.) on the Ebro R. While retreating, the rear guard, led by Roland (q.v.), was attacked and destroyed by the Basques (q.v.). An account of this event is given in the medieval French epic La Chanson de Roland ("The Song of Roland"). Charlemagne, however, secured part of Navarre (q.v.) and the portion of northeastern Spain known as the Spanish March. He returned to Spain, and between 796 and 811 he consolidated his earlier gains.

In a series of campaigns Charlemagne subjugated the peoples living along the eastern border of the Frankish kingdom. He gained control of Bavaria (q.v.) in 788; destroyed the resistance of the Avars (q.v.) in the regions of Carinthia and Croatia (qq.v.) between 795 and 796; and by 805 controlled most of the territory extending to the Oder R. Besides enlarging the bounds of Christendom, he fulfilled a self-appointed role as guardian of the Christian faith. In 799, when Pope Leo III (*see under* LEO) was driven from Rome by his enemies, Charlemagne helped put down the revolt and restore Leo to his papal throne. Charlemagne was at this time the most powerful ruler in Europe and protector of the Church in Rome; it seemed natural for the Church to revive the Roman Empire of the West under him.

On Christmas Day, 800, Charlemagne was crowned Emperor of the West by Pope Leo. In 812 the new emperor was formally acknowledged by Michael I Rhangabe (d. 845), ruler of the Byzantine Empire (q.v.). The coronation date is generally regarded as the beginning of the Holy Roman Empire (q.v.).

Charlemagne improved the administrative institutions he had inherited. The empire was divided into districts ruled by counts who defended the frontiers against attacks. Imperial unity was maintained by officers, the *missi dominici*, who were sent out in all directions as the instruments of the imperial will. Charlemagne was zealous in his attempts to promote education, agriculture, the arts, manufactures, and commerce.

Learned men from all parts of the empire were encouraged to come to his court, and he established a famous palace school for his own children and the sons of noblemen. He collected and preserved in his libraries original Greek and Roman manuscripts that might not have survived otherwise. He himself possessed an amount of learning unusual in his age. He could speak German, Latin, and Greek, and he attempted to draw up a grammar of his own language. He was succeeded as emperor by his son Louis, known as the Pious or the Debonair; *see* LOUIS I. *See also* EUROPE: *History: Medieval; FRANCE: History;* FRANKS; GERMANY: *History.*

**CHARLEROI,** town of Belgium, in Hainault Province, on the Sambre R. about 30 miles S. of Brussels, with which it is connected by canal. It is the center of the most important coal-mining region of the country. Metalworking, and glass manufacturing are also principal industries. The Spanish founded the town on the site of the village of Charnoy in 1666, during their occupation of what is now Belgium, and named it after Charles II, King of Spain (*see under* CHARLES). It was subsequently a French possession in the 17th and again in the 18th centuries. During World War I a furious battle took place between German and French troops at Charleroi in 1914, and the town was almost entirely destroyed. Pop. (1971 est.) 23,324.

**CHARLES,** river of Massachusetts, separating Boston and Cambridge. Rising in the S.W. part of Norfolk County, the river follows a winding N.E.

course of about 60 mi., flowing into Boston Bay between Boston and Charlestown (q.v.). The Charles R. joins the Mystic R., flowing from the N., to form inner Boston Harbor. Near the harbor the river has been dammed to form the Charles River Basin, and a system of locks controls the water flow.

**CHARLES,** name of several European rulers. Brief accounts of less important monarchs are included in this article under the name of the countries which they ruled. The more important rulers are described in separate biographical sketches, to which the reader is referred below.

From *Karl* in German and the Scandinavian languages, the Latinized as *Carlus* (*Karlus*) or *Carolus* (*Karolus*), come the spellings *Carlo* in Italian, *Carlos* in Portuguese and Spanish, *Carol* in Rumanian, and *Charles* in English and French. *See also* CARLOS; CAROL I; CAROL II.

### AUSTRIA

**Charles I** (1887–1922). *See* CHARLES I, Emperor of Austria.

### ENGLAND

Some historians list Charles I (r. 1625–49) and Charles II (r. 1660–85) as kings of Great Britain and Ireland rather than as kings of England, Scotland, and Ireland. Although the thrones of Scotland and England were united in 1603, when Charles I's father, James VI of Scotland (r. 1567–1625), became James I (q.v.), King of England (r. 1603–25), the legislative union of England and Scotland was postponed until 1707, when the two kingdoms officially were designated Great Britain.

**Charles I** (1600–49). *See* CHARLES I, King of England, Scotland, and Ireland.

**Charles II** (1630–85). *See* CHARLES II, King of England, Scotland, and Ireland.

### FRANCE

**Charles I** (823–77). *See* CHARLES II, Holy Roman Emperor.

**Charles II** (839–88). *See* Charles III, under *Holy Roman Empire*, below.

**Charles III,** called CHARLES THE SIMPLE (879–929), King of France (898–923), the posthumous son of Louis II (q.v.), King of France. Although Charles claimed the French throne during the reign of Eudes, Count of Paris (r. 888–98) he was not acknowledged king until 898. His reign was marked by raids of Norsemen to whom he finally ceded in 911 much of what later was called Normandy. Charles was deposed in 922 by his chief vassals and imprisoned in Péronne from 923 until his death.

**Charles IV,** called CHARLES THE FAIR (1294–1328), King of France (1322–28) and as Charles I, King of Navarre. He was the third son of Philip

IV (q.v.), King of France. In 1327 Charles helped his sister Isabella (1292–1358) to dethrone her husband Edward II (q.v.), King of England. During his reign Charles increased taxation, exacted burdensome duties, debased the coinage, and confiscated estates. Because he died without male issue, the direct line of the Capetian dynasty ended; *see* CAPET.

**Charles V** (1337–80). *See* CHARLES V, King of France.

**Charles VI,** called CHARLES THE WELL-BELOVED (1368–1422), King of France (1380–1422). He was the son of Charles V (q.v.), King of France. After the death of his father in 1380, he was under the guardianship of a ducal council until 1388, when he rejected its regency and began to reign in his own right. Charles ruled well until 1392, when he became insane. In the ensuing contest for control of the kingdom, France suffered grievously from civil wars between the Armagnacs (house of Orléans) and the Burgundians. The English took advantage of the internal strife by invading France. They won the Battle of Agincourt (*see* AGINCOURT, BATTLE OF) in 1415, conquered Normandy in 1417, captured Rouen in 1419 and Paris in 1420, and imposed on Charles the Peace of Troyes (1420). Under this treaty Charles was compelled to marry his daughter to Henry V (q.v.), King of England.

**Charles VII** (1403–61). *See* CHARLES VII, King of France.

**Charles VIII,** called CHARLES THE AFFABLE (1470–98), King of France (1483–98). He was the son of Louis XI (q.v.), King of France. His sister, Anne de France (1460–1522), served as regent from 1483 to 1491, when he began to reign in his own right. The chief event of his reign was his invasion of Italy in 1494 and his temporary occupation (1495) of Naples. As a result of that invasion and several subsequent French invasions of Italy, Italian cultural influences were introduced into France.

**Charles IX** (1550–74). *See* CHARLES IX, King of France.

**Charles X** (1757–1836), King of France (1824–30). He was the grandson of Louis XV (q.v.), King of France and younger brother of the French kings Louis XVI and Louis XVIII (qq.v.). Charles was known as Charles Philippe, Comte d'Artois, until he became king. During the French Revolution he led the émigrés (q.v.). He subsequently (1795–1814) lived in Great Britain. After the accession of Louis XVIII to the French throne (1814) Charles returned to France where he headed the ultraroyalist party of reaction. His attempts to rule as an absolute monarch aroused so much unpopularity that he was deposed by a revolution in July, 1830; see JULY REVOLUTION. Charles abdicated and went into exile in Great Britain. Later he lived on the Continent.

### GERMANY

The title King of Germany or King of the Germans was borne by several Holy Roman emperors named Charles, see below. See also HOLY ROMAN EMPIRE.

### HOLY ROMAN EMPIRE

**Charles I** (742–814). See CHARLEMAGNE.

**Charles II** (823–77). See CHARLES II, Holy Roman Emperor.

**Charles III,** called CHARLES THE FAT (839–88), Holy Roman Emperor (881–87), King of part of Germany (876–87), and as Charles II, King of France (884–87). He was the son of Louis II, King of Germany; see LOUIS: Germany. Charles was deposed from his three thrones in 887 by Arnulf (q.v.), Duke of Carinthia. His deposition marked the dissolution of the Frankish Empire.

**Charles IV,** known also as CHARLES OF LUXEMBURG (1316–78), King of Bohemia and of the Germans, Holy Roman Emperor (1347–78; crowned 1355). His reign was marked by his issuance of the Golden Bull (q.v.), a document establishing the method of Imperial election.

**Charles V** (1500–58). See CHARLES V, Holy Roman Emperor.

**Charles VI** (1685–1740). See CHARLES VI, Holy Roman Emperor.

**Charles VII** (1697–1745). See CHARLES VII, Holy Roman Emperor.

### HUNGARY

**Charles I** (1288–1342). See CHARLES I, King of Hungary.

**Charles II** (1345–86). See Charles III, under Naples, below.

**Charles III** (1685–1740). See CHARLES VI, Holy Roman Emperor.

**Charles IV** (1887–1922). See CHARLES I, Emperor of Austria.

### NAPLES

**Charles I** (1226–85). See CHARLES I, King of the Two Sicilies.

**Charles II** (1246–1309), King of Naples (1285–1309). He was the son of Charles I (q.v.), King of the Two Sicilies. A prisoner of the Spanish from 1284 to 1288, Charles succeeded to the throne while still in captivity. During his reign he waged an unsuccessful war (1296–1302) with Frederick II (q.v.), King of Sicily, for possession of that island.

**Charles III,** known also as CHARLES OF DURAZZO (1345–86), King of Naples (1381–86), and as Charles II, King of Hungary (1385–86). His reign was marked by his murdering his foster

mother Joanna I, Queen of Naples (1326?–82) and by his war (1382–84) with Louis I, the titular King of Naples (see LOUIS: Naples).

**Charles IV** (1716–88). See Charles III under Spain, below.

### NAVARRE

**Charles I** (1294–1328). See Charles IV, under France, above.

**Charles II,** called CHARLES THE BAD (1332–87), King of Navarre (1349–87). His reign was characterized by disputes with relatives, disregard for treaties, rupture of alliances, and interference in French and Spanish politics.

**Charles III,** called CHARLES THE NOBLE (1361–1425), King of Navarre (1387–1425). He was the son of Charles II, King of Navarre (see above). His reign was peaceful, and he increased the prosperity of his kingdom by construction of many public works.

**Charles IV,** usually called DON CARLOS and known also as PRINCE OF VIANA (1421–61). He was the son of John II, King of Aragón (see under JOHN) and Princess Blanche of Navarre (1385?–1441). Charles was expelled from Navarre in 1441 by his father, although his title to the kingdom, which he inherited from his mother, had been recognized by the Cortes. After nine years of civil war Charles was captured in 1452 and was imprisoned. Following his release he lived in France and Italy, then returned to Navarre, and again was imprisoned in 1459. New revolts compelled John II to recognize his son's succession in 1461, but within three months Charles died, perhaps of poison.

### NORWAY

The Norwegian kings named Charles were also kings of Sweden. See under Sweden, below.

### SPAIN

**Charles I** (1500–58). See CHARLES V, Holy Roman Emperor.

**Charles II** (1661–1700), King of Spain (1665–1700). He was the son of Philip IV (q.v.), King of Spain. Spain was controlled by a regency during the decade of his minority and then alternately by French or Austrian factions in his court. During his reign Spain rapidly declined as an international power. Charles willed the throne to Philip of Anjou, later Philip V (q.v.), King of Spain, precipitating the War of the Spanish Succession; see SPANISH SUCCESSION, WAR OF THE.

**Charles III** (1716–88), King of Spain (1759–88) and as Charles IV, King of the Two Sicilies (1734–59). He was the son of Philip V (q.v.), King of Spain. Charles became Duke of Parma as Charles I in 1731. In that capacity he conquered the Kingdom of the Two Sicilies, which he ruled as Charles IV. During his rule of Spain Charles assisted agriculture and commerce, established military academies, strengthened the navy, reformed the fiscal administration, curbed the Inquisition (q.v.), and expelled the Jesuits (q.v.) from Spain. His friendship with France and his dislike of Great Britain led to the alliance in support of the American Revolution.

**Charles IV** (1748–1819), King of Spain (1788–1808). He was the son of Charles III (see above). His wife, Princess Maria Louisa of Parma (1751–1819), and ministers, especially Manuel de Godoy (1767–1851), his wife's paramour, profoundly influenced Spanish foreign policy during his reign. Consequently, Spain became involved disastrously in the Wars of the French Revolution (1792–95) and was forced to cede to France (1800) the territory of Louisiana in America. In addition, the Spanish navy was destroyed at Trafalgar (see TRAFALGAR, CAPE) and France invaded Spain (1807). After his abdication in 1808 he lived in France and Italy.

### SWEDEN

**Charles I–VI.** These six kings are of dubious authenticity, their accounts being based mainly on early medieval legends.

**Charles VII** (d. 1167), King of Sweden (1161–67), the son of King Sverker (1134–55). Charles assumed the title King of Swedes and Goths in 1161. He was assassinated in 1167.

**Charles VIII,** known as KARL KNUTSSON (1408?–70), King of Sweden (1448–57, 1464–65, 1467–70), and as Charles I, King of Norway (1449–50). He served as regent of Sweden from 1436 to 1440. Charles' intermittent reign was marked by his flight into Germany in 1457, his temporary recovery of the sovereignty after the reign (1457–64) of Christian I (q.v.), King of Denmark and Norway, and his later recall to power in 1467.

**Charles IX** (1550–1611). See CHARLES IX, King of Sweden.

**Charles X Gustavus** (1622–60). See CHARLES X GUSTAVUS, King of Sweden.

**Charles XI** (1655–97). See CHARLES XI, King of Sweden.

**Charles XII** (1682–1718). See CHARLES XII, King of Sweden.

**Charles XIII** (1748–1818), King of Sweden (1809–18) and as Charles II, King of Norway (1814–18). He was the son of King Adolphus Frederick (1710–71) of Sweden and younger brother of King Gustavus III (q.v.). As high admiral, Charles defeated a Russian fleet in the Gulf of Finland in 1788. He was regent from 1792 to 1796 during the minority of King Gustavus IV (q.v.) and again in 1809 after Gustavus had lost his throne through revolution. During Charles'

reign Sweden lost Finland to Russia in 1809 but was united with Norway in 1814.

**Charles XIV John** (1763–1844). See CHARLES XIV JOHN, King of Sweden.

**Charles XV** (1826–72). See CHARLES XV, King of Sweden.

**Charles XVI Gustavus** (1946–  ), King of Sweden (1973–  ), the son of Prince Gustaf Adolph (1906–47) and grandson of King Gustavus VI (q.v.), whom he succeeded.

### WÜRTTEMBERG

**Charles,** full German name KARL FRIEDRICH ALEXANDER (1823–91), King of Württemberg (1864–91). He was the son of William I, King of Württemberg (see under WILLIAM). Charles aided Austria in the Seven Weeks' War (q.v.) but sided with Prussia and the other German states in the Franco-German War (q.v.). His reign was noted for liberal reforms.                    P.R.C-N.

**CHARLES I,** in full CHARLES FRANCIS JOSEPH (1887–1922), Emperor of Austria (1916–18) and, as Charles IV, King of Hungary (1916–18), born in Persenbeug, Austria. He was the eldest son of Archduke Otto (1865–1906), the nephew of Archduke Francis Ferdinand (q.v.), and grandnephew of Emperor Francis Joseph I (q.v.). Following the assassination of Francis Ferdinand and the death of Francis Joseph, Charles succeeded as emperor of Austria and king of Hungary in 1916. During World War I in a secret letter he supported the claims of France against those of the Austrian ally Germany in Alsace-Lorraine (q.v.) and proposed that Germany abandon Belgium. Charles disavowed the letter when it was published in April, 1918, but it had a disheartening effect on the Central Powers. Upon the collapse of Austria-Hungary on Nov. 11, 1918, Charles abdicated the throne of Austria, and two days later he abdicated the throne of Hungary. In March, 1919, he left Austria and in April the Austrian parliament formally deposed him. Twice in 1921 Charles launched unsuccessful attempts to regain the Hungarian throne. Banished from Hungary, he went into exile on the island of Madeira, where he died. He was the last of the Hapsburg (q.v.) rulers.

**CHARLES I** (1600–49), King of England, Scotland, and Ireland (1625–49), born in Dunfermline, Scotland. The second son of James I (q.v.), King of England, Charles became heir-apparent when his elder brother Henry died in 1612, and was made prince of Wales in 1616. In 1623, during the Thirty Years' War (q.v.), Charles visited Spain to negotiate his proposed marriage with the Spanish infanta. The proposal had been made in order to effect an alliance between Spain and England. When Charles failed in his

*Charles I of England, a portrait by the Flemish painter
Sir Anthony Van Dyck (1599–1641).*

mission, negotiations were begun for his marriage to the French princess Henrietta Maria
(q.v.), and England formed an alliance with
France against Spain. In 1625 Charles succeeded
to the throne and married Henrietta Maria, but
his marriage aroused the ill will of his Protestant
subjects because the queen consort was Roman
Catholic.

Charles believed in the divine right (q.v.) of
kings and in the authority of the Church of England. These beliefs soon brought him into conflict with Parliament and ultimately led to civil
war. He came under the influence of his close
friends George Villiers, 1st Duke of Buckingham
(*see under* VILLIERS), whom he appointed prime
minister in defiance of public opinion and
whose war schemes ended ignominiously.
Three Parliaments, convoked in four years, were
dissolved by Charles because of their refusal to
comply with his arbitrary measures. When the
third Parliament met in 1628, it presented the
Petition of Right (q.v.), a statement demanding
that Charles make certain reforms in exchange
for war funds. Charles was forced to accept the
petition. In 1629, although the assassination of
Buckingham had removed a parliamentary
grievance, Charles dismissed Parliament and

had several parliamentary leaders imprisoned. Charles governed without a Parliament for the next eleven years. The despotic Star Chamber and High Commission courts sanctioned forced loans, poundage, tonnage, ship money, and other extraordinary financial measure to meet governmental expenses; see HIGH COMMISSION, COURT OF; STAR CHAMBER, COURT OF.

In 1637 his attempt to impose the Anglican liturgy in Scotland led to rioting by Presbyterian Scots; see COVENANTERS. Charles was unable to quell the revolt, and in 1639 he convoked the so-called Short Parliament to raise an army and necessary funds. This body, which sat for one month, refused his demands, drew up a statement of public grievances, and insisted on peace with Scotland. Obtaining money by irregular means, Charles advanced against the Scots, who crossed the border, defeated his army at Newburn, and soon afterward occupied Newcastle and Durham. His money exhausted, the king was compelled to call his fifth Parliament, the Long Parliament (q.v.), in 1640. Led by John Pym (q.v.), it proceeded against the two chief royal advisers and secured the imprisonment and subsequent executions of the Archbishop of Canterbury, William Laud (q.v.), and Sir Thomas Wentworth, 1st Duke of Strafford (q.v.). In 1641 Charles agreed to bills abolishing the royal courts, prohibiting arbitrary taxation, and ensuring that Parliament would not be dissolved. The king also agreed to more religious liberties for the Presbyterians. Soon after, Charles was implicated in a plot to murder the Covenanter leaders, including Archibald Campbell, 8th Earl of Argyll (see under CAMPBELL). When Charles visited Scotland in August, 1641, he promised Campbell that he would submit to the demands of the Scottish Parliament. While still in Scotland, the king received word of the massacre of thousands of Irish Protestants by Irish Roman Catholics. When he returned to London in November, he tried to have Parliament raise an army, under his control, to put down the Irish revolt. Parliament, fearing that the army would be used against itself, refused, and issued the Grand Remonstrance, a list of reform demands, including the right to pass laws without royal approval. Charles appeared in the House of Commons with an armed force and tried to arrest Pym and four members. The country was aroused and the king fled with his family from London. Both sides then raised armies. The supporters of Parliament were called Roundheads (q.v.), and those of the king, Cavaliers (see CAVALIER). The first civil war of the Great Rebellion (q.v.), now inevitable, began at Nottingham on Aug. 22, 1642. The Cavaliers were initially successful, but after a series of reverses Charles gave himself up to the Scottish army on May 5, 1646. When he refused to accept Presbyterianism in June, 1647, he was delivered to the English Parliament. Later he escaped to the Isle of Wight, but was imprisoned there. By this time a serious division had occurred between Parliament and the army commanded by Oliver Cromwell (see under CROMWELL). Cromwell and his supporters, the Independents, compelled Parliament to pass an act of treason against further negotiation with the king.

The moderate Parliamentarians were forcibly ejected by the Independent commander Thomas Pride (q.v.), and the remaining legislators, who formed the so-called Rump Parliament (q.v.), appointed a court to try the king. On Jan. 20, 1649, the trial began in Westminster Hall. Charles denied the legality of the court and refused to plead. On Jan. 27 he was sentenced to death as a tyrant, murderer, and enemy of the nation. Scotland protested, the royal family entreated, and France and the Netherlands interceded, in vain. He was beheaded at Whitehall, London, on Jan. 30, 1649. Subsequently Oliver Cromwell became chairman of the council of state, a parliamentary agency that governed England as a republic.

**CHARLES II** (1630–85), King of England, Scotland, and Ireland (1660–85), born in London. He was the second, but eldest surviving, son of Charles I (q.v.), King of England, and was Prince of Wales from birth. He took his seat in the House of Lords in 1641 and held a nominal military command in the early campaigns of the first civil war of the Great Rebellion (q.v.). He later fled from England and went into exile at The Hague, the Netherlands, where he made two attempts to save his father. Upon the execution of Charles I in 1649, Charles II assumed the title of king and was so proclaimed in Scotland and sections of Ireland, and in England, then ruled by Oliver Cromwell (see under CROMWELL). After an acknowledgment of the faults of his father, Charles accepted the Scottish crown on Jan. 1, 1651, at Scone from the Scottish noble Archibald Campbell, 8th Earl of Argyll (see under CAMPBELL). He invaded England the following August with 10,000 men and was proclaimed king at Carlisle and other places along his route. His army was routed by Cromwell at Worcester (q.v.), on Sept. 3, 1651. After this battle Charles fled to France.

He spent eight years in poverty and dissipation while in exile on the Continent. In 1658, following the death of Cromwell and the succession of his son Richard Cromwell (*see under* CROMWELL) as Lord Protector, the demand for the restoration (q.v.) of royalty increased. In February, 1660, General George Monck (q.v.) led an army into London and forced the Rump Parliament (q.v.) to dissolve. In April, in the Declaration of Breda, Charles announced his intention to accept a parliamentary government and to grant amnesty to his political opponents; *see* BREDA. A new Parliament requested Charles to return and proclaimed him king on May 8, 1660. He landed at Dover on May 26, and was welcomed at Whitehall by Parliament three days later.

Charles was crowned on April 23, 1661. Noted for subservience and insistence on royal prerogative, his first Parliament was overwhelmingly Royalist, and gave him free rein. Edward Hyde (q.v.), 1st Earl of Clarendon, his companion in exile, was appointed chief minister. Clarendon restored the supremacy of the Church of England and English and Scottish Nonconformists (q.v.) and Presbyterians were persecuted contrary to the Declaration of Breda. Extravagant and always in want of money, Charles assented to the abolition of the feudal rights of knight service, wardship, and purveyance in consideration of a large annuity that, however, was never fully paid. On May 20, 1662, he married the Portuguese princess Catherine of Braganza (1638–1705) for her large dowry; *see* BRAGANZA. The failure of Parliament to produce the amount

*Charles II, King of England*    National Portrait Gallery, London

agreed on and the chronic mismanagement of the English finances brought the king to a desperate need of money. In return for subsidies from Louis XIV (q.v.), King of France, Charles formed a secret alliance with France, which in 1672 plunged England into a war with the Netherlands; *see* NETHERLANDS, THE: *History*.

The war was popular. Commercial and colonial rivalry had already brought about two wars between the two countries, the last one occurring between 1665 and 1667. The Dutch War of 1672 resulted in the English acquisition of the Dutch colony of New Netherland; *see* NEW YORK: *History*. Some knowledge of the negotiations with France, joined with efforts by Charles toward absolutism, brought him into conflict with Parliament. Aided by French subsidies, Charles dissolved his last Parliament in 1681. The struggle was heightened by enactment of the anti-Catholic Test Acts (q.v.) and by the so-called popish plot fabricated by Titus Oates (q.v.). From 1681 until his death, Charles ruled as an absolute monarch. Although a member of the Anglican Church, Charles received the last rites of the Roman Catholic Church. He was succeeded by his brother James II (q.v.).

**CHARLES V,** known as CHARLES THE WISE (1337–80), King of France (1364–80), born in Vincennes. He was the son of John II, King of France (*see under* JOHN). When John was captured in September, 1356, by the English at Poitiers during the Hundred Years' War (q.v.), Charles assumed the regency. The most significant event of his regency was the Jacquerie (q.v.), a peasant revolt. Upon the death of his father, in 1364, Charles ascended the throne. War with England raged for a number of years, but with results highly favorable to Charles, who stripped his enemies of most of their conquests in France. A generous patron of literature and the arts, Charles founded the first royal library in France in 1367. During his reign the Bastille (q.v.) was added to the fortifications of Paris. He was succeeded by his son Charles VI (*see under* CHARLES).

**CHARLES VII** (1403–61), King of France (1422–61), born in Paris. He was the eldest surviving son of Charles VI, King of France (*see under* CHARLES). When Charles VI died in 1422, the French throne did not pass to Charles VII but to the infant Henry VI (q.v.), King of England, a nephew of Charles. The English inheritance was stipulated by the Treaty of Troyes (*see* TROYES) of 1420, ending a phase of the Hundred Years' War (q.v.). Northern France was thereafter ruled by John of Lancaster (q.v.), regent for Henry, and southern France was governed by the

French king. During the next six years, the English, strenghtened by an alliance with the powerful Philip the Good, Duke of Burgundy (1396–1467), scored several major military victories. The tide of the war changed when Joan of Arc (q.v.) lifted the siege of Orléans on May 8, 1429. Charles was crowned king of France on July 17, 1429, in Rheims Cathedral. In 1435, when Philip abandoned the English cause and formed an alliance with Charles, a French victory seemed inevitable. The king entered Paris in 1436. In the following years the English lost all their French possessions except Calais. The last battle of the Hundred Years' War, a disastrous defeat for the English, was fought at Castillon (now in Gironde Department), on July 17, 1453. Charles was not a strong monarch, but he reformed the military, instituted sound fiscal policies, and encouraged trade. He was succeeded by his son Louis XI (q.v.), who had been in revolt against his father since 1446.

**CHARLES IX** (1550–74), King of France (1560–74), born in Saint-Germain-en-Laye. He was the son of Henry II and Catherine de Médicis (qq.v.). He succeeded his elder brother, Francis II (q.v.). During his minority and after 1563, when he assumed active rule, Charles remained under the domination of his mother. Intrigues and religious wars between Catholics and Huguenots (q.v.) marked the whole course of his reign; the barbaric Saint Bartholomew Massacre was the most memorable event (see SAINT BARTHOLOMEW'S DAY, MASSACRE OF). He was succeeded by his brother Henry III (q.v.).

**CHARLES I,** Holy Roman Emperor. See CHARLEMAGNE.

**CHARLES II,** known as CHARLES THE BALD (823–77), Holy Roman Emperor (875–77), and as Charles I, King of France (840–77). He was the fourth son of Louis I (q.v.), Holy Roman Emperor, by his second wife, Judith of Bavaria, born in Frankfurt-am-Main. The determination of Judith to secure a kingdom for her only son led to civil war with the other two surviving sons of Louis, Lothair I, Holy Roman Emperor (see under LOTHAIR), and Louis II, King of Germany (see under LOUIS). The war ended with the signing of the Treaty of Verdun in 843; see VERDUN. Charles received the western portion of the empire, which from this time may be called the Kingdom of France, or the West Frankish Kingdom. The government of Charles was weak; the great nobles were rapidly becoming independent, and the Northmen (q.v.) pillaged the country, almost without resistance from Charles, who bribed them to leave. Nevertheless, when Louis II, Holy Roman Emperor (see under LOUIS), died

in 875, Charles received the imperial crown through the favor of Pope John VIII (see under JOHN). He was succeeded as king of France by his son Louis II (see under LOUIS), but the imperial throne was vacant until 881. See CAROLINGIAN.

**CHARLES V** (1500–58), Holy Roman Emperor (1519–58), and as Charles I, King of Spain (1516–56), son of Philip I, Archduke of Austria (1478–1506), and Juana (1479–1555); maternal grandson of Ferdinand V of Castile and Isabella I (qq.v.); paternal grandson of Holy Roman Emperor Maximilian I (q.v.); and great-grandson of Charles the Bold, Duke of Burgundy (q.v.). He was born in Ghent (now in Belgium). Upon the death of his father in 1506, Charles inherited the Burgundian realm (see BURGUNDY); following the death of Ferdinand in 1516, Charles became ruler of the vast Spanish kingdom; and when Maximilian died in 1519, Charles gained the duchy of Austria and with his younger brother, Ferdinand, later Emperor Ferdinand I (q.v.), succeeded to the duchies of Hungary and Bohemia of the house of Hapsburg (q.v.). In 1519, Charles, having bribed the electors, was designated Holy Roman Emperor; he was crowned at Aix-la-Chapelle (now Aachen, West Germany), on Oct. 23, 1520.

Charles was now by far the most powerful sovereign in Christendom. His inherited lands far exceeded those of the Frankish emperor Charlemagne (q.v.). His territory included the Spanish kingdoms of Aragón and Castile; the Netherlands; the Italian States of Naples, Sicily, and Sardinia; Spanish conquests in America and Africa; and the Hapsburg lands. He ascended the imperial throne at a time when Germany was agitated by the religious reformer Martin Luther (q.v.). In an unsuccessful attempt to restore tranquillity, a great diet was held in Worms in 1521, before which Luther made a memorable defense of his doctrines; see REFORMATION. At this time rivalry between France and Spain over the Italian lands and Burgundy led Francis I (q.v.), King of France, to take up arms against Charles, whose attention was drawn away from the internal affairs of Germany.

The war between Charles and Francis, in which Charles was allied with Henry VIII (q.v.), King of England, and the powerful Charles, Duke of Bourbon (1490–1527), proved disastrous to France. Francis was taken prisoner in 1525 when the French were defeated at Pavia (near Milan, Italy). In January, 1526, he was forced to sign the Treaty of Madrid, relinquishing his claim to Italy and abandoning Burgundy. Soon after his release the following year, Francis re-

*Emperor Charles V with the symbols of the Holy Roman Empire, a sword and a crossed globe.*

newed the struggle, now aided by Henry VIII and Pope Clement VII (*see under* CLEMENT), who was anxious to rid Italy of the imperial armies. The pope was captured at Rome in 1527, and was kept a captive for seven months. The war ended with the signing of the Peace of Cambrai, by Charles and Francis in 1529. Francis again renounced the Italian lands, and Charles ceded Burgundy to France. In 1530 the pope crowned the victorious monarch in Bologna as Holy Roman Emperor, the last coronation of a German emperor by the pope.

Charles had been anxious to end the war with the French so that he could put down the religious revolt in Germany and prevent the Ottoman Turks from overrunning Europe; *see* TURKEY: *History.* The Turks controlled the Balkan Peninsula, and in 1526, the year that Ferdinand I laid claim to the Hungarian throne, Sultan Suleiman I (q.v.) swept over Hungary. Three years later the Turks laid siege to Vienna. In 1535 the Genoese admiral Andrea Doria (q.v.) in the service

of Charles, led an expedition to Africa, defeated the Turks at Tunis, and freed about 20,000 Christian slaves. In 1538 Charles formed an anti-Turkish alliance with Pope Paul III (*see under* PAUL) and the city-state of Venice. The alliance was unsuccessful, and in 1547 Ferdinand signed a five-year treaty with the Turks.

The failure of Charles to repel the Turks resulted in part from his inability to bring religious peace to his empire, particularly Germany. The spread of disorder during the Reformation emboldened the German princes to seek autonomy for their states. The peasants took advantage of the turmoil in 1524 and revolted; *see* PEASANTS' WAR. In 1530, shortly after his coronation, Charles convoked a diet in Augsburg to discuss the religious problem. The Protestant princes stated their creed in the Augsburg Confession (q.v.), which was unacceptable to Charles. Negotiations thereafter failed, and in 1531 the princes formed the Schmalkaldic League (q.v.). The domestic unrest and the continued war with the Turks forced the emperor to postpone his suppression of the Protestants and to grant them some liberties in 1532 in the Peace of Nuremberg.

In 1536 Charles was again at war with France. The war was terminated by the Treaty of Nice in 1538, granting Francis most of the Piedmont (q.v.) region of Italy. The war was resumed in 1542 and ended in 1544 by the Treaty of Crépy, which largely reaffirmed the earlier Peace of Cambrai. Charles, no longer fighting the French or Turks, turned his attention to the princes and the city-states of the Schmalkaldic League. In 1546 the emperor moved against the southern German principalities, and at Mühlberg, Saxony, on April 24, 1547, he scored a decisive victory against the Protestants. His success was temporary; in 1551 Magdeburg, a great stronghold of Protestantism, fell to Duke Maurice of Saxony (1521–53), but Maurice, who had previously supported the emperor, suddenly deserted Charles, allying himself with Henry II (q.v.), King of France. Charles fled before the Protestants. In 1552, through his brother Ferdinand, he concluded the Peace of Passau, by which the Lutheran states were allowed the exercise of their religion. In 1555 the settlement was reaffirmed in the Peace of Augsburg. Meanwhile, in 1552 Henry II seized the bishoprics of Toul, Metz, and Verdun, and an attempt by the emperor to reconquer Metz failed.

Weary of the constant struggles and heavy responsibilities of his scattered realms, Charles in 1555 resigned the Netherlands and, in 1556, Spain, to his son Philip II (q.v.). In 1557 Charles abdicated the imperial crown in favor of his brother, Ferdinand I (q.v.), and retired to the monastery of San Jerónimo de Yuste in Estremadura, Spain.

**CHARLES VI** (1685–1740), Holy Roman Emperor (1711–40) and, as Charles III, King of Hungary (1712–40), the son of Holy Roman Emperor Leopold I (*see under* LEOPOLD), born in Vienna, Austria. When Charles II, King of Spain (*see under* CHARLES), died childless in 1700, Leopold proclaimed his son king of Spain in opposition to Duke Philip of Anjou, who had been willed the Spanish throne. Philip became king as Philip V (q.v.), and thus precipitated the War of the Spanish Succession (*see* SPANISH SUCCESSION, WAR OF THE), which continued from 1701 to 1714. Charles had numerous allies and Philip was aided only by France, but after alternate successes and reverses Charles in 1714 renounced his claim to Spain in the Treaty of Rastadt and Baden. In 1711 Charles had succeeded his brother Joseph I (*see under* JOSEPH) as Holy

Roman Emperor, and in 1713 Charles issued the Pragmatic Sanction (q.v.) to secure the succession of his daughter Maria Theresa (q.v.) in the event that he should die without a male heir. In 1716 the emperor renewed an alliance with the city-state of Venice and entered into successful warfare against the Turks; *see* TURKEY: *History*. By the Treaty of Passarowitz in 1718, Charles gained control of Hungary and much of the Balkan Peninsula. As emperor, in 1733 Charles engaged unsuccessfully in the War of the Polish Succession; *see* SUCCESSION WARS. Under the Treaty of Vienna in 1738, which terminated that conflict, he ceded Spain the kingdoms of Naples and Sicily in exchange for the duchies of Parma and Piacenza. During a second war with the Turks from 1737 to 1739, Charles lost most of the territory he had won in 1718. Upon his death he was succeeded by Maria Theresa, but her succession was contested in the War of the Austrian Succession; *see* SUCCESSION Wars.

**CHARLES VII,** *or* CHARLES ALBERT (1697–1745), Holy Roman Emperor (1742–45), born in Brussels (now in Belgium). In 1726 he succeeded his father Maximilian II Emanuel (1662–1726) as Elector of Bavaria. During the War of the Spanish Succession (*see* SPANISH SUCCESSION, WAR OF THE), Charles was captured and taken to Vienna, where he was educated by the Jesuits. Released in 1714 after the Peace of Rastadt and Baden, Charles led the Bavarian branch of the imperial army in the war against the Ottoman Turks in 1717 (*see* TURKEY: *History*). Although he claimed to respect the Pragmatic Sanction (q.v.) by which the Austrian crown should pass to Maria Theresa (q.v.), he immediately contested the document after the death of Charles VI (q.v.), Holy Roman Emperor, in 1740. His claim, and those of Philip V (q.v.), King of Spain, and Augustus III, Elector of Saxony (1696–1763), led to the War of the Austrian Succession; *see* SUCCESSION WARS. He became king of Bohemia in 1741 and the following year was unanimously elected Holy Roman Emperor and crowned Charles VII. Even as the coronation was taking place, the Austrian army invaded Bavaria, and Charles VII held no real power during the greater part of his reign. He was reinstated by Frederick II (q.v.), King of Prussia, in October, 1744, but died a few months later. His son Maximilian III Joseph (1727–77) was forced to renounce his imperial candidacy; Charles was succeeded as emperor by Francis I (q.v.).

**CHARLES I,** also known as CHARLES ROBERT OF ANJOU, or CAROBERT (1288–1342), King of Hungary (1308–42), and founder of the Anjou (q.v.) dynastic house in Hungary. He was the son of Charles II, King of Naples (*see under* CHARLES) and the maternal grandson of Stephen V, King of Hungary (*see under* STEPHEN). Charles was the unsuccessful papal candidate for the Hungarian throne in 1301. He was elected king by the Hungarian nobles in 1308 and was formally invested in 1310. He levied direct taxes to support his army, encouraged trade and mercantile expansion of cities, and increased the territory of Hungary, thus making his country a major power. He was succeeded by his son Louis I (*see under* LOUIS).

**CHARLES I,** King of Spain. See CHARLES V, HOLY ROMAN EMPEROR.

**CHARLES IX** (1550–1611), King of Sweden (1604–11), the son of King Gustavus I (q.v.), born in Stockholm. In 1560 he became Duke of Sodermanland, and in 1569 he aided his brother John III (*see under* JOHN) in deposing their older brother Eric XIV (1533–77). In 1592 John died; he was succeeded by his son Sigismund III, King of Poland (1566–1632), and Charles became regent for his absent nephew. Charles, a Protestant, aroused the populace against his nephew, an ardent Roman Catholic. Sigismund landed in Sweden in 1598 and was defeated by Charles at Stångebro. Sigismund was formally deposed in 1599, and Charles in 1604 yielded to popular demand and was crowned king of Sweden. He was an ambitious, ruthless, but able leader, who was unpopular because of his costly wars with Poland, Russia, and Denmark. He was succeeded by his son Gustavus II (q.v.).

**CHARLES X GUSTAVUS** (1622–60), King of Sweden (1654–60), first ruler of the Palatinate dynasty, the nephew of King Gustavus II (q.v.), born in Nyköping. In 1654 his cousin Queen Christina (1626–89) abdicated in his favor; Charles succeeded to the throne of an almost bankrupt kingdom. Despite the unstable financial condition in Sweden, the king hoped to increase the territory of the country at the expense of nations already weakened by the Thirty Years' War (q.v.). In 1655, on the pretext of preventing his cousin, John II Casimir (q.v.), King of Poland, from seizing the Swedish crown, Charles invaded Poland. He formed an alliance with Frederick William (q.v.), Elector of Brandenburg, and was victorious at Warsaw. Soon thereafter Russia, Denmark, and the Holy Roman Empire all declared war on Sweden, and Brandenburg switched sides when the Poles agreed to recognize his territorial claims. Charles retired from Poland, but in 1658, leading his army across the frozen sea, he threatened Copenhagen. By the Treaty of Roskilde, Frederick II (q.v.), King of Denmark, ceded lands in

southern Sweden to Charles. Charles, now hoping for a total conquest of Denmark, attacked again, but was rebuffed by a stout Danish defense of Copenhagen. He died soon after and was succeeded by his son Charles XI (q.v.).

**CHARLES XI** (1655–97), King of Sweden (1660–97), the son of Charles X Gustavus (q.v.), born in Stockholm. During his minority the government was entrusted to a regency, and although the kingdom was kept free from foreign wars, it was misgoverned. The education of the young king was so neglected that he was nearly illiterate. In 1672 he assumed the reins of government. Under terms of an agreement made by the regency, Charles in 1674 entered the Dutch War as an ally of Louis XIV (q.v.), King of France. The Swedish army and navy were unprepared for war, and Sweden lost territory, although much of it was restored by the Peace of Saint-Germain-en-Laye in 1679. Charles, angered by the military failure, and supported by the burghers and peasants, instituted reforms that strengthened the armed forces and considerably reduced the power of the former regents and nobles. In 1682 the Riksdag, the Swedish legislature, granted the king absolute authority. By a judicious administration of revenues, he wiped out the public debt, reorganized the army and navy, and by 1693 was able to dispense with extraordinary subsidies. Although he had absolute power, he never imposed a tax without consent; and he published an annual account of revenues and expenditures. He was succeeded by his son Charles XII (q.v.).

**CHARLES XII,** known as the MADMAN OF THE NORTH (1682–1718), King of Sweden (1697–1718), the son of Charles XI (q.v.), born in Stockholm. Soon after Charles succeeded to the throne, Sweden, with extensive possessions on the Baltic, was threatened by a coalition of Frederick IV, King of Denmark (*see under* FREDERICK), Augustus II, King of Poland (1670–1733), and Peter I (q.v.), Czar of Russia. In 1700 Charles invaded Denmark and quickly forced Frederick to sign the Peace of Travendal (now Traventhal). Charles hastened to the Baltic, and rapidly brought his army of 8000 men to the Swedish stronghold, Narva (now in Estonian S.S.R.), which was beleaguered by 40,000 Russians. The disciplined Swedish troops, although they were wearied by forced marches, totally routed the Russians in November, 1700. Charles then turned to conquer Poland, which was overrun by the Swedish troops. Augustus was driven into Saxony, and Charles obtained the election of his ally Stanislas I Leszczyński (q.v.) as king of Poland in 1705.

*Charles XII, King of Sweden, in battle uniform at Altranstädt during the Swedish invasion of Saxony in 1706. Depicted at the height of his power, Charles sought throughout his reign to enhance the status of his country, often by means of radical military strategy.*

Charles then marched into Saxony, and Augustus, by the Treaty of Altranstädt of 1706, was forced to recognize Stanislas. Charles was at the height of his power, with a disciplined army holding Germany in awe, and spurning peace overtures from Peter. Charles, however, was determined to humble Russia, and began an invasion of Russia in September, 1707. He penetrated into the interior of Russia, his army harassed along the way, suffered through two severe winters, and turned south. On July 8, 1709, while besieging Poltava (now in Ukrainian S.S.R.), he was attacked by the Russian army. Within three days the entire fabric of his military success was shattered in one disastrous engagement. Charles barely escaped into Turkish territory. He induced Sultan Ahmed III (*see under* AHMED) to attack Russia. In 1711 Peter was able to escape from a precarious position on the Prut R. The Swedish monarch spent the next three years in intrigues to induce Turkey to attack Russia again. When he found that his plots were of no avail, he defied the Turkish power and was imprisoned. He escaped in 1714 and reached Stralsund, a Swedish possession in Pomerania (q.v.). The city was besieged by a combined force of Danes, Prussians, and Saxons

for a year before it surrendered. Charles again escaped, reached Sweden, and raised another army. He began an invasion of Norway in 1717. During this struggle he was killed at Frederikshald. He was succeeded by his sister Ulrika Eleonora (1688–1741), who began to negotiate a peace.

**CHARLES XIV JOHN,** originally named JEAN BAPTISTE JULES BERNADOTTE (1763–1844), King of Sweden and Norway (1818–44), born in Pau, France. He fought in the French Revolution, and in 1804 Napoleon I (q.v.), Emperor of France, created him marshal. Bernadotte distinguished himself in the victory of Austerlitz, Austria, in 1805, for which he was made Prince of Pontecorvo. He was also successful in the campaign against the Prussians in 1806–07. He was chosen by the Riksdag, the Swedish legislature, in 1810 to succeed King Charles XIII (q.v.), who had no heirs. Bernadotte agreed to become a Protestant, changed his name to Charles John, and soon began to exercise many royal functions. The crown prince resisted the efforts of Napoleon to involve Sweden in his designs against Great Britain. Sweden was soon engaged in war with France, and Charles contributed to the victory over the French at Leipzig in 1813.

He forced Denmark in the Treaty of Kiel to cede Norway, and in 1814 subjugated Norway. The reign of Charles XIV John was prosperous and peaceful. He founded the modern Swedish royal house of Bernadotte, and he was succeeded by his son Oscar I; see under OSCAR.

**CHARLES XV** (1826–72), King of Sweden and Norway (1859–72), the son of King Oscar I (see under OSCAR), born in Stockholm. During his liberal and popular rule, Charles instituted numerous reforms. The most important was in 1866 when he changed the Riksdag, the Swedish legislature, into a bicameral body with the upper house chosen by provincial representatives and the lower house by popular election. He was interested in literature and art, and wrote a volume of poems. Having no male heirs, Charles was succeeded by his brother Oscar II; see under OSCAR.

**CHARLES I** (1226–85) King of the Two Sicilies (1266–85). He was the posthumous son of Louis VIII, King of France, and the brother of King Louis IX (qq.v.). He was given the countships of Anjou (q.v.) and Maine by his brother, and through marriage in 1246, he became count of Provence (q.v.). In 1248 he accompanied Louis on the Sixth Crusade (see CRUSADES). In 1250 he was captured and briefly imprisoned, but later returned to Provence. By 1264 he controlled much of the Piedmont (q.v.). Charles agreed to aid the pope in his struggle against the Ghibellines (see GUELPHS AND GHIBELLINES) in return for the Kingdom of the Two Sicilies. In 1265 Charles invaded Italy; the following year the reigning monarch Manfred (1232?–66) was killed in battle and Charles became king. In 1268, Conradin (1252–68), nephew of Manfred and last of the Hohenstaufen dynasty, led a revolt against Charles but was captured and executed. The king firmly established himself in power by brutally suppressing the Ghibelline nobles and seizing their estates to pay his French soldiers. In 1270 Charles participated in the disastrous Seventh Crusade of his brother. In 1282, while he was preparing for another expedition, he learned of a revolt in Sicily against the French; see SICILIAN VESPERS. He tried to help his brother, but the rout of the French was completed when Pedro III, King of Aragón (1236–86) destroyed a fleet sent by Charles. The king died soon after, leaving his kingdom in a chaotic condition.

**CHARLES,** known as CHARLES THE BOLD (1433–77), last Duke of Burgundy, the son of Philip the Good, Duke of Burgundy, (1396–1467) and Isabella of Portugal (1397–1471), born in Dijon. In 1452 he became count of Charolais. He was ambitious, and when Louis XI (q.v.), King of France, forced Philip to cede some towns on the Somme R., Charles formed the League of the Public Weal, an alliance of noblemen. The forces of the league threatened Paris, and defeated the king at Montlhéry, near Paris, in 1465. The result was the Treaty of Conflans, by which the towns on the Somme were restored and the counties of Boulogne, Guines, and Ponthieu were granted to Charles. When he succeeded his father as duke of Burgundy in 1467, he became the ruler of the territories that comprise the Low Countries as well as the duchy of Burgundy and Franche Comté, or the Free County of Burgundy. In 1468, Charles married his third wife, Margaret of York (1446–1503), and formed an alliance with her brother Edward IV (q.v.), King of England. Richer and more powerful than any other prince, Charles planned to restore the old Kingdom of Burgundy, and fought a series of intermittent wars with France. In 1475 Charles made himself master of Lorraine. In March of the following year he invaded Switzerland and was defeated at Grandson. Three months later he suffered a still more severe defeat at Morat (now Murten). Nevertheless Charles refused to agree to peace terms and laid siege to Nancy in October, 1476. There he was defeated and killed on Jan. 5, 1477. His daughter and heiress, Mary of Burgundy (1457–82) soon thereafter married Maximilian I (q.v.), King of Germany, but Maximilian was forced to relinquish all of the Burgundian lands except Flanders.

See BURGUNDY.

**CHARLES EDWARD.** See STUART, CHARLES EDWARD LOUIS PHILIP CASIMIR.

**CHARLES LOUIS JOHN** (1771–1847), Archduke of Austria, third son of Emperor Leopold II (see under LEOPOLD), born in Florence, Italy. In 1796, during the French Revolution, he commanded the Austrian Army of the Rhine R., and in a major battle defeated a superior French force led by generals Jean Victor Moreau (1763–1813) and Jean Baptiste Jourdan (1762–1833). In 1799 he was again victorious over Jourdan, and in June defeated French Marshal André Masséna (1758–1817) at Zurich. Charles then became governor general of Bohemia, and formed a new army there. After a decisive Austrian defeat at Hohenlinden, in 1800, he reassumed the Austrian command. Five years later, during the Napoleonic Wars (q.v.), he defeated Masséna at Caldiero, Italy, but retreated to Croatia following Austrian losses elsewhere. This retreat was one of his greatest military achievements. Made field marshal of the Austrian forces, in 1809 he routed Napoleon I (q.v.), Emperor of France, at the battle of Aspern and

Essling (near Vienna). Charles, however, did not follow up his victory, and Napoleon, who reinforced his army, defeated Charles at Wagram. The archduke was compelled to retreat until he reached Znojmo (now in Czechoslovakia), where an armistice was concluded. He thereafter lived in virtual retirement.

**CHARLES MARTEL,** called CHARLES THE HAMMER (688?–741), Carolingian ruler of the Frankish kingdom of Austrasia (now part of Germany), son of Pepin of Herstal, ruler of Austrasia (*see under* PEPIN), and grandfather of the Frankish king Charlemagne (q.v.). Pepin was also mayor of the palace under the last Merovingian (q.v.) kings. When Pepin died in 714, Charles, an illegitimate son, was imprisoned by his father's widow, but he escaped in 715 and was proclaimed mayor of the palace by the Austrasians. A war between Austrasia and the Frankish kingdom of Neustria (now part of France) followed, which ended in Charles becoming undisputed ruler of all the Franks (q.v.). Although he was engaged in wars against the Alemanni, Bavarians, and Saxons, his greatest achievements were against the Saracens (q.v.), the Muslims invading from Spain, who threatened the Franks at the city of Tours. Charles overthrew the Saracens near Poitiers in 732 in a great battle in which their leader, the emir of Spain Abd-er-Rahman (q.v.), fell and their progress, which had filled all Christendom with alarm, was checked for a time. Charles drove the Saracens out of the Rhône valley in 739, when they had again advanced into the Burgundian territories as far as Lyon (now in France), and left them nothing of their possessions north of the Pyrénees beyond the Aude R. Charles died in Quierzy on the Oise R., leaving the kingdom divided between his two sons, Carloman (d. 754) and Pepin the Short (*see under* PEPIN). *See also* CAROLINGIAN.

**CHARLES OF ORLEANS.** *See under* ORLÉANS.

**CHARLES PHILIP ARTHUR GEORGE** (1948– ), Prince of Wales and heir apparent to the throne of the United Kingdom of Great Britain and Northern Ireland. He is the son of Elizabeth II (q.v.), Queen of Great Britain, and Philip Mountbatten, Duke of Edinburgh (*see* PHILIP, *Prince*). In 1958 Charles was created prince of Wales and in 1969 was invested as prince of Wales. He assumed his seat in the House of Lords in February, 1970, and became the first heir to the British crown to earn a university degree when he was graduated with honors from the University of Cambridge in June, 1970.

**CHARLES, Jacques Alexandre César** (1746–1823), French chemist, physicist, and aeronaut, born in Beaugency, Loiret. In 1783 he made the first balloon using hydrogen gas and ascended to a height of nearly 2 mi.; *see* BALLOON. He invented a thermometric hydrometer and a number of optical instruments. In 1787 he discovered the relationship between the volume of gas and temperature. The modern statement of the law is known variously as Gay-Lussac's Law (q.v.) or Charles' Law. He was elected to the French Academy in 1785, and later became a professor at the Conservatoire des Arts et Métiers.

**CHARLES, CAPE.** *See* CAPE CHARLES.

**CHARLESTON,** city in Illinois, and county seat of Coles Co., about 37 miles s. of Urbana. Charleston is a trade and rail center for the surrounding livestock, dairy, and agricultural region. The city has varied manufacturing. Railroad shops are located here. A Lincoln-Douglas debate was held here in 1858. Nearby are the Lincoln Log Cabin and Fox Ridge State parks. Charleston is the site of Eastern Illinois University, founded in 1895. Pop. (1960) 10,505; (1970) 16,421.

**CHARLESTON,** city and seaport in South Carolina, and county seat of Charleston Co., about 105 miles s.e. of Columbia. It is about 3 mi. from the Atlantic Ocean, on a low peninsula between the Ashley and Cooper rivers, which unite to form a broad bay. Almost entirely landlocked, the bay makes an excellent harbor, along the shores of which are noted bathing beaches and facilities for water sports. On two islands at the entrance to the bay are forts Moultrie and Sumter (*see* FORT SUMTER), just outside of the city is the Charleston Navy Yard, and 12 miles n.w. is the Charleston Air Force Base. In the city and its vicinity are a number of notable gardens, parks, and recreation centers. Charleston is a noted tourist center.

The second-largest city in the State, a network of rail, air, bus, and truck lines, and inland waterway, coastal, and transoceanic steamship lines connect Charleston with other cities on the Atlantic seaboard and in the interior, and with foreign ports. An important center of domestic and foreign trade, among the principal exports of the city are coal, textiles, tobacco, and wood pulp; imports include canned goods and cotton. Other industries include construction, printing and publishing, wholesale and retail trade, and the manufacture of apparel, chemicals, fertilizers, foodstuffs, lumber and wood products, and textiles.

The notable buildings of Charleston, some of historic interest, include a museum, founded in 1703 as the Old Powder Magazine; Dock Street

Theater, opened in 1736; Saint Michael's Episcopal Church, begun in 1752; the Unitarian Church, dating from 1772; the chapel of the Charleston Orphan House, erected in 1802; a number of fine 18th-century colonial homes; the City Hall, built in 1802; Market Hall, now a Confederate museum, erected in 1841; and the Beth Elohim Synagogue, built in 1840. Educational and cultural institutions include the College of Charleston, which was founded in 1770 and in 1837 became the first municipal college in the United States; the Medical College of the State of South Carolina, founded in 1824; the Citadel, a State military college, founded in 1842; the Porter Military Academy, an Episcopalian institution, dating from 1867; and Gibbes Art Gallery, constructed in 1905.

In 1670 English colonists came to Albemarle Point, on the west bank of the Ashley R., 3 mi. from the present city, and named their settlement Charles Town in honor of Charles II (q.v.), King of England. The city was moved across the river to the site of present-day Charleston in 1680 and was made the capital of the colony in the same year. Huguenots (q.v.) from France joined the colony in 1680 and other Huguenots after the revocation of the Edict of Nantes (q.v.) in France in 1685. Exiles from Acadia (q.v.), present-day Nova Scotia) increased the population of the town by about 1200 in 1755.

In 1775 Charleston was one of the chief cities and seaports in America, and it played a leading role in the American Revolution. On June 28, 1776, the garrison on Sullivan's Island, under Colonel William Moultrie (1730–1805), repulsed an attack by the British fleet; and in 1779 the city was again successfully defended; but on May 12, 1780, a garrison under General Benjamin Lincoln (1773–1810) was captured by a British force under Sir Henry Clinton (q.v.). On Dec. 14, 1782, the British evacuated the city and the Americans again took possession of it.

Incorporated as a city in 1783, Charleston was the capital of the State until 1790. Between the conclusion of the War of 1812 and the outbreak of the American Civil War, Charleston was the commercial and cultural center of the South. In 1832 Charleston was the center of the nullification (q.v.) movement; and the first ordinance of secession was signed in the city on Dec. 20, 1860. On April 12–13, 1861, the American Civil War was opened by the Confederate bombardment and capture of Fort Sumter. In 1863 a Federal fleet under Admiral Samuel Francis Dupont de Nemours (*see under* DUPONT) unsuccessfully attacked the fortifications of the harbor, and, although closely besieged and frequently bombarded, the city remained in possession of the Confederates until Feb. 17, 1865, when it was evacuated. On the following day the Union forces under General William Tecumseh Sherman (*see under* SHERMAN) took possession. On Aug. 31, 1886, Charleston suffered from an

*Fort Sumter in Charleston harbor was the scene of the first battle of the Civil War.*
South Carolina State Development Board

*The colonial and antebellum houses of Charleston are a major attraction for visitors.*

South Carolina State Development Board

earthquake; many persons were killed and more than $8,000,000 worth of property was destroyed. Pop. (1960) 65,925; (1970) 66,945.

**CHARLESTON,** city and capital of West Virginia, and county seat of Kanawha Co., at the confluence of the Elk and Kanawha rivers, about 45 miles E. of Huntington. One of the largest cities in the State, it is served by several railroads and airlines. In the surrounding region coal, natural gas, oil, and salt are produced. Charleston is a major producer of basic chemicals and a wholesale-distribution center. Other industries in the city include the manufacture of glass and metals. Among the principal points of interest are the State capitol, erected in 1932, and Morris Harvey College, founded in 1888.

In 1788 an outpost known as Fort Lee was built on the site of the present-day city; Scotch-Irish and German immigrants later settled in the vicinity of the fort. Charles Town (later changed to Charleston) was incorporated as a town in 1794; in 1870 it was incorporated as a city and made the State capital. Charleston lost this status in 1875, but regained it ten years later. Pop. (1960) 85,796; (1970) 71,505.

**CHARLESTOWN,** formerly a separate city, and, since 1874, a part of Boston, Mass., between the Charles and Mystic rivers. A large naval shipyard is in the S.E. part of Charlestown. Settled in 1629 by a small company from Salem,

Charlestown was organized as a town in 1634. Territory originally within the limits of the city has been divided up to form the towns of Woburn, Malden, Stoneham, Burlington, and Somerville, and parts of other nearby towns. The Battle of Bunker Hill (see BUNKER HILL, BATTLE OF) was fought in Charlestown in 1775, and is commemorated by the Bunker Hill Monument (q.v.). Charlestown was the home of the English clergyman John Harvard, the benefactor of Harvard University (qq.v.), and the birthplace of Samuel F. B. Morse, inventor of the telegraph (qq.v.).

**CHARLES UNIVERSITY,** coeducational institution of higher learning, located in Prague, Czechoslovakia, and under the jurisdiction of the ministry of education and culture. The university was founded in 1348 by Charles IV (1316–1378); in 1882 it was divided into Charles University and the German University. Both were closed in 1939 following the German occupation; in 1945 Charles University reopened, but the German University was abolished. The university has faculties of law, philosophy, mathematics and physics, natural sciences, education, journalism, physical education, medicine, pediatrics, and hygiene. Also part of the university are four specialized institutes and faculties of medicine located in Prague, Plzeň, and Hradec Králové. A professional title is awarded at the end of a five-year course of study, representing the equivalent of American baccalaureate-degree work. An additional three years of study and completion of the thesis leads to the *kandidát věd* (candidate of sciences), the equivalent of an American degree of master. The highest degree of *doktor věd* (doctor of sciences) is awarded upon presentation of a dissertation. The library has 1,900,000 volumes, including one hundred copies of the works of John Wycliffe. In 1972–73 student enrollment was 21,125; the faculty numbered 2812.

**CHARLEVOIX, Pierre François Xavier** (1682–1761), French historian and Jesuit missionary. He was born in Saint Quentin, the son of a deputy attorney general, and entered the Society of Jesus in 1698. As a missionary he was first sent to North America in 1705 and taught in Québec until 1709, when he returned to France. In 1720 Charlevoix was sent by the French government to Canada with the secret purpose of finding a new route from Acadia (q.v.), the French colony in New France, to the Pacific Ocean. He journeyed up the Saint Lawrence R. and through the Great Lakes, visiting military posts and missions and meeting with Sioux Indians. Thwarted in going farther west, he went down the Mississippi R. in 1721 to New Orleans, where he fell ill. From there he voyaged to Santo Domingo. After returning to France in 1722, he devoted himself to teaching and writing, completing historical works on Paraguay, Santo Domingo, and Japan. He is best remembered for his account of his travels in North America, *Histoire et description générale de la Nouvelle France,* also titled *Journal historique* (1744; Eng. trans., *History and General Description of New France,* or *Historical Journal,* 1761), which was the first general history of Canada to be published.

**CHARLOCK,** common name for the wild mustard plant, *Brassica kaber,* in the Mustard family (Cruciferae). This weed has rough, dentate leaves and small, yellow, four-petaled flowers. The seedpods are long, knotty, and tapering. The seeds are sometimes used as a substitute for table mustard. Charlock is an annual weed common in the United States and Europe.

**CHARLOTTE,** largest city in North Carolina, and county seat of Mecklenburg Co., about 130 miles s.w. of Raleigh, and about 20 miles N. of the South Carolina boundary. An important industrial and wholesale center, the city is served by several railroads and airlines. In the surrounding region cotton growing and dairy farming are the chief occupations. In Charlotte the

principal industries are printing, and the manufacture of chemicals, foodstuffs, machinery, metals, and textiles. Educational and cultural institutions in Charlotte include the Johnson C. Smith University, founded in 1867; Queen's College, established in 1857; the University of North Carolina at Charlotte, established in 1965; and the Mint Museum of Art, completed in 1936.

Charlotte was settled about 1750, chartered in 1768, and in 1774 was made the county seat. In September, 1780, during the American Revolution, the British general Charles Cornwallis (q.v.) entered the city and occupied it for several days. He referred to it as a "hornet's nest", a representation of which was later adopted as the city's emblem. The city was the last meeting place of the full Confederate cabinet, on April 10, 1865. Pop. (1960) 201,564; (1970) 241,178.

**CHARLOTTE AMALIE,** capital and chief port of the Virgin Islands of the United States (q.v.), on Saint Thomas Harbor on the southern shore of the island of Saint Thomas, 70 miles E. of San Juan, Puerto Rico. Rum, bay rum, woolens, jewelry, and sugar are exported. Local industries include boatbuilding, rum and alcohol distilling, and the production of handicrafts. A picturesque town built on three hills, Charlotte Amalie is a free port and a major tourist resort. Of special interest are Fort Christian, built in 1671; Beretta, the shopping area; and the Frenchtown section. Charlotte Amalie is the site of the College of the Virgin Islands and the Museum of the Virgin Islands. In 1672 the Danes founded the first permanent settlement on the site, naming it Amalienborg or Charlotte Amalia, after their queen. The city is also popularly known as Saint Thomas, which was the official name from 1921 to 1936. It became capital of the American territory of the Virgin Islands in 1917, when the former Danish West Indies were purchased. Pop. (1970) 12,220.

**CHARLOTTENBURG.** *See* BERLIN: *West Berlin.*

**CHARLOTTESVILLE,** independent city in Virginia, county seat of Albemarle Co., on the Rivanna R., about 69 miles N.W. of Richmond, in a rich farming, cattle-raising, and fruit-growing region. Industrial establishments in the city include woolen, silk, flour and planing mills, and plants engaged in the production of clothing, machinery, pens and pencils, and fruit wines and brandies. Monticello (q.v.), the home of Thomas Jefferson, third President of the United States, is 3 mi. to the E., and Ash Lawn, which was the home of James Monroe, fifth President of the United States, is nearby. The city is the site of the University of Virginia.

Charlottesville was settled about 1737 and named in honor of Charlotte Sophia, Queen Consort of Great Britain (1744–1818). It was incorporated as a town in 1762. In 1781, during the American Revolution, British troops under Sir Banastre Tarleton (1754–1833), raided the town in an unsuccessful attempt to capture Thomas Jefferson, then governor of Virginia. The town was chartered as a city in 1888. Pop. (1960) 29,427; (1970) 38,880.

**CHARLOTTETOWN,** city and seaport in Canada, and capital of Prince Edward Island Province, and county seat of Queen's County on Hillsborough Bay, on the s. central coast of the island, about 35 miles s.e. of Summerside. Industrial establishments in Charlottetown include textile mills, lumber mills, foundries, canneries, and the shops of the Prince Edward Island railway. Fishing is an important industry. Prince of Wales College and Normal School, founded in 1860, and Saint Dunstan's College (1831), a Roman Catholic educational institution, are located in the city. Founded by the French in 1750 as Port la Joie, Charlottetown was later renamed, under British rule, in honor of Charlotte Sophia, Queen Consort of Great Britain (1744–1818). It became the provincial capital in 1765. Pop. (1971) 19,133.

**CHARM,** any formula, act, or object supposed to have magical power to ward off danger or to bring good luck. Although the term originally meant the chanting of a verse, supposed to exert occult influence, by extension it came to mean an object worn or carried for protection or good fortune. *See* AMULET.

**CHARON,** in Greek mythology, the son of Night and of Erebus, who personified the darkness under the earth through which dead souls passed to reach the home of Hades (q.v.), the god of death. Charon was the aged boatman who ferried the souls of the dead across the River Styx (q.v.) to the gates of the underworld. He would admit to his boat only the souls of those who had received the rites of burial and whose passage had been paid with a coin placed on the lips of the corpse. Those who had not been buried and whom Charon would not admit to his boat were doomed to wander on the banks of the Styx for a hundred years. Although Charon would not ferry the living to the other world, he made an exception in the case of the Trojan hero Aeneas (q.v.).

**CHARPENTIER, Gustave** (1860–1956), French composer, born in Dieuze, Meurthe-et-Moselle Department, and educated at the Lille Conservatory and later at the Paris Conservatory under the French composer Jules Émile Frédéric Mas-

*Charon crossing the River Styx, 19th-century woodcut by the French painter Gustave Doré.* Bettmann Archive

senet (q.v.). Charpentier's fame rests mainly on the opera *Louise* (1900), for which he also wrote the libretto. *Louise* was an overwhelming critical and popular success when first produced at the Opéra Comique in Paris. Subsequently it was presented in all the leading opera houses of the world. The composer also set to music verses of the French impressionist poets Charles Baudelaire and Paul Verlaine (qq.v.). Two of his best-known compositions are an orchestral suite, *Impressions d'Italie* ("Impressions of Italy", 1890), and a cantata, *La Vie du Poète* ("The Poet's Life", 1892). His later works, which include the opera *Julien* (1913), never achieved the critical acclaim accorded *Louise*. In 1913 Charpentier was elected to the Académie des Beaux-Arts as Massenet's successor.

**CHARR.** *See* CHAR.

**CHARTER,** formal document by which rights or privileges are conferred. The term formerly applied to a written conveyance of land, and property held under such an instrument was, in Anglo-Saxon law, called "Charterland", "bookland", or "bocland". In this sense the term now used is deed. The term charter is used to describe a grant of land or special privileges by the state, or a solemn guaranty by the sovereign of popular rights. The Magna Charta (q.v.), or the Great Charter, issued by John (q.v.), King of England, in 1215, is one of the chief constitutional documents of Great Britain.

In American colonial history, three kinds of

charters were granted: 1. estates to companies for the purpose of establishing colonies; 2. to the inhabitants of colonies in general; and 3. to individual proprietors. Of the first sort were the charters granted to the Massachusetts Bay Company by Charles I (q.v.), King of England, in 1629, and the charter of Georgia, granted by George II (q.v.), King of Great Britain, in 1732. Of the second sort was the charter of Connecticut, granted to the people of the colony by Charles II (q.v.), King of England, in 1662. Of the third sort were the original charter of New York, granted by Charles II in 1664 to his brother the Duke of York, who later succeeded to the English throne as James II (q.v.), and the charter of Maryland, granted to George Calvert (*see under* CALVERT) by Charles I in 1632.

In the United States, corporations are chartered, as a general rule, by legislative acts of a State either by a special statute that confers upon a particular corporation the special powers and privileges named therein, or under a general law that provides the method to be pursued by persons who wish to organize a corporation. In the latter case the articles of association, taken in connection with the provisions of the general statute, constitute the charter. If the corporation is a public one, such as a city, county, or town, the charter may be changed at will by the legislature. Such a corporation is merely an agency of the State for the exercise of governmental powers within a particular area. It has no vested right to any powers or franchises. On the other hand, the charter of a private corporation is a contract between the State and the corporators. As such, it is protected from repeal or modification by the provision of the Federal Constitution that declares that "no state shall . . . pass any . . . law impairing the obligation of contracts" (Art. I, Sec. 10). The State granting the charter may, however, reserve the right to alter, amend, or repeal it. *See* CORPORATION.

In Great Britain, towns, universities, schools, banks, and joint-stock companies often derived their privileges from royal charters. Now, however, parliamentary sanction is generally obtained for grants of important privileges. In the case of companies, Parliament has passed a general act governing the procedure for incorporation. By complying with the provisions, any body can obtain the privileges of incorporation.

**CHARTERED COMPANIES,** companies created by a grant from a sovereign government to a portion of the people securing to them the enjoyment of certain rights set forth in the charter or document of grant.

The first employment of the word "company"

as a legal term was in connection with the great companies chartered by European nations in the 17th and 18th centuries. These companies grew out of the voyages of discovery and the desire of these nations for monopolies over the newly opened trade routes. The companies were given royal charters authorizing them to acquire and administer territory as well as to direct trade. It was the Dutch East India Company (q.v.), for example, that settled New Netherlands (now New York State). Late in the 19th century the British government chartered four such companies, the North Borneo (1881), the Royal Niger (1886), the British East Africa (1888), and the British South Africa (1888). As empires vanished with the rise of independent nations, this form of company vanished also. *See* EAST INDIA COMPANY.

**CHARTER OAK,** large white oak tree that stood in Hartford, Conn., until blown down in August, 1856, when it was computed to be nearly 1000 years old. Tradition has it that when Sir Edmond Andros (q.v.) was appointed governor general of New England, he went to Hartford in 1687 to procure the colonial charter. The colonists were loath to surrender the document, but, appearing to submit, carried it to the council chamber. During the debate the lights were extinguished and in the ensuing confusion the charter was carried from the room to its hiding place in the hollow of the tree. It remained there until 1689, when Andros was deposed, making further concealment unnecessary.

**CHARTIER, Alain** (1385?–1433?), French poet and diplomat, born in Bayeux, and educated at the University of Paris. He served the Dauphin, later Charles VII (q.v.), King of France, in various official capacities, including those of secretary and negotiator. After the crushing defeat in 1415 of France by England in the Battle of Agincourt (*see* AGINCOURT, BATTLE OF), Chartier wrote *Le Quadrilogue Invectif* (1422), a passionate appeal to all French classes to unite in support of their king. The appeal is written in the form of a conversation between France and the three estates of the realm, Nobility, Clergy, and the People. One of his most famous love poems, *La Belle Dame sans Merci* ("The Beautiful Merciless Lady", 1424), set a literary fashion and suggested the poem of the same title by the British poet John Keats (q.v.). Chartier wrote several patriotic works, but he is remembered chiefly for his allegorical love poems, especially *Lai de Plaisance* ("Poem of Pleasure"), written in 1413, and *Bréviaire des Nobles* ("Breviary of the Nobility"). The latter is a tale of unrequited love that was so greatly admired by his contempo-

*The Cathedral of Notre Dame can be seen from a side-street in Chartres.*   Standard Oil Co. (N.J.)

raries that court pages were required to memorize parts of it.

**CHARTISM,** political reform movement in Great Britain from 1838 to 1848. The word is derived from the term "People's Charter", which was applied to a legislative program submitted to Parliament in 1837 by the London Workingmen's Association. The Chartist movement, which the association sponsored, resulted from widespread dissatisfaction with the Reform Bill of 1832 and the Poor Law of 1834, legislation that workingmen considered discriminatory. *See* REFORM BILLS.

The People's Charter contained six specific demands, including suffrage for all male citizens twenty-one years of age and over, elections by secret ballot, and annual Parliamentary elections. When these demands were rejected by the House of Commons, the association launched a nationwide campaign for its program, and about 1,250,000 persons signed a petition to Parliament requesting that the charter be enacted into law.

When Parliament again rejected the charter, the Chartists planned direct action in the form of a general strike. The strike failed, but an insurrection broke out in Monmouthshire in November, 1839, and many Chartist leaders were arrested and imprisoned. Chartism was in a period of decline until 1848, when another petition was sent to Parliament. Despite a large public demonstration, the charter was again rejected because of insufficient and fictitious signatures. The Chartist movement gradually disintegrated thereafter, but all of the program, except the demand for annual Parliamentary elections, eventually became law.

**CHARTRES** (anc. *Carnutes; Autricum; civitas Carnutum*), city in France, and capital of Eure-et-Loir Department, on the Eure R., about 45 miles s.w. of Paris. Chartres consists of an upper and lower town connected by steep streets. The highest point of the city is crowned by the world-famous medieval Cathedral of Notre

Dame (12th and 13th centuries) noted for the beauty of its south spire, its statuary, its magnificent 13th-century stained glass, rose window, and its Renaissance choir screen. In 1594 Henry IV (q.v.) was crowned king of France in Chartres. The principal industries of the city are brewing, distilling, dyeing, the milling of flour, and the manufacturing of machinery, leather goods, hosiery, and stained glass. Chartres is a market center for the surrounding agricultural region. Pop. (1968) 35,335.

**CHARTREUSE,** liqueur named after the Carthusian monks of the monastery La Grande Chartreuse, near Grenoble, France. Chartreuse was first made at the monastery from a secret formula perfected by the monks about 1757. When the Carthusians (q.v.) were driven out of France in 1903 by anticlerical legislation, the secret of the preparation was taken with them to Tarragona, Spain. The monks were readmitted to France in 1940. The formula is said to be known only to the Father Superior of the order. It has never been discovered by analysis. The varieties of chartreuse, both green and yellow, are considered among the finest liqueurs in the world. They are officially designated *Liqueur des Pères Chartreux.*

**CHARYBDIS.** See SCYLLA AND CHARYBDIS.

**CHASE, Salmon Portland** (1808–73), American statesman, born in Cornish, N.H., and educated at Dartmouth College. As a lawyer in Cincinnati, Ohio, after 1830, he defended numerous fugitive slaves. He was a leading spokesman for the antislavery Liberty Party and helped to found the Free-Soil Party (qq.v.) in 1848. Chase was elected to the United States Senate in 1848 as a Democrat, but separated from the party in 1852 when it committed itself to slavery. In 1855 he was elected governor of Ohio as a Free Soiler, and in 1857 as a member of the newly formed Republican Party, which he helped to found.

From 1861 to 1864 he was secretary of the treasury in the cabinet of President Abraham Lincoln (q.v.). During his term in office Chase developed the national banking system and issued the first legal-tender paper currency not backed by gold. This currency, called greenbacks (see GREENBACK), was used to finance the Federal cause in the American Civil War. Chase resigned from the cabinet because he thought Lincoln's anti-slavery position was too moderate. In 1864, however, Lincoln appointed him Chief Justice of the United States Supreme Court. As Chief Justice Chase presided at the impeachment trial of President Andrew Johnson (q.v.), and wrote a dissent in the well-known Slaughterhouse Cases (q.v.) in 1873. Chase dis-

sented because he felt that this decision by the Federal government would endanger Negro rights in the South. He also took part in decisions that declared unconstitutional the issuing of greenbacks, a policy he had formerly supported.

**CHASE, Samuel** (1741–1811), American jurist, born in Somerset County, Md., and educated privately. He was admitted to the bar in 1761 and became a prominent figure in the American Revolution. As a member of the Maryland Assembly he opposed the Stamp Act (q.v.). He was a delegate to the Continental Congress from 1774 to 1778 and in 1784–85. In 1776 he was a member of the mission that sought unsuccessfully to induce the Canadians to declare war against Great Britain. That same year he signed the Declaration of Independence (q.v.). In 1791 he became chief judge of the Maryland General Court and in 1796 associate justice of the Supreme Court of the United States. Although impeached for his conduct in criticizing the administration of President Thomas Jefferson (q.v.) during a charge to a Maryland grand jury, he was strongly defended and ultimately acquitted by the Senate. Chase continued to serve as a member of the U.S. Supreme Court until his death.

**CHASIDIM.** See HASIDIM.

**CHASTELARD, Pierre de Boscosel de** (1540–64), French poet, born in Dauphiné. Chastelard was a courtier at the court of Francis II (q.v.), King of France. After the death of the king he accompanied Francis' widow, Mary, Queen of Scots (q.v.), to Scotland as a page. Hopelessly in love with the queen, he expressed his love for her in numerous poems. He became so rash that he was found in her bedchamber, seized, and sentenced to death the next day. He was executed in Edinburgh.

**CHASUBLE.** See VESTMENTS, ECCLESIASTICAL: *Vestments in the Roman Catholic Church: Sacrificial Vestments.*

**CHAT,** common name for a North American bird, *Icteria virens,* the largest species of the Wood Warbler family (Parulidae); see WOOD WARBLER. Known also as the yellow-breasted chat, it breeds in the eastern United States and winters in Mexico and Central America. It is about 7½ in. long and has a bright yellow breast and throat, a white abdomen, and olive-green upper parts. A variety of yellow-breasted chat found in the western States has a longer tail and is called the long-tailed chat.

The chat feeds on insects and builds its nest in thickets near the ground. The eggs, usually five in number, are white and spotted with brown. Like the mockingbird, the chat has a wide variety of imitative calls. The male has a clownish reputation. During the mating season he performs droll aerial gymnastics accompanied by a mixture of whistles, toots, and clucks.

The name chat is applied in Europe to several genera of birds belonging to the Thrush family (Turdidae).

**CHÂTEAU** or **CHÂTEL** or **CASTEL,** names applied in France and other parts of the Continent to residences of the feudal lords of the soil. The name *château fort* is applied to the fortified castles (*see* CASTLE) erected before the 15th century; the *château de plaisance* ("château of pleasure") refers to a residential château. Typical examples of the latter type are Chenonceaux (q.v.) and Chambord (*see* CHAMBORD, CHÂTEAU DE). In modern usage, the term "château" is also applied to the French country house when the proprietor is also the owner of extensive adjoining land.

**CHATEAUBRIAND, Vicomte François René de** (1768–1848), French writer and statesman, born in Saint-Malo, Brittany. He entered the French army in 1786, and was in Paris during the early years of the French Revolution. Refusing to join the Royalists or the radical revolutionaries, he came to the United States in 1791 supposedly to search for the Northwest Passage (q.v.). He traveled, however, only on the eastern coast. Learning about the arrest of Louis XVI (q.v.), King of France, Chateaubriand returned to France in 1792 and fought with the Royalist army for a short time. Several months later, wounded and ill, he became an émigré. He lived in England until 1800. There he published his first book in 1797, an essay on revolutions. Returning to France under a false name, he found favor with First Consul Napoléon Bonaparte, later Napoleon I (q.v.), Emperor of France, who gave him a diplomatic post. He resigned and turned against Napoleon in 1804, however, in protest against Napoleon's execution of Louis Antoine Henri de Bourbon-Condé, Duc d'Enghien (q.v.). After the Bourbon restoration Chateaubriand was made a peer of France in 1815, ambassador to Great Britain in 1822, and minister of foreign affairs in 1823–24. He was one of the most important French writers of the first half of the 19th century. He introduced new and exotic types of character and background, principally the Indians and scenery of North America, and emphasized introspection, generally of a pessimistic nature, as exemplified in his novels *Atala* (1801) and *René* (1802). These new literary elements mark him as a forerunner of the Romantic period in French literature; *see* ROMAN-

*Vicomte François René de Chateaubriand, prominent literary and political figure of the 19th century.*
Bettmann Archive

TICISM. In addition in *La Génie du Christianisme* (1802; Eng. trans., *The Genius of Christianity;* 1856) he asserted that Christianity was morally and aesthetically superior to other religions. This assertion had a profound influence on the religious and literary life of his time. Among his other important works are other defenses of Christianity, partly imaginary accounts of his travels in America, and his autobiography, *Memoires d'Outre-tombe* ("Memoirs from Beyond the Tomb", 1849–50).

**CHÂTEAU-THIERRY, BATTLE OF,** part of the Second Battle of the Marne, in World War I. It is notable in American history as the first victorious action of American troops in that war. *See* MARNE, BATTLE OF THE; WORLD WAR I: *The Campaigns and Other Events of 1918.*

**CHATHAM, Earl of, William Pitt, called the Elder.** *See under* PITT.

**CHATHAM ISLANDS,** small island group of New Zealand, in the Pacific Ocean about 536 miles E. of Christchurch, and forming the county of South Island, New Zealand. Chatham (or Wharekauri) Island, the largest of the group, is about 38 mi. long and has a maximum width of 25 mi. Of volcanic origin, it has elevations up to 1000 ft. above sea level and contains numerous small lakes. Pitt (or Rangiauria) Island, the next largest, has an area of 25 sq.mi. Waitangi, on Chatham Island, is the chief settlement. Sheep and cattle are raised on the Islands, and fishing is an important industry. Wool and frozen fish are exported. The islands were discovered in 1791 by a British naval commander. In 1831 the Maori (q.v.), a Polynesian seafaring people that began a great migration to New Zealand and other islands centuries earlier, took possession of the Chatham Islands, and killed most of the aboriginal inhabitants, a Polynesian people known as Morioris. The present population comprises Maoris, Europeans, and a few aborigines. Area, 372 sq.mi.; pop. (1971) 716.

**CHATTAHOOCHEE,** river of the United States, rising in the Appalachian Mts., in N.E. Georgia. About 410 mi. long, the Chattahoochee crosses the State in a southwesterly direction to West Point, Ga., where it turns S., forming part of the boundary between Georgia and Alabama and part of the boundary between Georgia and Florida. At the S.W. corner of Georgia it unites with the Flint R. to form the Apalachicola R. of Florida. The river is navigable for steamboats as far north as Columbus, Ga. Lake Lanier, N.E. of Atlanta, was formed by the Buford Dam on the Chattahoochee, and is a popular recreational area and storage reservoir.

**CHATTANOOGA,** city and port of entry in Tennessee, and county seat of Hamilton Co., on the Tennessee R., about 110 miles S.W. of Knoxville, and adjoining the Georgia boundary on the S. It is located in the area served by the Tennessee Valley Authority (q.v.), or T.V.A., which furnishes inexpensive, abundant hydroelectric power. Chattanooga, almost surrounded by mountains, lies within a coal-producing, farming, and timber-yielding area. The city is one of the leading industrial centers of the South and is served by several airlines and railroads. In Chattanooga the chief manufactures are chemicals, durable and nondurable goods, and textiles.

Among the principal structures of the city are the post office, which also houses the main headquarters of the T.V.A., and the Federal courthouse, a noted example of modern architecture, constructed in 1934; Union Station, erected in 1858; and Soldiers and Sailors Memorial Auditorium, in a modified Italian Renaissance style, dating from the early 1920's. Noteworthy educational institutions include the University of Chattanooga, founded in 1886, and Tennessee Temple College, founded in 1946.

Many historic landmarks and scenic attractions are located in Chattanooga and vicinity, making the city a popular tourist center. Several battles of the American Civil War were fought in the surrounding area; see CHATTANOOGA, BATTLE OF; CHICKAMAUGA, BATTLE OF. The sites of these battles are largely preserved in the Chickamauga and Chattanooga National Military Park, a beau-

tiful wooded tract covering 8190.39 acres. Situated mostly in Georgia, the park contains nearly 2000 battle-line tablets, regimental markers, and other guides inscribed with detailed descriptions of the military actions. Other features of the park include Signal Mt., site of a Confederate observation post; Orchard Knob, scene of the first Union success in the Battle of Chattanooga and headquarters of the Union commander, General Ulysses Simpson Grant (q.v.); Lookout Mountain (q.v.), on which was fought the second phase of the battle, known as the "Battle above the Clouds", and parts of Missionary Ridge (q.v.), where the fiercest and most decisive phase of the battle took place; the National Cemetery, with the graves of more than 5000 Confederate and Union soldiers; and a large Confederate cemetery. Access to the summit of Lookout Mt. is by an inclined railway, which attains a grade of 72 percent.

The name of the city is believed to be the Indian designation for Lookout Mt., that is, "rock rising to a point". Protestant missionaries were active among Indians living in the area as early as 1817, but the site of the present-day city was not permanently settled until 1835. Chartered as a town in 1839, Chattanooga later became an important river port. In the 1840's and 1850's the extension of railroads to Chattanooga spurred its development; in 1851 it was incorporated as a city. During the Civil War the city was extensively damaged. Pop. (1960) 130,009; (1970) 119,082.

**CHATTANOOGA, BATTLE OF,** major engagement of the American Civil War (see CIVIL WAR, THE AMERICAN) fought on Nov. 23–25, 1863, between a Union army of about 60,000 men under General Ulysses Simpson Grant (q.v.), and a Confederate force of approximately 40,000 under General Braxton Bragg (q.v.). Following an earlier defeat at Chickamauga (see CHICKAMAUGA, BATTLE OF), the Union Army withdrew to Chattanooga. The Confederates laid siege and cut off Union supply lines and communications. Bragg's army was entrenched on Lookout Mt. (q.v.), 3 miles S.W. of Chattanooga, and on parts of Missionary Ridge (q.v.), running parallel to Lookout Mt.

On Oct. 27–28 Union forces seized Brown's Ferry on the Tennessee R., west of Chattanooga, restoring a supply route into the city. Troops of the 11th and 12th Corps, under the Union general Joseph Hooker (q.v.), also seized the valley of Lookout Creek, west of Lookout Mt. Grant then halted further operations until the arrival of four reinforcement divisions under General William Tecumseh Sherman (q.v.). On Nov. 23

Union troops captured Orchard Knob, an elevation in the plain between Chattanooga and Missionary Ridge. Grant ordered an assault on Lookout Mt. at 8 A.M. on Nov. 24, and by the morning of the 25th Hooker had driven the Confederates from their positions.

The decisive phase of the battle began at 7 A.M. on Nov. 25, when Sherman's force, consisting of six divisions, attacked Confederate entrenchments on the northern slopes of Missionary Ridge. Unable to make headway, however, Grant ordered General George Henry Thomas (q.v.) to make a diversionary assault on the Confederate earthworks along the western base of the ridge. Simultaneously, Hooker's forces stormed the southern and eastern flanks of Missionary Ridge. Thomas' men, disregarding orders to advance no faster than the first line of earthworks, continued on up the steep slopes and, in one of the most remarkable charges known in military history, carried the enemy fortifications along the crest. The panic-stricken Confederates fled in disorder. During the night the remnants of Bragg's Army withdrew northward.

Grant's victory forced the Confederates to evacuate Tennessee and made possible Sherman's subsequent march through Georgia. Union casualties in the battle were estimated at about 5800; Confederate casualties, about 6700. The battlefield was established as the 8190-acre Chickamauga and Chattanooga National Military Park in 1890.

**CHATTEL,** in law, term nearly synonymous with personal property. As distinguished from real property, or real estate, the title to which passes directly to the heir, a chattel is property, the title to which, upon the death of the owner, passes to the executor or administrator of the estate. Chattel refers to those kinds of personal property that are movable and may be possessed. Thus, choses in possession (things) are chattels, but choses in action (legal claims for moneys due), although personal property, are not chattels in the technical sense.

Certain objects that are a part of real estate may become chattels upon being severed from it, as timber which has been cut, or ore mined and removed from the land; certain other objects that are still attached to and form a part of real property, such as growing crops, are for some purposes regarded as chattels. On the other hand, chattels that become attached to the land or are used as a part of the real estate generally lose their character as chattels and become real estate. Thus materials used in constructing a house or other structure forming a part of real estate are real estate. Chattels that are affixed to the real estate but capable of removal, like machinery and articles of furniture, retain their character as chattels for some purposes, but for other purposes they are deemed real estate. *See* PROPERTY.

**CHATTERTON, Thomas** (1752–70), British poet, born in Bristol, England, and educated at the Colston Free School. As a boy he learned to read from an old, Gothic-lettered Bible, and studied inscriptions and medieval manuscripts in the ancient Church of Saint Mary Redcliffe in Bristol. At fourteen he was apprenticed to an attorney, but devoted all his spare time to writing manuscripts in imitation of those he had studied. From 1765 to 1770 he wrote a series of poems in imitative Middle English, purporting to have been written by Thomas Rowley, an imaginary 15th-century monk. In 1768, when the new Bristol bridge was opened, Chatterton attracted attention by contributing to a newspaper an account of the opening of the old bridge in 1248. This account, his own composition, he claimed to have found in a 13th-century manuscript in Redcliffe Church. In 1769 he sent to the British writer Horace Walpole (*see under* WALPOLE) a manuscript containing several of his so-called Rowley poems. Walpole, at first enthusiastic, rejected the manuscripts when he found that they were not genuine.

Not finding the study of law congenial, Chatterton went to London in 1770 to engage in literary work. He wrote at a furious rate, producing squibs, political essays, satiric poems, tales, and letters. His work earned him little, however, and, despairing, he eventually committed suicide. The Rowley poems are characterized by rich invention, intensely romantic imagination, and sensitive feeling. They had considerable influence on the work of the British poets John Keats (q.v.) and Samuel Taylor Coleridge (*see under* COLERIDGE) and other poets of the British Romantic movement; *see* ROMANTICISM. Chatterton was also a hero to the British Pre-Raphaelite poets; *see* PRE-RAPHAELITES.

**CHAUCER, Geoffrey** (1343?–1400), first major English poet, born in London, and educated probably at Saint Paul's Cathedral School in London. In 1357 he was a page in the household of Lionel of Antwerp, 1st Duke of Clarence (1338–68), the youngest son of Edward III (q.v.), King of England. While serving from 1359 to 1360 during the Hundred Years' War with the English army in France, Chaucer was taken prisoner and later ransomed. By 1366 he had married Philippa de Roet, whose sister, Catherine Swynford, became the third wife of John of

Gaunt (q.v.), another of the king's sons and a patron of Chaucer. Between 1366 and his death Chaucer held a number of official appointments and traveled on diplomatic missions, so presumably he had become a substantial man of affairs. He journeyed to France and Flanders on government business and at least twice (1372–73, 1378) to Italy, where, it is supposed, he first came under the influence of the works of the Italian writers Dante Alighieri, Petrarch, and Giovanni Boccaccio (qq.v.). Chaucer held the important and lucrative post of controller of the customs of wools, skins, and hides for London from 1374 to 1386. For part of that time he had the use of a house above Aldgate, one of the gates of the city. He seems to have maintained residence thereafter mainly in Kent, for which he served as justice of the peace (1385) and member of Parliament (1386). In 1389 he was appointed clerk of the king's works, in charge of the building and repair of extensive royal establishments. This office proved to be hazardous, for he was assaulted once and robbed at least twice during a period of four days in 1390; he resigned in 1391. He then was appointed deputy forester of the royal forest of North Petherton. Toward the end of his life he apparently enjoyed the favor first of Richard II and later of Henry IV (qq.v.), kings of England, although records suggest that he was in financial difficulties. Chaucer is buried in Westminster Abbey (q.v.), in the Poets' Corner.

The works Chaucer wrote before about 1382 are dominated by a prevailing literary mode of the later Middle Ages. This is characterized by a symbolic interaction among allegorical or fanciful personages who often are in a garden closed off from the world or in a dream landscape. Most of these early poems are composed in the octosyllabic couplet characteristic of medieval narrative verse.

Chaucer's translation of the popular 13th-century work Le Roman de la Rose ("The Romance of the Rose") by the French poets Guillaume de Lorris (q.v.) and Jean Clopinel, known as Jean de Meung, belonged probably to this period. Another early work was The Book of the Duchess (1370?), a sensitive and evocative elegy in the form of a dream vision, written in honor of Blanche, the first wife of John of Gaunt. The unfinished poem The House of Fame (1372?–80?) was a partly humorous, very fanciful dream vision in which, in imitation of a more solemn scene in Dante's The Divine Comedy, Chaucer himself is carried by a talkative eagle from earth to a strange realm in which all our history and individual reputations are shown to depend on partly faulty information. In The Parlement of Foules (1380?–86?), or The Parliament of Birds, he is led in a dream into a garden, where he first enters a temple dedicated to the goddess Venus and devoted apparently to romantic and sensual love, and then sees the judgment of Dame Nature in distributing mates to various birds representing various kinds of people. Part of his intention was to portray love in marriage sympathetically.

Chaucer's later works, written between about 1382 and his death, generally depicted concrete individuals in the everyday world; they contained notable technical innovations. During this period he made extensive use of the rhyme-royal (a seven-line iambic pentameter stanza) in his conservative, formal, or religious narratives, and he introduced the iambic pentameter couplet into English verse, using it in his more secular or satirical compositions. See VERSIFICATION: English Versification.

At the beginning of The Legend of Good Women (1380?–86?) Chaucer again employed the dream vision but went on to the successive stories of famous women whose love was villainously betrayed by men. Troilus and Criseyde (1385?), a romance of ancient Troy, reflected another romance on the same subject by Boccaccio; Chaucer's work, however, differed in representing sensitively the psychological stages of the noble but inconstant Criseyde's love for and desertion of the warrior and prince Troilus. The poem related these occurrences to a larger view of man's fate, partly through the reactions of the worldly-wise, middle-aged character Pandarus. Chaucer's masterpiece, The Canterbury Tales, written probably after 1387, comprised a series of extraordinarily diverse tales and viewpoints tied together by revelations of the characters of a band of pilgrims. Chaucer exhibited in this work his mastery of story form and his understanding of the human condition. See CANTERBURY TALES, THE. He also wrote shorter poems, prose treatises, and other translations, some of which have been lost.

From his own time onward, Chaucer has been considered among the greatest of English poets. His breadth of human understanding and his loving and often jovial creation of individual human character are qualities which have endeared his work to generations of readers. He brought together in literary works of a new subtlety and urbanity the courtly and idealized view of life common to medieval romance, the spiritual insight common to medieval religious works, and the robust and lusty perception of human frailty common to medieval satire.

A Chaucer portrait illustrates the eulogy written for him by a contemporary, the poet Thomas Hoccleve. *Bettman Archive*

How þat þ[o] seruaunt was mayden marie
And sat his sone floure and fructifie

Al þogh his lyfe be queynt þe resemblaunce
Of him hath in me so fressh lyflynesse
þat to putte othir men in remembraunce
Of his psone I haue heere his lyknesse
Do make to þis ende in soothfastnesse
þat þei þt haue of him left þought & mynde
By þis peynture may ageyn him fynde

The ymages þt in þ chirche been
Maken folk þenke on god & on his seyntes
Whan þe ymages þei be holden & seen
Were oft vnsyte of hem causith restreyntes
Of þoughtes goode whan a þing depeynt is
Or entailled if men take of it heede
Thoght of þe lyknesse it wil in hym brede

Yit some holden oppynyon and sey
þat none ymages schuld i maked be
þei erren foule & goon out of þe wey
Of trouth haue þei scant sensibilite
Passe ouer þt now blessid trinite
Vppon my maistres soule mercy haue
ffor him lady eke þy mcy I craue

Moore othir þing wolde I fayne speke & touche
Heere in þis booke but such is my dulnesse
ffor þt al voyde and empty is my pouche
þat al my lust is queynt wt hevynesse
And heuy spirit commaundith stilnesse

From the Norman Conquest in 1066 to Chaucer's time, French and Latin were the languages of the upper classes of England. Subsequently his *The Parlement of Foules, Troilus and Criseyde,* and *The Canterbury Tales* proved most influential in establishing English as a literary language; see ENGLISH LANGUAGE: *History.* Chaucer's poetry set the style, vocabulary, and metrics of English and Scottish verse for more than a century after his death. It has been held in wide esteem in all succeeding ages, as attested by the adaptation of some of his works into Modern English by the poets John Dryden, Alexander Pope, and William Wordsworth (qq.v.). A.K.H.

**CHAUDIÈRE,** river of Canada, in Québec Province, rising in Lake Mégantic. Flowing generally N.W., it joins the Saint Lawrence R. about 7 mi. above the city of Québec. The Chaudière is about 120 mi. long. The falls of the same name are 2½ mi. above the mouth of the river.

**CHAULMOOGRA,** common name for any tree of the genera *Taraktogenos* and *Hydnocarpus,* growing in Burma and the East Indies. The large, soft fruit have a hairy surface and contain a few large seeds. From the seeds a clear, yellow oil, chaulmoogra oil, is obtained; the oil was formerly used in the treatment of leprosy and skin diseases. The principal active constituents of the oil are esters of chaulmoogric acid, $C_{18}H_{32}O_2$, and hydnocarpic acid, $C_{10}H_{28}O_2$.

**CHAU PHU,** formerly CHAUDOC, city in South Vietnam, and administrative center of Chaudoc Province, on the Song Hau Giang (Bassac R.), near the border with Cambodia, about 110 miles W. of Saigon. The city is linked with the port of Ha Tien on the Gulf of Siam by the Vinhte Canal. Chau Phu is the center of an irrigated area producing rice, corn, sugarcane, yams, castor beans, and kapok. Industries include silk weaving, boatbuilding, and distilling. Situated in an area of Cochin China (q.v.) formerly dominated by the Khmer people, Chau Phu was taken by the Annamese in the 18th century and by the French in 1867. The city's name was changed about 1965. Pop. (latest est.) 51,600.

**CHAUSSON, Ernest** (1855–99), French composer, born in Paris, and educated in law at the University of Paris. In 1879 he entered the Paris Conservatory and studied under the French composers Jules Émile Frédéric Massenet and César Auguste Franck (qq.v.). Franck especially influenced Chausson's works, which include operas, choral works, songs, chamber music, church music, and compositions for orchestra and for piano. Best known are his Symphony in B flat major, op. 20 (1890) and *Poème* for violin and orchestra, op. 25 (1896).

**CHAUTAUQUA,** movement in adult education. *See* EDUCATION, ADULT.

**CHAUVINISM,** excessive or blind patriotism. Chauvinism, like jingoism, is characterized as extreme patriotism often accompanied by a belligerent, aggressive foreign policy. The word is derived from the name of a French soldier, Nicolas Chauvin (fl. 1815), who continually talked of the achievements of Napoleon I (q.v.), Emperor of France, and of his own determination to take revenge for Napoleon's defeat at Waterloo. Vaudevillians of the day seized upon him as a subject for the comic stage, and thus the term chauvinist got its meaning.

**CHAVANNES, Puvis de.** *See* PUVIS DE CHAVANNES, PIERRE.

**CHÁVEZ, Carlos** (1899– ), Mexican composer and conductor, born in Mexico City. He studied piano with the Mexican composer and pianist Manuel María Ponce (1882–1948) but was largely self-taught in composition. In 1928 he was appointed director of the National Conservatory of Mexico, and in the same year he organized and became the permanent conductor of the Mexican Symphony Orchestra. He also conducted many orchestras in the United States and Europe. In 1960 Chávez organized the Composer's Workshop at the National Conservatory.

Chávez' most characteristic works, such as the ballet *El Fuego Nuevo* ("The New Fire", 1921) and the *Sinfonía India* (1935), employ the rhythmic figurations, melodic character, and percussion of Mexican-Indian music without actually quoting from folk sources. While most of his earlier pieces echo the pulsating rhythms of folk dance and contain harsh and percussive dissonances, or mixtures of discordant sounds, many later works bear little relationship to folk music (q.v.). His chamber music, in particular, contains intervals of various sizes as well as single points of sound arranged into nonrepeating patterns. Other works by Chávez include the ballet *HP* ("Horsepower", 1932), which represented a mu-

sical trend in the 1920's and 1930's toward glorifying machines; the opera *Panfilo and Lauretta* (1957); and several symphonies. Among his books are *Toward a New Music* (1942) and *Musical Thought* (1961).

**CHAVEZ, Cesar Estrada** (1927– ), American labor leader, born near Yuma, Ariz. He left school after the sixth grade, but having attended more than thirty elementary schools as a child migrant worker he was almost illiterate. He served in the United States Navy during World War II. From 1952 until 1962 he worked for the Community Service Organization, a self-help group. Then he began his efforts to create a farm workers union. Known at first as the National Farm Workers Association, the union was chartered in 1966 by the American Federation of Labor and Congress of Industrial Organizations (q.v.) as the United Farm Workers Organizing Committee, with Chavez as its president. Chavez gained much attention as leader of a nationwide boycott of California table grapes in 1968 in a drive to achieve labor contracts. In 1973, however, the rival International Brotherhood of Teamsters began to make inroads into the United Farm Workers membership.

**CHAYEVSKY, Paddy.** *See* DRAMA: *The New Drama.*

**CHAZARS.** *See* KHAZARS.

**CHEAT.** *See* BROME GRASS.

**CHEBOKSARY,** city and river port of the Soviet Union, in the Russian S.F.S.R., capital of the Chuvash A.S.S.R., 85 miles W. of Kazan' and 360 miles E. of Moscow. A rail-spur terminus on the Volga R., the city is a processing center for forest and farm products. It also produces leather goods, textiles, alcohol, electrical parts, bricks, and sunflower oil. Cheboksary is the site of a Chuvash regional museum, a 16th-century monastery, a 17th-century church, and teachers' and agricultural colleges. Inhabited since 1371, the area was taken by the Russians in 1552; the city was founded in 1556. Pop. (1970) 216,139.

**CHECHEN** or **TCHETCHEN,** people of the eastern Caucasus Mts. (*see* CAUCASIA), who speak a Caucasian or Japhetic language known as Chechen. Under their native Muslim chiefs, the Chechens fought against Russian aggression in the 18th and 19th centuries. In 1859, after the capture of the chieftain Shamyl (1797–1871), many of them fled to Armenia. Today the Chechens comprise about 55 percent of the population of the Chechen-Ingush A.S.S.R. *See* GEORGIAN LANGUAGE AND LITERATURE.

**CHECHEN-INGUSH AUTONOMOUS SOVIET SOCIALIST REPUBLIC,** administrative division of the Soviet Union, in the Russian S.F.S.R., on the N.E. slopes of the Greater Caucasus Mts. Chechen-Ingush is a major producer of oil in the Soviet Union. The capital city, Groznyy, the chief oil-refining center, is connected by pipelines with the Caspian and Black seas. Benzene is a major product. Engineering, food processing, wood, and the manufacture of chemicals and of wood products are important industries, as is agriculture. With the aid of irrigation in the Sunzha and Terek river valleys grains, fruits, and vegetables are produced. In 1934 the Chechen Oblast (formed 1922) and the Ingush Oblast (formed 1924) were united to form the Chechen-Ingush Autonomous Oblast, which became a republic in 1936. Dissolved in 1944 because the populace had collaborated with the Germans during World War II, it was reestablished in 1957. Area, 7350 sq.mi.; pop. (1970 est.) 1,065,000.

**CHECKERBERRY.** *See* PARTRIDGEBERRY.

**CHECKERS,** *or* DRAUGHTS, game played on a square checkered board, divided into sixty-four equal square spaces colored alternately black and red or any two strongly contrasted colors. The draughts, or checkers, are circular and flat. Other varieties of the game that differ somewhat in rules from American checkers are Chinese, English, Polish, Spanish, Italian, and Turkish checkers. A similar game was played by the Egyptians as early as 1600 B.C., and a form of it was popular in ancient Greece.

Two persons play the game, each having a set of twelve men, one set black, the other white, or red. The men may be placed either on the black or light squares, but they must all be placed on one color only. The men may be moved diagonally only, and one square at a time. If an opponent's man stands in the way, no move may take place unless there is a vacant square beyond

into which the piece can be lifted. The man leaped over is "taken" and removed from the board. If an opponent's man is in front of the new position, with an empty space beyond, the second man may also be taken; this is a double jump; longer jumps are possible.

When a man on either side has progressed to the last row on the opposite side, it is entitled to be "crowned", that is, made into a "king". A second man is placed on the first to indicate a king. Like other men, kings can move only diagonally, and only one square at a time except when jumping opponent's men; however, they may move either backward or forward. This additional power gives a great advantage to the player with the greatest number of kings.

The object of the game is to clear the board of all the opponent's men, or to hem them in so that they cannot be moved. If, when it is one player's turn to move, he has no piece he can move, he loses the game.

**CHECKS AND BALANCES.** *See* UNITED STATES: *Government: Division of Powers.*

**CHEDDAR,** Great Britain, town, of Somersetshire, England, on the S. side of the Mendip Hills, about 15 miles S.W. of Bristol. It lies at the entrance of the nearly 1 mi. long Cheddar gorge, noted for the stalactite caverns in its limestone cliffs. Prehistoric remains have been discovered in the caverns, and traces of Roman settlement have been found in the vicinity. Cheddar is noted for the cheese made there and named for it. *See* CHEESE. Pop. (1971) 3330.

**CHEEKTOWAGA,** unincorporated town of New York, in Erie Co., adjoining Buffalo on the E. Industries include paper milling, food canning, quarrying, and the manufacture of steel, machinery, wood products, and lenses. Pop. (1960) 84,056; (1970) 113,844.

*At a checkers world-championship meet in Moscow in 1962, grandmaster I. Kuperman of the U.S.S.R. is seen contemplating his next move.* UPI

American Dairy Assn.

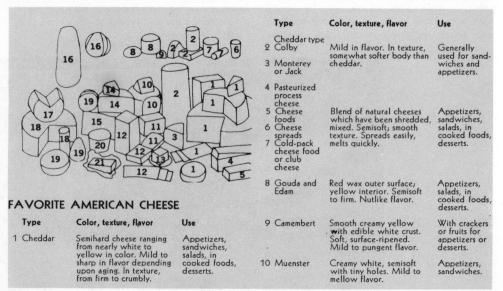

# FAVORITE AMERICAN CHEESE

| Type | Color, texture, flavor | Use |
|---|---|---|
| 1 Cheddar | Semihard cheese ranging from nearly white to yellow in color. Mild to sharp in flavor depending upon aging. In texture, from firm to crumbly. | Appetizers, sandwiches, salads, in cooked foods, desserts. |

| Type | Color, texture, flavor | Use |
|---|---|---|
| Cheddar type | | |
| 2 Colby | Mild in flavor. In texture, somewhat softer body than cheddar. | Generally used for sandwiches and appetizers. |
| 3 Monterey or Jack | | |
| 4 Pasteurized process cheese | | |
| 5 Cheese foods | Blend of natural cheeses which have been shredded, mixed. Semisoft; smooth texture. Spreads easily, melts quickly. | Appetizers, sandwiches, salads, in cooked foods, desserts. |
| 6 Cheese spreads | | |
| 7 Cold-pack cheese food or club cheese | | |
| 8 Gouda and Edam | Red wax outer surface, yellow interior. Semisoft to firm. Nutlike flavor. | Appetizers, salads, in cooked foods, desserts. |
| 9 Camembert | Smooth creamy yellow with edible white crust. Soft, surface-ripened. Mild to pungent flavor. | With crackers or fruits for appetizers or desserts. |
| 10 Muenster | Creamy white, semisoft with tiny holes. Mild to mellow flavor. | Appetizers, sandwiches. |

## FAVORITE AMERICAN CHEESE—Continued

| Type | Color, texture, flavor | Use | Type | Color, texture, flavor | Use |
|---|---|---|---|---|---|
| 11 Brick | Creamy yellow; semisoft with small holes. Mild to sharp flavor. | Appetizers, sandwiches, salads, desserts. | 17 Romano | Yellow-white. Hard, granular (brittle). Sharp, piquant flavor. | Grated in soups, breads, on spaghetti, in cooked foods. |
| 12 Swiss | Light yellow, large holes. Firm. Nutlike sweet flavor. | Appetizers, sandwiches, salads, in cooked foods. | 18 Parmesan | Yellow-white. Hard, granular. Sharp piquant flavor. | Grated in soups, breads, on spaghetti, in cooked foods. |
| 13 Limburger | Semisoft surface ripened cheese. Characteristic strong flavor and aroma. Creamy white interior. | Appetizers or desserts. | 19 Mozzarella and Scamorze | Unripened semisoft cheese. White stretchy cheese— when served hot it becomes chewy. Varying moisture content. Sometimes designated for pizza. Delicate, mild flavor. | Sliced, in cooked foods, on pizza, sandwiches. |
| 14 Blue | Blue-veined, crumbly. Semisoft to firm. Sharp salty flavor. | Appetizers, salads, salad dressings, in cooked foods, desserts. | | | |
| 15 Gorgonzola | Blue green-veined. Semisoft to firm. Sharp, salty flavor. Less moisture than Blue. | Appetizers, salads, salad dressings, in cooked foods, desserts. | 20 Cottage cheese | Soft, mild, white to creamy-white unripened cheese. May be small, medium or large curd. Creamed cottage cheese has added cream. | Appetizers, casseroles, main dishes, cheese cakes, sandwich fillings, salads. |
| 16 Provolone | Light yellow, semihard, smooth and somewhat plastic. Mellow to sharp, smoky flavor. | Appetizers, sandwiches, in cooked foods, desserts. | 21 Cream cheese | White unripened cheese. Soft and smooth. Mild, delicately flavored. | Appetizers, sandwiches, salads, in cooked foods, desserts. |

**CHEESE,** solid or semisolid food product prepared from milk. In the United States today cheese is almost invariably prepared from cows' milk, but the milk of ewes, mares, female goats, or other mammals is equally suitable for cheese making, and has been so used since prehistoric times.

The principal solid constituent of milk is casein (q.v.), a protein. The casein can be made to precipitate by the addition to milk of acid, or of rennet (q.v.) prepared from the gastric juice of calves. When milk is allowed to stand in a warm place, it sours because of the presence of bacteria that convert milk sugar into acid. This acid causes the casein to separate as a curd, leaving a thin, watery portion called whey. This was undoubtedly the earliest method of making cheese and is still used for making pot cheese and cottage cheese, although curd prepared with rennet is today preferred. The curd, however prepared, contains, in addition to protein, most of the other food value of the milk, including fat, minerals, sugar, and vitamins. Because it is compact, can easily be made solid, and can be preserved over long periods of time, cheese has certain advantages over milk that make it an important item in the diet of almost all primitive and many civilized peoples.

Cheddar, or American cheese, which amounts to about one third of U.S. cheese production, is manufactured from whole milk, and contains a small amount of fat. Cottage cheese and pot cheese, constituting about 45 percent of U.S. production, are made from skim milk and contain very little fat. Cream cheese, constituting about 3 percent of U.S. production, is made from cream or cream-enriched milk, and contains from 10 to 50 percent fat.

Cheese may be hard or soft, according to the amount of water left in it and the character of the curing. The action of various kinds of bacteria causes the ripening of cheese, on which the characteristic flavors of the different kinds depend. The principal hard cheeses are the common Cheddar cheese, the English Cheshire and Stilton, the Dutch Edam and Gouda, the Schweitzer (Swiss) or Emmentaler (French product, known also as Gruyère), and the Italian Parmesan and Gorgonzola. Among the soft cheeses are Brie, Camembert, Neufchâtel, Limburger, and Mozzarella. Roquefort is a semisoft French cheese made from sheep's milk.

In the U.S. cheese making was formerly a domestic operation conducted on farms. The first cheese factory was opened in Rome, N.Y., in 1851, and cheese factories have now virtually superseded the making of cheeses on farms. About two thirds of the total national production occurs in Wisconsin, and about half of the remainder in New York. The average annual production amounts to about 4,200,000,000 lb. In addition, between 136,000,000 and 180,000,000 lb. were imported yearly in the early 1970's.

**CHEETAH,** or HUNTING LEOPARD, distinctive species, *Acinonyx jubatus,* of the cat family, Felidae. The cheetah is about the same weight as the leopard, but has a relatively longer body and limbs, and a smaller head. The length of the head and body without the tail is about 4½ ft. Its claws are short and almost nonretractile. The color is yellowish brown with black spots. The cheetah takes its prey by running, rather than by leaping from ambush, and hunts by sight rather than by smell. It is the fastest animal on earth, being able to run at a speed of 70 m.p.h., swifter than the speed of a greyhound (q.v.) dog. It moves about during both daylight hours and bright moonlit nights, and antelope and gazelles are its chief prey. The cheetah was formerly trained and used for hunting in India. Once widely distributed in open and relatively dry parts of Africa and southern Asia, the cheetah has been much reduced in numbers and in range by shooting and alteration of habitat. Its presence in any part of India is now doubtful.

**CHEFOO,** city and seaport of China, in Shantung Province, on the N. shore of the Shantung peninsula, about 110 miles N.E. of Tsingtao, and about 100 miles S.E. of Lüta on the opposite shore of the Gulf of Chihli. Across the harbor on which Chefoo is situated is the village of Yentai, which is the actual port. Opened to foreign trade in 1863, Chefoo later became a center for the export of raw silk. In Chefoo representatives of Great Britain and China signed the Chefoo Convention in 1876, opening a number of Chinese ports to foreign trade. Chefoo remained a treaty port until 1943, when treaties with the United States and Great Britain ended foreign trading rights in China. Pop. (latest est.) 140,000.

**CHEJU,** city in South Korea, and capital of Cheju Province, on the northern coast of the island of Cheju, on Cheju Strait, 90 miles S. of Mokp'o. In an agricultural area producing grain, soybeans, sweet potatoes, and cotton, the city is a fishing port and produces woven goods, bamboo products, potash, and iodine. The city, a former penal colony, is the site of Cheju College. On the island of Cheju, the Mongol leader Kublai Khan (q.v.) built ships to invade Japan in 1273. The island was made a separate province in 1946, and the city was chartered in 1955. From the 17th century, the island was called Quelpart by Western geographers; and under Japanese rule from 1910 to 1945 the city was called Saishu. Pop. (1970) 106,456.

*Cheetah,* Acinonyx jubatus UPI

**CHEKA,** name of the first secret police organization of the Union of Soviet Socialist Republics. The term "Cheka" is a shortened form in Russian for an organization with the full title of All-Russian Extraordinary Commission for the Suppression of Counterrevolution and Sabotage. The Cheka was founded Dec. 20, 1917 to cope with sabotage and other counterrevolutionary activities against the Bolshevik government that had come into being by revolution in November. The Cheka was at first limited to making preliminary investigations of people suspected of counterrevolutionary activities. After the revival of terrorist activities against the government, including the wounding of the founder of the Soviet Union Vladimir Ilich Lenin (q.v.) in Moscow on Aug. 30, 1918, the Cheka was granted more extensive powers. These included the power of making summary arrests and of judging and executing those found guilty. Cheka activities, known as the Red Terror, claimed almost 50,000 lives. In 1922 the Cheka was reorganized as the G.P.U. (q.v.), from the initial letters of the Russian words for Government Political Administration.

**CHEKHOV, Anton Pavlovich,** or CHEKOV, Anton Pavlovich or TCHEKHOV, Anton Pavlovich (1860–1904), Russian dramatist and short-story writer, born in Taganrog, and educated in medicine at the University of Moscow. While still at the university he published humorous magazine stories and sketches. He rarely practiced medicine because of his success as a writer and because he had tuberculosis, at that time incurable. The first collection of his humorous writings, *Motley Stories,* appeared in 1886, and his first play, *Ivanov,* was produced in Moscow the next year. In 1890 Chekhov visited Sakhalin Island off the coast of Siberia, and later wrote *Island Sakhalin* (1891–94), an account of his visit. Chekhov's frail health caused him to move from his small country estate near Moscow to the warmer climate of the Crimea in 1897. He also made frequent trips to health resorts in western Europe. Near the end of the century he met the Russian actor and producer Stanislavski (q.v.), director of the Moscow Art Theater, which in 1898 produced Chekhov's famous play *The Sea Gull.* This association of playwright and director, which continued until Chekhov's death, led to the production of several of his one-act dramas and his other well-known plays, *Uncle Vanya* (1899), *The Three Sisters* (1901), and *The Cherry Orchard* (1904).

Modern critics consider Chekhov one of the masters of the short-story form in modern literature. He was largely responsible for the modern

*Anton Pavlovich Chekhov*          Bettmann Archive

type of short story depending for effect on mood and symbolism rather than on plot. His narratives, rather than having a climax and resolution, are a thematic arrangement of impressions and ideas. Using themes relating to the ordinary, everyday life of the landed gentry and professional middle class, Chekhov portrays the pathos of life in Russia before the 1905 revolution: the futile, boring, and lonely lives of people unable to communicate with one another. Examples of Chekhov's best known stories are included in the posthumously published *Darling and Other Stories* (1910).

In the Russian theater Chekhov is preeminently a representative of modern naturalism (q.v.). His plays, like his stories, are studies of the spiritual failure of characters in a society that is disintegrating. To portray these themes Chekhov developed a new dramatic technique, which he called "indirect action". He concentrated on subtleties of characterization and interaction between characters rather than on plot and direct action. In a Chekhov play dramatic events of importance take place off the stage. Although some of his plays were originally rejected in Moscow, his technique is very familiar to modern playwrights and audiences, and his plays continue to appear frequently in theatrical repertories.

**CHELAN LAKE,** lake in north-central Washington in Chelan County. It is about 50 mi. long and varies from about ½ to 1½ mi. in width. Located in a glacial gorge of the Cascade Range, the lake is fed by mountain streams and drained by the Chelan R., a tributary of the Columbia R. Chelan State Park borders on part of the lake. The 1419-ft. depth of the lake makes it one of the deepest in the United States; the bottom is 340 ft. below sea level.

**CHELSEA,** city of Massachusetts, in Suffolk Co., 3 miles N. of Boston. It is on a peninsula between the estuaries of Chelsea Creek and the Mystic R. On the N. it adjoins the city of Everett. It is connected with Charlestown by a bridge across the Mystic R., and with Boston by ferry and rail. Chelsea is principally a manufacturing city; its industries are lithography, fish canning, and the manufacture of shoes, elastic webbing, wallpaper, furniture, paints, chemicals, rubber goods, marine clocks, machine-shop and foundry products, and bakery products. It is an important center for trade in waste materials and junk. The city's principal buildings include the city hall, the courthouse, the United States naval and marine hospitals, the Massachusetts Soldiers' Home, and Ye Old Pratt House. The United States Coast Guard Station in Chelsea is a supply depot for lighthouses.

Founded in 1624 as Winnisimmet, Chelsea was a part of Boston until 1739 when it was incorporated as a township. In 1857 it was incorporated as a city. In 1908 a fire destroyed most of the city, which was rebuilt within two years. Pop. (1960) 33,749; (1970) 30,625.

**CHELSEA.** *See* KENSINGTON AND CHELSEA, ROYAL BOROUGH OF.

**CHELTENHAM,** urban township of Pennsylvania, in Montgomery Co., on Tacony Creek, adjoining Philadelphia on the N. It is composed of many chiefly residential villages and sections, including Edge Hill, Melrose Park, Cheltenham Hills, and Elkins Park. Manufactures include hosiery, wood products, paint, tape, ink, and cement. Cheltenham is the site of Beaver College, Faith Theological Seminary, the Curtis Arboretum, and a Quaker meetinghouse built in 1682. Pop. (1960), 35,990; (1970) 40,238.

**CHELTENHAM,** Great Britain, municipal and parliamentary borough of Gloucestershire, England, about 8 miles N.E. of the city of Gloucester. A resort town, Cheltenham is in a picturesque valley on the Chelt, a small stream which rises in the adjacent hills and flows into the Severn R. Among the numerous churches of the town is the parish church of Saint Mary, dating from the 14th century. Among the schools are the free

grammar school (1576); Cheltenham College (1843), a private school for boys; and Ladies' College, Cheltenham (1854), also private.

Roman remains have been discovered at Cheltenham. In the 13th century the town was noted for its fairs and markets. After 1716 when mineral springs were discovered, Cheltenham became known as a health resort. Festivals of contemporary British music and literature are held there each year. Pop. (1971) 75,500.

**CHELYABINSK,** city of the Soviet Union, in the Russian S.F.S.R., capital of Chelyabinsk Oblast, on the Miass R., in the S. foothills of the Ural Mt., about 900 miles S.E. of Moscow. Located on the Trans-Siberian Railroad, in a rich coal-mining area, Chelyabinsk is a major transportation and industrial center of the Soviet Union. One of the largest tractor plants in the U.S.S.R. is in Chelyabinsk. Other industries include iron and steel mills and plants manufacturing agricultural machinery, aircraft, and chemicals. The city was founded in 1658 as a fortress on the Russian frontier, and during the next century became an agricultural and coal-trading center. Industrial growth began with the building on the railroad in 1892 and the opening of a steel mill in 1928. Pop. (1972 est.) 910,000.

**CHELYUSKIN, CAPE.** *See* CAPE CHELYUSKIN.

**CHEMICAL ANALYSIS,** separation of complex materials into their constituents or specification of the composition in terms of simpler constituents, as opposed to chemical synthesis, which treats of the union of simpler materials to produce more complex substances. Chemical analysis is of two kinds: qualitative analysis, which determines the quality or nature of the ingredients of a sample; and quantitative analysis, which determines the exact proportion, by weight or volume, of each of the constituents. Corresponding to the divisions of inorganic chemistry and organic chemistry (*see* CHEMISTRY: *Divisions*), chemical analysis is also divided into inorganic analysis, which is concerned with investigation of the components of the atmosphere, water, soils, and rocks; and organic analysis, which isolates and identifies materials composed principally of carbon compounds.

Frequently the amount of only one ingredient or one kind of ingredient in a sample is of practical interest, for example, the amount of glutens and other materials in a sample of flour. In such cases, a proximate analysis suffices, that is, an estimate of groups of substances rather than of individual components. A proximate analysis of a sample of flour would reveal the amounts of glutens, starches, sugars, albumins, gums, oils, and minerals. Each of these ingredients is actu-

ally a composite of substances, but the distinction of one gluten from another is not necessary in this case. A complete analysis, specifying the nature and amounts of all the constituents of a specimen is termed an ultimate analysis.

Many different procedures prove valuable in chemical analysis, depending on the nature of the material being analyzed and the use that will be made of the findings. Volumetric analysis is based on determining what volume of a standard solution will react with a sample; gravimetric analysis depends on isolating a constituent from the sample and weighing it. In spectro-

*A chemist in a lubricant-research laboratory analyzes a sample of grease for its soap content. Grease is a mixture of petroleum by-products and graphite, with soap as a binding agent.* Standard Oil Co. (N.J.)

photometric analysis, the presence and amount of a constituent are revealed by the amount of light of a particular wavelength that is absorbed by the sample, perhaps after preliminary treatment. Other modern procedures of chemical analysis involve X rays, measurement of electrical potential (*see* POTENTIAL), conductivity, or dielectric (q.v.) constant, various spectroscopy methods (*see* SPECTRUM: *Applications of Spec-*

*trum Analysis*), and measurement of magnetic behavior in electric or magnetic fields and of molecular and submolecular properties.

Methods have been developed for the analysis of very small samples, such as those produced by complicated synthetic procedures. Such micromethods allow elemental analysis of amounts of material as small as a few micrograms, less than one millionth of an ounce. A related but separate development has been the devising of methods to detect trace constituents in proportions as low as one part per million (1 ppm). Powerful insecticides such as DDT must be detected in milk and other food products at levels below 1 ppm, and the impurity content of transistor materials must be monitored at similarly low concentrations. Many of these methods are based on spectrophotometry. Neutron activation analysis, in which artificial radioactivity is induced in certain elements by exposure to a beam of neutrons, is the most sensitive and specific of the modern instrumental methods of trace analysis.

**Organic Analysis.** The analysis of organic samples is more complicated than that of inorganic samples because of the great number of known organic compounds, about 2,000,000. The first step in the analysis of a complex organic material composed of known ingredients is separation of the sample into its constituent substances. Often this requires an elaborate process based on distillation (q.v.), extraction,

*Accurate measurements are basic to chemical analysis, especially in research in microbiology.* Torkel Korling

and fractional crystallization (*see* CRYSTAL). One very valuable means of extraction is chromatography (q.v.). In this procedure the sample, in the form of a vapor or a liquid solution, flows through a column or along a strip of properly chosen adsorbent material. The various constituents interact with the adsorbent with different intensity and thus emerge in a corresponding sequence from the column or strip; the component under study is caught as it emerges and can be subjected to further measurement or examination.

Quantitative analysis plays an important part in identifying a new compound, whether this compound is isolated from natural sources or is synthesized. The compound is always subjected to ultimate, or elemental, analysis to determine the proportions of carbon and hydrogen in the sample, as well as the proportions of nitrogen, chlorine, sulfur, and phosphorus, if they are present. In determining the amounts of carbon and hydrogen, the sample is burned in a stream of oxygen or air in the presence of heated copper oxide. The carbon forms carbon dioxide, which is then absorbed by a strong alkali, and the hydrogen forms water, which is absorbed by calcium chloride or a similar drying agent. The weights of the absorbents before and after absorption are used to calculate the amounts of carbon and hydrogen in the burned sample.

The amount of nitrogen in a sample may be determined by heating it with copper oxide in a stream of carbon dioxide, which converts the sample to water, nitrogen gas, and carbon dioxide. A solution of potassium hydroxide will absorb the carbon dioxide, and the nitrogen will collect over the solution, so that its volume can be measured. The known density of nitrogen then permits calculating the mass of nitrogen formed from the sample.

To help establish the identity of a new compound, its molecular mass is usually determined. One way the mass of a molecule can be determined is by observing the change that takes place in the boiling or freezing point (q.v.) of a solvent when the substance is mixed with it. Another way is by determining the behavior of the substance in a mass spectrometer.

Analysis of a compound also may involve characterization of the molecular structure, that is, the spatial arrangement of the atoms in a molecule. Molecular structure is usually inferred from the chemical behavior and the mode of synthesis of the substance, but very difficult problems of structure may be solved by two newer techniques, X-ray diffraction (*see* X RAY: *Properties of X Rays*) and mass spectrometry. X-ray diffraction may be used to reveal the relative positions of atoms in a crystal. When applied to complicated structures, it is far from simple, but it provided the first identification of the molecular structure of penicillin and of vitamin B-12, for which the British chemist Dorothy Crowfoot Hodgkin (1910– ) received a Nobel Prize in 1964. Mass spectrometry involves study of the fragmentation patterns produced when a substance passes through a mass spectrometer or mass spectrograph (see SPECTROGRAPH, MASS).

A final step in the proof of structure of a natural substance is often the synthesis of the compound, which may take a long time. Quinine (q.v.), for example, was originally identified in 1820 but was not prepared by synthesis until 1944. The question of whether a synthetic product is completely identical with a substance isolated from natural sources is usually answered by determining the melting points of the two separate substances and the melting point of a mixture of the two (mixed-melting-point method). If all three melting points are the same, the two substances are regarded as identical.

**Industrial Applications.** The general methods used in research laboratories have been adapted to meet the needs of industry. Many manufacturing processes require strict control of the composition of ingredients and strict monitoring of the composition of products. Very often small amounts of impurities affect adversely the usefulness of such products as metals, drugs, dyes, photographic materials, and plastics. In copper, for example, the presence of 0.01 percent of phosphorus or arsenic significantly lowers the quality of the metal as an electrical conductor. Recognizing and determining the proportion of trace constituents is often a major concern of industrial analysis.

Because complete chemical analysis of complex samples is often difficult, costly, and time consuming, simple procedures such as those listed below are widely used to provide practical answers for industrial problems.

SPECIFIC GRAVITY. The concentration of a liquid solution may be found by measuring its specific gravity (see DENSITY), which is done by observing the level at which a hydrometer floats in the solution. The acid used in automobile batteries and the fluid in automobile radiators are often analyzed in this way.

FLUORESCENCE. Many substances exhibit a characteristic glow when exposed to ultraviolet, or even to visible, light. For example, when dissolved in ligroin, margarine fluoresces a bright blue and butter fluoresces a faint yellow. Many minerals also fluoresce in characteristic ways; see FLUORESCENCE AND PHOSPHORESCENCE.

SOLUBILITY. Only rocks that contain carbonates effervesce and dissolve in hydrochloric acid, and in this way they can be distinguished in a few seconds. Brass dissolves in nitric acid, but gold does not. Oils and fats in foods dissolve in ether without affecting starches and proteins. Water, alcohol, and acetone may act as selective solvents and thus aid in other identifications.

MELTING AND FREEZING POINTS. The melting temperature of a substance is a characteristic that proves valuable in identification. At one time graphite was confused with lead, but the two materials, however much alike in some respects, show widely different melting behavior.

ROTATION OF THE PLANE OF POLARIZED LIGHT Many naturally occurring substances, including albumin, alkaloids, camphor, sugar, and turpentine (qq.v.), have the ability to rotate the plane of polarization of a beam of light; see OPTICS: *Polarization of Light.* This rotation is often sufficient to detect the presence of the substance causing it and to establish the proportion of the substance.

COLORIMETRY. Estimation of the depth of color of a complex sample may identify a particular ingredient if it is the only ingredient that exhibits color or produces color on addition of an appropriate reagent. Visual comparison with standard samples prepared for the purpose often suffices for identification, but a spectrophotometer gives more accurate results and extends the method to include ultraviolet and infrared radiation. These methods collectively constitute the field of colorimetry.

**Medical Applications.** Because good health is based on good body chemistry, chemical analysis can provide a kind of barometer for gauging the state of health. The detection of both normal and abnormal body constituents can help in detecting abnormal conditions and in monitoring the effects of treatment. Particularly important are analyses of blood, urine, and stomach fluids. Diabetes mellitus (q.v.) was one of the first diseases to be identified by means of a chemical test that detects the presence of reducing sugar in the urine. Many other chemical tests are now made routinely in hospital and clinical laboratories.

As the numbers of medical samples requiring prompt attention have increased, efforts have been made to improve the reliability and speed of the tests and to reduce the size of the required samples. Automated equipment makes it possible to analyze very small samples of blood and urine. A machine called the robot chemist

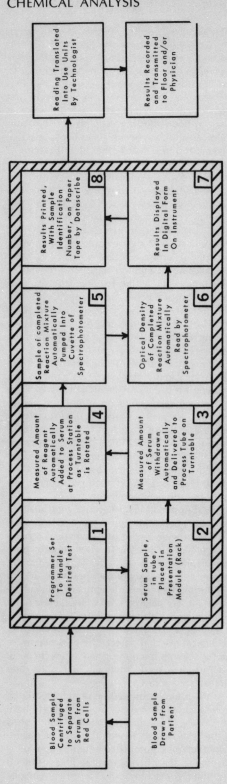

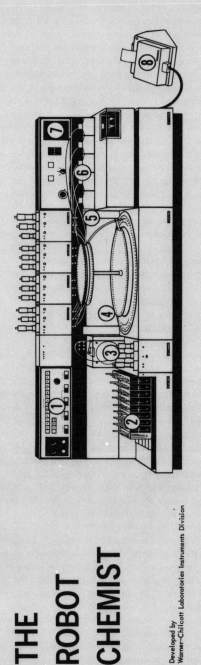

# THE
# ROBOT
# CHEMIST

Developed by
Warner-Chilcott Laboratories Instruments Division

*A computerized aid to modern medicine, the blood analyzer can be programmed to perform a variety of tests from small samples of blood.*

mixes a drop of blood with a drop of an appropriate reagent to determine automatically the levels of cholesterol (q.v.), creatinine, and transaminase (an enzyme), the sedimentation rate (speed of settling of red blood cells), hematocrit (a ratio of red blood cells to whole blood), and other factors that indicate the condition of various organ systems of the body. More complicated blood analyses are performed with the aid of a computer in which a mathematical model of blood composition has been programmed. Colorimeters and spectrophotometers are also used in medical analysis. S.Z.L.

# CHEMICAL COMPOUNDS, SYNTHETIC,

man-made substances that are the result of subjecting natural products to chemical processing. Many of these compounds are produced in great quantities by the chemical industry, and play an important role in the economy, affecting the standard of living, health, nutrition, and almost every human activity; see CHEMISTRY. See also separate articles on most chemical substances mentioned in this article.

The most important of the synthetic chemical compounds in use today are the solvents, soaps and detergents, automotive chemicals, plastics and elastomers, paints and coatings, pharmaceuticals, food additives, cosmetic and personal hygiene chemicals, and biocides.

**Solvents.** The majority of industrial and manufacturing operations require solvents for the purpose of introducing substances into systems in a form in which they can readily react with other substances, or for removing a reaction product, impurity, or undesired by-product from the system. The most common solvent is water, for several reasons: it is available in abundance at low cost, its molecules are highly polar and hence dissolve significant amounts of most polar and ionic substances, it is relatively volatile and can be easily eliminated by evaporation (and recovered, if desired, by condensation), and it is nontoxic and has a relatively low viscosity and high surface tension (qq.v.). Like water, the other common solvents are generally small, simple molecules, such as the following, listed in approximately the order of decreasing polar character: acetone $(CH_3)_2CO$; methanol, or wood alcohol, $CH_3OH$; isopropanol, or isopropyl alcohol, $(CH_3)_2CHOH$; benzene, $C_6H_6$; carbon tetrachloride, $CCl_4$; ether, $(C_2H_5)_2O$; and petroleum ether, $C_6H_{14}$, + other similar hydrocarbons. As the polar character of a solvent diminishes, its compatibility with, or ability to dissolve, polar substances decreases, and its compatibility with nonpolar substances increases. Kerosene is a mixture of hydrocarbons

containing 12 to 13 carbon atoms in the chain. The so-called aircraft dope, and the thinner for lacquers, nail polish, and printing compounds, is amyl acetate, $C_5H_{11}OOCCH_3$. The solvent most widely used in the dry cleaning and degreasing fields is perchloroethylene, $Cl_2C=CCl_2$. See ATOM AND ATOMIC THEORY; MOLECULE; SOLVENT EXTRACTION.

**Soaps and Detergents.** The special property that soaps have of wetting, emulsifying, and floating away dirt particles is the result of their molecular structure. A soap is a salt formed from the reaction of an alkali, such as sodium hydroxide, NaOH, with a long-chain carboxylic acid such as stearic acid, $C_{17}H_{35}COOH$, as follows:

$$C_{17}H_{35}COOH + NaOH \rightarrow C_{17}H_{35}COONa + H_2O$$
(soap)

Different carboxylic acids yield different soaps, the most commonly encountered soaps being based upon the acids that come from the hydrolysis of coconut oil, which yields stearic acid, and palm oil, which yields palmitic acid, $C_{15}H_{31}COOH$. The fundamental feature of the molecular structure of a soap is that it has a nonpolar end, the hydrocarbon chain, that causes it to be soluble in similar nonpolar oils, fats, and greases that are present in dirt and stains, and a polar end, the sodium salt part, $—COO^- Na^+$, that causes it to be strongly attracted to the polar molecules of water.

A detergent is a combination of two different classes of compounds, a wetting agent and a sequestering agent. The wetting agent is generally an alkylbenzene sulfonate; $C_6H_5CH_2 \ldots \ldots CH_2SO_3H$; the length of the hydrocarbon (alkyl) chain and whether it is branched or straight determines its affinity for oils and greases, as well as its biodegradability. The first synthetic wetting agents, introduced at the end of World War II, had a branched chain, but they were found not to be broken down and digested by bacteria, and have now been replaced by straight chain compounds that are readily degraded by bacteria. The sulfonic acid grouping, $—SO_3H$, makes the molecule water-soluble and provides the highly polar section that is essential for its affinity for water. The hydrocarbon end provides the nonpolar part that serves to attach the wetting agent molecule to the nonpolar dirt particles. See DETERGENT; SOAP.

The sequestering agent is a substance that forms complex ions (see ION; IONIZATION) with various species present in the water supply, thereby softening any hardness in the water and preventing the formation of scum or other deposits; see WATER: *Water Purification*. The most common sequestering agent in detergents today is sodium tripolyphosphate, $Na_5P_3O_{10}$. In an effort to reduce the water pollution (q.v.) problem created by discharge of large quantities of phosphates into natural water systems, an alternative sequestering agent, nitrilotriacetic acid, $N(CH_2COOH)_3$, or NTA, is now being used to replace a large part of the phosphate.

A recent addition to detergent products consists of one or more enzymes (q.v.), which are proteins that bring about the hydrolysis and breakdown of some of the macromolecules that produce stubborn stains. Two types of enzymes, both extracted from cultures of *Bacillus subtilis*, are used: proteases, which hydrolyze proteins, and amylases, which hydrolyze carbohydrates.

**Automotive Chemicals.** The chemical compounds that constitute automotive fuels are essentially pure hydrocarbons, the average gasoline being a mixture of six or more, including straight chain and branched chain molecules and a small proportion of unsaturated hydrocarbons. Most such fuels burn more efficiently in high compression engines if a small amount of a volatile lead compound, such as tetraethyl lead, $Pb(C_2H_5)_4$, is added. If lead compounds are present in the gasoline, a so-called scavenger compound is also added to prevent lead deposits from building up in the engine. Typical scavengers for lead are ethylene dibromide, $BrCH_2$—$CH_2Br$, and ethylene dichloride, $ClCH_2$—$CH_2Cl$. In the early 1970's in the United States, about 20 percent of the total annual consumption of lead and 85 percent of sodium was used in "leaded" gasoline and 75 percent of the bromine to make ethylene dibromide.

**Plastics and Elastomers.** The principal basic chemicals employed in the manufacture of plastics and resins (qq.v.) are unsaturated, or otherwise reactive molecules, and include acrylonitrile ($CH_2$=CHCN); ethylene ($CH_2$=$CH_2$); ethylene oxide ($CH_2$—$CH_2$) propylene oxide

$$CH_2\overset{\diagdown}{\phantom{x}}\underset{O}{\phantom{x}}\overset{\diagup}{\phantom{x}}CH_2$$

($CH_3CH$—$CH_2$); styrene ($C_6H_5CH$=$CH_2$); vinyl

$$\overset{\diagdown}{\phantom{x}}\underset{O}{\phantom{x}}\overset{\diagup}{\phantom{x}}$$

acetate ($CH_2$=CHOOCCH$_3$); vinyl chloride ($CH_2$=CHCl); formaldehyde ($H_2C$=O); methyl methacrylate ($CH_2$=CCOOCH$_3$); and methyl

$$CH_3$$

dichlorosilane (($CH_3)_2$ $SiCl_2$).

In each case, a molecule of the starting material, or monomer, is made to combine at each of its ends with one of the reactive ends of another monomer molecule, thus forming a long chain, or polymer, of units linked head-to-tail. The typ-

ical reaction scheme for the formation of a so-called linear polymer is as follows:

$$CH_2\!\!=\!\!CH + CH_2\!\!=\!\!CH + CH_2\!\!=\!\!CH \rightarrow$$
$$\phantom{xx}|\phantom{xxxxxx}|\phantom{xxxxxx}|$$
$$\phantom{xx}CN\phantom{xxxx}CN\phantom{xxxx}CN$$
$$-\!CH_2\!\!-\!\!CH\!\!-\!\!CH_2\!\!-\!\!CH\!\!-\!\!CH_2\!\!-\!\!CH\!\!-$$
$$\phantom{xxxxx}|\phantom{xxxxxx}|\phantom{xxxxxx}|$$
$$\phantom{xxxxx}CN\phantom{xxxx}CN\phantom{xxxx}CN$$
$$\text{(polyacrylonitrile)}$$

The polymer chain consists of a so-called backbone of hydrocarbon or similar groupings, to which are attached side groups, such as the —CN groups in the example above. The special properties of different polymers, such as their elasticity or rigidity, tensile strength, thermal deformability, optical properties, and susceptibility to softening or dissolution by various solvents, are determined by the nature of the backbone and of the side groups, and by the total length of the polymer chain, or, the degree of polymerization. Most elastomers and thermoplastic materials are linear polymers of the above type, or are copolymers, formed as above, but from a mixture of two different monomer molecules, so that in the polymer chain the backbone and the side groups alternate between the two types.

The rigidity and strength of synthetic materials can be increased, and their solubility decreased, by employing reactive side groups which can undergo chemical reaction themselves with the atoms of the backbones of adjacent polymer chains, thus binding together, or cross-linking, individual chains into a three-dimensional continuous network.

The typical molecular structures of some widely used plastics and elastomers are shown in an accompanying table.

A great variety of monomers and mixtures of monomers, or comonomers, can be employed, and there also exists great latitude in the degree of polymerization and in the amount of crosslinking. This permits the final properties of the polymer to be selected from a wide range.

In addition to the types of polymers listed above, others having useful properties include: polychlorobutadiene (Neoprene); polybutadiene-styrene copolymer (Buna S, GR-S); polyisobutylene (butyl rubber); polyvinyl chloride; polyvinylidene chloride (Saran, Velon); polymethylene polyphenylisocyanate (urethane plastics); polycarbonates; polytriazine (melamine plastics); and polyester (alkyds). In the U.S. over 5,000,000,000 lb. of plastics were used annually by the construction industry alone in the early 1970's; this includes the use of plastics in paints, coatings, adhesives, floor coverings, and resin-bonded wood, plywood, and Masonite.

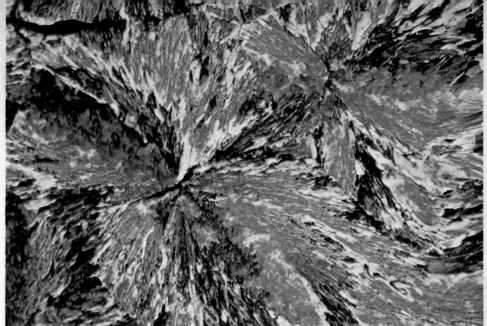

Dow Chemical Corp.

E. I. Du Pont De Nemours & Co., Inc.

**Chemical Compounds. Plate 1.**
*Above: Among the chemical compounds manufactured for pest control is one with the trade name Dursbane, here magnified 150 times. The active ingredient in the insecticide, used against cockroaches, chinch bugs, and mosquitoes, is known as chlorpyfiros.*

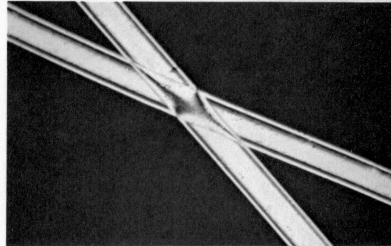

Allied Chemical Corp.

*Above, right: The nylon filament is here magnified 500 times.*

*Below, right: Plastics manufactured from synthetic chemical compounds are used today for the production of durable automobile parts, such as the distributor cap and components of the electrical and ignition systems.*

| Chemical Name | Trade Name | Type of Polymer | Backbone | Side Group |
|---|---|---|---|---|
| polyethylene | polyethylene polythene | linear | —C—C—C—C— | H— |
| polypropylene | polypropylene Escon 125 | linear | —C—C—C—C— | CH₃— |
| polystyrene | polystyrene Styrax Styrofoam | linear | —C—C—C—C— | C₆H₅— |
| polymethyl methacrylate | Plexiglas Lucite Perspex | linear | —C—C—C—C— | CH₃OOC— and CH₃— |
| polyamide | nylon | linear copolymer | —C—C—N—C—C— | O= |
| phenol-formaldehyde | Bakelite | cross-linked copolymer | —C₆H₄—O—C—O—C₆H₄— | H— |
| polytetrafluoroethylene | Teflon TFE | linear | —C—C—C—C— | F— |
| polyterephthalic ester | Dacron Mylar Terylene | linear copolymer | —C—C—O—C—C₆H₄—C—O— | H—, O= |
| polymethylsiloxane | silicone | linear and cross-linked | —Si—O—Si—O— | CH₃— |
| polyaminoalcohol | epoxy | linear | —C—C—N—C—C—N— | H—, HO— |

## Paints and Coatings.

A paint formulation consists of several different categories of chemical compounds. The so-called vehicle ultimately forms the adherent, flexible, skin-like coating; the pigment is dispersed throughout the vehicle and gives the final film its color and hiding power; and the solvent or thinner evaporates shortly after the coating has been laid. The vehicle can be an unsaturated, or drying, oil, which is an ester formed from the reaction of a long-chain carboxylic acid, such as linoleic acid, with a viscous alcohol, such as glycerine; or it can be a polymer such as any of those described in the preceding section.

The molecular structure of a typical drying oil, for example, linseed oil, is as follows:

$$CH_2—O—CO—C_7H_{14}—CH=CH—CH_2—CH=CH—C_5H_{11}$$
$$CH—O—CO—C_7H_{14}—CH=CH—CH_2—CH=CH—C_5H_{11}$$
$$CH_2—O—CO—C_7H_{14}—CH=CH—CH_2—CH=CH—C_5H_{11}$$

from glycerine    from linoleic acid

If this substance is exposed to the oxygen in the air, the unsaturated ends on the hydrocarbon chain, shown above at the locations of the double bond, —CH=CH—, are attacked, and an oxide, or ether, is formed, thereby cross-linking one molecule to another, to yield a tough, insoluble macromolecule with high molecular weight, as follows:

```
....CH=CH....              ...CH—CH....
    +                              |     |
    O₂          →                 O    O
    +                              |     |
....CH=CH....              ...CH—CH....
```

The drying oil, therefore, is a monomer when it is in the can, and becomes a polymer after being applied to an exposed surface.

If the vehicle is one of the synthetic polymers described in the previous section, it is dispersed in a suitable solvent, so that as the solvent evaporates the individual macromolecules come into contact and become enmeshed with each other, the latter process being helped along by the presence in the solvent of a polymerization catalyst, called a drier. The types of synthetic polymers most widely employed as paint vehicles are, for example, alkyd resins, which are polyesters of a polyhydric alcohol, such as glycerol, with a polybasic acid, such as phthalic acid, $C_6H_4(COOH)_2$; nitrocellulose, in which cellulose is depolymerized, the small molecules are nitrated, and the substance is then repolymerized (see RAYON); phenolic resins; acrylic resins; epoxy resins; polyvinyl acetate resins; and polyurethanes.

The pigment is a fine powder that either strongly scatters light, to yield a white effect, or absorbs certain wavelengths of light, producing a colored effect; see COLOR; LIGHT. Typical white pigments are the inorganic oxides: titanium dioxide, $TiO_2$; antimony oxide, $Sb_2O_3$; and zinc oxide, ZnO. Other white, insoluble, inorganic compounds are also frequently used, including zinc sulfide, ZnS; white lead (the hydroxycarbonate, hydroxysulfate, hydroxyphosphite, or hydroxysilicate of lead); and barium sulfate, $BaSO_4$. Typical colored pigments are the following inorganic oxides: iron oxide, $Fe_2O_3$ (yellow, red, or brown colors); chromium oxide, $Cr_2O_3$ (green); lead oxide, $Pb_3O_4$ (red). The chromates of lead, zinc, strontium, and nickel produce various shades of yellow and orange. A variety of organic solids is used for colors ranging from yellow through red to blue and violet.

The solvent or thinner for drying oil type paints is generally turpentine (q.v.), which is a mixture of cyclic hydrocarbons containing 10 carbon atoms, or the thinner may be a mixture of suitably volatile hydrocarbons derived from petroleum distillates. The solvent for most synthetic vehicles is of the alcohol, ketone, or ester types. Water can also serve as the thinner for some of the synthetics, in which case the vehicle is emulsified, or suspended as very tiny droplets in the water. More than 1,000,000,000 gal. of paint were being produced annually in the U.S. in the early 1970's.

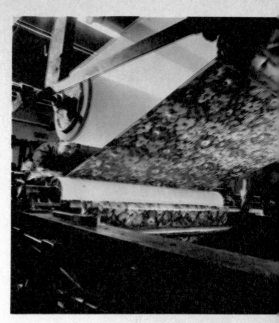

*Chemical Compounds. Plate 2.* Above, left: A common sight in supermarkets are the transparent and flexible packaging materials used to market foods. Above, right: After passing through calendering rollers, where the plastic substance is smoothed, glazed, and thinned into sheets, it is wound upon a paper core before packaging. Below, left: Colorful crewel embroidery in the side of this boot is done in synthetic vinyl fibers popular in fashion apparel. Below right: A curable liquid polymer is poured onto a platen to form a Letterflex plastic printing plate for the newspaper industry at lost cost, using modern photocomposition techniques.                W. R. Grace & Co.

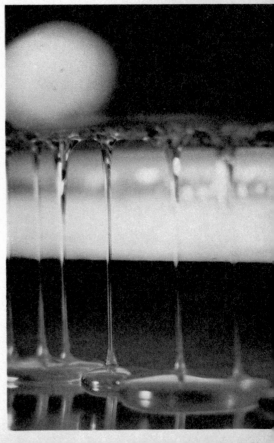

The increasing use of synthetic fibers in the home is reflected in the colorful elegance of a morning room designed by the American interior decorator Joseph Braswell. The entire color scheme is set off by the spring-green luxury of the shag carpet manufactured from the newly developed Source fiber.

Allied Chemical Corp.

*Chemical Compounds. Plate 3.*

Consumer interest in another area of synthetic textiles has been spurred by concern for the preservation of wildlife. These pile coats of Dynel fibers capture the realistic cheetah appearance at moderate cost. Union Carbide Corp.

**Pharmaceuticals.** Many diverse chemical compounds are included in the general class of pharmaceuticals; see PHARMACY. Classified according to the types of purposes for which they are intended, the most widely used types of pharmaceutical chemicals are: analgesics, or pain-killers; antacids; antiarthritics; antibacterials; antibiotics; antihistamines; antiobesity; antispasmodics; ataraxics, or tranquilizers; cardiovasculars, affecting the heart and blood vessels; cough and cold preparations; diabetic therapy drugs; dietary supplements; diuretics, or urination-promoters; hematinics, or blood improvers; hormones; muscle relaxants; psychostimulants; sedatives; and vitamins. Total annual sales of these pharmaceuticals in the U.S. in the early 1970's exceeded $8,000,000,000.

The molecular structures of the various types of pharmaceuticals do not have a common theme. Each compound molecule has a structure that permits it to interact with one or more of the biological molecules of the organism receiving therapy, and in many cases the substances involved in the reaction, as well as the nature of the interaction between them, are unknown. Furthermore, a number of methods probably exists, by which the same final physiological effect may be produced. The following, for example, are all anesthetics: ether, $(C_2H_5)_2O$; cyclopropane, $CH_2-CH_2$; chloroform, $CHCl_3$;

$$CH_2$$

nitrous oxide, $N_2O$; and novocaine, $H_2NC_6H_4COOC_2H_4N(C_2H_5)_2$, but they all have very different types of molecules, and although they produce similar pain-killing effects, each chemical affects a different part of the body, or works in a different way from the others.

**Food Additives.** More than 2500 food additives of all kinds are in use today, including both natural and synthetic compounds employed for the following purposes: colors, flavorings, preservatives and antibiotics, antioxidants to prevent rancidity by inhibiting the oxidative breakdown of fats and oils, sequestrants to separate and remove trace elements that would otherwise interfere with processing, stabilizers, thickeners, emulsifiers to maintain smooth, uniform texture, and surfactants or wetting agents. About 2,000,000,000 lb. of food additives were used annually in the U.S. in the early 1970's.

The principal preservative compounds used are benzoic acid, $C_6H_5COOH$, and its sodium salt, $C_6H_5COONa$, sodium metabisulfite, $Na_2S_2O_5$, and calcium propionate, $(C_2H_5COO)_2Ca$. These function by interfering with the metabolism of the microorganisms responsible for the spoilage of the foodstuff. See FOOD PRESERVATION.

The most widely used artificial sweetener in the U.S. is saccharin, $C_6H_4 \overset{\overset{\displaystyle CO}{\diagdown}}{\underset{\underset{\displaystyle SO_2}{\diagup}}{\phantom{x}}} NH$. Another sweetener that was for a time even more popular than saccharin, calcium cyclamate, $(C_6H_{11}NHSO_3)_2Ca\cdot2H_2O$, was declared unacceptable for unrestricted use by the Food and Drug Administration (q.v.) in 1969. About 21,000,000 lb. of these artificial sweeteners were used annually in the U.S. in the late 1960's. The molecular structures of both are very different, and differ enormously from the structure of the natural sugars. Because the chemical mechanisms of taste and smell are not yet fully understood, however, it is not possible to explain the source of the sweetness of these molecules.

The molecules of the surfactants and stabilizers employed in foods contain both polar and nonpolar, or hydrocarbon, sections, and function in the same manner as the wetting agents described before. For the chemical nature of the sequestrants, or complexing agents, see *Soaps and Detergents,* above.

**Cosmetic and Personal Hygiene Chemicals.** Substances that are applied externally to various parts of the body for hygienic or cosmetic purposes fall into the following categories: facial cosmetics, including cleansers, compacts, creams, lotions, astringents, eye makeup, lipstick, face makeup, face powder, and rouge; hand cosmetics, including creams, lotions, cuticle softener, nail polish, and nail-polish remover; hair products, including colorings, cream rinses, dandruff rinses, depilatories or hair removers, hair medicaments, permanent wave hair kits, hair tonics, shampoos, spray hair fixatives, wave-set preparations, and hair conditioners; oral hygiene requisites, including breath fresheners, dental floss, denture adhesives, denture cleaners, mouthwashes, and toothpaste; deodorants, shaving products, bath salts and oils, suntan preparations, talcum powder, perfume, and toilet water. Total annual sales of these products in the U.S. were worth about $5,000,000,000 in the early 1970's. See COSMETICS.

The chemical natures of the substances employed for these purposes are very diverse. The suitability of a given substance for a cosmetic use depends upon the combination in the chemical compound of certain physical properties with nontoxicity and with special chemical effects on parts of the human body. Some of these chemicals are inorganic substances; aluminum chlorhydrate, $Al_2(OH)_5Cl$, for example,

*A pharmacologist is seen isolating pure products of a multi-component reaction mixture using the column-chromatography process. The pharmaceutical value of the product is then determined by testing.* Pfizer Inc.

which is an astringent, causes a closing of the pores of the skin and interferes with the exudation of perspiration. Other chemicals are organic, such as thioglycollic acid, $HSCH_2COOH$, which is one of the active ingredients in permanent wave hair kits; it breaks some of the cross-links in the keratin macromolecules composing the hair fiber, permitting the fiber to be stretched into a new shape that becomes permanent when the effect of the thioglycollic acid is neutralized.

**Biocides.** Chemical compounds that interfere with the metabolic processes of living organisms are extensively employed to kill or otherwise control plants or animals that are considered pests. These include fungicides, insecticides, insect repellants, herbicides or weed killers, and antibiotics, which destroy virus, mold, and bacteria. About 400 basic ingredients are used in the several thousand pesticides on the market; *see* DDT; INSECTICIDE.

Insecticides consist of three main classes: (1) chlorinated hydrocarbons such as DDT, or dichlorodiphenyltrichloroethane, $(ClC_6H_4)_2$ $CHCCl_3$, benzene hexachloride, also called Lindane, $C_6Cl_6$, and dieldrin, $C_{12}H_8OCl_6$; (2) carbamates, which are compounds of the type $H_2NCOOR$, an example being the product known as carbaryl; and (3) organophosphates, which are compounds of the type $(RO)_3PO$ or $(RO)_3PS$, examples of these being parathion, $(C_2H_5O)_2(O_2NC_6H_4O)PS$, and DDVP, $(CH_3O)_2$ $(Cl_2C_2HO)PO$, sold as Shell No-Pest.

About six chlorinated hydrocarbons were on the market during the 1960's, and in 1964 accounted for 65 percent of all the insecticides in use in the U.S. About 100,000,000 lb. of DDT was produced by American manufacturers annually in the early 1970's, but because of the persistence of these chemicals, the use of the chlorinated hydrocarbons is declining, and they are being replaced by the more easily degradable carbamates and organophosphates. The use of DDT has been banned in several States in the U.S.

Herbicides include compounds chemically similar to the insecticides, and certain molecules that are especially toxic to plant physiology. Examples of the toxic substances are: 2,4,5-T, or 2,4,5-trichlorophenoxyacetic acid, $Cl_3C_6H_2OCH_2COOH$; 2,4-D, or 2,4-dichlorophenoxyacetic acid; PCNB, or pentachloronitrobenzene, $C_6Cl_5NO_2$; and 2,4-dichlorophenol, $Cl_2C_6H_3OH$. *See* AGRICULTURAL CHEMISTRY.

A widely used fungicide is the so-called Bordeaux mixture, composed of copper sulfate, $CuSO_4$, and lime, $CaO$. Common insect repellents are camphor; naphthalene, $C_{10}H_8$; and para-dichlorobenzene, $Cl_2C_6H_4$.                      S.Z.L.

**CHEMICAL ENGINEERING.** *See* ENGINEERING.
**CHEMICAL GARDENING.** *See* HYDROPONICS.
**CHEMICAL REACTION.** *See* REACTION, CHEMICAL.
**CHEMICAL SENSE IN ANIMALS.** *See* ANIMALS, CHEMICAL SENSE IN.
**CHEMICAL WARFARE,** the military use of flames, incendiary devices, smoke, toxic chemicals (*see* GAS WARFARE), and herbicides. Fire is the oldest chemical weapon. About 1200 B.C., the Trojans ignited flammable substances which they threw from the walls of Troy upon the attacking Greeks. In the 7th century A.D., the Byzantines hurled Greek fire, a mixture of sulfur, resin, pitch, oil, and quicklime, on their enemies. The modern portable flamethrower, which uses a thickened blend of petroleum products as a fuel, was first used by the German army in World War I. At the beginning of World War II, American chemists, searching for an effective gasoline thickener, developed an aluminum soap called napalm after its major constituents, *naphthenic and *palmitic acids, and the term was soon applied to the fuel itself. Napalm is very effective, as it burns evenly, sticks to flat surfaces, produces a compact stream of fire, and increases the range of flamethrowers. One-man portable napalm flamethrowers are widely used in combat. Napalm is also used for flamethrowers mounted on tanks and landing craft and in fire bombs dropped from aircraft.

Incendiaries are devices used to destroy buildings and other property by fire. They contain chemical substances that burn with an intense, persistent, and localized heat, igniting materials that normally do not burn. In World War II, 73 percent of the total quantity of bombs dropped on Japanese cities by the United States Air Force were incendiaries. One effective incendiary consisted of a magnesium shell filled with thermite (a mixture of aluminum and iron oxide) that burned for almost 10 min. and generated temperatures between 2500°–3500° F. Another widely used incendiary ejected a napalm filling on contact.

Smoke is used in battle to screen the movements of attacking or retreating troops and to mark positions. Mechanical smoke generators operate by vaporizing a mixture of water and certain petroleum oils. When the hot vapor strikes the cooler air, it condenses into tiny liquid droplets that produce a dense and persistent smoke. Smoke bombs, containing white phosphorus compounds, are fired from artillery and mortar firearms, sprayed from airplane tanks, or thrown as grenades.

Chemical defoliants and desiccants are used to prevent ambushes by decreasing the amount of cover available to the enemy, and to expose positions and trails camouflaged by vegetation. Defoliants prematurely remove leaves from plants by inducing and hastening seasonal abscission (leaf drop). Desiccants dry up plant foliage. They do not invariably lead to leaf drop, but usually change the color of the foliage within a few hours. This color change is readily apparent from the air and is used to mark targets, bomb release points, and parachute drop zones. Herbicides are sprayed from planes or portable hand sprayers to eliminate vegetation along roads and trails and expose the enemy's movements.                              M.B.

**CHEMIN DE FER.** *See* BACCARAT.

**CHEMISTRY,** study of the composition, structure, and properties of substances, of the interactions between them, and of the effects on them of the addition or removal of energy in any of its several forms. The substances of chemistry consist of all the types of materials found on or in the earth, oceans, and atmosphere, and include all the materials derived from them. These substances, and those produced as a result of other substances reacting with each other by the application of energy or for other reasons, and the starting materials themselves, are called chemicals, and the reaction is known as a chemical process. By the late 1960's more than 2,500,000 individual substances had been isolated or synthesized, purified, studied, and described by chemical scientists. All of these substances are composed of one or more of the 103 elements, which are the fundamental

building blocks of all matter in the universe; *see* ELEMENTS, CHEMICAL. See also separate articles on most of the chemical substances mentioned in this article.

**Elementary Substances.** A substance that involves only one element in its makeup is called an elementary substance; a given element may form a number of such elementary substances, which are called allotropes (q.v.) of each other. Carbon, for example, is the only constituent element present in diamond, graphite, and lampblack; the very pronounced differences in properties of these substances stem from different ways in which the constituent carbon atoms are linked together; *see* ATOM AND ATOMIC THEORY. Some elementary substances consist of individual atoms, unbonded to other atoms in the group. These are monoatomic substances such as the noble gases, helium, neon, and argon, and the vapors of most metals at high temperatures, the best examples being the glowing gases in sodium and mercury vapor lamps. Other elementary substances consist of molecules (*see* MOLECULE), with two, three, or more atoms, called diatomic, triatomic, or polyatomic molecules respectively. Oxygen ($O_2$), nitrogen ($N_2$), and chlorine ($Cl_2$) are diatomic, ozone ($O_3$) is triatomic, and phosphorus ($P_4$) and sulfur ($S_8$) are polyatomic.

The elementary metals such as iron, aluminum, copper, gold, and lead do not consist of discrete, individual atoms or molecules of the element, but the atoms are joined to each other in a three-dimensional network embracing the entire solid crystal (q.v.). Many of the nonmetallic solid elementary substances such as diamond, silicon, and germanium also consist of three-dimensional networks of interconnected atoms, though without the special type of interatomic binding that is responsible for the phenomenon of high electrical conductivity exhibited by the metals; *see* ELECTRICITY.

**Compound Substances.** An overwhelming majority of chemical substances consists of molecules containing two or more different elements. Although several elements compose the molecules of a compound, all the molecules have the same composition, a compound being a single substance and not a mixture of substances. Because of the great number and variety of types of chemical compounds, they are classified in several different ways, depending upon their notable characteristics. The principal categories into which chemical compounds are classified are based upon: (1) the origin of the compound; (2) the number of elements in it; (3) its properties; (4) its composition; (5) its binding or valence type; (6) its molecular size; and (7) its usage.

ORIGIN. Historically, chemical substances were regarded either as minerals (see MINERAL), or as products of the life processes of plants and animals. Today, minerals are those chemical compounds found in nature in rocks or sedimentary deposits, and biological chemicals or biochemicals are those chemical compounds found in, or produced by, living organisms. This classification originally grouped all substances as either inorganic or organic chemicals, but with the development of the science of chemistry it became clear that many compounds exist that are similar to the minerals, but do not occur in nature, and also many compounds identical with or related to the biochemicals exist, which can be made in the laboratory without the help of plants or animals. The term inorganic substance today applies to a chemical that is not composed principally of carbon combined with hydrogen or oxygen; an organic substance is one that contains carbon combined with hydrogen or oxygen as its main constituents.

NUMBER OF ELEMENTS. Substances composed of only two elements are called binary compounds; the two constituents may be present in a variety of ratios, as in $NaCl$, $H_2O$, $NH_3$, $Fe_2O_3$, and $Fe_3O_4$. A substance with three elements in its composition is a ternary compound, and one with more than three elements is known as a complex substance.

PROPERTIES. Chemical substances are classified as either metals or nonmetals on the basis of their electrical conductivity; as electrolytes or nonelectrolytes on the basis of their ability, when dissolved in water, to support the passage of an electrical current through the solution; as acids or bases, depending upon their respective ability to yield, or react with, hydrogen ions, or as salts if the substances have been formed as a result of the reaction between an acid and a base.

COMPOSITION. Compounds of an element with oxygen are called oxides; those formed with a halogen, such as fluorine, chlorine, bromine, or iodine are halides; those formed with sulfur are sulfides; and so on. Certain combinations of elements retain their identity from one compound to another and exhibit certain characteristic properties; such combinations are called radicals, examples of which are nitrate ($NO_3^-$), hydroxide ($OH^-$), sulfate ($SO_4^{2-}$), carbonate ($CO_3^{2-}$), phosphate ($PO_4^{3-}$), and acetate ($C_2H_3O_2^-$). Compounds containing these radicals are therefore named nitrates, hydroxides, sulfates, and so on.

Many of the metallic elements are grouped into families, the members of which have properties that are very similar; see PERIODIC LAW. Examples of these are the alkali metals, lithium, sodium, potassium, rubidium, and cesium, and the alkaline earth metals, magnesium, calcium, strontium, barium, and radium, and the noble metals, and rare earths (q.v.). A compound formed from the union of an alkali metal with one of the halogens is called an alkali halide; this family name applies to a group of twenty different individual compounds such as LiCl, NaCl, and NaBr. Because these compounds can also be made by allowing a base such as an alkali hydroxide to react with an acid, a hydrogen halide, as follows:

$$\underset{\substack{\text{potassium} \\ \text{hydroxide}}}{KOH} + \underset{\substack{\text{hydrobromic} \\ \text{acid}}}{HBr} \rightarrow \underset{\substack{\text{potassium} \\ \text{bromide}}}{KBr} + \underset{\text{water}}{H_2O}$$

they are salts. The common, nontechnical usage of the ancient term "salt" refers to only one member of the alkali halide family of salts, sodium chloride ($NaCl$), or common salt. The chemical usage of the term salt, however, can mean any member of a number of families such as the alkali halides, the alkaline earth nitrates, the noble metal sulfates etc.; see SALT.

Among the organic substances, individual compounds are classified according to the kinds of elements that are combined with the carbon, and also according to their manner of combination. If the compound contains only carbon and hydrogen, it is a hydrocarbon; there are several families within the category of hydrocarbons, such as the aliphatic and the aromatic, the straight-chain, the branched, and the cyclic, and the saturated and the unsaturated, the distinctions between which refer to different types of geometrical arrangements of the atoms within the molecule, or to different types of binding forces between the atoms. A compound containing carbon, hydrogen, and oxygen may belong to any of a number of categories, depending upon the nature of the binding of the oxygen atoms; these classes of organic compounds include the alcohols, aldehydes, ketones, esters, carboxylic acids, ethers, and others. Amines, amides, amino acids, and nitrocompounds are examples of organic compounds which include nitrogen in their makeup.

BINDING OR VALENCE TYPE. If the fundamental building blocks of a substance are ions (see ION), the substance is classified as an ionic, or electrovalent compound. Examples are the salts of the alkali and alkaline earth metals, such as sodium chloride, which, to emphasize this as-

**Chemistry. Plate 1.** *Above: "The Alchemist", a painting by David Teniers the Younger (1610–90). Below: A vacuum-fusion gas analyzer is employed by a research chemist to determine trace amounts of oxygen, nitrogen, and hydrogen in a metal sample.*

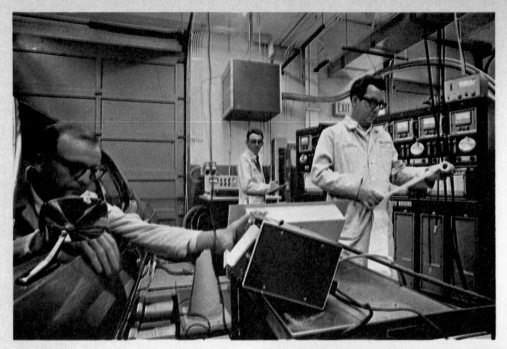

**Chemistry. Plate 2.** Air pollution by automobile exhausts has spurred research into control devices. Above: Exhaust fumes are checked in a laboratory, for hydrocarbons, carbon dioxide, carbon monoxide, and nitrogen oxide before and after insertion of a catalytic convertor. Below: A nuclear magnetic resonance spectrometer is used to determine the molecular structure of organic compounds. The superimposed console screen in the picture indicates the interaction between the strong magnetic field of an electromagnet and the weak magnetic fields within the molecules of a chemical sample. Right: A technician carries out the identification of a calcium sample, using atomic-absorption equipment. The absorption spectrometer sends a beam of light through the sample and analyzes it by recording the degree to which light has been absorbed, providing a specific absorption spectrum for every sample.

W. R. Grace & Co.

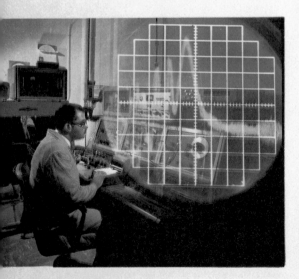

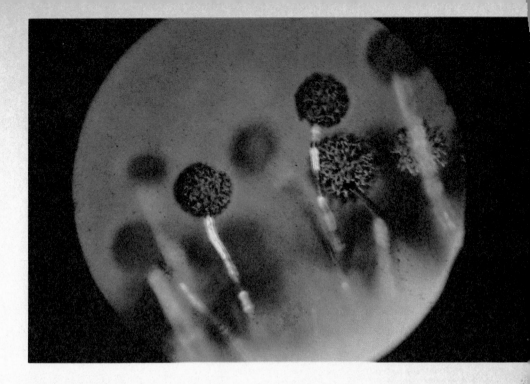

**Chemistry. Plate 3.** *Two photographs of Aspergillus niger, the black bread mold. This mold is used commercially in the production of citric acid, one of the most important and widely used industrial organic acids.* Pfizer Inc.

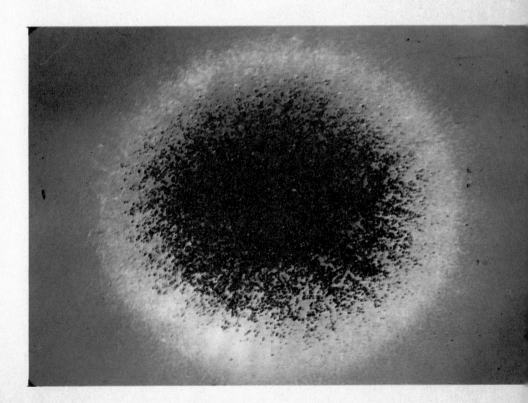

**Chemistry. Plate 4.** *Above, left: See-through educational aids such as this synthetic Polyox-resin apparatus allow students to observe germination of seeds and plant growth. A gel-forming polymer, Polyox also presents little resistance to the flow of fluids; it is used to coat the inside of pipes to make water flow faster and on boat hulls to make the boats move faster through the water. Above, right: Analog computers are widely used in the chemical industry to simulate refinery processes. This use permits the avoidance of any potential problems and the training of technical personnel before the chemical plant is actually finished. Below: Chemists discuss a model of the zeolite cracking catalyst employed in chemical refining processes.*

pect of its nature, would be represented by the formula $(Na^+, Cl^-)$, where $Na^+$ represents the sodium ion as equal to a sodium atom less one of its proper complement of electrons, and $Cl^-$ is the chloride ion, or a chlorine atom plus one extra electron. The binding force holding the entire substance together is the result of mutual electrical attraction between oppositely charged ions. See VALENCE.

Substances in which discrete molecules form the building blocks are called molecular compounds. To emphasize the concept that the individual molecules are held together internally as a consequence of pairs of electrons shared between adjacent atoms, these substances are described as covalent compounds. The covalent binding operates within the individual molecules; the forces between molecules which serve to hold the entire substance together are the result of small deviations from electrical neutrality of various regions of the molecules. The attractions between charged regions on one molecule and the oppositely charged regions of its neighbor are called van der Waals forces after the Dutch physicist Johannes Diderik van der Waals (q.v.).

Substances in which several radicals are joined to a central atom or ion, as for example, in the negative ion of the compound $(2K^+, PtCl_6^{2-})$ or the positive ion of the compound $[Zn(NH_3)_4^{2+}, SO_4^{2-}]$, are complex compounds; similarly, the ions just referred to would be called complex ions. Crystals of substances in which all the atoms are linked together to form a three-dimensional network within which individual, discrete molecules can no longer be distinguished, are said to form coordination structures.

MOLECULAR SIZE. Compounds composed of very large molecules are often distinguished from other simpler substances by classification of the former as macromolecular substances. Most macromolecules consist of chains of a large number of identical, simpler molecules linked together; the molecule is then called a polymer (q.v.), and the component links in the chain are monomers.

USAGE. Chemical compounds that are intended for laboratory use are called reagents; those that are employed in manufacturing processes are called industrial chemicals. An industrial chemical that serves as one of the ingredients in a synthesis is called an intermediate. An industrial chemical that is produced in very large quantities is called a heavy chemical. Substances used in large quantities in specialized fields are often designated by their final purpose; certain compounds, for example, are called pharmaceuticals (see PHARMACY) because they are employed in the manufacture of drugs, medicines and medications; agricultural chemicals are those compounds that are used as fertilizers and pesticides (see AGRICULTURAL CHEMISTRY); electrochemicals are those that are used in electroplating and electropolishing applications (see ELECTROCHEMISTRY); and photographic chemicals are those that are used in the manufacture or processing of photographic film and paper; see PHOTOGRAPHY. Compounds are also categorized in terms of the industrial methods of production; petrochemicals, for example, are those compounds derived from natural gas (see GAS: Natural Gas) or petroleum (q.v.), and naval stores are chemicals derived from pine trees.

For a survey of the most important individual chemical substances, see CHEMICAL COMPOUNDS, SYNTHETIC.

## HISTORY OF CHEMISTRY

The practical effects and applications of chemistry and chemical reactions have been known since the very ancient times, but they only became subjects of scientific study after the Renaissance (q.v.) in Europe.

**Ancient Period.** Among the earliest chemical operations consciously performed by primitive man were the production of fire, the tanning of skins, the firing of clay, the fermentation of fruit juices, and the making of glass, soaps, poisons, perfumes, cosmetics, and pigments. The handicrafts of primitive man led him to the discovery of rocks from which metals, chiefly copper, tin, and iron, could be extracted with the aid of fire. Steel was made as early as 1000 B.C. The first man known to have proposed a theory of the composition of substances was Thales (q.v.), of Miletus in Asia Minor, who in the 6th century B.C. upheld the idea that all things are composed of water. This theory was probably suggested to him by the observation that water is necessary for plant growth, that plants are moist within, that plants form the ultimate source of the food of animals, that soil is deposited from water, that water dries and turns into an atmospheric gas, and that water freezes into a hard solid. Philosophers who succeeded Thales identified the primary element of all things with air or breath; with fire; with a combination of earth, air, fire, and water; with undifferentiated matter; or with abstract concepts such as the infinite, number, and being. In the 5th century B.C., two Greek philosophers, Leucippus and Democritus (q.v.), anticipated the modern atomic theory by declaring that material bodies are composed of tiny, indivisible particles of different kinds, which, by combining in many ways, form all the substances of the universe, much as all the words of a language may be formed by different combinations of the same letters of its alphabet; see PHILOSOPHY: *Greek Philosophy: The Atomists.* Subsequent philosophers directed their attention to problems of the social, rather than the natural sciences, and further speculation on the composition of matter was abandoned until the Middle Ages.

**Medieval Period.**   The so-called alchemists in the medieval times were occupied chiefly with two problems, the transformation of other metals into gold, and the preparation of an elixir that would restore youth and prolong life. Most of their wizardry was futile, cryptic, and fraudulent. Their labors led, however, to the discovery of previously unknown substances. Among the acids, for example, they prepared oil of vitriol (the modern sulfuric acid), aqua fortis (nitric acid), and muriatic acid (hydrochloric acid), in addition to the oldest known acid, acetic acid (vinegar or sour wine). Soda and potash (now sodium carbonate and potassium carbonate) were their mild alkalis; caustic soda and caustic potash (now sodium hydroxide and potassium hydroxide), their caustic alkalis, produced by dissolving the mild alkalis in water and adding lime, a material obtained by roasting limestone or chalk. The alchemists learned that mixtures of acids and alkalis yielded salts upon evaporation, and they invented chemical apparatus of various types, and devised laboratory techniques. In the 16th century, the Swiss physician Philippus Aureolus Paracelsus (q.v.) sought to turn chemical investigations to the service of medicine, and thus founded the school of iatrochemistry. He and his followers adopted the theory, held by some alchemists, that the basic elements of all things are mercury, sulfur, and salt, rather than earth, air, fire, and water, as the people in ancient times had taught.

**Rise of Modern Chemistry.**   Modern chemistry began with the work and writings of the English scientist Robert Boyle (q.v.), who drew attention to the chief errors of alchemical theory impeding the development of a scientific chemistry. He held that the language in which the alchemists and the iatrochemists expressed their principles was so mystical as to be devoid of sense; that specific terms were employed in such a variety of meanings as to produce hopeless confusion; and that it was futile to try to analyze the composition of a large number of substances by limiting such analysis to a few elements chosen arbitrarily. He proposed definitions of compound and element: a compound

is a substance that can be decomposed into simpler ingredient substances, elements, and an element is a substance that cannot be separated into simpler components by chemical methods.

The erroneous phlogiston (q.v.) theory introduced by the German chemists Johann Joachim Becher (q.v.) and Georg Ernst Stahl (1660–1734) in the 17th century was an attempt to offer a single explanation for a multitude of observed facts. According to this theory, when a substance burns, an ingredient called phlogiston departs in the flame, leaving a calx or ash. As early as the 8th century the Arabian scientist Jabir ibn Haiyan (fl. 721–766), also known as Geber, reputedly observed the fact that lead or tin, when heated in air, is converted into a calx (now called oxide) which is heavier than the original metal; by the 17th century it was known that the extra weight came from the air, and also that the weight did not increase indefinitely.

Among the first scientists to study chemical changes by careful experiment, to produce evidence opposed to the phlogiston theory, and scientifically to establish chemical facts, was the British chemist Joseph Black (1728–99). Others, such as the British chemists John Mayow (1640–79) and Joseph Priestley (q.v.), established a number of important facts regarding the chemistry of combustion.

It was the French chemist Antoine Laurent Lavoisier (q.v.) who compelled the abandonment of the phlogiston theory and laid the foundation of modern chemistry. In 1770 Lavoisier, using accurate balances and weighing techniques, found that metals increased in weight when burned and that the increase in weight was equal to the air (oxygen) that disappeared. Phlogiston consequently would have to possess a negative weight. In the course of these experiments, Lavoisier enunciated the law of conservation of matter, which had been tacitly assumed by Black: that matter cannot be created or destroyed by human agency, and that there is an equal quantity of matter both before and after any chemical change.

A gas which bubbles up from metals immersed in dilute acids was named "inflammable air" by Priestley in 1781, after its most curious property. He noticed that the explosion of this gas in air formed dew, and the British chemist Henry Cavendish (q.v.), by burning large quantities of this inflammable air, proved that this combustion produced a liquid in no way different from water. Lavoisier, who also performed the experiment, renamed inflammable air hydrogen (Gr., "water-former"), and recognized water as its oxide.

**Chemistry. Plate 5.** *Above: Photograph of a petroleum-cracking catalyst magnified 80 times. The striking colors are obtained by use of color filters. Below: A segment of polystyrene foam magnified 10 times.*

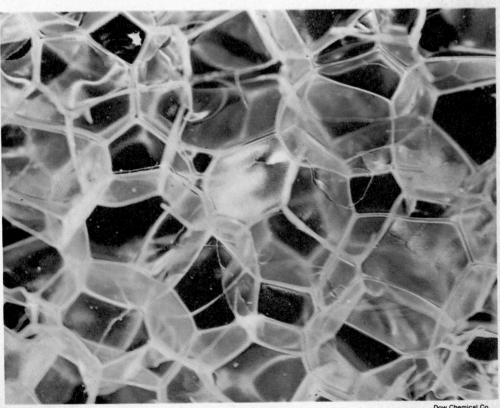

Neoprene latex is used to manufacture tough one-piece meteorological balloons for use by weather agencies, the U.S. armed forces, and some government and private research groups. W. R. Grace & Co.

**Chemistry. Plate 6.**

Below: Chemical technicians in a pharmaceutical plant keep a constant check on the reactors used in the production of antibiotics under the most highly sterile conditions. Pfizer Inc.

Pfizer Inc.

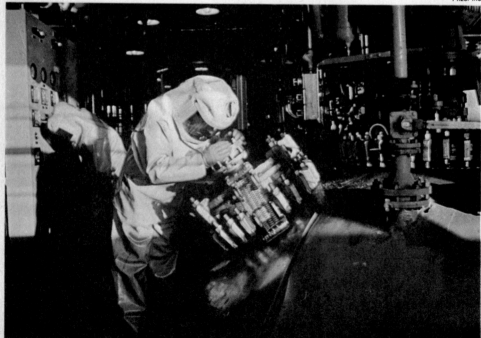

Pfizer Inc.

**Chemical Principles.** Early in the 19th century the French chemist Joseph Louis Proust (q.v.) distinguished and defined a compound, a mixture, and a solution: a chemical compound is a homogeneous substance in which the properties of its ingredient elements have disappeared, and in which new properties are found, unpredictable from those of its elements; a mixture is a substance in which the ingredients retain their properties, and the properties of the whole are the average properties of the ingredients; and a solution is a mixture in which the ingredients are distributed homogeneously. Proust also proposed the law of fixed proportions: that the proportions of the elements in any pure compound are invariable. A law of multiple proportions proposed by the British chemist John Dalton (q.v.) and a law of reciprocal proportions advanced by the German chemist Jeremias Benjamin Richter (1762–1807), maintained that every element can be assigned a so-called combining weight, in which, or in simple multiples of which, it combines with others.

These facts led Dalton to his atomic theory of the constitution of matter: that all elements are composed of tiny, invisible particles for which Dalton used the term "simple atoms". The simple atoms of an element join with those of other elements in definite ways, and thus form "compound atoms" of the resulting compound.

The combining weights of elements, that is, the ratios among the weights of elements which consistently enter into combination, could be determined experimentally. From these combining weights, however, the chemist could not deduce (nor did Dalton's atomic theory disclose) the atomic weights, or the relative weights of individual atoms, since it was uncertain how many of each kind of simple atom were joined in the compound atom. This knowledge was necessary to calculate mathematically the quantities of reagents and products involved in a chemical change. A clue to the problem was furnished by the French chemist Joseph Louis Gay-Lussac (q.v.), who observed that gases at the same pressure and temperature react in simple ratios by volume, and that if the product of the reaction is a gas, its volume bears a simple numerical ratio to those of its constituents, but is not the sum of these volumes. Thus, two volumes of ammonia gas can be decomposed into one volume of nitrogen and three of hydrogen. If the atoms of all gaseous elements, at equal pressure and temperature, were equally spaced, as Gay-Lussac thought, so that equal volumes of gases contained equal numbers of simple atoms, this could not be true also for compound

atoms. This difficulty was resolved by the Italian chemist Count Amedeo Avogadro (q.v.) by supposing each ultimate particle of an elementary gas to consist of two atoms joined together. He called such a combination a molecule, and applied this name also to the compound atoms of Dalton; see AVOGADRO'S LAW. On this assumption, the number of atoms which join in composing a molecule becomes obvious, and the relative atomic weights of elements can be determined. The hypothesis of Avogadro, however, was neglected for fifty years. During this time hopeless confusion characterized the subject of atomic weights, and some chemists regarded it as a mark of independent thought to have a personal, individual table of atomic weights. Finally, the theory of Avogadro was revived by his countryman Stanislao Cannizzaro (q.v.), who composed the first modern table of atomic weights.

**Chemical Symbolism and Equations.** Since medieval times, chemists have used symbols to denote the substances they considered elements. The symbols today consist of the initial letter, or initial two letters, of the Latin name of the element or, in the case of a recently discovered element, of its name in a modern language. The same symbols are adopted by all chemists throughout the world. A chemical reaction is expressed by an equation in which atoms of the reacting elements are expressed by symbols, with numerical subscripts following them to denote the numbers of each atom in the molecule. Numbers are prefixed to denote the least number of atoms or molecules which can be involved in the transformation. An arrow separates the reacting substances from their products. Thus, the combination of 1 volume of nitrogen, represented by the symbol N and molecular formula $N_2$, with 3 of hydrogen, represented by $H_2$, to form ammonia, $NH_3$, is represented thus:

$$N_2 + 3H_2 \rightarrow 2NH_3$$

An equation is balanced when the number of atoms of each kind in the reacting substances equals the number of atoms of that kind in the products. The 6 atoms in the 3 diatomic molecules of hydrogen, in the above example, thus, equal the 6 atoms of hydrogen in the 2 molecules of ammonia, each of which contains 3.

The proportionate weights of reagents and of products in a reaction depend upon the number of atoms of each kind involved and the relative atomic weights of each kind of atom. Such proportionate weights may be calculated by multiplying the number of each kind of atom by its atomic weight, and then adding the products to obtain the molecular weights of the compounds. In the illustrative reaction, nitrogen has an atomic weight close to 14, and hydrogen of very nearly 1, because whatever the actual weight of a nitrogen atom is, it is approximately 14 times as heavy as a hydrogen atom. Hence, 2 atoms of nitrogen have a proportionate weight of 28; 3 molecules of diatomic hydrogen, a weight of 6; and each molecule of ammonia, a weight of 14 plus 3, or 17. Thus, 28 parts by weight of nitrogen and 6 of hydrogen form 34 parts by weight of ammonia. *See* REACTION, CHEMICAL.

**Chemistry Today.** Today, chemistry is so widespread and important an activity that it touches the life of every individual in countless ways. The chemical industry is one of the largest enterprises in every industrialized country, and its technological development is intimately connected with the economic and cultural level of the lives of its citizens. In the late 1960's more than 400,000,000,000 lb. of industrial chemicals were manufactured annually in the United States alone, an average of about 2000 lb. of chemicals for every man, woman, and child in the nation. Over 1,000,000 persons were employed in chemical industry in the U.S., of whom about 100,000 were chemical technicians, and 35,000 were graduate chemists holding M.S. or Ph.D. degrees. An additional 20,000 chemists were employed in colleges, universities, and research institutes.

The tremendous volume of research activity may be judged from the fact that at a typical single meeting of the American Chemical Society in 1969, 12,000 chemists were present, and 2400 scientific papers were presented. American universities turned out 1800 Ph.D. chemists in 1967, nearly 10 percent of all the Ph.D.'s awarded in the other sciences, social sciences, humanities, and arts. In 1967 alone, more than 250,000 technical articles, research reports, and patents dealing with chemistry were published in journals and periodicals, and over 500 new chemical compounds were synthesized and put into practical use.

## MAJOR DIVISIONS OF CHEMISTRY

The field of chemical science has grown so vast and active that it has become differentiated into a number of specialties with well-defined characteristics. The broadest division is between the so-called pure and applied areas. Pure chemistry is concerned with the increasingly clear and detailed insights into the nature of chemical laws, the structure and behavior of molecules, atoms, and ions, and the relationship between constitution and properties (both chemical, such as

reactivities, and physical, such as color, viscosity, and volatility) of substances. Applied chemistry seeks to solve practical problems such as the development of new or better drugs, plastics, fertilizers, dyestuffs, and synthetic fibers, or the improvement of manufacturing processes, or the detection and elimination of pollutants.

The major divisions of chemical research within pure chemistry are analytical, biological, inorganic, organic, and physical chemistry.

**Analytical Chemistry.** The role of the analytical chemist is to develop and apply methods to determine the nature and quantities of chemical substances, whether they are present in a specimen as single, pure components, or in the form of mixtures. If a specimen for analysis consists of a single substance, the problem of identifying it is relatively simple. A characteristic physical property would be measured; if it is a liquid, for example, its boiling point (q.v.) might be determined, and if it boils at 100° C, it must belong to the relatively small group of liquids which boil at or near $100_8$ C. It could, for example, be water (b.p. 100.0° C.), isobutyl alcohol (99.8° C.), methyl methacrylate (100.0° C.), ethyl acrylate (99.8° C.), or methyl cyclohexane (100.2° C.). Measurement of a second property would then generally allow a definite identification to be made. For example, the densities (*see* DENSITY) of the liquids cited, all in grams per cubic milliliter, are: water (1.000), isobutyl alcohol (0.808), methyl methacrylate (0.936), ethyl acrylate (0.924), and methyl cyclohexane (0.786). These values are sufficiently different from each other so that the measurement of the density with only moderate precision would suffice to allow the identification of the specimen beyond reasonable doubt. In some cases, it is necessary to resort to the measurement of a third, independent property to confirm a doubtful identification, or to resolve any ambiguity.

The physical properties most commonly used for identification of chemical substances are the melting point, boiling point, density, refractive index, and degree of solubility in various solvents. Less commonly employed physical properties that are useful in special circumstances are the hardness, specific heat, viscosity (qq.v.), dielectric constant (*see* DIELECTRIC), magnetic susceptibility (*see* MAGNETISM), optical rotary power (*see* OPTICS: *Polarization of Light*), osmotic pressure (*see* OSMOSIS), vapor pressure (*see* VAPOR), crystal habit, electrical conductivity, latent heat of fusion or of vaporization, and thermal conductivity.

Since the end of World War II, the analytical methods used to identify a substance have been

The visual portion of the bright-line spectrum as photographed with a spectrometer and enlarged three times. Bausch & Lomb

greatly improved as a result of the development of a number of automated instrumental techniques that carry out a very large number of measurements of a given physical property over a standardized range of conditions. The following are some of the more typical instruments that have become standard analytical tools in modern chemistry.

ABSORPTION SPECTROMETER. This instrument sends a beam of light (q.v.) through the sample, and measures the degree to which the light has been absorbed. The wavelength of the light is caused to vary, and the amount of light absorbed by the specimen at each wavelength is graphed to yield an absorption spectrum. This chart of absorption as a function of wavelength is highly specific, and frequently serves as a rapid means of identification. It also provides a permanent record for future reference or for comparison between different investigators; see SPECTRUM: *Spectrometer*.

Absorption spectrometers have become indispensable instruments in most analytical chemistry laboratories. Three principal types of spectrometers are used, depending upon the range of wavelengths they are designed to cover. Infrared spectrometers cover the spectral range from about 0.8 to 200 microns or more, and are useful for the investigation of organic compounds of all kinds; see INFRARED RADIATION. Visible spectrometers cover the optical, or visual range, from approximately 0.4 to 0.8 microns, or 4000 to 8000 Angstroms (Å), blue to red light respectively; they are used for measurements of colored substances. Ultraviolet spectrometers cover the range from 4000 Å down to 1700 Å or less, and are particularly valuable in the analysis of certain kinds of organic substances, such as the unsaturated and aromatic compounds; see ULTRAVIOLET RADIATION.

A liquid scintillation spectrometer is used in cancer research to measure the amount of radioactivity in samples of blood or tissue extracts. Pfizer Inc.

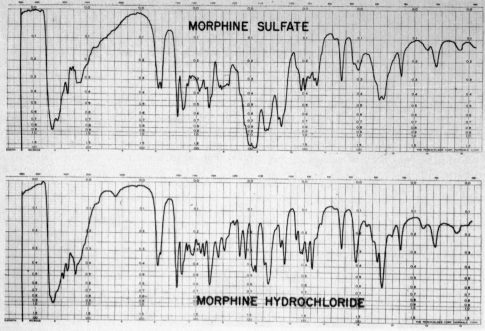

*Infrared spectra of morphine sulfate and morphine hydrochloride are recorded with Perkin-Elmer Model 21 double-beam infrared spectrophotometer.*  **Perkin-Elmer**

MASS SPECTROMETER. This device volatilizes, ionizes, and partially decomposes molecules, and charts the mass-to-charge ratio of the resulting mixture of fragments; *see* IONIZATION. This mass spectrum permits the molecular weight of the original compound to be determined, and also provides information about the way the molecule is put together, or the kinds of atomic groupings and radicals present; *see* SPECTROGRAPH, MASS.

MAGNETIC RESONANCE SPECTROMETER. This instrument measures the intensity of interaction of a strong magnetic field (caused by an electromagnet) with the weak magnetic fields that exist within certain kinds of molecules; *see* ELECTRICITY. A spinning electron (q.v.) has a small magnetic field as a result of its charge and spin (q.v.), and if this is not canceled by being paired with another electron spinning in the opposite direction, it can be affected by the field of an external magnet. An electron spin resonance (E.S.R.) spectrometer charts an electrical signal produced by the interaction between an unpaired electron in a molecule and a large electromagnet, between the poles of which the specimen is placed. Similarly, the nuclei of many (though not all) elements are also spinning charged objects (the others are charged, but do not spin), and have weak magnetic fields that can generate electrical signals if placed between the poles of an electromagnet. Instruments designed to detect these effects of nuclei are called nuclear magnetic resonance (N.M.R.) spectrometers. The magnetic resonance spectra produced by these instruments are very specific as to the molecular structure, and provide powerful tools for identification of the total composition and also the numbers and kinds of certain submolecular atomic groupings.

FLUORESCENCE SPECTROMETER. This instrument records the spectra of the radiations emitted by a substance that is irradiated by a source of radiant energy; *see* ELECTROMAGNETIC RADIATIONS; RADIATION. If the source is a high intensity X-ray tube (*see* X RAY), the sample is caused to emit its own type of X rays, and the chart of the wavelengths of these emitted, or fluorescent X rays permits the analyst to deduce the nature of the elements present in the specimen. Such devices are called X-ray spectrometer. If the radiant source is an ultraviolet lamp, the specimen emits fluorescent visible light. A Raman spectrometer, named after the Indian physicist Chandrasekhara Venkata Raman (q.v.), is an instrument of this type, yielding information that is very similar to that obtained from an infrared-absorption spectrometer. *See also* RAMAN EFFECT.

EMISSION SPECTROMETER. This instrument contains an arc or spark gap in which the specimen to be analyzed is subjected to such a high temperature or voltage that its atoms are stimulated to emit light. This light, consisting of a mixture of wavelengths characteristic of the atoms present in the specimen, is broken up into its components, and a chart of these wavelengths, a spectrum, is produced for the analyst.

OPTICAL ROTATION SPECTROMETER. This device records the degree to which the specimen affects polarized light beams of various wavelengths.

Although these sophisticated instruments have become essential in the modern analytical laboratory, simple qualitative tests also play an important role in the identification of substances. These consist of chemical reactions that result in a distinctive product, such as a colored solution or a precipitate, the occurrence of which (under defined conditions) is proof of the presence in the specimen of some specific substance or class of substances. For example, only three substances react with chloride ions ($Cl^-$) in an acidic medium to produce a precipitate, and only one of these precipitates, silver chloride, will dissolve in an excess of ammonium hydroxide solution. If a specimen is dissolved in water, therefore, and a white precipitate forms when some hydrochloric acid is added to that solution, and if that precipitate dissolves when an excess of ammonium hydroxide is added, it is evident that the original speci-

men was a silver compound. More or less elaborate schemes have been worked out along similar principles for the qualitative analysis of many kinds of specimens.

If the specimen is not a single, pure substance but a mixture of substances, the analytical problem is more difficult; the general analytical principles, however, remain the same. In many cases physical or chemical properties can be found that are sufficiently characteristic of one of the constituents to allow its presence to be established despite the presence of the other constituents. In a syrup or similar food preparation, for example, the extent to which the specimen rotates the plane of a polarized beam of light is almost entirely the result of the sugar content of the specimen, and this property can be utilized to reveal the presence (as well as the concentration) of the sugar regardless of the number and types of other substances.

Frequently, however, the several substances present in a specimen interfere with the detection of each, and a separation, or fractionation

*Sample of asparagus from field test plots treated with a weed killer are placed in an extraction apparatus and tested with precise analytical techniques to ensure that chemicals used on crops do not leave harmful residues.*
E.I. du Pont de Nemours & Co.

technique is used to free one of the components from the others. The most commonly used fractionation methods are: chromatography, distillation, ion exchange (qq.v.), extraction, precipitation, recrystallization, sublimation, dialysis, electrodeposition (*see* ELECTROCHEMISTRY; ELECTROPLATING), and electrophoresis.

In mixtures and solutions it is usually important to determine the precise proportions or concentrations of one or more of the constituents. This involves the methods of quantitative analysis, which are based upon a combination of the separation methods mentioned above with subsequent measurements of one or an-

other physical property by an appropriate accurate method. If the separation technique results in the precipitation of a single, pure compound that can be collected, dried, and weighed, the method is called gravimetric analysis, as the weight of the separated compound is related in a simple proportion to the weight of the original substance from which it was separated. In some cases a constituent can be caused to react with a standard solution (a solution containing a reagent in precisely known concentration), which is added in controlled amounts until the completion of the reaction is indicated by a change in color of an indicator substance. For example,

The complex deoxyribonucleic acid (DNA) molecule, which determines hereditary characteristics, is seen here in a floor-to-ceiling model. The chemical content of each nucleotide in the model is indicated by the white spirally ascending steps, representing the molecule's sugar-phosphate chains, and the horizontal pieces, representing the nitrogenous bases. UPI

litmus is a vegetable extract which is pink in an acidic solution, and blue in an alkaline solution; hence, it would indicate, by a change in color, when the last trace of an acid has been neutralized. This is an example of a volumetric analysis, because the quantity of the substance being analyzed can be calculated from the volume of the standard solution with which it reacts. The process of carrying out a controlled addition of a precisely measured volume of a standard solution is called a titration.

Analytical chemistry is necessary for the most basic understanding of the structure of molecules and the laws of chemistry, for it provides detailed quantitative measurements of the concentrations of substances and the ways in which observable properties are related to these concentrations, or the ways in which these concentrations are changed through the addition of energy or of other substances.

**Biochemistry.** The objective of the biochemist is to understand, on a molecular basis, the structures of the chemical compounds that are involved in the life processes of plants and animals, and the details of the reactions between these compounds. Biochemistry is thus on the one hand a branch of chemistry (particularly of organic chemistry) dealing with chemical compounds that are biologically significant, and on the other hand, it is a branch of biology (specifically of physiology, q.v.) dealing with those aspects of motion, metabolism, growth, and reproduction which are in essence merely chemical or physicochemical reactions. The limits of biochemistry are impossible to define because, being the connecting link between the biological and physical sciences, it draws upon the knowledge and techniques of all the so-called natural sciences.

Although many of the most dramatic advances of 20th-century science have been made in the realm of biochemistry, this study is only about a century old. Until 1824 it was believed that the reactions of life are unknowable, differing from reactions in the test tube by a subtle factor involving the so-called vital force of life; and until that time biochemistry could not exist as a science. In 1824, urea, a typical product of living animals, was synthesized in a test tube, but the concept of vital force was not finally abandoned until chemists had explained satisfactorily the structure of other physiologically important chemicals, notably benzene in 1865 and certain types of isomers in 1874. The realization that biochemistry could be investigated like any other science was followed by a great deal of research and culminated in such achievements as the synthesis and use of vitamins, hormones, amino acids, and the sulfa drugs. Compare BIOPHYSICS.

Biochemists study chemical substances in two ways: *in vitro,* in test tubes and similar apparatus, and *in vivo,* within the living organism. Penicillin, for example, was first shown to have bacteria-killing properties *in vitro* in 1929. Not until ten years later, however, was it shown to cure disease *in vivo* in laboratory animals, and not until two years after that was it shown to be effective in man. Numerous problems then appeared: biologists labored to grow penicillin-producing molds in large quantities; organic chemists developed methods of extracting and purifying natural penicillin and attempted to discover the structure of the penicillin molecule so that they might prepare it synthetically; and doctors studied the most effective methods of using this drug. Biochemists aided in all of these projects. Some of the great achievements of biochemical research are discussed in the text that follows.

The molecular structures of a large number of

*Electron microphotograph of a DNA sample that was successfully synthesized by scientists at Stanford University. An idea of the size of the substance can be obtained from the scale line of one micron, approximately four one-hundred-thousandths of an inch in length.* UPI

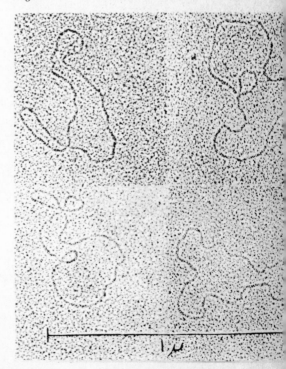

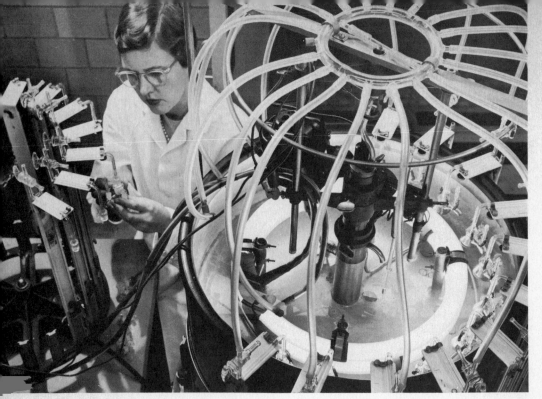

biological chemicals have been fully investigated, including the small but elusive molecules such as the intermediates, which play an essential role, but have very brief lifetimes, in photosynthesis (q.v.) and in the metabolic processes of digestion (*see* METABOLISM); the very complex macromolecules, such as enzymes, hormones, proteins, carbohydrates, and lipids have also been elucidated.

Methods have been developed for the synthesis of useful compounds through the control of the activities of yeasts, molds, and bacteria. Among the important substances now being produced industrially by fermentation techniques are ethyl and other alcohols, acetic and other acids, acetone, glycerol, antibiotics, vitamins, amino acids, enzymes, and steroids.

The detailed mechanisms by which living organisms convert foods into energy have been explained. The series of reactions by means of which fats are digested, absorbed, and stored are now understood, as is the way in which vitamins and hormones exert their physiologic influence. The chemistry of the reproductive cycle

is understood in considerable (though not yet complete) detail, and chemical methods have been developed for either assisting or interfering with it. The chemical processes by which some complex biological chemicals are produced in the living organism from the breakdown products of food metabolism have been discovered. The role of trace minerals in maintaining proper physiological balance has been clarified.

The chemical basis for the development of an entire organism from the collection of molecules present in a single germ cell is now understood. The molecular structures of deoxyribonucleic acid, or DNA and ribonucleic acid, or RNA have been worked out, and this has made it clear on a molecular level how hereditary characteristics can be transmitted from generation to generation, and how mutations and genetic damage occur; *see* HEREDITY; NUCLEIC ACIDS.

Despite the great and dramatic advances of biochemistry in the last two or three decades, many of the most important and intriguing problems remain to be solved. It is generally considered that biochemistry is now on the threshold of its most fruitful and significant era. **Inorganic Chemistry.** The field of inorganic chemistry comprises the study of all aspects of inorganic chemicals, or substances in which carbon combined with hydrogen or oxygen is not the principal ingredient. The carbon compounds are set apart because of the almost unique chain- and ring-forming properties of the carbon atom. A few carbon compounds, for example, carbon monoxide (CO), carbon dioxide ($CO_2$), the carbonates (such as $Na_2CO_3$), and the acetates (such as $NaC_2H_3O_2$), are commonly considered within the domain of inorganic chemistry. The elements silicon, boron, sulfur, and germanium form series of chain and ring compounds containing hydrogen and oxygen, quite analogous in many respects to the carbon compounds, but have generally been considered to belong to the field of inorganic chemistry. The silicones are examples of compounds that fall on the indistinct borderline between inorganic and organic chemistry.

Inorganic chemistry is too heterogeneous a subject to form a convenient unit of study; the term would be of little importance except for the tendency in schools to entitle courses "Inorganic Chemistry" when a better title would be "Elementary Chemistry". The subject matter of such courses includes the elementary laws of chemistry, its symbolism and nomenclature, and an introduction to the experimental method as applied to physical science, including practice in many of the laboratory manipulations that are important in experimental chemistry. The student is introduced to such fundamental chemical concepts as valency, ionization, activity, the atomic theory, and the kinetic theory (q.v.) of gases. The properties and reactions of substances in aqueous solution are given particular attention.

On the basis of their behavior in aqueous solution, most inorganic compounds can be conveniently classified as acids, bases, or salts (qq.v.). The properties of such compounds can usually be approximately predicted on the basis of their constituents; for example, ordinary table salt (sodium chloride, NaCl) has many properties in common with all sodium compounds on the one hand, and with all chlorides on the other. The most important inorganic element, geologically, biologically, and industrially, is oxygen, and its compounds with the elements, called oxides, can be classified as acidic and basic, inasmuch as the oxides of the metals form bases when combined with water, and the oxides of the nonmetals form acids.

The number of industries depending primarily on inorganic compounds is small in comparison with those depending on organic compounds, or on both. The number of professional chemists who call themselves organic chemists is large but relatively few call themselves inorganic chemists. A chemist confining himself to inorganic substances must further specialize, and may become, for example, an analytical chemist, an electrochemist, or a physical chemist. He may also specialize in a particular industry such as the manufacture of concrete, glass, ferrous or nonferrous metals, adhesives, or ceramics.

**Organic Chemistry.** The organic chemist tries to understand the properties of organic chemicals, to gain control over their reactivities, synthesize new molecular permutations and combinations, and elucidate the mechanisms of their reactions.

In view of the peculiar ability of carbon atoms to attach themselves to one another, there are a great many different types of organic compounds. Such compounds as the hydride of carbon, $CH_4$ (see METHANE), and the oxide of carbon, $CO_2$, are not essentially different from the hydrides and oxides of other elements. But carbon also forms hundreds of other hydrides; for example, two atoms of carbon may be combined to form a molecule of ethane, $C_2H_6$, ethylene, $C_2H_4$, or acetylene, $C_2H_2$. When more than two atoms of carbon are combined in a molecule, more variations are possible. Thus, there are two different compounds with the formula $C_4H_{10}$ and the name butane (q.v.), depending on whether the carbon atoms are combined in a straight or branched chain; these two compounds are called respectively *n*– (for normal) and *i*– (for iso) butane. In larger molecules, an almost infinite number of different chains or rings, with branches, of carbon atoms are possible, and an extremely large number of such different structures are found in nature, and have been prepared in the laboratory. *See* HYDROCARBONS.

Chemists have prepared and studied about 2,000,000 different organic compounds, approximately ten times more than the total known number of different compounds that contain any of the other elements but do not contain carbon. Although most of the elements may be present in organic compounds, the vast majority of these compounds contain only carbon, hydrogen, oxygen, nitrogen, sulfur, bromine, chlorine, and iodine. An organic chemist can easily prepare hundreds of new compounds, but unless time can be spent in studying their properties such research is unprofitable. Sulfanilamide, for example, had been known to organic chemists for many years before its germicidal properties were discovered. In the course of routine research, saccharin, which is hundreds of times sweeter than cane sugar, was prepared and its properties of sweetness were discovered only by accident. Tyrian purple, the royal dye of ancient times, was prepared by a chemist some years ago in accordance with the classical formula, but he then discovered that it was identical with a compound which had been previously synthesized and discarded as inferior to certain other synthetic dyes.

Because of the possible structural variations, organic chemical reactions rarely follow a single course. Ethylene ($C_2H_4$), for example, may react with chlorine in numerous ways: being unsaturated (because two of the valence bonds of each carbon atom are attached to one another), it may add HCl or $Cl_2$ to form $C_2H_5Cl$ or $C_2H_4Cl_2$ respectively; chlorine may substitute for hydrogen to form $C_2H_3Cl$, $C_2H_2Cl_2$, or other variations; there may be a combination of these two reactions; or two or more molecules may combine to form complex derivatives. The extent to which one or another of these reactions will predominate depends upon the relative concentrations, the temperature and pressure, the presence or absence of light, whether or not the reaction takes place in solution and the nature and concentration of the solvent, the presence of acids or alkalies, and numerous other factors. By controlling such factors the organic chemist may direct the reaction along desired lines, but the product nearly always requires purification. The organic chemist must not only control his reactions, but must also develop methods for purifying his products and for testing their purity. Moreover, he needs special methods for determining the structure of his compounds, and for proving the validity of his conclusions regarding structure.

DIVISIONS OF ORGANIC CHEMISTRY. Organic compounds are separated into two groups, the aliphatic, in which the carbon atoms in a molecule are connected to one another in chains, straight or branched, and the cyclic, in which the carbon atoms are connected in rings. The latter include: the aromatic, in which the rings are highly unsaturated, such as that of benzene ($C_6H_6$); the alicyclic, in which the rings are saturated, and the properties of the compounds are intermediate between the aliphatic and the aromatic; and the heterocyclic, in which atoms other than carbon, such as nitrogen, enter into the ring structure. For further details on all of these groups, *see* AROMATIC COMPOUNDS.

CLASSES OF ORGANIC CHEMISTRY. Like inorganic compounds which can be classified into acids, bases, and salts, organic compounds fall naturally into groups that contain similar radicals and have common properties. Organic acids contain the carboxyl radical, $-COOH$. The most familiar, and one of the simplest, of organic acids is acetic acid, $CH_3COOH$, the active principle of vinegar. The next member of this group is propionic acid, $C_2H_5COOH$, followed by butyric acid, $C_3H_7COOH$. The formula of successive members in a given group differs by the same amount of $C_1H_2$. Most organic acids, like acetic acid, are far weaker than such inorganic acids as hydrochloric or sulfuric. Some organic substances that do not have the carboxyl group may nevertheless have acidic properties; for example, phenol, $C_6H_5OH$, is sometimes called carbolic acid.

The organic analogs of bases are the aliphatic alcohols, such as ethyl (or ordinary) alcohol, $C_2H_5OH$, and the aromatic phenols, such as carbolic acid. The reaction of an organic acid with an alcohol yields an ester, the organic analog of a salt. In organic chemistry, however, such reactions are slow and incomplete, while in inorganic chemistry they are almost instantaneous. Other important classes of organic compounds are ethers, aldehydes, ketones, amines, nitro compounds, and sulfonic acids. Many compounds have two or more such active groups, and their properties comprise those of all the constituents. For example, the amino acids (q.v.) have both a carboxyl and an amine group.

COMPLEX COMPOUNDS. Although there is no clear dividing line, organic compounds with as many as fifty carbon atoms are usually considered simple. Many important organic compounds, however, have enormous molecules, of indefinite size, containing thousands of carbon atoms. The amine group of one molecule of an amino acid, for example, can combine with the carboxyl group of another, to form a molecule twice as large. Then the amine group of the second can combine with the carboxyl group of a third, and so on. In this way, protein (q.v.) molecules are built up within the bodies of both plants and animals. An identical chemical process under controlled conditions is responsible for such synthetic complex compounds as nylon (q.v.). Other textile fibers, both synthetic and natural, consist of complex, polymeric compounds formed by different reactions. Carbohydrates such as cellulose are similarly built up by the combination of many molecules of simple sugars. Rubber (q.v.), both natural and synthetic, and most plastics, resins (qq.v.), and gums (*see* GUM) consist of polymeric organic molecules.

Among the great achievements of organic chemical research are the synthesis of a great

variety of pigments and dyestuffs, providing a range of colors and degree of resistance to fading impossible to achieve with natural products; these are particularly useful in the textile and graphic arts industries.

The synthesis of monomers and the development of polymerization techniques have resulted in the availability of unlimited quantities of plastics, resins, elastomers, adhesives, and fibers at low prices; these synthetic substances can be given almost any desired combination of properties. The isolation and identification of the molecular structures of the active ingredients of useful natural products such as herbs, flavors, medicines, and perfumes has permitted these molecules to be synthesized and produced industrially, and has allowed the chemical scientists to modify the original molecular structures to produce new substances with special desirable combinations of properties. The development of improved fuels, solvents, explosives, detergents, food preservatives, and many other products, and the development of a comprehensive, detailed theoretical interpretation of the several modes in which carbon and its associated atomic partners are linked to each other, and of the factors which govern the reactivities of organic compounds, are among the most important contributions of organic chemical research.

**Physical Chemistry.** If the principal emphasis in chemical studies is on the application of the laws of physics (q.v.) to the elucidation of the properties of chemical substances, the disci-

*Many important chemical compounds for pharmacological studies and clinical testing are produced in the laboratory using the vacuum-distillation process.*
Pfizer Inc.

pline is known as physical chemistry or chemical physics. In general, no sharp distinction exists between these two terms, the difference being based more or less upon the degree of mathematical sophistication involved and the extent to which quantum and statistical mechanical reasoning are employed; *see* QUANTUM MECHANICS; STATISTICS. In other words, the term "physical chemistry" is usually applied to the study of the physical properties of substances, such as vapor pressure, surface tension, viscosity, refractive index, density, and crystallography, as well as to the study of the so-called classical aspects of the behavior of chemical systems, such as thermal properties, equilibria, rates of reactions, mechanisms of reactions, and ionization phenomena; *see* HEAT; HEAT TRANSFER; IONIZATION; REACTION, CHEMICAL. The term "chemical physics" is usually applied to: the analysis in terms of fundamental quantum theory (q.v.) of spectral properties; the interaction of energy with matter; the nature of chemical bindings; the relationships correlating the number and energy states of electrons in atoms and molecules with the observable properties shown by these systems; and the electrical, thermal, and mechanical effects of individual electrons and protons on solids and liquids. In addition, chemical physics embraces those activities that involve the application of the theory of statisti-

411

cal analysis to the explanation of the properties of bulk matter, as in statistical thermodynamics, where the thermal behavior of substances can be computed from a knowledge of nothing more than the energy states that can be occupied by an individual molecule of the substance. *See* THERMODYNAMICS.

The first formal recognition of physical chemistry as a distinct field of specialization within the broader discipline of chemistry dates from the founding, in 1887, of the first scientific journal devoted to this subject. In that year, the German chemist Wilhelm Ostwald (q.v.), one of the most important contributors to the new field, initiated the publication of the *Zeitschrift für physikalische Chemie* ("Journal of Physical Chemistry"). Physical chemistry grew rapidly during the next half century, and the number of research papers published by physical chemists increased sufficiently to necessitate the founding of additional specialized journals, such as the *Journal of Physical Chemistry,* published in the United States in 1896, and the *Zhurnal Fizicheskoi Khimii* ("Journal of Physical Chemistry") initiated in the Soviet Union in 1930.

In 1933 chemical physics acquired a form of separate status with the founding of the *Journal of Chemical Physics* in the U.S. Since the end of World War II, the field has grown enormously, as have many other fields of specialization within chemistry. The scope of current research activities in chemical physics can be judged from the names of some of the journals that are being published for research scientists active in this specialty: *Spectrochimica Acta,* (published in Oxford, England, in 1939); *Journal of Molecular Spectroscopy* (New York City, 1957); *Journal of Quantitative Spectroscopy and Radiative Transfer* (New York City, 1961); *Theoretica Chimica Acta* (West Berlin, 1962); *Journal of Physics and Chemistry of Solids* (London, 1963); *Molecular Crystals* (London, 1966); and *Macromolecules* (Murray Hill, N.J., 1968).

HISTORICAL DEVELOPMENT. The earliest phase of the development of physical chemistry as a specialized field of study was devoted to the investigation of the so-called problem of chemical affinities, or the widely varying extents and degrees of vigor with which various substances react with each other. Common examples are the easy corrosion of iron compared to gold, and the fact that oxygen supports combustion (q.v.) but nitrogen does not. It was first assumed that rapid reactions were those that proceeded to completion. It was soon realized, however, that these were independent factors; the degree of completeness of a reaction is determined by its

so-called equilibrium constant, a concept introduced in 1864 by the Norwegian chemists Cato Maximilian Guldberg (1836–1902) and Peter Waage (1833–1900) whereas the rate of a reaction is determined by the intimacy of contact between the reactants, the presence or absence of a catalyst (*see* CATALYSIS), and other factors.

John Dalton proposed his atomic theory in 1803 and it was placed on a firm footing in 1811 when Amedeo Avogadro made clear the distinction between atoms and molecules of elementary substances. At about the same time, the concepts of heat, energy, work, and temperature began to be clarified and made more precise. The first law of thermodynamics, according to which heat and work are mutually exactly interconvertible, was first clearly stated by the German physicist Julius Robert von Mayer (1814–78) in 1842. The second law of thermodynamics, according to which spontaneous processes occur with an increase in the degree of disorder in the system, was enunciated by the German mathematical physicist Rudolf Julius Emmanuel Clausius and the British mathematician and physicist William Thomson, later Lord Kelvin (qq.v.) in 1850–51.

These developments made it possible to begin to interpret the properties of gases, which represent the simplest of the states of matter, in terms of the behavior of their individual molecules. In the period 1860–75, Clausius, the Austrian physicist Ludwig Eduard Boltzmann (1844–1906), and the British physicist James Clerk Maxwell (q.v.) showed how to account for the ideal gas law in terms of a kinetic theory (q.v.) of matter. From this beginning have flowed all the subsequent insights into the kinetics of reactions and the laws of chemical equilibrium.

The important contributions to the field of physical chemistry were made toward the end of the 18th century by the French chemist Comte Claude Louis Berthollet (q.v.) who studied the rate and reversibility of reactions, and the Anglo-American physicist Benjamin Thompson (q.v.), Count Rumford, who attempted to deduce the mechanical equivalent of heat. In 1824 the French physicist Nicolas Léonard Sadi Carnot (q.v.) published his studies of the correlation between heat and work that established him as the founder of modern thermodynamics, and in 1836 the Swedish chemist Jöns Jakob Berzelius (q.v.) assessed the role played by catalysts in accelerating reactions. The application of the first and second laws of thermodynamics to heterogenous substances in 1875 by the American mathematical physicist Josiah Willard Gibbs (q.v.) and his discovery of the phase rule (q.v.) laid down the theoretical basis of physical chemistry. The German physical chemist Walther Hermann Nernst (q.v.), who in 1906 enunciated the third law of thermodynamics, also made a lasting contribution to the study of physical properties, molecular structures, and reaction rates.

The Dutch physical chemist Jacobus Hendricus van't Hoff (q.v.), generally regarded as the father of chemical kinetics, initiated the foundation of stereochemistry in 1874 with his work on optically active carbon compounds and three-dimensional and asymmetrical molecular structures. Three years later, he related thermodynamics to chemical reactions and developed a method for establishing the order of reactions. In 1889 the Swedish physical chemist Svante August Arrhenius (q.v.) investigated the speeding of chemical reactions with increase in temperature and enunciated the theory of electrolytic dissociation, known as Arrhenius' theory. The development of chemical kinetics has continued into the 20th century with the contributions to the study of molecular structures, reaction rates, and chain reactions by physical chemists such as Irving Langmuir (q.v.) of the U.S., Jens Anton Christiansen (1888–1969) of Denmark, Michael Polanyi (1891–1976) of Great Britain, and Nikolai Semenov (q.v.) of the Soviet Union, and important basic research continues today.

During the early years of the 20th century, studies of atomic and molecular structure, ionization, and chemical forces by the American chemist Kasimir Fajans (1887–    ) and the physicist Walter Kossel (1888–1956) of Germany aided the elucidation of electronic molecular structure and chemical binding. In 1923, the American chemist Gilbert Newton Lewis (q.v.) further clarified the principles of chemical thermodynamics enunciated by Gibbs.

The great watershed period for the development of chemical physics was 1900–30. In 1897 the German physicist Max Planck (q.v.) had proposed that energy in certain systems is "quantized", or occurs in discrete units or packages, just as matter occurs in discrete units, the atoms. In 1913, the Danish physicist Niels Henrik David Bohr (q.v.) showed how the concept of quantization served fully to explain the spectrum of atomic hydrogen. In 1926–29, the Austrian physicist Erwin Schrödinger and the German physicist Werner Karl Heisenberg (qq.v.) developed the picture of the wave function, a mathematical expression incorporating the wave-particle duality of electrons, and they

showed how to calculate useful properties from this formula. It is from these beginnings that modern concepts of the structures of atoms and the nature of the bindings between atoms have evolved.

SUBDIVISIONS OF PHYSICAL CHEMISTRY. The main subdivisions of the study of physical chemistry are as follows: chemical thermodynamics; chemical kinetics; the gaseous state; the liquid state; solutions; the solid state; electrochemistry; colloid chemistry; and photochemistry.

*Chemical Thermodynamics.* This branch studies energy in its various forms as related to matter. It examines the ways in which the internal energy, degree of organization or order, and ability to do useful work are related to temperature (q.v.), heat absorbed or evolved, change of state (for instance, from liquid to gas, gas to liquid, solid to liquid), work done on, or by, the system in the form of the flow of electrical currents, formation of surfaces and changes in surface tension, changes in volume or pressure, and formation or disappearance of chemical species.

*Chemical Kinetics.* This field studies the rates of chemical processes as a function of the concentrations of the reacting species, of the products of the reaction, of catalysts and inhibitors, of various solvent media, of temperature, and of all other factors that can affect the reaction rate. It is an essential part of the study of chemical kinetics to seek to relate the precise fashion in which the reaction rate varies with time to the molecular nature of the rate-controlling intermolecular collision involved in generating the reaction products. Most reactions involve a series of stepwise processes, the sum of which corresponds to the overall, observed reaction proportions (or stoichiometry) in which the reactants combine and the products form, but only one of these steps is generally the rate-controlling one, the others being much faster. By determining the nature of the rate-controlling process from the mathematical analysis of the reaction kinetics and by investigating how the reaction conditions (for instance, solvent, temperature, other species) affect this step, or cause some other process to become the rate-controlling one, the physical chemist can deduce the mechanism of a reaction.

*The Gaseous State.* This branch is concerned with the study of the properties of gases, in particular, the law which interrelates the pressure, volume, temperature, and quantity of a gas. This law is expressed in mathematical form as the "equation of state" of the gas. For an ideal gas (that is, a hypothetical gas consisting of molecules whose dimensions are negligibly small, and which do not exert forces of attraction or repulsion upon each other), the equation of state has the simple formula: $PV = nRT$, where P is pressure, V is volume, $n$ is the number of moles of the substance, R is a constant, and T is the absolute (or Kelvin) temperature. For real gases, the equation of state is more complicated, containing additional factors due to the effects of the finite sizes and force fields of the molecules. Mathematical analysis of the equations of state of real gases permits the physical chemist to deduce much about the relative sizes of molecules, as well as the strengths of the forces they exert upon each other.

*The Liquid State.* This field studies the properties of liquids, in particular, the vapor pressure, boiling point (q.v.), heat of vaporization, heat capacity, volume per mole, viscosity (q.v.), compressibility, and the manner in which these properties are affected by the temperature and pressure at which they are measured, and by the chemical nature of the substance itself.

*Solutions.* This branch studies the special properties that arise when one substance is dissolved in another. In particular, it investigates the solubility of substances and how it is affected by the chemical nature of both the solute and the solvent as well as the study of the electrical conductivity and colligative properties (the boiling point, freezing point, vapor pressure, and osmotic pressure) of solutions of electrolytes, which are substances that yield ions when dissolved in a polar solvent such as water.

*The Solid State.* This branch deals with the study of the internal structure, on a molecular and atomic scale, of solids, and the elucidation of the physical properties of solids in terms of this structure. This includes the mathematical analysis of the diffraction patterns produced when a beam of X rays is directed at a crystal. By using this method, physical chemists have gained valuable insights into the packing arrangements adopted by various types of ions and atoms. They have also learned the symmetries and crystallographies of most solid substances as well as their cohesive forces, heat capacities, melting points and optical properties. *See* CRYSTAL.

*Electrochemistry.* This branch is concerned with the study of chemical effects produced by the flow of electric currents across interfaces (as at the boundary between an electrode and a solution), and vice versa, the electrical effects produced by the displacement or transport of ions across boundaries or within gases, liquids, or solids. *See* ELECTRICITY. Measurements of electrical conductivity in liquids yield insights into ionization equilibria and the properties of ions.

In solids, such measurements provide information about the states of the electrons in crystal lattices and in insulators, semiconductors, and metallic conductors. Measurements of voltages (electric potentials) yield knowledge of the concentrations of ionic species, and of the driving forces of reactions that involve the gain or loss of electrons from various reactants. *See* ELECTROCHEMISTRY.

*Colloid Chemistry.* This branch studies the nature and effects of surfaces and interfaces on the macroscopic properties of substances. These studies involve the investigation of surface tension, interfacial tension (the tension that exists in the plane of contact between a liquid and a solid, or between two liquids), wetting and spreading of liquids on solids, adsorption of gases or of ions in solution on solid surfaces, Brownian motion of suspended particles (*see* BROWNIAN MOVEMENT), emulsification, coagulation, and other properties of systems in which tiny particles are immersed in a fluid medium. *See* COLLOIDAL DISPERSION.

*Photochemistry.* This branch concerns the study of the effects resulting from the absorption of electromagnetic radiations (q.v.) by substances as well as the ability of substances to emit electromagnetic radiations when energized in various ways. When X-radiation impinges on matter, electrons may be ejected from their places in the interiors of atoms, ions, or molecules, and measurement of the energies of these electrons reveals much about the nature of the electron arrangement within the atom, ion, or molecule. Similarly, investigation of the absorption of ultraviolet and visible light discloses the structure of the valence (q.v.), or binding electrons (*see* ULTRAVIOLET RADIATION); absorption of infrared radiation (q.v.) provides information about the vibrational motions and binding forces within molecules; and absorption of microwave, or radar (q.v.), radiation permits scientists to deduce the nature of the rotational motions of molecules, and from this the exact geometries (internuclear distances) of the molecules. The study of the interaction of electromagnetic radiation with matter, when that interaction does not result in chemical changes, is often designated as spectrochemistry, and the term "photochemistry" is then used only for those interactions that produce chemical changes. Examples of photochemical (that is, light-induced) reactions are the fading of dyes when exposed to sunlight, the generation of vitamin D in the human skin by sunlight, and the formation of ozone in the upper atmosphere by the ultraviolet radiation from the sun. *See* PHOTOCHEMISTRY.

SUBDIVISIONS OF CHEMICAL PHYSICS. The main subdivisions of chemical physics are statistical thermodynamics and mechanics, and quantum chemistry.

*Statistical Thermodynamics and Mechanics.* This branch is concerned with the calculation of the internal energy, degree of order or organization (entropy), ability to do useful work (free energy), and other properties, such as the equations of state of gases, the vapor pressures of liquids, the molecular shapes adopted by polymer chains, and electrical conductivities of ionic solutions. These calculations are based upon a model of the individual molecule or ion and the mathematical techniques of statistical analysis, which permit the mutual interactions of large numbers of randomly arranged particles to be evaluated.

*Quantum Chemistry.* This field deals with the interpretation of atomic and molecular structures in terms of the fundamental principles of quantum mechanics (q.v.). According to these principles, each system can be described mathematically by a so-called wave function, which includes all the experimentally knowable properties of the system, and from which any desired property can be calculated by certain mathematical operations performed on the wave function. Of major interest in this connection are the interpretation of spectra (*see* SPECTRUM), the explanation of the periodicities in the properties of the elements (*see* PERIODIC LAW), and the elucidation of the system of molecular orbitals involved in binding atoms together to produce molecules. *See* ATOM AND ATOMIC THEORY.

CURRENT STATUS. Physical chemistry and chemical physics are vigorously active fields of research in chemistry today. Electrochemistry, colloid chemistry and photochemistry are of great importance in many phases of modern industry. The current computer and communications (qq.v.) revolutions, for example, could not have occurred without the special chemicals, crystals, and devices developed in the course of research in these branches of physical chemistry.

In the area of fundamental research, as distinguished from applied research, the greatest emphasis today is on the theoretical analysis of spectra of all kinds, ranging from the X-ray region of the electromagnetic spectrum to the radio-wave region. Emphasis is also placed on the application of quantum and wave mechanics to elucidate the principles of molecular binding and structure. Valuable insights into these questions have been gained by studying the properties of substances under conditions both of extremely high and extremely low temperatures and pressures, as well as under the influence of strong electrical, magnetic, and electromagnetic fields.

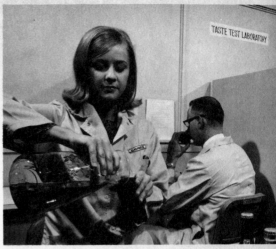

Tasters at a taste-test laboratory study samples of food and beverage products to see if any traces of the chemical sealing agent are discernible.   W. R. Grace & Co.

**Industrial Chemistry.** The field of industrial chemistry includes all of the branches of chemistry discussed before, the main difference in chemical work carried out industrially being its general direction toward the production of a substance for commercial purposes or for the solution of a specific practical problem. This work is carried on not only in strictly chemical industries, which generally produce bulk materials, but also in most other manufacturing industries that produce fabricated articles. The processes of synthesis and fabrication are combined under a single roof in some industries; thus, a typical plastics factory uses as raw materials chemicals such as formaldehyde and carbolic acid, or agricultural products such as cotton and corncobs, and turns out as finished products toothbrushes, electrical insulators, or rayon fabrics.

Industrial chemistry differs from laboratory chemistry principally in three points: cost, purity, and amount of the final product. A typical laboratory reaction yields at most a few ounces of product; in some cases where large amounts of material are unavailable, as in the original atomic-bomb experiments on plutonium, experiments must be done on less than a millionth of an ounce of material. In a typical industrial installation, on the other hand, production may reach many tons, or even thousands of tons, each day. The laboratory chemist, because of the negligible cost of the small quantities involved, uses materials of the utmost purity, and carries on his reactions in vessels of glass, platinum, or other substances which will not contaminate his products. He is interested in determining whether a particular product can be made or whether a particular reaction will take place. He assumes that if he can find a way to solve his problem, he can leave to the industrial chemist the method of its practical application. The industrial chemist, however, must bear costs constantly in mind; if the process is not economic, it cannot have widespread industrial applications. Ways must be found of using inexpensive, frequently somewhat impure, raw materials, employing reaction vessels of iron, wood, or similar inexpensive substances, and yet keeping contamination down to permissible limits. The industrial chemist arranges the reactions so that control will be simple and automatic, keeping labor costs at a minimum, and he must examine the effects of various irregularities in raw materials, climatic conditions, and numerous other factors, to insure uniform quality of the product.

Even after all of these problems have been solved in an industrial laboratory, the change of production from ounces to tons is difficult and requires extensive experimentation, for numerous unpredictable variations occur between small-scale and large-scale production. For example, a process for the manufacture of glue may have been evolved in the laboratory, in which the glue is boiled in a 1-gal. vessel. If the same reaction is now tried in a vessel of the same shape but 10 times as large in each dimension, it will be observed that although the volume of the vessel is 1000 times as great, the area of the surface is only 100 times as great. Under such circumstances, the formation of foam may exceed the rate at which the foam breaks down, and it may be impossible to boil the glue without it overflowing the vessel.

For similar reasons, after an industrial chemist has demonstrated a process to be practical in the industrial laboratory, an experimental plant of intermediate size, called a pilot plant, is built before a full-scale production plant is designed; with the experience gained in building and operating the pilot plant, it is possible to design a full-scale factory with some assurance that it will work satisfactorily. Generally, therefore, after the first test-tube experiment has been successfully performed, a period of from 5 to 10 years elapses before full-scale industrial operation can take place. In some recent developments, however, this period has been remarka-

bly shortened. In many cases, processes that seem to operate satisfactorily at the test-tube level have never become satisfactory for industrial production. For example, chemists in the 19th century knew how to make synthetically what is now called 100-octane gasoline; no practical industrial synthesis, however, has yet been developed, and this substance is still prepared from natural products; see PETROLEUM.

Among the most important industrial chemicals are the so-called heavy chemicals (chemical raw materials produced in large quantities), such as sulfuric acid, salt, caustic soda, ammonia, and chlorine. A list of all of the applications of industrial chemistry would contain virtually all the products of modern civilization, but among the more important products, both natural and synthetic, which industrial chemists have brought into existence, or for the processing of which they have invented improved methods, are: coke, alloys, rubber, glass, plastics, adhesives, paints, varnishes, lacquers, insecticides, fungicides, disinfectants, pigments, dyes, inks, photographic materials, food products, fertilizers, ceramics, refrigerants, cements, explosives, textiles, soap and detergents, hormones, sulfa drugs, antibiotics, and vitamins.

See separate articles on most of the industrial processes and products mentioned in this article. S.Z.L.

**CHEMISTRY, AGRICULTURAL.** See AGRICULTURAL CHEMISTRY.

**CHEMISTRY, ANALYTICAL.** See CHEMISTRY: *Major Divisions of Chemistry: Analytical Chemistry.*

**CHEMISTRY, BIOLOGICAL.** See CHEMISTRY: *Major Divisions of Chemistry: Biochemistry.*

**CHEMISTRY, INDUSTRIAL.** See CHEMICAL COMPOUNDS, SYNTHETIC; CHEMISTRY: *Industrial Chemistry;* ENGINEERING: *Chemical Engineering.*

**CHEMISTRY, INORGANIC.** See CHEMISTRY: *Major Divisions of Chemistry: Inorganic Chemistry.*

**CHEMISTRY, ORGANIC.** See CHEMISTRY: *Major Divisions of Chemistry: Organic Chemistry.*

**CHEMISTRY, PHYSICAL.** See CHEMISTRY: *Physical Chemistry.*

**CHEMNITZ.** See KARL-MARX-STADT.

**CHEMNITZ, Martin** or **KEMNITZ, Martin** (1522–86), German Lutheran theologian, born in Brandenburg and educated in Frankfurt-an-der-Oder and Wittenberg. He was placed in charge of the ducal library at Königsberg (now Kaliningrad, U.S.S.R.) in 1550 but returned to Wittenberg three years later to lecture on the *Loci Communes Rerum Theologicam* ("Commonplaces of Theology") by the German religious reformer Melanchthon (q.v.). The *Loci Communes,* an exposition of Lutheran doctrine, became the basis for Chemnitz's own posthumously published *Loci Theologici* ("Theological Arguments", 1591). In 1554 Chemnitz became a preacher in Brunswick, and in 1567 he was appointed superintendent there. He was influential in inducing the Lutherans of Saxony and Swabia to unite in accepting the Formula of Concord (*see* CONCORD, BOOK OF), which ended a split in the Lutheran movement. His other works include *Examen Concilii Tridentini* ("Examination of the Council of Trent", 4 vol., 1565–73).

**CHEMOTHERAPY,** the use of chemical agents in the treatment of disease. In its widest sense, chemotherapy includes the use of any therapeutic drug, but in general usage it is confined to those substances—especially synthetic chemicals, as well as certain isolated and purified natural products—which have a specific inhibiting effect against parasitic microorganisms (the causative agents of infectious disease) or against cancer cells, without serious toxic effect upon the host (the diseased individual).

**History.** The Swiss physician and chemist Philippus Aureolus Paracelsus (q.v.), who early in the 16th century tried to find specific chemical treatments for various diseases instead of the ancient herbal remedies, is generally recognized as the founder of chemotherapy. Also, it is known that cinchona (q.v.) bark, which contains quinine and other chemical agents, has been used to treat malaria (q.v.) since 1638.

The first synthetic chemotherapeutic agent was Salvarsan, discovered by the German bacteriologist Paul Ehrlich (q.v.) in 1909. Ehrlich had discovered that certain dyes, when injected into an animal, were highly selective, dyeing only a particular organ of the body. Later he discovered a dye, trypan red, which, when injected into a syphilitic animal, would dye the causative organisms without affecting the host. He reasoned that a suitable chemical composed of a combination of a dye such as trypan red (which would attach itself to the germ), and a poison such as arsenic (which would kill the germ), would comprise a "magic bullet" for the cure of syphilis. He prepared hundreds of such chemicals, and the 606th chemical was Salvarsan, also known as arsphenamine or 606. This drug effected almost miraculous cures of syphilis and related diseases.

**Sulfa Drugs and Antibiotics.** The next important advance in chemotherapy came with the discovery of the antibacterial action of sulfanilamide (*see* SULFA DRUGS), information on which was first published in 1935. Penicillin (q.v.) was first used to treat human beings in 1940. Since that time numerous other chemotherapeutic agents produced by microorganisms have been discovered; these substances are known as antibiotics.

Extensive research on chemotherapy was carried out in the United States during World War II, particularly on sulfa drugs, antibiotics, and antimalarials. Quinine, the traditional antimalarial drug, became unavailable early in 1942 when the Japanese conquered the cinchona-producing areas. The Germans, having experienced a similar situation during World War I, had done research on synthetic antimalarials, and had developed plasmochin in 1924 and Atabrine (q.v.) about 1930. Neither of these chemicals was entirely satisfactory, but both were useful, especially when combined with quinine. By the end of the Korean War various synthetic drugs had been developed for the prevention of most types of the disease; some strains, however, have been found to be resistant to treatment by synthetic drugs; *see* MALARIA.

During World War II the selective inhibitory effects of mustardlike drugs, or alkylating agents, on human leukemia and lymph-gland tumors was discovered. Thousands of potential anti-cancer agents were screened against a spectrum of animal tumors by government and private pharmaceutical research groups. This resulted in the apparent cure of some cancers disseminated by humans and in the suppression of tumor growth and subsequent prolongation of life in patients suffering from various malignant diseases. The simultaneous and sequential use of drugs acting by different intracellular mechanisms shows great promise for the field of cancer chemotherapy.

**Recent Developments.** In the mid-1950's drugs called tranquilizers (q.v.) were used in psychiatry as aids in the treatment of mental illness. Another group of drugs known as psychic energizers was introduced during the same period. Both groups of these drugs have palliative rather than curative value. Biochemical research is in progress to discover specific drugs for the cure of mental diseases; *see* MENTAL DISORDERS.

The ideal of a specific medicine for each disease has not been completely achieved, largely because the causative agents of disease are so numerous, so different in species and strain, and so various in their effect upon the tissues, cells, and chromosomes of the body. A drug that is found to be effective against a certain infection may also produce disturbing side effects. Moreover, strains of microorganisms resistant to established remedies may appear, necessitating a change in chemotherapy or instigating a search for new drugs, such as happened in instances of malaria contracted by soldiers in Vietnam and in instances of resistant gram-negative bacteria and resistant staphylococci.

Among major unsolved medical problems confronting chemotherapists are the numerous forms of cancer (q.v.) and many virus diseases.

In recent years, however, significant changes in the treatment of gout, cholera, psoriasis, and pulmonary embolism have been brought about by chemotherapy.                                    E.M.G.

**CHEMOTROPISM,** in botany, the orientation of plant cells or organisms as the result of chemical stimulus; see PLANT. If a plant organ turns toward the source of a chemical substance, it is said to be positively chemotropic to that substance; if it turns away from it, it is negatively chemotropic. The organ tends to orientate itself so as to be equally stimulated on all sides by the diffusing chemical substance; see DIFFUSION. In elongating organs, such as roots and fungus filaments, the reaction is one of growth; the curvature is brought about either by the retardation of growth on one side or by its acceleration on the other, or by both reactions operating together. The reaction is seen in the case of many gases, liquids, and solids when dissolved in water. The term "aerotropism" is applied to a similar response to stimulus from gases. An example of chemotropism can be observed if fungi are grown in a plate of moist gelatin, and

an excess of sugar is added to a certain part of the gelatin plate; the filaments will be seen to bend and grow from all parts of the medium toward the part which is richer in sugar. The diffusion of the sugar into the surrounding material causes the response.

**CHEMURGY,** branch of chemistry involving the use of farm and forest products and their residues in industrial manufacture and in the development of new types of plants for industrial use. The word "chemurgy" was coined in the United States in the early 1930's, when ways were being sought to utilize increasing farm surpluses. Plants, because they consist mainly of cellulose, starch, sugar, oils, and proteins, serve readily as raw materials for industrial and chemical products.

In 1938 Congress authorized the U.S. Department of Agriculture to establish laboratories at Philadelphia, Pa., New Orleans, La., Peoria, Ill., and Albany, Calif., for the purpose of finding new uses for farm products grown in their respective sections of the country. From these and other laboratories associated with the Department of Agriculture have come the first large-scale processes for producing penicillin and other antibiotics.

The development and promotion of new kinds of plants and their chemurgic uses led to the planting of safflower on some 300,000 acres in the U.S. in the late 1960's. Processed safflower oil is used as a food to reduce the amount of cholesterol (q.v.) in the diet. It is also used in the paint industry as a drying agent. Safflower meal is increasingly used as feed for livestock. The oil from the seeds of the guar plant is used in the manufacture of paper, textiles, and explo-

*Scientists test the properties of a newly developed cornstarch-based urethane foam designed for use in insulating homes and refrigerators. Left: The liquid foam is poured into a mold. Right: The resulting solid "bun" can be used to test applications of the foam.*
**U.S. Dept. of Agriculture.**

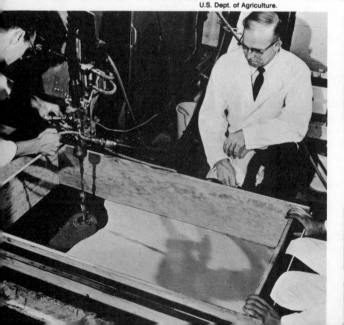
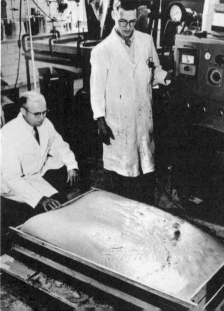

sives. Crambe, an oilseed containing more than 50 percent erucic acid, is an important industrial chemical used in the production of resins, plastics, fibers, and coatings. Crambe may be grown in wheat-growing areas and is therefore expected to serve as a replacement crop in countries that have annual surplus harvests of wheat. Industrial and governmental researchers have developed new applications for oils from soybeans, cottonseed, tung, and other plant sources. The discovery that the chemical ethoxyquin may be used as a long-lasting and effective preservative for carotene (provitamin A), vitamin E, and the xanthophylls in dehydrated forages has resulted in the establishment of important new markets for dehydrated alfalfa.

An early chemurgist, Charles H. Herty (1867–1930), developed an improved newsprint through experiments he conducted with the pulp of the southern pine tree. Another pioneer in chemurgy, George Washington Carver (q.v.), developed many products from such plants as the peanut and sweet potato.

**CHENAB,** river of Pakistan mainly in West Pakistan Province, about 675 mi. long. Rising in the Himalaya Mts. in Jammu and Kashmir State of India, it flows in a generally s.w. direction through the Punjab, a Pakistani region, to join the Sutlej R., a tributary of the Indus R. The waters of the Chenab are used in irrigation.

**CHENGCHOW,** city in China, and capital of Honan Province, an important rail junction near the Yellow R., about 350 miles N.W. of Nanking. It is an agricultural market center in an irrigated cotton-growing region and ships cotton, grain, food products, hides, skins, and salt. The important industries are cotton milling, food processing, flour and oilseed milling, and the manufacture of textile machinery. Also spelled Chengchou, the city was known as Chenghsien from 1913 to 1949. It became the provincial capital, succeeding Kaifeng, in 1954. Pop. (1970 est.) 1,500,000.

**CHENGTU,** city in China, and capital of Szechwan Province, on an arm of the Min R., about 175 miles N.W. of Chungking. The city is the commercial center of the fertile Chengtu plain, which is irrigated by canals built as extensions of the upper Min R. in the 3rd century B.C. Rail lines built in the 1950's and modern highways link Chengtu with the rest of China. In the surrounding region rice, sugarcane, tobacco, tea, wheat, sweet potatoes, and mushrooms are grown. The principal industries of the city are agricultural processing and the manufacture of silk and cotton textiles, matches, and railway equipment. A cultural center since ancient times, Chengtu is the site of a university, two medical schools, several technological institutes, and a music institute. During the 3rd century the walled city of Chengtu was the imperial capital of the Shu Han dynasty, which ruled w. China; see HAN. In the 9th century it was one of the places in China in which printing was first practiced. In the middle of the 17th century more than one half of the population in the area was massacred in a rebellion but the city soon was repopulated through immigration. A large airfield built near Chengtu during World War II was used as the principal base for United States bombing flights over Japan. Pop. (1970 est.) 2,000,000.

**CHÉNIER, André Marie de** (1762–94), French poet, born in Constantinople (now İstanbul), Turkey, and educated in France. From 1787 to 1790 he was attached to the French Embassy in London. Although he supported the objectives of the French Revolution (q.v.), he was alarmed by the excesses of the Reign of Terror. His writings antagonized the revolutionary leader Maximilien de Robespierre (q.v.), and Chénier was arrested. After four months in prison, he was guillotined.

Chénier is regarded as one of the most important French classical poets and as a forerunner of the French Romantic poets. Among his best-known poems are "Le Serment du jeu de paume" ("The Oath of the Tennis Court") and "La Jeune Captive" ("The Young Captive", 1795). The former was one of the two poems published during his lifetime; the latter was smuggled out of prison and published posthumously by his friends. In prison Chénier also wrote *Iambes* ("Iambics", 1794), a bitter denunciation of the Reign of Terror. The first complete edition of his collected works was published in 1819. An opera, *Andrea Chénier,* based on his life, was written by the Italian composer Umberto Giordano (1867–1948); it was first produced in 1896.

**CHENNAULT, Claire Lee** (1890–1958), American army officer, born in Commerce, Texas, and educated at Louisiana State University. In 1917, during World War I, he joined the United States Army Air Corps and pioneered in aviation pursuit tactics. He was one of the originators of the idea of using paratroopers. In 1937 he resigned from the army and became aviation advisor to the Chinese government, then at war with Japan. For the Chinese Air Task Force he organized volunteer American aviators into a corps known as the "Flying Tigers". The corps became famous for defending the Burma Road (q.v.), which was the Chinese supply route from India.

*Fishing boats line the harbor of Cherbourg.*

During World War II Chennault was recalled to American service as a brigadier general and in 1942 he was given command of the China Air Task Force. He became a major general in 1943, and from 1943 to 1945 when he retired, he led the 14th United States Air Force in China and the Chinese Air Force. After the war he returned to China and organized a commercial airline, which he later directed from Formosa. He wrote his autobiography, *Way of a Fighter*, in 1949.

**CHENONCEAUX,** small agricultural village of France, in Indre-et-Loire Department, on the Cher R., about 20 miles S.E. of Tours. The village is famous for the Château de Chenonceaux, a French Gothic and Italian Renaissance castle built on piles in the river. The foundations of the castle were laid in 1515, and it became crown property in 1535. The castle was expanded by Diane de Poitiers, mistress of Henry II, King of France, and later by Henry's widow, Queen Catherine de Médicis (qq.v.). The castle became private property in the 18th century and ownership later passed to the French government. The village has formal sculptured gardens. Pop. of village (1973 est.) 745. *See* CASTLE.

**CHENOPODIUM** (Gr. *chen*, "goose"; *pous*, "foot"), genus of herbs in the family Chenopo-diaceae, comprised of about 250 species, man, of which are weeds. The species, mostly annuals, are often mealy and emit strong odors. The plants, native to temperate regions, vary in height. *Chenopodium amaranticolor*, and ornamental species, grows up to 8 ft. tall and has red-striped and bright violet-red leaves. Lamb's-quarter, *C. album*, grows to about 3½ ft. high, has dark green or yellow leaves, and is sometimes used as a potherb. Good King Henry, *C. bonus-henricus*, reaches 2½ ft., is native to Europe, and is also used as a potherb. Mexican tea or wormseed, *C. ambrosiodes*, is a rank-scented plant used medicinally as an anthelmintic, a drug to destroy intestinal parasites. Other species include *C. botrys*, Jerusalem oak, an aromatic oak-leaved plant; and *C. vulvaria*, which is called stinking goosefoot because of its strong-smelling foliage.

**CHEOPS.** *See* KHUFU.

**CHERBOURG,** city and seaport of France, in Manche Department, on the English Channel, at the mouth of the Divette R., and about 190 miles N.W. of Paris. It is an important fishing and industrial center, with shipbuilding yards, iron and copper foundries, lumber mills, and rope factories. Cherbourg is a naval station and one of the principal ports of call for transatlantic steamers. Cherbourg harbor is protected by a breakwater more than 2 mi. long, thus making it accessible to the largest ocean-going vessels. The harbor includes a large roadstead, outer and inner basins for commercial shipping, and an extensive basin for naval craft. Among the naval installations, largely grouped in a section known as Port Militaire, are dry docks, barracks, magazines, a hospital, and heavy fortifications. The city's chief exports include eggs, butter, and paving stones; the chief imports are Algerian wine, phosphate fertilizers, and coal.

Cherbourg is built on the site of what was probably the ancient Roman camp of Coriallum. In the 11th century the town was known as Carusbar. Sacked by the English in 1295, it withstood several English sieges during the next two centuries. Projects for the fortification and improvement of the harbor were initiated in the 17th century. In 1758 Cherbourg was captured by the British, and its military installations were destroyed. A vast construction program, launched during the reign of Napoleon I (q.v.), Emperor of France, was finally completed late in the 19th century. During World War II, the city became a part of German-occupied France according to the terms of the Franco-German armistice of June 1940; its harbor installations, used by the German navy, became a frequent target of the Allied air forces. Following the invasion (June 6, 1944) of W. Europe by the Allies, the city was the scene of severe fighting before it was taken by the Allies. *See* WORLD WAR II: *Conclusion of the War in Europe: D-Day.* Pop. (1968) 38,020.

**CHEREMKHOVO,** city of the Soviet Union, in the Russian S.F.S.R., in s. central Siberia, near the Angara R., on the Trans-Siberian Railway, about 75 miles N.W. of Irkutsk. The surrounding area, known as the Cheremkhovo Basin, is noted for the production of coal and lime. The production of grain and livestock is also an important industry of the region surrounding Cheremkhovo. The city was built (1928–38) as part of the Soviet industrialization program of the first and second Five Year Plans. Following World War II, during the fourth Five Year Plan, the surrounding region was developed as the center of atomic energy production in the Soviet Union. Industry in the city is based on an abundance of coal, lime, and hydroelectric power. Pop. (1970) 99,000.

**CHERENKOV, Pavel Alexeyevich** (1904– ), Soviet physicist, born in Voronezh, and educated at Voronezh University. He joined the Institute of Physics of the Soviet Academy of Sciences in 1930. In 1932 he began to study the luminescence given off by certain liquids when

*Pavel Alexeyevich Cherenkov*          Sovfoto

they are irradiated by gamma rays and, in 1934, discovered a phenomenon known as the Cherenkov effect. This phenomenon (also called Cherenkov radiation) is the emission of a bluish light from a liquid when electrons or other charged atomic particles move through the liquid with a velocity greater than that of light in the same medium. Since the intensity of the light is proportional to the velocity of the particle, it is also possible to calculate the velocity with photoelectric particle detectors. In 1958 Cherenkov shared the Nobel Prize in physics with Ilya M. Frank and Igor Y. Tamm for the discovery and interpretation of the Cherenkov effect.

**CHERIMOYA,** or CHIRIMOYA or CHERI-MOYER, common names of the small, widely cultivated American tropical tree, *Annona cherimola,* of the Custard Apple (q.v.) family (Annonaceae). The tree, native to the mountainous regions of Peru, grows to a height of about 25 ft. and bears yellowish-brown flowers and edible fruit. Cherimoya is a Quechua, or native Peruvian, word meaning round, cold fruit. Both flowers and fruit emit a pleasant fragrance, but when the tree is covered with bloom the odor is so strong as to be almost overpowering. The fruit, also known as cherimoya, varies from 3 to 5 in. in length. Globular, conical, or heart shaped, the rind is sometimes nearly smooth but more often pitted. The flesh is white and juicy and has a somewhat acid taste.

**CHERNOVTSY,** or CZERŃOWITZ (Rum. *Cernăuţi*), city of the Soviet Union, in the Ukrainian S.S.R., capital of Chernovtsý Oblast, on the Prut R., near the border with Rumania, about 245 miles s.w. of Kiev. Before 1918 the city was the capital of the Austrian crownland of Bucovina; following the defeat of the Central Powers in World War I, it was the capital of the Rumanian provice of Bucovina from 1918 to 1940. After Bessarabia and N. Bucovina were ceded to the Soviet Union in 1940, during World War II, the city and the surrounding district were included in the Chernovtsy Oblast, except for an interval during the war when they were again held by the Rumanians. The chief industries of the oblast are the cultivation of cereal grains and general farm crops and the raising of cattle and sheep. Lumber is also produced. Pop. (1970 est.) 187,000.

**CHERNYSHEVSKI, Nikolai Garilovich** (1828–89), Russian writer and political leader, born in Saratov, and educated at the University of Saint Petersburg (now the Leningrad State University). He began his literary career as a critic with the influential radical periodical *The Contemporary.* Championing political and economic reform in Russia in the period of social unrest that followed the Crimean War (q.v.), he soon became prominent in the radical wing of the Russian reform movement. As a result of his attacks

*Cherokee wooden dance mask.*
Museum of the American Indian—Heye Foundation

on the government, he was arrested in 1862 and imprisoned in the Fortress of Saint Peter and Saint Paul in Saint Petersburg (now Leningrad). There he was permitted to write his best-known work, *What Is to Be Done?* (1863). This novel, expounding his ideas of how the true revolutionary should act, was very popular and is now regarded as a classic in the Soviet Union. In 1864 he was exiled to Siberia, where he was detained until 1883 when he returned to Saratov.

**CHEROKEE,** tribe of North American Indians, of the Iroquoian family (q.v.), originally one of the most powerful native tribes of the southeastern region of the.continent. Descendants of the original tribe consist today of a community of about 6000 living on a reservation in western North Carolina, and about 20,000 individuals living chiefly in Oklahoma.

When European colonization of North America began, the Cherokees inhabited the Allegheny and Appalachian mountain regions of what is now North Carolina, South Carolina, Tennessee, Georgia, and Alabama. Consisting of seven clans, the tribe lived in numerous permanent villages of substantially built log houses and subsisted by hunting and farming. During the struggles between the French and British for colonial supremacy in North America, the Cherokee sided generally with the British, and in 1730 the leaders of the tribe declared their allegiance to the British throne. Their relations with the colonists were marked, however, by occasional periods of warfare, especially between 1758 to 1761, when fierce fighting took place in South Carolina. In most instances hostilities resulted from seizure of Cherokee territory by the American colonial authorities. Motivated by hatred of the latter, the tribe aided Great Britain during the American Revolution. Representatives of the tribe negotiated a formal peace treaty with the United States in 1785, but Cherokee resistance to American sovereignty continued for ten years after the war.

Between 1790 and 1817 about 3000 of the tribe emigrated west of the Mississippi R., settling in what later became Indian Territory (now part of Oklahoma). In 1791 the tribal chieftains, confirming the previous treaty, ceded to the U.S. government part of their territory. This was the first of a series of similar cessions. The U.S. government, in return, recognized the ownership rights of the tribe in the remaining territory and established prohibitions against trespassing thereon.

Early in the 19th century, Christian missionaries began to work among the Cherokee, converting and educating many of them. In 1820 the tribe established a representative form of government, similar to that of the U.S., consisting of an elective principal chief, a senate, and a house of representatives. They also established a public-school system. Five years later the Cherokee adopted a syllabic alphabet of eighty-five characters, a system invented by Sequoya (q.v.), a member of the tribe. In 1827 they drafted a constitution, officially incorporating the tribe as The Cherokee Nation. About the same time the Cherokee began publication of a newspaper, the first Indian periodical to appear in the continental U.S.

Meanwhile, valuable gold deposits had been discovered in tribal territory, an area reduced by cessions and other losses to about 7,000,000 acres located in northwestern Georgia, southwestern North Carolina, and eastern Tennessee. In 1819 Georgia appealed unsuccessfully to the U.S. government to remove the Cherokees from its lands. Attempts were then made to purchase the territory, but The Cherokee Nation retaliated with a law making any such sale by one of its citizens punishable by death. Finally, between 1828 and 1830, in violation of U.S. laws which guaranteed the Indians possession of their lands, the Georgia State legislature enacted legislation that outlawed the Cherokee government, deprived its citizens of their fundamental rights, and confiscated their territory. Indian appeals to the U.S. government for protection were rejected by President Andrew Jackson (q.v.). In 1832 a majority of the United States Supreme Court, including Chief Justice John Marshall (q.v.), ruled that the legislation enacted by the Georgia State legislature was unconstitutional. Federal authorities, however, ignored the decision. Although a small group of leading Cherokee agreed in 1835 to cede the territory in exchange for $5,700,000 and land grants in the Indian Territory, their action was repudiated by more than nine tenths of the tribe and a number of the group members were put to death as traitors.

Troops of the U.S. government began military operations against the Cherokee in 1838, forcibly evicting them from their lands. In the confusion and fighting a substantial number of the Indians escaped. Later they settled in western North Carolina, where they purchased 56,000 acres of land, entailed the acreage to the tribe, and incorporated under the laws of the State. These settlements laid the foundations of contemporary Cherokee communities in North Carolina. Meanwhile most of the tribe, estimated to number 14,000, were driven west in a 300-mile forced march, known as "the trail of tears," that

took the lives of several thousand as a result of hunger and hardship. On their arrival in Indian Territory the survivors, under the leadership of their chief, John Ross (q.v.), reestablished their government, with Tahlequah (now county seat of Cherokee Co., Okla.) as their capital.

The Nation flourished until the outbreak of the American Civil War (1861), when fratricidal divisions and economic dislocations developed. The Cherokees provided large contingents of soldiers to both the Union and Confederate armies. After the war the Nation concluded a new treaty with the U.S., granting freedom and Cherokee citizenship to Negro slaves belonging to members of the tribe. Except for a few minor land disputes, the Nation thereafter maintained friendly relations with the U.S. In 1892 the Cherokee sold to the U.S. government their western territorial extension known as the Cherokee Outlet, and in 1906 they disbanded their Nation, becoming citizens of the U.S. Their residual tribal lands were forcibly broken up and parceled out by the government largely to whites. Today farming, forestry, factory work, and tourists (about 5,000,000 annually) provide income on the Cherokee Indian Reservation in western North Carolina.

**CHERRY,** common name for several trees of the genus *Prunus,* or for the edible fruit of these trees. The genus *Prunus,* in the Rose family, also contains the plums. Because many of these plants have been cultivated for thousands of years and widely hybridized, the classification is complex. Some botanists classify several species of plums and cherries in other, closely related genera, notably *Cerasus* and *Padus.*

The ancestors of most of the modern cultivated varieties of cherry are probably *Prunus avium,* the sweet or dessert cherry, and *P. cerasus,* the sour or pie cherry. The former plant attains a height of 40 or 50 ft., and has drooping leaves and peduncles, with small austere fruit. The latter has erect, smooth, shining leaves and a more juicy fruit, but is a much smaller tree. Both trees have white flowers in clusters or nearly sessile umbels, and both are generally regarded as natives of central and southern Europe, if not also of Great Britain, where both are naturalized. According to the Roman writer Pliny the Elder (*see under* PLINY), *P. cerasus* was introduced by the Roman general Lucullus (q.v.) from Cerasus in Pontus to grace his triumph after his victory (71 B.C.) over Mithridates (q.v.), King of Parthia. *Prunus avium* is frequently planted, not only because of its fruit and because it is exceedingly ornamental when in flower, but also for its value as a timber tree. It grows rapidly and has strong, close-grained wood, suitable for use by cabinetmakers, turners, and musical-instrument makers. Double varieties of both species are also grown.

The cultivated varieties of the cherry are very numerous, and differ considerably in size, color, and flavor. Among important varieties in cultivation are Mazzards, quick-growing trees used as stock for grafting other varieties; Hearts and Bigarreaus, sweet cherries, the latter being firmer and less juicy; Amarelles and Morellos, sugar cherries, the latter being darker colored and sourer; and Dukes, hybirds between the sweet and sour forms. Among the native species with very sour fruit that are occasionally cultivated is the chokecherry (q.v.), *P. virginiana.* The fruits of all these varieties are eaten fresh, or used for making preserves and liqueurs. A variety of cherry brandy made from fermented cherries with crushed pits (which give the brandy a bitter flavor) is known as *Kirschwasser.* It is made in several European countries.

Cherries are grown in many parts of the United States. Sweet cherries, more difficult to grow, are cultivated mainly in California, and sour cherries are common in the East. About 13,000,000 trees in cherry orchards in the U.S. produce more than 200,000 tons of cherries a year. The amount canned varies greatly from year to year, ranging from 2,000,000 to 4,000,000 standard cases of 24 No. 2½ cans.

Although all cherry trees are very attractive when in bloom, some species with inferior fruit are cultivated especially for their flowers. Most notable of these are the Oriental cherry, *P. serrulata,* and the Nanking cherry, *P. tomentosa.* Thousands of trees of these species, presented by Japan to the U.S. in 1912, have been planted in Washington, D.C., around the Potomac Basin, where the cherry blossoms attract considerable attention each year in April.

**CHERRY HILL,** urban township of New Jersey, in Camden Co., on the Cooper R. and the South Branch of Pennsauken Creek, 5 miles S.E. of Camden. Manufactures include electric products, pens, asphalt, aluminum products; electronic equipment, tools, and packed meats. The Garden State Racetrack is at Cherry Hill, and a part of Camden County Park lies along the Cooper R. The name of the area, formerly Delaware Township, was changed in 1961. Pop. (1960) 31,522; (1970) 64,395.

**CHERSO.** *See* CRES.

**CHERT,** or HORNSTONE, impure granular variety of cryptocrystalline quartz (q.v.). The stone is similar to flint (q.v.) but more brittle. In color it is commonly gray, white, yellow, or brown.

**CHERUB** (Heb. *Kĕrūbh*), in the Bible, a winged creature represented as in attendance upon Yahweh, and as belonging to the court of heavenly beings surrounding His throne. According to Exod. 25:18–22, two cherubim made of gold stood guard on top of the Ark of the Covenant (q.v.), and pictures of cherubim were woven into the veil of the Ark (Exod. 26:31, 36:35). In the first chapter of the book of Ezekiel (q.v.), four cherubim, represented as animals with the legs and feet of oxen; two pairs of wings; and four different faces, one each of a man, a lion, an ox, and an eagle, carry the vault of heaven on which rests the throne of Yahweh. Ezekiel's vision of the cherubim gave rise, in the early Church, to the symbolic figures of the four evangelists; the human countenance was associated with Saint Matthew, that of the lion with Saint Mark, that of the ox with Saint Luke (qq.v.), and that of the eagle with Saint John (*see* JOHN THE EVANGELIST). Cherubim are also mentioned in the Pseudepigraphical book of Enoch (q.v.).

In the developed system of Hebrew angelol-

*Pin cherry,* Prunus pensylvanica

ogy the cherubim form one of the ten highest classes of angels. Their function became more and more that of offering praise to God. Dwelling so near to the source of all knowledge, they also became examples of perfect knowledge; this characteristic was emphasized by the Jewish-Hellenistic philosopher Philo Judaeus (q.v.) and by many Christian teachers. In the hierarchical gradations established by theologians, the cherubim rank next to the seraphim (q.v.) as the second order of angels.

*See also* ANGEL.

**CHERUBINI, Maria Luigi Carlo Zenobio Salvatore** (1760–1842), Italian composer, born in Florence. He wrote a variety of church music and thirteen operas before moving to Paris in 1788. He became associated with the new Paris Conservatory of Music in 1795, becoming professor of music in 1816. As director from 1821 to 1841, he greatly influenced the music of his time. His music was classical in style and demonstrated a mastery of counterpoint. In 1808 he composed his greatest church work, the three-part Mass in F major. Other sacred music of importance includes the Mass in C major (1816), Requiem in C minor (1817), and Requiem in D major (1836). He wrote about thirty operas, including *Médée* ("Medea", 1797) and *Les Deux Journées* ("The Water-Carrier", 1800); many motets, cantatas, and choral works; and several string quartets. His treatise on counterpoint and the fugue, *Cours de Contrepoint et de la Fugue* (1835), was edited by the French composer Jacques Halévy (*see under* HALÉVY).

**CHERVIL,** common name for an aromatic annual herb, *Anthriscus cerefolium*, of the Parsley (q.v.) family (Umbelliferae). The species, native to Europe, grows to about 2 ft. high and bears deeply cut leaves about ¼ in. long. The plant is cultivated for the leaves, which are used as a potherb, as a seasoning in salads and soups, and as a garnish in the same way as parsley.

**CHESAPEAKE,** in United States naval history, a thirty-eight-gun frigate that figured in one of the episodes leading to the War of 1812 (q.v.) and in one of the memorable battles of that war. On June 22, 1807, the *Chesapeake*, en route to the Mediterranean Sea from Virginia, was stopped by the British man-of-war *Leopard*. The British demanded the surrender of four alleged deserters from the Royal Navy, but the American commanding officer, James Barron (1769–1851), denying the presence of deserters, refused to allow a British search party to board. The British then fired, disabling the ship and killing and wounding twenty-three of the crew of the *Chesapeake*. Barron was compelled to

Winged cherubs, in a 15th-century terra-cotta depiction of "The Adoration" by the Italian artist Andrea della Robbia.  Metropolitan Museum of Art— Bequest of George D. Pratt

submit to a search, and the four men, including three Americans, were seized. The *Chesapeake* turned back and finally reached Norfolk, Va. Barron was subsequently court-martialed for neglecting to clear his ship for action. The incident brought demands from the U.S. government for an apology and reparation, and public indignation in the U.S. contributed substantially to gradually worsening relations between the two countries. Great Britain, however, failed to take action on the American demands until the eve of the war, when the two surviving American sailors were returned.

On June 1, 1813, during the War of 1812, the *Chesapeake,* then under the command of Captain James Lawrence (q.v.), sailed from Boston to engage the thirty-eight-gun British frigate *Shannon*, which was blockading Boston. The first broadside from the *Shannon* killed several officers of the *Chesapeake* and heavily damaged the American vessel. Out of control, the *Chesapeake* drifted alongside the *Shannon*, enabling the British to board. The Americans fought fiercely and sustained heavy losses. Lawrence, although fatally wounded gave a final command: "Tell the men to fire faster and not to give up the ship; fight her till she sinks". Within

fifteen minutes after the battle began, the *Chesapeake* surrendered. American casualties in the engagement included 145 killed and wounded; British casualties were 82 killed and wounded.

**CHESAPEAKE,** city in Virginia, adjoining the cities of Portsmouth, Norfolk, and Virginia Beach. The chief industries are the manufacture of chemicals, wood products, and cement. The city was formed in 1963 by the consolidation of the city of South Norfolk and Norfolk County. Pop. (1970) 89,580.

**CHESAPEAKE AND OHIO CANAL NATIONAL HISTORICAL PARK,** area in Maryland and West Virginia surrounding one of the oldest and least altered canals in the United States. The park, the status of which was changed from that of a national monument in 1971, extends for 184½ mi. along the Potomac R. between Cumberland, Md., and Washington, D.C. One of the best-preserved waterways of early transportation in America, the Potomac Canal (1785–1828) was extended as the Chesapeake and Ohio Canal and was used from 1850 until its abandonment in 1924. With seventy-four locks, the canal varies from 60 to 80 ft. in width and from 6 to 7 ft. in depth. The land adjoining the 22-mi. route between Georgetown (a section of Washington, D.C.) and the Great Falls of the Potomac is now a nature preserve and recreational area. The entire historical park, covering 20,239.14 acres, is administered by the National Park Service (q.v.).

**CHESAPEAKE BAY,** large arm of the Atlantic Ocean on the E. coast of the United States. The bay extends in a northerly direction deep into Virginia and Maryland. It is about 200 mi. long and varies in width between 4 and 40 mi. The mouth, a passage between Cape Charles, Va., on the N., and Cape Henry, Va., on the S., is about 12 mi. wide. The bay is indented by many estuaries and streams, including the James, York, Rappahannock, Potomac, Patuxent, and Susquehanna rivers. The head of the bay is linked to the Delaware R. by the Chesapeake and Delaware Canal, a 19-mi.-long waterway providing access to the Camden-Philadelphia port area. The 17½-mi. Chesapeake Bay Bridge-Tunnel, completed in 1964, crosses over and under the entrance to the bay between Cape Henry, Va., and Cape Charles, Va. The Chesapeake Bay Bridge, built in the early 1950's, crosses the bay from Sandy Point, Md., near Annapolis, eastward to Kent Island, Md. Important ports on the bay, which is navigable by deepwater vessels throughout its length, are Newport News, Norfolk, and Portsmouth in Virginia and Baltimore in Maryland. The bay is an important source of oysters, crabs, and other sea food, and has several resort areas.

**CHESAPEAKE BAY RETRIEVER.** *See under* RE-TRIEVER.

**CHESHIRE,** Great Britain, county in N.W. England, bordered on the w. by Flint and Denbighshire in Wales, from which it is separated in part by the river Dee; and on the N.W. by the Irish Sea. The N.W. part of the county, the Wirral peninsula, is formed by the estuaries of the Dee and the Mersey rivers. The Weaver, a tributary of the Mersey, is the principal river within the county. Cheshire forms an extensive, nearly level plain between the Derbyshire and Welsh mountains and contains many grazing tracts and dairy farms. Cheese making is an important agricultural industry.

In addition to its river navigation, the county has an excellent system of canals, and contains part of the Manchester Ship Canal. The chief mineral products are rock salt and coal. The latter is mined near Chester and on the E.. borders of the county. In almost every part of Cheshire, freestone, limestone, millstone, and marl are quarried. The principal towns include Birkenhead, Stockport, Wallasey, Chester (qq.v.), and Crewe. Area, 1015 sq.mi.; pop. (1971) 1,542,624.

**CHESS,** game played by two players, or by two opposing groups of players, on a square board divided into sixty-four squares, called a chessboard, with thirty-two pieces, called chessmen. It is an intellectual contest with the element of chance reduced to a minimum. Although the essentials of chess are easily learned, mastery requires subtle and complex analysis of the dynamics of the game. Serious play is possible, therefore, only to players who devote a large part of their time and energy to the study and practice of the game.

The game probably originated in Persia (present-day Iran) in the 6th century A.D. From Persia chess spread eastward to India and, later, into the Near Eastern countries. Traders and other travelers are believed to have introduced the game into southern Siberia and China. The Arabs brought chess into Europe from the Near East late in the 10th century, and European colonists subsequently carried it to the New World.

Chess became stabilized shortly after its introduction into India; there were virtually no changes in rules thereafter until the 16th century, when the modern form of the game began to develop with several significant European modifications. Notable among these were the optional two-square first move of the pawns (see *Rules,* below) and, consequently, the *en passant,* or "in passing", capture; the introduction of castling as a means of removing the king to relative safety; and the extension of the bishops' and queens' moves. These changes not only quickened the play, but the last-named modification also altered the strategical objectives of the game. The queen, which had hitherto been the weakest piece, now became by far the most powerful, and the advance of pawns to become queens became correspondingly more important.

By the 18th century the new rules had gained general acceptance and masters of international fame had begun to emerge, first as the result of matches between individuals, and then from tournaments held among teams. For many decades chess competition and ratings varied in form from country to country. In Russia and Germany, for example, chess societies sponsored tournaments; players advanced by winning or placing well in higher and higher rated events until achieving the title of master. By contrast, tournament and match play were sponsored sporadically in the United States and Great Britain by various private groups, and the title of master was applied informally to players who won such matches or tournaments against outstanding competition.

The first major international tournament, held in London in 1851, was won by the German

*Chessmen in classic pattern. Left to right: King, queen, bishop, knight, rook, and pawn.* **CHESS REVIEW**

A chess game in progress in medieval Italy (from a
15th-century woodcut).
Bettmann Archive

Adolf Anderssen (1818–79). The first official U.S.
champion was the American chess genius Paul
Morphy (1837–84), who gained his title in 1857
by winning the Grand Tournament of the First
American Chess Congress, held in New York
City. Morphy then toured Europe for almost two
years, defeating all comers, and retired shortly
thereafter. In 1866 the Czech-Austrian Wilhelm
Steinitz (1836–1900) defeated Anderssen, proclaimed himself world chess champion, and was
generally recognized as such after winning
matches with the leading players of his time.
When Steinitz finally lost in 1894 to the German
Emanuel Lasker (1868–1941), the latter's claim to
the world chess title was universally recognized;
during the next half century, the world championship was won by a succession of chess masters.

In 1914, after a great international championship held in St. Petersburg (now Leningrad),
Russia, the Russian czar Nicholas II created and
bestowed on the five leading players in the
tournament the title "grand master". Among the
five grand masters named was the American
player Frank James Marshall (1877–1944). The
new title was later applied informally to winners
of tournaments open only to players recognized

as masters; by the 1930's the title had been
earned by three other Americans: Isaac Kashdan
(1905– ), Samuel Reshevsky (1911– ), and
Reuben Fine (1914– ). The four American
grand masters were mainstays of the American
teams that won the International Team Championship in 1931, 1933, 1935, and 1937. The
American title, succession to which had often
been disputed, was formalized in 1935 by the
establishment of a biennial championship tournament sponsored by the U.S. Chess Federation.
The first biennial tournament, held in 1936, was
won by Samuel Reshevsky.

World chess competition was severely cur-
tailed during World War II. In 1946 the world titleholder, the Russian-born, naturalized French
grand master Alexander Alekhine (q.v.), died undefeated, leaving the world championship disputed for the first time in fifty-two years. Subsequently, the International Chess Federation, the
world governing body, organized a multiple-
round world-championship tournament in
order to find a successor to Alekhine. The federation also set up a program of lesser tournaments designed to produce a challenger for the
world title at least once every three years. The
winner of the first world tournament, in 1948,
was the Soviet master Mikhail Botvinnik (q.v.).

During the postwar decade the International

Chess Federation assumed the responsibility of electing grand masters. By 1972 it had awarded the title to 88 of the world's outstanding players, including 11 Americans; 37, the greatest number from one country, were from the Soviet Union.

From 1945 on, the Soviet Union had dominated world chess play. A Soviet team entered and won the international team championship for the first time in 1952, and subsequently has won it every time. Soviet players have been preeminent in most major tournaments.

In 1972 in Reykjavík, Iceland, the Soviet titleholder, Boris Spassky (1937–   ), was defeated by the American grand master Bobby Fischer (q.v.). Television audiences followed every move as Fischer became the first American champion since 1859 and the first non-Soviet since 1948. In 1975 the International Chess Federation refused to meet Fischer's conditions for a match with the challenger, Anatoli Karpov (1951–   ) of the U.S.S.R., and the title was awarded to Karpov.

American grand master Bobby Fischer during a practice session in the summer of 1972 before his departure for Reykjavík, Iceland, where he defeated the Soviet world champion Boris Spassky in 21 games to win the crown.
UPI

## WORLD CHESS CHAMPIONS

| Player | Year |
|---|---|
| François André Philidor (France) | 1747–1795 |
| Alexandre Deschapelles (France) | 1815–1820 |
| Louis de la Bourdonnais (France) | 1820–1840 |
| Pierre de Saint-Amant (France) | 1840–1843 |
| Howard Staunton (Great Britain) | 1843–1851 |
| Adolf Anderssen (Germany) | 1851–1858 |
| Paul Morphy (United States) | 1857–1859 |
| Adolf Anderssen (Germany) | 1859–1866 |
| Wilhelm Steinitz[1] (Austria) | 1866–1894 |
| Emanuel Lasker (Germany) | 1894–1921 |
| José Raul Capablanca (Cuba) | 1921–1927 |
| Alexander Alekhine[2] (Russian-born) | 1927–1935 |
| Max Euwe (Netherlands) | 1935–1937 |
| Alexander Alekhine[2] (Russian-born) | 1937–1946 |
| Mikhail Botvinnik (U.S.S.R.) | 1948–1956 |
| Vassily Smyslov (U.S.S.R.) | 1957–1958 |
| Mikhail Botvinnik (U.S.S.R.) | 1958–1960 |
| Mikhail Tal (U.S.S.R.) | 1960–1961 |
| Mikhail Botvinnik (U.S.S.R.) | 1961–1963 |
| Tigran Petrosian (U.S.S.R.) | 1963–1969 |
| Boris Spassky (U.S.S.R.) | 1969–1972 |
| Bobby Fischer (United States) | 1972–1975 |
| Anatoli Karpov[3] (U.S.S.R.) | 1975– |

[1] First officially recognized world champion.
[2] Alekhine became a French citizen in 1927.
[3] By default when Fischer refused to play.

**United States Chess Champions.** As winner of the Grand Tournament of the First American Chess Congress in 1857, Paul Morphy of New Orleans became the first official U.S. champion. After his retirement the title was vacant until 1871, when George H. Mackenzie (1837–91) won the championship. From about 1875 to 1909 the title was frequently in dispute. Outstanding championship players of the period included Max Judd (1852–1906), Jackson W. Showalter (1860–1935), Simon Lipschuetz (1863–1905), and Albert B. Hodges (1861–1944). Frank J. Marshall defeated Jackson Showalter in 1909 and reigned as the acknowledged American champion until 1935, when he retired undefeated. The next American titleholder was Sam-

uel Reshevsky, who won in 1936, 1938, 1940, 1942, and 1946. Reshevsky did not compete in 1944, when the tournament was won by Arnold S. Denker (1914–   ). After the 1948 tournament, won by Herman Steiner (1905–55), the next two competitions were held triennially and won by Larry Evans (1932–   ) in 1951 and Arthur Bisguier (1930–   ) in 1954. Bobby Fischer won the championship eight times between 1957 (when he was fourteen years old) and 1967. Evans regained the title (1962–63 and 1968–69) when Fischer did not compete. Later champions were Samuel Reshevsky, again champion from 1969 to 1971; Robert Byrne (1928–   ) in 1973; and Walter Browne (1949– .  ) in 1974. In 1972 there was a tie between Reshevsky, Byrne, and Lubomir Kavalek (1943–   ).

**Rules.** The sixty-four squares of the chessboard are colored alternately light (usually white) and dark (usually black). The chessboard must be so placed that a white square is at each player's right. The rows of squares extending from left to right are called ranks. The rows of squares extending from a player to his opponent are called files. The rows of squares extending diagonally are called diagonals.

The chessmen consist of two sets of sixteen men, one set being light-colored and called White, the other being dark-colored and called Black. Each set of men consists of eight pawns and eight pieces.

| P | P | P | P | P | P | P | P |
|---|---|---|---|---|---|---|---|
| R | N | B | Q | K | B | N | R |

P, pawn; R, rook; N, knight; B, bishop; Q, queen; K, king.

The white queen is placed on a white square, and the black queen at the opposite end of the file; the kings are placed in the remaining vacant spaces.

The object is to capture the opponent's king. Regardless of the number of other pieces on the board, when the capture of one player's king becomes inevitable, he has lost the game. When a king is threatened with direct capture, it is said to be in check; it must then be moved out of check. This is done by removal to a safe square, by interposition, or by immediate capture of the attacking man. When none of these alternate defenses is possible, the king is checkmated and the game is over. If a player continues to check his opponent's king indefinitely, the game is drawn (tied) by perpetual check. If the king is the only legally movable man that a player has on the board, but is not in check but cannot be moved without moving into check, the game is stalemated and counted as a draw.

A player who has captured one of his opponent's pieces without sacrificing pieces of equal value has a definite advantage. For this reason much of the strategy of chess involves attempts to capture pieces other than the king. To make a capture a player moves one of his men to the square occupied by an opposing man and removes the opposing man permanently from the board. Except when capturing, a man may be

moved only to a square unoccupied by any other chessman.

White makes the first, or opening, move of each game. The players move alternately, and may move only one man at a time except in castling, as explained below.

The king is moved one square per move along any rank, file, or diagonal. Once in each game the king may make an alternate move: castling. In castling, the king is moved two squares to either side of its original position; simultaneously the rook on that side of the board is placed just to the other side of the king. A player may not castle if he has previously moved the castling rook or the king, or if, at the time, any of the squares between king and rook are occupied; nor may he castle if in so doing the king must move out of, into, or across a square under attack by an opposing man.

The queen can be moved one or more squares along an open file, rank, or diagonal.

The rook is similarly moved along either a rank or a file.

The bishop is similarly moved, but only diagonally.

The knight is moved one square along either a rank or file, and then one square diagonally to a square of a different color that is not adjacent to the square from which the move began.

All the foregoing pieces may be moved forward and backward across the board. Pawns alone may never be moved backward. A pawn may be moved only along its original file, and only one square per move, with two exceptions: when moved for the first time from its original position, it may be moved either one or two squares; a pawn may capture an opposing chessman only if the latter occupies a square diagonally adjoining that of the capturing pawn. When a pawn reaches the eighth rank it must be exchanged for a queen, rook, bishop, or knight of the same color, at the player's option. Thus a player may have two or more queens on the board at the same time. If, in being moved for the first time, a pawn is moved two squares and is thereby moved abreast of an opposing pawn on an adjoining file, it may be captured by the opposing pawn *en passant* ("in passing"), just as though it had moved only to the third rank. An *en passant* capture must be made on the player's very next turn to move.

Because of its mobility, the queen is the most valuable piece on the board. It is worth more than a rook and a bishop, but less than two rooks. Though the values of the chessmen, especially the pawns, vary somewhat as the game progresses, a practical scale of values is the fol-

*A typical opening sequence in chess. Each player has made his first move. White, who always moves first, advanced the pawn before the king (known as the king pawn) to the fourth square. Black did the same.*

CHESS REVIEW

*Here, each player has made his second move. First, White moved his knight as indicated, attacking Black's advanced pawn. Then Black protected that pawn by moving his queen pawn as shown on the board.*

CHESS REVIEW

lowing: queen, nine pawns; rook, five pawns; bishop, 3⅓ pawns; and knight. 3¼ pawns. The king is inexpendable, but has a playing value of three pawns.

Chessmen, with the exception of the knight, may not move over occupied squares. It is thus possible, in some cases, to defend a man under attack by interposition of another man between the attacking man and the man to be defended. Interposition as a means of defense against attack by a knight is impossible.

Chess play is divided into three general phases: the opening; the middle game; and the end game. In the opening, White, having the initiative, strives to bring his pieces into play rapidly, gain control of the squares in the center of the board to assure mobility for his forces, and construct a solid position as a base from which to launch an attack. Black's opening efforts are generally devoted to the development of an impregnable defense through the rapid deployment of men to hold the center, and to a concurrent search for opportunities to wrest the initiative from White and to pass from defense to attack.

Systems of opening play, the variations of which number several hundred, are called gambits (such as "Queen's Gambit", "Queen's Gambit Declined"), counter-gambits ("Center Counter-Gambit"), defenses ("Alekhine's Defense"), openings (English Opening), and games (Queen's Pawn Game). A number of these systems bear the names of the men who developed them. Opening play has been subjected to

persistent and exhaustive analysis, which has been embodied in a voluminous literature that is revised constantly. Success in opening play depends greatly on knowledge of this literature.

The middle game generally finds the opposing players locked in battle and striving to convert initial advantages into decisive ones. The middle game offers a practically, if not mathematically, unlimited field for the application of strategical plans, variations in tactical lines of play, subtle traps, and deliberate sacrifices of valuable pieces resulting in unexpected checkmates of the opposing king. Although the literature in this department of the game is considerable, it is neither as precise nor as extensive as that of the opening phase.

In the end game a player generally utilizes advantages won in the middle game to impose checkmate on his opponent, while the latter attempts to neutralize and overcome those advantages. Usually there are fewer pieces on the board in the end game; the king becomes an active and sometimes decisive factor, in both attack and defense; and the pawns greatly increase in value as they threaten to decide the issue by becoming queens. The utmost precision in calculating moves is required for successful play in this sphere. End-game play has been carefully studied and reduced to a series of rules in a literature that is more precise than but not so voluminous as that on opening play.

J.S.B.

**CHEST** *or* **THORAX,** in anatomy, the upper part of the body, lying between the neck and the abdomen. It is somewhat conical in form, flattened in back and in front. The apex is formed by the structures of the neck; the base is formed by the diaphragm. Backbone, sternum, and ribs form the framework of the chest; its walls are completed by the intercostal muscles. The principal organs enclosed in the chest are the heart and the great blood vessels, the lungs with the trachea and bronchi, the esophagus, and the thoracic duct, which is the terminus of the lymphatic system, collecting the chyle and lymph and discharging them into the blood. *See also* separate articles for the principal organs near and enclosed in the chest.

**CHESTER,** city and port of entry of Pennsylvania, in Delaware Co., on the Delaware R., 13 miles s.w. of Philadelphia. Served by three railroads and by steamship lines, the city is the trading and shipping center of a highly industrialized region. In Chester are extensive shipbuilding plants, steel mills and foundries, munition works, locomotive works, oil refineries, automobile assembly plants, and factories producing textiles, paper products, floor coverings, and chemicals. Pennsylvania Military College, founded in 1821, and the Crozer Theological Seminary (Baptist), founded in 1867, are in the city. Of historic interest are Pusey House, built in 1683; the Courthouse, built in 1724; and Washington House (1747), in which General George Washington (q.v.) wrote his account of the Battle of Brandywine for the Continental Congress.

Founded as Upland in 1644 by Swedish settlers, Chester is the second-oldest community in Pennsylvania. The Dutch controlled the settlement from 1655 to 1664, when it was placed under English sovereignty. William Penn (q.v.), founder of Pennsylvania, gave the settlement its present name in 1682. In 1701 Chester was incorporated as a borough, and from 1789 to 1851 it was the county seat of Delaware County. It was chartered as a city in 1866. Pop. (1960) 63,658 (1970) 56,331.

**CHESTER,** Great Britain, city and county borough in England, and county town of Cheshire, on the Dee R., about 16 miles s.e. of Liverpool. One of the most picturesque towns of England, Chester is on a rocky sandstone height and is still surrounded by ancient walls, nearly 2 mi. around, 7 or 8 ft. thick, and forming a promenade with parapets, on which two persons can walk abreast. Roman in origin, the city has a medieval atmosphere. The ancient gateways have been rebuilt, and of the 11th-century castle only the square Caesar's Tower remains. The two main streets cross each other at right angles, and were cut out of the rock by the Romans, 4 to 10 ft. below the level of the houses. These streets exhibit the curious arrangement called the "rows"; the front parts of their second stories, as far back as 16 ft., form a continuous paved promenade or covered gallery. Many picturesque old timber houses of the 16th century still exist, and many of the more modern buildings are in the same style of architecture. Cheshire Cathedral is a massive, irregular structure of red sandstone, 375 by 200 ft., with a tower 127 ft. high. It was formerly the church of the abbey of Saint Werburgh, which for 650 years was one of the richest in England. The present bishopric of Chester dates from the reign of King Henry VIII in the 16th century. About 3½ mi. from the city is Eaton Hall, seat of the duke of Westminster.

The tourist trade is important in the economic life of the city. Industry includes metalworking and the manufacture of food and tobacco products. Pop. (1971) 62,696.

**CHESTERFIELD,** Great Britain, town of Derbyshire, England, at the confluence of the Hip-per and Rother rivers, about 20 miles n.e. of Derby. Chesterfield is a town of great antiquity; it was mentioned in the 11th-century *Domesday Book* (q.v.). Among its notable buildings are the church of Saint Mary and All Saints, dating from about 1350; the grammar school, founded in 1574; and the Stephenson Memorial Hall, constructed in 1879. Lead and iron ores are mined, and slate and stone are quarried in the vicinity of Chesterfield. In the town are iron and brass foundries. Among the products that are manufactured are machinery, textiles, and earthenware. Pop. (1971) 70,153.

**CHESTERFIELD, 4th Earl of, Philip Dormer Stanhope** (1694–1773), British writer and statesman, born in London, England, and educated at the University of Cambridge. He was elected to the British House of Commons in 1715 as Lord Stanhope of Shelford. In 1726, after succeeding to the earldom of Chesterfield, he entered the House of Lords. A supporter of the British statesman Sir Robert Walpole (*see under* WALPOLE), Chesterfield served as ambassador to the Dutch Republic from 1728 to 1732 and also as lord high steward from 1730 to 1733, when he was dismissed by Walpole because he opposed the passage of an excise tax. Chesterfield then joined the opposition and acted as its leader in the House of Lords. His vigorous attacks on the government of George II (q.v.), King of England, appeared in the public press in a series of letters signed Geffrey Broadbottom. In 1743 a coalition government headed by the British statesman Henry Pelham (1695?–1754) became known as the Broadbottom Party. Chesterfield served as ambassador to the Dutch Republic again in 1744. As lord lieutenant of Ireland in 1745–46, he sought to effect peace among all the opposing factions. He later served as secretary of state to George II, with whom he enjoyed improved relations, and was one of those responsible for the passage of a bill for calendar reform (q.v.) in 1751.

Chesterfield's fame as a man of letters rests upon a series of letters, written in a graceful and witty style, that give a faithful account of the manners and customs of aristocratic society in 18th-century England. These *Letters to His Son,* posthumously published in 1774, were addressed to his illegitimate son, Philip Stanhope (1732–68). A second series, *Letters to His Godson,* which was not published until 1890, was addressed to another Philip Stanhope (1755–1815), a distant cousin and godson whom Chesterfield adopted as his heir after the death of his son. Chesterfield was a friend of many writers, including the French philosopher Voltaire, the

American chestnut, Castanea dentata U.S. Forest Service

British poet Alexander Pope, and the British satirist Jonathan Swift (qq.v.). One of the most famous letters of the British lexicographer Samuel Johnson (q.v.) was written to Chesterfield; the letter rejected an offer of patronage that had come when it was no longer needed, eight years after Johnson had applied for it.

**CHESTERTON, Gilbert Keith** (1874–1936), British writer, born in London, England, and educated at the Slade School of Fine Art and the University of London. He contributed regularly to British periodicals and achieved distinction as a poet and literary critic. Although originally a liberal in his philosophy, he later became a conservative. He formed a lasting friendship with the British writer Hilaire Belloc (q.v.), also a conservative, and the two men established a journal to expound their views. Because of his views, Chesterton was controversial, but his brilliant, vigorous, and witty style made him extremely popular. He did not become a Roman Catholic until 1922, but nearly all his works, before and after his conversion, are a defense of Catholicism and orthodoxy in general.

Among his more important writings are theological studies, polemics, critical studies of other writers, and volumes of poetry. Today Chesterton is perhaps most famous for his fiction, notably the novels *The Napoleon of Notting Hill* (1904), a fantasy of the future, and *The Man Who Was Thursday* (1908), a witty allegory; and for a series of detective stories relating the adventures of Father Brown, a mild-mannered Roman Catholic sleuth; *see* MYSTERY STORY: *The Detective Story.*

**CHESTNUT,** common name for trees of the genus *Castanea* in the Beech family (Fagaceae), or for the fruit of these trees. The American chestnut, *C. dentata,* is a magnificent tree, reaching a height of 100 ft., with a trunk diameter of 3 to 4 ft. Formerly one of the commonest trees in forests from Maine to Michigan and southward to Louisiana, it was much valued both for its nuts and for its timber, which was coarse grained, light, and durable. These trees have been attacked by a disease called chestnut blight caused by a fungus, *Endothia parasitica.* The disease, probably imported from the Orient, started near New York City about 1904 and spread rapidly throughout the country. No cure has been found, and virtually every American chestnut tree in the United States has been killed. Although young shoots spring up around the dead trunks, they are killed before they become old enough to bear fruit.

Several foreign chestnut trees, notably the European chestnut, *C. sativa,* the Japanese chestnut, *C. crenata,* and the Chinese chestnut, *C. mollissima,* have been cultivated in the U.S. These three species are comparatively resistant to blight. They are smaller than the American chestnut and have larger nuts, which, however, are less tasty. Some Japanese species with inferior nuts appear to be almost completely blight resistant. Several varieties of hybrid, blight-resistant chestnuts are now on the market.

The chinquapin, *C. pumila,* is a native American species, much smaller than any of the above. It is attractive but has a very inferior nut and has suffered extensively from blight.

*See also* BUCKEYE; WATER CHESTNUT.

**CHEVALIER, Maurice** (1889–1972), French singer and actor, born in the Ménilmontant district of Paris. He began his career singing in cafés at the age of twelve. At sixteen he was a music-hall star and at twenty-one a featured performer at the Folies Bergère in Paris. After serving in the French army in World War I, Chevalier returned to the operetta and music-hall stage in Paris and London. He signed his first motion-picture contract in 1928 and appeared in twelve American films in the seven years that followed. Among these were *The Love Parade* (1929), *The Smiling Lieutenant* (1931), *Love Me Tonight* (1932), and *The Merry Widow* (1934). Among the later films in which Chevalier appeared were *Gigi* (1958), *Can-Can* (1960), *Fanny* (1961), and *Monkeys, Go Home* (1967).

Chevalier's distinctive charm and insouciance were highly popular and widely imitated. He returned to France in 1935, made several films there and in England, and remained in seclusion during World War II. He toured the United States and Canada for the first time in his special one-man shows in 1947 and 1948, and he presented the last of these shows, which had taken him to many parts of the world, in Paris in 1968. He wrote the autobiographies *Ma Route et Mes Chansons* (1946; Eng. Trans., *Man in the Straw Hat,* 1949), *With Love* (1960), *I Remember it Well* (1970), and *My Paris* (published posthumously in 1972).

**CHEVIOT HILLS,** mountain range forming a boundary between the counties of Northumberland, England, and Roxburgh, Scotland, extending 35 mi. in a N.E.-S.W. direction. The highest point is Cheviot Hill (2676 ft.). Noted for the valuable breed of Cheviot sheep, the range was also the site of historic border warfare.

**CHEVROTAIN,** common name for the Tragulidae family, the smallest hoofed, ruminant animals in the world, intermediate between deer and swine, and native to the tropical jungles of western Africa and southeastern Asia. Because of their heavy hind parts they look like certain rodents, such as the agouti (q.v.). They are also often confused with musk deer (q.v.) because of their tusks, which they use for fighting. Chevro-

tains are hornless, and have reddish coats spotted with white. Several species inhabit southern India and Ceylon; one species inhabits the Philippine Islands. The best known are the kanchil, *Tragulus kanchil,* of the Malayan Islands, and the Indian chevrotain or mouse deer, *T. meminna.* The only African species, the water chevrotain, *Hyemoschus aquaticus,* lives near water and is a good swimmer. All are shy, walk with an odd, tiptoe gait, and stand about 12 in. high. They belong to a group that had been widely distributed in Middle Tertiary times and are traceable to the same ancestry as the deer.

**CHEYENNE,** tribe of North American Indians of the Algonquian (q.v.) linguistic family, formerly inhabiting an area that is now the State of Wyoming, but now living on reservations in Oklahoma and Montana. Originally from Minnesota, they were driven by the Sioux (q.v.) to the upper Cheyenne R. area and became one of the major tribes of the western plains. They had a typical nomadic plains culture and were noted as buffalo hunters and fierce warriors; *see* AMERICAN INDIANS: *Indians of the United States and Canada: The Plains Area.* By about 1830 they were divided into two groups, the Southern and Northern Cheyenne. The northern group joined with the Sioux in conflicts with the United States Army, in particular the Custer massacre (*see* LITTLE BIGHORN, BATTLE OF). The southern group, which formed an alliance with another Algonquian group, the Arapaho (q.v.), engaged in open warfare with the army because of treaty violations from about 1860 to 1878. Between that time and the turn of the century treaties with the U.S. were concluded and the Indians were settled on reservations.

**CHEYENNE,** city and capital of Wyoming, and county seat of Laramie Co., on a plateau, 6060 ft. above sea level, at the foothills of the Rocky Mts., about 150 miles S.E. of Casper. The largest city in the State, Cheyenne is served by several railroads and airlines, and is the shipping center for the surrounding region in which cattle and sheep are raised. In the city are airplane and railroad repair shops, a large construction industry, fertilizer plants, and oil refineries. About 10 miles west of Cheyenne is Francis E. Warren Air Force Base, the largest missile base in the world. Among the points of interest in the city are the old buildings of the Union Pacific Railroad, which date back to 1889; the Supreme Court building, which houses the State Historical Museum and the State Library; and the State capitol, designed in 1887. The Medicine Bow National Forest is west of the city. The city was first settled in 1867 when the Union Pacific Railroad

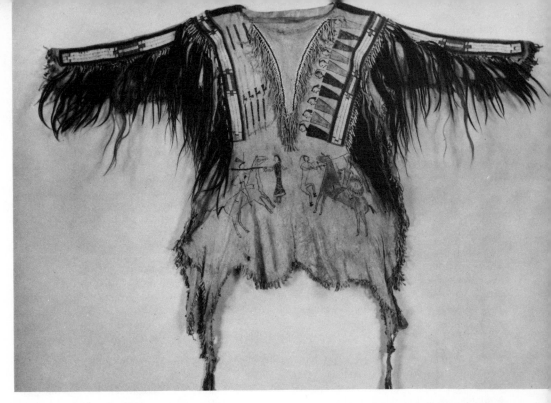

reached that point. In 1869 it was selected as the capital of Wyoming Territory. In 1890, when Wyoming was admitted to the Union as a State, Cheyenne became the State capital. Pop. (1960) 43,505; (1970) 40,914.

**CHIABRERA, Gabriello** (1552–1637), Italian poet, born in Savona, and educated in Rome. After studying at a Jesuit college in Rome, Chiabrera decided against a religious life. He became popular as a poet and enjoyed the patronage of the leading princes of Italy. Imitating classical metrical patterns, Chiabrera composed lyrics, odes, epics, satires, and pastoral and religious poems. In particular he used as a model the verse of the Roman poet Horace and the Greek lyric poet Pindar (qq.v.); Chiabrera eventually became known as the "Italian Pindar". Although considered conventional today, his poems exerted a great influence on the metrical forms used by modern Italian lyricists, particularly Giuseppe Parini (1729–99) and Giosuè Carducci (q.v.).

**CHIAI,** city in Taiwan, and capital of Chiai Co., on a coastal plain, 35 miles N.E. of Tainan. A major sugarcane and lumber center in an agricultural area, the city is also a road and rail junction; it has sugar mills, sawmills, and distilleries, and it manufactures cement and tile. The surrounding area grows rice, pineapples, sweet potatoes, and tobacco. The nearby Ali Shan lum-

*Painted, beaded, and quilled shirt of the Cheyenne Indians with scalp-lock decoration, collected about 1850.*
Museum of the American Indian—Heye Foundation

bering area is linked with the city by rail. Warm springs and Buddhist shrines are adjacent. The city dates from the 1700's. The name is also spelled Chiayi and Kiayi. Pop. (latest est.) 200,000.

**CHIANG KAI-SHEK,** name in childhood CHIANG CHUNG-CHENG (1887–1975), Chinese soldier and statesman, born in Chekiang Province and educated at the National Military Academy, Paoting (now Tsingyuan), and at the Military Staff College, Tokyo. During a visit to Japan in 1905 he became acquainted with the exiled Chinese revolutionary leader Sun Yat-sen (q.v.). Two years later, he joined the organization founded by Sun and known later as the Kuomintang ("people's party"). Following the outbreak (September, 1911) of the revolution against the Chinese imperial government he entered the revolutionary army as a regimental commander and participated in the capture of Shanghai. He remained in the military service after the establishment (1912) of the Chinese Republic, aided Sun's abortive attempt (1913) to overthrow the reactionary regime of President Yüan Shih-k'ai (q.v.), and fought in several of the ensuing civil wars and uprisings. Returning (1917) to civilian life, he engaged in various business activities until 1921, when he resumed his association with Sun, then president of the insurgent Southern Chinese Republic. In 1923 he was selected by Sun, who had close associations with the newly organized Soviet government to visit Russia and study its military and social systems.

In 1924, on his return to South China, he organized and became head of Whampoa Military Academy, training center for the Kuomintang army. As commander in chief after President Sun's death, he adhered to Sun's policies, notably the war policy against the northern Chinese regime. His forces overran two of the northern provinces during the final months of 1925, and in 1926 he led an expeditionary force through Hunan Province to the banks of the Yangtze R. and established Kuomintang headquarters at Wuchang. He was elected to the Central Executive Committee of the Kuomintang in 1926 and appointed chairman of the military affairs commission.

During the spring of 1927 Chiang assumed leadership of the conservative faction within the Kuomintang. In this capacity he removed the Kuomintang capital to Nanking, outlawed the Chinese Communist Party (then a part of the Kuomintang), and expelled the Soviet mission. In April Chiang's forces entered Shanghai,

thwarted an attempted Communist coup, and killed thousands of Communists. He retired to private life in August, 1927. Having previously divorced his first wife, he married (December) Soong Mei-ling, a sister of Sun's widow and a member of one of the wealthiest and most influential families in China. Through this marriage, Chiang formed valuable connections with important business interests. Originally a Confucianist, he was converted to Methodism, the religion of his wife's family, shortly after his marriage. Yielding to urgent appeals from the Kuomintang, he returned to his military command early in 1928. In October, after capturing Peking (called Peiping, 1928–37) and defeating the armies of the northern war lords, he was made president of the newly established Kuomintang government and generalissimo of the armed forces. His administration lasted nearly three years and was successful in eliminating various social evils inherited from the empire. Prosecution of the war against the Communists, however, imposed severe strains on national unity. In an effort to promote harmony among dissident groups within the Kuomintang, he again withdrew to private life in 1931, but continued to dominate the government.

Chiang was reappointed commander in chief

*In April, 1972, at the age of eighty-five, the venerable Chiang Kai-shek addresses the National Assembly of the Republic of China. He had just been elected to a fifth six-year term as president of Nationalist China.* **Wide World**

of the armed forces in 1932, during the crisis caused by the Japanese annexation of Manchuria (q.v.). Except for a stubborn defense of Mukden in 1931, the Kuomintang offered little more than token resistance to Japanese encroachments, however; and during the next few years Chiang was engaged chiefly in campaigns against the Communists. By the end of 1935 he had succeeded in driving them from their southeastern stronghold into northwestern China. Meanwhile Japan had begun to occupy sections of China proper.

Anti-Japanese sentiment was widespread in China during 1936, but Chiang, who had assumed the premiership in the previous year, made concessions to Japan, while attempting to organize the nation for an eventual decisive struggle. Acceding to Japanese demands for action against the Chinese Communists, Chiang ordered a general anti-Communist campaign early in December. To insure action in the province of Shensi, where members of the Kuomintang had been fraternizing with the Communists, Chiang flew to Sian, capital of Shensi. On Dec. 12 he was kidnapped and five of the generals in his entourage were executed. The Kuomintang government refused to negotiate with the insurgent leader Chang Hsueh-liang (1898– ) for Chiang's release, which was promised subject to an immediate declaration of war against Japan and readmission of the Chinese Communist Party to the Kuomintang. Private negotiations for his release were instituted and continued until Dec. 25, when Chang apparently capitulated.

In the half-year period following the Sian coup Kuomintang policy toward the Chinese Communists and Japan was reversed. Kuomintang-Communist agreements for united armed resistance to Japan were concluded early in 1937. Chiang took command of the national military establishment as the Sino-Japanese War began and led a brilliant defensive struggle during the next four years. For most of this period he also served as premier. In January, 1942, after Japan entered World War II on the side of the Axis powers, he was made supreme commander of all Allied ground and air forces in the Chinese theater of operations. He was elected president of China in September, 1943, and in November, 1943, he participated in the Cairo Conference (q.v.), which defined Allied war aims with respect to Japan.

During the final year of World War II, Chiang outlined comprehensive programs for the institution of representative government and for the social and economic rehabilitation of China. As a result, in April, 1948, he was elected the first constitutional president of China. Meanwhile Kuomintang-Communist rivalries had erupted into large-scale hostilities. As Communist victories mounted, the war-weary Chinese people lost confidence in Chiang's government. He resigned as president and commander in chief in January, 1949, but resumed the presidency on March 1, 1950. Late in 1949, after the collapse of their military resistance on the mainland, the Nationalists moved the government to the island of Taiwan (q.v.). The Taiwan regime was given economic and military aid by the United States, which was strongly opposed to the Communist regime for more than twenty years; see CHINA, PEOPLE'S REPUBLIC OF. Chiang, who periodically reiterated his determination to reconquer the Chinese mainland, was reelected director general of the Kuomintang in 1969, beginning his thirty-first year in that office. In 1972 he was elected to his fifth six-year term as president of the Republic of China.

His book *Soviet Russia in China* (1957) was reissued in 1965 in a revised edition translated by his wife, Madame Chiang Kai-shek (q.v.).

**CHIANG KAI-SHEK, Madame** (1898– ), Chinese sociologist and government official, born in Shanghai, and educated at Wellesley College, Mass. She was Mei-ling Soong of the noted Soong family before her marriage to the Chinese statesman Chiang Kai-shek (q.v.) in 1927. Her sister Ch'ing-ling (1890– ) was the wife of the statesman Sun Yat-sen (q.v.). Madame Chiang worked for the improvement of social and economic conditions in China. She assisted her husband in military campaigns and defense work, and frequently visited the United States to secure aid for the Chinese Nationalist cause. Among her writings are *China Shall Rise Again* (1941) and *Sure Victory* (1955), and she edited and translated the revised edition (1965) of *Soviet Russia in China* by her husband.

**CHIAROSCURO** (It. *chiaro,* "light"; *oscuro,* "shade"), in art, distribution of light and shade in a painting or drawing, whether in monochrome or color. In general the term refers to the skillful use of light and dark areas in a painting to create a harmonious effect. The word is usually restricted in use to paintings that are mostly dark in tone quality. In a narrower sense the word is often used to refer to the creation of the illusion of space behind objects in a painting by the skillful management of shadows on the part of certain Renaissance and modern painters. The three-dimensional use of light and shade can be seen in the works of the Italian painters Leonardo da Vinci, Raphael, and Michelangelo da Caravaggio (qq.v.), and of several painters of the Dutch school, especially Rembrandt (q.v.). Today the term "value" is often used in place of chiaroscuro to describe the relation of one part of a picture to another with respect to light and darkness.

**CHIBA,** city in Japan, and capital of Chiba Prefecture, on Honshu Island, at the N.E. extremity of Tokyo Bay, about 17 miles W. of Tokyo, of which it is a suburb. Chiba is the site of a medical university and has factories producing iron and steel goods, cotton textiles, and paper. Extensive fisheries are in the vicinity. Pop. (1972 est.) 533,027.

**CHIBCHA,** or MUYSCA, important South American Indian nation or confederacy centering, at the time of the Spanish Conquest, on the upper Magdalena R., around Bogotá, Colombia. Detached tribes of the same stock were found along the Central American isthmus and in Costa Rica. Culturally, the Chibcha resembled the Inca (q.v.), practicing agriculture with the aid of an extensive system of irrigation, weaving cotton cloth, and working gold with a high degree of skill, although they were ignorant of the use of copper and bronze. Next to the Inca the Chibcha had the largest, most politically centralized society in South America when the Europeans arrived. The Chibcha offered heroic resistance to the Spaniards but were finally subdued and nearly exterminated. *See also* AMERICAN INDIAN LANGUAGES: *Classification of Languages;* AMERICAN INDIANS: *Indians of South America: Andean Area.*

**CHICAGO,** city and port of entry in Illinois, and county seat of Cook Co., on the S.W. shore of Lake Michigan, about 175 miles N.E. of Springfield. Chicago is one of the principal industrial cities of the United States. The site of the city, 228.1 sq.mi. in area, is flat, crescent-shaped, and about 600 ft. above sea level. It extends along Lake Michigan for 26 miles N. to S. and is on both sides of the Chicago R. (q.v.), which divides less than a mile inland from its mouth into two branches, one extending N.W. and the other S.W. The river and its branches separate the city into three sections, known as the North, West, and South sides. These sections are connected by many bridges, a majority of which are movable, and by an underground rapid-transit system. Other transportation facilities are elevated and bus lines.

The city is a principal U.S. distribution center. Nineteen trunk-line railroad routes converge at Chicago, linking it with all major U.S. and Canadian cities, and about 13 percent of total annual U.S. rail carloadings are handled at Chicago ter-minals. Historically, its importance as a distribution point resulted from its position on the natural overland route between the industrial areas of the east and the agricultural regions of the west, and from its proximity to the Mississippi valley. Chicago has 149 railroad yards, with a total capacity of 180,350 cars. A belt-line railway system connects the various trunk-line systems, facilitating intracity freight transfer. Passenger terminals in the city include the Central, Grand Central, Dearborn, Union, La Salle Street, and North Western stations. Chicago is also served by many cross-country bus and truck lines, and by most major U.S. airlines. The city has three airports, the largest of which is O'Hare International. Chicago Midway Airport was, until the advent of large jets, the busiest air terminal in the world.

The principal business section of the city is at the north-south axis, near the lakefront, in an area known as the Loop, so named supposedly because it is encircled by the elevated-railway line. In this area are many of the leading railway passenger terminals, hotels, commercial firms, banks, theaters, newspaper-publishing plants, public buildings, and skyscrapers. The principal Loop thoroughfares include State, Clark, Dearborn, La Salle, and Madison streets. Nearby on Michigan Avenue is "the Magnificent Mile" of shops, hotels, and office buildings.

Notable Chicago buildings include the Standard Oil Co. building (1136 ft.); the 1127-ft. John Hancock Center; the 1st National Bank Building (850 ft.); the Civic Center (662 ft.); the Board of Trade building, a massive granite edifice 612 ft. high; the 24-story Merchandise Mart, a wholesale merchandising center covering two city blocks; the Tribune Tower; the Marshall Field and Co. department store; the U.S. Court House; the Pittsfield, Kemper Insurance, Prudential, and Palmolive buildings, all more than 550 ft. high; and the Conrad Hilton Hotel, one of the largest hotels in the world. Chicago has a reputation for innovational architecture, which originated with the construction there of the first American skyscrapers in the 1880's. The contemporary buildings are ultramodern; the most famous, Marina City, a skyline landmark with cylindrical towers, was completed in 1964. The 1454-ft. Sears Roebuck Building was the tallest in the world at the time of its completion in 1974.

Outside Chicago proper are suburban areas; residential neighborhoods within the city are concentrated in a narrow belt along the lakefront. The parks bordering the lake are separated from the city itself by Lake Shore Drive, which is lined with luxury apartment buildings.

The towers of Marina City (left), on the Chicago River rise dramatically at the northern edge of downtown Chicago.    Chicago Convention and Tourism Bureau

Several major freeways provide easy access to the Loop area for motorists. These include the Eisenhower, the John F. Kennedy, and the Dan Ryan expressways, from the west, the northwest, and the south, respectively. Although extensive slum clearance has been undertaken since World War II, Chicago still has many slum areas, especially on the South Side.

**Schools, Libraries, and Museums.** In addition to a modern public-school system, Chicago City Junior College, numerous parochial schools, and many privately operated art and technical-training institutes, the city has a number of outstanding schools of higher learning. These include the University of Chicago (see CHICAGO, UNIVERSITY OF), the Illinois Institute of Technology, Loyola University (qq.v.), Mundelein College, De Paul University, Chicago Theological Seminary, John Marshall Law School, Saint Francis Xavier College, Pestalozzi Froebel Teachers College, and Hebrew Theological College. The medical school of the University of Illinois (see ILLINOIS, UNIVERSITY OF) and the medical and other professional schools of Northwestern University (q.v.) also are in the city.

439

The Chicago Public Library, established in 1872, has about 3,500,000 volumes and maintains sixty-one branches. Other libraries include the Newberry Library, founded in 1887, which has a collection of about 850,000 volumes dealing with literature, music, philology, and archeology; the John Crerar Library, founded in 1889, with about 1,200,000 volumes, mainly on scientific subjects; the Library of International Relations, founded in 1932; and the libraries of the University of Chicago.

Other cultural and educational institutions are the Art Institute of Chicago (founded as the Chicago Institute of Fine Arts, in 1879), which has outstanding collections of paintings, prints, ceramics, medieval sculpture, Oriental art, and other art objects, and which maintains one of the leading art schools in the U.S.; the Field Museum of Natural History (founded in 1893), noted for its Hall of Babylonian Archeology and for its ethnological, botanical, zoological, and geological exhibits; the Chicago Academy of Sciences Museum of Natural History (founded in 1857), which contains habitat groups illustrating the natural history of the Chicago and other North American areas; the Chicago Historical Society (founded in 1856), with numerous exhibits and books relating to American history and an internationally famous collection of Lincolniana; the Museum of Science and Industry (founded in 1926), famous for exhibits emphasizing the relationship between science and industry in the modern world and for such displays as a large-scale model of a human heart that encourage audience participation; and the Adler Planetarium and Astronomical Museum (founded in 1930). Chicago is also the home of the Chicago Symphony Orchestra and the Chicago Lyric Opera, of several theaters, and of Hull House, the settlement house founded by Jane Addams (q.v.). Daily newspapers published in the city include the Chicago *Tribune, Daily News,* and *Sun-Times.*

Chicago is the seat of an archdiocese of the Roman Catholic Church, and has more than 1500 churches and synagogues. Notable among these are the Church of Saint Patrick, erected in 1856, the Second Presbyterian Church, built in 1874, and Temple Sholom, built in 1930.

**Parks.** The park system comprises about 430 parks and a number of beaches, recreation areas, and boulevards. Many of these occupy remarkably beautiful sites along the shores of Lake Michigan. The largest park in the city is Lincoln Park (1185 acres), which has many recreational facilities, a Zoological Garden, and a bird sanctuary. Grant Park is the site of the John

G. Shedd Aquarium, Buckingham Memorial Fountain (280 ft. in diameter), and a seated figure of Abraham Lincoln by the American sculptor Augustus Saint-Gaudens (q.v.). Adjoining Grant Park is Soldiers' Field, a stadium with a seating capacity of 100,000, which commemorates the Chicago war dead of World War I. Among other well-known Chicago parks are Burnham Park, Jackson Park, Union Park, and Garfield Park. Chicago Zoological Park, popularly known as Brookfield Zoo, is in Brookfield, 14 mi. southwest of the city. The Cook County Forest Preserve is a scenic and unspoiled woodland belt of 55,840 acres.

**Commerce and Industry.** Chicago is the largest grain market in the world; world grain prices are largely determined at the Chicago Board of Trade, a speculative trading organization established in 1848. The city ranks second in the nation in wholesale trade and third in retail trade. It is also a leading market in so-called commodity futures, agreements to transfer ownership of a specified commodity at some future time.

More waterborne cargo is handled at Chicago than at any other inland port in the world: about 80,000,000 tons annually. Most incoming shipments are bulk cargoes, notably iron ore, coal, coke, copper, and lumber. Outgoing cargoes include large quantities of grain, meat, and manufactured goods. The port is easily accessible to the waterborne traffic of the Great Lakes, and it is linked to the Mississippi R. and Gulf ports by the Illinois Waterway, a barge route completed in 1933. Since 1959, the port has been connected with international saltwater ports via the Saint Lawrence Seaway, for which it is the southwestern terminus. Most of the dock-terminal facilities of the port are concentrated at Calumet Harbor, in the southeast section of the city.

Chicago has many manufacturing industries. It ranks ahead of Pittsburgh, Pa., in the production of iron and steel, leads the nation in the manufacture of railway cars, and ranks second in the nation in manufacture of farm machinery. During World War II three airplane-engine factories, including the largest factory of this type in existence, were in operation in the city. Among other plants established in the city during World War II were two large airplane factories, a factory producing tank parts, and an aluminum-fabrication plant. Other industries include petroleum refining, printing, publishing, brewing, soapmaking, and the manufacture of telephone and radio equipment, refrigerators, motor vehicles and parts, men's clothing, musical instruments, foundry and ma-

Sears Tower, 110 stories and 1454 ft. high, at the time of its completion in 1974 the tallest office structure in the world.
Chicago Convention and Tourism Bureau

chine-shop products, furniture, paints and varnishes, confections, and bakery products. The city has approximately 14,500 manufacturing establishments, and the annual value of all manufactured products has been estimated at $35,500,000,000.

**Government.** The city is governed under the charter of 1872, adopted in 1875. Executive authority is vested in a mayor, elected for a four-year term. Members of the unicameral city council, one from each of fifty wards, are elected for four-year terms.

**History.** The name "Chicago" is probably derived from *She-kag-ong* (Ojibway Indian, "wild onion place"), a term applied originally to what is now the Chicago R. The first Europeans to visit the area were the French explorers Louis Joliet and Jacques Marquette (qq.v.), who arrived there in 1673. Later the area was visited by other French explorers, notably Robert Cavelier, Sieur de La Salle (q.v.). After 1684 the river and the surrounding territory were called Chekagou by the French, who controlled the region until 1763, when it was ceded to the British at the end of the French and Indian War. After the Ameri-

can Revolution the British ceded the region, along with the other western territories, to the U.S.

Jean Baptiste Point de Saible, a fur trader, built the first house on the site of the present city in 1779. In 1803 Federal troops established a stockade near the mouth of the Chicago R. The stockade was named Fort Dearborn after Henry Dearborn, the Revolutionary War general and U.S. secretary of war (1801–09). In 1804 the Canadian fur trader John Kinzie (1763–1828) acquired the property built by de Saible, becoming the first permanent settler of North American origin. While attempting to evacuate Fort Dearborn, in August, 1812, the garrison was ambushed, with many casualties, by hostile Indians, who burned the fort. It was rebuilt four years later. By 1830 a village consisting of twelve families had developed near Fort Dearborn. Chicago was incorporated as a town in 1833, when its population was 550. In March, 1837, when the number of inhabitants totaled 4170, it was incorporated as a city.

Chicago rapidly became one of the busiest ports on the Great Lakes, a process accelerated by the completion, in 1848, of the Chicago and Galena Union R.R., and of the Illinois and Michigan Canal (q.v.). The population was 29,963 in 1850, and within the next ten years it increased by about 360 percent. In 1860 Chicago was the scene of the historic National Convention of the Republican Party that nominated Abraham Lincoln (q.v.) for the Presidency of the U.S.

On Oct. 8–9, 1871, one of the most disastrous fires in the history of the nation swept through Chicago, destroying about 17,500 buildings and causing property damage of about $200,000,000. This destruction represented nearly one third of the city, an area of 3½ sq.mi. Hundreds of people perished and thousands were made homeless. Within a year the city had been largely rebuilt with the aid of contributions from the rest of the U.S. and from other countries. One of the few buildings that survived the fire was the Water Tower, today a popular point of interest.

The workmen of Chicago were among the first in America to attempt collective bargaining with employers, and the first to demand an eight-hour workday. Since 1877, when a walkout of railroad workers occurred, the city has been the scene of a number of major strikes. One of the more notable of these took place at the McCormick Harvester Company on May 3, 1886; several strikers were killed by the police, and the violence led to a protest demonstration, afterward known as the Haymarket Square Riot (q.v.), in which seven policemen were killed.

In 1893 the World's Columbian Exposition, commemorating the 400th anniversary of the discovery of America, took place in Chicago. By 1900 the population of the city was 1,698,575. Alternate periods of corruption and reform characterized the political history of Chicago for many years. After the election as mayor, in 1915, of William Hale Thompson (1869–1944), a long period of municipal graft and corruption ensued, for which both the Republican and Democratic organizations of the city shared responsibility. Violence was rampant in the city in the early 20th century. Bombings and murders marked an era of crime that followed the adoption of the 18th (Prohibition) Amendment to the Constitution of the United States, and Chicago was notorious for its bootleggers and gangsters. Anton Joseph Cermak (1873–1933), who was mayor from 1931 to 1933, initiated a reform movement that helped to reduce crime in the city; he was killed in Miami, Fla., by an assassin's bullet intended for President Franklin D. Roosevelt (q.v.). Violent race riots also marked this era. Another world's fair, the Century of Progress International Exposition, was held in

Chicago in 1933–34. In June, 1945, the voters of the city authorized the Chicago Transit Authority, a municipal body, to purchase the privately operated rapid-transit and streetcar systems. Since World War II Chicago has prospered and expanded. The construction of many new highways, buildings, O'Hare International Airport, and facilities such as the world's largest municipal water filtration plant, characterized the years from the mid-1950's onward. The predominant figure through most of this period was Richard J. Daley (1902–   ), first elected mayor in 1955 and reelected to a sixth term in 1975. The Democratic national conventions of 1952, 1956, and 1968 and the Republican national conventions of 1952 and 1960 were held in Chicago. The 1968 Democratic Convention was marked by disruptions between anti-Vietnam war demonstrators and police, causing a national debate on the issue of law and order.

**Population.** Between 1910 and 1950 the population of Chicago increased from 2,185,283 to 3,620,962. In 1960 it was 3,550,404; in 1970 it was 3,366,957.

**CHICAGO,**   river in N.E. Illinois, chiefly within the city of Chicago (q.v.). The river, formerly emptying into Lake Michigan and now an outlet for the lake, flows westward from the lake, separating into two branches about 1 mi. inland. The normal direction of flow into Lake Michigan was reversed during construction of the Chicago sewage disposal system, the principal feature of which was the Chicago Drainage Canal. The canal extends from a point on the South Branch of the river to a point on the Desplaines R. at Lockport, Ill., providing an outlet for effluence from the purification plants of the Chicago Sanitary District. Together with the canal the river forms a link of the Illinois Waterway, a system that joins the Great Lakes to the Gulf of Mexico via the Illinois and Mississippi rivers. The Chicago R. also is connected to the Illinois R. by the Illinois and Michigan Canal (q.v.), which extends from the South Branch, at a point in the Bridgeport section of Chicago, to La Salle, Ill., nearly 100 mi.

**CHICAGO HEIGHTS,**   residential and industrial suburban city of Illinois, in Cook Co., on Thorn Creek, 25 miles S. of downtown Chicago. The city, the earliest steel-producing center in northeastern Illinois, manufactures iron, steel, and other metal products, including machinery, tools, auto parts, and railroad and construction equipment. Other products are chemicals, asphalt, drugs, paint, building supplies, lumber and wood products, felt, and glass. The settlement of Thorn Grove was established in the

1830's, followed by the German settlement of Bloom (a name still applied to the adjoining township) in 1849. The city, renamed Chicago Heights in 1890, was incorporated in 1901. Pop. (1960) 34,331; (1970) 40,900.

**CHICAGO NATURAL HISTORY MUSEUM.** See FIELD MUSEUM OF NATURAL HISTORY.

**CHICAGO, THE UNIVERSITY OF,** coeducational, privately endowed institution of higher learning situated on the Midway Plaisance, between Washington and Jackson parks, on the south side of Chicago. Though the university is nonsectarian, its charter requires that one of the members of the board of trustees be a representative of the Baptist Theological Union. John Davison Rockefeller (see under ROCKEFELLER) founded the university in 1890. His own gifts amounted to $35,000,000 over a period of twenty years. The organizer and first president (1891–1906) of the university, Dr. William Rainey Harper (q.v.), divided the university year into four quarters rather than the usual two semesters thus instituting the summer school, sponsored the university press, emphasized graduate study and research, established an accredited home-study program, and forwarded the concept of junior colleges. In 1931, under Robert Maynard Hutchins (q.v.), who became president in 1929, Chicago University was reorganized according to a plan thereafter known as the Chicago Plan. Under this system, in place of the undergraduate college and the graduate school, the university established a college for general education, four graduate divisions for research and advanced study (one each for the social, physical, and biological sciences, and one for the humanities), and seven professional schools, including schools of business, divinity, education, library science, law, medicine, and social-service administration. To obtain a baccalaureate degree students were required to pass fourteen comprehensive examinations in the humanities, social sciences, and sciences. The examinations in a given field were taken after preparation which might consist either of undergraduate courses or of independent study. The guiding principle behind the Chicago Plan was that the baccalaureate degree represented the accumulation of a certain body of knowledge. The means and the time required to obtain that body of knowledge were of secondary importance. Thus, one of the most important features of the system was the so-called placement tests, administered on entrance to the college. If the placement tests indicated that a student already had sufficient knowledge to pass the comprehensive examination in a particular

field, he was automatically exempted from taking it. It was possible, therefore, for a student to earn the baccalaureate degree in less than four years. However, even if a student were exempted from all fourteen comprehensive examinations, he was required to complete at least one year of study, often on a graduate level.

Under the provisions of a change adopted in 1953 most undergraduates now complete four years of undergraduate study, although students are still eligible for advanced standing on the basis of placement tests. After the first year, students may choose to specialize in the humanities, the social, physical, or biological sciences, or in the New Collegiate Division (in which courses are offered in civilization studies, philosophical psychology, ideas and methods, history and philosophy of religion, and history and philosophy of science). The graduate divisions and professional schools of the university grant all advanced academic degrees. About two thirds of the student body consists of graduate students.

In connection with research on atomic energy, the university maintains the Enrico Fermi Institute and the Institute for the Study of Metals. It was on the campus of the university that the Italian-born physicist Enrico Fermi (q.v.) and a staff of scientists produced, on Dec. 2, 1942, the first controlled nuclear chain reaction; see NUCLEAR ENERGY.

Members of the department of astronomy staff the Yerkes Observatory (q.v.) and the McDonald Observatory of the University of Texas (q.v.).

In 1968 the libraries housed more than 2,700,000 bound volumes. The University of Chicago Press, established in 1892 to provide facilities for the publication of scholarly works, issues more than 30 journals and some 185 books a year. The total enrollment of the university in 1968 was about 10,500 students, the faculty numbered 1128 members, and the endowment of the university was about $182,000,000.

**CHICHÉN ITZÁ,** most important city of the Mayan Indians (see MAYA), now the site of archeological ruins, 18 miles S.W. of Valladolid, Mexico, in the N. part of the Yucatán peninsula. The name, meaning "Mouth of the Wells of Itzá", is derived from the Itzá tribe of Mayan Indians that formerly occupied it, and from the two natural wells that formed the water supply and around which the religious and cultural life of the city was centered. Chichén Itzá was founded early in the 6th century A.D. and abandoned about the year 670. Rebuilt about 300 years later, when the Itzá returned to the region,

*El Castillo at Chichén-Itzá is surmounted by the temple of Kukulcan, a Toltec god.*

it became the most important city of N. Yucatán and a center of Mayan culture. About 1200 the city was conquered by Toltec invaders from Mexico. Under their influence it developed even further. It was abandoned a century or more before the Spanish arrived.

The principal ruins cover an area of 1 sq.mi. The general structural type is that of the platform pyramid, ascended by means of broad stairways leading to vaulted chambers, the walls of which are covered with sculptured figures and hieroglyphic inscriptions or vividly colored paintings resembling the Aztec codices.

Each prominent structure is known by a distinct name, such as the Ball Court that was repu-

tedly used for playing symbolic religious games. It is formed of two parallel walls, each 274 ft. long and 30 ft. thick, standing 120 ft. apart. Projecting from each wall 25 ft. above the ground is a sculptured ring of stone in the form of two entwined serpents. During the game the players attempted to send the ball through the ring.

Another important ruin is El Castillo, a large temple on a pyramidal mound 1 acre in area and rising to a height of 100 ft., with staircases leading up to it on four sides. The Palace or Nunnery (*Casa de las Monjas*), the Sacred Well, the Temple of the Warriors, and the Caracol or Round Tower, probably an astronomical observatory, are among other notable ruins.

**CHICKADEE.** *See* TITMOUSE.

**CHICKAHOMINY** (Algonquin Indian, "river

of the coarse-pounded corn"), river of Virginia, about 90 mi. long. It rises N.W. of Richmond and flows in a generally S.E. direction, parallel for a number of miles to the James R., with which it merges about 8 miles W. of Williamsburg. In the American Civil War, during the Peninsular Campaign (q.v.) of 1862 to capture Richmond, Va., several battles were fought on or near the banks of the Chickahominy, as was the Battle of Cold Harbor in 1864; see COLD HARBOR, BATTLE OF.

**CHICKAMAUGA, BATTLE OF,** one of the major engagements of the American Civil War, fought on Sept. 19–20, 1863, near Chickamauga Creek, in northern Georgia, about 12 miles E. of Chattanooga, Tenn. The battle was fought between the Army of the Cumberland, numbering about 55,000 men, under the command of the Union general William Starke Rosecrans (q.v.), and a Confederate army, about 70,000 strong, commanded by General Braxton Bragg (q.v.). At stake was the possession of Chattanooga, which Rosecrans had occupied on Sept. 9, following Bragg's withdrawal from the city. In the mistaken belief that Bragg had begun a general retreat southward, Rosecrans ordered pursuit. Reconnaissance soon established the fact that the Confederate command was preparing to launch an enveloping movement, which, if successful, would cut the Union army off from Chattanooga. To meet this threat, Rosecrans met the Confederates on the upper Chickamauga at about 9:00 A.M. on Sept. 19. The battle began with a heavy Confederate assault on the Union left, held by troops under General George Henry Thomas (q.v.). Severe losses were suffered by both sides in the subsequent action, most of which took place at point-blank range in heavy underbrush. By sunset, Rosecrans had engaged his entire army in the action, while Bragg held in reserve three divisions, later reinforced by several brigades commanded by General James Longstreet (q.v.).

The battle was resumed, with a Confederate attack, early on Sept. 20. A tactical error by Rosecrans resulted in the weakening of his right flank, and a misinterpreted order caused the withdrawal of a division from his center. Confederate forces under Longstreet broke through the Union line, rolling back its right flank. This section of the Union line retreated to Chattanooga. Only Thomas, later known as "the Rock of Chickamauga", was able to withstand repeated attacks on the Union left, thus providing cover for the Union retreat. Later in the afternoon Thomas began a general withdrawal, occupying positions from which the Confederate pursuit was halted before nightfall. The Union army fell back to Chattanooga on the following day. This battle was in fact a great success for the Confederates, but Bragg did not consider it a victory and did not pursue the demoralized Union troops and make the victory decisive. His error led ultimately to the Confederate defeat at Chattanooga (see CHATTANOOGA, BATTLE OF) and his resignation. Chickamauga was the bloodiest battle of the war; Union casualties were 16,179 killed, wounded, and missing, and Confederate casualties, about 18,000. The percentage of casualties exceeded that of any other battle of the war. The battle site, covering 8190.39 acres, was established as the Chickamauga and Chattanooga National Military Park in 1890. It is administered by the National Park Service (q.v.).

**CHICKASAW,** North American Indian tribe of the Muskhogean (q.v.) linguistic family, closely related to the Choctaw (q.v.), formerly occupying what are now northern Mississippi and the adjacent part of Tennessee, and later as the Chickasaw Nation, the western part of Oklahoma. Originally they were a warlike people. Throughout the colonial period they supported the English against the French, who tried unsuccessfully to subdue them. After the close of the American Revolution, in which some of their warriors fought in the American army, they maintained friendly relations with the United States. In 1832 they sold their lands east of the Mississippi R. and moved to their present location in Oklahoma. They joined the Confederacy during the American Civil War, and after the war those Chickasaw who had acquired Negro slaves were obliged to free them and admit them to equal Chickasaw citizenship. The Chickasaw are now citizens of the U.S. *See also* AMERICAN INDIANS: *Indians of the United States and Canada: Southeastern Area.*

**CHICKASHA,** city in Oklahoma, and county seat of Grady Co., on the Washita R., about 40 miles S.W. of Oklahoma City. In the surrounding Washita Valley, cotton, corn, wheat, alfalfa, and sorghum are grown, and cattle are raised. The region contains large deposits of natural gas and oil, the Chickasha gas field being one of the largest in the world. In the city are textile mills and factories for the processing of dairy and poultry products. Chickasha is the site of the Oklahoma College for Women. Pop. (1960) 14,866; (1970) 14,194.

**CHICKEN.** *See* FOWL; POULTRY.

**CHICKEN CHOLERA.** *See* FOWL CHOLERA.

**CHICKEN POX or VARICELLA,** in medicine, an extremely contagious viral disease, chiefly of children, characterized by early fever, an eruption of papules and vesicles, and mild constitutional disturbances. In most cases fever is present twenty-four hours before the eruption appears. The eruption comes out on the face, scalp, or shoulders in crops of red, widely scattered papules, spreading slowly over the body, one crop maturing while another is appearing. Pitting is rare, generally occurring on the face, where the lesions may become infected with germs from the environment. No specific treatment for the infection exists, but antibiotic injections or ointments may be used to control secondary infections. Starch baths and calamine lotion sometimes are prescribed to relieve itching. Isolation of cases is necessary until all crusts on the skin separate and fall off. Chicken pox bears no relation to smallpox; it is very rarely dangerous, and complications or serious aftereffects are quite uncommon. Chicken pox is rare among pregnant women; the virus may be transmitted to the fetus, but no evidence exists of harmful effects to the unborn child from the disease.

**CHICKLING VETCH.** See LATHYRUS.

**CHICK-PEA,** common name for an herb of the genus *Cicer,* of the Pea family (Leguminosae). It has pinnate leaves, solitary axillary stalked flowers, and two-seeded pods inflated like bladders. The common chick-pea, *C. arietinum,* is native to western Asia and is cultivated in Europe and the United States. It is an annual, 1½ to 2 ft. high. About the size of common peas, the seeds are starchy and have a slightly bitter taste. The ripe seeds are eaten, either boiled whole or made into pea soup. They are sometimes roasted as a substitute for coffee. A red-seeded variety is grown both for table and stock food.

**CHICKWEED,** common name for any of several plants used as food for cage birds, especially those of the genus *Stellaria* in the Pink family (Caryophyllaceae). One of the common weeds of gardens and cultivated fields is *S. media,* the stitchwort or starwort. It is a native to most parts of Europe and Asia, and has been introduced into America. It is an annual with ovate leaves and a weak trailing stem, which is always marked with one or two lines of hairs. The leaves of chickweed afford an instance of the so-called sleep of plants, in that they close up on the young shoots at night. Although generally regarded as a troublesome weed, chickweed is a good substitute for spinach or greens. Some species of a related genus, *Cerastium,* also bear the name of chickweed, or mouse-ear chickweed, and the name is occasionally given to other plants, such as *Holosteum umbellatum,* the jagged chickweed.

**CHICLAYO,** city in Peru, and capital of Lambayeque Department and Chiclayo Province, in an irrigated oasis of the Lambayeque R. valley about 400 miles N.W. of Lima. On the Pan American Highway (q.v.), Chiclayo is connected by road and rail with the Pacific ports of Puerto Eten and Pimentel. The area produces the most rice of any area in the country and is second in sugar production; cotton is also grown. Industries in the city include rice and jute milling, cotton ginning, tanning, brewing, distilling, lumber milling, and fruit canning; furniture, shoes, glass, cement, chocolate, soap, and condensed milk are manufactured. Pop. (1972) 189,685.

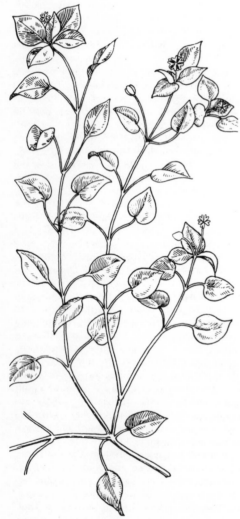

*Common chickweed,* Stellaria media

*Chicory,* Chichorium intybus

**CHICLE.** *See* GUM.

**CHICO,** city of California, in Butte Co., in the Sacramento Valley, about 82 miles N. of Sacramento. The city is a food-processing center for the surrounding agricultural area. Railroad shops and lumber mills are in the city. It is the site of Chico State College, founded in 1887. Lassen Volcanic National Park and Bidwell Park are nearby. Pop. (1960) 14,757; (1970) 19,580.

**CHICOPEE,** city of Massachusetts, in Hampden Co., on the E. bank of the Connecticut R. and at the mouth of the Chicopee R., 3 miles N. of Springfield. It is an industrial city, acquiring hydroelectric power from the Chicopee R. Manufactured products include textiles, textile machinery, firearms, automobile tires, and sporting goods. Chicopee was settled about 1652 and was a part of Springfield until 1848. It became a city in 1890, and was known for a time as Cabotville. The present city includes the separate sections of Chicopee, Chicopee Falls, and Willimansett, and is the site of the College of Our Lady of the Elms (Catholic, 1928) and of the Westover Air Base. Pop. (1960) 61,553; (1970) 66,676.

**CHICORY,** *or* SUCCORY, perennial herb, *Cichorium intybus,* of the tribe Cichoriae, in the family Compositae (q.v.), native to Europe, and naturalized in the United States. The plant has heads of large, bright blue flowers and dande-

lion-like roots. The roasted and pulverized root has been used in adulterating coffee, or as a substitute for it. The endive (q.v.) belongs to the same genus.

**CHICOUTIMI,** city and river port of Canada, in Québec Province, county seat of Chicoutimi Co., at the confluence of the Chicoutimi and Saguenay rivers, 120 miles N. of Québec. The city is a major producer of lumber, paper, and pulp, with large hydroelectric power plants nearby. It has aluminum works and tanneries and manufactures machinery, woolen textiles, furniture, cement, bricks, shoes, pottery, flour, liqueurs, and dairy products. Chicoutimi is a tourist center and a base for hunting and fishing enthusiasts. It is the site of Bon-Pasteur College, the Grand Séminaire Saint-Thomas d'Aquin, the Petit Séminaire de Chicoutimi (including the Saguenay Historical Society and Library), and the Chicoutimi Institute of Technology. A Jesuit mission was established here in 1670. Pop. (1971) 33,893.

**CHIEF JUSTICE,** in the United States judicial system, title of the presiding justice of the United States Supreme Court and of the presiding justices of the highest tribunals in most of the States. The Chief Justice of the U.S. is the highest judicial officer of the nation and is appointed for life by the President with the approval of the Senate; *see* SUPREME COURT OF THE UNITED STATES. He orders the business of the Supreme Court and administers the oath of office to the President and Vice-President upon their inauguration. According to Article I, Section 3 of the Constitution of the United States (q.v.), the Chief Justice is also empowered to preside over the Senate in the event that it sits as a court to try an impeachment of the President.

The chief justices of State supreme courts also order the business of the courts over which they preside. The method of selection of State chief justices varies from State to State. A State chief justice may be chosen by popular election or elected by the State legislature; appointed by the governor with the consent of the legislature or a judicial council; appointed or elected by the other justices of the State supreme court; appointed by a State judicial council; or appointed according to a method of court rotation, seniority of service, or the shortest length of time left to serve in an elected term.

In the British judicial system, the titles Lord Chief Justice and Chief Justice of the Court of Common Pleas (*see* COMMON PLEAS, COURT OF) are the equivalent of the U.S. title Chief Justice.

**CHIENGMAI,** *or* CHIANGMAI, city in Thailand, capital of Chiengmai Province, railroad

447

terminus on the Ping R. (Mae Nam Ping) 360 miles N.W. of Bangkok. It is the largest city of northern Thailand. Noted for the export of teak, the city also ships tobacco, rice, corn, soybeans, and cotton grown in the surrounding area. Manufactures include lac, lacquerware, handicrafts, pottery, silverware, and silk. Chiengmai is famous for the 14th-century Phra Singh and Chedi Luang temples and for the nearby Golden Umbrella (1383), a shrine believed to contain a relic of Buddha. It is also the site of the summer residence of the King of Thailand. The city was founded in 1296 on the site of an 11th-century settlement and was capital of an independent Lao kingdom until 1773. Rebuilt in the late 18th century, with the walls and ramparts of the 13th-century city preserved, it was made the capital of the Lao state of Chiengmai, the Bayap division of the Kingdom of Siam. The name is also sometimes spelled Chieng Mai. Pop. (1970) 89,272.

**CH'IEN LUNG** or **KIEN LUNG** (1711–99), fourth emperor of the Ch'ing dynasty in China (1736–96). His dynastic name was Kao Tsung. He succeeded his father Yung Chêng (1678–1735), and during his reign, the territorial limits of China were expanded to their greatest extent. Ch'ien Lung secured control of Tibet in 1751, and between 1755 and 1760 he substantially increased the imperial domain by conquering the western area now comprising the Sinkiang-Uigar Autonomous Region. An advocate of friendly policies toward the Western nations, he approved a trade agreement with the United States in 1784. Domestically, he encouraged development of the arts, notably literature and pottery making. In 1796 he abdicated in favor of his son, Chia Ch'ing (1760–1820).

**CHIGGER,** common name for the larva of any of several six-legged mites of the Trombiculidae family, particularly *Trombicula irritans,* which clings to the skin of men and animals and sucks blood. Chiggers, also called red bugs, jiggers, harvest mites, harvest lice, or harvest bugs, are common in the southern United States. They cling to grass stems and foliage and attach themselves to any animal that brushes against them. Their bite causes intense itching and irritation but is usually not dangerous. The term "chigger" is also applied to the chigoe (q.v.), but the chigoe is a different animal belonging to the Flea family. See also MITE.

**CHIGOE,** common name for a tropical American flea, *Tunga* or *Sarcopsylla penetrans,* of the order Siphonaptera. It is sometimes also called jigger, jigger flea, or chigger (q.v.), but a chigger is a mite (q.v.), a different kind of animal pest.

Chigoes are smaller than common fleas, but otherwise resemble them. The fertile female flea burrows under the skin of men and animals to lay her eggs. As the eggs develop, a painful and sometimes dangerous ulcer is formed. Chigoes are particularly likely to attack the skin of the feet.

**CHIHUAHUA,** type of toy dog descended from an ancient breed known to the Toltec Indians in Mexico in the 9th century. The modern breed was first discovered about 1850 in the state of Chihuahua, Mexico, from which it took its name. Two types of the breed exist, one with a smooth coat and one with a long-haired coat. Its ears, which usually are erect and large, tend to flare outward. The chief characteristics of both types are a well-rounded head, a slightly arched neck, a level back, and a moderately long tail. The Chihuahua weighs from 1 to 8 lb., may be of any color from white to black, and is alert and swift-moving.

**CHIHUAHUA,** city in Mexico, and capital of Chihuahua State, about 730 miles N.W. of Mexico City, and about 225 miles S. of El Paso, Texas. The city is at an elevation of 4635 ft. above sea level, in a plain surrounded by mountains on all sides except the N. It has a fine public square, in which stands a monument erected to Miguel Hidalgo (q.v.) and his generals, the leaders of the revolution of 1810. The city is the center of a mining district and contains important textile mills. Chihuahua was founded about 1704 and became a prosperous mining community. In 1864 it was, for a time, the provisional capital of Mexico, under President Benito Juárez (q.v.). Pop. (1970) 257,027.

**CHIKAMATSU, Monzaemon** or **NOBUMORI, Sugimori.** See JAPANESE DRAMA.

**CHILBLAIN.** See FROSTBITE.

**CHILD.** See AGE; CHILD LABOR; CHILD PSYCHOLOGY; CHILDREN, CRUELTY TO; CHILDREN'S LITERATURE; MATERNAL AND CHILD WELFARE; PARENT AND CHILD; PEDIATRICS.

**CHILD, Lydia Maria** (1802–80), American writer and abolitionist, born Lydia Maria Francis in Medford, Mass. She wrote her first novel, *Hobomok,* in 1821; started *The Juvenile Miscellany,* the first monthly magazine for children in the United States, in 1826; and conducted a private school in Watertown, Mass., from 1825 to 1828. After her marriage to David Child (d. 1874) in 1828, she and her husband became ardent abolitionists (q.v.). In 1833 her *Appeal for That Class of Americans Called African* (1833), was one of the first antislavery books published in the U.S. She also became editor and later coeditor with her husband of the *National Anti-Slavery Stand-*

*ard* (1840–49). As a result of their activities, which included using their home as a station in the Underground Railroad (q.v.), the Childs were ostracized, and Mrs. Child had to discontinue her children's magazine. Nevertheless she continued her campaign for both Negro and women's rights and wrote many fictional and nonfictional works devoted to these subjects.

**CHILDBIRTH.** *See* BIRTH; OBSTETRICS.

**CHILD LABOR,** designation formerly applied to the practice of employing very young children in factories, now used to denote the employment of minors generally.

The use of child labor was not regarded as a social problem until the introduction of the factory system into Great Britain during the latter part of the 18th century; *see* FACTORIES AND THE FACTORY SYSTEM. Owners of the cotton mills of that period collected orphans and children of poor parents throughout the kingdom, obtaining their services merely for the cost of maintaining them. In some cases children five and six years of age were compelled to work from thirteen to sixteen hours a day. Although British social reformers attempted as early as 1802 to obtain legislative restrictions against the worst features of the child-labor system, little was done even to enforce existing laws limiting work hours and establishing a minimum age for employment. Conditions as bad as those imposed on pauper children rapidly developed in enterprises employing nonpauper children. Often with the approval of political, social, and religious leaders, children were permitted to labor in hazardous occupations, notably mining. The resultant social evils included illiteracy, further impoverishment of poor families, and a multitude of diseased and crippled children. Popular agitation for reform steadily increased. The first significant British legislation dealing with the problem was enacted in 1878, when the minimum age of employees was raised to ten years and employers were required to restrict employment of children between the ages of ten and fourteen to alternate days or consecutive half days. In addition to making every Saturday a half holiday, this legislation also limited the workday of children between fourteen and

*Children working in a bean factory in 1890.*    UPI

eighteen years of age to twelve hours, with an intermission of two hours for meals and rest.

### CHILD LABOR IN THE UNITED STATES

Meanwhile the industrial system developed in other countries, bringing abuses of child labor similar to those in Great Britain. In the early years of the 19th century children between the ages of seven and twelve years made up one third of the work force in United States factories. The shortage of adult male laborers, who were needed for agriculture, was a contributing factor in the exploitation of child laborers. In addition, the majority of adults, imbued with puritanical ideas regarding the evils of idleness among children, cooperated with employers, helping them to recruit young factory hands from indigent families.

**Early Legislation.** The earliest feature of the factory system that caused concern among community leaders was the high rate of illiteracy among child laborers. The first effective step toward legislation governing the education of these children was taken in 1836 when the Mas-

sachusetts legislature adopted a law prohibiting the employment of any child under fifteen years of age who had received less than three months of schooling in the previous year. In 1848 Pennsylvania became the first State to regulate the age levels of youth employed in silk, cotton, or woolen mills by establishing a minimum age of twelve. Several other States also established minimum-age requirements, but none of the laws passed made provisions for establishing proof of the child's age or for enforcement.

The length of the workday for children was the next feature of the factory system to be regulated by legislation. By 1853 several States had adopted a ten-hour workday for children under twelve years of age. Despite these restrictions, the number of children in industry increased greatly in the U.S. after the Civil War, when industrial expansion resulted in unprecedented demand for manpower. By the end of the 19th century nearly one fifth of all American children between the ages of ten and sixteen were gainfully employed. By 1910, however, as the result of the public-enlightenment activities of various organizations, notably the National Child Labor

*A group of young miners, photographed in 1911.*
George Eastman House

Committee, the legislatures of several States had enacted restrictive legislation that led to sharp reductions in the number of children employed in industry.

Because of the lack of uniformity in child-labor standards established in the various States, a condition that placed industries in States with relatively high standards in a disadvantageous competitive position, the United States Congress, in 1916, passed a law that set a national minimum age of fourteen in industries producing nonagricultural goods for interstate commerce or for export. In 1918 the Supreme Court of the United States ruled, in a five-to-four decision, that the legislation was an unconstitutional infringement on personal freedom. Another child-labor law, enacted in 1918, was also declared unconstitutional by the Supreme Court in 1922. In 1924 both Houses of Congress passed an amendment to the United States Constitution, empowering Congress to limit, regulate, and prohibit the labor of persons under eighteen years of age. The number of State legislatures that ratified the proposed amendment was twenty-eight, eight less than the thirty-six then required.

**Federal Legislation.** Despite the reluctance of State legislators to ratify the child-labor amendment, legislative attempts to deal with the problem nationally continued, notably during the administration of President Franklin Delano Roosevelt (q.v.). The National Industrial Recovery Act (q.v.), passed by Congress in 1933, established a minimum age of sixteen for workers in most industries. In hazardous industries a minimum age level of eighteen was established. This law contributed to a substantial decrease in the number of young workers, but the U.S. Supreme Court ruled the act unconstitutional in 1935; *see* NEW DEAL. In the next year Congress passed the Walsh-Healey Act, which prohibits firms producing goods under Federal government contract from employing boys and girls under sixteen years of age.

The next important legislation on the problem was the Fair Labor Standards Act (q.v.) of 1938, better known as the Federal Wage and Hour Law. This act was declared constitutional in 1941 by the U.S. Supreme Court, which thereby overruled its former child-labor decision under a more liberal interpretation of the commerce clause of the Constitution (Article I, Section 8). The Fair Labor Standards Act, amended in 1949, applies to all workers engaged in interstate or foreign commerce. Under the child-labor provisions of the act, minors sixteen years of age and over may be employed in any occupation that

has not been judged hazardous by the secretary of labor. The minimum age for work in industries classified as hazardous is eighteen. There is no minimum age for nonhazardous agricultural employment after school hours and during vacation. Minors fourteen and fifteen years of age may be employed in a variety of nonmanufacturing, nonmining, and nonhazardous occupations outside school hours and during vacations for limited hours and under other specified conditions of work.

**State Legislation.** Every State today has child-labor laws. In most States employment of minors under sixteen in factories and during school hours is prohibited. Other provisions include a forty-hour workweek, prohibition of night work, and work permits for minors under eighteen. Children working on farms are not completely protected by Federal and State laws, which make no provisions for nonhazardous farmwork outside of school hours. The children of migratory workers, who move from harvest to harvest across the U.S., are usually not subject to State laws since they do not fulfill residency requirements, and they are often unable to attend local schools, which have no provisions for seasonal increases in school enrollment. Other children exempted from Federal and State labor laws are children employed as actors and performers in radio, television, and motion pictures, as newspaper delivery and sales boys, or as part-time workers at home.

**International Legislation.** The most important efforts to eliminate child-labor abuses throughout the world come from the International Labor Organization (q.v.), founded in 1919 and now a special agency of the United Nations. The organization has introduced several child-labor conventions among its member nations, including a sixteen-year minimum age for admission to all work, a higher minimum age for specific types of employment, compulsory medical examinations, and regulation of night work.

**CHILD PSYCHOLOGY,** study of mental, emotional, and social behavior of the child from birth through adolescence. Only in the 20th century were all facets of childhood distinguished from adulthood in systematic study. Through the ages, however, cultural and philosophic attitudes affected the raising of children.

**Early History.** In his pioneer work, *Centuries of Childhood,* the French cultural historian, Philippe Ariès (1914– ) reveals the variety of customs involving the treatment of children that have existed throughout history. Ariès shows in perspective that the concepts of childhood

*Charles Darwin, photographed about 1875.*
Bettmann Archive

ranged from that of the innocent Eros in Greek art to that of the child as a miniature adult and that these attitudes were reflected in practices that ranged from total devotion to infanticide. Ariès brings out the fact that medieval society possessed neither a definition of childhood nor a vocabulary to differentiate it from adulthood. It is necessary to emphasize historic concepts because these conflicting ideas have filtered through every period to the present. The child was considered on the one hand the embodiment of innocence and on the other the fountainhead of sin and depravity. These views evoked radically different methods of management, one permissive, the other authoritarian.

Although he was preceded by the English philosopher John Locke in the psychological approach to learning, the more gentle view was espoused by the 18th-century French philosopher, Jean Jacques Rousseau. In his books, notably *Émile* (1762), in which he anticipated the doctrine that foundations of adult life are rooted in childhood experience, that was enunciated by the Austrian psychiatrist Sigmund Freud, Rousseau argued that every child had the right to develop his abilities without abnormal constraint. The harsher view is epitomized by the 16th-century religious reformer John Calvin and the doctrine of original sin, which became the foundation of Calvinism (q.v.) and was brought to early America by the Puritans (q.v.).

The intellectual revival of the Renaissance and the later growth of humanism (qq.v.) resulted in a new attitude toward children and the initiation of inquiries into their nature and abilities. These inquiries were undertaken by the 17th-century Czech religious leader John Amos Comenius, who held the revolutionary belief that education could be pleasurable; by the Swiss educational reformer Johann Heinrich Pestalozzi, who formulated the equally revolutionary idea that learning should be adapted to a child's mental development; by the German philosopher and educator Johann Friedrich Herbart, who evolved a pedagogic theory of adjusting the child to society; and by the German educator Friedrich Fröbel, who suggested that the child's growth at work and play be uninhibited and encouraged. Another German educator, August Hermann Francke (1663–1727), had anticipated Rousseau's concern for youth with the establishment of his so-called ragged school for homeless children at Halle in 1695. The American scientist-philosopher Benjamin Franklin in 1751 established an academy in Pennsylvania, and the British social reformer Robert Owen in 1800 established schools for working children to implement his theory that character is formed by early environment and training. *See also* EDUCATION.

The interest of these pioneers lay more in improving the child's education than in studying him in all his aspects. The foundation of child psychology cannot be ascribed to a single individual; the movement was international. Some authors ascribe its origin to the British naturalist Charles Darwin, who in the 1870's recorded observations of his child, both to study the nature of childhood and elucidate his theory of evolution. Although much of later child study was based on biologic concepts, the tendency to regard the infant as a link between man and animal and the attempt to apply the results of experiments with laboratory animals to the learning processes of children delayed experimental studies of child psychology.

**Later History.** The foundations of child psychology are more accurately ascribed to the work of the German psychologist, Wilhelm Thierry Preyer (1841–1897), who progressed beyond Darwinism and genetics and assembled observations of the child by parents, teachers, and psychologists. The study of child behavior was concentrated thereafter in the United States, first under the leadership of the educator and psychologist Granville Stanley Hall. Hall adopted from Preyer the technique involving the use of a questionnaire to gather data about children. He also propounded the concept, derived from Herbart, that the child passes through phases in development that simulate the stages of evolution from animal to man. Although now discredited, the theory served to emphasize change in behavior as a characteristic of childhood. Hall's work also helped establish the modern view that the child is not mentally, any more than physically, a miniature adult whose intellectual capacities can be compared with those of adults. Hall's work and that of other contemporary investigators such as Gabriel Compayré (1843–1913) in France and Paola Lambroso in Italy inspired others to undertake studies of children's thinking, imagination, memory, and reasoning without regard to formal education.

**Development of Standard Tests.** The questionnaire, with its emphasis on objectivity, led to the development of tests that may be traced to the British scientist Sir Francis Galton; to Hermann Ebbinghaus (1850–1909), the German psychologist, who published in 1885 a summary of his experiments on memory; and to James McKeen Cattell (1860–1944), the American psychologist, who first used the term "mental test" and launched the technique of testing. Carrying on psychometry, the measurement of individual differences, the French psychologist Alfred Binet thereafter developed tests to differentiate normal from feeble-minded children and, with another French psychologist, Théodore Simon (1873–1961), applied these to retarded schoolchildren in 1905. The original test consisted of thirty graded verbal and linguistic problems and was thereafter rearranged at the suggestion of the German-American psychologist Louis William Stern (1871–1938). Stern arranged the tests by chronologic age and in this way was able to arrive at an evaluation of mental age. Often revised, this scale is still regarded as an effective measure of academic potential. It was based on the sometimes arbitrary assumption that a child of a given age should be conversant with certain areas of knowledge. On the basis of his test score, the child was ranked by his mental age (MA) which, divided by the chronologic age (CA), yielded an intelligence quotient (IQ). It was assumed that the IQ represented innate endowment, an inherited capacity distinguished from individual experience, a viewpoint no longer held by professionals. It was recognized that, however successful in classifying differences in mental capacity, such tests failed to take account of personality factors and regional, racial, and emotional distinctions. When the value of testing became apparent psychologists designed standard tests for every aptitude

a child might possess. Achievement against chronologic age became the standard; the performance of schoolchildren was compared with that of their peers.

The techniques of testing developed quickly after World War I, when tests measuring the abilities of soldiers were revised for schoolchildren of all ages. The purpose of these tests was to study development by determining changes in mental capacity and personality as the child matured. A further development occurred when the Swiss psychologist Jean Piaget (1896–    ) tested children by analyzing their solutions to real problems, rather than their responses to standard questions. Piaget attempted to follow their thought processes, especially in relation to the use of language. His work was significant because it gave precedence to the study of psychological processes over categories of achievement as a function of chronologic age; see PSYCHOLOGICAL TESTING: *Intelligence Testing.*

**Research into Behavior of Children.** The attempt to discover a method suitable for studying the child as a whole was a major problem confronting early researchers. The work of the American psychologist, John Broadus Watson, beginning in 1912, is of historic importance. On the basis of studies of animals, which, like babies and young children, cannot express their thoughts, feelings, and emotions in words, Watson suggested that observations of a child's behavior under controlled conditions would enable the experimenter to draw logical conclusions about basic psychological processes. This method, known as behaviorism (q.v.), prompted a variety of research studies of infants and children and launched a controversy about the determination of hereditary traits as distinguished from learned, or acquired, traits. It was assumed that characteristics present at birth were of genetic origin and that those achieved after birth were the result of learning, or conditioning. The theory of conditioning expressed by the Russian physiologist Ivan P. Pavlov had great appeal for American behaviorists because it offered a promise that the development of a child could be directed merely by controlling the circumstances of his environment.

An opposing theory was advanced by the American psychologist Arnold Lucius Gesell, who obtained his data first by using the moving-picture camera and later introduced the one-way vision screen through which an observer may watch the behavior of a baby or young child without distracting him. On the basis of observations, Gesell claimed that no amount of conditioning or training would accelerate the course of natural development in infants and thus initiated another controversy: maturation versus learning. The contradiction inherent in both the heredity versus environment and the maturation versus learning theories lay in the fact that each implied distinctly dual processes in child development. Gesell's maturation theory had a good effect, however, since it eliminated the burden of rigid schedules in management of young children advocated by behaviorists.

**The Influence of Freud upon Child Psychology.** Another psychological approach that affected attitudes toward childhood derived from the psychoanalytic concepts of Sigmund Freud in the 1920's. These concepts were based, not on direct observation of children, but on analyses of the neurotic behavior of adults. Freud's contention that adult neuroses have origins in early childhood experience focused attention on the child-parent relationship and, as did behaviorism, laid great responsibility upon parents for properly rearing their children. Whatever anxiety resulted was to some extent allayed by the cultural anthropologists, who contended that the general social and cultural milieu in which a child develops determines the development of his personality as much as environmental stimuli and his relationship to his parents.

The endeavor to explain the individual differences uncovered by testing, by anthropology, and psychiatry renewed the heredity-environment controversy. An offshoot of the attempt to allocate to each factor its proper weight was a study of twins by the British scientist Sir Francis Galton and later by Gesell; the child psychologist Myrtle B. McGraw (1899–    ); the geneticist Horatio Hackett Newman (1875–1957); and others. These revealed that identical twins have physical and mental characteristics more alike than those of nonidentical, or fraternal, twins. Identical twins may show differences especially in personality, in which the role of environment seems more important than in physical and

*Dr. Arnold Gesell examines an infant.*     Gesell Institute

Child psychologists and teachers often work together to combine special learning therapies with regular classroom studies, as at the McLean Hospital Children's Center, Belmont, Mass.    McLean Hospital Children's Center

mental development. Further studies of groups of senescent twins by the American psychiatrist Franz Josef Kallmann (1897–1965) reveal more clearly the influence of environment, showing that the similarities of identical twins persist as they grow, whereas those of nonidentical twins decrease; see HEREDITY.

**Developmental Studies of Children.** Early studies of development in children made use of the so-called cross-sectional approach, in which young children were compared with older children by age groups. It soon appeared that there were individual variations among children of the same age. A new method was therefore adopted; called the longitudinal approach, it traces the development over the years of the same children from the same age group. A pioneer longitudinal study of very bright children was begun by the American psychologist Louis Madison Terman (1877–1956); this investigation was carried on with the original subjects into middle age. Similar studies were made by Gesell, the American educators Walter F. Dearborn (1878–1956) and Nancy Bayley (1899–    ), and others.

These studies showed that children undergo a course of development at different rates of advancement, depending on physiologic and sociologic factors. Another result is that child psychologists have been able to divide the entire period of development into characteristic stages (see next column).

There have been two important outgrowths of longitudinal studies. The first is the establishment of standards for physical, motor, speech, mental, emotional, and social development at different ages. These make it possible to judge the development of individual children and determine how it compares with what is considered normal for their ages. The standards most widely used in this area are known as the "Gesell Norms". The second outgrowth of longitudi-

nal studies has been the construction of several series of developmental standards of what a child of a given age is expected to learn. The best-known series is that of the American psychologist Robert J. Havighurst (1900–    ). A new departure, evolving in the 1930's, was motivated

**Prenatal Stage**

From conception to birth, when the most important factor is physical growth, more pronounced in the head than elsewhere.

**Neonatal Stage**

From birth through the second week of life, when the infant does not gain weight or mature and when his behavior is characterized by reflexes.

**Infancy**

From two weeks to two years, when the major developments consist of the beginnings of speech and control over muscles. As his helplessness decreases, the baby tries to be more independent.

**Early Childhood**

From two to six years, when the child is learning skills to increase his independence, control his environment, communicate with others, and fit into family and social life.

**Late Childhood**

From six to ten or twelve years, when the child becomes integrated into society, associates with children of his own age, and learns to handle the symbolic and sophisticated ideas prevalent in his society.

**Puberty**

From ten or twelve to thirteen or fourteen years, characterized by onset of secondary sex characteristics and development of body structure.

**Adolescence**

From the puberty to sexual maturity and then to socially acceptable or legal maturity, which varies in each society. A relatively undefined stage, it is not recognized in some cultures.

by the rise in juvenile delinquency (q.v.). Profiting by techniques devised for the study of older children, important studies of adolescence presently use the longitudinal approach. The influence of physical changes on the mental, emotional, and social behavior of children in adolescence is highlighted by studies of maturing, especially those of Nancy Bayley and the American psychologist Mary Cover Jones (1896– ). Children who mature early are more precocious in their physical development than those who begin late, show better personality adjustments, and continue to mature during the early years of adulthood; see ADOLESCENCE.

**Current Trends in Child Psychology.** At present, all areas of adolescent behavior are being investigated. Drawing on research studies, child psychology has filled gaps in its knowledge of social behavior, "dating", and courtship. Contributions from applied psychology have added information about the vocational interests and work adjustments of the adolescent. Social psychology has yielded valuable data about adolescent leadership, popularity, religious attitudes, and moral behavior. With this help from other fields, the child psychologist has been able quickly to acquire a comprehensive understanding of typical adolescent behavior; see SOCIAL PSYCHOLOGY.

Recent studies of aging have thrown light on the importance of childhood as the foundation of life. Studies of normal adults have confirmed the fact that attitudes, interests, patterns of behavior, and personality and character traits can be traced to the early years. No longer is it assumed that childhood experiences are unimportant because they are not remembered. It is now recognized that child-training methods, discipline, early social relationships in and outside the home, and the methods used to teach skills and speech determine whether the child will develop into a happy, well-adjusted child or into a social misfit.

As research in child psychology advanced and brought to light information that could be used profitably in the rearing of children, it was disseminated through newspapers, magazines, books, and pamphlets written especially for parents. In recent years, their scope has extended beyond the preschool years into adolescence. Such writings give advice to parents on common problems arising at every stage of development. More importantly, child psychologists have recently written books directed to the adolescent himself in an attempt to explain growing up in terms of sexual changes and behavior patterns and to advise on the problem of becoming an adult.

See also ADOLESCENCE; KINDERGARTEN; NURSERY SCHOOL; PRESCHOOL EDUCATION; PSYCHOLOGY; and separate entries on most persons whose life dates are not given in this article.

**CHILDREN, CRUELTY TO,** intentional infliction of unnecessary pain on children; also applied to the neglect or abandonment of children by their parents or guardians. In the United States, the movement for the prevention of cruelty to children was begun in 1875 by the establishment of the New York Society for the Prevention of Cruelty to Children under the guidance of the American philanthropist Henry Bergh (1811–88). Sometimes a distinction is drawn between neglect of children and abuse of children. Neglect relates to the failures of parents in fulfilling the physical, medical, emotional, moral, and educational needs of their children. Abuse relates to the infliction of physical injuries. Neglected or abused children are protected through services provided by the Children's Division of the American Humane Association, a national association for child-protective agencies. The service is designed to help change negative or destructive attitudes on the part of parents. When the behavior of parents cannot be changed, or when the child is in danger of further mistreatment if he remains at home, the association invokes the authority of a juvenile or family court so that a temporary home may be provided for the child until he may be returned to his family.

Child-protective services are provided in a few areas by societies for the prevention of cruelty to children, principally in the northeastern U.S. In most States the service is included in a government-operated child-welfare program. The Children's Division of the American Humane Association conducts research, provides consultation services, drafts proposed corrective legislation, and publishes many books and pamphlets on child protective services. The association has its headquarters in Denver, Colo.

**CHILDREN, EDUCATION OF.** See EDUCATION; EDUCATION, ELEMENTARY; EDUCATION, SECONDARY; PRESCHOOL EDUCATION.

**CHILDREN, EMPLOYMENT OF.** See CHILD LABOR.

**CHILDREN'S BUREAU.** See HEALTH, EDUCATION, AND WELFARE, DEPARTMENT OF.

**CHILDREN'S COURT.** See JUVENILE COURT.

**CHILDREN'S CRUSADE.** See CRUSADE, CHILDREN'S.

**CHILDREN'S LITERATURE,** writings designed for children, or which children can read with interest, including fiction, poetry, biography, and history. Children's literature includes also riddles, precepts, fables, legends, myths, and folk poems and tales based upon spoken tradition. Primitive or very ancient literature, such as the Babylonian animal tales or the Homeric stories, is often adaptable to children's reading because of its simple narrative form.

Until the Renaissance the main sources of children's literature in the West were the Bible and the Greek and Latin classics. The expansion of literacy following the invention of printing in the 15th century increased the range of children's literature, and subsequently, national history became a fresh source. After the 18th century archeologists, philologists, and anthropologists added material from Oriental and primitive cultures and European folklore. The developments in English and American literature for children were generally typical, and these developments will be the subject of the present article with occasional references to works and influences originating in other countries.

**The Middle Ages.** In England the earliest forms of oral literature, shared from generation to generation by young and old alike, were simple folk tales, usually of Celtic and Anglo-Saxon origin. These tales included the hearty folk ballads, among them the Robin Hood (q.v.) group, and the narratives sung by wandering bards about King Arthur and his knights (*see* ARTHU-RIAN CYCLE) and other heroes of chivalry.

The first books intended for the young were Latin collections of the 7th and 8th centuries. The best-known works, written by such outstanding ecclesiastical scholars as Aldhelm, Alcuin, and Bede, were used as lesson books in the monastery schools.

**The Renaissance.** With the development of vernacular literature, particularly after the invention of printing, more children's books appeared. Among the publications of the first English printer, William Caxton, was the *Book of Curtesye* (1477), a collection of rhymes which set forth rules of conduct for a "goodly chylde". Eight years later Caxton printed the English translator and compiler Sir Thomas Malory's *Le Morte d'Arthur*, which became the basis for later treatments of the Arthurian legends. Caxton also issued the *Fables* of Aesop, translated from the French, and the beast fable *Reynard the Fox*, translated from a Flemish version.

A new type of children's book, called the hornbook, appeared during the 16th century. It consisted of a printed page covered by a transparent sheet of horn and mounted on a square of wood with a handle at one end for the child to hold. Used for elementary instruction, the hornbook contained alphabets, the Lord's Prayer, Roman numerals, and the like. The chapbook, an unstitched pamphlet consisting usually of about seventy folded pages, appeared in the 17th century. Chapbooks, which were peddled from door to door throughout England, contained versions of poular literature ranging from nursery rhymes to medieval romances.

**The 17th and 18th Centuries.** Works of moral and religious instruction directed to children long had been in circulation, but under the influence of Puritanism in the 17th and 18th centuries such works became more important than any other type of writing for the young. *The New England Primer,* printed (1690) in Boston, Massachusetts Bay Colony, by the English-born publisher and journalist Benjamin Harris (fl. 1673–1716), is typical. It contained a rhymed alphabet, tables of syllables, the Lord's Prayer, the Apostles' Creed, the Ten Commandments, and an account of the burning of a Protestant martyr at the stake. Preparation for possible sudden death and departure to the next world was a feature of the rhymes and stories in earlier editions of the *Primer.* Among verses that became well known through their inclusion in the *Primer* was the prayer "Now I Lay Me Down to Sleep" and the "Cradle Hymn" by the English

T  Young TIMOTHY
Learnt fin to fly.

U  VASTHI for Pride,
Was fet afide.

W  Whales in the Sea,
GOD's Voice obey.

X  XERXES did die,
And fo muft I.

Y  While youth do chear
Death may be near.

Z  ZACCHEUS he
Did climb the Tree
Our Lord to fee.

*A page from* The New England Primer, *published in Boston in 1690.*

churchman Isaac Watts (1674–1748). Editions of *The New England Primer* were issued as late as the 19th century. The title of another contemporary children's book, *Spiritual Milk for Boston Babes,* further indicates the religious tone of most of the children's literature of the period.

One of the most significant developments in children's literature was the use of illustrations. *Orbis Pictus* ("The World in Pictures"), the first known children's picture book, was issued in 1657 by the exiled Czech Protestant educational reformer John Amos Comenius. An English translation appeared a year later. Its subject was natural history and the illustrations were woodcuts.

Among the classics of children's literature are adult books that appeal to children as well, or have been adapted for children. One is the simple but forceful allegory of man's conflict between good and evil, *The Pilgrim's Progress* (published in two parts, 1678 and 1684) by the English author and preacher John Bunyan. Another is Daniel Defoe's *Robinson Crusoe* (1791), the story of an ingenious and self-reliant castaway. This masterpiece served as a basis for another children's favorite, *The Swiss Family Robinson* (1812; Eng. trans., 1814) by the Swiss writer Johann David Wyss. Jonathan Swift's *Gulliver's Travels* (q.v.; 1726), which adults enjoyed for its satire, is enjoyed by children for its fantasy. The first significant French children's book was *Histories ou Contes du Temps Passé avec des Moralités* (1698), a collection of traditional fairy tales, known also as *Contes de Ma Mére l'Oie,* by Charles Perrault. The tales included "Sleeping Beauty", "Cinderella", "Red Riding Hood", and "Bluebeard". These stories were soon afterward translated into English. "Mother Goose", however, became a lasting name in England and America as applied to nursery rhymes.

In the 18th century the British publisher John Newbery (1713–67) became the first to print attractive, inexpensive books for children. Containing stories, verses, puzzles, riddles, maxims, and lessons, the books sold in England for sixpence each in little paper-covered editions. Newbery's moral precepts were gentler and less forbidding than those of the previous century. His best-known publications are *The History of Goody Two Shoes* (erroneously credited to the British author Oliver Goldsmith); *A Little Pretty Pocket Book*; and *Mother Goose's Melody,* reprinted (1785) in Boston.

Until late in the 18th century no clear distinction had been made between instruction and entertainment in children's literature. Most stories and poems written for children were de-signed to convey useful information or moral advice. Largely because of growth of religious freedom, especially in Great Britain and in the newly established American nation, and because of the egalitarian principles spread by the French Revolution, children's literature eventually became less didactic in purpose. A major influence in this development was Jean Jacques Rousseau. In his *Émile* (1762) Rousseau became the first to point out that the mind of a child is not merely the mind of an adult in miniature and that it has to be considered in its own terms.

One effect of the ideas expressed in *Émile* was a tendency in the children's books influenced by it to overemphasize the guiding role of the wise and benevolent adult. In England *History of Sandford and Merton* (3 vol., 1783–89) by Thomas Day spread this portion of Rousseau's influence in the story of pampered little Tommy Merton who was reclaimed by good, rugged Harry Sandford under the wise supervision of a clergyman, Mr. Barlow. The story is constantly interrupted by lengthy sermons that stress its educational purpose. A similar product of the Rousseau movement was the work of the

*A page from* Songs of Innocence *by the 18th-century British artist and poet William Blake.* Bettmann Archive

Irish novelist Maria Edgeworth, who wrote two collections of short stories for children, *The Parent's Assistant* (1796) and *Moral Tales* (1801). A preachy and highly moral tone is maintained throughout these volumes, but it does not greatly interfere with the author's keen understanding of children and her skill in describing scenes and characters.

The *Songs of Innocence* (1789) and *Songs of Experience* (1794) by the British artist, poet, and mystic William Blake provide the first example of literature concerned with the essential goodness of children in the spirit of Rousseau's educational philosophy. Blake's ideas on children's innocence and on corruption of children by adult standards of belief and behavior derive less from Rousseau directly than from a blend of German mysticism, English Protestantism, and the political ideas of the French Revolution. Blake believed that passion, or feeling, according to the individual conscience, was superior to all intellectual rules. However, his writings and engravings were much too difficult for a youthful audience; instead of children, they influenced, long after Blake's death, other authors and artists in the field of children's literature. Blake, like William Wordsworth in the same years, made childhood seem a happy and virtuous time, and growing up a saddening and complicated process. Blake's work, ignored during his own time, became generally known only during the latter part of the 19th century.

## THE 19TH AND 20TH CENTURIES.

The Romantic wave that swept Europe early in the 19th century also affected children's literature. In England the writings of the novelist Sir Walter Scott, noted for his tales of chivalry, were read with delight by older children. A revival of interest in William Shakespeare gave children one of their most fascinating books, *Tales from Shakespeare* (1807), consisting of versions of the Shakespeare stories by the essayist Charles Lamb and his sister Mary Ann Lamb. Two American authors of the same period, Washington Irving, and James Fenimore Cooper, wrote with similar historical vividness about the more recent American past. Irving developed the legends of the Dutch country in New York State in *The Sketch Book of Geoffrey Crayon, Gent* (1819), which contained "Rip Van Winkle" and "The Legend of Sleepy Hollow", and Cooper wrote about early American frontier life in his series known as the Leatherstocking Tales, the most famous of which is *The Last of the Mohicans* (1826).

Renewed interest in folklore, a tendency of the romantic movement, led to the enrichment of children's literature with myths, legends, and wonder stories. The German philologists, the brothers Jacob Ludwig Karl Grimm and Wilhelm Karl Grimm, made notable contributions in their volumes of stories known collectively as *Grimm's Fairy Tales*. Published between 1812 and 1815, and circulated in translations throughout the world, the volumes include such tales as "Hansel and Gretel", "Snow White and the Seven Dwarfs", "The Valiant Little Tailor", and "Rapunzel". More creative and stylized versions of the folk tale were written by the Danish author Hans Christian Andersen, whose collections appeared between 1835 and 1872. Some of the more famous Andersen stories are "The Snow Queen", "The Nightingale", "The Red Shoes", "The Ugly Duckling", and "The Constant Tin Soldier". The classic myths of Greece were retold in *A Wonder-Book for Girls and Boys* (1852) and *Tanglewood Tales for Boys and Girls* (1853) by the American novelist Nathaniel Hawthorne. In Great Britain, toward the end of the century, the man of letters Andrew Lang wrote one of the best-known collections of European fairy tales in a series of volumes beginning with the *Blue Fairy Tale Book* (1889).

The avid response of children to myth and fairy story made it clear that their minds have an unlimited range of imagination and that they do not distinguish sharply between reality and unreality. Edward Lear, the British painter and author of limericks and nonsense verse, was among the first to appreciate these truths. His *A Book of Nonsense* (1846) and *More Nonsense* (1870) are landmarks of children's literature. The supreme combination of fantasy and humor was achieved by the British author and mathematician Charles Lutwidge Dodgson (Lewis Carroll) in *Alice's Adventures in Wonderland* (1865) and *Through the Looking Glass* (1871). According to some theories, the success of these works is to be accounted for by the mathematical logic underlying their fantasy; according to others, by the profound psychological perceptions in the fantasy. In any case it is generally agreed that the two books constitute the ultimate masterpiece of children's literature. The drawings of the original illustrator, Sir John Tenniel, are so apt that his name has become almost as well known as that of the author.

Another British writer who continued the creative fairy-tale tradition was Oscar Wilde in *The Happy Prince and Other Tales* (1888). Two other notable late-19th-century British writers for children were Robert Louis Stevenson and Rudyard Kipling. Stevenson's *Treasure Island* (1883), *A Child's Garden of Verses* (1885),

*An illustration from* The Tale of Mrs. Tiggy-Winkle, *one of the series of children's books written and illustrated by Beatrix Potter.* Frederick Warne & Co., Inc.

and *Kidnapped* (1886) have become classics, as have Kipling's animal stories in *The Jungle Book* and *The Second Jungle Book* (1894–95) and *Just So Stories for Little Children* (1902), based upon the folk traditions of India. Separate lyrics by Kipling are to be found also in poetry anthologies for older children. In the United States during this period the most notable stories about animals were the dialect tales of Joel Chandler Harris in his *Uncle Remus* books (published between 1880 and 1906), which relied upon Negro folk traditions.

Fantasy continued to be a major mode of imaginative literature for children in the early 20th century. From his successful stage play *Peter Pan* (1904), a fantasy about a boy who would not grow up, the British novelist and dramatist Sir James Matthew Barrie adapted *Peter Pan in Kensington Gardens* (1906) and *Peter and Wendy* (1911). Another fantasy that has become a classic is the British writer Kenneth Grahame's *The Wind in the Willows* (1908), recounting the adventures of Rat, Mole,

Badger, and their pompous friend Toad. A distinguished contribution to children's poetry was made by Walter de la Mare in his *Songs of Childhood* (1902) and other collections. His anthology of children's poems *Come Hither* (1923) remains the most comprehensive of its kind.

Among foreign children's classics which have enriched English and American children's literature also are *Heidi* (1880; Eng. trans., 1884) by the Swiss writer Johanna Spyri (1827–1901), whose heroine is a spirited little girl living in the Swiss Alps; *The Adventures of Pinocchio* (1882; Eng. trans., 1892) by the Italian writer Carlo Lorenzini (1826–90), better known as Carlo Collodi, whose hero is an irrepressible wooden marionette; and *The Wonderful Adventures of Nils* (2 vol., Eng. trans., 1906–07) by the Swedish author Selma Ottiliana Lovisa Lagerlöf, whose hero is a boy who rode over Sweden on the back of a goose. In another vein are the science popularizations by the French naturalist Jean Henri Fabre, whose books, especially those about wasps, bettles, mason bees, and spiders, are models of their kind.

**Illustrated Children's Books.** A tradition of clear, colorful, and simple drawing for children in various styles gradually developed, especially in Great Britain. Among the more famous artists were Walter Crane, whose series of picture books was initiated in 1873 with *The Frog Prince*; Catherine (Kate) Greenaway, whose lovable children on flower-bedecked pages appeared in *Kate Greenaway's Almanacs* (1883–97) and other books; and Randolph Caldecott (1846–86), whose works include *Farmer's Boy, Diverting History of John Gilpin, Three Jovial Huntsmen,* and *Come Lassies and Lads.*

Among other outstanding British illustrators are Leonard Leslie Brooke (1862–1940), best known for *Johnny Crow's Garden* (1903), *Johnny Crow's Party* (1907), *Johnny Crow's New Garden* (1935), and the collection *The Golden Goose Book* (1905) and *Ring O'Roses* (1922). Beatrix Potter (1866–1943) wrote and illustrated books that have been called "classics in miniature", among them *Peter Rabbit* (1902) and *Squirrel Nutkin* (1903). The character of Peter Rabbit was adopted in stories written by Thornton Waldo Burgess (1874–1965), the American author of children's books on animals and wildlife. *Little Black Sambo* (1899) by Helen Bannerman (1866?–1946), a British writer, is perhaps the classic example of text integrated with pictures.

**Early Children's Magazines and Contributors.** Magazines such as the American publications *Youth's Companion,* founded in 1827, and *St. Nicholas,* founded in 1873, were significant in the development of children's literature, and they continued their influence into the early years of the 20th century. The contributors included British writers, such as Kipling; the Americans Louisa May Alcott, Howard Pyle, who was noted also as an illustrator, Oliver Wendell Holmes, Lucretia Peabody Hale (1820–1900), and Samuel Langhorne Clemens (better known as Mark Twain); and the Canadian-born illustrator and author Palmer Cox (1840–1924).

Three of the American contributors became famous for their children's books. In *Little Women* (1867), Louisa May Alcott began a series of children's books about New England family life that have remained popular favorites. Mark Twain's *The Adventures of Tom Sawyer* (1876) provides a lively picture of boyhood escapades in a Missouri town on the Mississippi River in the period when frontier life was still a recent memory. The companion volume *The Adventures of Huckleberry Finn* (1884) is considered by critics the greatest book for boys ever written by an American and an enduring contribution to the national literature. Howard Pyle, although a lesser writer, made a notable contribution to children's literature by retelling English legends, especially in *The Merry Adventures of Robin Hood* (1883) and *The Story of King Arthur and His Knights* (1903). Both are illustrated with his own distinguished drawings.

**Fiction for Older Boys and Girls.** Various works of fiction written specifically for older boys and girls appeared in the mid-19th century and became increasingly popular during the 20th century. Among the best known of such books are those by Horatio Alger, such as *Ragged Dick* and *Brave and Bold,* based upon the theme of success achieved through hard work and thrift. Other examples of popular books for boys include the series about a schoolboy athlete named Frank Merriwell, written by Gilbert Patten (1866–1945) under the pen name Burt L. Standish, and the series of adventure stories, *Onward and Upward* by William Taylor Adams (1822–97), who wrote under the pen name Oliver Optic. Love stories designed for teen-age girls also first became popular in this period, notably *Ramona* (1884) by Helen Hunt Jackson and a series entitled *What Katy Did* by Sarah Chauncey Woolsey (1835–1905), who wrote under the pen name Susan Coolidge.

**The Period after World War I.** Notable among postwar English children's books were those by the writer and illustrator Hugh Lofting (1886–1947), whose *Doctor Dolittle* series, begun in 1920, has for its hero a doctor who prefers to treat animals rather than humans. The

book of poems, *When We Were Very Young* (1924) and *Now We Are Six* (1927) and tales of whimsy in *Winnie-the-Pooh* (1926) and *The House at Pooh Corner* (1928) by the poet and playwright Alan Alexander Milne have become classics. The *Mary Poppins* books (1934–52) by Australian-born Pamela Travers (1906–  ), have a nursemaid as their heroine.

The distinction between works written expressly for children and those which children could share with adults became more precise in the period after World War I, particularly in the United States. Important reasons for this development were the spread of compulsory education and psychological testing; thus it became possible for authors to write for children within specific age and intelligence groups. Under these influences and that of the educational theories of the American philosopher, psychologist, and educator John Dewey, children's literature began to emphasize the real world in terms of the child's experience.

The volume and quality of reading material for children increased tremendously after World War I, and school and public libraries made books, magazines, and reference works available without cost. The American Library Association was increasingly helpful to educational organizations in the selection of reading material for children. The annual observance of Children's Book Week, begun in 1919, acquainted the general public with the importance of books for the young. Annual prizes such as the Newbery and the Caldecott awards, for the best American children's books, and the best picture books, respectively, focused attention on quality in children's literature. Encyclopedias for children were issued, among them the *World Book Encyclopedia* (19 vol., first published in 1917–18 as the *World Book*) and *Britannica Junior* (12 vol., 1934). Newspapers inaugurated regular departments in which children's books were reviewed. The *Horn Book* magazine, established in Boston in 1924, evaluates only children's books and related subjects.

Imaginative tales, based on the prowess of such legendary figures as Paul Bunyan, Pecos Bill, John Henry, Mike Fink, and Tony Beaver and on episodes in the life of the American pioneer David Crockett, continue to captivate the American children. An outstanding collection of such tales is *America Sings* (1942) by the poet and novelist Carl Lamson Carmer (1893–  ).

With the publication of *Millions of Cats* (1928) by the American artist and writer Wanda Gág (1893–1946), the picture narrative, in which text is reduced to a minimum, became a favorite

*Some of the "wild things" in* Where the Wild Things Are, *a modern children's classic by Maurice Sendak.*
©1963, Harper & Row, Publishers, Inc.

with pre-school children. Until 1930 most illustrated children's books were in black and white, but new printing developments made color illustration universal. Among leading color illustrators, Ludwig Bemelmans, Roger Duvoisin (1904–  ), Leonard Weisgard (1916–  ), and others produced volumes of high craftsmanship, sometimes writing their own texts.

**The 1940's and 1950's.**  Notable among American children's writers of the 1940's and 1950's were James Grover Thurber, whose fantasies *Many Moons* (1943) and *The White Deer* (1945) were illustrated with his own drawings; and E(lwyn) B(rooks) White, whose *Stuart Little* (1945) and *Charlotte's Web* (1952) won praise and popularity. Other books of unusual interest were *A Hole Is to Dig* (1952), by Ruth Krauss (1901–  ), a delightful attempt to recreate childhood experience through subtleties of language; *The Wheel On the School* (1954) by Meindert DeJong (1906–  ), a writer of keen perception; *Impunity Jane* (1954) by Rumer Godden (1907–  ), who writes for children with all the resources of a practiced novelist; and *The Cat in the Hat* (1957) by Theodore Seuss Geisel (1904–  ), who writes under the pen name Dr. Seuss. The last-named book is an extravagant fantasy, conceived as a supplementary reader for schoolchildren and illustrated with boldly comic drawings.

**The 1960's and Early 1970's.**  Informational books, especially those relating to science and social studies, became predominant in the children's books of the 1960's, and 1970's. Outstanding collections of poetry were published, however. These include *Cricket Songs* (1964), translations of a particular form of Japanese verse by the American poet Harry Behn (1898–1973); and *Reflections on a Gift of Watermelon Pickle* (1967), compiled by Stephen Dunning and others.

In fiction, despite such works of fantasy as *A Wrinkle in Time* (1962) by Madeleine L'Engle (1918–  ) and *The High King* (1968), the fifth volume in the Prydain cycle by Lloyd Alexander (1924–  ), the emphasis was upon realism. Two books, *Harriet the Spy* (1964) by Louise Fitzhugh (1928–74) and *Dorp Dead* (1965) by Julia Cunningham (1916–  ), were controversial because of the unconventionality of their heroes. Both white and black authors explored the problems of minority groups, as Natalie Savage Carlson (1906–  ) wrote about school integration in *The Empty Schoolhouse* (1965), and Julius Lester, in *To Be a Slave* (1968), employed the slaves' own words to describe Negro slavery in the United States. A young high-school dropout, John Steptoe (1950–  ), began his career and a new literary trend with *Stevie* (1969), a brilliantly colored picture book written in the language of the ghetto. A Newbery award winner, *Sounder* (1969), by William Armstrong (1914–  ), provoked discussion as to the feasibility of white authors' writing about the black experience; the controversy was renewed when the book became a successful motion picture (1972).

*Trumpet of the Swan* (1970) proved that the veteran E(lwyn) B(rooks) White had not lost the skill demonstrated in his earlier books. Another veteran, Isaac Bashevis Singer, continued to produce such allegorical works as *The Wicked City* (1972). One engrossing novel about the love of a young girl for the wolves of Alaska, *Julie of the*

*Wolves* (1972), won a Newbery medal for the author, Jean George (1919–  ). One of the most provocative (and to many critics the most talented) new author-artists was Maurice Sendak (1928–  ). Among his hauntingly imaginative picture books are *Where the Wild Things Are* (1963) and *In the Night Kitchen* (1970).

Paperback books for children were firmly established by the early 1970's; many popular works of the past were being reprinted in this cheaper form. Children's literature was also being offered in a wide variety of nonprinted forms, such as recordings, films, and tape cassettes. In 1974, however, of the total number of books published in the U.S. (40,846), more than 2592 were books for children.

**Modern Children's Magazines.** Periodicals dedicated to young readers continue to be a vital aspect of children's literature in the U.S. As noted above, the *Youth's Companion* began in 1827. It merged with *The American Boy* in 1929, but by 1941 it had ceased publication. *St. Nicholas,* begun in 1873, suspended publication in 1940, was revived briefly, and then ceased in 1943.

Two early magazines, however—*Boys Life* (begun 1911) and *The American Girl* (begun 1917)—with their combination of stories, articles, and how-to-do-it features, continued into the 1970's as official publications of the Boy Scouts and Girl Scouts of America, respectively. The most successful independent magazines of the 1970's were those designed for six- to twelve-year-old children, including *Jack and Jill, Children's Digest,* and *Humpty Dumpty.* In 1970 a new magazine named *Kids* appeared, written and illustrated by children themselves; and in 1974 two new periodicals were born: *Ebony Jr.,* the first magazine for black children, and *Cricket,* patterned somewhat after the classic *St. Nicholas.*

*See also* COMIC BOOK, and separate articles on many of the authors mentioned above whose life and death dates are not provided.

**CHILD WELFARE.** *See* MATERNAL AND CHILD WELFARE.

**CHILE,** republic of South America, bounded on the N. by Peru, on the E. by Bolivia and Argentina, and on the S. and W. by the Pacific Ocean. It lies between about lat. 17°25′ S. and lat. 55°59′ S. (Cape Horn) and long. 67° W. and long. 75° 30′ W. With an extreme length of approximately 2650 mi., Chile is longer in a north-to-south direction than any other country in the world. Its width, ranging between 46 and 221 mi., averages about 110 mi. The total area of the country is 286,396 sq.mi., making it the seventh-largest South American republic. This total includes the chief islands and island groups, which extend along the coast from Chiloé Island to Cape Horn. Among these are Chonos Archipelago, Wellington Island, and part of Tierra del Fuego (q.v.); the E. part is Argentine territory. Other islands belonging to Chile include the Juan Fernández Islands, about 400 miles W. of the coast, and Easter Island (q.v.), in the South Pacific. Chile also claims a section of Antarctica (q.v.).

### THE LAND

Chile can be divided into three general topographic zones: the lofty Andean cordillera on the E., the low coastal mountains on the W., and the plateau area, which includes the Central Valley in the central region. The dominant physiographic feature of Chile is the Andes mountain system. The W. cordillera of this system, known as the Cordillera de los Andes, extends from the great Bolivian plateau in the N., southward along the E. boundary of Chile into Tierra del Fuego. The cordillera is volcanic in origin, has several active volcanoes, and contains structural faults that result in severe earthquakes. In the N. portion of the cordillera average altitudes range from 12,000 to 15,000 ft., but many peaks exceed 20,000 ft. Among the notable mountains are Ojos del Salado (22,572 ft.), the highest peak in Chile, and Llullaillaco (22,057 ft.). Aconcagua (22,831 ft.), the highest elevation in the world outside Central Asia, lies in Argentina close to the Chilean border. Uspallata Pass, the principal pass in the central cordillera, crosses the Andes at 12,000 ft. The cordillera is generally broad in the N., exceeding 100 mi. in places. South of lat. 33° S., the cordillera is complicated by spurs and chains, and elevations decrease from the extreme at Aconcagua to about 6000 ft. at the S. extremity. This section of the range is considerably narrower than in the N., and many passes, which seldom exceed 5000 ft., provide access to Argentina. The peaks are perpetually snow-capped and, below 1500 ft., heavily forested.

An extensive plateau begins from the base of the N. portion of the cordillera. The plateau, particularly N. of lat. 28° S., is desert country. This is the area of the great Atacama Desert, which contains vast nitrate fields and rich mineral deposits. The plateau extends S. into a 600-mi.-long valley, known as the Central Valley, which begins at about lat. 38° S. and ends submerged in the Pacific Ocean in the S. The valley drops from an altitude of about 2300 ft. to sea level and is approximately 25 to 50 mi. wide. It is fertile between the Aconcagua and Bío-Bío rivers.

In the extreme N., Andean spurs and the coastal mountains join, forming a series of pla-

*Aconcagua, the highest mountain of the Andes (22,831 ft.), towers over the Chilean border with Argentina.*
Ewing Galloway

teaus separated by deep valleys. A distinct mountain range, called the Cordillera Marítima, begins somewhat s. of Valparaíso. Elevations of this chain, which slopes steeply on the w. and gradually on the e., seldom exceed 6000 ft. South of Chiloé Island the range sinks into the Pacific. Its peaks constitute the long chain of islands and archipelagoes that project beyond the Strait of Magellan; fiords reach into the range at about lat. 42° S.

Numerous rivers traverse Chile from the Andes to the sea; among the most important are (from N. to S.) the Loa, Elqui, Aconcagua, Maipo, Maule, Bío-Bío, and Imperial rivers. Although of limited value to navigation because of cascades and great waterfalls, the rivers are vital to the economy of the country for irrigation and hydroelectric power.

Remarkably few natural harbors are situated on the Chilean coast N. of Chiloé Island. The chief exception is Concepción Bay, where several good harbors, notably that of Talcahuano,

are located. North of Concepción Bay safe anchorages have been constructed at San Antonio, Valparaíso, and several N. mining ports. The principal harbors s. of Concepción Bay are Coronel and Lota, near the mouth of the Bío-Bío R.; Corral, at the mouth of the Valdivia R.; Puerto Montt, on Reloncaví Sound; and Ancud, on Chiloé Island.

**Climate.** The climate of Chile is as diversified as its physiography. The region N. of lat. 28° S., situated in the rainless zone of the s.e. trade winds, is one of the driest areas in the world. Some precipitation occurs along the w. slopes of the cordillera during the summer months, occasionally creating serious flood conditions; the rivers, with only one or two exceptions, are dry throughout the remainder of the year. In the coastal regions, monthly average temperatures range between 60° F. and 73° F. during the summer months and seldom fall below 52° F. in winter. Temperatures decrease about one degree for each 300 ft. of altitude in the Andes. The Central Valley has a Mediterranean climate, with mild wet winters (average, 52° F.) and long dry summers (average, 63.5° F.). Temperatures in

# INDEX TO MAP OF CHILE

**Continued on page 468**

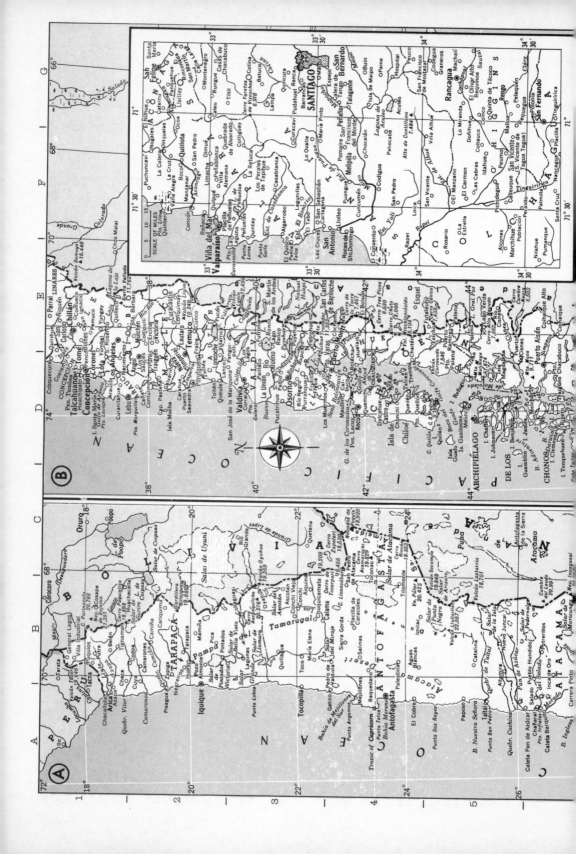

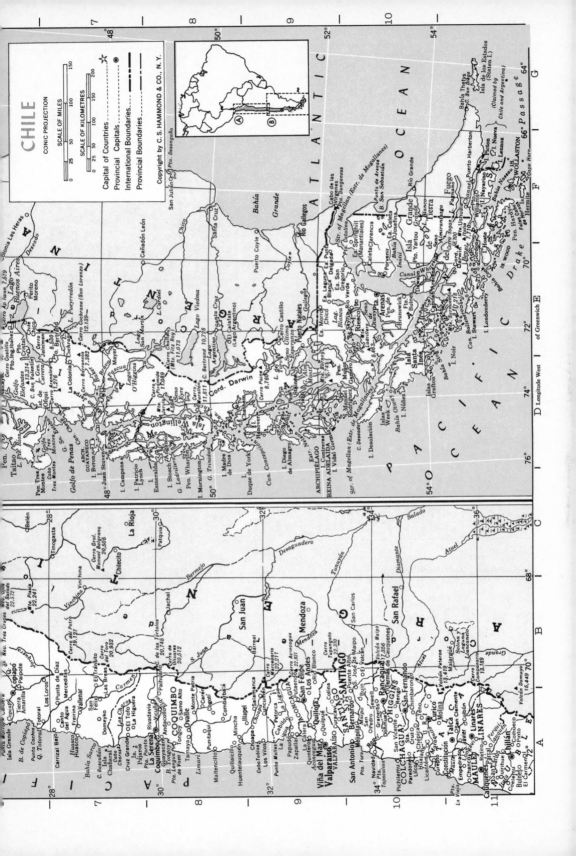

the regions s. of lat. 45° S. are considerably lower. South of lat. 28° S., precipitation, confined mainly to the winter months, increases from about 5½ in. annually at La Serena to more than 100 in. in the vicinity of Valdivia, although the interior plateau region of this area is dry as far s. as Santiago. Precipitation reaches a maximum of about 200 in. near the Strait of Magellan, where violent storms frequently occur. Heavy rainfalls also occur in the w. slopes of the southern extensions of the Andes.

**Natural Resources.** Mineral deposits, located chiefly in the N. in Atacama and Tarapacá provinces, constitute the principal source of national wealth. Chile has 40 percent of the total world reserve of copper. The country does not produce enough food to meet its own needs, although it is slowly introducing modern farming methods that are expected to increase the productivity of existing farmland.

**Plants and Animals.** The indigenous plant life of Chile differs in the various climatic zones. The northernmost coastal and central regions, largely devoid of any vegetation, constitute the closest approach to an absolute desert in the world. The Central Valley, with its considerable rainfall, supports several species of cactí, the espino (a thorny shrub), and the Chilean pine, which bears edible nuts. In the s., where the rainfall is heaviest, are dense forests containing laurel, magnolias, and various species of false beech and conifers. Native food plants include the potato, bean, and pepper.

Many animal species found throughout the rest of South America could not traverse the Andes into Chile. Mammals found in Chile include the puma; vicuña; guanaco; the Andean wolf; numerous species of rodents (including the chinchilla); the huemal, a large deer; the pudu, smallest of deer; and some distinct types of marsupials. Smaller species of birds abound, but most of the larger common Latin American types are absent. Aside from trout, which were introduced from North America, few freshwater fish inhabit Chilean streams and lakes. The coastal waters abound in fish and marine animals, including whales and seals.

**Soils.** Soil conditions in Chile vary from the barren soils of the N. desert to the rich alluvial central plain, which supports the production of cereals and vegetables and, in its N. section, subtropical and temperate fruits, including the renowned Chilean grape. To the s. Chile is heavily forested. The fjords and mountains on the Pacific side of the extreme s. are barren, but the sheltered pampa regions of Magallanes and Tierra del Fuego on the Chilean E. side provide

*The fast-flowing Rapel River in the central part of Chile is not navigable, but it has great potential as a source of hydroelectric power.* United Nations

excellent grazing lands. Recently, the government has begun programs designed to increase land productivity through soil restoration and irrigation.

**Waterpower.** The fast-flowing rivers that descend from the Andes into the heavily populated Central Valley are potentially rich sources of hydroelectric power. Although only 6 percent of these vast reserves has been developed, this proportion is larger than that of any other South American country.

In 1971 total electric power output was about 8,524,000,000 kw hours a year, yet only slightly more than half of this was produced by waterpower. Efforts are being made by the government to increase hydroelectric production.

### THE PEOPLE

Until the middle of the 19th century, immigration into Chile was limited to Spanish citizens, whose language is the official language of Chile

*The Avenida Bernardo O'Higgins, one of the main boulevards in Santiago, with San Cristóbal rising in the background.*                    Grace Line

today. The early settlers intermarried with the Indians, mainly of the Araucanian (q.v.) tribe, and their descendants, the mestizos, constitute about 68 percent of the current population. When immigration policies were eased, a movement was initiated to attract German immigrants. The influence of this movement is evident in the s., particularly in the Valdivia–Puerto Montt area. Italy, Austria, Switzerland, Great Britain, Yugoslavia, and France also made important contributions to the immigration to Chile. Today 30 percent of the Chilean population is of European stock. Only 2 percent of the population is pure Indian.

**Population.** The population of Chile (census April, 1970) was 8,834,820; the 1972 estimate was 10,440,900. The overall population density is about 33.6 persons per sq.mi. (U.N. est. 1970).

Nine tenths of the people live in the central region between Concepción and La Serena, an area which constitutes one third of the territory of the country. About 66 percent of the Chileans live in urban centers. In the desert regions of N. Chile the population is clustered chiefly in mining towns, river valleys, and the mineral-exporting ports; vast unpopulated stretches lie between the settlements. In s. Chile, between Puerto Montt and Punta Arenas, the population is dispersed in isolated settlements; in between are unpopulated stretches of rain forest, glaciers, fjords, and rain-soaked islands.

About 100,000 pure Araucanians and 200,000 culturally allied people of mixed blood live mostly in the forest region s. of Bío-Bío R. Their numbers have increased in recent decades. A few small Indian groups of other stock are found in the far N., including the Changos. The Yahgans and the Onas, who once populated Tierra del Fuego, are virtually extinct.

**Political Divisions.** Chile is composed of twenty-five provinces; they are Aconcagua, Antofagasta, Arauco, Atacama, Aysén, Bío-Bío, Cautín, Chiloé, Colchagua, Concepción, Coquimbo, Curicó, Linares, Llanquihue, Magallanes, Malleco, Maule, Ñuble, O'Higgins, Osorno, Santiago, Talca, Tarapacá, Valdivia, and Valparaíso. Chile also lists an antarctic territory among its subdivisions.

**Principal Cities.** The major cities of Chile, with their 1970 populations, are Santiago, the capital and financial center (2,661,920); Valparaíso, the principal seaport (292,847); Concepción, the agricultural center (196,317); and Viña del Mar, one of the most popular resort areas of Latin America (153,085).

**Religion.** Roman Catholics constitute about 90 percent of the population of Chile, although the church was disestablished in 1925. The seat of the archdiocese is at Santiago. The remaining 10 percent of the population is composed of Protestants, Jews, and Indians who still practice their ancient religions.

**Education.** Chile has both a free public school system and numerous private schools. All children between the ages of seven and fifteen must attend school. The school system is controlled by the national government under the minister of education, and even the private schools, which enroll about 30 percent of all students, are government-approved. The effectiveness of this system is reflected in the literacy rate, about 84 percent, one of the highest in Latin America.

ELEMENTARY AND SECONDARY SCHOOLS. In the early 1970's about 2,000,000 students were enrolled in some 5000 primary schools, 300,000 students in 550 secondary schools, and 89,000 students in 200 commercial, technical, and vocational schools. Since then a major drive to increase educational facilities has added substantially to school rolls.

UNIVERSITIES AND COLLEGES. The University of Chile at Santiago, an institution highly respected throughout the world, had an enrollment in the early 1970's of nearly 51,000 students. Other centers of higher learning include Concepción University, two Catholic universities, technical universities at Valparaíso and Santiago, and a number of colleges maintained in the provincial capitals.

**Culture.** Two lively and contrasting cultural strains predominate in Chile: the cosmopolitan tastes of the urban upper class, educated in a European tradition, and the popular culture of the peasants, which is predominantly Spanish but contains traces of their Araucanian heritage.

*Children from a poor community in Santiago, the capital of Chile.* United Nations

Folk dances are colorful and rhythmic and resemble Spanish tap dances. Guitars and bright costumes accompany the dances, the most popular of which is the cueca, a dramatic dance of love or conquest. The folk music too has a distinctly Spanish beat, although some of the Indian instruments and songs have been preserved and give Chilean music its unique sound.

LIBRARIES AND MUSEUMS. The largest library in the country is the National Library in Santiago, with about 1,200,000 volumes. The University of Chile possesses about 1,000,000 volumes. Chile has over 500 public libraries. Museums include the National Historical Museum, the National Museum of Fine Arts, and the National Museum of Natural History in Santiago, and the Natural History Museum in Valparaíso.

ARCHEOLOGY. See PERUVIAN ARCHEOLOGY.

LITERATURE. Since the 1840's Chile has produced outstanding poets, novelists, historians, and essayists. World-famous poets include two Nobel Prize winners for literature, Gabriela Mistral, who won in 1945, and Pablo Neruda (qq.v.), who won in 1971. See SPANISH-AMERICAN LITERATURE.

ART. Chile has not been as active in the visual

arts as some of the other Latin American countries. Among the best-known painters of Chile are Pedro Lira (1842?–1912), a naturalist of the 19th century, and Nemencio Antúñez, Robert Matta, Pablo Buchard, Jr., Luis Herrera Guevara, José Perotti (1898–1956), and Israel Roa (1909–    ), all 20th-century painters.

MUSIC. *See* LATIN AMERICAN MUSIC.

## THE ECONOMY

Since World War II the industry of Chile has been expanding rapidly, although inflation has somewhat slowed this growth. Today Chile is one of the leading industrial nations in Latin America and its largest mineral producer. Industrial output exceeds agricultural output. Efforts are being made to create a more balanced economy and to become less dependent upon the importation of food.

The government plays a dominant role in the economy of Chile, controlling foreign trade, operating most of the transport and communications systems, and promoting new enterprises such as hydroelectric plants, petroleum exploi-

tation and refining, and steel manufacturing. In 1939 the Corporación de Fomento de la Produción (CORFO) was founded by the government to plan and organize the industrial development of the country. In 1961 CORFO announced a ten-year $10,000,000,000 development plan designed to double the industrial capacity of the country and to raise living standards. In 1966 a Chileanization policy was enacted to lessen domination of the copper mines by American-owned companies. Under this policy Chile first took a controlling share of the industry; by 1971 nationalization was complete. Similarly Chile nationalized the country's iron, coal, and nitrate mines.

Annual budget figures in 1970 estimated $1,470,000,000 in revenue and $1,954,000,000 in expenditures.

**Agriculture.** Agriculture and stock raising provide about 16 percent of the national income of Chile and employ nearly 30 percent of the labor force. Except for sheep raising, which is conducted in the far s., agricultural enterprises are concentrated in the Central Valley. The country has about 73,980,000 acres of potential farmland,

*Merrymakers on a day of national celebration.*
United Nations

but only 4,050,000 acres are under cultivation. The chief crops include wheat, potatoes, corn, oats, barley, beans, rice, lentils, and chickpeas. Sugar beets, flax, hemp, onions, tobacco, alfalfa, clover, and nuts also are raised. The leading fruit crops are grapes (from which about 100,000,000 gallons of wine are produced in an average year), apples, melons, peaches, apricots, plums, and cherries.

Until recent years, 1.5 percent of landowners held 70 percent of the land, while 500,000 peasants lived on less than 4 acres per family. As a result of recent agrarian-reform laws the number of small holders has increased substantially.

Sheep are raised in large numbers in Tierra del Fuego and the Magallanes pampas, where ranch acreage totals about 15,000,000. Flocks comprised about 6,800,000 head in 1971. Annual wool output is about 22,000 tons. Other livestock in the country includes about 3,000,000 cattle, 1,150,000 pigs, 440,000 horses, and 950,000 goats.

*Grinding copper ore. The mining and refining of copper, the most important source of foreign revenue, is a keystone of the Chilean economy.* The Anaconda Company

Chile must import a substantial amount of food products, particularly wheat, beef, pork, and milk. It is, however, engaged in improving its agriculture with the aid of foreign experts and funds from various international agencies. Modern farming methods have increased agricultural productivity by 2 percent per year.

**Forest and Fishing Industries.** Extensive forested areas are located in the s. part of Chile, mainly in the region extending from Valdivia to Aysén. The total forest area in Chile is about 40,000,000 acres. About 290,000,000 cu.ft. of roundwood were being cut each year in the early 1970's. Exports of forest products amount to about $3,000,000 annually. Paper and cardboard production in 1971 was about 242,000 tons. Cellulose production started in 1959.

More than 200 varieties of fish are found within 30 mi. of the Chilean coast. The country

473

*Mechanization has not yet revolutionized Chilean agriculture. Here a farmer hoes his field.* Paul Conklin — PIX

has one of the largest fishing industries in Latin America. Whaling in the s. brought in about 250 whales in 1970–71. Seals and otters are hunted in Magallanes. Processing plants pack a good part of the fish catch and also produce and export fertilizers, fish meal, and other by-products. Recently Chile began exporting frozen langostino, a rock lobster, to the U.S.

**Mining.** Chile ranks third as a world producer of copper, although the copper deposits in Chile are the largest in the world. Copper is the most important source of foreign exchange (about 75 percent) and accounts for over 30 percent of government revenues. About 723,000 metric tons were produced in 1972.

Iron ore has overtaken nitrate as the second mineral of Chile. High-grade deposits, estimated at more than 1,000,000,000 tons, exist in the provinces of Atacama and Coquimbo. Pro-

duction of iron ore in the early 1970's was estimated at approximately 9,200,000 metric tons annually.

Prior to the development of synthetic processes of manufacturing nitrates, nitrate of soda was the chief export of Chile. More than 500,000 tons were still being exported each year in the early 1970's. A by-product of the nitrate production is iodine; Chile produces about 60 percent of the world supply of iodine. The government has made efforts to increase the production of copper and nitrates. In addition to the Chileanization policy, additional investments are expected to increase the output of copper. To enable the nitrate industry to be more competitive vis-à-vis the synthetic nitrate industry, new production methods have been developed, including solar evaporation, a method particularly suited to the rainless nitrate areas. A by-product of this process is potassium salts. Plans are under consideration to establish chemical industries in the N., where the population and the economy of the cities that grew with the production of nitrate have declined.

Chile also has large deposits of sulfur and coal and significant deposits of silver, gold, cobalt, molybdenum, tungsten, mercury, zinc, manganese, and bauxite.

Petroleum was discovered in the Magallanes in 1945. This state-owned industry is developing quickly. In the early 1970's some 1,650,000 metric tons of petroleum were produced annually. About 4,640,000,000 cu.yd. of natural gas were also produced. Two petroleum refineries, one at Concón, north of Valparaíso, and the other near Concepción, process domestic and imported crude oil.

**Manufacturing.** Mineral, forest, and agricultural resources provide the basis for a wide range of manufacturing industries in Chile. Industrial production increased by 45 percent between 1940 and 1950 and by an almost equal amount during the next five years. Subsequently various economic problems, including inflation, slowed growth. Industrial output exceeds agricultural output in value. Roughly 700,000 workers, almost 30 percent of the labor force, are employed by industry.

Chile is one of seven Latin American nations that produce steel. A nationally owned steel plant in Hauchipato, near Concepción, produced about 550,000 metric tons of steel ingots in 1970. On a per capita basis Chile ranks first in Latin America in the production of electric power, second in the production of shoes, and third in the production of cement. Other important manufactures include plate glass, plywood, textiles (cotton, wool, rayon, nylon), clothing, chemicals, glassware, chinaware, explosives, processed foods, metal goods, beverages, pharmaceuticals, cosmetics, paints, paper and cardboard, cordage, cigarettes, and electrical equipment. There has been an increase in the production of household appliances and of tires, tubes, and other rubber goods. In many consumer items Chile now supplies most of its own needs.

Industrial growth in Chile has been actively stimulated by the government through tariff protection and subsidies. In late 1970 the government nationalized the textile industry and assumed a controlling stock interest in the largest tire-producing plant.

**Currency and Banking.** The monetary unit of Chile is the escudo, which was introduced on Jan. 1, 1960, to replace the peso. The escudo, consisting of 100 centesimos, then had an official rate of about U.S.$0.90. Steady inflation forced the abandonment of an official rate of exchange in 1962, but continued inflation lowered the value of the escudo, and in 1973 the unofficial rate of exchange was U.S.$0.0040.

The Central Bank of Chile, established in 1926, and nationalized in 1970, controls the lending operations of the other Chilean banks and has exclusive power to issue bank notes.

**Commerce and Trade.** In 1973 total exports were valued at more than $1,200,000,000, with minerals constituting over three fourths of the value. Besides mining products, Chilean exports included agricultural products and animal products. The principal markets of the export trade of Chile were the U.S., West Germany, Great Britain, and Japan. The major imports consisted of machinery, chemicals, drugs, and transportation equipment from the U.S., West Germany, and Great Britain; foodstuffs from Argentina; and cotton and raw sugar from Peru. Imports in 1972 were valued at about $941,100,000.

**Transportation.** The railroad lines of Chile total about 5200 mi. and are entirely confined to the N. two thirds of the country. The main system is connected by spur lines to important coastal towns and by trans-Andean lines to points in Bolivia and Argentina. Electrification of the railroads is proceeding. Of the approximately 36,000 mi. of roads, about 6 percent are first-class roads. According to the latest United Nations statistics, Chile had about 194,000 passenger cars and 152,000 commercial vehicles in 1971. Several international air-transport systems provide service between Santiago and major world points, and a government-owned airline furnishes domestic and foreign service. Because of Chile's long coastline and few through roads or railroads, coastal cities are linked by shipping. About one half of the ports are used principally for national coastal shipping. Passenger travel between Chile and all parts of the world is facilitated also by a number of steamship lines, which operate passenger vessels on regular schedules from Valparaíso.

**Communications.** Chile has a federal postal service which operates about 1150 post offices. It has 4 government-controlled television stations. The American-owned telephone company, with some 370,000 telephones, was nationalized in 1971.

**Labor.** About one third of the Chilean population comprised the labor force in the early 1970's. One out of every five nonagricultural workers was a member of a union. The trade union movement started in the latter half of the 19th century, but it was not until the 1930's that its influence became significant. About 90 percent of Chilean unions were members of the Central Unica de Trabajadores de Chile (CUTCH), a federation led by Communist and Socialist officers, until it was outlawed in late 1973.

## GOVERNMENT

The government of Chile was based on the constitution of 1925 until it was suspended following the 1973 coup d'etat.

**Central Government.** The constitution vests executive power in a president, popularly elected for a six-year term, and a cabinet, which is appointed by the president. If no candidate for president receives a majority of the popular vote, the congress chooses between the two leading candidates. The president cannot serve two consecutive terms. He has certain veto powers, which may, however, be overridden by a two-thirds vote of the congress. All literate citizens twenty-one years of age or older are eligible to vote in national elections. Women received full voting privileges in 1949. Foreign residents may vote in elections.

**Health and Welfare.** Social welfare legislation was first enacted in the 1920's. Today the welfare program of Chile ranks as one of the most extensive in the world. Workers insured under the Workers' Compulsory Social Security Fund receive health, maternity, and unemployment benefits; life insurance; old-age pensions; and disability and funeral expenses. Improved health services have substantially lowered the infant and maternal mortality rates.

**Legislature.** Under the 1925 constitution, legislative power is vested in the Congress, a bicam-

*Commercially exploitable forests cover about one fourth of the area of Chile and have great economic potential.*                    **Ewing Galloway**

eral body consisting of a Chamber of Deputies, whose members are elected for four-year terms on the basis of 1 for each 30,000 inhabitants or fraction of not less than 15,000, and a Senate of 50 members. Senators are elected for eight-year terms and represent either a single province or a group of provinces.

**Political Parties.** Among the political parties of Chile are the Conservative and Liberal parties, which have been dominant in Chilean history; the Radical Party, which first gained political power in 1938 in a popular front with the Communists and Socialists and was the first party to represent middle-class interests; the Christian Democratic Party, which was formed in 1957 and was the ruling party from 1964 to 1970; and two Socialist parties. The political pattern has been fluid; elections have increasingly seen realignments of new and old groups,

sometimes under new names. Labor's role in politics is important. The Communist Party was banned in 1948, but regained its status as a legal party in 1958. Socialists and Communists have been allied since 1958 in the Popular Unity front, which in 1966 was the major congressional opponent of the Christian Democrats, and the parties won the presidential election in 1970; see *History: Postwar Governments,* below.

**Local Government.** The governmental structure of Chile is highly centralized, with the president appointing the administration heads of the 25 provinces and of the provincial subdivisions, or departments. These administrators are called intendents and governors, respectively. Municipalities, however, are governed by popularly elected officials, except for the mayors of large cities, including Santiago and Valparaíso, who are presidential appointees.

**Judiciary.** Judicial authority is vested in a High Court of Justice, appointed by the president;

ten courts of appeal; departmental courts; and various minor courts.

**Defense.** In Chile military service is compulsory for all able-bodied men, although exemptions may be obtained. Recruits are called up in their twentieth year and must serve twelve months of active duty. They remain in the reserve until the age of forty-five. The active army enrollment numbers about 23,000 men. Naval strength stands at about 20,000 men. The air force consists of 8000 men and 200 aircraft.

On April 9, 1952, Chile signed the Military Assistance Pact with the U.S., promising access to armed support and raw materials in defense of the Western Hemisphere.

## HISTORY

The first European to visit what is now Chile was the Portuguese explorer Ferdinand Magellan (q.v.), who landed at Chiloé Island following his voyage, in 1520, through the strait that bears his name. The region was then known to its native population as *Tchili,* an Indian word meaning "snow". At the time of Magellan's visit, most of Chile south of the Rapel R. was dominated by the Araucanians, an Indian tribe remarkable for its fighting ability. The tribes occupying the northern portions of Chile had been subjugated during the 15th century by the Incas of Peru. In 1535, after the Spanish under Francisco Pizarro (q.v.) had completed their conquest of Peru, Diego de Almagro (q.v.), one of Pizarro's aides, led a gold-hunting expedition from that country overland into Chile. The expedition spent nearly three fruitless years in the country, and then withdrew to Peru. Pedro de Valdivia (q.v.), another of Pizarro's officers, led a second expedition into southern Chile in 1540. Despite fierce resistance from the Araucanians, Valdivia succeeded in establishing several settlements, including Santiago in 1541, Concepción in 1550, and Valdivia in 1552. However, in 1553 the Araucanians organized a successful uprising, killing Valdivia and many of his followers and devastating all of the towns except Concepción and La Serena. The rebellion was the initial phase of warfare that lasted nearly one hundred years. The Araucanians were the only important Indian people who did not quickly succumb to Spanish attack. Strife continued intermittently during and after the Spanish colonial period and did not end until late in the 19th century.

In the Spanish colonial organization Chile originally was a dependency of the viceroyalty of Peru and later had its own government. Chile developed slowly because it did not have important silver or gold deposits to attract the Spanish, or natives who were willing to labor.

Moreover it was far from the main centers of Spanish colonization in Peru and was difficult to reach. Farming in the Central Valley was the chief occupation, and Chile supplied Peru with foodstuffs, especially wheat. The townspeople lived by trade.

**Independence from Spain.** In 1810 Chile joined other Spanish colonies in breaking political ties with Spain. On Sept. 18, celebrated thereafter as the Chilean independence day, the Santiago town council deposed the colonial governor of Chile, delegating his powers to a council of seven. Although this act marked the formal establishment of Chilean independence from Spain, intermittent warfare against Spanish troops, dispatched from Peru, continued for more than fifteen years. A royalist army was decisively defeated at Chacabuco on Feb. 12, 1817, ending Spanish control of northern Chile. One year later Bernardo O'Higgins (q.v.), one of the revolutionary leaders, proclaimed the absolute independence of Chile. However, royalist forces controlled nearly all of southern Chile until 1818 and were not completely expelled from the country until 1826.

**Conservative Rule.** O'Higgins, who had been named director general of Chile in 1818, ruled the country with dictatorial powers until 1823, when popular hostility to his regime forced his resignation. A liberal constitution, establishing a republican form of government, was then adopted, but political strife among numerous organizations contending for power kept Chile in turmoil until 1830. In that year conservative elements, headed by General Joaquín Prieto (1786–1854), organized a successful rebellion and seized control of the government. In 1831 Prieto became president, but the leading person in the government was Diego José Victor Portales (1793–1837), who filled various cabinet posts during Prieto's administration. A new constitution, vesting immense powers in the executive department of the government, was adopted in 1833. Abortive armed attempts to remove the Conservatives from power were made by liberal groups in 1835, in 1851, and in 1859.

Despite its reactionary character, the Conservative Party government fostered domestic policies that contributed substantially to the commercial and agricultural development of Chile. In addition, steps were taken to exploit mineral resources, railroads were constructed, and immigration was encouraged. A school system and cultural institutions were established. The chief development in Chilean foreign relations during the period of Conservative dominance was a series of boundary disputes with

Argentina, beginning in 1843. Armed hostilities were narrowly averted on several occasions in connection with this problem, which was not settled until 1881. In that year a treaty was signed, granting half of Tierra del Fuego to Chile.

**Growing Liberal Opposition.** Divisions resulting from disagreements with the Roman Catholic Church had taken place, meanwhile, within the Conservative Party. Beginning in 1861 its liberal wing, in coalition with the Liberal Party, instituted a number of constitutional reforms, including prohibition of consecutive presidential terms. Endeavors to promote public welfare and the further development of national resources were intensified, notably by new railroad and highway projects and the creation of a postal system. In 1865 Chile and Spain became involved in a war that continued sporadically until 1869.

Chilean interests subsequently began the exploitation of the immensely valuable nitrate deposits in the Atacama Desert. Rejecting Bolivian claims to the region, the Chilean government in February, 1879, ordered its military forces into the Bolivian port of Antofagasta. Two months later Peru, an ally of Bolivia, declared war on Chile, precipitating the War of the Pacific. As a result of its victory in this conflict, terminated in 1883, Chile acquired considerable territory, including the province of Antofagasta from Bolivia and the province of Tarapacá from Peru. Peru also yielded Tacna and Arica to Chile, on condition that after ten years a plebiscite be held. Although the two countries failed to agree on conditions for a plebiscite, disposition of the disputed areas was achieved in 1928 by peaceful negotiation, Tacna becoming a possession of Peru and Arica going to Chile. See TACNA-ARICA DISPUTE.

In 1891 political forces closely allied with the Roman Catholic clergy organized a revolt against the administration of President José Manuel Balmaceda (q.v.), a Liberal Party leader. Under the leadership of Captain Jorge Montt (1847–1922), a naval officer, the rebels, who termed themselves "Congressionalists", seized the Chilean fleet and the rich nitrate provinces in the north. In August they defeated a government army near Valparaíso. This city fell to the rebels, as did Santiago, virtually ending the war. More than 10,000 lives had been lost, and considerable property destroyed. Balmaceda committed suicide in September. Shortly thereafter Montt became president, and Chile entered an extended period of peaceful reconstruction. As a concession to liberal sentiment in the country,

Montt instituted several reforms, notably democratization of the executive department. The following years were marked by increasing participation of the Chilean people in politics, and by mounting political turbulence.

In August, 1906, a disastrous earthquake virtually destroyed Valparaíso and extensively damaged Santiago, killing more than 3000 people and making about 100,000 homeless. The damaged areas were rapidly rebuilt, however.

Chile was neutral in World War I. After the war great strife developed in the country between liberal and conservative elements. The Liberals gained power with the election in 1920 of former minister of interior Arturo Alessandri Palma (see ALESSANDRI PALMA, ARTURO), but he was unable to gain adoption of his proposals for reform. In 1924 a group of military figures accomplished a coup d'etat, ostensibly for the purpose of forcing liberal reforms, drove Alessandri from office, and established a military dictatorship. The dictatorship was overthrown early in 1925 in another military coup. Alessandri was restored to the presidency, but his term lasted for less than a year. Under the next president, Emiliano Figueroa, governmental authority was actually wielded by an army officer, Carlos Ibáñez del Campo (1877–1960), who ruled as president from 1927 until 1931. Following additional coups and changes of administration, Alessandri was elected president again in 1932 and served until the end of his term in 1938.

In the election of 1938 a liberal government, with Radical Party member Pedro Aguirre Cerda (1879–1941) as president, was elected by a coalition of democratic groups united in a popular front. His ambitious "New Deal" program was disrupted by a devastating earthquake that occurred in 1939, killing about 50,000 people. This coalition was successful again in 1942, when Radical Party member Juan Antonio Ríos (1888–1946) was elected president, governing moderately amid the political tensions engendered by pro-United States and pro-Axis elements during World War II. Ríos led his country into a pro-Allied position, entering the war on the side of the U.S. in 1944. During the war the Communist Party emerged as one of the strongest political organizations in Chile. The country became a charter member of the United Nations in June, 1945.

**Postwar Governments.** The 1946 presidential election was won by Gabriel González Videla (1898–    ), the Radical Party leader who was supported by a left-wing coalition consisting mainly of the Radical and Communist parties. Although González Videla appointed three

Housewives in Santiago, protesting food shortages and steadily rising prices, bear witness to the political unrest that rocked Chile in 1973.　　　UPI

Communists to his cabinet, thereby establishing a precedent in the politics of the Western Hemisphere, the coalition endured for less than six months. The Communists, frequently at loggerheads with others of the government, were removed from the cabinet in April, 1947.

Chile was represented at the International Conference for the Maintenance of Peace and Security, held at Petropolis, Brazil, in 1947. It approved the Inter-American Treaty of Reciprocal Assistance drafted by the conference. *See* RIO TREATY.

In the same year diplomatic relations with the Soviet Union were severed. During 1948 hundreds of Communists were incarcerated in concentration camps, and the Communist Party was outlawed from political activity. A military revolt led by Ibáñez was suppressed. Manifestations of social and labor unrest were frequent in 1949–50. In 1951 strikes occurred in almost every sector of the economy.

Industrial strife, the high cost of living, and nationalism with strong anti-U.S. overtones provided the backdrop for the 1952 presidential contest. A popular reaction against the traditional parties resulted in the election of Gen. Ibáñez. He restored some order but did not effectively cope with the economic and social problems. In 1958 former Senate member Jorge Alessandri Rodríguez (1896–　　), the candidate of a Conservative-Liberal coalition, was elected to the presidency on a platform favoring free enterprise and the encouragement of foreign investment. In response to strong opposition from the newly legalized Communist Party and the newly formed Christian Democratic Party, he proposed a ten-year plan that included tax reforms, building projects, and some agrarian reform. Natural disasters, an earthquake and resulting tidal wave, hindered his efforts, and in 1961 the opposition parties increased their strength in Congress.

Diplomatic relations with Cuba were broken in August, 1964, but later that year diplomatic ties with the U.S.S.R. were resumed. In the presidential election of 1964 former Senate member Eduardo Frei Montalva (q.v.), candidate of the Roman Catholic-supported center party, the Christian Democratic Party, won over a leftist coalition; and in the following year the party won a majority of the seats in the Chamber of Deputies. Frei introduced a number of major reforms, including partial government ownership of the copper industry. These measures, however, failed to satisfy the left wing of his own party, and large-scale defections ensued. At the same time the moderate reform policies antagonized the conservative sections of the population. Subsequently, political opposition, at times marked by violence, mounted; the situation was aggravated by inflation and drought.

As the presidential election of 1970 approached, leftist opposition united to form a Popular Unity coalition, which nominated Dr. Salvador Allende Gossens (1908–73), a Marxist-Leninist physician and senator. Allende waged his campaign on a platform that promised the reestablishment of diplomatic relations with Cuba and full nationalization of all basic industries, banks, and communications. In the elections of Sept. 4, 1970, Allende received a plurality but not a majority of the votes. On Oct. 24, a joint session of the Congress voted 153 to 35 for Allende over his rightist opponent, former President Alessandri. The winner attracted many Christian Democratic votes and received the solid support of the Socialist and Communist parties. Allende became the first president elected in a Western Hemisphere non-Communist country on a Marxist-Leninist program.

Allende quickly began to implement his campaign promises. The opposition parties, however, were working more closely together, winning by-elections, and gaining support in the universities and some unions. Political violence became increasingly common, as did strikes and student protests. The cost of living rose by more than 160 percent in 1972, and critical shortages of food and many consumer items arose.

The completion of nationalization of the copper industry in 1971 brought retaliatory measures by the former U.S. owners. Chile also found its credit standing severely damaged both in the U.S. and in Europe.

Legislative elections in March, 1973, resulted in gains of seats in both houses for Allende's coalition government; however, the opposition coalition retained its majority in the Congress. Spring and summer of 1973 witnessed much economic and political upheaval in Chile. Strikes (particularly that of the transportation-business owners) and other obstructions to orderly government culminated in September in a military takeover. In the course of the coup, President Allende was killed or committed suicide; subsequently, General Augusto Pinochet Ugarte (1915–  ) was selected as president of a four-member junta to rule the country with a fifteen-member cabinet. The new government ruled dictatorially, suspending the 1925 constitution and banning political parties. Steps were taken to reduce the high rate of inflation and to improve Chile's international economic position.

**CHILE, UNIVERSITY OF,** autonomous, coeducational institution of higher learning, located in Santiago, Chile. It was founded in 1738 by Philip V (*see under* PHILIP: *Spain*) of Spain as the Universidad de San Felipe and was reorganized in 1839; it assumed its present name in 1842. The university comprises faculties of law and social sciences, fine arts, philosophy and education, economics, music, and the Latin American faculty of social sciences. There are also faculties of architecture, mathematics and physics, chemistry and pharmacy, dentistry, medicine, veterinary medicine, and pharmacy. In addition, a great many specialized schools and institutes are affiliated with the university. The degree of *licenciado* or a professional title is awarded upon the completion of a course of study that may vary from three to seven years, depending upon the field of study. A degree of at least four years' duration may be considered the equivalent of an American baccalaureate degree. The libraries of the University of Chile contain about 1,000,000 volumes. In the early 1970's students numbered about 22,600 and the faculty comprised some 1200.

**CHILI.** See CAPSICUM.

**CHILLÁN,** city in Chile, and capital of Ñuble Province, about 56 miles N.E. of Concepción. It is the commercial center of a rich agricultural region. Industries include brewing and flour milling. Chillán was founded by Spanish settlers in 1594. Pop. (1970) 80,270.

**CHILLICOTHE,** city in Ohio, and county seat of Ross Co., in the foothills of the Allegheny Mts., on the Scioto R., about 50 miles S. of Columbus. It is the trade center of a farming and grazing region, and is an industrial city, containing railroad shops. Paper products, shoes, dairy and other food products, furniture, chemicals, and concrete are manufactured in the city. Chillicothe was founded in 1796, and in 1800 became the seat of government of the Northwest Territory. It served as the first capital of the State of Ohio (1803–10; 1812–16). Near the city is the Mound City Group National Monument. Pop. (1960) 24,957; (1970) 24,842.

**CHILLON,** ancient castle in Switzerland, at the E. end of Lake Geneva. The castle dates from about the 8th century. For centuries the castle was the stronghold of the dukes of Savoy (*see* SAVOY, HOUSE OF), and it long served as a state prison. The Swiss patriot François de Bonnivard (1496–1570) was confined for six years in the dungeon of the castle. His captivity was immortalized by the poem *The Prisoner of Chillon* (1821) by the British poet George Gordon Byron, Lord Byron (q.v.).